Site Server 3.0

Personalization and Membership

Robert Howard

Wrox Press Ltd. ®

Site Server 3.0
Personalization and Membership

| First Published | November 1998 |
| Reprinted | April 2000 |

Published by Wrox Press Ltd, Arden House, 1102 Warwick Road,
Acocks Green, Birmingham, B27 6BH, UK
Printed in the United States
ISBN 1-861001-9-40

Trademark Acknowledgements

Credits

Author
Robert Howard

Technical Reviewers
Robert L Barker Jr
Bob Beauchemin
J Boyd Nolan
Gary Falis
Charles Fichter
Marc Kuperstein
Stephen Leonard
Craig McQueen
Dave Sussman
Marco Tabini
Richard Whitcomb
Andrew Zack

Development Editor
Anthea Elston

Editors
Joanna Mason
Ian Nutt

Design/Layout
Frances Olesch

Cover
Andrew Guillaume
concept by Third Wave

Index
Julian Skinner

About the Author

Robert Howard is a Technical Evangelist for Microsoft's Developer Relations Group. He advises organizations on how best to implement Microsoft products, and he writes and reviews code and provides technical support to said organizations.

Acknowledgements

I'd like to thank all the people that helped me write this book:

First and foremost, I'd like to thank my wife Courtney for allowing me to spend mornings, nights and weekends writing this book (even as we moved into our first home). I promise to make up for it!

Thanks are also due to the editorial team at Wrox – especially Anthea, for providing me with the opportunity, and Ian and Joanna, for combing through all my gibberish and turning it into prose. I'm also indebted to the technical reviewers and editors, who provided me with the critical feedback I needed to help make this book as informative and accurate as possible – thanks!

Thanks also to my Microsoft DRG team members, for their support during the time I spent on this book. In particular, I want to mention Hans Hugli – an incredibly talented developer whom I could always count on to help me work through any problems and hardships I had while writing and coding. Jon Nicponski, Steve Fell, Leo Artalejo, Frank Strobel, Howard Greenstein and Mike Culver are the evangelists who always pushed my limits and helped me grow. And finally, a special thanks to one of the greatest managers I've ever worked for – Naseem Tuffaha.

Finally, to all my friends who seem to think I dropped off the face of the earth – yes, I finally finished!

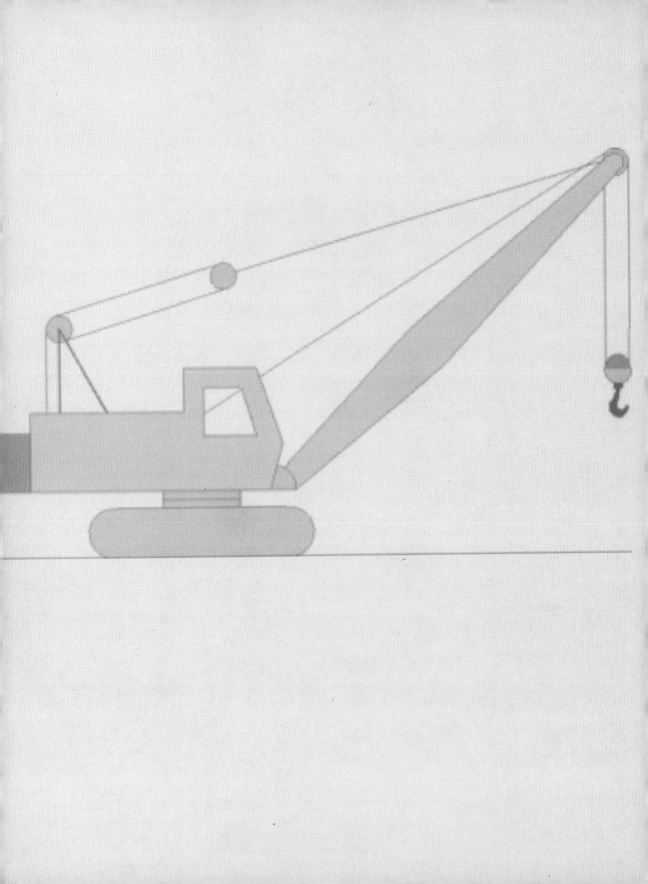

Table of Contents

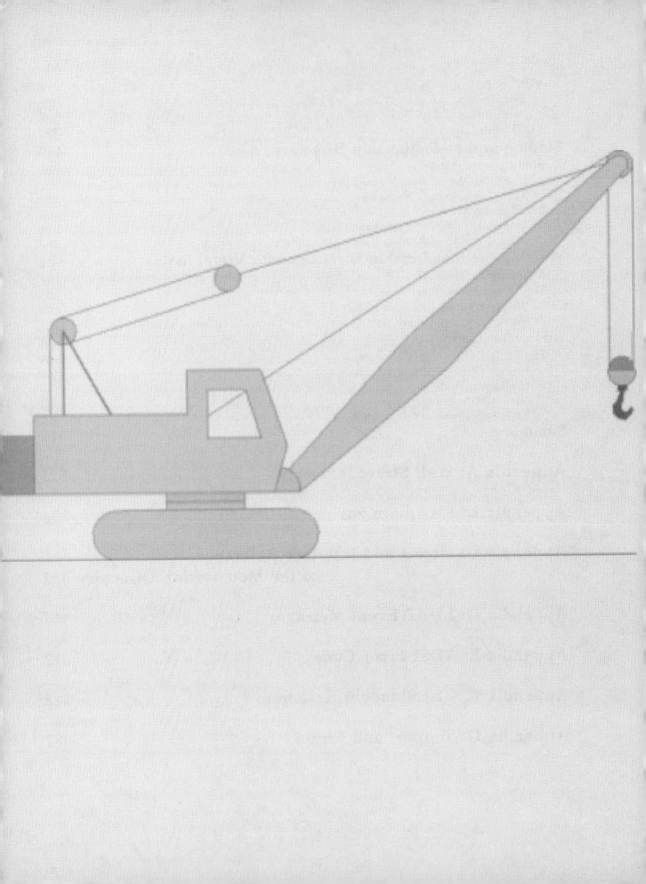

Foreword

The days of viewing a web site as a purely promotional vehicle or information catalogue are long behind us. With the explosion of Internet users and content available on the World Wide Web, businesses are now beginning to confront the challenges they face in other mass-market mediums. These challenges include understanding the needs and interests of their customers, analyzing their behavior and purchasing patterns, and building customers' profiles so they can be better targeted with the messages and information that will resonate with them.

The good news is that, in many ways, web-based technologies can address these challenges in a more efficient and more complete way than ever before. Beyond collecting simply demographic information, companies can build richer profiles of their customers by tracking many variables. The most obvious examples include the pages their users visited, the products they viewed, and previous purchases they made. And while tracking this information and matching it to unique customers is the first step to building stronger customer relationships, the real business value comes to fruition only when companies can efficiently act on this information and leverage it as competitive asset across their sales and marketing processes.

This is precisely what Site Server Personalization and Membership enables. Robert Howard's book is a must-read for those companies who are considering using Site Server P&M to tackle the critical challenges of building successful online businesses. Leveraging his experience assisting leading Internet companies to deploy Windows NT-based solutions, the author is able to give both a broad and deep view into P&M and its related technologies. While the critical concepts are distilled succinctly throughout the book, the author excels in providing a very specific and practical guide to optimally using P&M. For the beginner who is looking get started with P&M, the developer who wants to build advanced personalized services, or the administrator who needs to understand the details of securing and scaling their web application – Site Server 3.0 Personalization And Membership is the ideal one-stop resource.

Anthony Bay
General Manager
Commercial Systems Division
Microsoft

Introduction

What is this Book About?

Did you ever try to create an integrated, dynamic web site that supplied value information to many different types of user? Was it capable of supplying secure custom information based on whether the user was a prospective customer, a recognized customer, a business partner or a supplier? Did it have a dedicated data store for your users' data, that was optimized for that purpose, compatible with the industry standards and fully extensible and scalable? Was your data storage layer capable of distributed storage? How easy was it to extend the system by building your own customized components, or by integrating third-party applications?

Designing a corporate Internet or Intranet site with all these capabilities is highly desirable, and there are a number of high-end sites like this in existence. However, if you plan to develop such a site from scratch then you should be aware that the overhead is huge – they are complex animals, and the development, testing and debugging involved will make for a costly and time-consuming process.

And what about the future? If you're going to this expense, then you can't just plan your system for today and tomorrow – you want to be sure that your system is scalable to the needs of your company next year, and beyond. That means dealing with an ever-growing community of users, and integrating with technologies that are presently undreamed-of.

What can a developer do? The ideal is appealing, yet the cost is high. Microsoft have released a solution, in the form of **Site Server 3.0**, and **Site Server 3.0, Commerce Edition**. These comprehensive Intranet and Internet solutions enable the developer to implement effective web sites that give immense functionality, are vastly scalable and use the accepted industry standards. Moreover, Site Server's **Personalization and Membership** solution makes it easy to provide a personalized service to each user, and control web-user access to system resources, based on a system of user authentication and authorization.

With Site Server, sites with this kind of capability are now a feasible proposition – because it takes care of the costs and risks of developing a custom solution from the ground up. This book is an introduction to Site Server, and to its Personalization and Membership solution – it will explain the architecture and technology, help you to plan, build and configure your site, and show you how to maintain and extend your system.

What Does this Book Cover?

In order to get the best out of Site Server P&M, it's helpful to understand the architecture underlying Site Server 3.0 itself. It's important to plan ahead of building your P&M site, so we'll think about the kind of site you want to build and how Site Server P&M can help you to attain your goals. Once Site Server is installed, we can start using the tools and wizards provided with the product to get a really good feel for what's happening on the inside – and we can begin to configure the set-up to our own demands. We'll look at how to integrate Personalization and Membership with other products, and how to automate tasks through code. The emphasis is on giving you reusable examples that you can download and adapt for your own purposes.

In order to address the issues outlined here, we've organized the book into four sections.

Section I: Planning and Architecture (Chapters 1–5) is an introduction to Site Server 3.0 Personalization and Membership – we'll overview the important concepts and how Site Server 3.0 provides solutions. We'll talk about how Site Server uses a dedicated data store – the Membership Directory – to store membership information, and how Site Server integrates with Windows NT, Internet Information Server and database servers. The Membership Directory is accessed through an open, standards-based protocol called LDAP – we see how this allows us to integrate Site Server P&M with other applications. We'll understand the architecture underlying Site Server Personalization and Membership, and explain the considerations behind designing and scaling your Personalization and Membership site. This section also considers the choices that you need to make as you step through Site Server's installation process.

Section II: Configuring Personalization and Membership (Chapters 6–8) consists of three chapters, in which we'll see how to set up and configure the three principal components of Personalization and Membership, using the snap-ins in the Microsoft Management Console. First, we'll set up and configure a Membership Server; second, we'll examine the Membership Directory Manager; and third, we'll configure and map our Internet Information Server. All these tasks are essential to getting the best out of Personalization and Membership.

We'll start **Section III: Using Personalization and Membership** (Chapters 9–13) by looking at the Active User Object, which is a special COM object used by Personalization and Membership. We'll also learn how to apply Personalization and Membership to Active Server Pages, Site Server Commerce Edition, and Windows Media Technologies. Finally, we'll cover some of the other COM objects installed by Site Server 3.0 (related to P&M), and an in-depth discussion of security.

Finally, in **Section IV: Advanced Personalization and Membership** (Chapters 14 and 15), we'll look at some advanced Personalization and Membership topics, building on what we've learned about P&M objects and interfaces: managing the Membership Directory through script, and using Visual Basic and C++ through Active Directory Service Interfaces to gain access to the Membership Directory. By the end of this section you'll be in a position to start building your own application components for use with P&M.

There are also a number of **appendices**. We'll examine a demo site, and review the `PMAdmin.vbs` tool that's used to manage Site Server Personalization and Membership from the command line. You'll find a complete listing of the interfaces to all the objects that we discuss in the book, and a listing of error codes with brief explanations. We've also collected together all the useful URLs and further reading resources mentioned in the book, and you'll find them in Appendix F.

Who is this Book For?

There are two types of developer, in particular, who will benefit from using this book:

❑ Program managers and product managers who are interested in furthering their web endeavors and wish to evaluate Site Server or plan their strategy using the product. Planning is a key element in any large-scale Internet or Intranet development effort, and the first part of the book is devoted to planning, machine requirements, and development time frames.

❑ Developers and consultants whose responsibility is to implement and solve real-world problems with Site Server 3.0. The book is weighted towards using the Personalization and Membership features of Site Server 3.0, and the latter part of the book in particular has a distinct P&M flavor.

The book contains a great deal of reusable code, that developers can apply to their own real-world web applications and test sites. All the code in the book is available as a download from the Wrox Press web site – more on that in a moment.

How to Use this Book

I doubt that every reader of this book will sit down with an evening or two to spare, and wade through all 500+ pages from cover to cover. Therefore, I've tried to structure the book to anticipate your motive for buying it.

If you're evaluating Personalization and Membership with a view to making a business decision, I suggest that you attack the book in this order:

❑ Chapter 1 is an overview of the technologies – it's not too detailed, and should give you a good idea of what's possible

❑ Chapter 2 discusses the benefits of using a directory service and LDAP, relative to other data storage mechanisms

❑ Chapter 3 discusses the Personalization and Membership architecture, and how all the different components are integrated

❑ Chapter 4 provides detailed information on how to scale the architecture outlined in Chapter 3

❑ Chapter 13 is considerably more technical, but outlines how the security system of Membership works with Windows NT 4.0

❑ Appendix A – The Wall Street Investor demo – discusses a demonstration site that uses Personalization and Membership to show off ideas and features

However, if you've already decided on Personalization and Membership, and you want to know more about how to install and use it, then try this order:

❑ Chapter 1 to give you an overview of the technologies

❑ Chapter 5 describes the installation of the product, what is required, and what to expect

- ❑ Chapter 6 discusses the Personalization and Membership snap-in, which is a Site Server tool used to administer a P&M Membership Server. Most of the configuration options are exposed through this snap-in

- ❑ Chapter 7 discusses the Membership Directory Manager snap-in, which is used to provide a visual representation of the Membership Directory

- ❑ Chapter 8 shows how to configure your Internet Information Server 4.0 settings so that you can use Personalization and Membership directly from IIS 4.0

- ❑ Chapter 9 presents a COM object, called the Active User Object, which is used from an ASP page served by an IIS 4.0 server to retrieve member information from the data store, and hence provide a personalized service to the user

- ❑ Appendix A demonstrates features of Personalization and Membership through the Wall Street Investor demonstration site

If you're developing with Site Server Personalization and Membership, then I hope that you'll find the whole book useful! My priority in writing this book was to provide code that you can use immediately. Therefore, you'll find reusable code samples – along with explanation – right through the book (especially from Chapter 6, where we begin to get into managing and configuring your new Site Server site).

A lot of the code in this book is presented in the form of functions. The language of choice for most of these is VBScript, although we also look at Visual Basic and C++. VBScript enables the code in this book to be used in Active Server Pages, Windows Scripting Host, and can easily ported to Visual Basic. Additionally, Visual Basic provides a mechanism for error handling. We won't be looking at JavaScript for server-side code; however, we will see some JavaScript for client-site code in Appendix A. All of the code in the book is available as a download from the Wrox Press web site, at

http://webdev.wrox.co.uk/books/1940

I've emphasized understanding the underlying structure of what is happening through ADSI and the Active User Object, rather than discussing the web-based administration tools or Design Time Controls (although I'm sure that developers who've used DTCs find them wonderfully useful). My aim was to separate and explain methods that will enable you to build your own customized solutions.

In addition to the code, I have tried to provide insights and concepts throughout the book to stimulate your thinking on how Personalization and Membership can be applied to your organization.

Advanced Concepts

You'll find special topic areas at the end of some chapters, under the heading *Advanced Concepts*. The purpose of this material is to provide additional information (usually related to the chapter) that you might find useful down the line.

Conventions

We have used a number of different styles of text and layout in the book to help differentiate between the different kinds of information. Here are examples of the styles we use and an explanation of what they mean:

Advice, hints, and background information comes indented and italicized, like this.

Important information comes in boxes like this.

Bullets are also indented, and appear with a little box marking each new bullet point, like this:

- ❑ **Important Words** are in a bold type font
- ❑ Words that appear on the screen in menus like the <u>F</u>ile or <u>W</u>indow are in a similar font to the one that you see on screen
- ❑ Keys that you press on the keyboard, like *Ctrl* and *Enter*, are in italics
- ❑ Code has several fonts. If it's a word that we're talking about in the text, for example when discussing the **For...Next** loop, it's in a bold font. If it's a block of code that you can type in as a program and run, then it's also in a gray box:

```
Set oCars = CreateObject("WCCCars.Cars")
Set recCars = oCars.GetAll(RegistryRestore("Showroom", "Not Set"))
```

- ❑ Sometimes you'll see code in a mixture of styles, like this:

```
If IsMissing(ConnectionString) Then
    varConn = RegistryRestore("Showroom", "Not Set")
Else
    varConn = ConnectionString
End If
```

The code with a white background is code we've already looked at and that we don't wish to examine further.

These formats are designed to make sure that you know what it is you're looking at. We hope they make life easier.

Tell Us What You Think

We've worked hard on this book to make it useful. We've tried to understand what you're willing to exchange your hard-earned money for, and we've tried to make the book live up to your expectations.

Please let us know what you think about this book. Tell us what we did wrong, and what we did right. This isn't just marketing flannel: we really do huddle around the email to find out what you think. If you don't believe it, then send us a note. We'll answer, and we'll take whatever you say on board for future editions. The easiest way is to use email:

feedback@wrox.com

You can also find more details about Wrox Press on our web site. There, you'll find the code from our latest books, sneak previews of forthcoming titles, and information about the authors and editors. You can order Wrox titles directly from the site, or find out where your nearest local bookstore with Wrox titles is located.

Customer Support

If you find a mistake, please have a look at the errata page for this book on our web site first. If you can't find an answer there, tell us about the problem and we'll do everything we can to answer promptly! Appendix G outlines how can you can submit an errata in much greater detail. Just send us an email:

support@wrox.com

or fill in the form on our web site:

http://www.wrox.com/Contacts.asp

What is Site Server Personalization and Membership?

Microsoft Site Server 3.0 is a collection of utilities, tools and NT services that help developers rapidly respond to the needs of web users. There are two editions: **Site Server** is the regular edition, and **Site Server, Commerce Edition** is an extended edition that also features Commerce Server and Ad Server. In this book, we'll focus on the Personalization and Membership features of Site Server 3.0.

What makes the Personalization and Membership features such a great tool set? Arguably, its main strength is its integratability – with the other pieces of the Site Server suite, with the Windows NT Option Pack, with Windows NT services, and with other third-party products.

In this first chapter, we'll introduce some of the concepts of personalization and membership by considering the problems faced by organizations that tried to provide these services without Site Server 3.0 Personalization and Membership. We'll also look at how Site Server Personalization and Membership solves these problems.

So, here's what we'll be discussing in this chapter.

- ❑ **Before Site Server Personalization and Membership.** We'll start with a general overview of some of the thought processes that developers had to wade through, in the days before Site Server 3.0 Personalization and Membership.
- ❑ **Membership.** We'll discuss some of the inherent problems with trying to implement membership, and look at how Site Server Membership solves these problems. We'll also take a brief look at the different authentication methods provided with Site Server 3.0 – we'll be coming back to them in later chapters.
- ❑ **Personalization.** We'll look at what we mean by personalization – how to utilize your member data to enrich your users' experience. We'll also take a preview of some of the delivery mechanisms and applications that are provided by Site Server 3.0.

By the end of this chapter we'll have a better understanding of the problems faced by developers implementing a personalization and membership solution before Site Server 3.0. We'll also have a solid understanding of how easily Site Server 3.0 Personalization and Membership solves these issues.

All of the topics mentioned in this chapter will be looked at in more detail in later chapters of the book.

Life Before Site Server 3.0 Personalization and Membership

Before the introduction of Site Server 3.0, developers had two choices if they wanted to personalize the user's experience. First, they could rely upon a data store to persist user properties and settings. This data store could be anything from a text file or a database. Second, they could use a complex set of cookies to store settings on the user's computer.

Whenever a user visited the site, he had to be authenticated, and this happened in one of two ways: either the user had to log on, or the site could authenticate the user by pulling a cookie off the user's machine. This logon information or cookie could be used to look up a record in the data store that contained the information required to provide the customized view for the user.

Home-Grown Systems

Needless to say, building this system from the ground up is quite an undertaking. Home-grown personalization and membership sites need to be concerned with data store design requirements, how the system could scale to meet growing demands, and all sorts of other problems, long before integrating with the Web. There are some custom systems in existence – and many are highly successful – but the resources required to build such a system are time-consuming and costly. And we all know that when an application (or web site) is unavailable, incomplete or inaccessible, it can cost your organization money *and* users.

Of course, the designers of these home-grown systems had plenty of design considerations to chew over. How would the personalized member information be delivered? Will it peek into a database and retrieve a new recordset of information, every time a 'personalized' member visits the site? This method can quickly become expensive to the system. (I once provided some support to just such a system – it used proprietary database technology to connect to and look up records in a database. The system worked well, but as the needs of the organization changed, the system was not extensible enough and had to be replaced.)

Should the delivery method be the same for every application that uses our data? If so, then it's possible to develop an object model that represents the data structure, knows how the data is represented and how to interact with it. But if the data structure changes, it might break the object model – which causes all kinds of headaches for the application designers.

Further, what protocol will be used to access the data, and what level of dependency is placed on that protocol? Is it necessary to develop a new, proprietary protocol specifically for communicating with the data structure? If the data store is to be some form of relational database, should ODBC calls be used directly, or is it acceptable to use the ActiveX Data Object?

Another curious phenomenon is the number of developers that start planning a personalization and membership system by establishing how the data will be delivered. Really, this consideration should come well down the list: data collection and storage are by far the greater concerns.

Site Server to the Rescue

Site Server Personalization and Membership has addressed all of the concerns that a developer is likely to come across when building his P&M site. In this book, we'll learn how we can use Site Server 3.0 Personalization and Membership to rapidly and cost effectively build solutions.

We'll spend the rest of this chapter examining personalization and membership. We'll look at some real-world scenarios, and provide some references to other parts of the book, where you can find more information on some of these topics.

Just before we do that, I want to mention an important ethical data collection consideration.

Do Not Abuse Customer Data

The Internet has become a real business tool; its users expect to be treated accordingly. Don't allow your marketing department to use your customer data to drown users with floods of junk email. Do the extra work and determine the needs of your customers; become familiar with usage patterns and online behavior by using tools like **Site Server Analysis** and **Site Server Personalization and Membership** to better serve your customers; but don't abuse their data.

Use Customer Data to Serve the Customer Well

The information that your customers volunteer is valuable material, and just as important are the log files that your users generate to help your business better determine customers' needs. Use this information to better your site and your customer relations.

If a customer has visited your New Products site 10 times in a single day, then it's probably safe to say that they are looking for your latest hot new product. So, shoot this customer an email: let them know some more information about this product. Get personal!

Don't Share Customer Data

If you disclose your customer data – and your customers or users find out about it – then very soon you won't have many web users left. People don't mind giving data if they feel there is some value behind sharing it, and they usually realize the benefits that their demographic information can provide to a business.

Don't sell your customer data to any marketing company, or any other business. Sure, the information is valuable; but consider it an investment, rather than a product to sell business to business.

Think About Privacy

Things are afoot in government concerning privacy on the Internet. Be smart: use customer data to serve your customers better. If your customers or users make a request to view the information that you've collected about them, be honest, they'll appreciate it!

OK, that's enough preaching. Let's roll up our sleeves and get stuck into Site Server. We'll begin with Membership.

Membership

Before we can personalize settings for each user that visits our site, we have to know who the user is – only then can we match the user to his personalization settings. **Membership** is the process of establishing the identity of the user (authentication), and whether or not this user should gain access to our resources (authorization). In fact, membership can also take this one step further: it can encompass the ability to authenticate and authorize a request before granting access, *and* after performing the authentication, keep the context of the requester for use with personalization.

Before we examine what Site Server Membership provides, let's look at some of the problems that developers have encountered when trying to implement their own membership systems.

Membership Problems

When a user visits our web site, what method should the site use to authenticate – that is, determine whether or not the visitor is valid? Then, if our authenticated user is a personalized user, how do we determine whether they are authorized to view the data they have requested?

How will secured access to resources be provided? If we're using Windows NT, then we already have an excellent security system for working with the Internet; but integrating with this system is no small task.

If we are to build a membership solution, then we first need to provide some mechanism for authenticating the user; for checking that the credentials presented by the user are valid; and for authorizing access to the resource that the user requested.

The bottom line is this: we need to make sure that the right user gets the right data.

Authentication

On the Web today, there are several proprietary solutions for authenticating users; however, they all boil down to two scenarios for determining the user's identity: authentication against a database, and platform-specific solutions (such as Windows NT accounts).

Database Authentication

A database-based authentication system is certainly one way to solve the authentication problem. This involves using the **database** to store all the user information for the site, and authenticating via Active Server Pages (or some other technology) – and it's a complex task. Of course, you have to manage the database; but the database must also be capable of efficiently handling the volume that the site generates from logins and lookups.

Another major negative with database authentication methods is that they can't tap into the Windows NT security system to authorize which users or groups have access to what system resources (unless, of course, you were to roll your own impersonation system for validating users against a Windows NT account – yuck!).

Windows NT User Accounts Authentication

Instead, we could use a platform-specific solution – such as entering all the web users into the Windows NT Security Accounts Manager (SAM) database, which is used to authenticate Windows NT users. Thus, we create a **Windows NT user account** for each of our Internet users. This should be perfect! Windows NT knows how to handle and grant access permissions to users; Internet Explorer can use challenge/response authentication, and other browsers can use Clear Text/Basic authentication; for systems with many users, we could even use Windows NT groups to aggregate common permission for system resources – problem solved!

Ah, not so fast – now we have encountered several new problems. First, when the number of users or groups starts to grow (which it *will!*), or we need to expand the system to support multiple sites, the NT User Manager tool becomes the bottleneck for the system. The User Manger is great for administering domains, groups and users; but when the number of users grows, the User Manager tool becomes extremely difficult to work with. All users and groups are viewed together, and there's no logical organizational structure provided to allow us to view just selected groups or members. (It's not a design flaw; it's just that this is a simple, unconventional use that the User Manager's developers never accounted for. Before the advent of the Web, who would have imagined that a single organization might have millions of users?)

Moreover, the security risks associated with creating a new system account for each and every web user far outweigh the perceived benefits of Internet authentication and personalization. You have the potential for a huge number of unknown Internet users – each of which has an NT account on your system. What happens if the system is improperly engineered? Do Internet users now have access to the domain? Yikes! Try explaining that one to your CEOs when your security is breached!

What's the Solution?

Despite the problems that we've listed above, these two systems both offer some sensible features, and could provide great solutions if they were properly engineered. So what about a hybrid?

Site Server 3.0 Membership

Site Server 3.0 Membership offers the capability for storing member credentials, either in the Windows NT SAM, or a directory; and for authenticating members from either of these sources. More importantly, Site Server *always* uses a valid Windows NT account to access system resources – so that we can still control authorization.

If you haven't come across the concept of a directory before, don't worry – we'll spend the next chapter getting up to speed on how Site Server stores its member data, and exactly what a directory is.

What Site Server Membership Provides

One of Site Server's greatest features is that Site Server Membership is easily integrated with Microsoft's **Internet Information Server 4.0** (IIS 4.0). In fact, the integration is so smooth that all authentication is handled by the system: in order to enable users to authenticate on a resource requested from IIS 4.0, there's no need to write a single line of code! We'll examine the integration between Site Server and IIS 4.0, in Chapter 8.

This can all be set and modified in the safety of the point-and-click environment of the **Microsoft Management Console** – which we'll do in Chapters 6 and 7. Alternatively, you can choose a more maverick approach, by writing all your own administrative tools programmatically – we'll do that in Chapter 14.

> *In fact, everything that you could ever need to do to enable authentication and authorization can be managed programmatically.*

Site Server provides several different features for membership. We'll mention each briefly here, with the understanding that we'll go into much more detail in later chapters.

Data Storage

Site Server uses a directory service, called the **Membership Directory**, to store all member information. When appropriate, the Membership Directory is also used to store member credentials. The Membership Directory is a hierarchical organized structure that logically groups similar items together – we'll get into the directory services in Chapter 2, and the Membership Directory in particular in Chapter 3.

The Access Mechanism

In order to create a more open and standards based system, Microsoft chose the **Lightweight Directory Access Protocol** (LDAP) as the interface for communicating with the Membership Directory. LDAP can be used to communicate between the Membership Directory and other LDAP-friendly applications, including non-Microsoft applications and platforms. We'll read in detail about LDAP in Chapter 2, and throughout the rest of the book.

Authentication

When we set up our Site Server Membership Directory, we choose one of the two authentication types that are used to protect resources in the Windows NT system and in the Membership Directory:

- ❑ **Membership authentication** mode uses the Membership Directory to store the usernames, credentials and passwords that are used to access both Windows NT system resources and Membership Directory resources.
- ❑ **Windows NT (Intranet) authentication** mode uses the Windows NT Security Accounts Manager (SAM) to store user credentials; but all other user information is stored in the Membership Directory.

Shortly, we'll look into the Membership Directory's two authentication modes a little more. In Chapter 8 we'll look at how to apply authentication through IIS 4.0, and in Chapter 11 we'll learn how to apply authentication and membership to custom solutions like the Windows NT NetShow Services (yes, this is a *highly* extensible solution!).

The Active User Object (AUO)

Site Server provides a special COM object, called the **Active User Object** (AUO), that is specifically used to communicate with the Membership Directory through ASP pages. Chapter 9 looks in great detail at what the AUO does, and how to use it. For now, it's sufficient to say that, after the user has been authenticated, we can use the AUO (via ASP pages) to retrieve requested data from the Membership Directory.

Security

Under Membership authentication mode, Site Server provides a secure means for controlling access to the Windows NT system without needing to create an NT account for each user. This is known as **impersonation**. A single Windows NT account is used by all members of the site (the default NT impersonation account is called MemProxyUser). Under Windows NT authentication mode, the account used is that of an existing user in the Windows NT Security Accounts Database. We'll begin to explore all these concepts in Chapter 3.

Let's take a moment to look at how Site Server authentication is provided through IIS 4.0.

Site Server Authentication

Windows NT 4.0 already provides a very secure form of web-based authentication, called the **Windows NT LAN Manager** (NTLM). The NTLM allows clients coming from machines that are already part of the domain to access the site through a series of challenge/response messages.

Site Server's Windows NT authentication mode (which we mentioned above) integrates well with this method, by allowing users to store data in the Membership Directory and mapping that information against valid NT accounts created in the Membership Directory.

Site Server's other authentication mode, Membership authentication, doesn't depend upon Windows NT accounts to validate users. Instead (as we've already mentioned), Membership authentication uses an impersonation account to impersonate a Windows NT user.

Windows NT (Intranet) Authentication

When Site Server is used on an Intranet and Windows NT users are already mapped to the file system resources, integrating with Site Server is straightforward. Windows NT authenticates users either through the NTLM or via an anonymous account.

Anonymous Authentication

Internet Information Server 4.0 supports an anonymous account, called IUSR_*[server_name]*, which can be used as a catch-all impersonation account for anonymous users. The user is assigned to resources on the file system and users that access the system without authenticating are allowed in and assigned to this account. Note that we can't provide personalization for this account.

Windows NTLM Challenge/Response Authentication

In order to provide a more secure method of accessing a Windows NT system over the Internet, without ever sending the user's password, Microsoft integrated a challenge/response system into IIS. When a Windows NT user has been authenticated, his Membership information is read from the Membership Directory.

> Note that, in NTLM authentication, the user's password is never sent across the wire.

Clear Text/Basic Authentication

NTLM authentication provides a very secure means of providing credentials; however, it's only supported by Microsoft's Internet Explorer browsers. In order to allow other clients to authenticate, the Windows NT authentication mode also supports Clear Text/Basic authentication, which is a widely-supported authentication method.

In Clear Text/Basic authentication (and unlike NTLM authentication), the user's logon credentials are sent in *clear text* rather than in an encrypted format. However, we can use Secure Sockets Layer (SSL) encryption, to encrypt the transmission of the username and password between the client and the server during authentication. On the other hand, Clear Text/Basic authentication is similar to NTLM authentication in that, once authenticated, the user's Membership information is read from the Membership Directory.

Using Windows NT authentication with Site Server is a great solution for sites that have already put Windows NT authentication mechanisms in place, but still want to leverage Site Server 3.0's Membership Directory for data storage. However, if an organization is planning for a large amount of web traffic, then they should take a close look at Site Server's Membership authentication mode, which 'abstracts' the web members from the Windows NT account database.

Membership Authentication

Membership authentication mode arranges for member credentials to be stored in the Membership Directory (unlike Windows NT authentication, where they were stored in the Windows NT SAM). Additionally, Membership authentication provides four methods of authenticating the user, plus the IIS 4.0 anonymous user account.

Anonymous Authentication

Anonymous access through Membership authentication is handled in just the same manner that Internet Information Server uses. The IUSR_*[server_name]* account is used as a catch-all impersonation account for anonymous users, and the impersonation account is not used. This user is assigned to resources on the file system and users that access the system without authenticating are allowed in and assigned to this account.

Automatic Cookie Authentication

Automatic Cookie authentication stores a small amount of data, called a cookie, on the user's computer. The cookie can be used for identification when navigating around a site. Each user logging on under Automatic Cookie authentication remains anonymous – Membership automatically creates a new anonymous account that is distinguished only by its GUID (globally unique identifier). In Chapters 8 and 14, we'll look at how we can manage this member, and the required cookie used for identification, programmatically.

HTML Forms Authentication

HTML forms authentication uses HTML forms to allow visitors to enter a username and password to verify their member status:

This member information is sent to an ASP page via the POST method, and passed to a Site Server Membership object that can authenticate the user. If the user authentication information is accepted then the user is given access to the requested resource; otherwise the user is denied access.

The HTML Forms authentication mode can use Secure Sockets Layer (SSL) to encrypt data that is sent during the exchange of username and password information. We'll learn more about HTML Forms authentication in Chapter 8, and in Chapter 12 we'll look at the Membership.VerifUsr object, that is used to verify user credentials.

Clear Text/Basic Authentication

Clear Text/Basic authentication is a standard authentication method that passes the username and password information across the Internet in clear text form (i.e. non-securely). It is a text-based protocol that sends data as UUEncoded strings that represent the username and password. Clear Text/Basic authentication is best used on resources that are not highly secure, yet require a form of authentication that is stronger than cookie-based authentication. Again, we can use SSL encryption to encrypt the transmission of the username and password between the client and the server during authentication.

Under Clear Text/Basic authentication, the user is prompted for authentication details with a dialog box that requests username and password:

```
Enter Network Password                           [X]
   ____
  | ?? |   Please type your user name and password.
   ‾‾‾‾
           Resource:   WROX

           User name:  [|_____]

           Password:   [_____]

                              [   OK   ]  [ Cancel ]
```

Distributed Password Authentication

Distributed Password authentication (DPA) is rather similar to the NTLM challenge/response method (under Windows NT authentication – see above), in that the user's password is never sent across the wire. Instead, the client machine creates a response ID that is composed of a hash of the user's password, plus a random challenge that was sent by the server: all this is packaged up and returned to the server. If the server approves of the response ID then the user gains access to the system.

The dialog for DPA is different from that of Clear Text/Basic authentication:

```
Sign In                                       [?][X]
  ┌──────────┐  ┌─Sign in───────────────────────────┐
  │          │  │  Realm:      WROX                  │
  │          │  │                                    │
  │          │  │  Member ID:  [_____]  │
  │          │  │  Password:   [_____]  │
  │          │  │                                    │
  │          │  │       [ ] Remember my password     │
  └──────────┘  └────────────────────────────────────┘
  ┌────────────────────────────────────────────────┐
  │ Type your member ID and password to connect to this Internet site. │
  └────────────────────────────────────────────────┘

  [    OK    ]      [  Cancel  ]      [  Help  ]
```

> **The Distributed Password authentication method is supported for Internet Explorer browsers only.**

When a user requests access, the system automatically authenticates the user through the selected method and (if successful) provides access to the underlying Windows NT system through an impersonation account (so authorization is based on Windows NT permissions to resources). Once you decide to use Personalization and Membership in your site, you don't need to write one line of code to authenticate a user. Site Server 3.0 provides this functionality out of the box!

Membership Scenarios

Before we move on to Site Server Personalization, let's look at some possible scenarios in which Site Server Membership can be employed.

An Internet Service Provider

In this scenario, it's easy to provide levels of security for all users – we can use the familiar Windows NT security system, but we don't need to add hundreds or thousands of users to the Windows NT SAM. Instead, the Site Server system can use a Windows NT impersonation account, in Membership authentication mode, to *dynamically* grant each individual web user permissions to resources – without the need to assign each member his or her own Windows NT user account.

An Internet Content Provider

Here, content can easily be provided on a pay-per-view basis. For example, suppose that a particular content provider wishes to sell Microsoft Streaming Media or Real Streams over the Web. A willing customer can purchase a stream, and would then be added to the proper group to access the stream for a predetermined amount of time. When the time allocation has elapsed, the user's permissions will expire (and if the user wants more, they'll have to pay to view the content again). We'll look further into this scenario, in Chapter 11.

An Intranet or Enterprise Site

Most Intranets already use the existing Windows NT SAM to provide accounts for their user base. Intranet sites can keep their existing user base and still reap the other benefits of Site Server by storing only their member attributes in the Membership Directory.

So, we've tickled the surface of Site Server Membership. Now let's have a look at Site Server Personalization.

Personalization

Site Server 3.0 **Personalization** is the technology that enables the developer to acquire and store properties as they relate to a specific user or object, and to persist them in the Membership Directory. Various systems (such as IIS 4.0 Active Server Pages) can access the Membership Directory, in order to expose these user attributes for the purposes of personalization.

Once we've authenticated and authorized the user with Site Server Membership, we can easily access the user's properties to affect the service that we provide via the ASP pages.

Why Personalize?

Personalizing a web site is not a new concept. Several successful Internet companies have implemented techniques that track what an individual user has done in the past, and use this information to influence what data is presented to them in the future. Amazon, the Seattle bookstore, is one such organization – you can visit their web site at http://www.amazon.com. They have done such a tremendous job of personalizing their site that other organizations want to follow suit.

However, designing and engineering the backend solution to support such a site is no small task. Moreover, limitations on the available developer resources has made it difficult for many organizations to design, architect, and implement their own solutions.

Although it's difficult to implement a system like Amazon's, there's still a huge demand for such systems. Relationship management is quickly becoming the newest buzzword on the Internet, as an increasing number of sites compete for users' attentions. In addition, as electronic commerce becomes a major driving force, organizations want to serve their users as best they can.

> *There are many books that discuss electronic commerce. A complete definition of electronic commerce can be found in* Professional Active Server Pages 2.0*, Wrox (ISBN 1-861001-26-6).*

The developers and program managers that drive the web project are not necessarily the same people who drive relationship management of the web site. Instead, business units such as Sales and Marketing are quickly becoming the major organizational driving forces behind web sites. The motivation for this comes from the earning capabilities that can potentially be derived from successful web stores or ad revenue-generating sites.

Because of these potential revenue streams, organizations are re-designing web interfaces to be as user-friendly as possible. This 'user-friendly' feature tends to be a personalization (or relationship management) of the user's needs, based upon the information that the user volunteers or frequently requests.

Let's see what Site Server provides for accomplishing these objectives.

Site Server 3.0 Personalization

Site Server Personalization accomplishes relationship management objectives through a number of tools and objects. Active Server Pages can be used to display personalized web content, email can be used to 'deliver' personalized content, and Internet Explorer channels can be used to 'push' content. We can also extend the personalization services to other applications, such as the Windows Media Player, to dynamically build personalized streaming content – and we'll look at this in Chapter 11.

> *In addition to these services, Site Server provides a tool called the Rule Builder, and some functionality, the Site Vocabulary, to ease the implementation of a Personalization site. The Rule Builder and Site Vocabulary go hand-in-hand and are more focused on the publishing side of Personalization.*

Collecting Member Data

The Personalization feature of Site Server 3.0 allows users to explicitly add information about themselves, through HTML forms, ActiveX controls and Java Applets, and other systems that aren't necessarily Internet-related. You might be familiar with this type of explicit profiling if you've visited http://home.microsoft.com recently. In Chapter 10, we'll learn just how easy it is to profile member data explicitly, and to add it to the Membership Directory.

Additional information can be added implicitly by the administrator or site owner, using script and other applications and tools, and through the Microsoft Management Console. For example, this information may include the number of visits to the site, the user's favorite page, and the types of ad to which the user has clicked through.

Storing Member Data

All of this user information is collected and stored in the Membership Directory. From there, the user information is easily accessible to any application that supports the Lightweight Directory Access Protocol, LDAP.

Site Server Personalization Utilities

We can write ASP pages using users' attributes to control the display that the end user views. For example, this can be as simple as greeting the user by his or her first name each time they visit the site, or dynamically remembering the positioning of objects on the page (to allow the user to set his own layout of the content).

We can also associate information stored in other data sources with the specific attributes stored for each user. This archived data is known as a **secondary data source**. We can use such data for personalization purposes, by accessing it through the Personalization and Membership system as a secondary provider to the Active User Object. For example, consider a bank that uses a database system to store information about its customer accounts. The bank can associate this information with a membership account that exists for the user. When a user accesses a members-only area of the bank's site, account information can be displayed to the user via a secondary provider that associates an attribute of the member with a record in the database.

Site Server Personalization makes delivering personalized content easy. Microsoft has provided several methods and tools for delivering and structuring the information. Components such as the **Active Directory Service Interfaces** (ADSI) can also be used to write new directory tools to serve other purposes. We'll introduce ADSI formally in Chapter 2, and we'll write our own directory tool in Chapter 15.

Using **ASP pages** to build personalized web pages and using **Direct Mail** to send personalized mail are not complicated, and are tightly integrated with the rest of Site Server Membership and Windows NT.

Delivery Mechanisms

Out of the box, Site Server provides three simple delivery mechanisms for custom content.

Personalized Web Pages

Using Microsoft Active Server Pages (ASP) with the Active User Object (AUO), we can build web pages dynamically and deliver *just* the relevant information to the user. The information displayed is derived from the user attributes (properties about the user) that express just what the user is interested in. These user attributes are persisted in the Membership Directory, and are immediately available when a user first visits a Site Server Personalization and Membership site.

We can also design personalized data – such as a user's favorite product – so that it can be used in combination with other technologies such as Site Server 3.0 Commerce Server or Microsoft NT NetShow Services, to target ads or customize streams dynamically.

*There are additional utilities, known as **Design Time Controls** (DTCs), provided with Site Server. DTCs are ActiveX controls that allow the developer to use Personalization and Membership at an even higher level of abstraction. Many developers find the DTCs useful, but they're out of the scope of this book. If you'd like to know more about them, have a look at the Site Server Documentation that comes with Site Server 3.0 installation.*

Direct Mail

The concept of sending personalized email is not new. There was a time when developers spent hours writing Perl scripts on UNIX machines, for guest book applications that would send a personalized email back to each guest's email address, thanking them "for visiting our wonderful site" and leaving their stamp. These simple Perl scripts used SendMail in UNIX.

Site Server's **Direct Mail** application can read a list of users out of the Membership Directory, and send the appropriate email to each user, custom-tailored from the user's attributes or usage patterns. These custom emails are built from Active Server Pages, that are executed to generate the custom message in the context of the user. Thus, logic can be built into the ASP pages to display certain content to specific users based on their attributes.

Personalized Channels

A channel is used to deliver information directly to the user. Personalized channels are installed with Site Server and can be used with Personalization and Membership. However, we won't dwell on the subject for long in this book – if you can write a personalized ASP page, then you have the knowledge necessary to create a personalized channel.

Users can express interest in certain types of content, and have that content delivered to them in a pre-determined manner. This pre-determined content is delivered by a Site Server 3.0 service called the Active Channel Multicaster. These channels can supply users with information, as it becomes available, and download it to their desktop.

Tools for Customizing Content and Delivery

In addition to these delivery mechanisms, Site Server provides several tools for working with the directory and providing targeted content. The Site Vocabulary and Rule Builder are two of these tools.

The Site Vocabulary

The **Site Vocabulary** is simply a pre-defined data structure in the Membership Directory, that is used by other applications and objects in the Membership Directory to help define information. It's a hierarchical structure that defines a limited set of values, which can be used as the set of possible values for a given attribute.

For example, if we were running a sportswear store, we can create a set of values in the Site Vocabulary that corresponds to different sports that represent our stock: soccer, baseball, basketball. We can ask each site member to select the sports in which he or she is interested, from our predefined list of sports – and the selected sports are contained as values in a member attribute called favoriteSport. Thus, the members can only choose from those sports on our pre-prepared list, and this ensures that the attribute always contains valid values.

The Site Vocabulary is similar to the functionality gained in code by using constants to equate to the integral values allowed for a given field. In fact, we can use the Site Vocabulary to replace these constants with actual data strings that are stored in the Membership Directory.

The Rule Builder

The **Rule Builder** provides a unique interface for building Visual Basic Script to take a specified action based on requirements defined in the rule. It makes use of tools such as the Site Vocabulary, and other Membership Directory attributes, to build rules. These rules can then be applied to a site to personalize content if a user attribute matches some criteria that the rule defines.

More specifically, the Rule Builder can conditionally display content, sort through an analysis database for users with particular attributes, or perform some kind of action defined by custom Visual Basic Script.

We could write a whole separate book on these tools, and you'll find lots more about them in the Site Server documentation. We'll be concentrating on how we can access and use member information in the Membership Directory for personalization.

Personalization Scenarios

Let's quickly consider a few example scenarios, to give our previous abstract discussion a little more solidity.

An Internet Service Provider

If a user needs a higher level of service, he may have permissions or attributes that allow him to view reports and menus that are customized to his particular needs. For instance, the Internet Service Provider can design an ASP page that displays site usage data, and uses personalization to generate the appropriate report for the customer requesting the information.

An Internet Content Provider

Information can be sorted and ordered based on settings that the user sets explicitly. A site visitor can go to the site with prior knowledge of what kind of information he will see. Alternatively, a visitor can enter the site unaware that the information delivered to them is tailored to their profile – but the visitor will enjoy the fact that the resulting site is easier and more 'familiar' to navigate. For instance, a search site can track the last five items that a user has searched for, and use this information to cut down the time that the user spends trying to find common information. A good real-world example of this is www.msnbc.com; here, the site requests the viewer's zip code and then displays localized news to the user.

An Intranet or Enterprise Site

Suppose that all users belong to one of the following groups: marketing, development, administration. These groups determine what content the user can view, and perhaps also update the user with new information relative to their area of expertise. Personalization can provide the capability for developers to author a single set of ASP pages that personalize themselves according to the group membership of the user.

Summary

We began this chapter with an overview of a few of the problems that developers face when implementing home-grown personalization and membership in a web site. We've talked about how Site Server solves nearly all of these complex business problems with Personalization and Membership.

The main points that we've learned include:

❑ Membership provides the process of determining the identity of a user.

❑ Personalization allows the developer to provide each user with a personalized view of the web site, based on properties that might be set either by the user or by the developer. Thus, the developer and content provider work together to provide targeted data to their user base.

❑ The principal data storage tool for storing Membership and Personalization information is the Membership Directory.

❑ There are two authentication modes. Under Windows NT authentication, users are authenticated against data contained in the Windows NT Security Accounts Database. Under Membership authentication mode, users are authenticated against data contained in the Membership Directory, and access to the Windows NT system is gained via an impersonation account.

❑ Each of the two authentication modes offers a number of different methods for authenticating users.

Together, Personalization and Membership provide a powerful infrastructure for managing and nurturing relationships and community among a user base.

In the next chapter we'll cover LDAP – the protocol used to connect to the Membership Directory, and we'll also introduce ADSI – the Active Directory Service Interfaces.

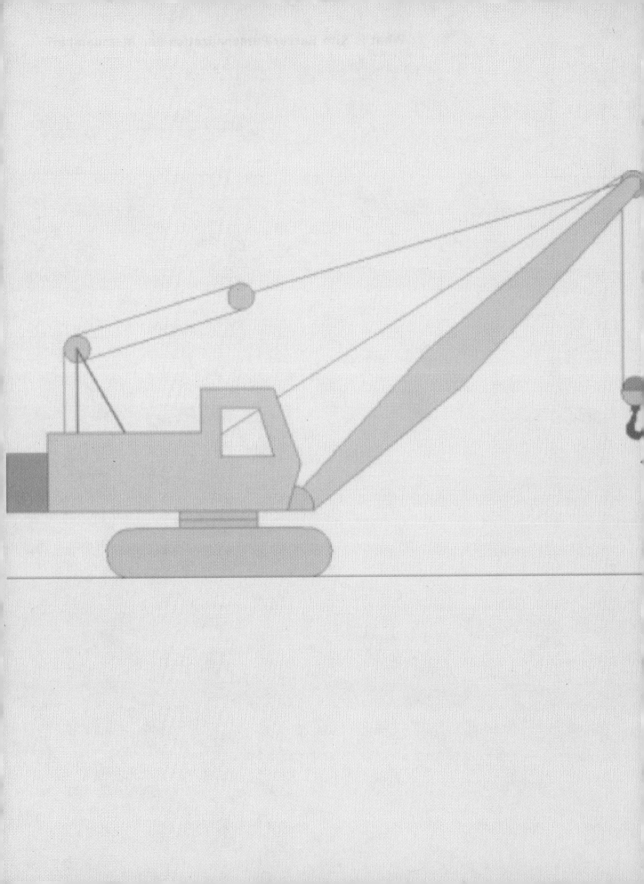

LDAP and Directory Services

Suppose you want to call your best friend on the 'phone, but you don't have the number handy. You can get the number by calling the operator. All you need to do is provide the operator with some basic information, such as your friend's name. The operator looks up the name in a namespace directory – the phone book – and tells you the 'phone number (or connects you directly). Here, the operator is playing the role of the interface between the caller and the directory.

Similarly, Personalization and Membership uses an operator to handle requests and supports the electronic equivalent of a phone book to look up the requests. In Site Server, this electronic phone book (or directory service) is called the **Membership Directory**, and the operator is the **Lightweight Directory Access Protocol** (**LDAP**) server. We use the LDAP service to ask the Membership Directory for information, in the same way you asked the operator for your friend's number.

Before we can effectively use Site Server Personalization and Membership, it's important that we have a sound understanding of the *why* and *how* of directory services and LDAP. So in this chapter, we'll take an in-depth look at what a directory is, and how LDAP is used to access a directory.

So here's what we'll be covering in this chapter:

- ❑ **What is a Directory Service?** We'll start this chapter with an in-depth look at what a directory service is. We'll also discuss the history of directory services and how they have evolved from proprietary systems to the standards based directory of X.500. Additionally, we'll discuss the Directory Access Protocol (DAP) and its evolution into the Lightweight Directory Access Protocol (LDAP).

- ❑ **Why Use LDAP and Directory Services?** It is critically important to understand why Site Server uses directory services and LDAP in preference to other data storage solutions (such as relational databases). We'll compare directory services and databases, and consider where each should be used and what should be stored in each type.

❑ **The Roles of a Directory Service – Some Examples.** In this section we'll look briefly at some of the different roles of a directory service.

❑ **The Membership Directory.** Here, we'll talk about Site Server's data store – the Membership Directory. In particular, we'll look at its object-oriented nature, its authentication configuration and some access considerations.

❑ **The LDAP Service.** We'll discuss the Site Server LDAP, which is the protocol used to access the Membership Directory; and we'll say a few words about the naming convention that it uses to impose on the organization of data within the Membership Directory. We won't provide all the specifics here, but we will see how the LDAP service can be distributed, we'll also talk about how the Membership Directory is accessed programmatically through Active Directory Service Interfaces (ADSI) and Active Directory providers.

By the end of this chapter, you should have a firm grasp on directory services and the LDAP protocol that is used to access directory services. We can apply this knowledge to our Site Server Personalization and Membership solution's design, architecture and implementation.

What is a Directory Service?

A **directory service** is a highly-organized resource that makes itself available on a computer network – in much the same way that a phone book can be used to look up a person's name or address. People can use a directory service to look up information on the network. However, there are three major differences between a printed directory and a directory service:

❑ **Updating.** In order to remain relevant, a printed directory must be regularly reprinted and redistributed. A digital directory service is a dynamic entity that exists only to grow, change, and adapt as its environment changes.

❑ **Flexibility of searching.** To facilitate searching, a printed directory has a fixed (and inflexible) index. A directory service on the other hand, can be searched for any value – this is done using LDAP queries, which are similar to SQL queries.

❑ **Security.** A directory service can take advantage of encryption and other security technologies to control access to the resources in the directory.

Many of the companies listed in *Fortune 1000* (the top 1000 companies in the world, as listed by *Fortune* magazine) use directory services as a central location in which to store corporate information that needs to be shared throughout the organization. However, many small businesses are also finding that directory services provide the necessary data storage model in which to share information across network boundaries – and the most notable network, of course, is the Internet.

In these business applications the directory services serve as the repositories, or knowledge centers, of the organization. They play an essential part in navigating the complex array of organizational data, available resources and user information. All this is made available on the LAN or WAN, and can be accessed by anyone who has the appropriate credentials for accessing and viewing the directory.

Let's take a quick look at the evolution of directory services and LDAP.

A Brief History of X.500 and LDAP

In the beginning there was **DAP** (**Directory Access Protocol**), and DAP was good. Unfortunately DAP was overweight, and didn't fit comfortably into the lean and mean architecture known as the Internet – or PCs either, for that matter. Fortunately, the University of Michigan had the foresight to put Directory Access Protocol on a diet. The result of this exercise was the **Lightweight Directory Access Protocol** (LDAP). We'll look at LDAP in a moment, but first take a step back in time.

The Birth of Directory Services

The lights flash and we're feeling dizzy... and we find ourselves back in the mid-1980s, in the good old days of terminals and mainframes! At this stage, application developers were starting to use network directories as a resource for individual applications. Applications that knew how to talk to the directory could request and receive information.

Sharing the data in these early directories was an oft-considered idea, but there was no real incentive or necessity to share the data. And even if data *was* to be shared, these early directories were highly proprietary and no common structure or protocol could be used to access them. Moreover, developers didn't necessarily need to share resources with one another because each system was entirely unique to its own situation; so although integration was a desired feature, it wasn't a high priority.

But as always, the demands of users were to change all that. The business needs and possible potential behind directories meant that users wanted to share their data with one another. Their idea was to share this common data store, and – as long as one had the necessary permissions – control over this directory could be distributed.

After a couple of standards bodies kicked this around, it eventually became a directory service called X.500, and the access methodology was Directory Access Protocol.

X.500 and the Directory Access Protocol (DAP)

The **X.500 directory service** is a set of standards for a directory service. It was developed in 1988 and modified again in 1993. Many larger organizations still use X.500 directories as the organizational tool of choice for the logical organization of corporate information.

The **Directory Access Protocol** (DAP) was the protocol set forth in the standard for X.500 for connecting to these directories. This protocol works well for large complex directories. However, smaller organizations found that DAP was a protocol that could not be implemented easily, because of its overall complexity:

- ❑ DAP requires proprietary networking software. Therefore, in order to understand how to optimize DAP network traffic, an organization needs the services of both a network technician *and* an engineer.
- ❑ DAP queries are very large. This translates to large network traffic and processing power requirements.
- ❑ X.500 encodes requests in a very complex manner. Consequently, it takes time to decode and encode these requests.
- ❑ DAP methods are complex, and hard to program against.

With the introduction of PCs and the Internet came the need for a directory and access protocol that was more flexible and easier to implement.

The Lightweight Directory Access Protocol (LDAP)

The University of Michigan designed the **Lightweight Directory Access Protocol** – usually known as LDAP. It's a lighter version of DAP, and is used to access an X.500-compliant directory. LDAP was designed to work over TCP/IP networks, and has become an Internet standard for accessing user information in directories.

Directory applications use LDAP to communicate with a directory in the same way that a web browser uses HTTP as the protocol communicating with a web server:

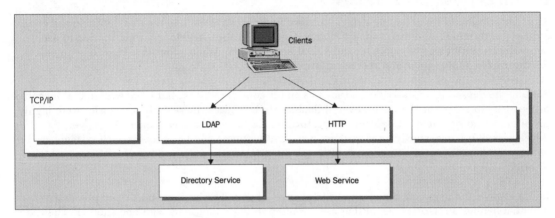

In both cases, TCP/IP is the network protocol used to communicate between different services (LDAP defaults to port 389, and HTTP defaults to port 80).

LDAP, like HTTP, is an open, standards-based protocol; and LDAP is supported by any directory service. This means that when a vendor, company or developer writes a directory service, they must architect it in such a fashion as to allow LDAP to communicate with that directory service. *Vice-versa*, if you're writing an application that wishes to use a directory service to store commonly-accessed information, then you must design the application architecture such that the application uses LDAP (or another object that abstracts the LDAP access) to communicate with a directory service.

> **LDAP is an IETF standard. To review the document LDAP IETF RFC-1777, see http//info.internet.isi.edu/in-notes/rfc/files/rfc/1777.txt.**

Why Use LDAP and Directory Services?

I was at a meeting in Redmond, WA, when a delegate posed this question to a speaker. Specifically, the question put to the speaker was, "Can you explain why I would want to use a Directory Service, instead of a normal relational database?" It's a very valid question – one that developers, program managers, and IT executives all face – and that's why I'm taking a section of this book to answer it.

So what *are* the most attractive benefits to be gained by employing a directory service and LDAP? We can summarize them as follows:

❑ **LDAP is an open, standards-based, cross-platform protocol.** Hence, any client or service that supports LDAP can use this technology to share information across network, operating systems, and application boundaries. Cross-platform interoperability means that two distinct operating systems – such as Windows NT and UNIX – can both use the same LDAP directory to share information.

❑ **The schema is exposed.** Although the schema is modified, the base schema remains the same for any application that uses LDAP and the directory. With the base schema of the directory, we define how entries are created in the directory and what their relationship to one another is.

❑ **The directory service is simply a database that is optimized for reads.** The directory is designed around the desire to provide storage for common information that does not change regularly. Since a large number of the requests for the directory are for data, a higher importance is placed on optimizing for reads.

❑ **Directory services and LDAP are designed for distribution.** Both the directory and the LDAP service are network services that can reside on different network segments and separate machines. The only requirement is that the machines can find each other and clients can find the LDAP service. What this really means is that directories are extremely scalable.

❑ **Directory services are designed with a highly organized structure.** The directory is designed around an object-oriented architecture that uses instances of objects and containers to organize information in a logical manner. You can compare it to the way that a phone book organizes data – objects are stored in containers, in the same way that the name *Fell* is stored under the letter *F* in a phone book. The structure of the directory and LDAP lends itself to simplified maintenance, scalability, and distribution.

❑ **Open security standards such as SSL.** Security standards such as Secure Sockets Layer can be used as long as the client knows how to use them. Using SSL enables us to provide a secure mechanism for exchanging information with the directory.

❑ **Many organizations are moving to directory services to organize and expose their data.** As the Internet grows and evolves, many organizations and software developers are using LDAP Services and directories to share information more easily.

We'll be expanding these points in this chapter, and throughout the rest of the book. But let's try to fashion an answer to the question that we posed at the beginning of this section.

Directory Services versus Databases

Directory services provide some useful services, such as hierarchical namespace organization, security services, and the role of a data store. Realistically, is it possible to use a relational database to solve most of these problems? Well, the answer is both "yes" and "no". If you want to develop a proprietary system that doesn't need to share information in an open format – or if you don't mind writing every application around a specific architecture – then a SQL database works just fine.

One might argue that a directory becomes a proprietary system once the schema has been modified for the organization. But this modified schema still relies on the underlying structure of the directory for organization. Entries may be organized in a highly specific manner, but the naming convention and logic behind any directory remains similar. This is not the same for a database, where the relationship between tables and records is specific to a particular problem.

Let's not fool ourselves: a directory service is (with apology to the purists) just a fancy database schema – it's optimized for reads, it's incredibly extensible, and it's easily distributed. This doesn't mean that directory services can entirely replace databases – indeed, there are some kinds of information that don't belong in a directory service at all. For example, large data resources and resources that change frequently should generally be stored in a database.

Databases

Specifically, as it applies to the Internet technologies, accessing a database isn't as easy as accessing a directory service. Most Internet-related database requests are made through ODBC, and this requires a data source name (DSN) to be configured in the ODBC applet on a server machine, or code that defines the data source programmatically.

Moreover, databases need to be secured, and most access to secured data is performed through database security methods with one logon id. In a highly secure environment, this doesn't work too well.

In addition, all access to system resources should be tracked, and logged. This can't be done effectively when a single username and password is used for the data access for each user. (There are further complications for users who access databases through badly-written server-side applications (e.g. ASP pages) that store username and password information in the ASP page! When these security holes are discovered – like the ::$DATA **hole** that was recently found in Internet Information Server 4.0 – this information is publicly available!)

> *To find out more about* ::$DATA *security issue, and other security-related issues with Microsoft products, see* http://www.microsoft.com/security.

From a security perspective, the ideal solution is to create multiple implementations of the same logon id for each user per application. However, this would mean maintaining user credentials for the application *and* the database, and would require some form of a broker account to access and perform the authentication check for the username and password provided by the user.

Directory Services

Directory services meet these needs. Multiple logon ids and passwords are not necessary since the directory can provide security services – such as credential authentication and password validation.

Additionally, directory services don't require ODBC Data Source Names, since they rely on the LDAP service to provide the protocol and use TCP/IP as the transport. The LDAP Services can be scattered around the network and have the necessary knowledge about the directory service that they serve and can provide the required services to the client.

This is truly the advantage of using a directory service versus a database. The Membership Directory is stored in a SQL Server (or Access) database, but we use LDAP – which is a standards-based protocol – to abstract the communications away from the database and let LDAP translate all requests into SQL.

Before we move on, consider an example. Instead of storing database information (the database name, and the usernames and passwords) in a web application's global.asa, why not store them in the directory? Then, the application becomes more 'extensible' – since the information used to access the data is abstracted from the application. If necessary, the data source information can be changed in a single place – and every client gets the effect. Access to the directory will be controlled through the member authentication system provided by Site Server Membership.

While we're evaluating directory services, there are a few other concepts that we should chew over.

A Directory Service for Personalization and Membership

In the first chapter, we covered some of the more common problems that are faced by developers who want to implement Personalization and Membership – and how it makes more sense to use a well-developed product rather than a home-grown solution. The motivation for this includes our preference for a scalable, extensible, open architecture that other applications can use across the internal network or the Internet.

Site Server Personalization and Membership uses a directory service – the **Membership Directory** – to store most of the user's 'personalization' information for the Personalization system. If we use the Membership Directory, we can gain all the advantages of Site Server's Personalization and Membership features – including member management tools, authentication mechanisms, and a slew of available tools and technologies used to manipulate the data.

The Membership Directory is available across the network to any application that supports LDAP.

> *We'll have a more formal introduction to the Membership Directory later on in this chapter, and we'll be discussing it throughout the book!*

Distributed Authentication

The LDAP Service does not have to reside on the machine requiring the LDAP services. In fact, the LDAP Service does not even have to be in the same sub-network. The LDAP Service can be used for authentication as long as it is available *somewhere* on the network.

Later on in this book (Chapter 11), we'll discuss a Windows NT NetShow Services plug-in (which is similar to an ISAPI filter for IIS) that authenticates members requesting a Windows Media Stream against a Membership LDAP Service that resides elsewhere on the network. In my experience, businesses and organizations use this filter to take advantage of distributed directory-based authentication. The LDAP Service can be exposed – and secured – as an available resource on the Internet in one location, and the Windows NT NetShow Services can use these LDAP Services to authenticate access to their resources – Windows Media Streams. For example, take a look at the diagram:

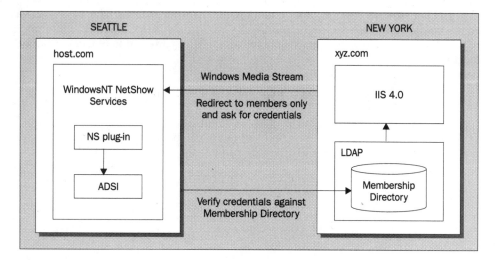

In this diagram, a request is made for a Windows Media Stream from the Internet and the Windows NT NetShow Services authenticates the request for this stream against a Membership Directory in another location.

This is different from the normal security model, in that all member and security information is provided on site – where it can be easily controlled and managed – while the content can be hosted off site.

Business Reasons

The Microsoft Corporation appears to be betting pretty heavily on the Active Directory in Windows NT 5.0. The **Active Directory** is the directory service that Windows NT 5.0 will use to store all users and most system information for Windows NT 5.0 domain architecture. Microsoft seems to think that using LDAP and directory services will not only improve the way you do your business, but make it simpler. It is, it seems, all part of the *Digital Nervous System* (that's another Microsoft Marketing buzzword).

Personally, I believe that this is a great decision – not least because a directory service is a great solution for sharing multiple resources over a network such as the Internet.

Moreover, database administrators don't like to open up their databases to the Internet, although there's a need for data stores to be made available to store the wealth of information collected on the Web. Directory services are perfectly suited for this role: they solve some of the basic information-sharing problems that organizations have, since they are intrinsically accessible on TCP/IP networks with the LDAP protocol.

This is not to say that databases will become obsolete; in fact, they still have a definite role in the provision of data storage on the Internet. Web site content and regularly-changing data is the kind of stuff that should be stored in a database, and not in the directory. Directory services provide a more flexible means for organizing and distributing user or application-specific information in a hierarchical data structure that can be distributed throughout the network.

For example, consider a web site that provides secured content to users. The site administrator should use a directory to provide the user and application-specific data – such as user security and credentials, and information about the database where the content is stored. The administrator should use a database to store large amounts of information – such as web site content. The information that describes the database – such as the data source name (DSN) or table and field name – can be stored in the directory.

What the Directory is Best Used For

The directory is best used as a data store for common information. It can also be used as a reference to access other information. This reference could be to the database where the information for the web content is stored or a listing of servers that can provide the required information.

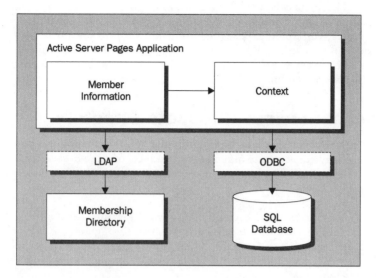

Using a database alongside a directory service is a great solution. Member information can be stored in the directory service, where it can be read and accessed and acted upon. Information that relates to the web site or is highly specific to the user – such as content, resumes, or portfolios – can be stored in the database and accessed via a key (such as a primary key in the database) stored as an attribute of the user in the directory.

> *In Appendix A, Wall Street Investing, members can specify what types of content they are most interested in through the page* MemberProfile.asp. *This information is then used to 'profile' the content towards the user. Users that select an interest in technology will be shown technology-specific data. This data is stored in a SQL Server 6.5 (or Access) database and is requested via the appropriate matching key in the type field for that data.*

Now that we've laid the foundation for directory services and the Lightweight Directory Access Protocol, let's take a look at some example roles of directory services.

The Roles of a Directory Service – Some Examples

A directory service can serve a variety of roles within the organization. In this section, we'll look at some of these possible roles.

A Corporate Employee Directory

Within organizations, the most common use of a directory service is as a store for employee data. The directory service has a highly organized structure – hence, it easily lends itself to the personnel charts of large and small organizations. This simple but flexible design allows for division of data into logical categories that represent the structure of the organization. We could easily accomplish the same thing with a database, but we would also have to implement security mechanisms and any application wishing to use the data would have to be designed around the proprietary design of the database.

For example, consider a business called DirectSystems, Inc., which has offices in Dallas, New York and London. This organization can create representations of these branches within the directory. By opening the Dallas branch, you would expose the staff details that are specific to the Dallas office, arranged into containers that represent the company's organizational structure. By opening the New York branch, you could expose the same organizational arrangement; but now it contains staff details that are specific to the New York office.

An Organizational Services/Products Directory

Any organization exists to provide products or services, and this information can also be represented in a directory. The directory can logically organize the products that the organization sells, and the services that the company provides – and it can share this information with external and internal users.

Let's consider the case of DirectSystems, Inc., again. We can allow the Dallas office to connect to the organizational products and services directory (which is shared throughout the organization) to find the product inventory levels among the other divisional branches. If certain stocks are available in the London branch, they could be shipped to the Dallas branch and made available there – all based on the information in the directory.

We can also allow users to consult the directory – for example, to find out about available delivery methods and details. The advantage of the directory (over a database) is that the information is designed to be accessible over the Internet and across multiple platforms and applications.

Directory Integration

The directory can easily be integrated with any application; we simply need to ensure that the application knows how to communicate with the directory. The application and the directory will communicate via LDAP. All directory services support LDAP for the purposes of communication: so if an application needs to communicate with the directory service, then it must *also* support LDAP:

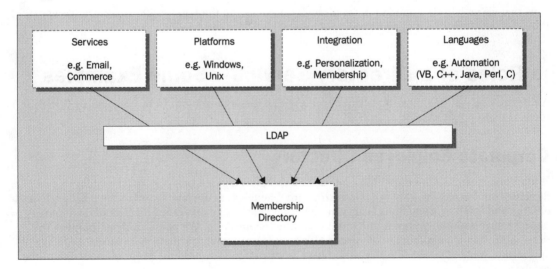

Site Server provides a high level of integration between the Membership Directory and Internet Information Server 4.0. IIS 4.0 uses the Membership Directory to store information about users. Then, if (for example) a developer needs to change the behavior or security within the IIS 4.0 web server, he does so by changing the information contained in the Membership Directory.

Windows NT NetShow Services can make use of a directory to authenticate users: we'll cover integration of the Membership Directory with Windows Media Technologies in Chapter 11. We'll include a C++ Windows NT NetShow Services plug-in, that can be used to authenticate Windows Media streams against the Site Server Membership Directory.

Corporate Security Services

Organizations can use a directory service to provide corporate security services. User credentials can be stored in a directory that is made accessible throughout the organization. Then, when a user starts up an application, the application can communicate with the directory to authenticate the user (i.e. to ask whether the user's credentials are valid), and to authorize the user (i.e. to ask whether the user has the appropriate permissions for accessing the requested information).

The Site Server Membership Directory provides such a service. The Membership Authentication portion of the Site Server Personalization and Membership directory in Membership Authentication mode stores all user credentials in the directory.

> *There's more about directory security – as it applies to the Membership Directory – in Chapter 13.*

Two key facts that we've established so far are as follows: first, that directory service is a highly organized structure that we can use to organize information and provide secured generic storage mechanisms. Second, any application that wants to communicate with a directory service must do so via LDAP. Later in this chapter, we'll look at LDAP, but before that we need to delve into the world of the Membership Directory.

The Membership Directory

Although Microsoft entered the directory service market fairly late in the game, the expectations are high. Developers and organizations are anxiously awaiting the Active Directory, which will make its debut in Windows NT 5.0. This is not to say that Microsoft has not been in the directory service arena; but the Active Directory will be a super-set of the features found in the directory services of Exchange 5.5 and Site Server.

The directory service provided by Site Server 3.0 – the most recent directory Microsoft has released, and half the topic of this book – is the **Membership Directory**. The Site Server Membership Directory, like most directories, provides a central and open standards data store for user information. This directory is used by the Site Server Personalization and Membership system (and other applications) to share information – rather than allowing each application to persist its own data in a proprietary data store.

The primary role of Site Server's Membership Directory is to store the user data used by the Membership and Personalization system. This data is made up of email addresses, phone numbers, and other common attributes that are used to store information about users. Moreover, custom attributes and classes can be created in addition to the predefined attributes and classes, to provide extended capabilities for the Membership Directory. (So, if your organization's marketing department wants the Site Server Personalization and Membership system to start tracking member demographic information – say, favorite coffee brand – it's easily done by creating a new custom attribute which is added to the existing list of attributes allowed by the member class.)

The Membership Directory can be used to store other information, such as network resources and database information. We've learned that directory services can also contain lists of physical resources on the network and the services that these resources provide. This knowledge can be exposed to applications and users, as a way of discovering information when it is needed. In fact, storing resource information in the directory is a great idea!

In fact, sharing resources through the Membership Directory is easy. For example, databases that store the content for large sites usually store access credentials and database schema information in some sort of global resource file for the site (the `global.asa` *in IIS scenarios). Rather than storing this information in the global resource file, it can be stored in the Membership Directory – where only those users with the appropriate security permissions will ever be exposed to the information.*

Some Common Uses

The Membership Directory can store data for any number of applications, but is most often used for the following types of data:

- ❑ **Member properties.** These are also known as attributes. Every member instance has attributes that represent items to be tracked for the member. These attributes include username, password, first name, last name and any other relevant information. Custom attributes can also be created and tracked for members.

- ❑ **Member permissions.** Members' permissions only apply within the Membership Directory. Every item in the Membership Directory has an Access Control List (ACL): the ACL defines the permissions that different users and groups have to the resource.

- ❑ **Groups.** The Membership Directory supports one of two authentication modes: Membership or Windows NT (we'll learn about these later). Under the former, the Membership Directory contains NT shadow groups that provide an abstraction for real Windows NT groups, whose security IDs are used to provide the security context for the user when accessing Windows NT system information. Under the latter, members are real NT users that exist in the Windows NT Security Accounts Manager (SAM), and directory groups are also real groups that exist in the SAM.

- ❑ **Microsoft NetMeeting.** Microsoft NetMeeting can use the Membership Directory for accessing the users that are on-line. NetMeeting looks for users in the ou=dynamic container of the Membership Directory. (We haven't formally introduced containers yet – for now, it's enough to understand that a container is used to 'contain' data. The ou=dynamic container persists its data in RAM on the machine providing the LDAP Service, and allows for requests to be served much more quickly.)

You've probably noticed that we've started using the term **member** to refer to a user in the directory. This makes sense, because the Membership directory uses an instance of the member class to store each member's information. Members and membership make up the primary use of the Membership Directory – hence the name!

Object-Oriented Design of Membership Directory

The Membership Directory is an **object-oriented** service. An **object** is a collection of one-or-more pieces of data (called **properties**, or **attributes**) and elements of functionality (called **methods**). Central to this, of course, is the concept of a class. A **class** is like a template, in that it describes just what an object should look like – that is, it determines exactly what attributes and methods each object should contain.

For example, one of the most commonly used objects in the Membership Directory is the member object – each member object represents a real-life site member. Let's say, for the sake of argument, that every member object contains a username, real name, a unique ID, address string, phone number and email address – this list of attributes is dictated by the member class. When we create a member object, we are taking an instance of the member class – we give the new object a name, and fill its attributes with values. We can create lots of member objects and they are all similar because they have the same attributes, although their attributes probably contain different values!

> *If you're not familiar with object-oriented design, then there are many introductions to the subject – you could try Wrox's* Beginning Object Oriented Analysis and Design with C++ *(ISBN 1861001339).*

The Membership Directory also has classes that represent other entities, such as containers.

mustContain Attributes and mayContain Attributes

So an object is an instance of a class, and the class defines exactly what attributes the object should contain. The attributes themselves come in two varieties – mustContain and mayContain:

❑ A **mustContain** attribute is an attribute that *must* always be populated, in every instance of the class.

❑ A **mayContain** attribute is an attribute that *may* be populated at any time, or never.

Some classes are predefined, and all their attributes are already set to either mustContain or mayContain. Other classes (such as the member class) are created when the Membership directory is created (see Chapter 7), and we can determine whether the attributes of these classes are mustContain or mayContain when we create the class.

For example, each of our member objects (in the example above) have six attributes. Of these, it's likely that the username, real name, a unique ID and email address will be mustContain attributes, while the address string and phone number will be mayContain attributes.

The attributeSchema Class and the classSchema Class

This is where it starts to get fun! As we've already mentioned, every entity in the Membership directory is an object. This also means that every attribute is an object, and every class is an object. In fact, this makes good sense.

Let's focus on the attributes first. One attribute looks very similar to another – that is, every attribute has a name; it has a syntax; it's either single-valued or it's not. Thus, it makes sense that an attribute is created as an instance of a class – the attributeSchema class. The attributeSchema class is used to define attributes in the cn=Schema, ou=Admin, o=*[organization]* container. When we modify a class by creating a new attribute (see the **New Attribute Wizard** in Chapter 7), we actually create an instance of the attributeSchema class and add values to its properties.

The mustContain properties (or attributes) of an attributeSchema object include:

❑ **cn** – The common name (the name of the entry)
❑ **attributeSyntax** – Determines what values this attribute can contain
❑ **isSearchable** – Boolean; dictates whether or not searches can be performed on this attribute
❑ **isSingleValued** – Boolean; dicatates whether or not this attribute can hold multiple values

Similarly, one class looks very much like another – in the sense that every class has a name; it has at least one mustContain attribute; it's either a container, or it's not. So, every class in the Membership Directory is created as an instance of the classSchema class. Every instance of the classSchema class contains the following mustContain attributes:

❑ **cn** – The common name (the name of our new class)
❑ **isContainer** – Boolean; determines whether or not the class can act as a container for other classes
❑ **isSecurityPrincipal** – a special attribute that dictates whether or not the class can be treated as a security principal on a resource in the Membership Directory
❑ **mustContain** – defines the mustContain attributes of this class
❑ **possSuperiors** – defines the possible containers that might contain instances of this class
❑ **rdnAttID** – the naming attribute of our class (it's the relative distinguished name attribute ID). It must be one of the mustContain attribute types of the class and is treated as the index in a container. The must common rdnAttID we'll see is cn.

With all that said, object-oriented design in the Membership Directory is fairly simple. In particular, there is no object inheritance. For now, we'll move on to look at how information is stored in the Membership Directory.

Directory Storage

The data storage medium for representing the Membership Directory comes in the form of **Microsoft SQL Server 6. 5**, or SQL Server 7.0 (with **Service Pack 1**), or **Microsoft Access**. LDAP requests are translated into this data structure by the Microsoft LDAP Service, which is shipped as part of the Site Server suite.

The Underlying Data Structure

If an application needs to use the directory as an information storage resource, then it should support Active Directory Service Interfaces (ADSI) and access the directory through LDAP. This is transparent to the users and applications that use or provide services for the Membership Directory.

In Chapter 3, we'll take a look at the tables and relationships that the database representing the directory uses.

Don't Modify the Data Directly

Since the underlying structure of the Membership Directory is a database, it's reasonable to expect that this database could be accessed directly – e.g. for services using ADO or some other database access technology. Though this is possible, it is definitely not recommended. In fact, direct modification of the database could potentially constitute a huge security hole – because directory permissions and SQL Server permissions are not equal. If a user or application gains direct access to the SQL Server database representing the Membership Directory, there's no telling what kind of security issues can arise.

It's tempting to modify or remove tables and indexes that we think aren't being used – but again, this could be disastrous for the directory. If it is necessary to delete an item from the Membership Directory, then this deletion should be done in one of two ways:

❑ Through the Membership Directory Manager – a Microsoft Management Console snap-in which we'll cover in Chapter 7.
❑ Through code that uses Active Directory Service Interfaces (ADSI) – which we'll cover in Chapter 9.

The reason for this is that since the LDAP is responsible for maintaining the relationships, modifying the database could damage data integrity or the relationships that tables and data are used to represent.

Viewing the Data Model

Having delivered this stern warning, it isn't a bad idea to *view* the tables in the Membership Directory, so that you can get a better understanding of how information is stored and how optimizations can be made while still using Active Directory Service Interfaces to access the directory. But beware – *don't* modify anything directly! In Chapter 3's *Advanced Concepts* section, we'll take a look at these databases, what they store, and the relationships between them.

Authentication Configuration

The Membership Directory can be configured in one of two authentication modes: **Membership authentication** or **Windows NT (Intranet) authentication**. We must configure the authentication mode when we create the Membership Directory – and our choice of authentication configuration affects the way security is managed within the site, so we need to understand the differences in advance. We'll go into much more detail as to the differences and nuances of the Membership and Windows NT authentication modes in Chapter 13, but for now – so that we can start creating directories – we'll hit the highlights of both.

Windows NT Authentication

Windows NT authentication takes advantage of Site Server Personalization, but does not make use of the membership features (such as storing member credentials in the Membership Directory). In Windows NT authentication, all the member credentials (which are used to verify the member) are stored in **the Windows NT Security Accounts Manager (SAM)**, and *associated* with a corresponding account in the Membership Directory. This corresponding account is used to store personalization information (e.g. the user's email address or favorite web site) that can be stored as part of the user's profile.

All access to the system or resources is done via the Windows NT user's account. Windows NT authentication is based on the existing system. In contrast, Membership authentication uses impersonation and stores the credentials used to gain access in the Membership Directory.

Membership Authentication

Unlike Windows NT authentication, **Membership authentication** stores all member credentials – username and password – in an instance of a `member` object, stored in the **Membership Directory**. Members live in the Membership Directory and cannot log in to the Windows NT system – but they can authenticate against the directory and gain access to Windows NT resources through impersonation.

Site Server's primary use of members is for the integration of Membership with IIS 4.0. When a user requests a resource from an IIS 4.0 web that is protected by Membership authentication, the user is prompted for a login. This login is performed using cookies, HTML forms, Basic/Clear Text or Distributed Password Authentication (this is similar to NTLM authentication). The credentials given by the user are compared against those stored in the Membership Directory. If the credentials match, the user will be 'mapped' to the impersonation account (the default impersonation account is called the MemProxyUser). The MemProxyUser is a special Windows NT account, that is used solely for impersonation purposes – in much the same way that the IUSR_*[server_name]* anonymous impersonation account is used for IIS anonymous access.

Resource Security

In Membership authentication mode, users gain access to Windows NT- and NTFS-protected resources through group permissions. The member belongs to certain groups within the Membership Directory – these groups correspond to actual Windows NT groups in the SAM. The MemProxyUser is given the security ids (SIDs) of these groups, and allowed access to resources. If the user requests a protected resource whose security matches the access type requested (and the SID of the thread) then access is allowed. This is based on the standard Windows NT security system – to read more see Chapter 13.

NTFS is the Windows NT File System.

Site Server Membership provides for a potentially large user base 'living' in the Membership Directory, with one impersonation account in the SAM (and, of course, the additional NT groups needed to control access to resources).

This "potentially large user base" could consist of millions of members, each of which has its own account in the Membership Directory. If the user base is huge, then it's possible to ease the system by providing services through multiple machines, and multiple LDAP services – each web server would have its own MemProxyUser Windows NT account. We'll talk more specifically about the scalability of this system in Chapter 4.

Access and Security for the Membership Directory

Access to the Membership Directory is gained in one of two ways – either via an **anonymous account** or via a **valid member account**. Security configurations will vary, depending on the configuration of the directory (that is, whether we chose Windows NT authentication or Membership authentication).

Although most architectural issues of your site should be planned before you build your site, security considerations can be implemented at any time *after* you've got the site up-and-running. Having said that, it's a good idea to ensure that your Membership Directory is properly secured *before* it's used in a production environment! To read more about securing the Membership Directory, see Chapter 13.

Access under Windows NT Authentication

If the Membership Directory employs Windows NT authentication, we must gain access to it in one of two ways: we either provide the **credentials of a valid Windows NT user**, or we provide **no credentials**. If no credentials are provided, then the Windows NT `LDAP_ANONYMOUS` account is used to access the directory.

Under Windows NT authentication mode, there are only four groups that have access to the Membership Directory:

Windows NT User Groups	Description
SiteServer Administrators	Users in this group have full permissions to all Site Server 3.0 secured items – including the Membership Directory.
SiteServer Directory Administrators	Users in this group have full permissions to the Membership Directory.
SiteServer Knowledge Administrators	Users in this group have full permissions to the Membership Directory
Everyone	This group contains all valid Windows NT users.

> The Membership Directory should be 'secured' before the site is in general usage. This involves removing the Access Control Entry (ACE) that allows "full permissions" to members of the **Everyone** group (i.e. every user!). Among other things, this process ensures that members of the **Everyone** group don't automatically have access to the Membership Directory. A full discussion of this is contained in Chapter 13.

Following this 'securing' of the site, any user or group that needs access to the Membership Directory must be in one or more of the Windows NT groups listed above (excluding **Everyone**, of course).

Access under Membership Authentication

Membership authentication also allows access to the Membership Directory for both known and unknown (anonymous) accounts. If the user provides **no credentials**, then a member account is used to provide anonymous access to the directory.

When a new Membership-authenticated Membership Directory is created, the only groups to have access to the Membership Directory are the following Windows NT groups:

Windows NT User Groups	Description
Administrators	This is the main Windows NT Administrators group.
SiteServer Administrators	Users in this group have full permissions to all Site Server 3.0 secured items – including the Membership Directory.
SiteServer Directory Administrators	Users in this group have full permissions to the Membership Directory
SiteServer Knowledge Administrators	Users in this group have full permissions to the Membership Directory

In addition, there are just two Membership groups:

Membership User Groups	Description
AdminGroup	This group is a group in the Membership Directory that is granted full permissions within the directory. Members of this group should be Membership Directory members that will need to administer the Membership Directory but doesn't need an actual Windows NT account.
Public	This group is similar to the Windows NT Everyone group, except that it represents all members in the Membership Directory.

As we described above, the Membership Directory should be 'secured' before the site is in general usage (that is, the Access Control Entry (ACE) that allows "full permissions" to members of the Everyone group should be removed). This ensures, among other things, that members of the Windows NT Everyone group don't automatically have access to the Membership Directory. We're deferring full discussion of this until Chapter 13.

The beauty of Membership authentication is that the users – known as members in the Membership Directory – don't need to exist in the Windows NT SAM. This means that members of our site don't have a Windows NT user account on our system. If a member were to somehow gain access to the server providing the various Internet services – e.g. through PC Anywhere or RAS – they can't use their member account to gain access to the Windows NT system.

The four Windows NT Groups (i.e. excluding the Everyone and Public groups) are given access to the directory, so that members who belong to these groups gain both the Windows NT ACEs and the ACEs for the Membership Directory.

The LDAP Service

We now have a clear picture of what the Membership Directory is used for; but so far we've skirted around the issue of how to access it. We know that LDAP is used – but what provides the services for using LDAP against the directory? The Membership Directory itself is only a data structure – it's the **LDAP service** that represents the functionality of this data structure.

When servicing requests, Site Server Personalization and Membership uses the LDAP service to communicate with the Membership Directory. For example, Membership uses the LDAP service (in Membership authentication mode) to verify credentials – all member credentials (username and passwords) are stored in the directory. Personalization uses the LDAP service to retrieve (and to set) member attribute values.

LDAP Service Network Location

The Site Server LDAP Service can live anywhere on the network, as long as it can communicate with the Membership Directory and be available for clients:

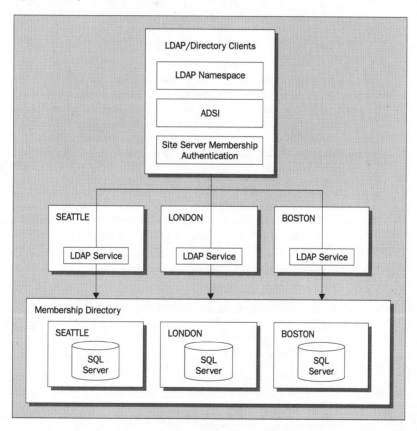

There's plenty in this figure that we haven't covered yet, but the point is to illustrate that applications, LDAP services and the Membership Directory can all exist and work together location-independently.

Attribute Naming Prefixes

As you flicked through this book, or through other Site Server documentation, you probably noticed that the names of objects are often written with a prefix – c=, o=, ou= or cn=. These prefixes are labels that indicate the types of attributes that are being used to identify these objects. This naming convention is enforced in the X.500 directory standard, and is supported by LDAP.

When we come to look at the internal structure of a Membership Directory (Chapter 3), we'll see that the directory's architecture is given in the form of a Directory Information Tree (DIT). The DIT is a hierarchy of containers and leaves – in order to access objects in the Membership Directory, we specify the unique path that is determined by the DIT hierarchy. The DIT also supports the X.500 directory standard, and we'll see that these prefixes are used to label the entries of the DIT.

The four common attribute prefixes, used in the standard directory structure, are:

Prefix	Notes
c= (country)	In most directories, c=*[country]* is the root container. When we come to create our Site Server Membership Directory, we could build a c=*[country]* container near to the root of the directory's DIT.
o= (organization)	However, the default root container of the Membership Directory's DIT is o=*[organization]*.
ou= (organizational unit)	ou=*[organizational_unit]* is a type of container, that is used to organize all containers underneath o=*[organization]*. In this book, we'll be making particular use of an organizational unit container called ou=Members – this container is part of the default Membership Directory DIT, and is used to contain member objects. We can create sub-containers of an ou=*[organizational_unit]* container. For example, we can subdivide all the members in our ou=Members container, into three sub-containers – say, ou=Marketing, ou=Sales and ou=Production.
cn= (common name)	The cn=*[common_name]* is the common name of an object, and is unique within its container. It's also known as the relative distinguished name (RDN). These objects are usually (but not always) leafs.

Let's have a quick illustrative example. Consider the following (very simple) DIT:

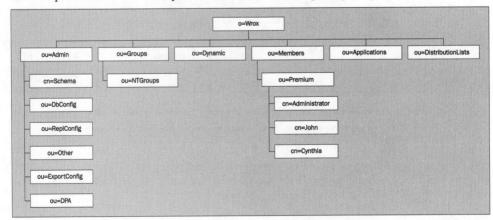

In this example,

❑ The LDAP path to the root container is LDAP://localhost/o=Wrox or simply LDAP://localhost
❑ The LDAP path to the members container is LDAP://localhost/o=Wrox/ou=members
❑ The LDAP path to the member cynthia is
LDAP://localhost/o=Wrox/ou=members/ou=premium/cn=cynthia

We'll talk more about DITs, LDAP paths and namespaces in Chapter 3.

Programmatic Access to the Membership Directory

How does Site Server Membership retrieve information from the Membership Directory? We've said that the Membership Directory must always be accessed via LDAP, but how does LDAP fit into the system?

Active Directory Service Interfaces

Site Server uses **Active Directory Service Interfaces** (**ADSI**) to communicate with the Membership Directory. ADSI is a set of well-defined application programming interfaces (APIs), which are designed for accessing OLE-Directory Service (OLE-DS) data sources. ADSI is based on Microsoft's implementation of Open Directory Services Interfaces (ODSI) and – of course – communicates with the Membership Directory using LDAP.

ADSI is comparable to ODBC – Open Database Connectivity – which is an open standard (originally developed by Microsoft) that allows transparent access to data stores such as databases. Like ODBC, ADSI provides a 'generic' view or means of accessing a data store (in our case, a directory) either locally or across the network. (In fact, ODBC data sources can be accessed via ADSI, because the objects that provide the ADSI interfaces can be configured to 'read' ODBC data sources and can treat information as though it came from a directory service.) One notable difference is that ADSI uses LDAP as the protocol for communications, but ODBC does not.

The Active User Object

Where do these ADSI interfaces live? Site Server uses an **Active Directory provider**, called the **Active User Object** (**AUO**), to take care of this. The AUO is a server-side COM object, and (for the purposes of this discussion) does two things: it implements the functionality that can determine the context of the user, and it provides the ADSI interfaces that bind to the Membership Directory.

What makes the AUO particularly important to Personalization and Membership is that it works in conjunction with the Membership authentication system to pass context of the user accessing a Membership-enabled IIS 4.0 web server. Using this context, the AUO can bind to the correct user in the correct Membership Directory – either Windows NT or Membership authentication modes.

What Site Server LDAP Does (and Doesn't) Support

As you can see, LDAP is a crucial part of Site Server's mechanism for accessing the Membership Directory. Site Server's own version of LDAP supports the following capabilities

❑ **Adding** entries to the Membership Directory
❑ **Modifying** existing Membership Directory entries
❑ **Deleting** entries from the Membership Directory

❏ **Dynamic data** – that is, storing entries dynamically in a node of the directory service that is in memory
❏ **Referrals** to other directory services
❏ **Rich Search Filters** – we can build complex search queries to search the Membership Directory
❏ **Standard Authentication and Access Control** – users accessing the directory are authenticated before gaining entry, and access control for these users can be controlled on attributes, containers, and entries specific to members

There are also a few things that Site Server LDAP doesn't support:

❏ **Client session control** – this allows clients to do a search and then order by a particular attribute. In Site Server, client RecordSets support paging; but the client is still responsible for sorting the order of entries returned from an LDAP query
❏ **Connectionless LDAP over UDP** – Site Server LDAP does not support connections to directory services using User Datagram Protocol (UDP). UDP is a connectionless network transport protocol that is a non-guaranteed protocol. UDP is unlike TCP – which guarantees that *either* data will be delivered *or* an error will be reported

Modifying the LDAP Service

The LDAP service can be configured in one of three ways:

❏ Via the graphical tool provided by Site Server Personalization and Membership Microsoft Management Console Snap-in (see Chapter 6)
❏ Through the command line tools that use COM objects, provided by Site Server, to administer the LDAP Service programmatically. This is known as PMAdmin.vbs
❏ Programmatically, through custom code using the same COM objects that are employed by PMAdmin.vbs

We'll look at the command line implementation of this in Appendix B and review some of the objects used in Chapter 12.

If you want to do more background reading on LDAP, you could look at the IETF RFC-1777, which is available at http://info.internet.isi.edu/in-notes/rfc/files/rfc1777.txt.

Summary

Together, directory services and LDAP provide an open, non-proprietary solution for sharing information across network, platform, and application boundaries. We've seen that we can think of the operator–phone book scenario as an analogy of how directory services and LDAP work together to provide access to services: the LDAP service is like an operator that allows applications to consult the directory.

Here's a summary of other main points of the chapter:

- ❑ A directory service is a highly organized structure that we can use to organize information and provide secured generic storage mechanisms through LDAP. If an application wants to use a directory service for storing or reading information, then the application must support LDAP.

- ❑ DAP is a protocol that was used as the standard for gaining access to X.500-standard directory services. LDAP is an improved, lightweight protocol – developed by the University of Michigan – that has superceded DAP as the protocol of choice for accessing directory services. We compared LDAP and HTTP, showing how both use TCP/IP to access services on directories and web services respectively.

- ❑ LDAP is an open, standards based, cross-platform protocol. Both LDAP and directory services are designed for implementation over distributed systems.

- ❑ The Membership Directory is an object-oriented system, whose underlying directory structure is a database. There are two authentication configuration options for the Membership Directory – Windows NT authentication and Membership authentication – these authentication types dictate where membership credentials are stored.

- ❑ Site Server's LDAP service provides the front-end to the Membership Directory. The LDAP service is available from anywhere on the network.

- ❑ The X.500 standard defines certain naming attributes that are used to provide organization within the directory.

- ❑ Site Server uses objects which implement ADSI interfaces to communicate with the Membership Directory, via the LDAP protocol.

Now we can move on to look at the internal structure and architecture of the Membership directory itself.

Personalization and Membership Architecture

The architecture of Site Server Personalization and Membership is immensely flexible, and can be adapted to meet the demands of nearly every site. For example, the target use of your web site will affect the ideal security configurations: if your web site serves internal customers, you can choose to build your Membership Directory with Windows NT (Intranet) authentication – this allows you to build on your existing Windows NT Security knowledge. However, if the goal is to provide services on the Internet, then you can build your Membership Directory around Membership authentication – so that you can still take advantage of your Windows NT Security knowledge, without having to give a Windows NT account to each Internet user.

In this chapter, we'll look at the key aspects of Site Server P&M architecture. The knowledge presented here (and in all of these early chapters) is crucial to understanding how your application can be scaled to meet the expected traffic demands. In addition, we'll talk about the IIS configuration and the debugging configurations that are used in the remainder of the book.

In this chapter we'll be covering the following topics:

- ❑ **A High-Level Overview of P&M Architecture.** We'll begin the chapter by looking at the broad picture of Site Server Personalization and Membership architecture. One concept that we'll focus on is the number of dependencies that exist within a Personalization and Membership system.
- ❑ **The Directory Information Tree.** Next, we'll consider the Directory Information Tree (DIT). The DIT is a representation of all the information in the Membership Directory as a hierarchical structure, or tree, of objects.
- ❑ **Data Caching.** Site Server Personalization and Membership uses a number of services, and each service provides data caching to some degree or other. By understanding how the caching system works, we'll be able to design a more robust and scalable system.

❑ **Internet Applications Development Strategy.** After reviewing the architecture, the DIT and the various forms of data caching, we'll spend some time fine-tuning IIS 4.0. We'll also discuss some development strategies and tips, and end with a short discussion of COM.

❑ **Advanced Concepts.** Here, we'll look at the database tables that represent the Membership Directory.

The Personalization and Membership architecture isn't trivial, but by the end of this chapter you should be clearer how the system works to provide services for managing user relationships. Let's start with the 50,000-foot view of Personalization and Membership architecture.

A High-Level Overview of P&M Architecture

From way, way up above, the architecture of Personalization and Membership is quite simple. The view of the engineers, down in the trenches slinging the code and putting the pieces together, is rather more complex – but it makes sense to take a look at the architecture from a distance, to get a better understanding of what's happening in a Personalization and Membership scenario. Take a look at the following diagram:

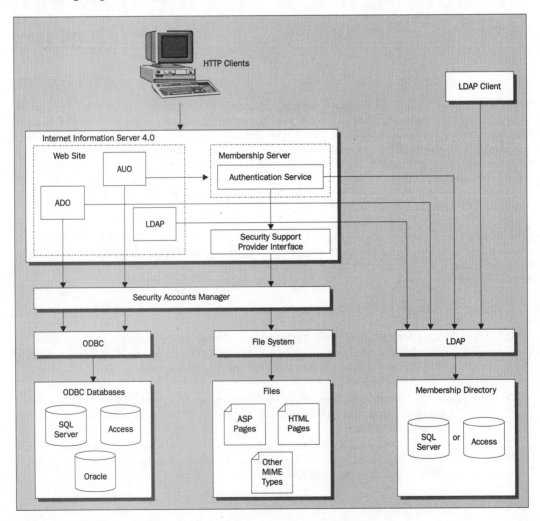

Site Server Personalization and Membership is an n-tier solution. Site Server uses three tiers to represent the distinct separation between the presentation (HTTP browser) layer, the business logic (COM, IIS, Site Server) layer and the data storage (SQL Server, Membership Directory) layer. An n-tier architecture allows the system to be extensible and segregated – each layer is responsible for its own specific set of duties, and distinct layers can exist on different machines.

Our three-tier architecture is divided up as follows:

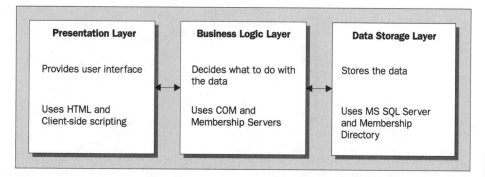

The **presentation layer** is what the client uses to access the system. In Personalization and Membership, the presentation level usually comes in the form of a web browser, which displays information to the client. The client uses the browser to communicate with the business rules, and (indirectly) with the data itself.

The **business logic layer** includes services such as Internet Information Server and the Site Server LDAP Server, and COM objects such as Active Data Objects (ADO) and the Active User Object (AUO). The objects and services provide the means of accessing and formatting the data for the presentation layer.

The **data storage layer** contains the repository for our information – it might be the Membership Directory, Message Queuing or databases. The data itself has no business logic (e.g. stored procedures, etc) built into it – instead, the data relies upon the business logic layer to determine where and how the data should be acted upon.

Let's take a more detailed look at these three layers, and how they apply to Site Server Personalization and Membership.

The Presentation Layer

The presentation layer in our architecture is an HTTP client, such as Internet Explorer or Netscape Navigator (although some pieces of Site Server require IE 4.0 for best viewing). The responsibility of the presentation layer is simply to provide the user with a means of interacting with the business logic layer. We rely on the capabilities of the browser to format and display information (such as HTML, DHTML and client side scripting) that is provided by the business logic layer.

Avoiding Client-Side Business Logic

In some environments (such as Client/Server), some basic distributed client processing is acceptable. In such an environment, enabling client-side processing (through Java applets or ActiveX controls, for example) will result in a better service for clients.

In an n-tier architecture, however, we should be careful that we don't rely on the presentation layer to handle business logic functionality. The following diagrams illustrate the problems that can arise when the client is given business layer functionality:

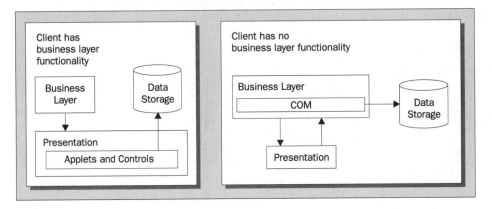

By allowing the client this level of interaction, the rules of n-tier architecture are broken. The potential problems are immediately clear. From the administrator's point of view, the client is the only variable in the equation. The danger lies in the dependency upon the client: if you don't know what form the client will take, then you can't predict how it will behave. Developers should never rely on client-side utilities (such as ActiveX controls or Java applets) that have the responsibility of providing business logic, if the client has the option to refuse them.

Even if you monitor every single browser that enters your site, there are problems in store. If the code or business logic changes, then each client must be updated to properly apply the new logic – which is highly inconvenient (if not impossible) to implement.

The good news is that, in Personalization and Membership, there is *no* client-side business logic processing. All of the business logic objects are server-side COM objects that depend upon user-interactions via Active Server Pages (ASP) or Internet Information Server (IIS). And, as we'll learn in later chapters, we can use these COM objects in Visual Basic or C++ to build other applications.

The Business Logic Layer

Site Server's business logic layer consists of code provided by Site Server, code written by the developer, and various services that are necessary for communicating with the Membership Directory. It's the business layer that really reflects the differences between Site Server's two authentication modes: Membership authentication and Windows NT authentication.

The Business Logic Layer under Membership Authentication

In a Personalization and Membership site, authentication is the first thing to occur. The following diagram illustrates the process:

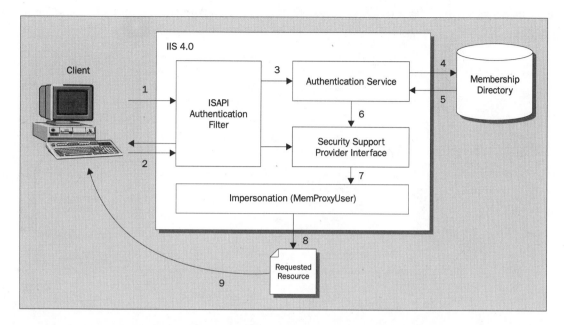

In Membership authentication mode, an ISAPI authentication filter traps requests (1), and attempts to authenticate (2). The Authentication filter then hands the user's authentication credentials to the authentication service (3), which attempts to bind (4) to an object representing the member in the Membership Directory. If this fails then authentication is denied. If it succeeds (5), the thread servicing the request is switched by the Security Support Provider Interface (6) to the context of the Windows NT impersonation account (7) – the default impersonation account is called **MemProxyUser** – and Windows NT security services take over for authorization (8). Finally, if authorization is approved, the requested document is supplied to the client (9).

> **Note the difference between authentication and authorization.**
> **Authentication (Step 5) is the act of confirming the user's identity.**
> **Authorization (Step 8) determines whether or not the authenticated user is**
> **permitted to access the requested resources.**

If the user is properly authenticated (Step 5) then he is given a unique Security ID (SID), as the **MemProxyUser** Windows NT account. In addition, the authenticated user will belong to certain groups in the Membership Directory; and the **MemProxyUser** is assigned the SIDs of those Windows NT groups that map to these Membership Directory groups. This is known as **group impersonation**. The SID mappings are performed through the Security Support Provider Interfaces that impersonate users coming through IIS 4.0. Once the appropriate SID token is generated, the thread (on which the process is running) is switched to the context of the impersonation account, **MemProxyUser**. All other security privileges (in relation to resources) are granted or denied in accordance with the permissions assigned to the Windows NT groups through the Windows NT security system.

The important thing to remember is that the user accessing the Windows NT file system is an authenticated Windows NT user; therefore the only permissions available to the user are the permissions available through the group mapping done through the Membership Directory. (We'll explore this in more detail in Chapter 13.)

The Business Logic Layer under Windows NT Authentication

Under Windows NT authentication, this is how P&M's business logic layer looks:

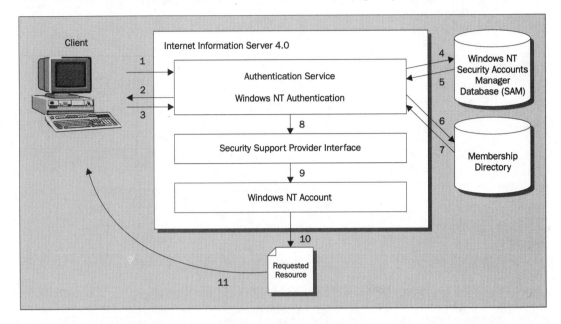

The client requests a resource from the IIS (1). If the resource is protected by Windows NT Access Control Entries and IIS is configured to authenticate all requests, the client will be authenticated (2). When authentication is complete (3), the IIS 4.0 authentication system verifies the user in the Windows NT SAM (4). If successful (5), the Site Server Authentication Service binds to the appropriate member (6) in the Membership Directory (7) and then hands off to the SSPI (8) so that the authenticated account (9) gains access to the resource (10). Finally, the client obtains the requested resource (11); all subsequent requests are performed with the authenticated user context.

> *Note (unlike Membership authentication) that resources won't be accessed with an impersonation account. For a 'member' to gain access to resources, actual NT accounts are used. In Chapter 8, we'll review the various authentication types supported by IIS 4.0 for Windows NT authentication, and in Chapter 13, we'll look at the Membership authentication system in more detail. Remember, Windows NT authentication is best for Intranets, and Membership authentication is best for the Internet.*

As a final note, observe that the process described here is entirely contained within the business logic layer of the Personalization and Membership system. The presentation layer has no part in decision-making – the only role of the presentation layer is as the interface that assists the client in providing authentication credentials.

The Data Storage Layer

The data storage layer of Site Server Personalization and Membership exists in the form of the Membership Directory. The Membership Directory is accessed through an LDAP Service (as we learned in Chapter 2). The beauty of the LDAP Service abstraction of the SQL Server database is that the data storage layer is now available to any client that can talk LDAP.

If you've spent some time digging around in the SQL Server 6.5 databases, you'll know that the SQL database uses stored procedures – pre-compiled, reusable objects that live in the database and execute on the server. Doesn't this break the n-tier design? Well, yes and no. Although the data is stored in a database, our applications are not dependent upon the database. Rather, our applications are dependent upon the ability of the LDAP Service to allow us to see it as a directory service. Remember that we shouldn't attempt to use the Membership Directory as a database – *all* access to the Membership Directory should be done through the LDAP Service.

In the next section, we'll focus in some more on the Membership Directory – and in particular, on the Directory Information Tree.

The Directory Information Tree

The storage system for Personalization and Membership is the Membership Directory, and the schema – the logical, hierarchical organization of the directory – is known as the **Directory Information Tree** (DIT). The Membership Directory is configured with a default DIT containing six sub-containers. Each of these containers holds more containers or classes:

Each item displayed in the figure is a **container** – an object that is capable of containing other items. Administering the Membership Directory involves close work with these containers. The screenshot on the next page gives a preview of the Membership Directory Manager, which we'll use in Chapter 7 to view the DIT:

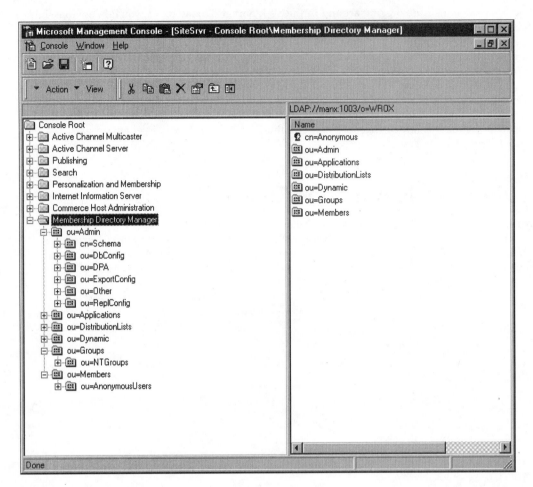

In order to bind to a particular container in the Membership Directory, we must specify the LDAP path to the container. For example, to bind to the ou=AnonymousUsers container, we'd use an LDAP path that follows this syntax:

```
LDAP://[server]:[port]/o=[organization]/ou=Members/ou=AnonymousUsers
```

The default DIT is configured so that the tools and utilities provided with Site Server (such as the Membership Directory Manager snap-in, above) know where to look for particular types of information. For example, we know that the Membership Directory stores all of the authentication information necessary to authenticate a user in Membership authentication mode. When a user is presented with a challenge to authenticate, the authentication system knows that it will find the necessary logon information in the ou=members container of the Membership Directory.

Limitations of the Membership Directory

The Directory Information Tree supports a maximum of 20 levels of containers. The first level is the root container (o=*[organization]*); the default second- and third-level containers are shown in the diagram on the previous page.

In fact, the number of levels that your DIT can *usefully* hold is restricted by another factor: namely, that the length of any distinguished name is limited to 1024 characters. So, for example, the distinguished name LDAP://[server][port]/cn=MikeC, ou=members, o=Wrox fits comfortably within this limitation; however, if your DIT contains many levels of containers, and some of your containers have excessively long names, then you might have difficulty accessing them with a distinguished name! In fact, these limitations are important, as we'll find out in the next section.

Data Caching

Data caching is a way of storing frequently-used data in memory, in such a way that it can be accessed quickly. Of course, if an application can read such data in this way (rather than reading from a disk or across the network) then the application will run more efficiently. Site Server Personalization and Membership takes advantage of data caching on two separate levels of our n-tier model, to optimize performance.

The business logic layer handles authentication caching, by allowing user properties to be stored in memory on the system. This cache is also commonly referred to as the **authentication cache** and caches all authentication requests (for example, binding to a member). Additionally, when Active Directory Service Interfaces (ADSI) is used to access a Membership Directory, an **ADSI cache** is used to cache information other than the initial authentication cache, such as member attributes. By caching member attributes, the system can handle any request that relates to member attributes by reading the data from the cached memory, rather than from the Membership Directory; and thus the request is handled more efficiently.

In addition to ADSI caching, and somewhere between the business logic and data storage layers, the **LDAP Service cache** stores the DIT container structure – so that requests for objects in the DIT can be handled more rapidly. Moreover, the LDAP service also caches all the entries in the dynamic (ou=dynamic) container.

> *We've already talked about the size limitations that are placed on the DIT – namely, that a maximum of 20 levels of containers are permitted, and that the distinguished name should be at most 1024 characters in length. These restrictions allow us to cache the DIT on the same machine that supplies the LDAP service. If the restrictions were not enforced, and the DIT were allowed to be rather larger with many sub-containers, then it would be difficult to cache all this information – and performance could degrade.*

Finally, the data storage layer provides caching in the database (although this caching only occurs on SQL Server – and not in Microsoft Access databases). Caching in Microsoft SQL Server is out of the scope of this book – if you want to know more, try the Microsoft SQL Server 6.5 documentation. However, we will complete this section by taking a closer look at the other caching activities mentioned above.

The ADSI Cache

With ADSI caching, the system can efficiently provide the attributes and properties of a member authenticated to the page for system requests. The precise way that ADSI caching works is dependent on whether the Membership Directory is configured to use Windows NT authentication or Membership authentication. We'll look at both scenarios.

ADSI Caching under Membership Authentication

When a user visits an IIS 4.0 web site that is mapped against a Site Server Personalization and Membership Server, the authentication process is the first thing to kick into action. The user is authenticated through Membership system. The Membership Authentication Service talks to the Membership Directory through the Membership Broker, via LDAP. During the authentication service, the Broker (which has permissions to all items in the Membership Directory) checks the username and password against the username and password in the Membership Directory; the broker then returns all of the information about that user – including the password – to the authentication cache. When a request is made by the authenticated member, the ADSI cache is populated with all the attributes of the member.

> *This is rather different from previous versions of Microsoft's Membership System – older versions didn't support pass-through authentication, since the Membership system didn't receive a copy of the user's password. Pass-through authentication was chosen to make the system work with other platforms that can talk LDAP. This open design allows for other services to use LDAP to verify username and password information.*

Behind the Scenes

What's happening behind the scenes? HTTP clients connect to the IIS 4.0 web, and are initially denied access – the request is then trapped by the Membership Authentication filter. The filter begins the process of authenticating the user, by calling the appropriate authentication method (via cookies, forms, or basic/clear text):

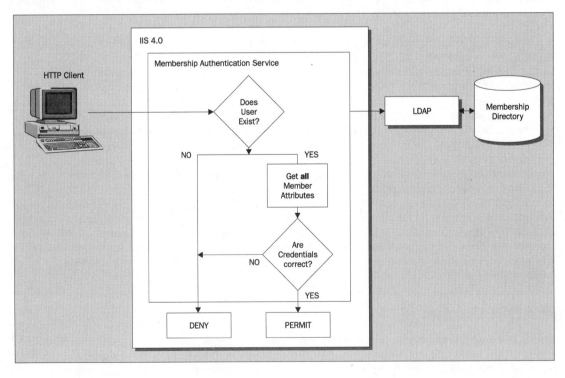

This information is passed to the Membership Authentication service, which performs the lookup in the Membership Directory and determines whether or not the user is granted or denied access. If access is granted, then *all* of the member's attributes are passed back to the calling membership server and are cached.

What is Cached, and Where

All member information – including the user's password – is passed back to the authentication service and cached. Note that the password is encrypted when it is sent between the Membership Directory and the LDAP Service. Note also that the cached data includes the Access Control Entries (ACEs) that specify the client's access permissions to his *own* member information. Thus, if the user (whose thread is executing the ASP page) requests access to his own logon information, access is either granted or denied without having to query the Membership Directory.

> *This is especially useful since the user will be denied access to those attributes to which he does not need access. For example, suppose Company A is supplying business services to Company B. Then Company B only needs to be able to access the service – in particular, they* don't *need access to the discount rate applied to their purchases (which just happens to be stored as part of their profile in the directory). Although this 'account information' will be brought across the wire with all the other user attributes, an ACE can be set to ensure that the user is denied Read access to this attribute.*

ADSI Caching under Windows NT Authentication

For sites using Windows NT authentication, there's no need for the Membership Broker when connecting to the Membership Directory. Instead, the username and password are passed to the Security Support Provider Interface (SSPI), which maps the Windows NT LAN Manager (NTLM) login to a real account in the Security Accounts Manager. The client is able to connect to the Membership Directory using this account (if he has the appropriate permissions), and can retrieve all of the relevant information – which is then stored in the ADSI cache.

Behind the Scenes

So what's happening? HTTP clients connect to an IIS 4.0 web site and are passed to the Membership Server, which hands the information to the SSPI, since the authentication service is handled by one of the authentication methods provided by Windows NT (i.e. NTLM or Clear Text/Basic Authentication).

The SSPI then attempts to validate the user information against the Security Accounts Manager; if the authentication is validated then the thread begins running under the validated user's context. This information is passed back to the authentication service, which then uses the information to connect via LDAP to the Membership Directory, and pulls back all of the attributes associated with that user.

What is Cached, and Where

The situation is rather similar to what we described in the Membership authentication case. The user's attributes are cached on the authentication service; thus, if and when the Active User Object is instantiated, it doesn't have to make a trip out to the Membership Directory to retrieve the user information:

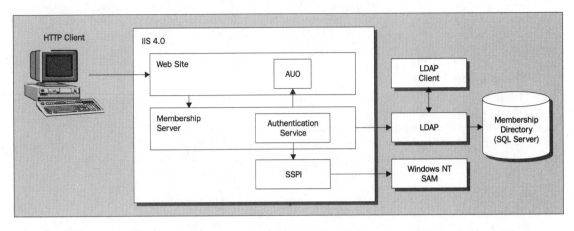

In the figure, once the Authentication Service communicates with the LDAP Service, and ultimately the Membership Directory, the returned data is cached in the ADSI cache on the Membership Server.

Direct LDAP Access

Site Server Membership abstracts direct LDAP access away from the user; however, the credentials used to access LDAP are initially those of a 'broker' account, whose **DS-PRIVILEGES** attribute is set to **SUPERBROKER**. With this setting, the LDAP system ignores the Access Control Lists that control user access permissions, and gives the broker account access to the entire Membership Directory.

This is necessary because the broker is responsible for initial communications with the Membership Directory, and for obtaining all of the attributes of any member who requests authentication. Thus, the information can be cached when it arrives back at the authentication service of the Membership Server that made the initial request.

Subsequent requests use the context of the 'authenticated' Membership user to access the Membership Directory through the LDAP service. The LDAP service also authenticates every request that connects to it.

However, clients that don't depend on the Membership Authentication Service (such as clients using the LDAP namespace to access the directory) will make a round trip to the Membership Directory for every request. This is because the client can't use the cached information in the authentication service that the Membership Server uses to bind with.

Handling DNS Round Robin Scenarios

The situations described above cover the case where all requests are made to the same machine. If multiple machines are being used – for example, behind a DNS round robin or other load balancing utility – each machine has its own cache. How can we ensure that the cache is always up-to-date?

Suppose that we have a system with two servers, ServerA and ServerB, which both authenticate via the same Membership Directory. Suppose that a user is working on ServerB – so that ServerB's ADSI cache contains information about this user, cached from the Membership Directory. Now suppose that the user clicks across to ServerA, and runs a script there, which changes ServerA's ADSI cache and updates the information in the Membership Directory.

Finally, suppose that the user now clicks on another link and is directed back to ServerB:

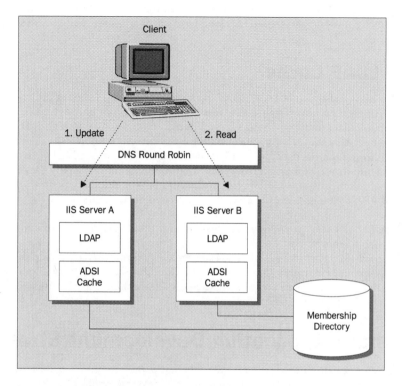

Since the Membership Directory was updated when the user was working on ServerA, we could reason that the cache on ServerB now contains dirty data (we refer to a cache as being **dirty** when the cache does not reflect the correct values in the Membership Directory).

In fact, this shouldn't happen – provided the user has agreed to accept cookies. When the user makes the update to the Membership Directory via ServerA, a cookie called MemRightsChanged is written back to the browser:

When the user clicks on the link that directs him back to ServerB with the stale cache, the MemRightsChanged cookie is passed along in the header, and tells the cache to refresh itself with new data.

The LDAP Cache

Site Server also provides an LDAP caching mechanism, which is designed to assist in user requests. LDAP caching never caches any member information or entries in any containers, except for dynamic data (most commonly stored in the ou=dynamic container). Dynamic information – transient data that is only appropriate for the current session – is cached in the LDAP service, since its information needs to be readily accessed and easily shared between other LDAP services. Such dynamic data that might include information that would normally be stored in a session in ASP, or a list of users currently logged on. The LDAP cache is initially updated when the LDAP service starts. If the DIT changes, the LDAP cache is updated accordingly.

The LDAP cache provides a very fast way for the LDAP Service to know whether or not it can service a request. For example, suppose the user requests an item in a container that doesn't exist (say, ou=Member instead of ou=Members). Then, the LDAP Service can consult the LDAP cache for this information, rather than querying the Membership Directory – and thus the query is more efficient. This saves us the performance hit of searching the Membership Directory for information that does not exist.

Internet Application Development Strategy

I often hear about architectural mistakes that people make when designing Internet applications. Since a solution built with Personalization and Membership is an Internet application, we'll discuss some suggestions for building these applications, starting with Active Server Pages.

Active Server Pages Tuning

All too often, ASP pages are used to house the business logic functionality of applications – generally, complex ASP code should really be built into COM objects. This compiled code does add complexity to your Internet application, but it also provides for faster and more reusable code.

ASP should be seen as the glue that binds services – such as Personalization and Membership – to Business Logic objects – such as the Active User Object. We'll discuss COM a little more shortly; first, let's look at some other ASP design considerations.

Session State

Internet Information Server provides a means for storing information specific to a **session** – the period during which a user accesses resources – this is called **session state**. Before the existence of Personalization and Membership, it made sense to use session state to maintain information about a user during a session, or while the user was navigating between forms. However, with P&M available, the smarter decision is to use the AUO, and persist the session data as dynamic objects in the Membership Directory (or to save the data in the form of member attributes).

> *To find out more on the subject of using the Membership Directory and the AUO for session state data, have a look at the white paper at*
> http://www.microsoft.com/workshop/server/nextgen/sessiondata.asp.

In addition to using the Membership Directory for storing session or member related data, you'll get further performance enhancement by disabling session state. When session state is enabled in IIS, requests are served in the order they are received (which means that they can get queued up); by disabling session state, it's possible for IIS to serve a request immediately.

> *To read more about the performance enhancements of disabling session state, take a look at the* IIS 4.0 Resource Kit *(Microsoft Press, ISBN 1-572-31-6381).*

Determining Whether Session State is Enabled

So how do you tell whether session state is enabled? From the MMC, open up Internet Information Server, right-click on an IIS 4.0 web, select Properties, and then select the Home Directory tab:

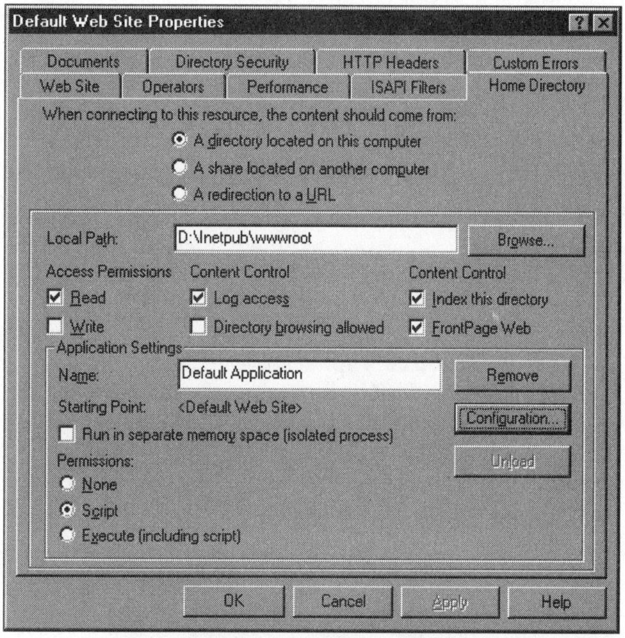

Now select the Configuration... button (in the Application Settings panel) to display the Application Configuration dialog, and finally select the App Options tab; there, we can note the setting of the Enable session state checkbox:

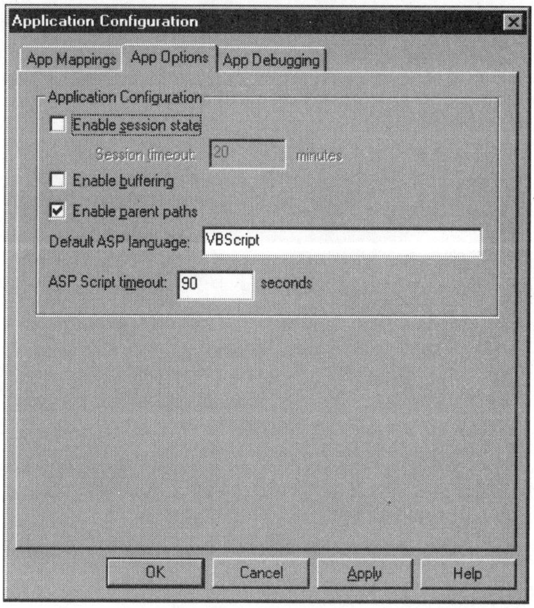

More often then not, developers abuse the session state by allowing references to objects and database recordsets to be stored in memory on the server! There are two good reasons why this is a mistake: first, it reduces the amount of system memory available for the rest of the server application, and second, the performance will degrade exponentially with the number of session instances consuming memory.

Recently, for example, I was assisting a developer with his new Internet application. It appeared, on face value, that he was having data storage problems – however, after a closer examination of the site architecture, we discovered that the site was configured to create and connect to a database, and assign that connection to a session variable. Consequently, every user that came to the site would get a database connection and object representing the connection, which is expensive on the system – so much so that it prevents any effort to scale the system beyond the available memory, and consumes too many connections to the database.

Internet Information Server 4.0 Application Mappings

IIS uses **application mappings** to determine how a file request should be handled. For instance, we all know that an ASP application has the extension `.asp` – this is mapped to `%windir%\system32\inetsrv\asp.dll`. The mapping ensures that any ASP page will be processed by `asp.dll`.

If you have any *unnecessary* application mappings on your system, then they should be removed. Such tidy housekeeping will help to optimize the rate at which IIS 4.0 can serve pages. To remove an application mapping, we need to adjust the details on the Application Configuration dialog again. Bring up this dialog as we did in the previous section (fire up the MMC, open Internet Information Server, right-click on the selected web site and select Properties; then select the Home Directory tab of the resulting dialog, and click the Configuration... button) and this time select the App Mappings tab:

Deleting an application mapping is simple: just highlight the application mapping to be removed and press the <u>R</u>emove button!

I almost always delete the following extensions: .htr, .htw, .ida, .idc, .idq, .shtm, .shtml, .stm. However, if you're using Front Page Server extensions, you might want to double-check that none of these are being used.

For more information on ASP and IIS 4.0 performance, see the IIS 4.0 Resource Kit.

Error Trapping and Debugging

Two of the least-known, and most under-used, features of ASP technology are **error trapping** and **debugging**. We'll be using these techniques throughout the book, so it's important that we understand how to configure and use them.

Error Trapping

Although error handling is not usually a big concern for most ASP developers, it should be made a higher priority. We'll make extensive use of error trapping in this book – there are some errors that we will expect, such as requests for attributes that don't exist.

The number one language choice for server-side script development should be **VBScript**, if only for one reason – it supports error handling.Error handling with VBScript is handled through the statement On Error Resume Next – this is just as in Visual Basic error trapping. The On Error Resume Next statement tells the script engine it should continue executing whenever it encounters an error.

On its own, this statement can cause complete havoc in an ASP page! But used correctly, in conjunction with the script debugger and advanced error trapping and handling techniques, it makes quite a nice feature.

Code Sample – Error Trapping

For example, whenever you use the Set directive to set a variant to an object in VBScript, *always* trap any errors that occur – as in the following code sample:

```
<%
Option Explicit
On Error Resume Next

Dim blnDebuggerOn
Dim objADOConn

blnDebuggerOn = true          ' Not production - script debugger is available

Set objADOConn = Server.CreateObject("ADO.Connection")  ' Should be
                                              ' ADODB.Connection
If Err.Number <> 0 Then
  If blnDebuggerOn = true Then
    stop
  Else
    ' handle error here
    Response.Write "Unable to create the objADOConn object"
  End If
End If
%>
```

I recommend that you develop your own method, that can be called to handle error events. However, calling unknown methods from the sample code in later chapters in this book is likely to prove confusing, so – for the course of this book – we'll only use inline error handling.

> **The best choice for server-side scripting is VBScript – if only because it supports error handling. For more information on error trapping in ASP, refer to the Wrox books _Professional Active Server Pages 2.0_ (ISBN 1-861-00-1266) or _Professional ASP Techniques for Webmasters_ (ISBN 1-861-00-1797).**

Now we know how to trap errors, the next step is to learn how to use the debugger.

The Script Debugger

Error handling alone is not enough. Developers should also make use of the **script debugger**, to step through code before it ever goes into production.

Enabling the script debugger is simple. We need to go back to the Application Configuration dialog box (in the MMC, open the Internet Information Server snap-in, right-click on a web application and select Properties; then select the Home Directory tab, and press the Configuration... button). This time, select the App Debugging tab; to enable the script debugger, check the Enable ASP server-side script debugging and Enable ASP client-side script debugging checkboxes:

After setting these properties and applying them, close all your applications and reboot the machine. Alternatively, you can stop and restart all Internet Information Server 4.0 related services, from the command line. First, stop the iisadmin service, by typing:

```
net stop iisadmin
```

Now, restart the services by typing:

```
net start w3svc
```

Now, with <u>E</u>nable ASP server-side script debugging checked, you will be able to step through ASP code as it executes, by including a `stop` directive in the code (as we saw in the code sample). When we access the application, the debugger will open and allow us to step through the ASP execution:

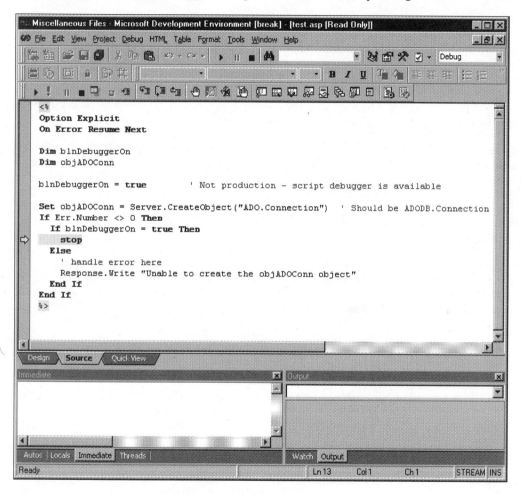

OK, I said we'd return to mention COM, and here it is.

The Component Object Model (COM)

You may have heard of the `$DATA` security hole that was recently discovered in the Windows IIS platform – the hole exposed the source code of ASP applications using a secondary data stream. We won't cover the details here – there's more information at http://www.microsoft.com/security. But of course, if users can view the source code of your ASP pages then you're in for problems – especially if the source code exposes valuable information such as the username and password, the data source names of database connections, or proprietary business logic.

The intrinsic ASP `Server` object, and its `CreateObject()` method, together form one of the most powerful tools in the ASP developer's toolbox. The `CreateObject()` method is used to create instances of COM objects, which can then expose their properties and methods in the executing context of the ASP page. However, a common mistake among novice ASP developers is the use of `CreateObject()` for the ActiveX Data Object (ADO), to connect to databases. This is particularly bad design architecture, since the database connection information must be passed on the ASP page, and thus can be exposed to anybody with access to the ASP file.

Another common error is to write the business logic for the purpose of an ASP page *directly* into the ASP file. This is not as problematic as using the ADO directly from the ASP page; however, it can lead to the same sort of security problems.

The best way to avoid these errors is by implementing COM components to encapsulate business logic. **COM** (the Component Object Model) is a standard for writing components that expose their methods and properties so that they may be 'discovered' at run time. All COM objects support the idea of interfaces – logical collections of methods and properties.

For instance, the ADO supports several different interfaces, including `Connection` and `Command`. The `Connection` interface supports several methods and properties, including `Open()`, which (unsurprisingly) is used when opening a connection. I've already mentioned the improper use of the ADO object to access databases directly from an ASP – with COM, you can encapsulate all of the necessary connection information, SQL queries, and expose the methods you need. Wrapping ADO like this is a good habit – it prevents the exposure of the database connection information directly through the ASP.

Developers can easily design their own COM objects and encapsulate their business logic and database connections inside these objects. Rather than exposing the ADO object directly through ASP, a wrapper COM object can be used to encapsulate and call ADO thus protecting access to SQL queries and database usernames and passwords.

> *This is just a single instance of how COM can be applied to your application design and architecture. If you don't know about COM, then I recommend* Inside COM *(Microsoft Press, ISBN 1-572-31-3498), for getting getting a grip on the foundations of COM;* Beginning ATL COM Programming *(Wrox, ISBN 1-861-00-1401), for learning how to write ATL based COM objects, and lots of great code; and* Essential COM *(Addison Wesley, ISBN 0-201-63-4465) for a whirlwind tour of COM.*

Advanced Concepts

In this section, we'll take a look at the database table that is used to represent the Membership Directory. If you decide to explore a Membership Directory for yourself, then I recommend that you create a *new* Membership Directory using Microsoft Access (as described in Chapter 6). Use your Windows NT Explorer to navigate to the Microsoft Site Server/Data directory, and look for the file mpinst1.mdb. Do open this file, but *beware*, Microsoft warns you that (as with the registry), any modifications are unsupported – if you modify *any* values or information stored in this database, your Membership Directory may no longer work!

Exploring the Membership Directory Database

Exploring existing Membership Directories for yourself is definitely *not* recommended! That said, we can look at a Membership Directory database through the following screenshots. In particular we'll be able to see that the Membership Directory database is deep but not wide – that is, the table used to store the data consists of very few columns but (potentially) very many rows.

Table Relationshipships

Although there's much more in the database, the Relationships view – accessible from Tools | Relationships... – displays the relationships amongst the different tables in the database:

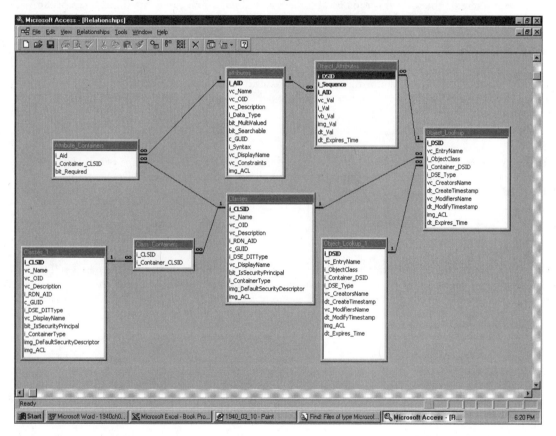

The tables are described below.

Attribute_Containers

The **Attribute_Containers** table maintains the relationship between attributes and classes. If we examine this table, we'll see three columns:

- ❑ i_Aid represents the attribute id
- ❑ i_Container represents the container id
- ❑ bit_Required determines if the attribute is a required attribute of the class.

This table defines the attributes that a class may or must have.

attributes

The **attributes** table stores all of the attributes that exist in the cn=Schema, ou=Admin container of a Membership Directory. If we examine the columns of this table, we'll see a vc_Name column that represents the name of the attribute. We can also see the img_ACL column, which is used to store the Access Control Lists for the attribute – which we'll see in Chapter 13.

Class_Containers

The **Class_Containers** table represents the relationship between classes that can act as containers of other classes. An example of this is the ou=Members container which can contain instances of the members class.

Classes and Classes_1

The **Classes** and **Classes_1** tables, both shown in the relationship diagram, represent the same table: Classes. The table provides the information about classes in the Membership Directory. As with the attributes table, its values are accessible from the cn=Schema, ou=Admin container of the Membership Directory.

Configuration

Although not displayed in the relationships view, the **Configuration** table contains two columns with one important entry: the value of the password encryption key (PEKey). The PEKey contains a key value used to encrypt data stored in the Membership Directory. Later on (in Chapter 13), we'll learn more about how communications between the LDAP Service and the Membership Directory are encrypted.

Object_Attributes

The **Object_Attributes** table contains the values of the attributes belonging to class instances. If we create a member object in the Membership Directory, and find the i_DSID value in the Object_Lookup table we can find the populated value of an attribute – to determine which attribute's value you're looking at examine the i_AID entry for the row.

Object_Lookup

Finally, we've already mentioned the **Object_Lookup** table, which contains the naming attribute of an object. For example, if we looked in this table for the cn=Administrators:

I_DSID	vc_EntryName	i_ObjectClass	i_Container_DSID	i_DSE_Type	vc_Cre	dt_CreateTimestamp
2127	cn=Hold	26	2124	8		
2128	cn=SampleSite	26	2013	8		
2129	cn=Products	26	2128	8		
2130	cn=AutomaticRockingChair	26	2129	8		
2131	cn=DisposableRocketLauncher	26	2129	8		
2132	cn=ElectronicBirdWarbler	26	2129	8		
2133	cn=FusionCar	26	2129	8		
2134	cn=MarsCrawler	26	2129	8		
2135	cn=MoonWalker	26	2129	8		
2136	cn=SelfCleaningHouse	26	2129	8		
2137	ou=DPA	7	2	8		
2138	cn=SiteServer DirectMail Administrators	12	2009	8		
2139	cn=GRPBRKRAccess	12	56	8		
2140	cn=MBSBRKR2_MANX	13	55	1		
2141	cn=4ab0bba4-18c8-11d2-b58d-0080c7b87	33	2139	1		
2142	cn=GRPTMAccess	12	56	8		
2143	cn=SiteServer Ad Manager Administrators	12	2009	8		
2144	cn=SiteServer Analysis Administrators	12	2009	8		
2145	cn=SiteServer Commerce Operators	12	2009	8		
2146	cn=SiteServer DirectMail Operators	12	2009	8		
2147	cn=SiteServer Directory Administrators	12	2009	8		
2148	cn=SiteServer Knowledge Administrators	12	2009	8		
2149	cn=SiteServer Membership Administrators	12	2009	8		
2150	cn=Administrators	12	2009	8		
2151	cn=SiteServer Publishing Administrators	12	2009	8		
2152	cn=SiteServer Search Administrators	12	2009	8		
2153	cn=SiteServer Administrators	12	2009	8		
2154	cn=DPASharedAuthKey	50	2137	1		
2156	ou=SiteA	7	55	8		
2157	ou=SiteB	7	55	8		
2158	ou=AnonymousUsers	7	2156	8		
2159	ou=AnonymousUsers	7	2157	8		
2160	cn=MBSBRKR3_MANX	13	55	1		
2161	cn=4ab0bca3-18c8-11d2-b58d-0080c7b87	33	2139	1		

Record: 166 of 177

Datasheet View

We could find the i_DSID of the object, which could then be used to find the related values in the Object_Attributes table.

Summary

In this chapter we learned about the architecture of Site Server Personalization and Membership. The key points were:

❑ Site Server P&M is an n-tier architecture, which uses caching to optimize performance. There are many dependencies that exist within a Personalization and Membership system.

❑ Data caching involves copying frequently-accessed data to a location where it can be accessed efficiently. Each of the services used by Site Server P&M uses caching to improve performance. Object-level information is cached by the requestor, and DIT level information is cached by the LDAP Service. Also, some caching does take place within SQL Server.

❑ The Directory Information Tree (DIT) represents the logical structure of the Membership Directory. The size of the DIT is limited – these limitations make it possible for the LDAP service to cache DIT level information, and hence optimize performance.

❑ We can tune our ASP settings to get improved performance from our ASP applications – by disabling session state and deleting redundant application mappings. Also, the importance of error trapping and debugging techniques are not to be underestimated. We can use COM technology to avoid including our business layer logic within ASP pages – and the accompanying potential security nightmare!

❑ In the data storage layer, the Membership Directory database is a deep, narrow table with many relationships.

In the next chapter, we'll see how Site Server Personalization and Membership architecture can be scaled to handle millions of users.

Scaling Personalization and Membership

One of the most powerful features of Site Server Personalization and Membership is that we can easily scale the system to store data for millions of users. However, this does require a certain amount of planning and forethought. This chapter will present you with the knowledge you need to properly and effectively scale your architecture, so that it won't baulk as an increasing number of users access your site.

So, here's what we'll be discussing in this chapter:

- ❏ **Selecting the Database for the Membership Directory.** Here, we'll discuss the two databases that can be used to represent the Membership Directory – Microsoft Access and Microsoft SQL Server. We'll begin by examining a table, to compare and contrast some of the more obvious differences.

- ❏ **Scaling the Membership Directory.** This is the crux of this chapter: we'll look at partitioning the Membership Directory, which allows us to distribute the storage load across multiple SQL Servers.

- ❏ **Scaling the Architecture.** We'll look at four configurations that make up the evolutionary process of a typical Personalization and Membership site. In the first stage of evolution, all services are provided by a single Windows NT Server platform; in the most advanced stage of evolution, services are distributed among multiple Windows NT Server platforms.

- ❏ **Advanced Concepts.** Here, we'll talk about how to bypass Access Control Lists in the Membership Directory, in order to speed up user access times. We'll also cover an ASP script that populates a Membership Directory with any number of users – a useful tool for testing a directory installation.

This chapter is by no means intended to replace the knowledge of the system administrator or database administrator; however, it should provide supplementary knowledge that will help you to better understand how to scale these products with Site Server. By the end of the chapter, we'll be ready to build a Site Server Personalization and Membership system that is capable of scaling to handle millions of users.

Selecting the Database for the Membership Directory

We've already seen that the Membership Directory is simply a database with a pre-determined schema, optimized to store structured information. We've also seen that the Membership Directory should only be accessed through the LDAP Service, to preserve the integrity of the Membership Directory.

Although the LDAP Service provides a platform-independent manner of communicating with the Membership Directory, there are only two database types – Microsoft **Access** and Microsoft **SQL Server** – that support the data storage for the Membership Directory. In other words, at some time during the planning process for our P&M site, we must decide whether we want to use an Access database, or a SQL Server database, to represent our Membership Directory.

Site server provides a tool – the New Membership Server wizard – that we can use to create a new Membership Server. The following screenshot, from that wizard, illustrates that we must make the choice of Membership Directory database type *before* we finish creating the Membership Server:

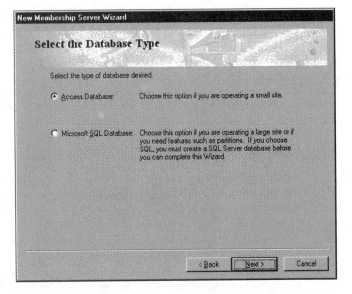

We'll look at the wizard in full in Chapter 6. The point is that we must appreciate the differences between these two database types, from a Membership Directory point of view, if we are to make a wise decision.

One important factor in all of this is the fact that there is no conversion tool available for converting a Membership Directory, either from an Access database to a SQL Server database, or vice-versa. Although the Microsoft Upsizing tool can export the data structure from an Access database to a SQL Server database, it can't create the necessary stored procedures in SQL Server, upon which the LDAP Server depends.

It's not too difficult – if you're a whizz with databases – to write a tool that migrates data from one Membership Directory to another by reading one Membership Directory programmatically, and mirroring its data to another. There's a code sample in Chapter 14 that programmatically creates attributes and classes in the Membership Directory's schema – it could be re-purposed to examine one Membership Directory, read out the entire schema, compare this with the contents of another Membership Directory and recreate any missing classes and attributes by examining its properties. After mirroring the Schema, it would also be necessary to mirror all the objects.

But it's a whole lot easier simply to understand the benefits and shortcomings of Access-based Membership Directories and SQL server-based Membership Directories at the planning stage, than to attempt to go back and correct your mistakes later. In this section, we'll discuss the most important aspects of each database solution, but we can abridge the discussion as follows:

	Access	SQL Server
Size limitation?	1 GB	None
RDN length limitation?	230 characters	250 characters
Search feature supports % and _ characters?	No	Yes
Distributed LDAP Service?	One LDAP Service must reside on each computer with an Access database.	LDAP Service and SQL Server can exist on separate computers; therefore multiple LDAP Services may be used to support a Membership Directory.
Must shut down LDAP Service to back up the database?	Yes	No
Attribute value length limitation?	4095 characters	None

Let's look at Access-based Membership Directories first.

Access-Based Membership Directories

A Microsoft Access database is a great choice if you're prototyping a Personalization and Membership system, or if you're running a small-scale Personalization and Membership site. Obviously, it's very simple to use, and it offers more of a 'black box' approach to the Membership Directory. This can present both advantages and disadvantages. Let's weigh up the pros and cons of using an Access-based directory.

The Advantages

Definitely the greatest strength of selecting an Access database for the Membership Directory is its **simplicity**. You don't need to know a thing about database devices, or how to configure the database with the proper number of users and memory. If you're getting up to speed with Personalization and Membership, then it's much faster to use an Access-based Membership Directory – simply because you avoid all the configuration considerations that come with using SQL Server. You can spend your time learning the platform – rather than configuring it.

Installing and setting-up an Access-based Membership Directory is simple. In fact, this simplicity is reflected in the New Membership Server Wizard screenshot, that we saw earlier in the chapter. If we choose Access, Site Server will automatically create a new Access database on your server and build the Membership Directory structure within it. Moreover, you don't actually need to have Microsoft Access (the product) installed on your computer! And you don't need to known a thing about database management to make it work. We'll see the wizard in action in Chapter 6.

If you're working with an Access Membership Directory, you do have the option of opening the file and **taking a peek** at the database schema. Although this has its obvious dangers (especially in a real-life production environment), this is quite useful if you're learning the ropes of Site Server P&M, because it allows you to get a better understanding of the relationships within the database. There's a review of the architecture of an Access database Membership Directory – along with the appropriate health warnings! – in the *Advanced Concepts* section of Chapter 3.

Backing-up an Access-based Membership Directory is much simpler than backing up a SQL Server database. This is because the Microsoft Access database is simply a file – we can copy the file and instantly have a ready-to-roll backup in case something happens to our original.

The Disadvantages

While it's easy to use, if you're working in a real-life production environment you'll probably find that Access's disadvantages far outweigh its advantages.

Probably the most important disadvantage is that an Access-based Membership Directory **can't be partitioned**. We haven't discussed partitioning in detail yet – we will a little later in this chapter. For now, it's enough to know that partitioning is what allows us to extend and scale the Membership Directory across multiple machines and multiple databases – it's our big scalability tool. Moreover, partitioning a large Membership Directory allows for faster searches, because the index of a set of multiple small databases is smaller than the index of a single large database.

Access databases have a physical **size limitation** of 1 gigabyte. Since the database is not a true Relational Database Management System (RDBMS), the physical size of the database will always be a hindrance. As the database grows the performance decreases. We'll come back to performance considerations later in this chapter, when we talk about the estimated storage requirements for the Membership Directory.

We've already mentioned that backing up an Access database is easy – however, if you're **backing up** an Access-based Membership Directory then it's necessary to stop the LDAP Service. Of course, you can't service requests as long as the LDAP Service is stopped, and during this back-up period all applications dependent upon the Membership Directory are rendered useless.

Every entry in the Membership Directory must have a Relative Distinguished Name (RDN) – it's the unique naming characteristic that identifies the entry in the Membership Directory. In Microsoft Access-based Directories, the RDN has a **naming limitation** – namely, that each RDN must have fewer than 230 characters (SQL Server-based Membership Directories give us a little more scope). It doesn't sound much like a limitation, but in some instances it can be.

Microsoft Access does not support the use of the % and _ symbols in **search strings**. When we come to look at SQL Server, shortly, we'll see why they're useful.

So Access-based Membership Directories have their place, but they also have important and unsurprising limitations. Let's take a look at what a SQL Server-based Membership Directory can do.

SQL Server-Based Membership Directories

The Site Server Personalization and Membership documentation suggests that an Access database be used for prototyping, and that a SQL Server database be used for production. While it's more complicated to install and to use, it's so much more powerful that it's usually the natural choice for a production environment. Let's have a look at the pros and cons.

The Advantages

The main advantage of SQL Server over Access is that it provides the ability to partition the Membership Directory across multiple databases. However, there are quite a few other advantages as well. Let's look at why SQL Server is better for the Membership Directory than Access.

A SQL Server Membership Directory is not limited to one physical database (as we've seen is the case with Access). In fact, we can use **partitioning** to span a Membership Directory across multiple SQL Server databases, in multiple locations. Multiple databases means smaller index sizes on tables, and more efficient searching; and if hardware becomes a bottleneck, your Membership Directory can be distributed across multiple machines. Thus, partitioning capability is by far one of a SQL Server-based Directory's most important design features.

SQL Server provides its own services to service database requests – unlike Access, which is accessed directly by LDAP Service. This means that the SQL Server and LDAP Service can reside on the same machine, or we can use SQL Server's flexibility to set up the LDAP and SQL Server services **on separate machines**.

It's possible to use multiple LDAP Services to access SQL Server across the network. Thus, as an extension of the above, we can create a **distributed LDAP Service** by building a system in which multiple LDAP Services communicate with a Membership Directory that is provided by multiple SQL Server databases. We'll see how to architect such a solution later in this chapter.

SQL Server's **search facility** is stronger than that of Access. In particular, SQL Server uses the % and _ characters as wildcards to aid data search – % represents any number of characters while _ represents a single unspecified character. Finally, we mentioned that Access-based Membership Directories are limited to 1 GB in size, and impose a limit of 230 characters on the RDN. By contrast, a SQL Server Directory has **no physical size limit** – partitioning takes care of that – and each RDN may be up to 250 characters in length.

The Disadvantages

We can't really call it a disadvantage as such, but it is true to say that the Microsoft SQL Server product must be installed in order to configure and manage a SQL Server-based Membership Directory. It's also necessary to configure the Directory manually. Moreover, it's important to install SQL Server, Site Server and the various Option Packs and gizmos in the correct order – we'll cover that in Chapter 5.

Although Microsoft Access works well for understanding and prototyping a Site Server Personalization and Membership solution, you'll probably want to take advantage of the performance and scalability with a SQL Server database in your final business solution.

In Chapter 3, we made the assumption that SQL Server was the platform used to provide the Membership Directory. In Chapter 5 (when we install our Membership Server) and Chapter 6 (when we create a new Membership Server), we'll make the same assumption – this will allow us to cover the more complex installation options that come with installing a SQL Server-based Membership Directory.

Partitions in the Membership Directory

One of the oft-trumpeted strengths of Site Server 3.0 Personalization and Membership is that the Membership Directory is massively scalable – that is, we can design our Membership Directory in advance so that it is ready to store the data of huge numbers of members. We do this by distributing the Directory over a number of SQL Server databases. To begin with, these databases might all live on a single SQL Server machine; but as your system grows, you can migrate individual databases to their own dedicated SQL Server machine.

By using a sufficient number of SQL Servers, and sufficiently many databases, you can allow yourself enough memory to cope with just about any number of members you can throw at it, and room for further expansion.

Partitions and the DIT

So how do multiple databases manifest themselves within the Membership Directory? The answer is **partitioning**. We use the logical structure of the Directory Information Tree (DIT) to determine what type of data goes into which database. There are two types of partitions – **namespace partitions** and **value partitions**. Let's look at each of these, and find out how they work.

Namespace Partitions

We use a namespace partition when we want to create a dedicated database to store all the data within a given container. For example, we could use one database to store everything in the ou=Members container:

The ou=members container, and all its leaves and sub-containers are contained in SQL Database B, while the remainder of the Membership Directory is contained in SQL database A. Note, however, that the LDAP Service works with the logical structure of the DIT, and therefore sees the *entire* Membership Directory.

Namespace partitions give us the capability to use a different database for each container, if we so choose. For example, if an ISP host uses a single Membership Directory to host many customers, it's possible to set up one ou=*[customer]* container per customer, each with its own dedicated database.

Value Partitons

We use a value partition to distribute the contents of a container across two or more physical databases. The distribution is more-or-less even. We can only value-partition a container at the time we create our Membership Server. However, we can create a number of value partitions on a single machine to begin, and – as the size of the container grows – we can migrate each value partition to its own dedicated SQL Server machine.

Thus, we can allow a large degree of scalability for each container – by spreading it over multiple databases and ultimately over multiple machines, provided we plan the partitions in advance.

In the following (very small) example, the ou=Members contains five members, and is value-partitioned into two physical databases so that one contains three members and the other contains two:

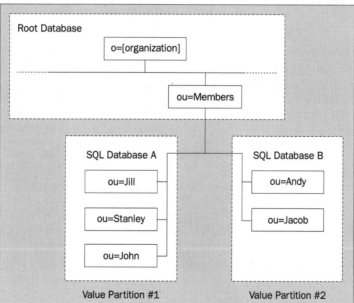

The value partitions of a container are distinguished by the hashing value – as in partitions #1 and #2 in the figure above. The Membership Server decides where a member will be stored, and does its best to distribute members evenly across the two value partitions. Value partitions, like namespace partitions, are transparent to the LDAP Service, which sees the entire Directory.

How Partitions Affect LDAP Caching

You'll recall from Chapter 3 that the entire DIT is cached at the LDAP Service when the LDAP
Service is first started. If you decide to partition your Membership Directory, this will have an effect
on how the Directory information is cached. Consider the following diagram, which shows a
namespace-partitioned Membership Directory:

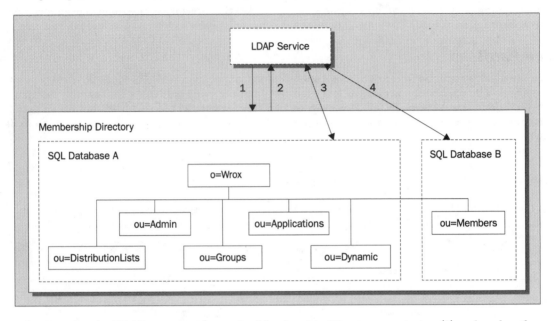

In the diagram, the LDAP service accesses the Membership Directory on startup (1) and caches the
DIT structure (2). Later, if a request is made to bind to the o=Wrox container, then the LDAP service
consults the cached DIT structure information and establishes that it needs to direct the request to
Database A (3). If a request is made to bind to the ou=Admin, o=Wrox container, then the same
process occurs. However, if a request is made to bind to the ou=members container, then the LDAP
service consults the cached DIT structure and redirects the request to Database B.

All this logic is accomplished by the LDAP Service – not by a Site Server method.

Planning your Partitions in Advance

As we've mentioned, it's vital that you plan your site requirements in advance. Site Server 3.0 doesn't
allow you to re-partition your Membership Directory once you've started using it, so you should plan
your partitions in advance. If you don't have the hardware available when you create the site, then
it's essential to estimate the amount of traffic you expect you see in 1 or 2 years, and create the
partitions when you create the Directory. Once you've prepared your partitions, you can always
obtain hardware and migrate databases later on.

How Many Partitions Do I Need?

The answer to this question depends upon the number of objects that you will eventually create in the
Membership Directory.

There's a useful paper on Site Server Capacity and Performance Analysis, which you can find at http://www.microsoft.com/siteserver/intranet/Update/performance.asp.

Unfortunately, this white paper doesn't make a recommendation regarding the optimal size of the object_Attributes table, that is used to store the object attribute values. As a rule of thumb, I reckon that around 15–20 million rows is optimal for an object_Attributes table. This is by *no* means enough to stress SQL Server, and it gives us enough room to grow and ensures that the table indices remain small for faster lookups.

Row Number Estimation – An Example

Let's go through an example that attempts to estimate the number of table rows needed to store member information for all the members that we expect at our site. Note that this example is based on estimating the number of member class instances, but you can apply it to any class.

To begin, each instance of the member class requires nine rows in the Membership Directory. These nine rows are used to store for system data – things like the creation timestamp, the modify timestamp, the name attribute of the class, the class instance type, and so on.

In addition, every member instance has a number of attributes, and each attribute is represented by one row. Every time a member is assigned membership of a particular group, this is also represented by one row of the table.

Finally, when the Membership Directory is first installed there are around 1760 rows that are used to describe the Membership Directory structure. These rows contain information for the default DIT, attributes and classes that already exist in the cn=Schema, and the default containers (ou=Members, ou=Admin, ou=Groups, etc.).

So, if N represents the anticipated number of members, A is the average number of attributes per member, and G is the average number of groups per member, then the number of rows we need to accommodate all our members is:

Rows = [N * (9 + A + G)] + 1760

Let's work with a real example, in which we anticipate a total of 500,000 members, with $A = 25$ and $G = 5$. Then the estimated number of rows will be:

Rows = [500,000 * (9 + 25 + 5)] + 1760 = 19,501,760

In our example case, you should consider partitioning the Membership Directory, since our 15-million-row threshold may be breached.

Now, Microsoft's *Membership Directory Capacity and Performance Analysis* white paper *does* recommend 1080 MB of disk space per 100,000 members in the Membership Directory. This is calculated with very small overhead for containers, and this number can change based on number of attributes stored for each member, the number of groups created, and the number of containers created. So we can also get an idea of the total amount of storage space we'll need:

Estimated Storage Requirement = 500,000 * (1.080/100,000) = 5.4 GB

Another Example

Consider a subscription site with 20,000 users and an expected maximum of 2 million users. By planning ahead, they can estimate for the future requirements and calculate how much space would be required to store all this information:

Estimated Storage Requirements = 2,000,000 * (1.080/100,000) = 21.6 GB

If the site estimated 15 attributes per member, and 3 groups per member, we could also estimate the number of value partitions required of the ou=Members container:

Rows = [N * (9 + A + G)] + 1760
Rows = [2,000,000 * (9 + 15 + 3)] + 1760 = 54,001,760

Therefore,

Estimated Partitions = 54,001,760 / 15,000,000 =~ 3.6

Partitioning Scenarios

In the following scenarios, we'll look at one example each for applying namespace and value partitions, and in the last case we'll use both.

Internet Service Provider

An Internet Service Provider that would like to provide Personalization and Membership features to its customers has two options: It can either build a new Membership Directory for each customer, or it can work with a single Membership Directory and create a series of namespace partitions. These namespace partitions could then be mapped to independent LDAP servers that could be created for each site. Obviously, a series of namespace partitions is much easier on the administrator, but it requires more planning initially.

Internet Content Provider

Internet Content Providers that plan on growing their user base should use value partitioning on the ou=Members container. Thus, as the number of members increases, additional SQL Server machines can be added to absorb and scale the site transparently.

Intranet or Enterprise Site

Choosing whether to implement a namespace partition or a value partition comes down to how the Membership Directory of your Intranet site is to be configured. That is, will each business unit be represented by a group or by a container? If the organization's members are to be divided by containers under the ou=Members containers (such as ou=Marketing, ou=Administration, etc.) then it makes more sense to create namespace partitions and ask the users to log in as Marketing*[user name]*. It's like logging into a domain, but the domain name is replaced by the name of the appropriate container. Additionally, we could then create value partitions of the namespace partitions if there are many members, i.e. use multiple databases to represent ou=Marketing.

Scaling the Architecture

By coupling Site Server Personalization and Membership with Internet Information Server 4.0 and SQL Server databases, we have an extremely scalable architecture. When it comes to using this scalability to extend our system, there are a number of routes that we could take. In this section, I've tried to provide a series of snap-shots that suggest how the configuration of a site might evolve over time in order to respond to demands on the system to grow and maintain performance levels. You won't find these levels of configuration documented in any of the Site Server documentation, and it's not the only way to evolve your site – but I hope that it provides some illumination.

In our evolutionary process, partitioning plays a crucial role so we'll assume that the Membership Directory is represented as an aggregation of SQL Server databases. Here's an overview of the four configurations we'll see here:

❑ **Stage 1** – In this basic configuration, a single machine provides all the various services that are necessary for Site Server Personalization and Membership. We would expect to find this configuration in a development environment, or for a prototype.

❑ **Stage 2** – Here, multiple web servers – or machines – share a Membership Directory based on a single SQL Server machine. The single SQL Server machine might contain multiple databases that represent any value and/or namespace partitions within the Membership Directory.

❑ **Stage 3** – Here, multiple machines are used to provide web services, and these in turn rely upon multiple SQL Server machines to provide the Membership Directory. This is the most common configuration to be found in a production environment.

❑ **Stage 4** – Finally, multiple machines are used to provide the web services and service the Personalization and Membership LDAP requests. These LDAP requests are funneled through a DNS round-robin – or other IP routing solution – to multiple LDAP Services (also distributed across multiple machines), and finally to the Membership Directory which is also value- and/or namespace-partitioned over multiple machines.

The evolution of your particular solution may take a different route – or it may be appropriate to skip a configuration level. Let's look a little more closely at each of these configurations.

The Single-Machine Web Site

The configuration outlined in Stage 1 is great for a site that has just a single web server, responsible for serving content to the Internet or Intranet. In this configuration, IIS 4.0, Microsoft Site Server 3.0 LDAP Service and the Membership Directory all reside on a single machine. All Personalization and Membership services rely on the ability of these separate technologies to communicate efficiently using TCP/IP and LDAP. This configuration is good for developers, or sites where one machine is capable of handling the load.

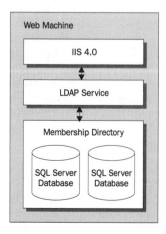

If it's a test site, then an Access database is probably the most suitable way of providing storage for the Membership Directory. However, if you're thinking of scaling this configuration later on, then it's best to start out with a SQL Server database that is appropriately partitioned to suit your organization and anticipate the growth of the site (as shown in the diagram). Of course, in this case the partitions mean that you're using multiple databases – but they're all contained on the same machine.

If you're using this configuration to service a small real-life Internet or Intranet site, the you need to ensure that the single machine that provides all the services is sufficiently powerful to handle the demands placed on it by the three Microsoft server technologies.

Multiple Web Servers

The Stage 2 configuration supports a single SQL Server and multiple IIS 4.0 servers. We can use routing technology (software or hardware) to manage the web server's load (i.e. requests served) by distributing requests across the available machines:

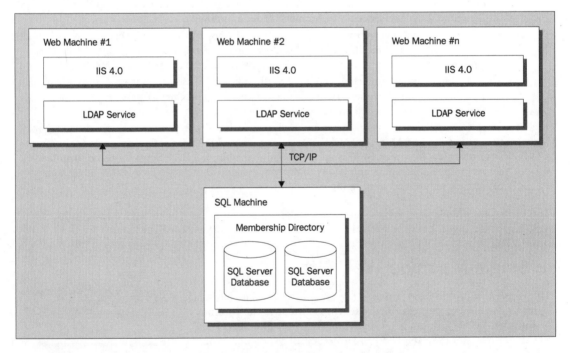

For example, suppose you're expecting your site to receive, say, 500 requests per second, yet a single web server is only capable of serving 200 requests per second (of course, this figure is dependent upon the configuration and hardware). In order to maintain a reasonable performance for your users, you need to implement this kind of multiple-web server configuration that can evenly handle the load required.

This configuration is likely to be a common design among sites where the focus is on the web services rather than the data services. The web server machines handle the web requests, and a single SQL Server machine provides the data storage that serves all of these requests. This design allows us to continually scale the number of web servers upwards – as long as the ability of the single SQL Server machine does not bottleneck the system.

Migration from Stage 1

The migration path from Stage 1 to Stage 2 is simply a case of moving the SQL Server database (or databases, if you've anticipated growth by implementing partitions) to another machine. SQL Server 6.5 provides tools for this – you can find them in the **SQL Enterprise Manger** tool using the **Database/Object Transfer** tool.

Multiple Web Servers and Multiple SQL Servers

In the Stage 3 configuration, the databases representing the value partitions and/or namespace partitions of the Membership Directory are spanned across multiple SQL Server machines. This configuration usually occurs when the ability of the SQL Server to service requests can no longer handle the number of requests by each web server. By moving these databases to their own dedicated machines, we can improve performance:

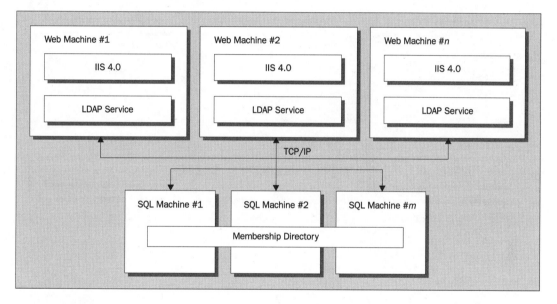

As we mentioned in Chapter 3, the Membership Directory is capable of spanning multiple SQL Servers – and indeed, this gives us the flexibility to house different parts of the Membership Directory in different physical locations. The most important thing to understand is that the system sees the Membership Directory as a *single* directory through the LDAP Service, and not as a collection of databases.

Requests for data from the Personalization and Membership system are routed through the LDAP Services provided on the web server machines. The LDAP Service knows which SQL Server to communicate with, in order to fulfil its request – because the entire DIT structure is cached on the LDAP Service.

Migration from Stage 2

Ideally, we should consider moving to Stage 3 when we have more than five web servers in our environment (we'll learn why 'five' is the magic number later), or when the single machine providing SQL Server services becomes a bottleneck for the system. As long as the directory has been partitioned across multiple SQL Server databases, we can dedicate a separate machine for each database.

The migration process itself is simple: we use the SQL Server SQL Enterprise Manger tool, employing the Database/Object Transfer tool functionality to move each database to its new machine.

Multiple LDAP Services

The Stage 4 configuration reflects how we can really begin to optimize performance in our system, as the system grows. In this configuration, the LDAP Services now live on their own dedicated machines:

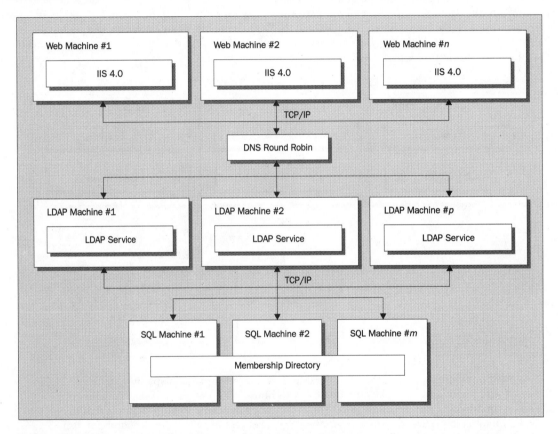

By moving each LDAP Service to its own dedicated machine (or adding more LDAP Services on new dedicated machines), we can provide multiple LDAP Services for each web server using Personalization and Membership. So, when is it necessary to have multiple LDAP Services available for the web servers?

We know that it's possible to scale the Membership Directory to store the information of millions of users. However, if a system is to handle many *concurrent* users in an efficient manner, then the answer is multiple LDAP Services. Let's consider a sample calculation.

We'll start with some component expectations. A Membership Directory using SQL Server can handle around 1000 requests per second. An LDAP Service can handle around 200 requests per second.

Now, suppose the ou=Members container of our Membership Directory is value-partitioned across three SQL Server databases on three separate machines. Based on the assumptions above, is it fair to assume that this architecture can handle around 3000 requests per second (assuming all machines were on the same network segment and were dedicated to the Membership Directory)?

The answer depends (in part, at least!) on the number of LDAP Services that are being used to access the Membership Directory. If we're using only a *single* LDAP Service, then our system will be bottlenecked at the LDAP Service. Although the Directory can handle 3000 requests per second, the LDAP Service can only supply 200 requests per second – so the Membership Directory is only running at 200/3000 = 6.7% of its potential performance.

To solve this problem, we should add more LDAP Services. (Note that adding LDAP Services does add its *own* overhead: by default, each LDAP keeps 10 connections open to the SQL Server database, and each open connection on the database consumes 37KB of memory.) With these assumptions, it's easy to deduce that the optimal strategy for scaling the LDAP Service is to provide **five** LDAP Servers per SQL Server partition. (How did we arrive at that? Simply that each SQL Server partition handles around 1000 requests per second, and each LDAP Server handles around 200 requests per second. In order to satisfy each SQL Server Service, there must be 1000/200 = 5 LDAP Services. It's a rough-and-ready calculation, but it's a good starting point.)

Migration from Configuration 3

The migration path from Stage 3 is to provide additional machines to provide the LDAP Service. Configuring an LDAP Service via the New Membership Server Wizard is covered in Chapter 6.

Advanced Concepts

In this section, we'll just take a look at a script that allows us to populate a Membership Directory.

Scaling Script for Membership Authentication

The following script is a useful little tool for populating a Membership Directory that uses Membership authentication. Simply set the number of users to be populated, and the LDAP server that you're using, as in the following example:

```
Const LDAP_SERVER = "LDAP://manx:1003"
Const NUM_POPULATE = 98
```

Code Example – ScalingScript.asp

Here's the code:

```
<%
Const LDAP_SERVER = "LDAP://manx:1003"
Const NUM_POPULATE = 98

Const POPULATEDS_BAD_LDAP = 10
Const POPULATEDS_BAD_MEMBERS_CONTAINER = 9
Const POPULATEDS_FAILED_CREATE_GUIDGEN = 8
Const POPULATEDS_FAILED_CREATE_MEMBER = 7
Const POPULATEDS_FAILED_MEMBER_SETINFO = 6
Const POPULATEDS_SUCCESS = 1
```

```
' Call the appropriate function
' *****************************************************
Select Case PopulateDS(LDAP_SERVER, NUM_POPULATE)
  Case POPULATEDS_BAD_LDAP
    Response.Write ("Failed: Unable to connect to LDAP server.<BR>")
    Response.Write ("Suggestion: Please ensure LDAP_SERVER ")
    Response.Write ("constant points to a valid LDAP Server<BR>")

  Case POPULATEDS_BAD_MEMBERS_CONTAINER
    Response.Write ("Failed: Unable to connect to ou=members container.<BR>")
    Response.Write ("Suggestion: Please ensure user has correct ")
    Response.Write ("permissions to get this container.<BR>")

  Case POPULATEDS_FAILED_CREATE_GUIDGEN
    Response.Write ("Failed: Unable to create GUID generator object. <BR>")
    Response.Write ("Suggestion: Make sure this machine has Site ")
    Response.Write ("Server 3.0 installed.<BR>")

  Case POPULATEDS_FAILED_CREATE_MEMBER
    Response.Write ("Failed: Unable to create new member in members ")
    Response.Write ("                  container.<BR>")
    Response.Write ("Suggestion: Please ensure user has correct ")
    Response.Write ("permissions to create this object.<BR>")

  Case POPULATEDS_FAILED_MEMBER_SETINFO
    Response.Write ("Failed: Unable to call SetInfo for new member.<BR>")
    Response.Write ("Suggestion: Please ensure user has correct ")
    Response.Write ("permissions to create this object.<BR>")

  Case POPULATEDS_SUCCESS
    Response.Write ("Success: " & NUM_POPULATE & " new members created.<BR>")
    Response.Write ("Suggestion: Filter on *1 through *9 to view ")
    Response.Write ("in Membership Directory Manager.<BR>")
End Select

Public Function PopulateDS(strLDAPServer, nNumPopulate)
  On Error Resume Next

  Dim objLDAPRoot
  Dim objMembersContainer
  Dim objGUIDGen
  Dim strGUID
  Dim objNewUser

  ' Connect to the LDAP Server and get the root object
  ' ************************************************************
  Set objLDAPRoot = GetObject(strLDAPServer)
  If Err.Number <> 0 Then
    PopulateDS = POPULATEDS_BAD_LDAP
    Err.Clear
    Exit Function
  End If

  ' Use root to get the members container
  ' ************************************************************
  Set objMembersContainer = objLDAPRoot.GetObject("organizationalUnit", _
                                            "ou=members")

  If Err.Number <> 0 Then
```

```
   PopulateDS = POPULATEDS_BAD_MEMBERS_CONTAINER
   Err.Clear
   Exit Function
 End If

 ' Get object to generate guids
 ' ************************************************************
 Set objGUIDGen = Server.CreateObject("Membership.GUIDGen.1")
 If Err.Number <> 0 Then
   PopulateDS = POPULATEDS_FAILED_CREATE_GUIDGEN
   Err.Clear
   Exit Function
 End If

 ' Loop appropriate number of times and create new members
 ' ************************************************************
 For nLoop = 1 to nNumPopulate

   ' Use GUID generator object to generate a new guid
   ' ************************************************************
   strGUID = objGUIDGen.GenerateGuid

   ' Create new members in members container
   ' ************************************************************
   Set objNewUser = objMembersContainer.Create("member", "cn=member" & nLoop)
   If Err.Number <> 0 Then
     PopulateDS = POPULATEDS_FAILED_CREATE_MEMBER
     Err.Clear
     Exit Function
   End If

   ' Add values for new member
   ' ************************************************************
   objNewUser.Put "GUID", CStr(strGUID)          ' Must contain attribute
   objNewUser.Put "userPassword", "password"     ' May contain attribute

   ' Call SetInfo to commit to DS
   ' ************************************************************
   objNewUser.SetInfo
   If Err.Number <> 0 Then
     PopulateDS = POPULATEDS_FAILED_MEMBER_SETINFO
     Err.Clear
     Exit Function
   End If

 Next

 ' Clean Up
 ' ************************************************************
 Set objLDAPRoot = Nothing
 Set objGUIDGen = Nothing
 Set objMembersContainer = Nothing
 Set objNewUser = Nothing

 ' All Done!
 ' ************************************************************
 PopulateDS = POPULATEDS_SUCCESS

End Function
%>
```

For a Membership Directory that has multiple value partitions, this script is useful for populating these partitions and then moving the partitions to ensure that the partitions can be distributed across multiple machines.

Summary

This chapter has presented you with an overview of how to scale a Personalization and Membership Site. Here's what we covered:

❑   First, we discussed the two databases that may be used for the Membership Directory – Microsoft Access and Microsoft SQL Server. We examined the advantages and disadvantages of each.

❑   Next, we discussed partitioning the Membership Directory. We formally introduced the two types of partitions that may be created – namespace and value partitions. We discussed how partitioning affects the way the LDAP Service caches the Membership Directory's Directory Information Tree.

❑   We examined how it's possible to scale the Personalization and Membership architecture. We examined four different configurations of the Web, LDAP and Membership Directory services.

❑   Finally, in the *Advanced Concepts* section of this chapter, we examined an ASP script for generating members, useful for testing a Membership Directory installation.

We've done all our homework, and now we're ready to create our first Personalization and Membership site! On to Chapter 5...

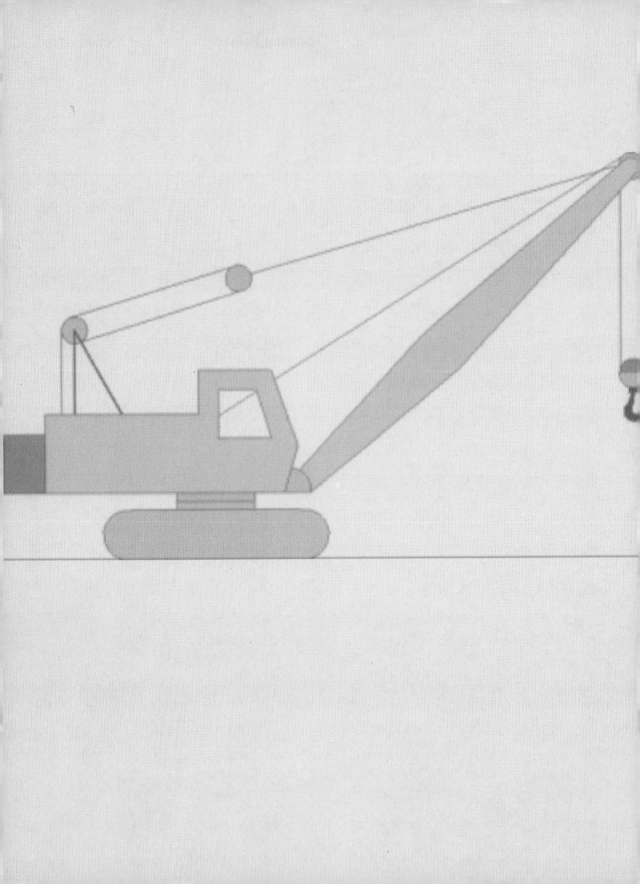

Installing Site Server

The most important thing to remember about the Personalization and Membership system is that planning is critical. The system can become inflexible and difficult to engineer if the proper precautions are not taken – such as partitioning the Membership Directory, or understanding how the site will scale to accommodate the expected growth. Without the foundation and knowledge laid out in Chapters 3 and 4, you may encounter difficulties later on. In other words, if you've skipped ahead to this chapter, it's worth reviewing Chapters 3 and 4 before you install the product. Don't misinterpret this introduction – installing and configuring Site Server Personalization and Membership is not difficult. However, the software installation is only half the job; understanding the installation and platform configuration is just as important.

Here's what we'll be looking at in this chapter.

- ❑ **Software Installation.** When we install Site Server, the platform needs to be properly configured to 'accept' the installation. Additionally, we'll cover an installation checklist as well as a software installation order for products that reside on the server. We'll also step through each section of the wizard – we'll talk through the different screens and explain what's happening.
- ❑ **Fine-Tuning the Site Server Installation**. Here we'll take a look at the different services we can configure to fine tune the machine providing the services for Site Server Personalization and Membership.
- ❑ **Site Server 3.0 Service Pack 1**. We'll take a look at the installation process for Site Server 3.0 Service Pack 1, as well as where to find the executable. We'll also mention what documents to browse after installation to find out what modifications the service pack performs.

By the end of this chapter you will be able to successfully install Site Server 3.0 and Site Server 3.0 Service Pack 1, so that you can use the following chapters to configure it for Personalization and Membership. We'll also have completed the first section of the book: *Planning and Architecture*. By now we should have the necessary knowledge to plan, architect, install and configure a Site Server 3.0 Personalization and Membership solution.

Software Installation

The software installation for Site Server is simple – as long as we have properly prepared the platform for the installation first and understand all of the requirements. Remember, Site Server 3.0 is not one application, but rather a collection of tools, utilities, and objects all tightly integrated with each other, and with the Windows NT platform. My personal recommendation is to start with a clean machine when you can – i.e. a hard drive that has been formatted. This will allow us to install the software in the proper order to insure that our Site Server installation is successful. However, if this is not an option, make sure that the hard drive serving the web documents is formatted to NTFS. Also, run through the checklist for a new machine making sure your configurations match as closely as possible. So, before we start with Site Server, let's look at the following installation checklist to ensure that we meet the necessary requirements.

The Installation Checklist

Before we begin the installation of Site Server 3.0, we should make sure that the following conditions have been met. We can set up both Site Server itself and the data store for the Membership Directory on the same machine, or set up one machine to act as a web server (where Site Server would be installed) and another machine to act as the data store. We'll cover machine requirements for two machines, as this is the configuration you would probably want to implement for best performance. You can follow the same installation checklist even if you're installing onto one machine. We'll also use SQL Server rather than Access as the database for the Membership Directory, based on our discussions in Chapter 4. If you want to use Access (say, if you're setting up a test site) you need to make sure it is installed, but you don't have to create a database – Site Server can handle that, as we'll see in the next section of the book. We'll call the web server **Web Server Machine** and the Membership Directory machine **SQL Server Machine.**

Web Server Machine and SQL Server Machine

Both the Web Server Machine and the SQL Server Machine should have as much hardware resource available as possible. Ideally, the Web Server Machine would have two Network Interface Cards (NICs) and the SQL Server Machine should have at least one. The machines should then be configured in a daisy-chain fashion where the Web Server Machine would have one NIC dedicated to servicing requests and another dedicated to communicating with the SQL Server Machine for requesting information. We'll look at a diagram of this in a moment, but first let's take a look at the hardware and software requirements for our servers.

Hardware

Following on from our discussion in Chapter 4 of the different stages of scaling the architecture, we'll be looking at how we would configure two machines for Stage 2 – one machine dedicated to Web services and another machine dedicated to SQL services. If you're installing on to one machine just aggregate the requirements.

1   **Memory** – Both machines should have a substantial amount of memory available; the cost of memory is lower now than it has ever been. The Site Server documentation recommends 128 MB, but plan for at least 256 MB with room to grow on the Web Server Machine. For the SQL Server Machine, we should also provide plenty of memory since SQL Server is a memory-intensive application, and the more memory we can allocate to SQL, the better.

2   **Processor** – Put as much horsepower here as you can – the best configuration being a dual-processor Pentium with as much onboard cache as possible. With prices as low as they are, you shouldn't settle for anything less that a 266 MHz.

3   **Network Card** – Definitely don't skimp here – two 100-BaseT NICs (with the other proper network equipment, of course). For our Web Server Machine, we should dedicate one NIC for the requests (i.e. web traffic) and one for communicating with the Membership Directory. For our SQL Server Machine, at least one NIC should be dedicated to requests from our Web Server Machine:

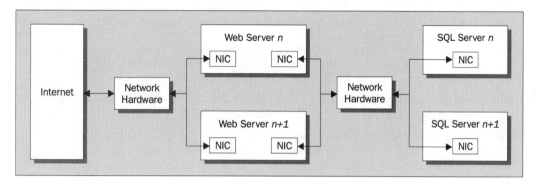

A configuration such as this allows for a dedicated network connection for data requests so that the number of collisions – attempts by machines to communicate on the network – is reduced, thus giving us better performance between our SQL Servers, our Web servers and the Internet (or Intranet).

Software

In Chapter 4 we discussed the various stages of the architecture and how we could best scale it. As in the above discussion of hardware, we'll be looking at configurations for two machines: the Web Server Machine and the SQL Server Machine. Although these services can exist together on one machine, it makes more sense to distribute them, across two machines at least. If you're installing onto one machine you will need to install all the software below on to your single machine. In any case, you should install the software in the order listed below.

1   **Windows NT Server** – Site Server can only be installed on Windows NT Server 4.0. This machine can be a Primary Domain Controller (PDC) if necessary, but a stand-alone server is recommended. Format the drives as NTFS (NT File System). We need NTFS to enforce security checking on file resources when requested. TCP/IP must be configured as a supported network protocol.

> **Although a PDC and a domain do make a lot of sense for Windows NT authentication, the focus of this book is more towards Membership authentication – storing all user accounts in the Membership Directory. Therefore, the only benefit a domain would provide – with Membership authentication – is the ability to have shared groups and impersonation accounts. However, the overhead associated with communicating with the domain controller to verify accounts from each standalone server is not worth the central domain management provided.**

2   **Windows NT Server 4.0 Service Pack 3** – Service Pack 3 adds some enhancements and fixes some bugs – we'll need this before we can install the Windows NT Option Pack.

3   **Internet Explorer 4.01** – Also necessary before the option pack can be installed – IE 4.01 updates drivers and other system files on the machine that have dependencies on libraries in the Window NT Option Pack.

4   **SQL Server (single machine install only)** – If we're installing all services on to one machine, we should skip ahead to Steps A and B below, for installing SQL Server – and then go to Step 5. Otherwise, we go straight to Step 5.

5   **Windows NT Option Pack** – Installs Internet Information Server 4.0, and some other services (such as the SMTP service, or the Certificate Server). Ideally, we should also install FrontPage Server Extensions (if you plan to use them – we don't in this book), and the Windows Scripting Host. If you're unfamiliar with the Windows Scripting Host (WSH), you don't know what you're missing. With WSH, we can run command line utilities similar to Active Server Pages to perform configurations, all in the comfort of our favorite scripting language.

6   **Site Server 3.0** – Finally, we're ready to install Site Server 3.0. We'll walk through the wizard in detail, later in the chapter.

7   **Site Server 3.0 Service Pack 1** – After installing Site Server 3.0, you should apply the Site Server 3.0 Service Pack 1 (SP1). SP1 fixes several outstanding issues and adds some functionality as it relates to Personalization and Membership. We'll cover installation of the service pack at the end of the chapter.

8   **SQL Server (multiple machine install only)** – At this point, if we're installing all services onto a single machine, then our installation is complete. On the other hand, if we're using a separate machine for SQL Server, now's the time to install SQL Server onto our dedicated SQL Server machine (Steps A and B).

For our SQL Server, we should install:

A   **SQL Server 6.5** – If the role of the machine is to provide the Membership Directory, such as the case with our designated SQL Server Machine, we need to install SQL Server 6.5. However, once we have installed Site Server 3.0 Service Pack 1, we can use SQL Server 7.0.

B   **SQL Server Service Pack 4** – Additionally, if we install SQL Server 6.5, we also need to install the most recent SQL Server Service Pack. At the time of writing, this is SQL Server Service Pack 4.

> **TCP/IP must be one of the selected network protocols for the LDAP Service to communicate with the SQL Server databases.**

Before continuing from this point, take a look at the Site Server 3.0 documentation – specifically the setup instructions available from the first screen of the setup wizard. The documentation goes into lavish detail on each of the above requirements – including minimum requirements – about how to set up and properly configure each of the above hardware and software configurations.

Configuring SQL Server 6.5

Before we move on to installing Site Server 3.0, let's prepare some foundations we can use when we come to configure Personalization and Membership in the next section of the book. We won't be going into the details of configuring SQL Server as that is out of the scope of this book, but we need to make sure that we have enabled TCP/IP and that we have a database to hold the Membership Directory.

Enabling TCP/IP

Since all communication is done via TCP/IP for the architecture, we need to ensure that TCP/IP is one of the supported protocols that SQL Server has enabled. To ensure that SQL Server 6.5 has TCP/IP enabled as a network protocol, select Programs | Microsoft SQL Server 6.5 | SQL Setup. After navigating through several opening screens (by pressing Ok or Continue) you will be presented with the Microsoft SQL Server 6.5 – Options:

Make sure Change Network Support is highlighted. Next, press Continue and select TCP/IP Sockets. You may choose to leave Named Pipes checked as a supported protocol if the particular SQL Server will be servicing requests for other applications.

After pressing OK from the Select Network Protocols dialog you will be presented with the TCP/IP Socket Number dialog:

TCP/IP Socket Number

SQL Server will listen on the following TCP/IP port number:

Port Number: | 1525 |

[Continue]
[Back]
[Exit]
[Help]

To enter a different TCP/IP port number, use the BACKSPACE key to delete characters, and then type the TCP/IP port number you want SQL Server to listen on.

The TCP/IP Socket Number dialog allows you to choose which TCP port SQL Server will service requests on. The default port is 1433, and since this is a well-known port, it is strongly advised that you select another port.

Creating Databases

SQL Server is now ready to service requests via TCP/IP, but we also need to create a database to act as the Membership Directory, which we'll be creating in the next chapter. In the previous chapter, we read why it is important to partition the Membership Directory so that the site can be scaled more easily. Depending on the demands that you will place on the Membership Directory (remember this depends upon the number of groups and the number of attributes) you should have at least one partition per five million estimated rows in the Object_Attributes table of the database. As a rule of thumb, I reserve three databases in SQL Server for my Membership Directory: one namespace partition for the main DIT, and two value partitions for the ou=Members container.

Now that we've discussed the pre-installation process, let's look at the actual Site Server 3.0 installation.

Installation Wizard

Believe it or not...we're all ready to go, four and a half chapters from where we started and now we are ready to begin the installation process!

Installation Options

When we run setup.exe from the Site Server 3.0 CD, the first screen we see is the installation options screen.

Microsoft®
Site Server 3.0

Setup Instructions
Server Installation
Tools Installation
SDK Installation
Introducing CSSs
Readme Files

Exit

Choose this option to install the complete Microsoft Site Server software feature set, including all server, administration, client, and tools software. Use this installation for your primary installation sites and any other sites that require all Site Server functionality. If you choose this option, you do not need to perform the Tools Installation.

The installation options screen presents us with several options: we can read over the setup instructions (which I highly recommend), run the server installation, install the Site Server 3.0 tools, install the SDK, read about the CSSs (Customizable Starter Sites), view the Readme files, or exit. You will need the SDK later on in the book when we use Visual Basic and C++ with Personalization and Membership, but we won't cover installing it here, as it will be simpler to download all the SDKs that we need when we come to that topic. You could choose to install just the Site Server tools if you wanted to administer Site Server from a client computer running Windows 95 or Windows NT. The details of which tools are installed with this option are covered in the Site Server documentation, so we won't repeat them here. We'll see all the Site Server tools as they are included in the option we will be focusing on, Server Installation.

The Customizable Starter Sites are excellent resources for learning not only the Personalization and Membership features of Site Server, but some of the other tools and services as well.

System Requirements

We'll only see the system requirements screen of the installation if we don't meet the necessary system requirements, or don't meet the system recommendations:

We'll get a system recommendation error if we don't have FrontPage Server Extensions, or if we have below 128 MB of RAM. Since we spent four chapters talking about planning, architecture, and the system, as well as spending the first part of this chapter reviewing the system requirements, we'll assume that the only issues we'll encounter are system recommendations, which we can choose to ignore.

Setup Wizard

After ensuring that the system requirements are met, the Setup Wizard starts off with the Setup Wizard Splash Screen. We've shown every screen of the wizard, but if you're familiar with Microsoft setup style you'll want to move on through some of them fairly quickly.

Site Server 3.0 Personalization and Membership

Screens 1 and 2: Splash Screen and End-User License Agreement

The first screen of the Microsoft Site Server Setup Wizard simply explains what the wizard does and what requirements the wizard has. The only requirement is that all applications that could potentially use files that Site Server will write over need to be free; in other words, close all other applications before starting the installation process.

The End-User License agreement is the agreement between the end user and Microsoft on how the product is to be used. In order to continue the installation, the license agreement must be accepted.

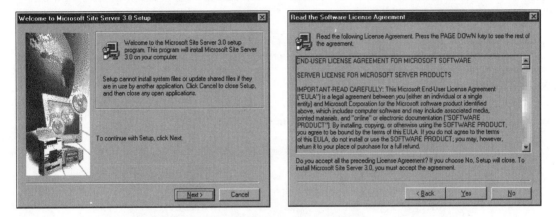

Screen 3: Specify Product and User Information

The product and user information is entered into the registry, but only the CD key needs to be completed to install the product. This information, such as the admin email address, might be useful later on when the application is available. In later chapters, we'll look at some ways to access information from the registry through Active Server Pages.

Screen 4: Specify Microsoft Site Server 3.0 Folders

Screen 4 of the wizard is used to specify the target destinations of the application executables, data and samples to install. Ideally, we should install the defaults of the program, site, and data folders – there is no good reason not to. Estimate upwards of 120 MB for the full installation, with SQL selected as the database of choice for analysis. Make sure that the applications are installed to an NTFS drive to ensure that the application security is properly configured by the installation process.

The fields here are:

- ❑ Program folder – The Program Folder is where the main executables for all the Site Server features will be installed.
- ❑ Data folder – The Data Folder is where the data for each of the different features of Site Server store their application specific data. For Personalization and Membership, all Membership Directories created in Microsoft Access will be created in this directory by default.
- ❑ Site folder – The Site Folder is where the sample and administrative sites for each of the different features of Site Server are created. All the Personalization and Membership samples and sites are installed in this directory under the samples\knowledge\membership subdirectory.

Screen 5: Choose Installation Type

The fifth screen of the Site Server Setup Wizard prompts for the installation type. Although 3 options are presented, we should always choose custom to have more control over what the setup process will be installing. For a product such as Site Server there should rarely be a typical installation.

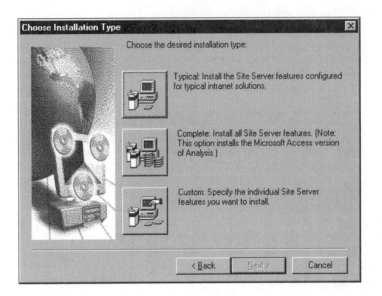

The three options here are:

- ❏ Typical – Selecting typical installation installs the Publishing and Analysis services, but does not install the Active Channel multicaster.
- ❏ Complete – Selecting the complete installation installs the entire services suite, but configures the Analysis tool to use Microsoft Access rather than SQL Server.

> **Although not the topic of this book, the Analysis tool really requires Microsoft SQL Server to achieve the maximum performance and usage.**

- ❏ Custom – Selecting the custom installation – the recommended choice – will allow us to selectively choose which features of the product are to be installed. Additionally, we should select custom so that we can view and discuss the remaining screens encountered during installation.

To read more about Typical and Complete installation options, as well as silent installation, see the Site Server documentation.

Screen 6: Select Features

Assuming we selected the Custom installation in Screen 5, Screen 6 presents us with the three solution categories that Site Server provides through a tree view:

Select Features

Select the features you want to install; clear the
features you do not want to install.

☑ Knowledge : [28013k]
☑ Publishing : [6378k]
☑ Analysis : [22158k]

Description:

Analysis provides you with a tool to
analyze content, site structure, links,
and site usage and enables you to
convert your analysis data into usable
reports.

Folder: Space
                 available/required:

[C:] Site Server   317 M / 130976 K

[C:] Data   317 M / 782 K

[C:] Sites   317 M / 2606 K

Select All   Clear All

< Back   Next >   Cancel

Expanding this tree further reveals the granular options
for each solution category:

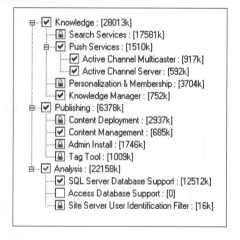

The lock symbols in some of the categories represents services that are part of the base installation,
and must be installed. Let's review each of these three sections:

- ❑ Knowledge – Includes features such as Search, Push, Knowledge Manager, and Personalization
  and Membership. In order for Personalization and Membership to be installed, Knowledge must
  be selected. However, the other features may be unselected if they are not used.

- ❑ Publishing – Includes features such as Content Deployment, Content Management,
  Administrative tools for Publishing and finally the tag tool. The publishing features may be seen as
  a 'document management system' in environments where multiple content submitters need to be
  monitored to maintain site integrity.

- ❑ Analysis – Analysis will be installed whether we want it or not, the only option is whether the
  install should use SQL Server or Access. However, the services used by Analysis may be disabled.

Site Server 3.0 Personalization and Membership

To read more about the different features and options included in Site Server – other than Personalization and Membership – see the Site Server 3.0 documentation. Later in this chapter we'll also cover the different services that can be stopped, in order to tune Site Server Personalization and Membership.

Screen 7: Specify a Program Folder

After making the installation selections, the Setup Wizard will prompt for the Program Folder to install the links to the product. Once Site Server is installed, we'll use this folder to find the various programs installed.

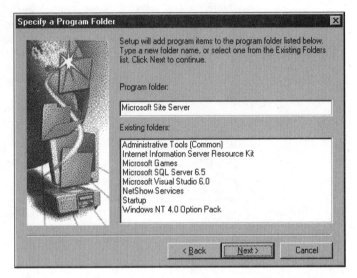

Screen 8: Configure User Accounts

If installing any Publishing or Search features, a Windows NT account with administrative privileges needs to be used to properly configure these services. Both features can be configured together by selecting one, pressing *Shift*, and selecting the other.

Clicking the Set User Account... button, from the Configure User Accounts screen, displays the Set User Account dialog box:

Set User Account ⊠

Type the user name, password, and domain information for the
Site Server Service user account.

User name: [   ]

Password: [   ]

Confirm password: [   ]

Domain: [MANX   ]

[OK] [Cancel]

This dialog is used to select the username, password, and domain of the account to use to configure these services. If you want these services to run under a special account, create a new Windows NT user that is part of the appropriate domain, and is a member of the Administrators group.

Screen 9: Stop Services

After configuring the accounts to use for setting up the Publishing or Search features, the Setup Wizard will announce that it is going to stop several services:

Stop Services ⊠

Setup will stop the following services:

World Wide Web Publishing Service
FTP Publishing Service
Microsoft NNTP Service
Microsoft SMTP Service
IIS Admin Service
Content Index

[< Back] [Next >] [Cancel]

The services that need to be stopped are the services directly related to Internet Information Server 4.0:

- ❑ **World Wide Web Publishing Services** – Services for providing HTTP capabilities
- ❑ **FTP Publishing Services** – Services for providing FTP capabilities
- ❑ **Microsoft NNTP Services** – Services for providing news services
- ❑ **Microsoft SMTP Services** – Services for providing mail services
- ❑ **IIS Admin Services** – The main service for Internet Information Server
- ❑ **Content Index** – The service for Index Server

Site Server 3.0 Personalization and Membership

Screen 10: Start Copying Files

After stopping the services, the Site Server Setup Wizard displays the features to be installed. At this point the installation can be cancelled, or the installation options can be confirmed and installation will begin.

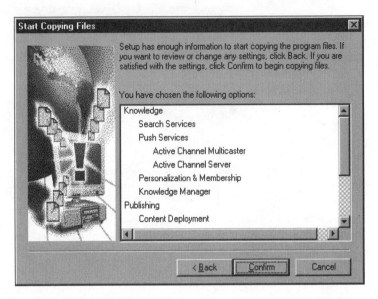

Screen 11: Setup Complete

The final screen simply confirms that the installation is complete, and offers the option to peruse further documentation:

Now that we've completed the installation, let's look at how we can fine tune the installation for Site Server Personalization and Membership by configuring the different Windows NT services that were installed.

Site Server NT Services

Site Server 3.0 installs several new NT services to the Windows NT server that it is installed on. Not all of these services are required depending on how Site Server will be used. However, after installation, all these services are set to automatic startup by default. Any service that is started and running in the Services dialog that is not necessary is consuming precious resources. Stopping services and configuring services not to start up automatically is a great way to increase system performance without any costs. In this section we'll take a look at some of the Site Server Specific Services and Windows NT specific services we can configure to better 'optimize' our system, again as it relates to our Web Server and our SQL Server.

Let's start with a brief summary of Windows NT Services. Again, if you're familiar with them already just skip forward.

Windows NT Services

A Windows NT Service is an executable application that has no user interface and is used to provide services, as the name implies, for other applications. A service that you might be familiar with is the World Wide Web Publishing Service (**W3SVC**), which is a service for Internet Information Server. This particular service is always running (if started) in the background and monitors certain ports and IP addresses waiting for HTTP requests. All services are started by and run under the system (unless otherwise specified) and are controlled by the Service Control Manager (SCM). The Windows NT services dialog is found by double clicking on the services icon in the control panel.

Scrolling through the Services dialog, we eventually find the Site Server services installed.

For more in-depth information about Windows NT Services, I recommend the Windows NT Resource Kit *(Microsoft Press, ISBN 1-572-31-3447) and* Professional NT Services *(Wrox, ISBN 1-861-00-1304).*

Site Server Services

Site Server installs a total of 8 new services all available from the Services applet in the Control Panel (if all options are selected during installation – we'll assume they are for the sake of covering each in detail). Let's examine what each of these services provide.

The only services required for Personalization and Membership are:

- **Site Server Authentication Service** – The Site Server Authentication Service is used by Site Server Membership to authenticate users from Internet Information Server 4.0. This service also provides the cache, or memory, for storing user information that is pulled from the Membership Directory when the user first authenticates. The Authentication Service offers four main features: password validation, security contexts to support Windows NT's security model, the mapping of Membership Directory groups to Windows NT groups, and retrieving user properties from the Membership Directory.

- **Site Server LDAP Service** – Site Server LDAP Service provides the LDAP service to allow applications to connect to Membership Directories on the same machine or on different machines. The LDAP service is similar to the W3SVC service – the service used by Internet Information Server to service web requests – in that clients connect to it via TCP/IP and request information and the service is responsible for servicing the request.

Two additional Services may be enabled if you want to use Personalization and Membership with Direct Mail functionality:

- **Site Server List Builder Service** – The Site Server List Builder Service provides the capability to impersonate the various members from a distribution list. The distribution list is stored in the Membership Directory, and the impersonation account is used to access an Active Server Page. The Active Server Page generates a personalized document that is then handed off to the Site Server Message Builder Service, which then mails the personalized document to a member via email.

- **Site Server Message Builder Service** – The Site Server Message Builder Service accepts data passed by the Site Server List Builder Service to generate an email. The mailing is performed by an SMTP service – ideally the SMTP service installed with the NT Option Pack – which then can communicate with a mail server to send the mail.

The following services are not necessary, and should be disabled (though I've included a description of each, for information):

- **Site Server Active Channel Multicaster** – The Site Server Active Channel Multicaster service is used to deliver Internet Explorer channels to subscribers. It uses the Channel Definition Format (CDF) – an XML based format – to push information only to users that request it. The service is used as the process that generates the CDF and makes it available to requestors.

- **Site Server Content Deployment** – The Site Server Content Deployment Service, or SSCD, is often used as a type of document management system to control site integrity and monitor developer's additions to a site, as well as communicating with other Content Deployment servers.

- **Site Server Gatherer** – The Site Server Gatherer service works in conjunction with Site Server Search. The Gatherer writes log files related to the building of new search catalogs. Additionally, the Gatherer service works to collect all the files – as the name implies – to be used by Site Server Search when searching for data.

❑   **Site Server Search** – The Site Server Search service is used to service requests for searches. Whenever a search request is performed, the Search Service is responsible for processing the request and returning the information. Additionally, the Search service validates security permissions and only returns content to the requestor that the requestor has permissions to view.

In addition, the following Windows NT services can also be disabled depending on the requirements of the machine used by Personalization and Membership:

❑   **Content Index** – Content Indexer indexes content on the local machine that can later be searched. Disable this service if the machine is going to be a dedicated Membership Directory, or does not have any content that needs to be indexed. Do not confuse the Content Index service with Site Server Search. Index Server – another searching utility – distinct from Site Server Search – uses the Content Index service.

❑   **FTP Publishing Service** – The FTP Publishing Service is the Internet Information Server 4.0 service to provide FTP capabilities for the local machine. If FTP is not going to be used, the service should be disabled.

Special Cases

Depending on our architecture here are the other services that we should have running for Personalization and Membership:

❑   **World Wide Web Publishing Service and IIS Admin Service** – Both services related to IIS 4.0 and are required for serving web content. We should have these services running for our Web Server machine configuration.

❑   **MSSQLServer and SQLExecutive** – Both services relate to providing services for SQL Server 6.5. We should have these services running for our SQL Server machine configuration.

Site Server only depends on SQL Server to act as a data storage mechanism, and performs all access via TCP/IP to SQL Services on other machines. For more information on these services see the IIS 4.0 Resource Kit or the product documentation for SQL Server 6.5.

We've learned how to install Site Server 3.0 and looked at how to optimally configure the different Windows NT services for our needs. Let's now take a moment and look at Site Server 3.0 Service Pack 1.

Site Server 3.0 Service Pack 1

We won't be going through the installation in detail, as the procedure is the same as the one we've already seen. At the time of writing, the Site Server 3.0 Service Pack 1 installation file can be found by navigating to http://www.microsoft.com/siteserver and selecting the appropriate product. The Service Pack (SP1) provides some fixes for the SQL Server based Membership Directories, and some fixes for the PMAdmin, and Web based Administration.

After downloading the service pack, we can start the executable and simply follow the screens. After the service pack stops all of the necessary services, the files will be copied and installed, and the services will be restarted with the service pack applied. The updates and bug fixes performed by the service pack are documented in readme_sp1.htm and readme_kb.htm. Please review these files after installing the service pack to review what modifications have been made, as well as what modifications you need to perform.

The SQL Server modifications installed by the service pack are not performed automatically, and must be run. Here are the instructions included in the Service Pack:

1 Copy **mcis2upd.sql** from \Site Server 3.0 SP1\Scripts to a location accessible from your SQL Server computer.

2 On the Start menu of the SQL Server computer, point to Programs, point to Microsoft SQL Server 6.5, and then click SQL Enterprise Manager.

3 Click the plus sign (+) next to the name of the SQL Server computer that is hosting the Membership Directory, click the plus sign (+) next to Databases, and then click the Membership Directory database.

4 On the Tools menu, click SQL Query Tool.

5 In the Query window, click the Load SQL Query icon, and then in the Open File dialog box, open mcis2upd.sql from the location to which it was previously copied.

6 The mcis2upd.sql script is loaded into the Query window. Click the Execute Query icon.

Summary

This chapter provided us with the necessary information to install and configure Site Server 3.0. The installation was geared towards Personalization and Membership and what we needed to get it up and running optimally. 95% of the problems related to installation are from poor resource allocation or incorrect configuration options on the platform – all of which we covered either in this chapter or previous chapters.

Here's what we covered in a little more detail:

❑ **Software Installation.** We read about installing Site Server and what the Windows NT 4.0 platform should look like before we install the product. Additionally, we covered an installation checklist as well as a software installation order for products that reside on the server. Next, we went step by step as we used the Setup wizard to install the Site Server 3.0 system.

❑ **Fine Tuning The Site Server Installation**. After reading about the installation, we looked at how we could fine tune the installation by configuring the different services that Site Server 3.0 provides. In addition, we looked at some of the other services required by Site Server.

❑ **Site Server 3.0 Service Pack 1.** We reviewed the service pack and where to look for information for what the service pack installed.

In the next section of the book, *Configuring Personalization and Membership*, we'll look at how to set up the site and configure its properties to suit our particular needs.

The Personalization and Membership Snap-In

There are many tasks involved in building a complex site to authenticate and manage stored information for users, and some of the more difficult ones are abstracted into a series of **snap-ins** that are found within the Microsoft Management Console (MMC). From the MMC, you can administer almost all settings using just *two* of the new snap-ins that come with Site Server 3.0. In fact, Site Server installs a total of six new snap-ins (or seven, if Site Server Commerce Edition is installed). In this book, however, we'll only cover those that relate to Personalization and Membership – the Personalization and Membership snap-in and the Membership Directory Manager snap-in.

In this chapter we will discuss the Personalization and Membership snap-in, which is used to administer and configure the Membership Servers that are available either on the local machine or on remote machines.

Here's an overview of how this chapter is organized:

- ❑ **The Basics.** In this first section, we'll begin with a high-level overview of the Personalization and Membership snap-in. We'll explain where to find the snap-in, and mention some other administrative possibilities.

- ❑ **Creating a New Membership Server.** In this section we'll look at how to configure a new Membership Server. A Membership Server is a collection of items (such as an LDAP Service) that is 'mapped' or associated with another service, such as Internet Information Server. The items of the Membership Server don't necessarily need to be on the same machine as the services – for example, it's possible to use an LDAP Service from another machine. We'll run through three of the most common configuration options using the New Membership Server wizard.

❑ **Properties of the Membership Server.** We'll take a detailed look at the properties of the snap-in and of the services that it provides. These include the Authentication Service, the Active User Object Providers, and the LDAP Instance. Each of these has various settings and configurations – some specific to the Authentication type – that change the behavior of the Membership Directory as well as system-level security and Membership Directory security.

❑ **Partitioning the Membership Directory.** We discussed the 'why's of partitioning in Chapter 4; in this section we'll discuss the 'how's. The Personalization and Membership snap-in provides a wizard – the Membership Directory Partition wizard – for creating the new partitions. We'll step through the various screens of the wizard to see just how to create the necessary partition type for our Membership Directory.

❑ **Advanced Concepts.** Finally, we'll look at how to change the broker account used by the Membership Server for authenticating and validating members in the Membership Directory. We'll also look at how we can change the proxy user account used by the Membership Authentication system for a Membership Directory in Membership Authentication mode.

The Basics

The **Personalization and Membership snap-in** is used to view and manage Membership Server instances. Each instance of the Membership Server is a virtual representation of the aggregated services that the Membership Server provides – including the LDAP service and the Direct Mail service. The **LDAP service** provides services for accessing the Membership Directory, while the **Direct Mail service** provides services that interact with an SMTP server for sending personalized email. We can't just stop and start the Membership Server, but we *can* stop and start the services running within the Membership Server.

> **A Membership Server is the virtual representation of the aggregation of the services provided by the LDAP Service & Direct Mail.**

We use the Membership Server to associate these services with other applications – such as Internet Information Server 4.0. Once another service – such as IIS 4.0 – has a Membership Server mapped to it, it can take advantage of the capabilities provided by the Membership Server – such as access to the Membership Directory, and authentication. In Chapter 8 we'll learn more about how IIS can use the services provided by the Membership Server.

Finding the Snap-In

So how do you find the Personalization and Membership snap-in? Once you've installed Site Server 3.0, look under the program group Microsoft Site Server, select Administration, and select the Site Server Service Admin (MMC) option. This will open the **Microsoft Management Console** (MMC), and display all of the appropriate snap-ins that Site Server provides.

The Personalization and Membership snap-in should be available in the left-hand portion of the screen:

Expanding this snap-in will reveal a small icon that looks like a computer – this should be labeled with the name of your machine. In fact, this icon is a representation of the local computer, and is necessary since multiple computers can be administered through this central utility. If we only wanted to administer the services on remote machines – e.g. if access to the physical machines were restricted – we could install only the Site Server Tools (from Site Server Setup) as we saw in Chapter 5.

To find the Membership Servers available on the local computer, simply expand the icon – this displays each of the available Membership Servers, identified by an icon that shows a folder and a small globe (as in the screenshot above). To view the services that a Membership Server supports, just expand the Membership Server icon. Expanding this icon will reveal the available services – LDAP and/or Direct Mail.

> *One of the default snap-ins that you can view immediately is the **Intranet (Windows NT Authentication) Membership Server**. This is the Membership Service that you will be using if you decide to use enterprise or NT authentication as the default authentication method for your site.*

Other Administration Possibilities

You can accomplish many tasks through the MMC, but it's not the only way to perform your administrative duties. We can perform all of the same tasks through any application that can use automation objects: Active Server Pages, Windows Scripting Host, and all the automation enabled languages (Visual Basic 5.0-6.0, Visual C++ 5.0-6.0) and this is just what we'll do, starting in Chapter 9.

However, let's not dive into the code just yet. The best approach is to learn how the Personalization and Membership snap-in works, so that we can take advantage of the rich feature set. Once we've looked at all the possible uses here, we'll take a look at some code to see how we can do the same things directly through programs.

Creating a New Membership Server

There are three ways in which we can create a new Membership Server:

❑ Via the **New Membership Server** wizard from the Personalization and Membership snap-in
❑ Via the PMAdmin tool from the command line
❑ programmatically using the appropriate COM objects

The PMAdmin *tool is a Visual Basic Script utility. It provides a method that uses the necessary COM objects to create new Membership Server instances from the command line. To read more about the* PMAdmin *tool, see Appendix B.*

In this section, we'll describe how to create new Membership Servers with the New Membership Server wizard.

Finding the New Membership Server Wizard

To start the New Membership Server wizard, select the computer icon that represents the computer on which you want to create the new Membership Server; right-click on this icon, and select New | Membership Server Instance....

Using the New Membership Server Wizard

The New Membership Server wizard is a simple way to create a new Membership Server. Each screen in the wizard represents a different configuration option for the Membership Server, and the services it will represent. We'll walk through the wizard and take a detailed look at each screen, using two example procedures. Also, since creating a Membership Server in SQL Server is more complex, all screens will be 'directed' towards SQL Server. In order to create a new Membership Directory that uses SQL Server, we need to have already created and configured a SQL Server database for that Membership Directory.

> *See Chapter 5 for more information about creating an SQL Server 6.5 database for the Membership Directory.*

A New Membership Directory (with Microsoft SQL Server)

The New Membership Server wizard can create a *new* Membership Directory along with the new Membership Server instance; or it can configure the new Membership Server to use an *existing* Membership Directory. First, we'll step through the procedure for creating a *new* Membership Directory for the new Membership Server.

Screen 1: The Splash Screen

The initial screen we're presented with is the splash screen, which lists the functions of the wizard:

Screen 2: Selecting the Configuration Mode

In Chapter 3, we explained how we can configure and devote an entire machine to the Membership Directory, and configure multiple machines to share that Membership Directory through individual Membership Server instances.

Screen 2 of the wizard presents us with the option of how we want to configure this Membership Server instance:

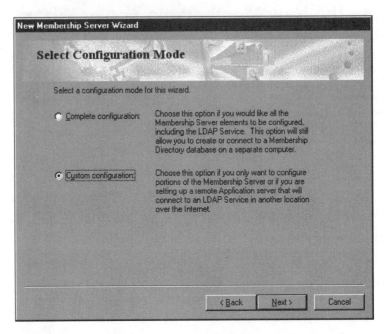

In this run-through, we will select the Custom configuration – this will allow us to examine the other available settings.

Screen 3: Select Configuration Options

Assuming that you selected the Custom configuration option in Screen 2, then Screen 3 presents you with the following three configuration options:

Let's look at each of these options in turn.

The Active User Object. You'll recall from Chapter 2 that the Active User Object (AUO) is a wrapper for a lower level set of interfaces (called the Active Directory Service Interfaces, or ADSI); these interfaces are used to navigate and manage a directory – in our case the Membership Directory. In addition to navigation and management, the AUO also captures the context of the user when used in an ASP page run from an IIS 4.0 web with a Membership Server mapped to the web. When a user accesses a site mapped to a Membership Server, they are first authenticated before gaining access to resources. The AUO can grab this authenticated context, to bind to the appropriate member in the Membership Directory.

If you don't plan on scripting against your directory server instance, and all you care about is using the membership (or authentication) features of the Personalization and Membership system, them you won't need the AUO.

However, if you do want to customize your pages based on your attributes, or dynamically interact with the Directory Service, then you definitely want to select the AUO.

> If you select *only* the AUO from this screen, the wizard will assume that the AUO will be using an existing Membership Directory.

The LDAP service. You should select the LDAP Service checkbox *either* if you need to create a new Membership Directory, *or* if you need to connect to an existing directory. The LDAP service provides the ability for applications to communicate with the Membership Directory through the LDAP protocol.

There are only two cases when you would *not* want to add the LDAP service:

- ❏ If separate LDAP services were used from Internet Information Server. In this case, we must specify the LDAP Service for the Membership Server to be used later in the wizard.
- ❏ If the computer is dedicated for the Site Server 3.0 Direct Mail. We can create a Membership server containing the Message Builder Service and then map that service to a particular web server.

The Message Builder Service. Selecting the Message Builder Service option dictates that email can be used from web pages, and allows for the direct mail service to email to users. In the wizard, it states that the Message Builder service should be run on its own computer to optimize performance. This is especially true if the direct mail feature is intended to be used to build and send customized emails to users, since it uses a large amount of system resources.

For the sake of this current example, we'll select all three of the above components. However, if you choose *not* to check the LDAP Service checkbox, then the wizard jumps straight to Screen 5, so let's quickly see what you would see there…

Screen 5: Connect to LDAP Service

Here, you would be asked to connect to an LDAP service on another machine. For this, you would need to specify the IP address or Domain Name Server (DNS) name, as well as the TCP port of the LDAP Service:

By default, Site Server installs the Membership NT Authentication Membership Directory on port 1002 and each new Membership Directory on 1002 + *n*, where *n* is the number of additional Membership Directories. The default TCP port for an LDAP service is 389, but can vary – depending on the setup options chosen for the LDAP Service installation.

OK, that's what happens if you don't select the <u>L</u>DAP Service checkbox in Screen 3. Now let's get back to our real example – if you check the <u>L</u>DAP Service checkbox in Screen 3, along with either (or both) of the other services, then the wizard moves straight on to Screen 4.

Screen 4: Select the Membership Directory

This screen allows you either to create a *new* Membership Directory, or to connect to an *existing* Membership Directory:

By electing to create a *new* Membership Directory, the wizard will apply the Membership Directory schema to a database, specified later in the wizard, which will provide the services of the Membership Directory. By connecting to an *existing* Membership Directory, the wizard simply allows for the creation of a new LDAP Service or Active User Object to use against the Membership Directory selected later in the wizard.

For this example we're going to create a new Membership Directory, which will take us to Screen 6.

Screen 6: Select Authentication Mode

The next step is to select an authentication mode:

The Membership feature of Personalization and Membership refers to user credentials that are stored *either* in an existing NT user base (this is Windows NT Authentication mode), *or* in the Membership Directory (this is Membership Authentication mode). There is a fuller discussion of the details of these two authentication types in Chapter 13. In this run-through, we'll select Membership Authentication.

> *If you want to create a Membership Server with Windows NT authentication, you should choose* Windows NT Authentication *here – this will bring up Screen 10 as the next screen. Screen 10 is only different from Screen 9 in one respect – namely, that you're not asked to create an account for the Membership Directory Administrator. This is because, under Windows NT authentication, the administrator of the Membership Directory will be the local NT Administrator account. All other screens for creating a new Membership Directory will be the same, regardless of the authentication mode chosen.*

Let's plough on, selecting Membership Authentication here. The resulting screen is Screen 9.

Screen 9: Name the Membership Directory and Create Account

Our next step is to create a name for the new Membership Directory. The Membership Directory Name is used as the realm for authentication. The **realm** is the value for the organization name (o=) used when building a Distinguished Name to an entry. The organization container represents the root container in the Membership Directory. The realm is displayed in the Clear Text/Basic and Distributed Password Authentication, and is a simple way of letting the user know what they are providing credentials for.

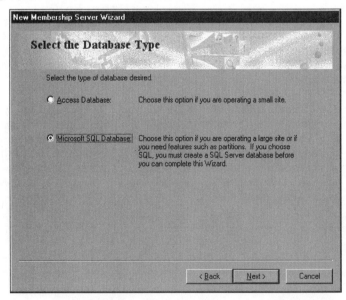

The <u>P</u>assword for the Membership Directory Administrator account is the password for the first account that the directory manager should use. The Administrator account should be used for Administration purposes only – i.e. when first connecting to the Membership Directory through the Membership Directory Manager snap-in, and for creating other users with proper permissions for appropriate tasks. The Administrator account will be given the SUPERBROKER privilege in the Membership Directory.

We'll be seeing more about the Membership Directory Manager snap-in in the next chapter.

Screen 11: Select the Database Type

The Membership Directory is nothing but a database schema. Therefore, we need to create a database in which this schema, and the corresponding tables, will exist:

At the time of writing (that is, pre-Service Pack 1 for Site Server), the only databases that are supported for Membership Directories are Microsoft Access and Microsoft SQL Server 6.5. Site Server Service Pack 1 should allow for Personalization and Membership to make use of SQL Server 7.0, which is a more robust database. Unfortunately, the Membership Directory does not support other databases, such as Oracle or Sybase.

Screen 12: Type SQL Database Information

When you create a new Membership Directory that uses SQL Server 6.5, you don't need to bother with creating an ODBC DSN. However, you *do* need to make sure that TCP/IP is one of the supported protocols for SQL Server 6.5 – otherwise the wizard will return an error.

The **S**erver name is the name of the machine that has the new SQL Server 6.5 database that is to be used for the Membership Directory. The **D**atabase name corresponds to the name of the database that we created to store the Membership Directory, and the SQL **u**ser name and **p**assword should be equivalent to the **sa** permission level.

See Chapter 5 for more information on SQL Server 6.5 and Site Server Personalization and Membership.

Screen 13: Create Local LDAP Service

The next step is to create a new LDAP service for the new Membership Directory. When a new LDAP service is created on a machine, a port number and IP address must be assigned to it.

If you are using Microsoft DHCP on your network, leave the IP address selection drop-down set to [All Unassigned] – this way, the machine can support Domain Name Service resolution and will only be dependent upon the port number. However, if a specific IP is used for the Network Interface Card (NIC), assign that IP address to the LDAP service as well.

Microsoft DHCP is an application that implements dynamic allocation of IP addresses.

Screen 14: Message Builder Configuration

You will only see this screen if you have selected to install the Message Builder server, back on Screen 3. In order to use the Direct Mail feature of Site Server Personalization and Membership, an SMTP mail server must be provided. The SMTP server installed with IIS 4.0 suits this role quite well: it can reside on any machine along with IIS, and is installed from the Windows NT 4.0 Option Pack. However, the IIS 4.0 SMTP Server is only a relay server, and requires another server (such as Exchange 5.5, or the POP3 Server that is provided with MCIS) to send email.

To configure Site Server to use an SMTP server, simply enter the name of the server that SMTP services are running on.

Screen 15: Complete the Configuration

Once we have provided all the information needed the wizard presents the most important screen of all. The Complete the Configuration screen provides the user with some of the most critical information that should immediately be consigned to memory (or better still, written down!).

```
New Membership Server Wizard

        Complete the Configuration

        You are now ready to complete the New Membership Server Wizard.

        For this instance you have chosen to:
        - Enable Membership Authentication
        - Configure the LDAP Service
        - Configure the AUO
        - Configure the Message Builder Service

        The following accounts will be created automatically for you. Unique passwords
        will be generated automatically for each of the accounts.

            Membership Directory Accounts:
                Authentication Service Account: MBSBRKR3_MANX
                Message Builder Account: MBSDM3_MANX

            Windows NT Accounts:
                Windows NT Impersonation Account: MemProxyUser3

                                          < Back      Finish      Cancel
```

This screen gives a brief overview of the Membership Server features installed by the wizard, and the accounts that are used for system and authentication purposes. The Membership Directory accounts correspond to accounts in the Membership Directory that fulfill certain 'system' roles.

❑   **Membership Directory Accounts** are accounts that exist in the Membership Directory:

> The **Authentication Service Account** is only necessary for a Membership Directory configured for Membership Authentication mode. The LDAP service uses this account to connect to the Membership Directory and retrieve user information, which is compared with logon information submitted when a client is challenged.

> The **Message Builder Account** is another special account that is added when Message Builder services are installed for the Membership Server. The account is used to access the Membership Directory and impersonate users or perform the necessary actions to generate content for personalized mailings

❑ **Windows NT Accounts** are accounts created for impersonating the Membership User when accessing the Windows NT file system through the Personalization and Membership system. This account is only created for Membership Directories that use Membership Authentication; they are not necessary for Membership Directories that use Windows NT authentication.

The **Windows NT Impersonation Account**, MemProxyUser, is a special account used by the Personalization and Membership system to impersonate the user currently accessing the IIS web, where the IIS web is mapped to a Membership Server in Membership authentication mode.

Whenever a request is made for a file system resource, the MemProxyUser is granted the Security IDs of the membership groups (corresponding to Windows NT groups) that it belongs to. Never assign any resource permissions directly to the MemProxyUser, or every membership user will have access to these resources.

The placeholder represents the Membership Server Instance ID (in the screenshot above, it's set to the value 3). Each Membership Server on the machine is assigned a unique ID. This ID is the value for the AUO instance number in the registry. You can view this through the path HKEY_LOCAL_MACHINE\SOFTWARE\Microsoft\Site Server\3.0\P&M\AUO, as shown in the next screenshot:

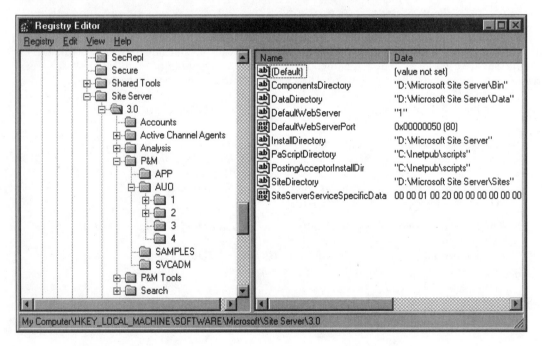

Connect to an Existing Membership Directory

Now, let's look at a different example. We'll create a Membership Server that will connect to an *existing* Membership Directory. We might do this, for example, if we wanted to create additional LDAP Services to scale the site. Each LDAP instance will still be represented by a unique Membership Server instance. The first steps are exactly the same as those in the example above:

❑ **Screen 1.** Splash Screen

❑ **Screen 2** Select Configuration Mode – Custom Configuration

❑ **Screen 3** Select Configuration Options – AUO, LDAP and/or Message Builder

❑ **Screen 4** Select the Membership Directory – Connect to an existing Membership Directory

This time, in Screen 4 we choose the second option, Connect to an existing Membership Directory. This option takes us directly to Screen 7.

Screen 7: Connect to an Existing Directory

You are prompted to select the Microsoft Access or Microsoft SQL Server database in which the Membership Directory exists:

The values entered here must correspond to a database that has already been created or built by another Membership Server. You can find the database details of an existing Membership Server by opening the Properties dialog of the LDAP Service for that Membership Server (we'll cover this in the next section).

From here, the wizard takes us to Screen 13 – Create Local LDAP Service – which we've already seen. From there, we're guided onto Screen 8.

Screen 8: Log on to the LDAP Service

When connecting to an existing Membership Directory, the Administrator account (or any other account for that Directory with DS-PRIVILEGES of the SUPERBROKER attribute) must be used.

New Membership Server Wizard

Name the Membership Directory and Create Account

Type a name for the Membership Directory and choose a password for the Administrator account.

Type a name for your Membership Directory. This name will be used as the Realm in the DS. Choose a name that identifies your service or your community of users.

Membership Directory name:

Type a password for the Membership Directory Administrator account of this Membership Directory.

Password:

Re-enter password to confirm:

Make a note of the password you choose for this account. This is the most powerful account in the Membership Directory and you will need it later in the configuration process.

< Back | Next > | Cancel

This is necessary since a new broker account will be created in the Membership Directory for the new LDAP service, and it's only possible to create an account with the SUPERBROKER privilege from an *existing* account that also has the SUPERBROKER privilege.

There are two more screens that tie up this session of the wizard, namely Screens 14 and 15:

❏ **Screen 14**   Message Builder Configuration (only if Message Builder service was selected in Screen 3)
❏ **Screen 15**   Complete the Configuration

These are identical to those screens that we saw in our first example.

Properties of the Membership Server

So we've seen how to create a new Membership Server; now we can look at how to configure its properties. Next we'll look at the properties of the LDAP instance for a Membership Server. By expanding any of the Membership Servers (such as the Intranet (Windows NT Authentication) Membership Server, which is the default installed with Site Server) we can administer the LDAP Service instance and the Direct Mail Service instance.

Continue by right-clicking on the Membership Server itself, and selecting Properties from the menu; this presents us with a property dialog box for configuring the Membership Server instance. We can use this dialog box to make a number of selections, which affect how the Membership Server instance behaves. You will find that there are either one or two tabs in this dialog box, depending on whether the Membership Server is configured to use Membership or Windows NT authentication.

> If the Membership Server has been configured to use Windows NT Authentication, then we'll only see one tab – the **Active User Object (AUO) Providers** tab. This is because Windows NT Authentication uses the existing Windows NT Authentication architecture – so we don't need to make any configuration changes for authentication. This is the case for the default Membership Server, the Intranet (Windows NT Authentication) Server.
>
> If the Membership Server has been configured to use Membership Authentication, then a second tab – the **Authentication Service** tab – is also provided.

The Authentication Service Tab

This tab presents us with the option to change settings for the Membership Directory connection, HTML Forms Authentication, and the Windows NT impersonation account. You can see these three sections in the example dialog box:

We'll deal with each of the three sections in turn in the following paragraphs. To read more on the authentication settings covered here, refer to Chapter 13.

The Membership Directory Connection

The Membership Directory connection dictates the configuration settings for connecting to the Membership Directory. This includes the name of the LDAP Service that we will connect to, the TCP port that should be used, and the Membership Broker account username and password. Let's look at these more closely:

❑ **LDAP host**. This is the name of the machine on which the LDAP service is running. The LDAP host can be run on any machine that has Site Server 3.0 installed and makes its LDAP service available. This can be especially useful since multiple LDAP services can be configured on different machines to scale the site, and LDAP Services can easily be changed.

❑ **TCP Port.** Since LDAP is a protocol that talks TCP/IP, there needs to be a port on our LDAP server that looks for LDAP requests. This option allows us to set which port will be used to talk the LDAP protocol over TCP/IP in order to communicate with our Membership Directory.

❑ **User name.** The user name points to a special user, called the **broker**, that exists in the Membership Directory. The broker acts as a liaison between a user that wishes to be authenticated and the Membership Directory. The broker account is a special account that exists in the Membership Directory (in Membership Authentication mode) or in the Windows NT SAM (in Windows NT Authentication mode). The broker account has full privileges to the Membership Directory, and is used to bind to the Membership Directory and verify member credentials for Membership Authentication. The broker is granted these permissions by a special attribute, DS-Privileges, with the value SUPERBROKER.

❑ **Password.** The password is simply the password for the Membership broker account. Note that if a Membership Directory has not removed the group ACE public from the root container then it runs the risk of users being able to access this password, since the public group is granted full permission by default. (The public group is set by default when a new Membership Directory is created.) We'll learn how to resolve this in Chapter 13.

HTML Forms Authentication

The second section in the Authentication Service tab is HTML Forms Authentication. The HTML Forms Authentication options determine settings for web sites that will use HTML Forms authentication. More specifically, the single parameter here determines the session expiration time-out value:

❑ **Session expiration.** The session expiration determines the time (in minutes) that a particular user session lasts if Forms authentication is used to verify the user when accessing a Personalization and Membership web site. Whenever the user requests a new resource – after being authenticated – the session time is either reset, or the member is re-authenticated if the session has timed out.

We'll talk more about HTML Forms, and other authentication methods, in Chapters 8 and 13.

The Windows NT Impersonation Account

The final section of the Authentication Service tab manages the Windows NT impersonation account. The settings in this section pertain to the impersonation account that is used by Windows NT when a Membership-authenticated user requests access to the file system.

You'll recall that a Membership-authenticated user's credentials are stored in the Membership Directory. This is in contrast to Windows NT authentication, which uses the Windows NT Security Accounts Database to store users' credentials.

The parameters that we can control here are as follows:

❑ **User name.** This is the user name that will be used to access the Windows NT file system when requesting secured resources. The user account MemProxyUser, shown in the screenshot on the previous page, will assume the access permissions of the user or the group permissions assigned in the Membership Directory when accessing any NT resources.

❑ **Password.** The password of the MemProxyUser is set through the Windows NT User Manager tool. We'll look at how to change and reset this password in the *Advanced Concepts* section, at the end of this chapter.

The Active User Object (AUO) Providers Tab

The Active User Object (AUO) Providers tab enables us to add additional providers that the AUO will aggregate into one collection or namespace. The idea is that ASP – or any other application – can use the AUO to connect to multiple data sources and retrieve records that can be accessed as a single item, transparently to the user. AUO providers are listed in the table below.

In this screenshot we can see the default AUO provider. This is the provider for the ou=Members container, which interacts with actual members in this container. The table lists the AUO alias and ADS provider type for each secondary provider. We need to specify an alias for each provider we use – here the alias is Default. The AUO uses this alias to access the data for that provider. The Active Directory Services (ADS) provider field shows the type of provider to be used. Here it is LDAP since the secondary provider points to the Membership Directory. There are four types of ADS provider:

ADS Provider	Description
IIS	The ADSI path to use as a starting point in the Internet Information Server Metabase.
LDAP	Used to connect to containers and objects within a directory service..
SimpleDBDS	Used to connect to databases through a Data Source Name (DSN). These databases must provide a primary key that is unique for each item and can be used to access the associated data.
WinNT	Used to connect to exposed properties in Windows NT. This provider, or one quite similar, will be one of the providers that is used for accessing the Windows NT 5.0 Active Directory.

In addition, if your provider is using Novell's Directory Service (NDS) or NetWare 3.0 (NWCOMP) you will have the option of selecting these as your ADS provider type.

In order to view the properties of an AUO provider in detail, double-click on its entry in the table to bring up the AUO Provider properties dialog with the values of the AUO Provider you have selected. If you want to add a new provider you can click the A<u>d</u>d... button – this in fact brings up the same dialog as you get by double-clicking on a table entry, but this time the fields are blank to be filled in. We'll look at these fields in a moment by adding an example secondary provider.

Secondary AUO Providers

Secondary providers are best used for accessing data to which you would otherwise have to build a connection programmatically each time you needed to retrieve some information. For instance, if the ou=dynamic container was intended to be an intermediate location for storing some member data that would expire after a certain period, this information should be accessed through a **secondary Active User Object provider**. This secondary AUO Provider would point at the ou=dynamic container, and we could then create new member objects in the ou=dynamic container using this secondary provider. An example application of this would be to use member objects in the ou=dynamic container for a simple way of tracking which members are currently on the system.

The secondary provider must be accessed using the root provider. For instance, if we want to specify the secondary provider programmatically then we call a method for that secondary provider with the following syntax:

```
PrimaryProvider("SecondaryProvider").Method()
```

The following code fragment gives a brief example of how we would use this syntax if we wanted to use a secondary AUO provider to create new objects in the ou=dynamic container:

```
' Create main Active User Object (root Provider)
' **************************************************
Set objAUOUser = Server.CreateObject("Membership.UserObjects.1")
' Use Secondary provider pointing to the
' dynamic container called dynamic that will
' live for 15 seconds
' **************************************************
objAUOUser("Dynamic").Put "userComment", "Hello World!"
objAUOUser("Dynamic").Put "ttl", "15"
objAUOUser("Dynamic").SetInfo
```

We'll see how to use code like this further on in the book when we have completed our configuration of Site Server. Let's take a brief look at how we set up a secondary AUO provider through this tab.

The documentation for Site Server gives an example of creating a secondary provider using the HTML admin pages – in our example here we'll use the dialogs from the MMC.

We click on the A<u>d</u>d... button from the AUO Providers tab as discussed above, to bring up the following dialog:

We'll continue with the example of creating a secondary AUO provider that points to the ou=dynamic container to look at the fields in this dialog. The first value we need to specify is an alias for the provider – we'll call ours dynamic. Next we need to specify where the provider will look for objects. We want to set the path to point to the ou=dynamic container, and the ADS provider type will be LDAP as the provider will need to access the Membership Directory.

Under the Path suffix: label, we need to indicate how objects in the secondary provider are to be identified. In order to retrieve secondary data from a secondary provider we must use primary keys that are unique in the primary provider, and identify information in the secondary (such as the common name (cn) of a user). The secondary provider is a dependent provider to the one that supplies the primary key. For example, while most member information is stored in the Membership Directory, we might also want to use member data from a legacy database. We can use a secondary provider to access the appropriate data in the legacy database and associate it with a member account in the Membership Directory.

Finally, in order to be able to create new objects in the dynamic container we have to define the schema that the new provider will use.

Supported Secondary Providers

There are a number of supported directory services that can be used by the secondary provider; these include Novell's Directory Service (NDS), NetWare 3.0 (NWCOMP), Microsoft's Internet Information Server, and Microsoft's WinNT Active Directory. In addition, ODBC databases can be used as providers – although they cannot be authenticated against, nor can they be used as a root AUO provider.

> **Only the Membership Directory can be used to provide the credentials used for Membership authentication.**

In order to use an ODBC data source as a secondary provider, a connection must be made: to do this, it is necessary to build a System Data Source Name (DSN) for the data source, using the **ODBC** applet in the **Control Panel** (shown below). For data in the database to be associated with the root AUO, the object to be associated with the database must have a corresponding attribute in the database.

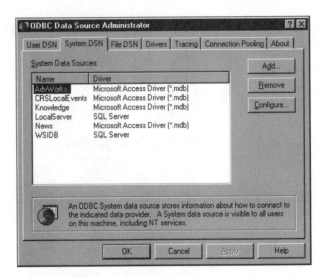

Non-ODBC databases may also be used as secondary providers; however, in order to do this you must create a custom ADS provider, which is beyond the scope of this book.

The LDAP Instance

OK, so we've looked at the properties of the Membership Server. Now let's expand the Membership Server icon in the MMC, and right-click on the LDAP instance and select **Properties**. This will bring up the LDAP Properties dialog:

The LDAP Properties dialog box defines configuration settings for the LDAP instance used by the Membership Directory. As you can see, there are six tabs presented in this dialog: General, Root Database, Dynamic Directory, Directory Properties, Membership Directory Security and Logging. We'll complete this section by discussing each of these tabs in turn.

The General Tab

The General tab of the LDAP Properties dialog box provides the user with the configuration options for some of the administrative features of the LDAP instance. The server instance, connection and search settings can be configured here.

The Server Instance

There are four fields to consider here:

- ❑ **Server name.** The server name corresponds to the name of the machine on which the LDAP service is running. Note that the LDAP service doesn't necessarily have to run on the same machine as the Membership Server. The LDAP Service can live on any machine available on the network – this configuration option is set in the New Membership Server wizard.

- ❑ **IP address.** An LDAP instance can be assigned a particular IP address. Alternatively, if you're using DHCP on your network, you must use this field to set the LDAP Service IP address to [All Unassigned].

- ❑ **TCP port.** This is identical to the port we saw defined on the Authentication Service tab of the Membership Server's Properties dialog. We use the TCP port because LDAP is a TCP/IP protocol. If you've set the IP address field to [All Unassigned] then you should define unique TCP ports. Alternatively, if you're using a unique IP address (or if there is only going to be one LDAP Service instance for this machine) then use port 389 – this is the default LDAP service port. Finally, if accessing the LDAP service through a firewall is a concern then the LDAP service can be on a separate machine from the web server and expose port 80.

- ❑ **SSL port.** If Secure Sockets Layer is to be supported through LDAP, use port 636 (which is reserved for SSL communication and should not be used by any other TCP/IP service on the computer). Also, note that you can only have one SSL service per LDAP Service or IP address.

> **Unless otherwise specified, LDAP Services default to port 389. Secure Sockets Layer for LDAP should talk over port 636, which is reserved for SSL.**

The LDAP Connections Settings

Under the Connections section of the General tab three parameters may be set:

- ❑ **Max connections.** This option sets the maximum number of current sessions that a particular LDAP instance will support.

- ❑ **Connection timeout.** This defines the timeout period (in seconds); in other words, how long a connection will be kept open with no requests.

- ❑ **Read-only mode.** If an LDAP instance is set to Read-only then any connection is only allowed to read from the Membership Directory. The Membership Directory is optimized for reads, but this is a way to enforce a read-only Membership Directory.

The Searches Settings

The Searches section defines how LDAP will treat searches in the Membership Directory.

❑ Limit searches to initial substring only. When this box is checked, the only searches permitted are those that are of type *Begins with*. Searches of type *Contains* and *Ends with* are thus disallowed. This is just a simple way of ensuring that a search doesn't completely bottleneck the system. Searches that begin with **search-value* are more expensive than *search-value** (where * is a wildcard). The type *Begins with* is meant to include *search-value**.

❑ Max query time. This defines the maximum length of time that a query can exist – the query expires after this period of time. This is another way of avoiding system bottlenecking.

❑ Max page size. When a search is performed and a result set is returned, the Max page size limits the number of records that can exist per page of that result set.

❑ Max results set. This specifies the maximum number of entries that can be contained in a query. Any item in the Membership Directory is an entry, so if a search for a specific user is performed, and the result is (say) 1000, then either the entire amount could be returned (which would be expensive for the network services), or a limited number of entries could be returned. The options are:

Unlimited: Specifies that an unlimited amount of entries can be returned by a search. For large results, this could degrade system performance.

Limited to: Limits the number entries that can be contained in a record set. A correctly formed query should circumvent any problems that could occur from the Max Results Set being limited to a reasonable amount (the default is 500).

> **All views of a container are treated as queries. Hence, if we have 1000 entries in a container and we attempt to enumerate through these entries we will only work with the first 500 (the default) unless the Max Result Set option is changed.**

The Root Database Tab

Since a directory service is nothing more than a highly structured database optimized for reads, the developer or administrator has the option of using either an **Access database** or a **SQL Server database** to store the Membership Directory Schema data. Under the Root Database tab, we can make this selection and configure different settings for each database.

Microsoft Access

If you're using a Microsoft Access database, there's just a single field to complete:

- ❑ File name. This points to the location of the Microsoft Access .mdb file.

Microsoft SQL Server

If you're using a Microsoft SQL Server database, there are four fields that you need to complete:

- ❑ Computer name. This is the name of the machine on which SQL Server is installed.
- ❑ Database name. This is the name of the database that is used for the Membership Directory. The Membership Directory is stored in a SQL database on the machine specified in the Computer name field defined above.
- ❑ User name. This is the username used to access the SQL Server database. Note that in the screenshot above, the username sa is used to access the database. In a production environment you should create a unique username and password that has the necessary permission to access the SQL database.
- ❑ Password. This is the password of the user that is accessing the database (specified in the User name field).

Microsoft Access is a great database for prototyping a Personalization and Membership site. However, in any production environment it's definitely preferable to use Microsoft SQL Server. There's more on this issue in Chapter 5.

The Dynamic Directory Tab

The dynamic directory is the only container in the Membership Directory that is never written to disk. The dynamic directory lives in memory on the machine which runs the LDAP service, and should be used for entries that need fast access, or items that are guaranteed to expire (such as session variables).

There's an excellent white paper from Microsoft, which addresses how to use the dynamic directory to manage session state. This is especially useful for web sites that are load-balanced, since it's not possible to guarantee what server the user will use next. The dynamic directory supports replication among other dynamic directories, so that multiple machines can share this container. The white paper is available at
http://www.microsoft.com/workshop/server/nextgen/sessiondata.asp.

Let's have a look at the settings on this tab:

❑ Enable Dynamic Directory. This checkbox determines whether or not the LDAP service will support a dynamic directory. The dynamic directory only exists in memory; if it's turned off, this will release any memory that it held.

❑ Minimum client time to live. This specifies the minimum time-to-live (TTL) for which an object will exist in the dynamic directory. Entries created in the dynamic directory will then default to this time-to-live value, unless another is expressly set programmatically.

❑ Maximum dynamic entries. This specifies the maximum number of objects that can exist in the dynamic container at any one time (as with any other container, this will be true for all users).

❑ Enable NetMeeting 1.0 support. This specifies whether or not Microsoft NetMeeting will be supported. In order to support Microsoft NetMeeting, the LDAP service must reside on port 389 – the default LDAP service port. In addition, no other LDAP Service (supporting the same Membership Directory) can have NetMeeting support turned on.

Membership Directory Support for NetMeeting is a carry-over from Microsoft Internet Locator Service.

❑ Enable dynamic data replication. When selected, this checkbox specifies that this Membership Directory is set to replicate the dynamic directory with any other LDAP Services that connect to the same Membership Directory and also support dynamic data replication. In the table below this checkbox, you need to list the LDAP Services with which you want to replicate data. For each LDAP Service, specify the name of the computer on which it is running, and the Membership Server with which it is associated. Whenever a write is made to an LDAP Service's dynamic directory with replication enabled, a remote procedure call (RPC) is performed to the other LDAP Services and the data is copied.

The Directory Properties Tab

The Directory Properties tab specifies the properties of the Membership Directory to which this LDAP Service connects.

Let's have a look at the fields included in this tab.

- ❏ **Root distinguished name (DN) o=.** This is the root distinguished name of the Membership Directory (as discussed in Chapter 2). The value of this text box cannot be edited once the directory is created.

- ❏ **DN prefix (optional).** For the Membership Directory the Distinguished Name prefix is set to none, but it can be set, if so desired, to support multiple organization types under one directory service (so, for example, it can be changed to support the X.500 Distinguished Name prefix.) When the value is set, it defines the root node of a directory service to specify the country (c=) value in the directory information tree. The DN Prefix should be left to <None> unless the Membership Directory needs to be re-purposed for very specific situations that are outside of the scope of this book.

Selecting a Partition to View Underlying Databases

In order to make the Directory Service as scalable as possible, it is possible to partition individual containers. There are two kinds of partitioning, as we discussed in Chapter 4. **Visible** or **namespace partitioning** involves using a dedicated database to store all the information for a particular container. Value partitioning involves distributing the contents of a container evenly over two or more databases.

> **Remember: a Membership Directory can by partitioned only if it uses SQL Server.**

Later on in this chapter, we'll see how to implement partitions using the Member Directory Partition wizard. The fields in the second half of this tab enable you to view (and modify) the existing partitions of any container:

❑ **Container partition.** This is the container whose database partition details are displayed in the Master databases table.

❑ **Value partition.** If the container in the field above is *not* value-partitioned, then this value is 0. If the container *is* value-partitioned, then this integer indicates the number of the value partition whose details are displayed in the Master databases table.

❑ **Master databases on this partition.** In this table, there are three fields display the details of each database in the partition:

> **Server Name:** The server name of the database.
>
> **Database Name:** The name of the database that contains the specified directory service partition.
>
> **Database Type:** Determines whether the database can be written to and/or read from.

Editing Databases

Ideally, we would create a Membership Directory with multiple partitions to handle the growth of the Membership Directory across multiple SQL Server databases. As the number of members and the amount of data stored grows, we can expand the table index size; and as I/O issues become a bottleneck for the system, databases can be moved to other machines.

If a database is moved to another machine, we'll also need to change the database server properties. We can change these settings by clicking the Edit... button on the LDAP Properties dialog:

Before you change the database that a particular container points to, you must first ensure that the database has the correct data for the container you have chosen.

❑ **Server name.** This is the name of the server where this database is found.
❑ **Database name.** This is the name of the database that this container refers to.
❑ **User name.** This is the username used to access the database.
❑ **Password.** This is the password corresponding to the username that is used to access the database.

❑   <u>M</u>aximum connections. This is the maximum number of connections that the directory service
will use when connecting to the database. Each LDAP Service will use 10 connections to the SQL
Server database, by default. This means that SQL Server needs to have the appropriate number of
user connections available.

❑   Default <u>t</u>imeout. This is the time (in seconds) before a connection will be released due to
inactivity.

The Membership Directory Security Tab

The Membership Security tab defines what
security methods will be used when access to the
Membership Directory is requested.

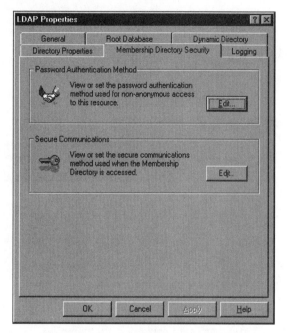

It is important to remember that if the Membership Directory has the public group enabled with the
full permissions ACE, then *any* user can read *all* properties in the Membership Directory, including
passwords. Securing the Membership Directory is an important issue, which we'll cover in
Chapter 13.

There are two sections to this tab – Password Authentication Method and Secure Communications.
Let's have a brief look at them now.

The Password Authentication Method

The Password Authentication Method determines how LDAP will access the Membership Directory.
This is especially important when the Membership Directory and the LDAP service exist on different
computers. However, the method chosen will not affect how members are authenticated from IIS. For
example, if we choose to disable <u>A</u>llow anonymous from this dialog, then we are simply telling the
LDAP Service that anonymous access to the Membership Directory is not allowed.

If our LDAP Service is accessing a Membership Directory that uses Windows NT authentication,
we'll be presented with options for binding to the Membership Directory using the appropriate
methods:

Since Windows NT Authentication validates members from the Windows NT Security Accounts Manager (SAM), we need to specify the types of access that are allowed into the Membership Directory based on Windows NT credentials.

If our LDAP Service is accessing a Membership Directory that uses Membership Authentication, we'll be presented with options for binding to the Membership Directory using Membership authentication methods:

- ❑ **Allow anonymous.** If this option is turned off, only authenticated members will be allowed access to the Membership Directory.
- ❑ **Clear Text/Basic Authentication.** Clear Text/Basic Authentication is required for most applications, such as Personalization and Membership, to authenticate with the Membership Directory. Although clear text/basic is used, the password information is encrypted using the value/key pair when it is sent back and forth between the LDAP Service and the Membership Directory. The encryption keys are stored on the LDAP Service and the Membership Directory, and can be modified. To read more about the keys used for encryption by LDAP and the Membership Directory, see Chapter 13.
- ❑ **Distributed Password Authentication (DPA) (Membership 1.0 Compatibility).** Note that DPA is disabled by default. This setting doesn't apply to the Membership authentication method (i.e. cookie, forms, clear text/basic, distributed password); instead it is specific to how the LDAP Service communicates with the Membership Directory. Distributed Password Authentication is only provided for backward compatibility with Membership 1.0, and doesn't need to be used since the passwords passed back and forth between the LDAP Service and the Membership Directory are encrypted. To activate DPA authentication, use the PMAdmin.vbs command line tool:
  `PMAdmin Set LDAP /LdapAuth:4 /ID:[Id of Server Instance]`
- ❑ Once Distributed Password Authentication is turned on, anonymous users will no longer be able to gain access to the Membership Directory.

Secure Communications

If the Directory Service needs to be locked down entirely, secure channel or SSL sockets can be required so that any user or program that accesses the Membership Directory will be encrypted.

The Logging Tab

To turn on logging for the directory service, simply check the Enable logging option under the Logging tab in the LDAP properties.

The logging feature can write *either* to an Internet Information Server log format *or* to an ODBC database, to enable logs to be imported into an analysis engine in order to write reports based on member information.

Partitioning the Membership Directory

As we recall from Chapter 4, in order to scale a Personalization and Membership site properly it is important that we create enough partitions to handle the planned load of the system throughout its life. Once data is entered into the Membership Directory, the directory cannot be further partitioned unless we move the data temporarily. For example, if we needed to repartition the ou=Members container we must remove all of the existing members and then re-add them afterwards. In order to partition a container, it must be empty – the only exception is the main directory information tree, which can only be partitioned when the Membership Directory is first created. In this section, we'll walk through the Membership Directory Partition Wizard to see how to create partitions.

> Remember, a Membership Directory can be partitioned only if it is created on SQL Server.

Understanding Partitions

A **partition** is a division of a storage unit. Many of us are already familiar with hard drive partitions – where a single hard drive is separated into many logical partitions, each of which can be treated by the system as an independent hard drive.

A Membership partition is much like a hard drive partition, in that it is a logical division (which can be further physically divided to separate machines) of the Membership Directory between many SQL Server databases. This logical division allows for an unprecedented amount of scalability, since each SQL Server added can drastically improve the performance of the Membership Directory.

Creating New Partitions

If any data has been added or modified in the Membership Directory prior to attempting the partitioning, you will be unable to partition the directory. Assuming that the databases to represent the partitions have already been created in SQL Server and that the Membership Directory has not yet been partitioned, highlight the appropriate Membership Server, right-click and select New | Partition to start the wizard.

Screen 1: Splash Screen

The splash screen for creating partitions is pretty boring. Unlike the other wizards, it gives no details as to what actions it is going to perform.

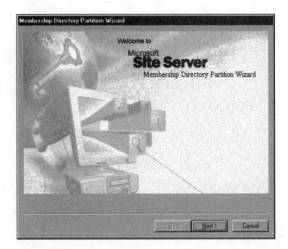

Screen 2: Select Membership Directory Container to Partition

The container to be partitioned must be selected by typing its Distinguished Name. In addition, the container can be divided into a number of partitions, and this number determines whether the container is a namespace partition or a value partition.

> **Membership Directory Partition Wizard**
>
> ## Select Membership Directory Container to Partition
>
> Specify which container in the Membership Directory you wish to partition.
>
> Type the full Distinguished Name (DN) of the Membership Directory container you would like to partition. The container you choose must be empty (i.e. contain no user defined object) and you may not add any object to this container until the wizard is completed.
>
> Directory container: [   ]
>
> Select the number of value partitions you would like to create for this container.
>
> Number of partitions: [1]
>
> [< Back] [Next >] [Cancel]

Screen 3: Database for value partition #n

There's a screen like this for each new partition – *n* represents the number of the value partition. In this screen the Server name, Database name, user name and password information must be entered for the databases to be used for the partitions.

> **Membership Directory Partition Wizard**
>
> ## Database for value partition #1.
>
> Specify the computer name, database name, user name, and password for this partition.
>
> You must have an empty SQL Server database already set up on your SQL Server.
>
> Server name: [   ]
>
> Database name: [   ]
>
> SQL Server database user name: [sa   ]
>
> SQL Server database password: [   ]
>
> [< Back] [Next >] [Cancel]

Screen 3 will be repeated for each of the partitions to be created.

Advanced Concepts

There are further changes we can make to Membership Server settings. In this section we'll look at how to change the settings for two user accounts within the Authentication Service: the Membership Server **broker** account is a user inside the directory service, while the Windows NT **impersonation** account is an actual NT user created in the Security Accounts Manager (SAM). You shouldn't change the settings for these user names and passwords, unless it's absolutely necessary: there shouldn't be any reason to change them, unless the users get renamed, accessed, or you're performing a system password change. With that said, we *can* change or reset these users if we need to.

Some of these steps require knowledge of how to use the Membership Directory Manager (Chapter 7), so you may want to come back to this section when you're familiar with all the P&M components.

The Broker Account

The user name and password created for the Membership Directory connection points to a member of the directory service that is created automatically when the New Membership Server wizard is run. This member – the **broker account** (or **superuser**) – has the necessary permissions to connect to the directory and perform any and all service-related tasks, including accessing all user permissions.

If you need to create another user to perform these tasks, perform the following steps:

1 Use the Membership Directory Manager snap-in to connect to the appropriate directory service, with the user name and password of the Administrator account that was created with the New Membership Server wizard.

2 Create a new user in the appropriate container. The appropriate container should be *either* the members container *or* a container under the members container.

3 Assign the attribute DS-privileges, with a value of SUPERBROKER, to the new member. This tells the Membership Directory that this user has all rights and permissions to the directory and will bypass ACL checking.

4 Add this new user to the GRPBRKR*[Site Name]* group.

5 Assign the new member a user-password attribute and enter a new password for the value.

6 Use the Personalization and Membership snap-in to view the properties of the Membership Server instance (right-click on the folder and select Properties).

7 Change the user name settings to the Distinguished Name (DN) of the new member. For a new member called MyBroker in the members container, and in a Membership Directory with an organizational name of Membership, this would look like:

```
cn=MyBroker, ou=members, o=Membership
```

8 Finally, change the password value to the password entered for the new member.

The Windows NT Impersonation Account

The Windows NT **impersonation account** is a Windows NT account that is created by the New Membership Server wizard when completing a new directory service creation.

The purpose of the impersonation account is to provide a Windows NT security principal that can be used to access NT resources, and can be dynamically granted group Security Ids (SIDs) to access secured resources in Membership authentication mode. We'll read more about the role of the MemProxyUser in Chapter 13.

This user should never be directly assigned to any resource. Instead, the specific Site Server NT shadow groups should be granted the access rights on the system, and the impersonation account will be dynamically added to (or removed from) the corresponding membership server groups, depending upon the request by Site Server.

To replace the NT impersonation account user:

1   Run Windows NT User Manager and create a new user, either in the domain or on the local machine –depending on whether you're using domain accounts or local accounts for NT system access. This assumes that the user logged onto the Windows NT system has administrator-level access.

2   Set the user properties:

- ❑   <u>P</u>assword – enter a password that would be difficult to guess.
- ❑   User Cannot Change Password – this checkbox should be checked.
- ❑   Password Never Expires – this checkbox should also be checked.
- ❑   Groups –add this member to the guest group *only*.

3   Use the Personalization and Membership snap-in to view the properties of the Membership Server instance (right-click on the folder and select Properties).

4   Change the user name settings of the Windows NT impersonation account to the user name of the new user created in User Manager.

5   Change the password value to the password entered for the new user.

6   Finally, press the Check Password button to ensure that the password is valid.

Summary

The Personalization and Membership snap-in is used to administer multiple Membership Directory Services on different machines through a single user interface. Through the Personalization and Membership snap-in, we can configure a large majority of the various services for the Membership Server and the LDAP Service.

We've studied the Personalization and Membership snap-in in some depth:

❑   The P&M snap-in provides the **New Membership Server** wizard, which is used to create new Membership Servers, LDAP Services, Membership Directories, to attach to existing LDAP and Membership Directories.

❑   The P&M snap-in also provides the **Membership Directory Partition** wizard, which is used for partitioning the Membership Directory. We expanded on our knowledge from Chapter 4 of why the Membership Directory needs to be partitioned, and examined how it's done using this wizard.

❑   The P&M snap-in provides a logical grouping of Membership Servers and services.

There are two services that can be configured through the Membership Server Properties dialog:

❑   The settings of the **Authentication Service** (applicable only to servers with Membership Authentication) configure the usernames and passwords used to bind to the Membership Directory, and the impersonation account used for gaining access to the Windows NT file system.

❑   The **Active User Object (AUO) Providers** are used to access various data structures through ADSI interfaces. The root AUO is used by the Membership system to work with member objects in the Membership Directory. Other providers can be used, and custom ADS Providers can be built to work with other data structures.

The LDAP Service provided by Site Server 3.0 is used to access the Membership Directory. This service can be configured through the LDAP Service Properties dialog, as can the following components:

❑   The Root Database used by the Membership Directory
❑   The Dynamic Directory (a special container of the Membership Directory)
❑   The Membership Directory
❑   Membership Directory Security
❑   Logging

In the next chapter, we'll learn about the Membership Directory Manager snap-in used to view and manage a Membership Directory.

7

The Membership Directory Manager Snap-In

The Membership Directory Manager is a tool used to view and manipulate a Membership Directory. It allows the user to view the actual Membership Directory schema, and provides the ability to add, remove, and modify entries in the directory. Most of this functionality is provided through wizards each of which we'll examine in more detail. A solid understanding of the Membership Directory is key to taking full advantage of Site Server Personalization and Membership, and the Membership Directory Manager is the best place to start. Later in the book we'll see how to accomplish in code many of the tasks we cover in this chapter.

Here's what we'll be covering in this chapter:

- ❑ **The Basics.** We'll start with the basics, such as finding the Microsoft Management Console snap-in known as the Membership Directory Manager. We'll then cover connecting to the Membership Directory and authenticating with either Membership authentication credentials or Windows NT authentication credentials.

- ❑ **Navigating the Membership Directory.** In this section, we'll show you how to navigate through the Directory Information Tree of the Membership Directory. We'll take a detailed look at all the default containers, and learn how to apply filtering in containers.

- ❑ **Modifying the Membership Directory.** Next, we'll cover some of the tasks involved in managing the Membership Directory. This will include the wizards for new classes, attributes, members, and groups, as well as those for adding attributes to classes and adding members to groups.

- ❑ **Advanced Concepts.** Finally, we'll talk about how to have multiple Membership Directory Manager snap-ins in the Microsoft Management Console (MMC) to manage multiple Membership Directories, as well as talk about the valid names for new class instances in the Membership Directory.

By the end of this chapter, we'll be able to administer the Membership Directory, and we'll have a better understanding of what the directory provides.

The Basics

The Membership Directory Manager is a powerful tool. No matter what authentication type we choose (Membership authentication or Windows NT authentication), the Membership Directory Manager allows us to manage all aspects of the classes, attributes, and objects represented in the Membership Directory. This tool is perfect for any level of user needing to administer the Membership Directory. It is capable of many of the tasks that an engineer would usually do through code, and other tasks that are simple enough not to require code. For example, if a member informed us through email that they forgot their password or username, we could easily open up the Membership Directory Manager, filter by the givenName attribute (which we'll read about later in the chapter), find the member and either reset their password or email them their username.

However, the Membership Directory Manager is not so great for adding many values (such as a large number of users), or if you want to reproduce a Membership Directory on multiple machines. In spite of the splendor of the GUI and the functionality of the wizards, the performance of the Membership Directory Manager cannot compete with code that does identical tasks. In Chapter 14 we'll learn how to do many of the tasks performed in the Membership Directory Manager through code.

Finding the MMC Snap-In

To find the Membership Directory Manager snap-in (assuming you've already installed Site Server 3.0), look under the program group **Microsoft Site Server**, select **Administration**, and select the **Site Server Service Admin MMC** option. This will open the Microsoft Management Console with all of the appropriate snap-ins that Site Server provides. In particular, the Membership Directory Manager snap-in should be available in the left-hand portion of the screen:

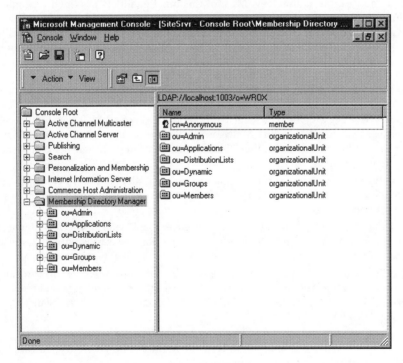

By expanding this snap-in, you will reveal six items that resemble folders. These folders are called **containers**, and each container can contain more folders. This is the Directory Information Tree we read about in Chapter 3. If you opted for the default installation of Site Server 3.0, then expanding the Membership Directory Manager should reveal the Membership Directory for the Windows NT user accounts.

> **The Directory Information Tree you will see by default in the Membership Directory Manager is that of the Membership Directory created during the installation of Site Server 3.0 for the Intranet (Windows NT authentication) Membership Server. If in the previous chapter you created a new Membership Server with a new Membership Directory, you will need to modify the properties of the Membership Directory Manager, as described below, in order to view the Directory Information Tree of that new Membership Directory.**

Connecting to a Membership Directory

The Membership Directory Manager uses LDAP to connect to the LDAP Service providing the Membership Directory. Therefore, using the Membership Directory Manager, we can connect to any Membership Directory whose LDAP Service is accessible from our computer. If we created a new Membership Directory in the previous chapter we can connect to that. Remember, if your computer is behind a firewall, and you need to be able to manage a Membership Directory across the Internet, create an LDAP Service on port 80 – most firewalls leave this port open. To specify which LDAP Service to connect to, we need to modify the properties of the Membership Directory Manager snap-in.

Setting the Properties

The Membership Directory Manager properties tell the Membership Directory Manager which LDAP Service to connect to, and thus which Membership Directory.

Finding the Membership Directory Manager Properties

Right-click on the Membership Directory Manager snap-in and select Properties. This should give you the following dialog box:

This dialog box contains the values for logging on to a Membership Directory with an organization name of Wrox, accessible via LDAP on port 1003. If you look at this screen for default Membership Directory (i.e. the one that's included when you install Site Server 3.0), you'll see that its organization name is Microsoft and the port number is 1002.

> *If, at any time, a dialog box prompts for logon while configuring the snap-in, press* OK. *This dialog box is prompting for us to login to the Membership Directory. Assuming the Membership Directory has not been secured, we can login anonymously. We'll cover this dialog box in more detail a little bit later in the chapter.*

From the Membership Directory Manager Properties dialog, enter the name of the server and port number of the LDAP Service configured for the Membership Directory you wish to view. If the Membership Directory is on the local machine, you can use localhost as the server name. Alternatively you can enter the actual name of your machine. The port number corresponds to the TCP port of the LDAP Service instance to be connected to. In Chapter 6, we learned that we can view these settings from the Personalization and Membership snap-in: to determine the port number, right-click on the LDAP instance for the appropriate Membership Server, select Properties, and look under the General tab for the TCP port value. You can see this in the following screenshot:

After entering the appropriate TCP port number and server name for the LDAP Service on our Membership Directory Manager dialog box, click the OK button. If we haven't yet logged in this session to the Membership Directory whose details we've just filled in, and this directory isn't using Windows NT authentication, we should get the following dialog box:

> **We'll only be prompted for authentication at this point if the Membership Directory to which we are connecting uses Membership authentication.**

A Membership Directory using Windows NT authentication uses the context of the user running the Membership Directory Manager to connect to the Membership Directory from the Membership Directory Manager. If we were to configure the Membership Directory Manager to connect to a Membership Directory that used Windows NT authentication, and we were connected to the Windows NT machine as the Administrator, we would be logged in as the Administrator in the Membership Directory Manager. However, we may be prompted to log in to the Membership Directory even under Windows NT authentication if we are accessing the Membership Directory through a program, as we will do in the third section of the book. For this reason we will include Windows NT authentication in our discussion of how to log in to the Membership Directory and be authenticated.

Authenticating Against the Membership Directory

When we access a Membership Directory and are being prompted to log in we have two options: we can log on anonymously, or we can log on using a username and a password.

Logging on Anonymously – Membership Authentication

Logging on anonymously for a Membership Directory that uses Membership authentication uses the cn=anonymous member account in the root container of the directory. This member is highlighted in the next screenshot:

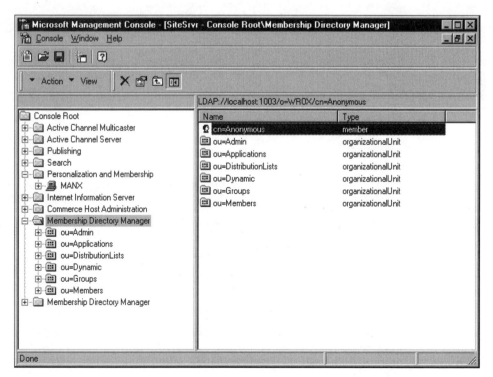

This member doesn't belong to any groups apart from the public group, which all members belong to, and so the only permissions it has are those of the public group. The public group is similar to the everyone group in Windows NT, except it applies only to the Membership Directory. However, when a new Membership Directory is created in Membership authentication mode, the public group has full permissions throughout the entire directory by default. This means the cn=anonymous member will have full access to anything in the Membership Directory, including adding members to Windows NT groups.

> **Before the Membership Directory is used in a production environment, it should be secured to prevent the anonymous user from having full access. We'll read about how to do this in Chapter 13.**

Logging on Anonymously – Windows NT Authentication

On a Membership Directory that uses Windows NT authentication, an anonymous logon is performed through the LDAP_ANONYMOUS account (an account that is automatically created by Personalization and Membership) in the Windows NT Security Accounts Manger database. This user account is highlighted below:

When a new Membership Directory is created in Windows NT authentication mode, the everyone group has full permissions throughout the entire directory. This gives the LDAP_ANONYMOUS user full access to anything in the Membership Directory, including adding users to Windows NT groups.

Logging on Using a Username and Password – Membership Authentication

To log on to a Membership Directory that authenticates through Membership authentication, we need to provide the username and password of a member account in the Membership Directory. The security permissions of that member are then applied to the Membership Directory Manager. We can view or modify any objects or entries for which we have permissions; any objects and entries for which we don't have permissions are not visible.

We'll cover how to create new users in the Membership Directory later in the chapter. If this is a new Membership Directory we'll only have the user accounts that were created as part of the setup process (as discussed in the previous chapter). One of these will be the Administrator account, so we can log in now as the administrator. Once the Membership Directory is secured the Administrator account should only be used for administration purposes.

Logging on Using a Username and Password – Windows NT Authentication

To log in to a Membership Directory that authenticates through Windows NT authentication we need to provide the username and password of an existing user in the Windows NT Security Accounts Manager. The NT user will be added automatically to the Membership Directory the first time that the user account is modified, for instance if you add a value to that user. Additionally, if the user is a domain user, a new container is auto-magically created under the ou=Members container with the name of the domain. If the machine you are working on is the primary domain controller the user will be added into the members container. You may need to exit and re-enter the Membership Directory Manager in order to see the icons appear.

Now that we know how to connect to another Membership Directory, let's navigate through the Membership Directory and look at the various containers available.

Navigating the Membership Directory

Navigating within the Membership Directory is much like navigating a file system with the Windows NT Explorer. The left-hand window represents the containers and presents a broad overview, while the right-hand window presents the details of each container. To view the contents of a container, let's say the ou=Members container, expand the root container in the Membership Directory Manager snap-in to view all of the available containers in the left-hand window. Next, left-click or select the ou=Members container and view the members listed in the right-hand window.

When it's first created, the Membership Directory is populated with a pre-determined Directory Information Tree. Within this Directory Information Tree, a default set of containers, objects, and attributes are added during installation. Understanding the purpose of these containers is important, because some containers, like the ou=Members container or the ou=Admin container, contain important entries – such as members and the schema.

Containers

When the Membership Directory is first created, the default Directory Information Tree (DIT) contains six containers under the root. We looked at the structure of the Membership Directory when we discussed the architecture of Personalization and Membership in Chapter 3. Each container in the DIT has a specific purpose. The containers created include: ou=Admin, ou=Members, ou=Groups, ou=Dynamic, ou=Applications and ou=DistributionLists (in no particular order):

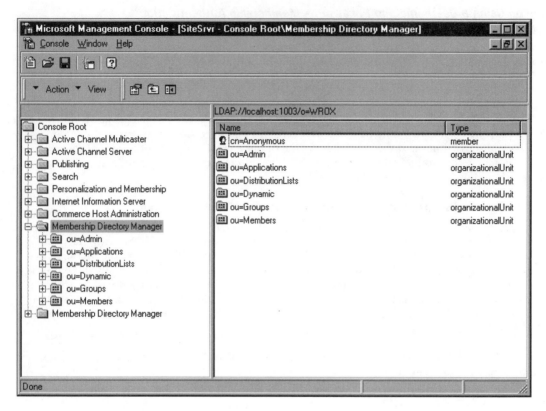

Let's start by examining the ou=Admin container.

The Admin Container (ou=Admin)

The ou=Admin container is used for holding information that relates specifically to the Membership Directory, such as administrative settings and configuration information. In this container we'll find the cn=Schema, ou=DbConfig, ou=ReplConfig, ou=Other, ou=ExportConfig, and finally ou=DPA sub-containers. Let's examine each in more detail, starting with cn=Schema.

cn=Schema, ou=Admin

The schema container is a special container used to hold the cn=attributeSchema and the cn=classSchema entries that define the Membership Directory. Also, the schema container is the only common-name (cn=) container in the Membership Directory. This is where the schema that represents the relationships between objects is exposed in the Membership Directory. The schema provides the ability for any application to connect to the Membership Directory and view the available schema – i.e. the design of the directory. We'll learn how we can use the entries in the cn=Schema later in the book.

ou=DbConfig, ou=Admin, and ou=DPA, ou=Admin and ou=ReplConfig, ou=Admin

After much digging through the documentation and finally speaking with some of the developers of the product, I've learned that ou=DbConfig, ou=DPA and ou=ReplConfig do not serve any purpose. The documentation for Site Server 3.0 stating that they provide information related to configuration information is incorrect. However, they are part of the main DIT, and cannot be deleted.

ou=Other, ou=Admin

The ou=Other container below ou=Admin is a container for three further containers. Within these subcontainers we define content types – such as ODBC datasources – and tag terms used by the Site Vocabulary. The three containers are:

- ❏ **ou=ContentClasses, ou=Other, ou=Admin** is used for defining content types that can integrate with the Rule Builder.

- ❏ **ou=TagTerms, ou=Other, ou=Admin** is a hierarchical definition of logically related items – such as products – otherwise known as the Site Vocabulary. The Site Vocabulary can be used to specify a range of values for attributes. If we wanted to define a new member as having an attribute that specified which of our products was their favorite, we could define a number of products as values for that attribute in ou=TagTerms. We would then be able to view these values through the Membership Directory Manager:

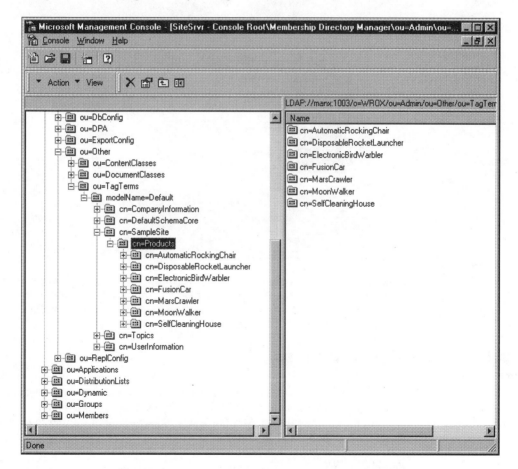

In this example, we could define the favorite product attribute for a member to have the value "FusionCar".

- ❏ **ou=DocumentClasses, ou=Other, ou=Admin** stores entries that we can use to describe content. It's primarily used by the Tag Tool – another Site Server tool, but one we won't be looking at – to add HTML meta tags to content for Site Server Search.

ou=ExportConfig, ou=Admin

The ou=ExportConfig container defines the data to be exported to the Analysis engine for interoperability with Personalization and Membership. Within this container the ou=Users subcontainer identifies the user data to export.

❑   **ou=Users, ou=ExportConfig, ou=Admin** identifies the actual attributes to be exported. By default, it has one entry: cn=Default of type exportConfig. This has one multi-valued attribute, Exported Properties, that lists the member class properties to be exported. These are listed in the following screenshot:

These exported properties are actually exported the first time the Rule Manager is used to build a rule that interacts with the Analysis engine. All Analysis data from that point forward will be able to interact with the Personalization and Membership system, but only with the attributes defined in the cn=Default ExportedProperties attribute.

Members Container (ou=Members)

The ou=Members container is the default container used to store all members of a Personalization and Membership site. Additionally, many of the tools used with Site Server, such as the default AUO provider, are configured to look in this container for members. If we want to keep members in another container we would have to modify the ADsPath value of any tool that wanted to access that other container. To modify the default AUO Provider, that we saw in the previous chapter, to look in a new subcontainer that we had created called SiteAMembers, we could change the ADsPath value from LDAP://localhost:1003/o=Wrox/ou=Members to LDAP://localhost:1003/o=Wrox/ou=Members/ou=SiteAMembers.

In Chapter 4, we discussed how to scale your site, and in particular we mentioned the advantages of partitioning – and you may have considered partitioning your ou=Members container into value and/or namespace partitions. It is possible to support multiple Internet Information Server sites from one Membership Directory – by running one Membership Directory and storing the members in a container other than the ou=Members container. (This is discussed further in the *Advanced Concepts* of Chapter 8.)

The Members container I supplied with one default subcontainer: the anonymous users container.

ou=AnonymousUsers, ou=Members

The ou=AnonymousUsers container, underneath ou=Members container, is a special container that is used by Membership for all users that authenticate using Automatic Cookie Authentication, but that the site does not recognize. These members, known as anonymous members, are assigned a new globally unique identifier (GUID), for both their common-name and GUID attribute values. The members' mustContain attribute specifies that new members must have these values.

> **Automatic Cookie Authentication is an authentication method supported only by Membership authentication – this container serves no purpose for Windows NT authentication.**

Anonymous members can personalize information and retain state and be recognized by Automatic Cookie Authentication. If one of these users becomes a member we can make sure they don't lose any of their information with a few lines of code which we'll see in Chapter 9 when we read about the MoveHere() method.

The Groups Container (ou=Groups)

The ou=Groups container is used to hold Membership groups that site members can belong to. In Membership authentication mode these groups correspond to Windows NT impersonation groups, and in Windows NT authentication mode, these groups only affect permissions to items in the Membership Directory not on the NT system. Groups created in this container are created in the Windows NT SAM automatically as long as auto group creation is turned on – which it is by default. We can choose whether or not groups are to be created automatically and whether these groups are to be created as domain groups through the PMAdmin.vbs tool – see Appendix B. The ou=Groups container has one subcontainer.

ou=NTGroups, ou=Groups

Windows NT groups are created in the Membership Directory automatically as part of the default DIT. Members can belong to these groups – we'll cover how to create groups and add members later in this chapter – and when they authenticate through IIS 4.0, the impersonation account receives the Security Id of the Windows NT group that corresponds to this Membership Directory group. Resources can then be authorized using the Windows NT security system. We'll read more about security in Chapter 13.

The Dynamic Container (ou=Dynamic)

The Dynamic container holds entries in memory – on the LDAP Service, as we read about in Chapter 3 – and is used by applications to share information. The dynamic container is different from all the other containers, in that objects created in this container have a specified time to live.

Any object created in the container whose time to live is not periodically updated will expire. The default expiration of entries in the ou=Dynamic container is configured through the Personalization and Membership snap-in's LDAP Service properties (see Chapter 6) from the Dynamic Directory tab:

Additionally, the ou=Dynamic container provides about 2 or 3 times the performance of the LDAP Service, since it does not access the Membership Directory to read information.

The Application Container (ou=Applications)

The ou=Applications container is used for defining attributes specific to an application. If you design an application that uses the Membership Directory to store application-specific data, the data should be stored in the ou=Applications container. Entries in this container are of class type **application** and simply store attributes about the application. After the creation of a Membership Directory, you should have one application installed and configured – MS-NetMeeting. This application is a dynamic container used by Microsoft NetMeeting clients.

The Distribution List Container (ou=DistributionLists)

The last of the six root containers in the Membership Directory DIT, the ou=DistributionLists container, is used to contain distributionList entries used by Direct Mail. These distributionList entries define users to receive a Direct Mailing. If we examine one of the default entries inside the ou=DistributionLists container, cn=KmBriefList, we'll notice that it allows us to enter members:

The Direct Mail tool uses a distributionList entry, specified when we use the tool, to read out the member distinguished name entry and generate a Personalized page using each individual member's attributes. We'll read more about Direct Mail and how it works in Chapter 11.

Now that we've read about the containers, let's learn how to filter the entries in the containers.

Filtering Containers

Since the Membership Directory can potentially hold millions of entries, filters are necessary to 'filter' through what is visible in the Membership Directory Manager. If the number of entries for any one container is greater than or equal to the defined value in the Membership Server of the maximum number of entries that can be displayed, the container will display a message stating that there were too many objects to display:

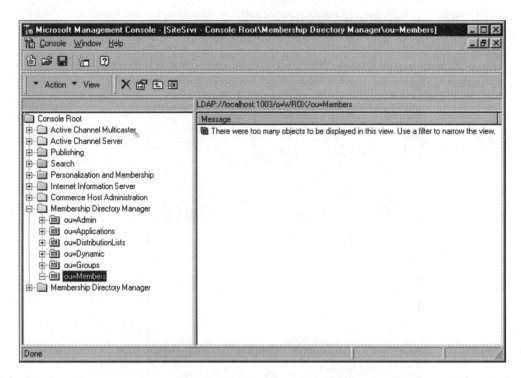

If the number of entries is greater than the max results value, we'll need to configure a filter so that we can view only a sub-set of entries, i.e. less than max results value.

> **The default maximum number of entries is 500. To change this setting see the max results set parameter in the LDAP Service properties general tab (Personalization and Membership snap-in, Chapter 6).**

Configuring Filters

To set up or remove a filter on any container in the Membership Directory Manager, right-click on the container and select Task | Filter. A filter dialog will then appear. This presents us with three options: No filtering, Standard filtering, and Advanced filtering.

We'll look at each of these below. Before that, note that there are a number of caveats we should be aware of when applying filtering to the Membership Directory:

- ❏ The cn=Schema, ou=Admin, o=[*organization name*] container cannot be filtered.
- ❏ Wild card filters, those that use the *, can only be applied to attributes that are of type string.
- ❏ For attributes that have a type of Date/Time, if a time is part of the attribute a search on the date alone will return no data.

No Filtering

By default, all containers have filtering set to No filtering. To filter a container, we need to select from one of the two options from the Filter dialog. To remove a filter from a container, we simply need to set the filter type back to No filtering.

Standard Filtering

A standard filter can be used to filter only on the object class type and the common name value (cn) of an object. Configuring a new standard filter is simple. Once we've determined the class type of object that needs to be filtered – more than likely it is a member class type – we select that class type from the available list of class types in the object class drop-down box. Next, we need to determine how the filter is to be applied to these classes. The easiest way to filter objects is with a **wildcard**. Just like in most other applications, the wildcard is the asterisk *. We can use the asterisk wildcard to filter objects that have common properties – for example, by listing all members whose cn starts with a*:

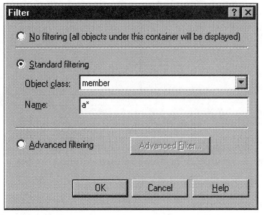

After applying this filter to the members container, we should see listed those members whose common name value begins with an a:

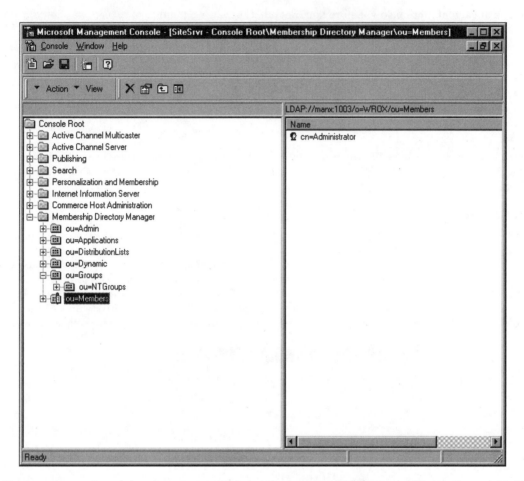

You may have noticed that the icon representing the ou=Members container changed once the filter was applied. This provides us with a quick reference to know whether or not a filter is being used on a container.

In Chapter 6 we discussed how we could select the Limit searches to initial substring only option from the LDAP Service properties general tab. If this option is selected, we will not be able to use filters such as: *a. Remember, this is done to help improve LDAP performance.

Advanced Filtering

Advanced filters can be configured to search only on attributes within the container. Unlike standard filters, advanced filters are also able to filter on multiple attributes. These attributes can be configured in a similar way to the common-name search in the standard filter, i.e. using wildcards. For example, if we wished to find all the members that had the attribute DS-PRIVILEGES value of SUPERBROKER, we could apply the following advanced filter to the ou=Members container:

After applying this filter, we should only see the following members in our ou=Members container:

Next, let's look at how we can modify information in the Membership Directory.

Modifying the Membership Directory

Entries in the Directory Information Tree can be modified, added, removed (and so on) through the Membership Directory Manager. Using the Membership Directory Manager can be a slow, cumbersome process when you're working with large amounts of data or adding multiple users; but it still provides a simple, intuitive interface that any user can become comfortable with. My recommendation is that you write your own administration tools – customized for your business – to manage objects and entries in the Membership Directory, and only to use the Membership Directory Manager for the most basic of tasks. In Chapter 14, we'll learn how this can be done through ASP, and in Chapter 15 we'll learn how we can use the Membership Directory from Visual Basic and C++.

Creating New Attributes

In Chapter 2 we defined an attribute as a describing property for a class – member classes in the Membership Directory are composed of a series of attributes that describe a member, such as givenName, telephoneNumber, and so on. If the member object doesn't have representation of an attribute that we wish to use – such as modemSpeed – we need to create a new attribute used to store this value for our member. An attribute is defined in the cn=Schema as an attributeSchema class type. To create a new attribute, we need to create a new instance of the attributeSchema type populating its attributes with the definitions for our new attribute. All attributeSchema classes are stored in the cn=Schema, ou=Admin, o=[*organization name*] container, and this is where we must create all new attributes. We can view existing attributes in this container through the Membership Directory Manager:

We'll use the New Attribute Wizard to create new attributes in the Membership Directory. However, it is also possible to create new attributes programmatically (see Chapter 14).

The New Attribute Wizard

The New Attribute Wizard can be found by right-clicking on the cn=Schema, ou=Admin, o=[*organization name*] container and selecting New | Attribute.

Screen 1: Splash Screen

The splash screen for the New Attribute Wizard describes what the purpose of the wizard is, and what it is used for.

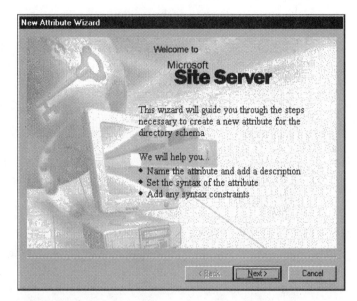

Screen 2: Type the Name of the New Attribute

In the second screen of the New Attribute Wizard, we describe the new attribute:

The only required item on this screen is the N<u>a</u>me, which represents the common-name value – one of the mustContain attributes of an attribute class. Once the new attribute is created it will be referred to as cn=modemSpeed in the cn=Schema. The display name and the description are both used to provide a more 'user friendly' means of labeling an attribute. We'll see these values a little bit later on when we add the attribute to the member class. Note the Multi-<u>v</u>alued checkbox, near the foot of the screen. If we check the box, the attribute created will be able to store multiple values stored as an array. We'll learn more about how to work with this special attribute type in Chapter 9.

Screen 3: Select the Attribute Syntax

The syntax of the attribute determines the type of the value to be stored by the new attribute:

The possible attribute types are as follows:

- **String.** String attribute values consist of one or more characters, and can include spaces. String values are typecasted as UnicodeString in the attribute definition represented by the attributeSyntax attribute.

- **Integer.** The integer attribute values are the positive and negative whole numbers, and zero. For example, -1 and 10 are integers, but not 0.5. Integer values are typed as Integer in the attribute definition represented by the attributeSyntax attribute.

- **Date/Time.** Date/Time attribute values contain the year, month, day, and time. Date/Time values are typed as GeneralizedTime in the attribute definition represented by the attributeSyntax attribute. An example Date/Time value would look like: 19981008135944Z otherwise known as October 8th, 1998 1:59:44pm.

- **Distinguished Name.** Distinguished Name attribute values refer to a unique object in the Membership Directory. Distinguished Name values are typed as DN in the attribute definition represented by the attributeSyntax attribute. When we add a member to a group, we're actually creating another object type: memberof. The memberof object uses a DN attribute that points to the member. The system can use this DN value to later bind to the member.

❑ **Binary**. Binary attribute values consist of arbitrary binary data. Use this syntax when data cannot be represented in any other syntax. Binary attribute values cannot be searched. Binary values are typed as Binary in the attribute definition represented by the attributeSyntax attribute.

Both String and Integer have an additional screen to the New Attribute Wizard for specifying syntax constraints:

Screen 4: Specify the String Syntax Constraints

If the syntax selected is of type string, one final screen will be presented that allows for syntax constraints to be put on the string value stored by this attribute:

The possible choices are as follows:

❑ **None**. No syntax constraints, any data can be entered for the value of this attribute.

❑ **Length**. Specifies the minimum and maximum length that acceptable values for the data must be. If we wanted to specify that a password had to be longer than 5 characters and less than 15, we would modify the userPassword attribute to reflect this range.

❑ **Site Vocabulary**. Values that are stored in a tag term model under ou=TagTerms, ou=Other, ou=Admin, o=[*organization name*] and are entries that can represent valid values for the string. Using the site vocabulary as a syntax constraint is a great idea if a site is to support constants in the Membership Directory rather than in the code.

Screen 5: Specify the Integer Syntax Constraints

If the syntax selected is of type integer, one final screen will be presented that allows for syntax constraints to be put on the integer value stored by this attribute.

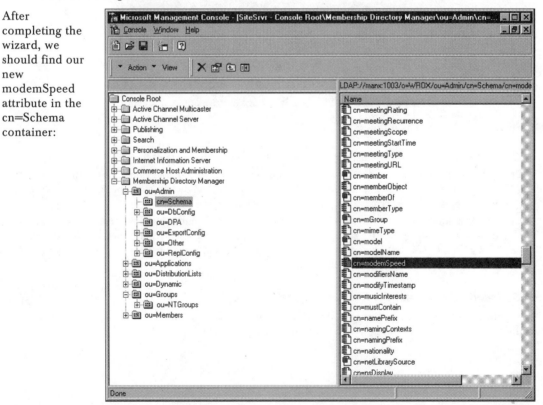

There are just two options here:

❑ **None.** No syntax constraints, any data can be entered for the value of this attribute.

❑ **Range.** Specifies the minimum and maximum range of acceptable values for the data. If our modemSpeed attribute used numbers to signify acceptable ranges, we could use 28 as the minimum (for 28.8) and 1000000 as the maximum – just in case any of our members happened to have a T3 or greater at home.

After completing the wizard, we should find our new modemSpeed attribute in the cn=Schema container:

Before we move on and look at how we add our new modemSpeed attribute to the member class – which we must do before a member can use it – let's first examine how we create new classes in the Membership Directory.

Creating New Classes

Creating new classes for the Membership Directory is as easy as creating new attributes. The only difference is that now we'll be creating a new classSchema rather than a new attributeSchema object. In Chapter 2 we defined a class as a collection of attributes, that together define an object. For example, every member is an instance of the **member class** – the member class defines the attributes that any member may have. Like new attributes, new classes must be created in the cn=Schema, ou=Admin, o=[*organization name*].

The New Class Wizard

To create a new class in the Membership Directory, we need to right-click on the cn=Schema, ou=Admin, o=[*organization name*] container, the same as for attributes except we'll select New | Class. Let's step through the New Class Wizard now. To create this new class I'll use my cat Scully as an example. Before we can represent Scully in the Membership Directory we need to create a new classSchema object called Cat.

Screen 1: Splash Screen

The splash screen for the New Class Wizard describes the purpose of the wizard.

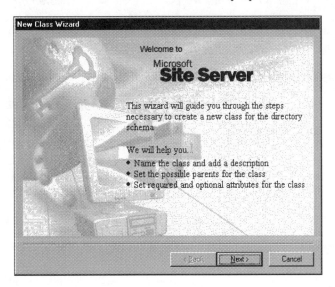

Screen 2: Type the Name of the New Class

Similar to the New Attribute Wizard, the second screen of the New Class Wizard is used to describe the class that we're creating.

The only required item on this screen is the N<u>a</u>me, which represents the common-name value – one of the mustContain attributes of a class. The <u>D</u>isplay name and the <u>D</u>escription are both used to provide a more 'user-friendly' means of labeling a class. Note the A<u>l</u>low children option, near the foot of the wizard screen. This determines whether or not the class can be paternal, or the ability to have children. If the class is allowed to have children we call it a container. An example of a container class is the organizationalUnit – instances of which include ou=Members, ou=Admin, etc.

Screen 3: Add Parent Classes

New instances of this class can only exist under the types of classes set as its parents – such as organizationalUnit (ou=Members) and organization (o=Wrox). This means that if a new class is created that can contain sub-classes, these sub-classes need to re-define their parent class attribute to support the new parent class.

The Add... button brings up a dialog listing all available classes. Classes can be selected and added as parents of this class. The Remove button removes class types from the current list Parents.

Screen 4: Select the Attributes for the Class

The final screen in the New Class wizard is for adding the attributes that make up the class. We can add any attribute we want to this new class. However, we do need to choose one of these attributes that we add to the class, as a mustContain attribute.

To add a new attribute to the class, we use the Add... button and select from the list of available attributes. The list presented is the entire contents of the cn=Schema, ou=Admin, o=[*organization name*], and any number of attributes can be added to the new class to represent member values. The attributes chosen are recorded in the Attributes table. In Chapter 2 we explained that a class must have some attributes, and may have other attributes. If we want to specify an attribute as a mustContain attribute for the class, check the box to the left of the Display Name of the added attribute. The most common type of mustContain attribute for a new class is the common-name attribute. One of the mustContain attributes *must* be selected in the Naming Attribute field to identify the class. Again, the most common attribute used as the Naming Attribute is the common-name.

After pressing the Finish button, we'll find our new class created in the Membership Directory's cn=Schema:

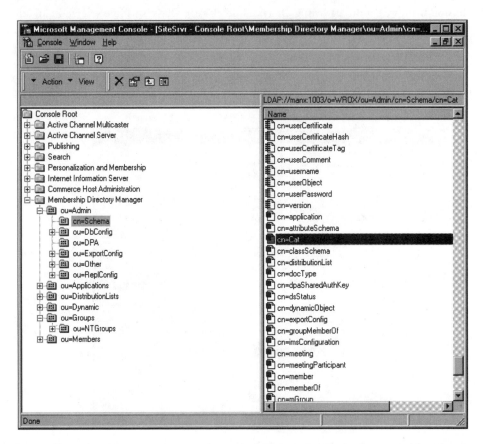

Now that we know how to create new attributes and classes, let's learn how to add and remove attributes from existing classes – such as adding our modemSpeed attribute to the members class.

Adding and Removing Attributes from Classes

A common task we will have to repeat often when working with the Membership Directory is adding and removing attributes from classes. This is especially true when we're working with the member class. Often, we need to add new attributes to the cn=members class to track information about members that isn't part of the default member attribute configuration.

Adding Attributes to a Class

To add a new attribute to a class open the cn=Schema, ou=Admin, o=[*organization name*] container and find the appropriate class to modify. Entries in the Schema container are identified by icons. An attributeSchema icon shows a page with four horizontal colored bars. A classSchema icon shows a page with a green square:

After selecting the appropriate class – in our case we'll view the cn=members class – double-click on the class to view its properties. Next select the **Class Attributes** tab from the class properties dialog box.

Next, to add an attribute press the **Add** button. A list of available attributes from the cn=Schema container will appear allowing us to select any attribute that we have not already selected:

We should find our modemSpeed attribute in this list of available attributes. If we select it we'll return to the previous dialog. By default, this attribute will be a mayContain attribute. As we saw when we created a class, to define an attribute as mustContain or mayContain we can check or uncheck the box to the left of the **Display Name** column. You don't want to modify the cn=member class' default mustContain attributes. These attributes are used by the Personalization and Membership system to identify the member.

Removing Attributes from a Class

To remove an attribute from a class, view the class's properties and highlight the attribute you want to remove, then press the Remove button.

Now that we've learned how to create new attributes, classes, and modify the mustContain and mayContain attributes of a class, let's use the wizards to create a new member.

Creating New Members

Creating new members can be done through the Membership Directory Manager; in fact a wizard, the New User Wizard, is provided just for this purpose. However, for creating large numbers of members, it is much easier to do so programmatically. Remember that we don't need to create members in the Membership Directory if that directory is using Windows NT authentication. As we saw when we looked at logging on to the Membership Directory, user accounts in the Windows NT SAM will be mapped across into the Membership Directory when we first update them.

To read more about how to create new members programmatically, see Chapter 14.

The New User Wizard

To bring up the New User Wizard we have to right click on the ou=Members, o=[*organization name*] container and select New | User. We'll walk through the wizard – the steps are straightforward.

Screen 1: Splash Screen

The splash screen for the New User Wizard tells us what it will do. After running the wizard we will have named a new user, populated attributes for the new user, and added group permissions for the new user.

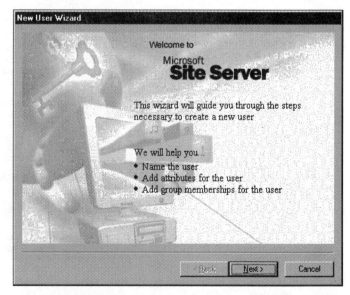

Only the name of the new user is required. The name represents the common mustContain naming attribute value for the new member. The GUID value, another mustContain value for a new member, is automatically generated by the wizard. We'll learn how to create our own GUIDs programmatically in Chapter 9.

Screen 2: Type the Name of the New User

The name value is the only required value for a new member. The name value will be the value that the member uses when authenticating, so we need to choose a username that the user will remember.

> **New User Wizard**
>
> **Type the Name of the New User**
>
> The user name must consist of at least one non-white-space character. Single spaces are allowed in user names. Leading and trailing spaces, and adjacent spaces, are not allowed.
>
> N_ame: `Robert Howard`
>
> [< _B_ack] [_N_ext >] [Cancel]

Screen 3: Add Attributes for the User

From the third screen in the New User Wizard we can add values for any attribute assigned to the member class. We can also populate attributes that are multi-valued by using the Add Value button.

> **New User Wizard**
>
> **Add Attributes for the User**
>
> Attributes that appear in italic require a value.
> Click Add Attribute to add additional attributes for this user.
> For multi-valued attributes, click Add Value to add additional values.
>
> A_ttributes:

Attribute	Value
description	This is a multivalued
	attribute!
Modem Speed	28.8
user-password	xxxxxxxxxxxxxxxxx

> [_A_dd Attribute...] [_D_elete Attribute] [Add _V_alue...] [Delete Va_l_ue]
>
> [< _B_ack] [_N_ext >] [Cancel]

Screen 3: Add the User to Groups

We can also add the new user to groups, from the third wizard screen:

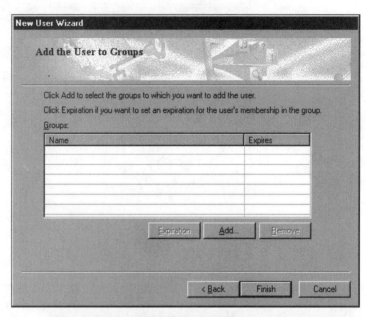

To add the new user, click the Add... button and select the group or groups to add members to:

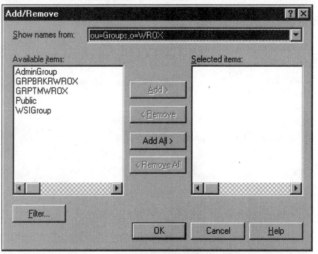

Groups are container classes. Each group that a member belongs to has a separate **memberof** class that represents the relationship between the group and the member. In Chapter 13 we'll explore more about the importance of groups when we look at security. Having chosen a group, on the original screen we can click the Expiration button to add an expiration value for the group membership.

The ability to set an expiration date for groups is a great tool for administrators. Members can belong to a group only until a specific date. Access can be granted to an item, such as a NetShow stream, for a specified period of time, after which the group Membership will expire. After completing the group selection and pressing Finish, the new member is created:

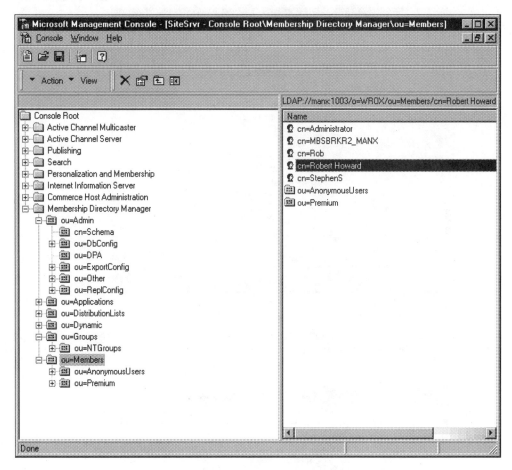

Now that we've learned how to create new members – and add them to groups – let's see how we create new groups in the ou=groups container.

Creating New Groups

Creating new groups is as simple as creating new members. The Membership Directory Manager provides us with another wizard specifically for groups: New Group Wizard.

The New Group Wizard

Similar to the New User Wizard only being available from the ou=Members container, the New Group Wizard is only available from the ou=groups container. Let's take a look at how we use it.

Site Server Personalization and Memership

Screen 1: Splash Screen

Again, similar to the New User Wizard, the New Group Wizard splash screen merely tells us what the wizard does.

Screen 2: Type the Name of the New Group

Each group has a naming value that is a mustContain attribute used to identify the new group. If we enter Premium as the value for the name, the name of the group in the ou=groups container will be cn=Premium.

Screen 3: Add Attributes for the Group

Somewhat similar to attributes for a member, we can add attributes for a group. We can add an attribute that provides us with a description of the group to help group members know the purpose of the group.

Screen 4: Add Members to Group

Finally, after selecting the attributes for the group, Screen 4 asks us to select the members of the new group:

Pressing the <u>A</u>dd... button brings up the
Add/Remove dialog that lets us select
new group members from the members
container:

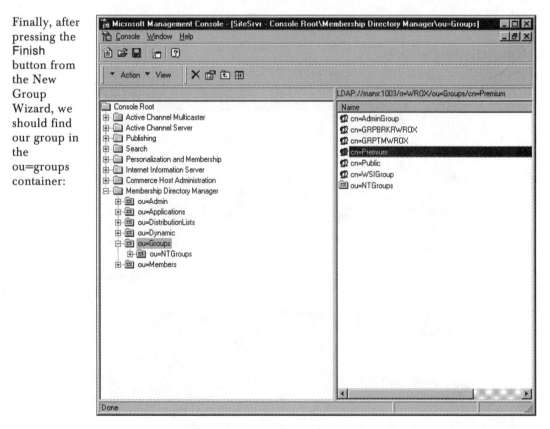

After selecting the members of the group, we can also choose to filter group members. Applying a
filter to a group, is identical to applying a filter to a container, since a group class instance is a
container for memberof objects (objects used to point to members of the group via the members'
DN). The ability to apply filters to the group is extremely useful once we have a large number of
members.

Finally, after
pressing the
Finish
button from
the New
Group
Wizard, we
should find
our group in
the
ou=groups
container:

Advanced Concepts

In this Advanced Concepts section, we'll look at how we can have multiple Membership Directory Manager snap-ins available to administer multiple Membership Directories from the MMC. Additionally, we'll look at the valid names that can be used for new attributeSchema and classSchema entries in the cn=Schema of the Membership Directory.

Multiple Membership Directory Manager Snap-ins

If you're managing multiple Membership Directories, or need to compare two directories without continually switching back and forth between them by changing the Membership Directory Manager properties, you can do so by adding another Membership Directory Manager snap-in into the MMC.

To add a new Membership Directory Manager snap-in, open the Microsoft Management Console for Site Server, and select Console | Add/Remove Snap-in. A dialog box should display the snap-ins:

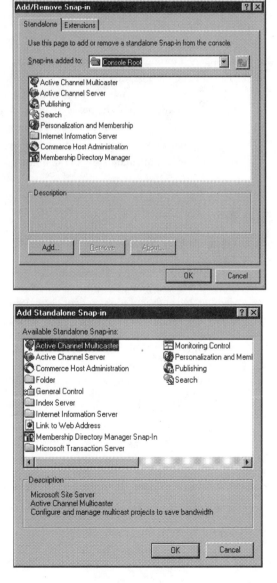

To add another Membership Directory Manger snap-in press Add…. You should see the Add Standalone Snap-in dialog:

The Add Standalone Snap-in dialog allows us to select another snap-in to be added. To add the Membership Directory Manager Snap-in, select the appropriate icon in the dialog, and press OK.

We can just as easily delete other snap-ins that we don't use. To remove a snap-in, navigate to the Add/Remove Snap-in dialog, highlight the appropriate snap-in and press the Remove button.

Rules for Creating Valid attributeSchema and classSchema Names

There are some specific naming rules that must be followed when choosing names for new attributeSchema or classSchema entries. Remember that the naming value is the name of the new attribute or new class – such as cn=modemSpeed. The name of any new entry created in the cn=Schema must be chosen in accordance with the following rules:

❑ The name may **include** the alphabetic characters a through z, and A through Z, and the numeric characters 0 through 9, and the whitespace character

❑ The name may **begin** with any of the alphabetic characters a through z, or A through Z

❑ The name of a new attributeSchema or classSchema **must not begin** with a numeric character (0 through 9). However, for the name of a new class instance, this rule does not apply

❑ The name **must not begin** or **end** with a whitespace character

❑ The name **must not contain** two consecutive whitespace characters

❑ The name **must not contain** any of the following characters: \ ( ) * % - / , + = ; | #

Summary

This was a long chapter, but we covered a lot of important information.

❑ We started by finding the Membership Directory Manager snap-in, in the Microsoft Management Console. We saw how to connect to the Membership Directory and authenticate with either Membership authentication credentials or Windows NT authentication credentials.

❑ We've learned how to navigate through the Directory Information Tree of the Membership Directory. We took a detailed look at all the default containers, and learned how to apply filtering in containers.

❑ We've covered some of the common wizards in the Membership Directory and some other common tasks – including the wizards for creating new classes, attributes, members, and groups, and those for adding attributes to classes and adding members to groups.

❑ In the Advanced Concepts section, we learned how to have multiple Membership Directory Manager snap-ins in the Microsoft Management Console (MMC) to manage multiple Membership Directories, and we reviewed the valid names for new class instances in the Membership Directory.

In the next chapter, we'll talk about how to configure our Internet Information Server.

Internet Information Server

Before we can use Site Server Personalization and Membership with Internet Information Server (IIS) 4.0, we need to associate (or **map**) the Membership Server to an IIS 4.0 web. This association does several different things – for example, it adds a new virtual directory, and if the Membership Server is for a Membership Directory in Membership authentication mode, installs several Security Support Providers, and also installs an ISAPI filter.

The good news is that the mapping process is easier than it sounds. In fact, it is just a two-step process, using the Microsoft Management Console. Once we've mapped the Membership Server, we can configure different authentication methods for each item in the IIS 4.0 web. However, depending on the Membership Server, the authentication methods will be different.

This chapter is all about mapping a Membership Server, and the various authentication methods provided by a Membership Directory (whether it's using the Windows NT (Intranet) authentication type or the Membership authentication type); we'll also look at the virtual directory, _mem_bin, that is added during the mapping.

Here's a high-level overview of the chapter:

- ❑ **Mapping a Membership Server to IIS 4.0.** We'll begin the chapter by looking at how we get Internet Information Server 4.0 and Site Server Personalization and Membership to work together. As I mentioned in the introduction, we do this by associating a Membership Server with an IIS 4.0 web – we'll learn how to 'map' a Membership server to an IIS web site.

- ❑ **IIS Authentication Configuration.** Here, we'll take a look at IIS's authentication configuration options. First, we'll discuss the options available to IIS when the Membership Directory employs Windows NT (Intranet) Authentication – we'll take a detailed look at the three different authentication methods and how they apply to the Site Server Membership Directory. Then we'll move onto discuss IIS's configuration options under Membership authentication. Membership authentication provides four different methods for authenticating members. We'll take a look at each of these authentication methods, and discuss how we use these authentication methods in the Membership Directory.

❑   **The _mem_bin Web Application.** With the two authentication types under our belts, we'll look at the _mem_bin web application – this is added to any IIS 4.0 web that is mapped to a Membership Server. The _mem_bin application provides a number of files for authentication and troubleshooting authentication logons, and is installed as a separate web application (this means that we can configure settings for the _mem_bin separate from the web it lives under).

❑   **Advanced Concepts.** Finally, we'll cover supporting multiple web sites with one Membership Directory, how to change the base distinguished name of a Membership Server, how to configure the Internet Information Server 4.0 MMC Admin to use Site Server extensions, and how to script against the IIS 4.0 metabase.

This chapter will complete the section on *Using Personalization and Membership*. By the end of the chapter, we should have enough knowledge to successfully plan, architect, configure, scale, develop and manage a Personalization and Membership application.

Mapping a Membership Server to IIS 4.0

So, before we can use Site Server Personalization and Membership with Internet Information Server, we need to map a Membership Server to an IIS 4.0 web. Once we've done this, the IIS 4.0 service knows which Membership Server to use in order to take advantage of the features of Site Server.

Site Server Membership is applied on a per-server instance for IIS 4.0. We'll use the term **IIS 4.0 web** to represent an IIS 4.0 server, whether its virtual or not – the Membership Server mapping won't apply to the entirety of IIS 4.0, only the select IIS 4.0 webs we map.

> **Personalization and Membership will not work with Internet Information Server versions earlier than 4.0. Moreover, an IIS web instance can only have one Membership Server mapping (remember IIS can support multiple web servers).**

As part of the process of mapping a Membership Server to an IIS 4.0 web, a virtual directory called _mem_bin is installed. If our Membership Server is to be used to serve a Membership Directory in Membership authentication mode, then the mapping process also installs an ISAPI filter (for catching access-denied errors) and the Security Support Providers (SSPs) for Membership authentication mode logins.

> *Security Support Providers (SSPs) work with the Membership authentication system to allow IIS 4.0's SSP Interface to switch the context of the thread serving the request to the Windows NT impersonation account. If properly authenticated, the thread serving the request will switch to the impersonation account for the Membership Server mapped. There are four SSPs provided by Site Server Personalization and Membership: Cookie Authentication, HTML Forms Authentication, Clear Text/Basic Authentication and Distributed Password Authentication.*

We'll learn how to apply these SSPs later in this chapter, and in Chapter 13 we'll take a more in-depth look at these Membership Directory-related security issues. For now, let's get on with looking at how we map a Membership Server to an IIS web.

Mapping a Membership Server

Before we map a Membership Server, we need to consider which type of authentication type our Membership Directory should use. If the Membership Directory uses **Membership authentication**, then member credentials are stored in the Membership Directory. Alternatively, if the Membership Directory uses **Windows NT (Intranet) authentication**, then member data is stored in the Membership Directory, but uses the Windows NT Security Accounts Manager database for user authentication.

Chapters 6 and 7 talk all about creating Membership Servers and Membership Directories.

The process of performing the mapping is simple. First, we select the Internet Information Server 4.0 web that needs to be mapped; second, we select the Membership Server that it should be mapped to. The rest is handled by Site Server. So, Site Server adds the _mem_bin virtual directory, and deals with various authentication issues. If the Membership Server points to a Membership Directory in Membership authentication mode, then Site Server installs the Authentication Filter that traps and handles authentication, and (as we mentioned above) also installs the SSPs that are used to authenticate members. On the other hand, if we're dealing with a Membership Directory in Windows NT (Intranet) authentication mode then Site Server simply allows the Membership authentication system to use the Windows NT Security Accounts Manager database.

Let's take a look at the process of mapping a Membership Server to an IIS 4.0 web site just a little more closely.

Steps for Mapping a Membership Server

We'll start by assuming that you've already created a Membership Server – if you're not in that position yet, then the preceding chapters will guide you into this position. OK, so now you're ready to map the Membership Server to the Internet Information Server 4.0 web. We'll use the Microsoft Management Console (MMC) to manage both the IIS 4.0 server and the Membership Server that need to be mapped. To remind you, you'll find the MMC under the Start menu, in Programs | Microsoft Site Server | Administration | Site Server Service Admin (MMC).

You should beware if you're accessing the MMC through the Internet Admin link from the NT Option Pack 4.0 installation. In this case, you won't be able to use the installed Site Server 3.0 features until you've associated the Personalization and Membership extension with the Internet Information Server snap-in. To read how to do this, see the Advanced Concepts section at the end of this chapter.

Within the MMC, open the Internet Information Server snap-in. Now choose the IIS 4.0 web that is to be mapped (in the screenshot on the next page, you'll see that Default Web Site is chosen), right-click on it and select Task | Membership Server Mapping...:

This selection brings up the following dialog box, which lists all the available Membership Servers on the local machine:

Using this dialog, we can select the Membership Server that represents our desired Membership Directory (i.e. the Directory that is to be used with the IIS 4.0 web to be mapped). The drop-down menu lists the Membership Servers available in the Personalization and Membership snap-in.

Note that it's only possible to map Membership Servers that live on the same machine as the Internet Information Server, so this list will only include Membership Servers that live on the local machine. This is in contrast with a Membership Server's LDAP service (or the Membership Directory to which the LDAP service points), which can be on a different machine.

When you've made the selection, press OK; you'll have to wait for a few seconds while Site Server completes the Membership Server mapping. Then, you can configure the Membership authentication methods for the IIS 4.0 web.

IIS Authentication Configuration

Configuring authentication for an IIS web is simply a matter of selecting the authentication method to use for the resource. It's certainly possible to make modifications to the Internet Information Server 4.0 metabase programmatically (we'll examine how we access the metabase in Chapter 15). However, it's a straightforward task to set the authentication types through the Microsoft Management Console, and that's what we'll cover here.

As we've mentioned, there are two choices for the authentication type: Windows NT (Intranet) Authentication and Membership Authentication. Your choice of authentication type will affect how IIS 4.0 authenticates members.

IIS Authentication Properties under Windows NT (Intranet) Authentication

You'll recall, back in Chapter 6, how we used the New Membership Server wizard to set up our new Membership Server – and that in Screen 6 of the wizard we configured our Membership Directory to use one of the two available types of user authentication. If you chose Windows NT (Intranet) authentication, then you've effectively told the Membership Directory that it must authenticate users based on the accounts in the Windows NT Security Accounts Manager (SAM). Windows NT (Intranet) authentication with Site Server is a great solution for sites that already have Windows NT (Intranet) authentication mechanisms in place but want to leverage Site Server 3.0 personalization.

Where does the Membership system get its user information from? Well, it takes copies of the appropriate Windows NT account entries from the SAM, and stores these copies in the Membership Directory. Note that all authentication is performed against the Windows NT SAM database – regardless of whether or not the account exists in the Membership Directory.

> *In fact, both forms of authentication – Windows NT (Intranet) authentication and Membership authentication – use Windows NT accounts to authorize access to system resources. Membership authentication adds a layer of abstraction, by storing credentials in the Membership Directory and using a Windows NT impersonation account for authorization. It's important to understand that all system-level security is done with the Windows NT 4.0 security subsystem.*

Using the Authentication Methods Dialog Box

In this section we'll go through the configuration for the Windows NT authentication types for Windows NT. The dialog for configuring Windows NT authentication from an IIS 4.0 web is easy to find. Within the Internet Information Server snap-in representation of the MMC, simply choose a web site object (e.g. the web site itself, a directory or an individual file), and right-click; then select Properties. The number and types of tabs on the resulting dialog depends on the type of web site object you're configuring. Then select the Directory Security or File Security tab (again, depending on the type of object you're configuring). In either case, the tab itself looks like this:

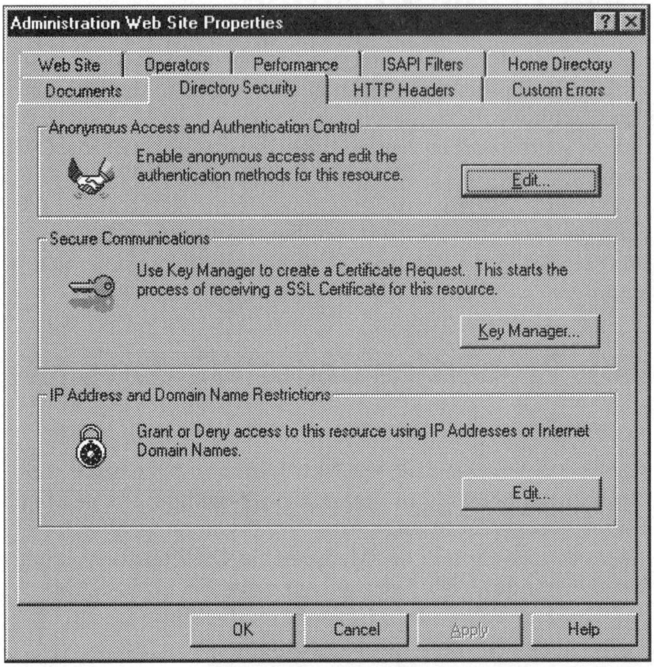

Finally, select the Edit button of the Anonymous Access and Authentication Control frame. We are presented with the Authentication Methods dialog box:

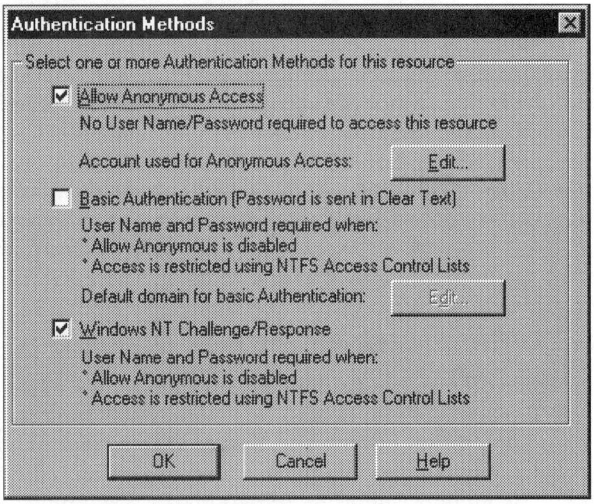

The dialog presents us with three options: Allow Anonymous Access, Basic Authentication and Windows NT Challenge/Response. We'll look at these in a moment.

Note that when you reconfigure the Windows NT authentication settings, hit the OK *button, and then leave the* Properties *dialog, you'll be presented with the following dialog:*

This dialog tells you that the pages and virtual directories listed in the Child Nodes box have default authentication settings, and your changes will not apply to those nodes. The _mem_bin provides authentication, configuration, and assistance for the authentication process (as we'll see later in this chapter) – so it's generally not a good idea to over-write their default authentication settings – just hit the Cancel button. You can use this dialog to over-write them if you want, but it's not recommended.

OK, let's take a look at the three authentication options that we saw just now in the Authentication Methods dialog box, and how they interact with the Membership Directory.

Allowing Anonymous Access

With the Allow Anonymous Access option selected, the Security Support Provider Interface uses Windows NT's special anonymous user account, IUSR_*[server_name]*, for any user that the system does not recognize.

The Security Support Provider Interface is what provides IIS 4.0 with the ability to use credentials given by a member and create a Windows NT user thread context. If properly authenticated, the thread serving the request will switch to the user whose credentials were passed by the Security Support Provider.

In fact, when a new web site is created with IIS's New Web Site Wizard, the Allow Anonymous Access option is selected by default, as you can see from the screenshot on the next page:

Why would we use this option? For example, on a large public web site it's often the case that only *some* of the available information needs to be authenticated and/or personalized. This is the case if most of the stored information is general product information, or other information that is intended to be accessible by *any* user. By using Site Server to provide Personalization and Membership services to the site, the administrator can mark these 'general information' pages with the Allow Anonymous Access method. Thus, any user attempting to access this information can do so without providing user credentials.

So what actually happens when this access method is selected? Whenever a client requests access to a resource, IIS and Windows NT check the user's permissions to determine whether or not access should be granted. Anonymous access will be granted *only* if the discretionary ACL of the requested resource has the IUSR_[*server_name*] account (or has either the Guest group or the Everyone group), with Read/Execute ACEs for both the directory and file.

> *You can view the permissions and user information of the* IUSR_[*server_name*] *account, by using the local machine's Windows NT User Manager. To start the User Manager tool, use the command* usrmgr \\[*machine_name*] *in the* Start | Run *dialog box.*

Since the IUSR_[*server_name*] is the *anonymous user* account, there's no way of associating it with any particular user. Hence, Site Sever is unable to store member information in the Membership Directory, and so Site Server itself doesn't handle the IUSR_[*server_name*] account.

> *In fact, it's not possible to store member information for the* IUSR_[*server_name*] *under the Membership authentication configuration, either. However, Membership Authentication does provide a way to handle anonymous users separate from the* IUSR_[*server_name*] *account – we'll cover this in the* Membership Authentication *section, below.*

IUSR_[*server_name*] is the default anonymous user account. You can change the Account used for Anonymous Access by hitting the first Edit... button, which you saw on the Authentication Methods dialog box a couple of pages ago:

In the resulting dialog, you can enter your chosen anonymous user account and password (after it has been created in the Windows NT SAM). Once we've selected the appropriate user (and if the Enable Automatic Password Synchronization box is checked), this facility synchronizes the password with the Windows NT SAM automatically.

Using Basic Authentication (Password is sent in Clear Text)

If the Basic Authentication checkbox is checked, then the user will be authenticated against a Windows NT SAM database each time he requests a resource. When the user requests a resource, he is challenged by the following authentication dialog:

The user must supply his username and password. If the user's credentials match those in the SAM user database, then access is granted – and the corresponding account in the Membership Directory is made available as the current 'member', along with all the attributes and values. If access is denied, then the user is redirected to the IIS 4.0 page that is displayed for 401.1 server access-denied errors.

By default, the domain members are the users from the Windows NT Server SAM providing the web service (for example, manx in the dialog above). However, the administrator has the ability to specify the domain from which users are authenticated. This is done by selecting the second Edit... button from the Authentication Methods dialog box, which results in the following dialog:

The Clear Text/Basic Authentication method is supported by a number of applications, including Netscape, and most clients should be able to use it. Indeed, HTTP clients such as Netscape can *only* access the Site Server site through the Basic Authentication and Anonymous Authentication methods (there's more on this at the end of this section). However, the Basic Authentication method passes the user's authentication credentials back to the server as clear text, in base 64 UUEncoded format. The existence of network sniffing tools, that can easily detect and decode information that is transported in base 64 UUEncoded format, means that this is an important security concern.

Indeed, if you take another look at the default checks in the Authentication Methods dialog box above, you'll see that, by default, the Basic Authentication box is *not* checked. If you check the box, then IIS displays the following warning:

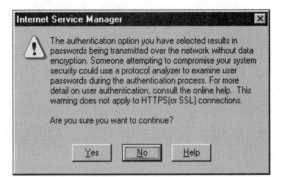

The solution to this is to implement Secure Sockets Layer (SSL). This is a 40-bit or 128-bit encryption protocol, which can be used to encode authentication information as it's sent. With SSL implemented, a higher level of security can be achieved.

> *If you want to know more about using SSL with IIS 4.0, then you should refer to the* IIS 4.0 Resource Kit *(ISBN 1-572-31-6381).*

If a user account is authenticated using Clear Text/Basic Authentication, the account is written to the Membership Directory automatically. A user can log into any domain, simply by specifying the domain as part of the username when sending the logon credentials (that is, by specifying the domain and username, separated by a backslash, in the form *domain\username*). When the user account is authenticated, and if the credentials are not from the root domain, the domain for the user is created as a container under the BaseDN.

> *Recall that the base distinguished name (BaseDN) represents the container from which members will be authenticated. By default the BaseDN is the ou=Members container, but can be changed through the PMAdmin.vbs tool. When a member passes credentials for authentication a path is built to that member using the BaseDN. We'll read more about the BaseDN, as well as how to change its value, in the* Advanced Concepts *section at the end of this chapter.*

Let's consider a brief example. Suppose we have a user who is a member of a domain that has access to resources on the network. Suppose that the user accesses the domain by authenticating himself with Clear Text/Basic Authentication, and that the user is visiting the site for the first time. Since our site is mapped to a Membership Server that uses Windows NT (Intranet) authentication, a new member instance will be created for the member in the Membership Directory. Moreover, if the domain is *not* the base domain for the site, then a new container under the BaseDN container of the directory will be created with the name of the domain. With all this set up, the P&M system is now in a position to store personalized data about this member.

Clear Text/Basic Authentication provides us with some of the functionality that we need to secure a site. Used in conjunction with Secure Sockets Layer encryption, the Basic Authentication method can provide us with a viable solution that works for all browsers.

However, for users accessing the site via a browser that supports NTLM, we can make use of the **Windows NT Challenge/Response** (also known as **Windows NTLM**) method to handle authentication. It's the third option on the Authentication Methods dialog box, and we'll look at it next.

Using Windows NT Challenge/Response (NTLM)

The beauty of this method is that – unlike Clear Text/Basic Authentication – there's no need to send user credentials across the network. Instead, Windows NT (or whatever clients are accessing the resources) sends a series of challenges and responses back and forth between itself and Internet Explorer.

First, the server challenges the client. To do this, the server applies a series of numerical algorithms (called **hashes**) to the username and password, and sends the encrypted result to the client. The client then creates a response. The response is constructed as a hash of the user's password, plus the random challenge that was originally sent by the server – these two items are packaged up and sent back to the server. The server examines the response, checking that the user's credentials match – if so, the user is authenticated and the Security Support Provider Interface maps the thread to the user's security ID in the SAM. As long as the session is active, any further requests are made with the authenticated thread. The real beauty of NTLM, is that the user's password is never sent across the wire, only the hashes.

If an account is authenticated in this way, Site Server handles it in just the same way as if it had been validated through Clear Text/Basic Authentication. Thus, the user account is written to the Membership Directory automatically, and the domain for the user is created as a container under the BaseDN (if the credentials are not from the root domain).

Using Combinations of Authentication Methods

Of course, it's possible to select both Allow Anonymous Access and Basic Authentication simultaneously. In this case, when a user attempts to access content without the appropriate group or user ACEs for the IUSR_[server_name] account, then he sees only a Basic Authentication dialog box.

By marking resources as supporting Allow Anonymous Access with either Basic Authentication or Challenge/Response, we can manage the resource's security from the normal Windows NT security mechanisms.

A Note on Netscape and Trusted Domain Authentication

We've already mentioned that HTTP clients such as Netscape Navigator can only access Site Server through Anonymous Authentication or Clear Text/Basic Authentication. When a user tries to access a particular domain through a browser that *doesn't* support Challenge/Response authentication, and IIS is on a *separate* trusted domain, then the client will be denied access to the resource:

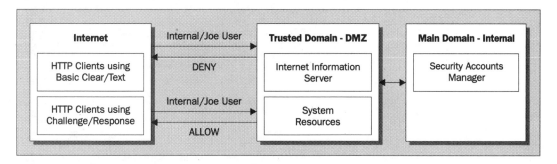

The only exception is when domain users that need to access the site are added to the users group (or another appropriate group) on the trusted domain.

IIS Authentication Properties under Membership Authentication

Having covered the IIS authentication configuration options for a Membership Server under Windows NT authentication, let's move on to consider the configuration options for a Membership Server under Membership authentication. To revise: if you chose the Membership Authentication option (back in Screen 6 of the New Membership Server wizard, in Chapter 6) then you've told the Membership Server that it should use the user credentials that are stored in the Membership Directory. Once a member has been authenticated, a security context is created with a Windows NT impersonation account (the default impersonation account is called MemProxyUser) – and the member gains access to the system via an instance of the impersonation account. The system creates an in-memory copy of the impersonation account, and assigns a unique Security Id (SID). Thus, many members can be signed on simultaneously, and these members will have different SIDs that don't conflict.

> **Under Membership authentication, access to the Windows NT system is always gained through a Windows NT impersonation account. To read more about security under Windows NT with Membership authentication, see Chapter 13.**

The configuration steps for Membership Authentication are a little different to those that we've seen for Windows NT (Intranet) Authentication.

Configuring Membership Authentication

In order to configure IIS authentication properties under Membership Authentication, fire up the MMC and right-click on the appropriate web object (e.g. web site, directory or resource file) in the Internet Information Server snap-in; then select Properties. Again, the number of tabs on the resulting dialog is dependent on the type of web object you're configuring – however, there is always a Membership Authentication tab and you should select it.

This presents you with the supported Membership authentication methods:

The dialog box shows the name of the Membership Server that the IIS 4.0 web site is mapped to, and also displays the possible authentication options. Remember, we can only map one Membership Server to any IIS 4.0 web site. However, we can support multiple sites on one machine, so each site can use a different Membership Server.

So what do all these methods do? Let's start with the Anonymous Authentication type.

Allowing Anonymous Authentication

If the Allow Anonymous checkbox is checked, then the IIS 4.0 web will allow unrecognized users to access the site as the IUSR_[*server_name*] account.

Note that the Allow Anonymous checkbox in this dialog is not related to the anonymous membership accounts created in the ou=AnonymousUsers container in the Membership Directory. This is a very common cause of confusion. The following table should help to clarify what account is used in what situation:

Data source	Under Windows NT authentication	Under Membership authentication
IIS web	IUSR_[server_name]	IUSR_[server_name]
Membership Directory	LDAP_ANONYMOUS	cn=anonymous

The Allow Anonymous checkbox represents Internet Information Server's IUSR_[server_name] *anonymous access method. The account used to access the Membership Directory anonymously (in Membership authentication mode) is the* cn=anonymous *account. Members in the* ou=AnonymousUsers *container are created when we use* Automatic Cookie Authentication. *We'll come onto the latter in a moment.*

What's the purpose of the Allow Anonymous checkbox? If part of a Membership-enabled web needs to allow access to all users, and doesn't need to be concerned with personalization, we can use Allow Anonymous to remove the necessity to provide authentication.

Let's expand on this a little. Obviously, there are some sites that *do* need to authenticate every member that visits the site. However, there are also many sites for which this isn't a necessity – there's no reason why these sites should suffer the overhead associated with Membership authentication (i.e. cookie creation, Membership Directory new member instance creation) when their resources don't need these services. We can mark resources like this as Allow Anonymous – as long as the resource's Discretionary ACL carries the appropriate ACEs, e.g. Guests.

If Allow Anonymous Fails – Having the Correct ACEs

Access to a resource will be denied if the requested resource's Discretionary ACL does not have the appropriate ACE for the Windows NT anonymous user (just as if we were using the Windows NT (Intranet) authentication method). In this event, the authentication process will default to a Membership Security Support Provider that has to be used in conjunction with Allow Anonymous. A possible order of events is demonstrated in the figure:

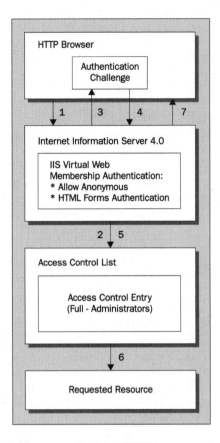

- ❑ **(1) Resource is requested anonymously** – An HTTP browser attempts to access a resource on an IIS 4.0 web (the IIS4.0 web is using the Membership authentication method, but supports A̲llow Anonymous). The client attempts to access the resource via IIS's IUSR_*[server_name]* anonymous account.

- ❑ **(2) Access is requested via the anonymous account** – The Windows NT security system attempts to access the resource as the anonymous account. If the proper ACEs are not available for the security principal performing the request (i.e. IUSR_*[server_name]*), access is denied.

- ❑ **(3) Membership authentication** – If access to the resource is denied, the Membership system attempts to authenticate the user with the Security Support Provider selected.

- ❑ **(4) Membership credentials** – Based on the information provided by Membership authentication, access is either granted or denied. If access is granted, the member accesses the resource as the impersonation account (MemProxyUser) and receives the Windows NT group security ids that match the corresponding groups in the Membership Directory.

- ❑ **(5) Access is requested via the impersonation account** – If the impersonation account has the necessary security ids that match the access type supported in the ACE, then access is allowed. Otherwise, access is denied.

- ❑ **(6) The resource is exposed** – The resource is now available to the requesting account.

- ❑ **(7) Displayed to the browser** – Finally, the resource is processed by IIS and served to the HTTP browser.

Providing only Allow Anonymous

There is a little known secret that we can use to force anonymous authentication. By selecting Allow Anonymous and Other Password Authentication, but not selecting an Other Password Authentication method such as Clear Text/Basic Authentication, we force only anonymous. In some cases, such as using ASP to generate content that we don't want to be directed through the ISAPI, this is extremely valuable.

Now that we've covered Allow Anonymous – which is identical to the Allow Anonymous Access option for Windows NT (Intranet) Authentication – let's talk about the new authentication methods provided by Site Server, the Security Support Providers.

Security Support Providers

There are four Security Support Provider authentication methods provided by Site Server Membership:

- ❑ Automatic Cookie Authentication
- ❑ HTML Forms Authentication
- ❑ Distributed Password Authentication
- ❑ Clear Text/Basic Authentication

> **We can use a combination of different authentication types on resources, depending upon the amount of security that the resource demands.**

The SSPs work with IIS 4.0's Security Support Provider Interface (SSPI) and the Membership authentication type, to map Membership Directory accounts to a Windows NT impersonation account (by default, this is the MemProxyUser account). Let's walk through these SSPs now.

Automatic Cookie Authentication

Cookie authentication provides us with a quiet and discreet authentication method for both anonymous users and registered members. Cookie authentication uses two cookies – SITESERVER and MEMUSER – to store information on the user's computer. If the user doesn't accept cookies then they will not be able to access the site. As long as the user is prepared to accept cookies, we can authenticate and track the member throughout the site.

When Automatic Cookie Authentication is selected, the ISAPI filter (which was installed by the mapping of the Membership Server) parses the headers of the client and looks for the SITESERVER and MEMUSER cookies. There are three possibilities. If the cookies exist then the information found therein is used to authenticate and bind to a member. If the cookies are invalid then the member is redirected to an ASP page in the _mem_bin virtual directory; we'll come back to this shortly. If the cookies don't exist then the ISAPI filter creates and binds to a *new* member in the Membership Directory, in the ou=AnonymousUsers container. Once bound to this user, two new cookies are written to the browser. These two new cookies SITESERVER and MEMUSER will be used in future sessions to identify the member uniquely.

> **If a user is to be authenticated via Automatic Cookie Authentication then he must have agreed to accept cookies. All authentication methods except for Allow Anonymous (which can't be personalized), Basic/Clear Text and Distributed Password Authentication (DPA) rely upon cookies to maintain member state.**

In addition to tracking members, Automatic Cookie Authentication accommodates each new member by sending cookies to the new member and automatically creating a new account in the Membership directory, under ou=AnonymousUsers, ou=Members, o=[*organization name*]. This anonymous account can be used to personalize information about the visitor, and later to provide the functionality for migrating the anonymous member (and all its member information) to a new account in the ou=Members container (or some other container).

> *We'll cover 'anonymous-to-member' migration in Chapter 9 – it's done by using the* IADsContainer's MoveHere() *method, which is designed to move objects from one container to another.*

Let's have a look at the two cookies that Automatic Cookie Authentication uses. The SITESERVER cookie represents the GUID (or Globally Unique Identifier), and corresponds to the value of the member GUID attribute. When the user is asked whether he is prepared to receive a cookie, he sees the following dialog:

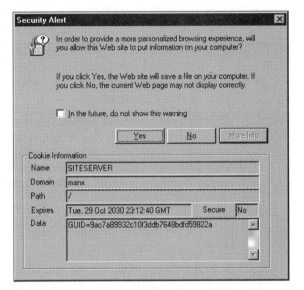

In this case, the data stored in the SITESERVER cookie is GUID=9ac7a89932c10f3ddb7648bdfd59822a.

The MEMUSER cookie represents the distinguished name (DN) of the member represented – this value should be the same as the name of the member in the Membership Directory:

In this case, the accepted cookie will contain the data string `Administrator`.

The values contained in the `SITESERVER` and `MEMUSER` cookies are used to look up the corresponding member information in the Membership Directory – and to use that member (and its corresponding Windows NT group security Ids) to access resources on the Windows NT Server. In the HTTP headers `HTTP_COOKIE` value, these cookie values appear together as

```
SITESERVER=GUID=9ac7a89932c10f3ddb7648bdfd59822a; MEMUSER=Administrator;
ASPSESSIONIDGQQQQQBB
```

Notice the normal GUID decorations (curly braces and dashes) are not stored in the cookie GUID value.

Although the ISAPI AuthFilter creates and/or manages these cookies for us, we can programmatically modify, send, or delete them ourselves. We'll defer a discussion of this until Chapter 14.

> **A brief note about security: Automatic Cookie Authentication is a useful form of authentication. However, it's not the most *secure* form of authentication. Cookies can easily be copied and emailed, and used in any other similar browser type. Automatic Cookie Authentication works best for displaying non-secure personalized content to the user.**

So, suppose we want to write some simple personalization into a web page (such as greeting the member). Suppose also that the contents of our web page are not highly confidential. In this case, Automatic Cookie Authentication would be quite suitable – and we'll cover this scenario in Chapter 10. However, if the page contained more sensitive information – such as financial data – then we would want to use a more interactive authentication method.

Automatic Cookie Authentication with Allow Anonymous

We can use Automatic Cookie Authentication and Allow Anonymous simultaneously. In this case, IIS first determines whether the user has access to a resource, by attempting to use IIS's anonymous account, the IUSR_*[server_name]*, to access a resource (you'll recall this from our diagram in the *Allowing Anonymous Authentication* section of this chapter). If access is granted, then the user accesses the resource through the IUSR_*[server_name]* account.

If access is denied, the Membership system will attempt to authenticate the user by requesting the Site Server 3.0 cookies. If the `SITESERVER` cookie exists, but the `MEMUSER` cookie is blank, it is assumed that the member will be found in the ou=AnonymousUsers container. Alternatively, if the `MEMUSER` cookie *does* exist then the information is used to bind to a member whose GUID attribute value matches the `SITESERVER` cookie, and whose member RDN matches the value of the `MEMUSER` cookie.

If the system is able to bind to the appropriate member then the Security Support Provider Interface will handle the impersonation process and mapping of the member to the Windows NT impersonation account (you'll recall that the default impersonation account is called MemProxyUser).

HTML Forms Authentication

To provide a more secure (but equally simple) form of authentication, we can use HTML Forms Authentication. This method of authentication uses HTTP's POST method to send the user's credentials to an ASP page, which handles the submission – the credentials are sent via the headers of the page. Then, the ASP page makes use of a special COM object – the VerifUsr object – to verify the user's credentials.

Moreover, it's possible to combine HTML Forms authentication with Secure Sockets Layer (SSL), so that data is encrypted as it is sent across the wire.

HTML Forms Authentication also makes use of the ISAPI Membership Authentication filter – you'll recall that this filter is installed when a Membership Server, using Membership authentication, is mapped to an IIS 4.0 web site. When a user makes a call to a page that uses HTML Forms Authentication, ISAPI traps that call and redirects it to a special ASP page called FormsLogin.asp.

The FormsLogin.asp page is provided in the _mem_bin web application. We can modify this page; or supply our own version of the FormsLogin.asp page – it should be placed in the same directory as (or a parent directory of) the requested resource. The authentication filter will look for the FormsLogin.asp page – first in the same directory, then in each successive parent directory, and finally in the _mem_bin virtual directory web application.

> *HTML Forms Authentication sets a 120-character limit on the number of characters in the password. It's possible to enter up to 256 characters – but only the first 120 characters are significant.*

In order to gain access to the resource, the user must complete the `FormsLogin.asp` HTML form and hit the Login button. This submits the contents of the form to an ASP page called `VerifPwd.asp`. This page creates an instance of the `Membership.VerifUsr.1` COM object, which accepts the username and password, and the HTTP path of the URL resource that has been requested. (In fact, this URL is used only for redirecting back to the original page – it does not have any bearing on the security context).

We'll explore the `VerifUsr` *object in Chapter 12.*

Code Sample – VerifPwd.asp

If you wish, you can replace the code in the existing `VerifPwd.asp` with the following code, which is a little clearer and more efficient:

```
<%
Option Explicit
On Error resume next

' ************************************
' Use the Membership.VerifUsr object to
' verify the Member's credentials
' ************************************

Dim objVerif
Dim strURL
Dim strUserName
Dim strPassword

' Grab passed form items
' ************************************
strUrl = Request.Form("URL")
strUsername = Request("Username")
strPassword = Request("Password")

' Create the VerifUsr object
' ************************************
Set objVerif = Server.CreateObject("Membership.verifusr.1")
If Err.Number <> 0 Then
  Response.Write "Authentication failed. Please try logging in again.<br>"
  Response.Write "The URL " & strUrl & " cannot be accessed.<br>"
  Response.Write "Use the back button on your browser to try again."
  Response.End
End If

' Call the VerifyCredentials method
' to validate the account
' ************************************
strUrl = objVerif.VerifyCredentials(strUsername, strPassword, strUrl)

' Handle errors or redirect
' ************************************
If (Err.Number <> 0) Or (strURL = "") Then
  Response.Write "Authentication failed. Please try logging in again.<br>"
  Response.Write "The URL " & strUrl & " cannot be accessed.<br>"
  Response.Write "Use the back button on your browser to try again."
Else
  Response.Redirect strUrl
End if
%>
```

Compare this with the following code, which is the version of `VerifPwd.asp` provided with _mem_bin:

```
<%
  On Error resume next
  set x = Server.CreateObject("Membership.verifusr.1")
  strUrl = Request.Form("URL")
  strUsername = Request("Username")
  strPassword = Request("Password")
    REM VerifyCredentials verifies that the username/password
    REM specified is correct. If the credentials are valid,
    REM VerifyCredentials issues the FormsAuth cookie to the user.
    REM VerifyCredentials returns the URL to which a redirect
    REM must be sent.
  y = x.VerifyCredentials(strUsername, strPassword, strUrl)
  if y = "" Then
    Response.Write "Authentication failed. Please try logging in again.<br>"
    Response.Write "The URL " & strUrl & " cannot be accessed.<br>"
    Response.Write "Use the back button on your browser to try again."
  Else
    Response.Redirect y
  End if
%>
```

As you can see from the code above, HTML Forms authentication makes use of `VerifyCredentials()`, which is a method of the `Membership.VerifUsr.1` COM object. The `VerifyCredentials()` method has three arguments: *user name, password* and *URL to access*. `VerifyCredentials()` performs the calls to the Security Support Provider Interface, to map the running thread to the appropriate impersonation account and adds the appropriate Windows NT Security Ids that correspond to the Membership group mappings.

> *Any ASP page called* `FormsLogin.asp` *can be used; the only condition is that it must call* `/_mem_bin/verifpwd.asp` *(or some other ASP page that provides identical functionality by calling the* `Membership.VerifUsr` *COM object).*

HTML Forms Authentication uses just a single cookie, called FORMSAUTH. The FORMSAUTH cookie controls the length of the HTML Forms authentication session. The session length determines whether or not the current session is valid. This value is set under the properties of the Membership Server through the Personalization and Membership snap-in, and defaults to 10 minutes. The member must accept the FORMSAUTH cookie, otherwise he will not be authenticated:

The cookie will always be set to expire after the default time period specified in the Membership Server and is reset on every subsequent visit to the site.

The main advantage of HTML Forms Authentication over Automatic Cookie Authentication is that HTML Forms Authentication forces the member to authenticate before gaining access to content. (Automatic Cookie Authentication authenticates based on the cookie alone, so no password is required.) This eliminates the chance that security will be compromised through Members sharing cookies, since we require an authentication regardless of the cookie credentials.

Further, unlike other methods of authentication, HTML Forms Authentication can take advantage of the look and feel of the web site. It's possible to handle the logon process through a set of ASP pages with which the user is familiar – instead of relying on login dialog boxes as used in Distributed Password Authentication or Clear Text/Basic Authentication.

Finally, it's possible to provide other login credentials that we can check after calling the `VerifyCredentials()` method – for example, it may be convenient to include an attribute to store the user's `lastVisit`.

There are two other authentication methods, that provide a more elegant 'under the covers' solution than we've seen so far. These two authentication methods are provided within the Membership Authentication tab, under the Other Password Authentication option. Both are, to a large extent, similar to the corresponding settings under Windows NT (Intranet) authentication – therefore we'll mention them only briefly here.

Distributed Password Authentication (DPA)

Distributed Password Authentication (DPA) works for Membership authentication in much the same way as Challenge/Response works for Windows NT authentication. You can probably guess the main difference: for DPA, users are authenticated against the Membership Directory (rather than the Windows NT Security Accounts Manager database). It's only possible for Windows Internet Explorer clients to use DPA, and usernames and passwords are hashed with a challenge sent by the server.

Here's what the user sees when he attempts to gain access through DPA:

Clear Text/Basic Authentication

When we select **Basic Authentication**, we authenticate any user that requests a resource against the credentials stored in the Membership Directory. We can also specify extra information with the username, from which to authenticate users. But here lies a difference between Basic Authentication under Windows NT (Intranet) authentication and Basic Authentication under Membership authentication: in the former case this extra information is in the form of a domain, and in the latter case the information represents a sub-container.

This 'extra information' specifies the container below the base distinguished name (BaseDN) container, from which authentication occurs. If no sub-container is specified, then the authentication will assume that all accounts live in the BaseDN of the Membership Directory. For example, suppose that the BaseDN value of our Membership Directory is **ou=Members**, and that the user information passed from the authentication dialog box is **Premium\Robert**. Then members will be authenticated from the **ou=Members\ou=Premium** container.

> *The BaseDN, or Base Distinguished Name, represents the container that members will be authenticated from. By default the BaseDN is the ou=Members container, but can be changed through the PMAdmin.vbs tool. To read more about how to change the BaseDN of a Membership Server see the Advanced Concepts section at the end of this chapter.*

The Clear Text/Basic Authentication method is supported by a number of applications, including Netscape, and most clients should be able to use it. (As we mentioned earlier, this is also true for Clear Text/Basic Authentication under the Windows NT (Intranet) authentication method.)

A Few Final Remarks

DPA and Clear Text/Basic Authentication can be selected simultaneously. In this case, the server will first attempt to issue a DPA authentication challenge. If (and only if) the client cannot interpret the challenge, the server will offer the Clear Text/Basic Authentication request.

If Allow Anonymous and Clear Text/Basic Authentication have been selected simultaneously, then the user will see a Basic Authentication dialog box *only* if the anonymous user account access has been denied to the resource.

As we've mentioned before, Clear Text/Basic Authentication provides us with some of the functionality that we need to secure a site. If we use it in conjunction with Secure Sockets Layer encryption, we can provide a viable solution that works for all browsers. However, by restricting to Internet Explorer browsers, we can use Site Server Distributed Password Authentication to handle more secure Membership Authentication. DPA works similarly to Windows NT Challenge/Response, and the username and password is never sent across the wire.

Personalization and Membership Web Application

When an IIS 4.0 web site is mapped to a Membership server, the Personalization and Membership web application, _mem_bin, is automatically created as a virtual directory on the web site. (This is true whether the Membership server supports the Membership authentication method or the Windows NT (Intranet) authentication method.) The virtual directory _mem_bin maps to \bin\P&M\html, under the Site Server 3.0 installation point. _mem_bin contains 17 files in the base directory, and two further sub-directories: one of these directories stores images, and the other contains 19 files that handle various authentication errors.

In this section, we'll explain why the _mem_bin virtual directory is necessary. We'll also find out about some of the functions (and the limitations) of the files provided in _mem_bin.

The _mem_bin Virtual Directory

The _mem_bin web application is added when a Membership Directory is first mapped to an IIS 4.0 web site or virtual directory. The purpose of the _mem_bin web application is to provide a set of HTML and ASP pages for HTML Forms authentication, error handling, and a number of other services. We can break up the capabilities of the _mem_bin web application into five discreet parts:

- ❑ HTML Forms Authentication pages
- ❑ Membership Management pages
- ❑ Logon Error pages
- ❑ Troubleshooting pages
- ❑ Other pages

It's worth noting at the outset that we can modify any of these pages in any way, as long as the required functionality remains the same.

Let's take a more detailed look at each of these service groupings, as well as the files used by each.

HTML Forms Authentication Pages

We've already discussed HTML Forms Authentication in some depth in this chapter – basically, it allows us to authenticate member credentials through HTML forms. HTML Forms Authentication is very convenient since we can modify the HTML to represent the look and feel of our existing site. Moreover, we can adapt our HTML forms so that they are supported by any browser type. In fact, this is an important consideration: if your sales depend on your web site, and your authentication method doesn't recognize half of the client browsers in existence, then you're throwing away a substantial percentage of your market. HTML Forms Authentication provides the most access to the greatest percentage of users.

The _mem_bin web application provides two files that are central to the implementation of HTML Forms Authentication, namely FormsLogin.asp and VerifPwd.asp. These files don't necessarily need to be stored in the virtual directory, but if they are not found in or above the file requiring the authentication then the Authentication Filter will default to the _mem_bin.

FormsLogin.asp

The ASP page, FormsLogin.asp, passes three values to VerifPwd.asp – the username, the password, and the Request.ServerVariables("QueryString") value stored in the URL, which is a hidden form value. These values are passed by the POST method of the HTML form. When the Authentication Filter is called by a page that uses HTML Forms Authentication, the name of the requested URL is passed to the FormsLogin.asp page through the QueryString.

If the user passes an incorrect username and password to FormsLogin.asp, they will be prompted for credentials again – and this is repeated until the correct credentials are passed. This makes it very easy for a hacker to 'work' on a site that uses HTML Forms Authentication. Since it is possible to POST from any page, the hacker can (theoretically) design an application that repeatedly POSTs username–password–URL combinations to VerifPwd.asp, until access is gained.

> *To resolve this security problem we need to use the blacklisting feature of Personalization and Membership. We'll read about this in Chapter 13.*

Any version of *FormsLogin.asp* page can be used, as long as it calls */_mem_bin/verifpwd.asp* – or another ASP page that provides the identical functionality.

VerifPwd.asp

The `VerifPwd.asp` does just one thing – it passes the username, password, and URL values mentioned above to the `VerifyCredentials()` method of the `Membership.VerifUsr.1` COM object. This method returns the URL for a `Response.Redirect`.

> *It is suggested that you use the modified version of* `VerifPwd.asp` *that we saw earlier in this Chapter – it contains useful comments and is clearer and more efficient than the version supplied with _mem_bin. Also, I recommend that you use* POST *rather than* GET, *and seriously consider using SSL to secure the transmission.*

Membership Management

It's a little known fact that the _mem_bin web application provides several useful ASP pages for managing user membership information. We can use these pages within our site to help members remember their passwords, cancel their membership, or use methods provided by the `DTCLib.inc` file.

> *In Chapter 14, we'll cover several methods that provide similar functionality to the methods in the* `DTCLib.inc` *file – and hopefully make them a little clearer!*

Cancel.asp

The `Cancel.asp` page, as supplied with _mem_bin, is an example page that is used to cancel a user's membership. The page doesn't remove the user (although it could do so very easily – we'll explore this in Chapter 14). However, it does reset the `accountStatus` attribute to 0.

If you use `Cancel.asp`, you should first make a number of modifications to the file. First, if you take a look at the contents of `Cancel.asp` you'll see that the username and password are stored in the ASP page:

```
' You must set the username and password here for this script to use
' in connecting to the directory.

  gMemUserScriptID = "cn=administrator,ou=members,o=microsoft"
  gMemUserPassword = "password"
```

Storing the username and password within the ASP page itself is a huge security risk – it's safer, and just as easy, to store the information in the registry. You can arrange this by using a modified version of the `RegistryLookup()` method:

Code Sample – Registry Lookup

```
' ****************************************************
' FUNCTION: RegistryLookup
'
' PURPOSE:  Look up values in the registry
```

```
'
' PARAMETERS:
'     varItem - Item to look up, this can be
'               a predefined contant or the path to a
'               key in the registry
'
'
Public Function RegistryLookup(varItem)
  On Error Resume Next

  Dim objAdminRegistry

  ' Assume failure
  ' *********************************
  RegistryLookup = ""

  ' Create Admin Registry object
  ' *********************************
  Set objAdminRegistry = Server.CreateObject("Commerce.AdminRegistry")
  If Err.Number <> 0 Then
    Err.Clear
    Exit Function
  End If

  RegistryLookup = objAdminRegistry.GetValue(varItem)
  If Err.Number <> 0 Then
    Err.Clear
    Exit Function
  End If
End Function
```

Storing information in the registry can be expensive, but the pay-off in terms of security can make any storage overhead worthwhile. Even then, care should be taken because, although this script doesn't give away the username and password, it does give away the fact that you have a component that can access the registry.

Once we've become more familiar with Membership security (Chapter 13) we will be able to create a user that only has permission to make these modifications. Even then, it would be very *risky to store such information within the ASP page.*

A little known alternative is to store the data in the **IIS 4.0 metabase**. The metabase is stored in memory, and can provide faster access method than is achievable using the registry. To set this up, you need to add a new attribute to the `IIsVirtualWeb`, to represent the value; the value can then be accessed and read through ADSI. We'll explore this in Chapter 15, and you'll find more information in the *IIS 4.0 Resource Kit* (Microsoft Press, ISBN 1-57231-638-1).

There are further changes that you should make to your `Cancel.asp` code. `Cancel.asp` sets an undocumented value for the `accountStatus` attribute: it's important to change the line `User.accountStatus = 0` in `Cancel.asp`, so that the attribute is instead set to the value 3 or 4.

Setting the `accountStatus` attribute to 0 does disable the account; however, the defined values for this attribute are 1=active, 2=pending, 3=disabled, and 4=to be removed. If you fail to set a value for the `accountStatus` attribute, then the attribute will default to the value 1.

DTCLib.inc

The DTCLib.inc file includes a plethora of methods used for managing objects, attributes, and members in the Membership Directory. Most of the functionality provided by this include file is covered in Chapter 14. However, we can very easily use the #include directive to include the file in an ASP page, and then use its methods.

Remind.asp

What happens if a member loses his password? In such a case, help is at hand: we can use the functionality provided by Remind.asp. The idea is simple: each user has an attribute called passwordReminder – its value is set by the user, and is intended to help the user to remember his password. When the unfortunate (or careless) user forgets his password, he can call on Remind.asp, which simply delivers the value of the passwordReminder attribute – after asking for a password hint.

There are two significant advantages to making Remind.asp available. First, the user who would usually call (or email) the site administrator – requesting a new password – can use Remind.asp and hence avoid bothering the administrator. Second, the user who would simply decide not to bother with the site – since they can't get access without their password – instead has a chance to recover his password, and hence you don't lose a valuable customer.

Remind.asp is a useful concept; however, if security is a serious concern then you might choose not to implement the page. However, you can also make modifications to Remind.asp, to make it fairly secure.

> **In order to use the Remind.asp, the user must have previously supplied his password hint and stored it in the passwordReminder attribute.**

Logon Error

If you work with the Membership Directory for any length of time then you're likely to come across some error messages. In Site Server, all error pages are in fact ASP pages. In the case of a logon error – such as an authentication problem or a cookie conflict – the ISAPI authentication filter delivers a **logon error page**, by redirecting the browser to an ASP page that is contained within the _mem_bin virtual directory.

All of Site Server's error pages are ASP pages. In fact, this is a great feature, because it allows developers and administrators to add extra functionality to the existing error pages – for example, to redirect or to provide additional options to the user when he encounters the error.

Let's have a look at the ASP error pages that are supplied within the _mem_bin virtual directory.

IntError.asp

IntError.asp is the general 'catch-all' error page. If an error occurs, and the ISAPI Authentication Filter doesn't know how to deal with it, then the user is directed to the IntError.asp page.

InvalidCookie.asp

When the Authentication Filter attempts to authenticate the member with Cookie Authentication, and the account specified in the MEMUSER cookie (the distinguished name of the member, or the Name property of the AUO) is invalid, then the user is redirected to the InvalidCookie.asp error page.

This is a fairly basic error page – we can use it as an example of how to add further functionality to ASP error pages. Ideally, Site Server should handle the 'invalid cookie' error by providing the user with the opportunity to re-authenticate and to reset the values of the MEMUSER and SITESERVER cookies. In order to set this up, we can add to the default behavior of InvalidCookie.asp. One method is to add a link to InvalidCookie.asp – this link will redirect the user to a page which employs an authentication method (such as Clear Text/Basic), creates the AUO as g_objAUO and calls the SendCookiesToExistingUser() method.

Sending Cookies – SendCookiesToExistingUser()

Here's the code for the SendCookiesToExistingUser() method:

```
' ********************************************************************
' SendCookiesToExistingUser
'
' Purpose:
'       Sends the user the cookies to id them
'
'
' ********************************************************************
Public Function SendCookiesToExistingUser()
  Dim strVUGuid
  Dim strVUCn

  ' Retrieve User values
  ' ***********************************
  strVUGuid = g_objAUO.Get("GUID")
  strVUCn = g_objAUO.Get("cn")

  ' Remove decoration from GUID
  ' ***********************************
  strVUGuid = Replace(strVUGuid, "-", "")
  strVUGuid = Replace(strVUGuid, "{", "")
  strVUGuid = Replace(strVUGuid, "}", "")

  ' Send the cookie
  ' ***********************************
    Dim objNewCookie
    Set objNewCookie = Server.CreateObject("Membership.verifusr.1")

    If Err.Number <> 0 Then
      DisplayErrorMessage("Unable to verify user.")
      Err.Clear
    Else
    ' Everythings looks good...set the cookies
    ' ***********************************
    objNewCookie.IssueCookie "SITESERVER", "GUID=" & strVUGuid
    objNewCookie.IssueCookie "MEMUSER", strVUCn
    End If

    ' Release VerifyUser Object
    ' ***********************************
    Set objNewCookie = Nothing
End Function
```

We'll talk more about this in Chapter 12, when we discuss the methods of the VerifUsr object.

NoCookie.asp

The `NoCookie.asp` page is encountered when a user has specified that he does not wish to accept cookies. In such a case, it's possible to employ the Cookie Munger utility (provided in Microsoft's *IIS 4.0 Resource Kit*) to pass the cookie data in the QueryString. The Cookie Munger is out of the scope of this book – for further reading you could consult the *IIS 4.0 Resource Kit*.

PrivilegedContent.asp

`PriviledgedContent.asp` is encountered when a user provides Membership Authentication information that is authenticated (i.e. the user's identity has been confirmed) but not authorized (i.e. the user doesn't have adequate permissions to access the resource).

In the example below, the user `StephenS` (1) enters his user credentials and requests the resource `Admin.asp`. The ACL (2) of this resource contains only two ACEs – for the Administrator and for the System. Since `StephenS` entered the correct credentials, his authentication is successful and he is allowed access to the site. However, in this example `StephenS` is not the administrator or the system (3). Therefore, he is not granted access to the resource; instead he is redirected (4) to `PriviledgedContent.asp`, which explains (5) that he has been authenticated, but not authorized.

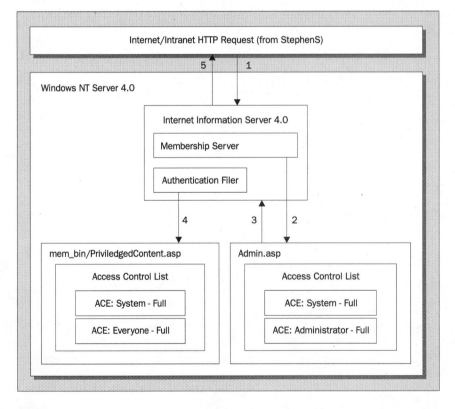

Troubleshooter

If the user provides incorrect authentication credentials for Clear Text/<u>B</u>asic Authentication or <u>D</u>istributed Password Authentication, then he is redirected to the **troubleshooter**. The troubleshooter helps the user to fix his authentication problem, whether the problem is software-, account- or security-related.

The pages of the troubleshooter follow a certain logic – largely in the form of a series of questions, whose answers are either "yes" or "no". This is outlined in the following diagram:

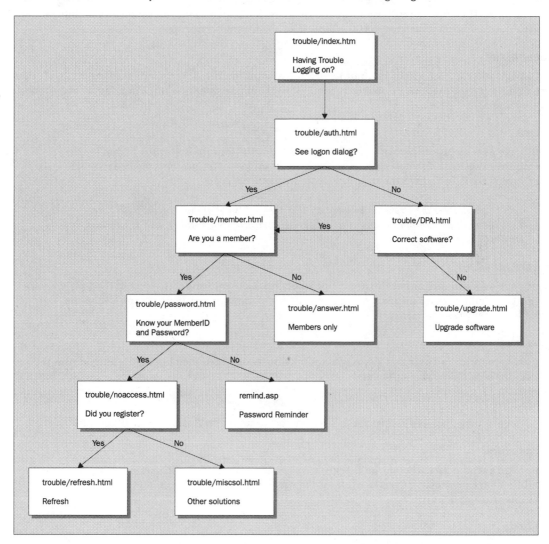

All the files here are found in the `trouble` directory, under the `_mem_bin` web application. Of course, the system is extendible, and if you choose to extend the existing system then it's likely that you'd want to replace the code provided in these files. Let's have a quick look over the files that are supplied.

index.htm

This is the first page of the troubleshooting wizard – it is designed to suggest some alternative ideas to the user, before the troubleshooter itself is called to action.

auth.html

The troubleshooter begins in earnest, by asking the user a basic question – Did you see a logon dialog box or form? If the user's response to `auth.html` is "yes", then the troubleshooter presents `member.html`; if the user's response is "no", then the troubleshooter presents `dpa.html`.

member.html

This page asks the user whether or not he is a member of the site. If the user's response is "yes", then the troubleshooter presents `password.html`; if the user's response is "no", then the troubleshooter presents `answer.html`.

dpa.html

This page asks the user whether or not he is working with software that is supported by the Membership system. If the user answers "yes", the troubleshooter presents `member.html`; if the user's response is "no", then the troubleshooter presents `upgrade.html`.

> `dpa.html` *makes the erroneous assumption that the user is not authenticating with Clear Text/Basic Authentication (or any other supported authentication method), and is only using DPA authentication.*

password.html

This page asks whether or not the user remembers his username and password. If the user answers "yes", the troubleshooter presents `noaccess.html`; if the user's response is "no", then the troubleshooter presents `remind.asp`.

answer.html

This page informs the user that some content may be available to members only, and advises the user to register with the service provider.

upgrade.html

This page advises the user to upgrade his system, by visiting http://www.microsoft.com!

noaccess.html

This page asks the user whether he is registered to use the service. If the user answers "yes", the troubleshooter presents `refresh.html`; if the user's response is "no", then the troubleshooter presents `miscsol.html`.

remind.asp

This page is designed to help the user remember their password – it does this by providing the user's 'password hint'. `remind.asp` resides in the root of the _mem_bin web application – we discussed it earlier in this section.

refresh.html

This suggests three further possibilities that the user might pursue, if all other options have been exhausted.

miscsol.html

Finally, this page attempts to explain why the user is unable to log into the site, by providing a number of possible causes.

Unused Files

The `trouble` directory also contains a few files – `os.htm`, `deferror.htm` and `content2a.html` – that aren't used in the troubleshooter wizard. These files were used in earlier incarnations of Site Server, but are now essentially defunct.

> *When the user encounters an HTTP 401 error on a site mapped to a Membership Server, then troubleshooter is configured to start automatically. It's possible to change this behavior by removing the mapping from the Custom Errors tab of the web site's Properties dialog. If you want to disable troubleshooter altogether, you could point the 401 error to the page* `fixpassw.html` *– this page simply directs the member to contact customer service.*

Other Files in _mem_bin

There are a few other files in the **_mem_bin** virtual directory, that we'll mention just briefly here:

`AUOConfig.asp`	Returns the available secondary providers for the Membership Server.
`DMMP.asp`	Returns information about a mailing list created with the Direct Mailer that may be edited, additionally displays debugging information.
`DMSP.asp`	Provides a means for editing a mailing once a package has been created in the Direct Mailer.
`DSExport.asp`	Is used to export and associate member data with the log files generated by IIS 4.0. Once member data has been associated with these log files, it's possible to track member behavior implicitly, and to link directly to the member in the Membership Directory.

Advanced Concepts

In this section, we'll examine how to support multiple web sites with a single Membership Directory; how to configure the Internet Information Server snap-in to use Site Server; and we'll look at a programmatic method for creating web sites for IIS 4.0 using ADSI interfaces.

Supporting Multiple Web Sites in one Membership Directory

Site Server allows us to support any number of web sites, and with Membership Directory technology it's possible to ensure that the membership information for each site is kept separate and distinct from the others. This topic is particularly relevant to organizations such as Internet Service Providers, that host multiple web sites.

The beauty of Site Server is that it's not necessary to have one Membership Directory for each web site – you can support the membership information for *all* of your web sites using just a *single* Membership Directory. The idea is to create a separate Membership Server for each web site – each Membership Server authenticates against a different container within the Directory. We do this by specifying a different base distinguished name (BaseDN) value for each Membership Server.

The BaseDN represents the container from which members will be authenticated. In Site Server Membership, the default BaseDN is the ou=Members container – but it's easy to choose a different BaseDN, by using the `PMAdmin.vbs` tool. When a member passes credentials for authentication, a path is built to that member using the BaseDN.

> In order to support multiple web sites on a single Membership Directory, it's essential that the Membership Directory hardware is scaleable to the number of connections and requests-per-minute required by each web site. See Chapters 3 and 4 for more on determining requirements for scaling and planning.

Configuring the Membership Directory

How do we configure a Membership Directory to host multiple web sites? First, we need to prepare a new Membership Directory and create new containers (under the ou=members container, ideally) for each web site. We must also set up new ou=AnonymousUsers containers, underneath these new members containers. The path for the two new sites, from the ou=AnonymousUsers container, should look something like:

```
LDAP://localhost/o=[organization name]/ou=members/ou=SiteA/ou=AnonymousUsers
```

```
LDAP://localhost/o=[organization name]/ou=members/ou=SiteB/ou=AnonymousUsers
```

Creating New Membership Servers

Next, we need to create new Membership Servers – one for each web site. The easiest way to do this is by following the **New Membership Server** wizard scenario in Chapter 6: in Screen 4, choose the option **Connect to an existing Membership Directory**. In addition, select **Custom Configuration** in Screen 2, and select both **LDAP** and **AUO** in Screen 3. The directory to which we are connecting is the Membership Directory configured with multiple containers, underneath the ou=Members container.

Next, we must configure the BaseDN for each Membership Server. The BaseDN represents the container information that is to be appended to the front of the member name, when binding to the directory. By default, the BaseDN is the ou=members container. Any Membership authentication will be performed using this BaseDN information to build the path to the member.

In order for a single Membership Directory to support multiple sites, we must set up multiple containers. Each site has a corresponding container – there will be a distinguished name in the container for each member of that site, and the site's members will be authenticated against the DNs in the appropriate container. In order to authenticate members against each Membership Server's appropriate BaseDN path, we must use the PMAdmin.vbs command line tool.

> *The* PMAdmin.vbs *tool is a command line utility. To use* PMAdmin.vbs, *navigate to the* [installation path]\Microsoft Site Server\bin\P&M *directory through the command line.*

For each container, this procedure requires that we pass a Membership Instance ID to PMAdmin.vbs – this is how it knows which Membership Server to modify. There are two ways to determine the instance ID:

❑ The PMAdmin.vbs tool can be used to return a list of the available Membership Servers, with their names and instance IDs. To do this, use the list verb with the instance value, like this: PMAdmin list instance. Then find the instance id that corresponds to the name value.

The Membership instance ID of 1 usually corresponds to the Windows NT (Intranet)
Authentication Membership Server instance.

```
C:\WINNT4\System32\cmd.exe                                    _ □ ×

D:\Microsoft Site Server\Bin\P&M>pmadmin list instance
Microsoft (R) Windows Scripting Host Version 5.0 for Windows
Copyright (C) Microsoft Corporation 1996-1997. All rights reserved.

Site Server P&M Administration
Copyright (C) 1998 Microsoft Corporation. All rights reserved.

Server: localhost

Instance ID#: 1
Name: Intranet (Windows NT Authentication) Membership Server
Authentication Mode: Windows NT

Instance ID#: 2
Name: WROX
Authentication Mode: Membership

Instance ID#: 3
Name: Membership Server #3
Authentication Mode: Membership

D:\Microsoft Site Server\Bin\P&M>_
```

❑   Alternatively, we can review the properties of the MemProxyUser that is created for each
     Membership Server.The Membership Server ID corresponds to the number at the end of the
     MemProxyUser ID.

Associating Membership Server BaseDN

Once we've obtained the Membership Instance Ids for each Membership Server, we can again use
PMAdmin.vbs to modify the BaseDNs for the Membership Servers. To associate a Membership
Server with the appropriate container (SiteA and SiteB in our example), we'll use PMAdmin.vbs
to change the BaseDN for each LDAP service instance. The BaseDN tells the Membership Server
(from the root) which container to use when authenticating new users.

The usage is as follows:

```
PMAdmin Set authsvc /basedn:[from_the_members_container]
/ID:[Membership_Instance_ID]
```

The BaseDN defaults to ou=members and should be changed to:

```
ou=[New_Container_Name], ou=members
```

To read more about the PMAdmin.vbs *command line tool, see Appendix B.*

Mapping the Appropriate Membership Server to IIS

Finally, we need to map each Membership Server to Internet Information Server. This procedure was
covered at the beginning of the chapter.

Configuring the IIS Admin MMC to use Site Server

If you've tried to use Site Server features through the Administration MMC of IIS 4.0, you may have noticed that the Site Server services are unavailable. To make these services available, the proper extensions must be enabled.

To enable the Site Server 3.0 extensions, open up the IIS Admin MMC and select Console | Add/Remove Snap-in. In the resulting dialog box, select the Extensions tab:

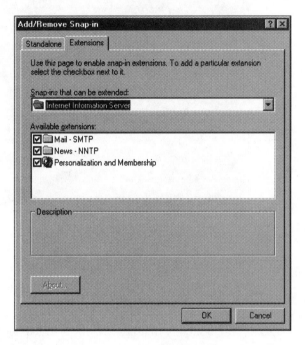

Select Internet Information Server as the snap-in to be extended, and mark the checkbox for each service that should be supported. To support the Site Server Personalization and Membership system, we need to select the Personalization and Membership option – this allows the MMC to provide the correct behavior for mapping Personalization and Membership sites. Checking the other extensions – SMTP and NNTP – ensures that these services are supported from IIS 4.0.

Scripting Against IIS 4.0

We can use Active Directory Service Interfaces (ADSI) for IIS 4.0. With ADSI, we can create web sites and manage existing web sites programmatically.

> *IIS 4.0 has an Active Directory Service Interface namespace provider, ProgID =* IISNamespace. *When we use the moniker* IIS:// *to perform a bind from a* GetObject() *method call, we pass the path to bind to the* IISNamespace *object. There's more about ADSI in Chapter 12.*

Code Sample – Creating New Virtual Directories with ASP

We can use the following method, CreateNewVirtualDir(), to create a new virtual directory that can be browsed and read. We must pass the name of the virtual directory and the path of the new directory to the method.

```
<%
Public Function CreateNewVirtualDir(strName, strPath)
  On Error Resume Next

  ' Assume failure
  ' **********************************************************
  CreateNewVirtualDir = false

  Dim objServer
  Dim objRoot
  Dim objVirtualDir
  Dim nWebInstance

  ' Obtain the number that corresponds to this web instance
  ' **********************************************************
  nWebInstance = Request.ServerVariables("INSTANCE_ID")

  ' Connect to the web instance
  ' **********************************************************
  Set objServer = GetObject("IIS://localhost/W3SVC/" & nWebInstance)
  If Err.Number <> 0 Then
    Exit Function
  End If

  ' Connect to the root of this web
  ' **********************************************************
  Set objRoot = objServer.GetObject("Root")
  If Err.Number <> 0 Then
    Exit Function
  End If

  ' Create a new virtual dir
  ' **********************************************************
  Set objVirtualDir = objRoot.Create("IIsWebVirtualDir", CStr(strName))
  If Err.Number <> 0 Then
    Exit Function
  End If

  ' Set values for new virtual dir
  ' **********************************************************
  objVirtualDir.path = CStr(strPath)
  objVirtualDir.EnableDirBrowsing = true
  objVirutalDir.AccessRead = true

  ' Call set info make changes
  ' **********************************************************
  objVirtualDir.SetInfo
  If Err.Number <> 0 Then
    Exit Function
  Else
    CreateNewVirtualDir = true
  End If
End Function
%>
```

We'll see a little more of the IIS:// *namespace in Chapter 15. For a more detailed reference, see the* IIS 4.0 Resource Kit *(Microsoft Press, ISBN 1-572-31-6381).*

Summary

In this chapter, we've pulled the covers off and taken a detailed look at how Site Server 3.0 and Internet Information Server 4.0 integrates. Here are the key points that we've covered:

❑ We learned about how to map a Membership Server to an IIS 4.0 web site and examined the steps required to make the mapping. We mentioned that Site Server 3.0 would not work with versions of IIS earlier than 4.0.

❑ We covered the Windows NT (Intranet) Authentication methods. In studying the Allow Anonymous Access option with the IUSR_*[server_name]* anonymous account, we discussed how to grant access to resources and learned that Site Server couldn't personalize information for the anonymous account since all users would share it. We also covered Clear Text/Basic Authentication and Windows NT Challenge/Response. Again, we discussed how Site Server uses these authentication types and discovered that Site Server creates the accounts in the Membership Directory automatically, but still authenticates against the Windows NT Security Accounts Manager.

❑ We introduced Membership Authentication, and contrasted it (at a high level) with Windows NT (Intranet) Authentication. We saw how we can still provide IUSR_*[server_name]* anonymous access to the system, and that it is not possible to personalize this account. We introduced the Security Support Providers that are installed with Site Server 3.0, and studied them in some detail, comparing and contrasting the differences and advantages between the various Membership Authentication techniques.

❑ We looked at the _mem_bin virtual directory that is installed when we map a Membership Server to an IIS 4.0 web site. We looked at the various services provided by the _mem_bin, and how to tweak it to work for specific situations.

❑ Finally, we looked at how to support multiple web sites with a single Membership Directory. We saw how to configure the Internet Information Server 4.0 Admin MMC to use Site Server 3.0 services, and we learned how to use Active Directory Service Interfaces to work with the IIS 4.0 metabase.

The Active User Object

When you visit a bank to withdraw funds, it's not just a simple case of walking in and taking the money – even if the money's yours. There are certain formalities: you need to speak to a bank teller to verify your credentials and the transaction needs to be approved. Only then will the funds be handed over. Using the Active User Object (AUO) works in a similar fashion. Once the membership system authenticates the user – acting as our bank teller to verify credentials – we can gain access to the gold mine of member data stored in the Membership Directory by using the AUO.

If we want to personalize an ASP page, we can use an instance of the AUO. The AUO is able to gain access to the context of the member account that we used to authenticate ourselves – remember the first thing that happens in a P&M enabled IIS 4.0 web is member authentication. Before we can personalize anything, we need to know what user to personalize for! The AUO enables us to access this information in the Membership Directory. We don't have to bind to or authenticate against the Membership Directory with direct Active Directory Service Interfaces (ADSIs) as the AUO takes care of this for us, and we'll see how in this chapter.

Let's take a look at exactly what we'll be covering in this chapter:

- ❑ **The Active User Object.** First, we'll introduce and discuss the Active User Object (AUO), and – in advance of learning about the AUO's interfaces – we'll cover how to create instances of the AUO. Creating the AUO is as simple as creating any other server-side COM object; however, to use it properly we need to understand what the AUO requires of us.

- ❑ **Active User Object Interfaces.** The AUO provides three interfaces. Namely, these are the IADs (for working with directory entries); the IADsContainer (for working with directory containers); and the IUserObjects (for providing the interaction with the Site Server Membership system and other directory binding services). We'll examine each of these three interfaces in great detail, along with code examples to help you understand why and how we use their methods and properties.

❑ **The Membership GUIDGen Object.** The GUIDGen object provides services for creating a GUID. We use Globally Unique Identifiers (GUIDs) throughout the Membership Directory: every class object has a GUID, and instances of the Member class define GUID as an attribute a member must have. This simple object becomes very important later on in the book.

❑ **IGUIDGen Interfaces.** The GUIDGen object has one interface, called IGuidGen, which has three methods. The method that is most important to us is the GenerateGuid() method. We'll use the GenerateGuid() method to return a GUID that we can the use. We'll only be taking a look at this one method, since the other two are identical – in theory – to ones covered in the AUO interface definition for IUserObjects.

When we've finished this chapter, we should be able to create an instance of the Active User Object and use its properties and methods effectively to get to member information in the Membership Directory. In addition, we will have gained familiarity with another Membership object – the Membership.GUIDGen object – which is used for creating Globally Unique Ids (GUIDs). Finally we'll be well on our way to having a firm understanding of the role that ADSI plays in the scope of the Membership Directory.

The Active User Object

The AUO is a server-side COM object that implements three interfaces into one complete object, and also adds some functionality which allows us to determine the context of the user. The three interfaces are IADs, IADsContainer, and IUserObjects. They give the AUO the ability to bind to the Membership Directory and manage objects within it. Each interface serves a special purpose, and we'll discuss each in-depth in their respective areas of this chapter. First however we'll briefly put these interfaces in context.

ADSI Interfaces

Two of the AUO interfaces, IADs and IADsContainer, are Active Directory Service Interfaces. We defined Active Directory Service Interfaces early in the book, but let's have a brief review. ADSI is an application-programming interface for working with directory services. More specifically, ADSIs are COM objects that we can use to bind to and work with a variety of data services: the Membership Directory, the IIS 4.0 metabase, and the upcoming Windows NT 5.0 Active Directory. We call them interfaces because other objects (such as the AUO and LDAPNamespace objects) expose them as interfaces of their own. However, these interfaces can also be used independently – for example, we can use an IADs object to point to the same member as the AUO, using code like this:

```
' If we authenticate as the Administrator, both the
' Active User Object and the new objIADs object
' will point to the cn=Administrator
' **************************************************
Set objAUO = Server.CreateObject("Membership.UserObjects.1")
Set objIADs =
GetObject("LDAP://localhost:1003/o=Wrox/ou=Members/cn=Administrator")
```

We'll be looking at how these objects are created in more detail below. IADs and IADsContainer are not the only ADSIs that can work with the Membership Directory. Indeed, we'll be looking at some other ADSIs that we can use with the Membership Directory when we get to Chapter 12.

AUO Interfaces versus Raw ADSI

As we said in the introduction, using the AUO means that we don't have to implement individual ADSIs directly. The main advantage of using the AUO is that unlike other ADSI providers, the AUO – when used from an IIS 4.0 web mapped to a Membership Server – knows who the member is once the object is instantiated. It does this through the `OnStartPage()` method. This is an event called by ASP when starting a COM object, which allows for context to be passed from the ASP page to the object.

Binding is the process of locating an object by its name or moniker, starting it (if it has not already been started), and returning an interface pointer to the object. The AUO works in conjunction with the Membership Authentication system, so when it is created it knows which member account it needs to use to bind to the Membership Directory. Remember, whenever we connect to a directory we have to provide credentials to access the directory. Before we can use the AUO, we have to be authenticated – otherwise, how would the AUO know who we are?

We could use a different ADSI provider. A moniker we use for the Membership Directory is the name space path to an object – LDAP://localhost/o=Wrox/ou=Members/cn=Administrator. If however we wanted to use the LDAPNamespace object and bind as a valid member, we'd have to use another ADSI to pass the correct username to the Membership Directory.

> *Several other resources are available for reading about the Active User Object. The Site Server 3.0 documentation and the Site Server 3.0 Software Development Kit are places to start.*

Notes for Running the Code Examples

Most of the code examples are designed to run from an ASP page. For more information on running ASP pages, please refer to the Introduction. We'll use a standard set of HTML headers and footers, and define the variables we're going to need, at the beginning of each code sample. Where this is the same in every example the code will be on a white background, so that the section of code we are discussing is easily visible on a gray background.

Before you can bind to the Membership Directory from an ASP page, you need to map the IIS 4.0 web under which the ASP page is running to your Membership Server. You'll need to refer to Chapter 8 if you haven't yet done this. In this chapter, the code samples will focus on using the AUO from an ASP page running under an IIS 4.0 web (such as the **Default Web Site**) mapped to a Membership Server (such as the **Intranet (Windows NT Authentication) Membership Server** installed by default). You can easily map a site to a Membership server by using the MMC, selecting the site, and selecting **Tasks | Membership Server Mapping...** from the **Action** menu. You can only map whole sites, not virtual directories. Later on in the chapter, we will see how to use the AUO from an ASP page where the IIS 4.0 web is not mapped to a Membership Server, and from outside an ASP page altogether when we look at the **IUserObjects** interface. However, to run the majority of the code examples you will need the configuration described above.

You will only be able to retrieve attributes of an AUO instance if you have bound to the Membership Directory as an authenticated member. In a given session, the first time you run a code example in which you need to bind to the Membership Directory (e.g. the first script in this chapter, `FindUsersCN.asp`) you will be prompted for a username and password to authenticate yourself against the Membership Directory. If the Membership Directory is using Windows NT authentication, you will need to provide the username and password of a valid user account in the NT User Manager. If the Membership Directory is using Membership authentication, you will need to provide the username and password of a user account in the Membership Directory. You won't need to authenticate yourself again unless you log off your IIS session by exiting your browser.

If the Membership Directory is set to allow anonymous access, any scripts in this chapter that try to retrieve properties of an AUO instance will fail with the following error:

> The user could not be identified so the Active User Object (AUO) could not be initialized. Enable authentication for this page

This is because you will have accessed the Membership Directory as an anonymous member, and therefore there are no properties stored for you. In order to disable anonymous access you need to change the properties of the IIS 4.0 web under which you are running your ASP page – see Chapter 7 for more details.

Using the Active User Object

We can use the AUO both from within an ASP page and independently. To use the AUO from an Active Server Page, we need to create the object. If the ASP page is not on an IIS 4.0 web mapped to a Membership Server we will have to initialize the object ourselves, otherwise it will be initialized automatically. Then, if the Membership Server we are mapped to uses authentication, the object will be bound to the member that was authenticated. However, if the Active Server Page creating the AUO is *not* authenticated – or is set to allow the IUSR_[*server_name*] anonymous account – then we have to tell the AUO explicitly which member it should bind to. We'll see how to use the AUO outside an ASP page further on in the chapter when we look at the IUserObjects Interface Init() method.

We'll look first at the most common scenario: using the AUO from an ASP page, where we have mapped our IIS to a Membership Server and set up authentication, as we saw how to do in the previous section of the book, *Configuring Personalization and Membership*. Member authentication is always the first event that occurs when a user accesses a Membership Server mapped site. The AUO instantiation takes care of binding to the appropriate member in the appropriate directory, with the OnStartPage() method called when the object is created – ASP will always attempt to call the OnStartPage() method of any COM object that is created from an ASP page. With the AUO, this method retrieves the context of the authenticated user, and we can then ask the AUO for any information that exists for a member through the properties and methods provided by the ADSI IADs and IADsContainer interfaces of the AUO.

Creating an Instance of the Active User Object

So how do we create an instance of the AUO from an Active Server Page? We'll use the CreateObject() method. CreateObject() is a method of ASP's Server object. Using CreateObject(ProgID) returns a pointer to a new instance of the object specified by ProgID. The programmatic ID (ProgID) is a readable name for a binary object, that maps to the real name of the object (or CLSID, which stands for 'class ID') in the registry.

We'll only need to know the CLSID for an object when we're working with C++, and even then only in specific cases.

The ProgID for the Active User Object is Membership.UserObjects. The complete syntax for creating the AUO in a VBScript/ASP is:

```
Dim objAUO
Set objAUO = Server.CreateObject("Membership.UserObjects")
```

This is all we need to create an AUO object. Once the object is created, its `OnStartPage()` method grabs the context of the user that was authenticated from the Membership Server, so we can use the object's interfaces to view additional member information. For instance, to access the current user's common name (cn) we simply ask for it. Before we see some code that uses the AUO to view a member's cn value let's define an example user that we can use throughout all the code samples in this chapter. Assuming that the Membership Directories' root container is Wrox, and that the LDAP Service is available on port 1003, our user will have the following attributes:

- **Common name (cn)**: StephenS
- **Password (userPassword)**: password
- **Path to the member**: LDAP://localhost:1003/o=Wrox/ou=Members/cn=StephenS

Code Sample – Finding the User's Common Name

Now that we've defined these values, let's see how we find the user's common name. This code sample can be run on any IIS 4.0 web. However, if the web server is not mapped to a Membership Server, or if it uses the IIS anonymous account, then we'll only see an error message when we try to display member information.

```
<HTML>
<BODY BGCOLOR=WHITE>
<FONT FACE=ARIAL SIZE=3>
<B>
Finding the User's Common Name
</B>
<HR SIZE=1>
</FONT>
<FONT FACE=ARIAL SIZE=2>
<%
On Error Resume Next

' Dimension variables
' ********************************************************
Dim objAUO                  ' AUO object
Dim strCommonName           ' cn property of user

' Create the AUO object
' ********************************************************
Set objAUO = Server.CreateObject("Membership.UserObjects.1")
If Err.Number <> 0 Then
  Response.Write (Err.Number & "<BR>" & Err.Description)
Else
  Response.Write ("Created AUO successfully.<P>")
End If
```

Here, we've set up the variables we're going to need and created our AUO instance. Next, we use the `Get()` method to store the cn value of the current user in our local variable `strCommonName`:

```
' Assign the cn value to strCommonName
' ********************************************************
strCommonName = objAUO.Get("cn")              ' can also use objAUO.cn

' Handle any errors
' ********************************************************
If Err.Number <> 0 Then
```

```
  Response.Write "<FONT COLOR=RED>"
    Response.Write "<B>Error Number</B> -" & Err.Number & "<BR>"
    Response.Write "<B>Error Description</B> -" & Err.Description & "<P>"
    Response.Write "Advice - Make sure that the machine you are "
    Response.Write "working on has Site Server 3.0 installed, and "
    Response.Write "the web server you are accessing is mapped to "
    Response.Write "a Membership Server instance."
  Else
    ' Display strCommonName
    ' ********************************************************
    Response.Write "The cn of the current user is: " & strCommonName
  End If
%>
</FONT>
</BODY>
</HTML>
```

If we requested the above ASP page and authenticated as StephenS, we would see the following output:

> Finding the User's Common Name
> Created AUO sucessfully.
>
> The cn of the current user is: StephenS

Now that we've seen how to create the AUO, let's take a detailed look at the different interfaces available.

The Active User Object Interfaces

The Active User Object exposes three interfaces, and each of them has distinct methods and properties. Two of these interfaces, IADs and IADsContainer, are Active Directory Service Interfaces – they're used for working with directory objects, and can also be used independently of the AUO. The third interface of the AUO is IUserObjects, which provides methods for binding and connecting to the directory.

The diagram below shows the relationship of the two ADSIs to the Membership Directory. The IADs interface represents entries in the directory and can be used to work with instances of classes. The IADsContainer is used to work with special directory objects that can act as containers for IADs objects.

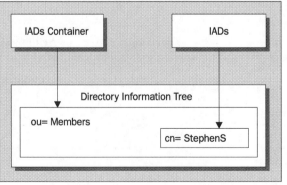

In the diagram, we use an IADsContainer for working with the ou=Members container, and an IADs for working with a specific member – in this case StephenS.

As we go on to discuss these interfaces below, you may notice that some methods are not mentioned for the IADs and IADsContainer per the interface definitions. Apparently, these are unsupported or unavailable when working with the Membership Directory.

Let's start with a look at the ADSI IADs interface.

The IADs Interface

The IADs interface exposes and supports six properties:

Property	Description
Name	Returns the relative distinguished name of an object
Class	Returns the class type of the object pointed to
Guid	The Globally Unique Identifier (GUID) – every object class in the Membership Directory has one
ADsPath	Returns the Active Directory path string of the object, which uniquely identifies the object
Parent	Returns the parent object's Name property of the current object pointed to
Schema	Returns the ADsPath string of the object that represents this schema class in the schema

It also supports the following six methods:

Method	Description
GetInfo()	Used to refresh or retrieve the information in the ADSI cache
SetInfo()	Used to update the values that have been modified in the ADSI cache
Get()	When passed the name of an attribute, it returns the value that the attribute contains.
Put()	Allows for the value of attribute to be modified in the ADSI cache
GetEx()	An extended version of the Get() method providing the ability to return multi-valued attributes
PutEx()	An extended version of the Put() method that allows for adding multi-values to an attribute and for deleting attributes

The complete interface definition is given in Appendix C.

We'll spend the rest of this section taking a closer look at IADs's properties and methods, starting with the Name property.

The Name Property

The Name property returns the relative distinguished name (RDN) of an object. The RDN uniquely identifies the object within a container. With this property a Membership Directory that supports multiple webs can easily handle users with the same names for different sites. As long as each site uses its own container for members, the name for each member will be unique relative to its container.

```
o= Wrox
  ou= Members
    ou= SiteA
      cn= StephensS

    ou= SiteB
      cn= StephensS
```

Code Sample – The Name Property of IADs

In the sample for this property we'll ask for the Name of an instance of the Active User Object. The call will return the member's RDN:

cn=StephensS (non-anonymous or authenticated member)

Alternatively, if the member has been assigned to the ou=AnonymousUsers container (i.e. the system has failed to identify them) then a GUID is returned:

cn=1f7540522441142053c3751f48dc4c4d (anonymous member)

Note that if we have logged into the Membership Directory anonymously (i.e. if anonymous authentication is enabled for that IIS 4.0 web) we will not be able to retrieve any cn value.

Here's the code:

```
<HTML>
<BODY BGCOLOR=WHITE>
<FONT FACE=ARIAL SIZE=3>
<B>
IADs - Name
</B>
<HR SIZE=1>
</FONT>
<FONT FACE=ARIAL SIZE=2>
<%
On Error Resume Next

Dim objAUO

' Create the Active User Object
' ********************************************************
Set objAUO = Server.CreateObject("Membership.UserObjects.1")
If Err.Number <> 0 Then
  Response.Write "Unable to create the AUO."
  Response.End
End If
```

```
' Use the Name
' ***********************************************************
Response.Write "The name method displays the "
Response.Write "naming attribute and value of "
Response.Write "the object type.<P>"
Response.Write objAUO.Name
%>
</FONT>
</BODY>
</HTML>
```

After running this ASP, this is what we would see:

> IADs - Name
> The name method displays the naming attribute and value of the object type.
> cn=StephenS

Another example use of the Name property is in issuing cookies. In Chapter 8, we learned that Membership authentication uses Automatic Cookie Authentication to store the RDN in the MEMUSER cookie. Site Server uses this value to bind to a member building the path from the base distinguished name (BaseDN). If we needed to send the user a new MEMUSER cookie – such as when the member deletes their original – then we can send them the value of the Name property of the Active User Object.

Remember, the base distinguished name (BaseDN) represents the container that members will be authenticated from. By default the BaseDN is the ou=Members container, but can be changed through the PMAdmin.vbs tool – which we read about in Chapter 8.

Code Sample – Send a New MEMUSER Cookie

We could use the following ASP fragment to reset the MEMUSER cookie for the current user. Note that before running this code we would need to set the authentication method for this ASP to use either HTML Forms or Basic/Clear Text authentication if the cookie used for Automatic Cookie Authentication is no longer available.

```
<%
On Error Resume Next

Dim objAUO
Dim objNewCookie

' Create the Active User Object
' **********************************
Set objAUO = Server.CreateObject("Membership.UserObjects.1")
If Err.Number <> 0 Then
  Response.Write "Unable to create the Active User Object"
End If

' Send the user a new MEMUSER cookie
' **********************************
Set objNewCookie = Server.CreateObject("Membership.VerifUsr.1")

If Err.Number <> 0 Then
  Response.Write "Unable to create the Membership.VerifUsr Object"
Else
```

```
      ' Everythings looks good...set the cookies
      ' **********************************
  objNewCookie.IssueCookie "MEMUSER", objAUO.Name
End If
%>
```

This snippet of code has no output and ideally should be encapsulated in a method rather than a plain ASP page. In Chapter 14, we'll explore the necessity of sending the user new cookies in more depth – as well as examine the complete method.

We can also use an object's relative distinguished name for a direct bind on an object in conjunction with the Class property. Talking of which, the Class property is next.

The Class Property

The Class property returns the class type of the object pointed to. In the case of the Active User Object, the Class property should always return 'member', since an instantiated AUO is used for managing a member.

Code Sample – The Class Property of IADs

In this sample, we use the Class property of the IADs interface to return the class of the object pointed to.

```
<HTML>
<BODY BGCOLOR=WHITE>
<FONT FACE=ARIAL SIZE=3>
<B>
IADs - Class
</B>
<HR SIZE=1>
</FONT>
<FONT FACE=ARIAL SIZE=2>
<%
On Error Resume Next

Dim objAUO

' Create the Active User Object
' ********************************************************
Set objAUO = Server.CreateObject("Membership.UserObjects.1")
If Err.Number <> 0 Then
  Response.Write "Unable to create the AUO."
  Response.End
End If

' Use the Class
' ********************************************************
Response.Write "The class method displays the "
Response.Write "class type of the object pointed "
Response.Write "to.<P>"
Response.Write objAUO.Class
%>
</FONT>
</BODY>
</HTML>
```

After running this ASP, we should expect to see:

> IADs - Class
> The class method displays the class type of the object pointed to.
> member

Now, we have enough information about the Name and the Class to build a small sample. We can use the AUO's Name and Class properties to bind a separate IADs object to the current AUO member. This sample does present some new concepts; however, reading through the code we can see how we would use the Name and Class properties to do direct binds.

Code Sample – IADs Binds

Here's the code:

```
<HTML>
<BODY BGCOLOR=WHITE>
<FONT FACE=ARIAL SIZE=3>
<B>
IADs - Binds using properties
</B>
<HR SIZE=1>
</FONT>
<FONT FACE=ARIAL SIZE=2>
<%
On Error Resume Next

Dim objAUO
Dim objLDAP
Dim objIADs

' Create the Active User Object
' ******************************************************
Set objAUO = Server.CreateObject("Membership.UserObjects.1")
If Err.Number <> 0 Then
  Response.Write "Unable to create the AUO."
  Response.End
End If

' Bind to the LDAP Members directory directly
' ******************************************************
Set objLDAP = GetObject(objAUO.Parent)

' Do a bind based on AUO properties
' ******************************************************
Set objIADs = objLDAP.GetObject(objAUO.Class, objAUO.Name)
%>
</FONT>
</BODY>
</HTML>
```

In this particular code sample, we're using the values of the AUO provided by the Name and Class properties to use the GetObject() method provided by the IADsContainer interface to bind an ADSI object directly to the object.

We won't really need to use the Class *property until we start using the* LDAPNamespace *object and compare objects to one another. We'll see another good example of the need to compare object types in Chapter 13, when we talk about Access Control List canonicalization in the Membership Directory.*

Next, we'll take a look at the GUID property, which provides a unique identification for an object class.

The GUID Property

Every object class in the Membership Directory has a **globally unique identifier** (GUID). Just as the name implies, a GUID is a number that is guaranteed to be unique. Entities that need to be uniquely identified – such as interfaces or objects in the Membership Directory –have a GUID. Towards the end of this chapter, we'll look at another object – Membership.GuidGen – that we can use to generate GUIDs for ourselves.

Unlike most properties, we need to be careful how we ask for the GUID property. The member class not only has its own GUID as a class identifier, but it uses an attribute called GUID as a member instance identifier! The values for many objects can be requested implicitly, for example we can retrieve the cn with objAUO.cn, rather than objAUO.Get("cn"). However, this convenience can lead to confusion when asking for properties with the same name as an attribute of the object itself, such as GUID. If we ask explicitly for the GUID attribute for a member, i.e. objAUO.Get("guid"), we will receive the value of the GUID attribute for that particular instance of the class. However, if we perform an implicit request for the GUID, i.e. objAUO.guid, we will be asking the IADs interface for the GUID value of the class to which the object points.

Let's look at a diagram that better displays the relationship:

We can see in the figure that using `objAUO.Get("GUID")` returns the GUID attribute of the member – much like we used cn to return the common name of a member. We can also see that `objAUO.GUID` asks for the GUID property of the IADs interface returning to us the GUID of the class, in this case cn=member.

Code Sample – The GUID Property of IADs

In the following code sample, we show the different results of the GUID property vs. the GUID attribute.

```
<HTML>
<BODY BGCOLOR=WHITE>
<FONT FACE=ARIAL SIZE=3>
<B>
IADs - Guid
</B>
<HR SIZE=1>
</FONT>
<FONT FACE=ARIAL SIZE=2>
<%
On Error Resume Next

Dim objAUO

' Create the Active User Object
' ********************************************************
Set objAUO = Server.CreateObject("Membership.UserObjects.1")
If Err.Number <> 0 Then
  Response.Write "Unable to create the AUO."
  Response.End
End If

' Use the Guid
' ********************************************************
Response.Write "The guid property displays the "
Response.Write "guid of the object class pointed "
Response.Write "to.<BR>"
Response.Write "objAUO.Guid Property: " & objAUO.Guid & "<P>"

Response.Write "While the guid attribute "
Response.Write "displays the guid of the class "
Response.Write "instance.<BR>"
Response.Write "objAUO.Get(""Guid"") Attribute: " & objAUO.Get("Guid")
%>
</FONT>
</BODY>
</HTML>
```

We make the two different calls and write the output to the screen. You can see this output and the two different GUID values in the screenshot on the next page:

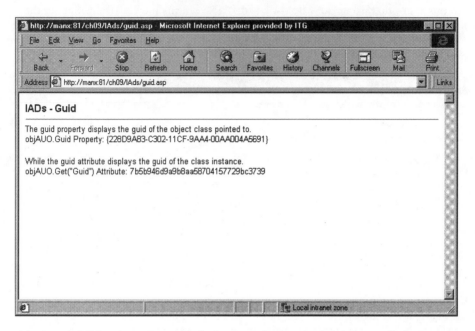

Again, like most of the properties covered, the GUID property of the class only becomes important later in the book. In particular, in the context of security in Chapter 13, we'll also discuss **granularity** – how security is applied to unique objects. If we have the GUID representation of a class, we can specify more granular security in the Membership Directory for this object, such as only read permissions on a particular class type. This granular security will determine if access is either granted or denied for class types, and if granted, it determines what permissions are given to the security principal attempting to use the class.

The ADsPath Property

The ADsPath property is used to return the Active Directory service (ADs) path, or namespace path, of the current object. We can use this hierarchical namespace path to bind directly to the object. For example, the ADsPath – or LDAP namespace path – to our StephensS member is LDAP://localhost:1003/o=Wrox/ou=Members/cn=StephensS. Using this path, we can bind directly to this member through a GetObject() method call.

Don't confuse the ADsPath with the distinguished name for the entry. The ADs path is merely the LDAP namespace path to the entry, while the distinguished name uniquely identifies the object in the directory. However, the ADsPath can be translated into a distinguished name through a method provided by another object we'll look at in Chapter 12. The code sample below will retrieve the ADs path for the current user and write it to the screen.

Code Sample – AdsPath

Here's the code:

```
<HTML>
<BODY BGCOLOR=WHITE>
<FONT FACE=ARIAL SIZE=3>
<B>
```

```
IADs - ADsPath
</B>
<HR SIZE=1>
</FONT>
<FONT FACE=ARIAL SIZE=2>
<%
On Error Resume Next

Dim objAUO

' Create the Active User Object
' ********************************************************
Set objAUO = Server.CreateObject("Membership.UserObjects.1")
If Err.Number <> 0 Then
  Response.Write "Unable to create the AUO."
  Response.End
End If

' Use the ADsPath
' ********************************************************
Response.Write "The ADsPath returns the  "
Response.Write "full LDAP path to "
Response.Write "the object in the directory.<P>"
Response.Write objAUO.ADsPath
%>
</FONT>
</BODY>
</HTML>
```

With the full LDAP path to the object, we can bind to the object at any time – whether or not the object is already instantiated. We can do this with the GetObject() method. The GetObject() method is a method of the IADsContainer interface which we'll look at in the next section of this chapter. For the moment we'll just say that it starts or binds to a running object with the information passed.

For example, we could pass a full LDAP path – such as
LDAP://localhost/o=Wrox/ou=Members/cn=StephenS – through the GetObject() method. This starts the LDAPNamespace object. The LDAPNamespace object translates the LDAP path and attempts to bind to the directory entry. If the GetObject() succeeds, it returns a pointer to a IADs object in the directory. If it fails it returns nothing. Since the full LDAP path is returned when we retrieve the ADsPath property, the call to perform the bind we've just described would look like this:

```
Set objIADs = GetObject(objAUO.ADsPath)
```

The LDAPNamespace object bind will be performed through the LDAP moniker, since we are binding to a directory entry. As with most of the other properties and methods provided by the Active User Object, we use the ADsPath property when we're working with both the Active User Object and other Active Directory Service Interface objects.

Next, let's take a look at the Parent property.

The Parent Property

The `Parent` property provides the name of the parent container of the current object. If the instantiated AUO points to a member, we can use the `Parent` property of this object to return the ADsPath to the container containing the member. By default this will be the ou=Members container which is the container that members are created in.

Code Sample – The Parent Property of IADs

In this code sample we retrieve the parent property of the AUO and write it to the screen.

```
<HTML>
<BODY BGCOLOR=WHITE>
<FONT FACE=ARIAL SIZE=3>
<B>
IADs - Parent
</B>
<HR SIZE=1>
</FONT>
<FONT FACE=ARIAL SIZE=2>
<%
On Error Resume Next

Dim objAUO

' Create the Active User Object
' *******************************************************
Set objAUO = Server.CreateObject("Membership.UserObjects.1")
If Err.Number <> 0 Then
  Response.Write "Unable to create the AUO."
  Response.End
End If

' Use the Parent
' *******************************************************
Response.Write "The Parent returns the  "
Response.Write "full distinguished name to "
Response.Write "the object above the current "
Response.Write "object in the directory.<P>"
Response.Write objAUO.Parent
%>
</FONT>
</BODY>
</HTML>
```

In this sample, we would expect the HTML display to contain the following output:

IADs – Parent
The Parent returns the full distinguished name to the object above the current object in the directory.
LDAP://MANX:1003/o=WROX/ou=members/OU=AnonymousUsers

Once the Membership Directory is secured, we can't just anonymously bind to any container or entry. We need to bind and pass member credentials with a `OpenDSObject()` method call (we'll look at this in detail in Chapter 12). This makes it much more expensive for every bind, due to all the overhead involved for processing a secured bind. Instead of binding afresh every time we can use the `Parent` property to navigate through the directory. Here is some example code to do just this:

```
On Error Resume Next

' Loop to get ldap root
' ***********************************************
Do While Not (objEntry.class = "organization") OR (Err.Number <> 0)
   Set objEntry = GetObject(objEntry.parent)Loop
```

We start from the current object we have bound to, and 'walk' up the directory tree until we find the root organization container. This is less expensive than repeated binds.

Next, we'll take a look at the Schema property.

The Schema Property

The Schema property returns the ADsPath to the base class of the object we're working with, in the cn=Schema, ou=Admin, o=[organization name] of the Membership Directory. While the ADsPath property returns the path to the instance of the class, the Schema property returns the path to the class itself. We use the ADsPath of the Active User Object to bind an IADs object to a member. We use the Schema property, which also returns an Active Directory Path, to bind to the class definition stored in the Schema container.

Code Sample – The Schema Property of IADs

This is how we retrieve the value of the Schema property:

```
<HTML>
<BODY BGCOLOR=WHITE>
<FONT FACE=ARIAL SIZE=3>
<B>
IADs - Schema
</B>
<HR SIZE=1>
</FONT>
<FONT FACE=ARIAL SIZE=2>
<%
On Error Resume Next

Dim objAUO

' Create the Active User Object
' **********************************************************
Set objAUO = Server.CreateObject("Membership.UserObjects.1")
If Err.Number <> 0 Then
   Response.Write "Unable to create the AUO."
   Response.End
End If

' Use the Class
' **********************************************************
Response.Write "The schema property displays the "
Response.Write "ADsPath to the class in the schema "
Response.Write "of the object pointed to.<P>"
Response.Write objAUO.Schema
%>
</FONT>
</BODY>
</HTML>
```

For our AUO, the Schema property should return:

LDAP://localhost:1003/schema/member

If we know the ADsPath to the class in the Membership Directory schema, we can bind to this classSchema object and look at its available attributes. This is very useful for determining what attributes a member instance has and for displaying all populated attributes of the member. Since a member is not a collection, we can't enumerate through all the populated attributes. We need some way to associate the attributes that a member may or must have with the populated values of the member instance attributes, and this is what the Schema property provides.

In the code sample below, we bind to the members container, and for each member that we find we use the Schema property to retrieve the path to the class for that member. We can then enumerate through the properties for that class. We test to see if that property is populated for the current member, and if it is we print out the name of the property and the current value.

Code Sample - Enumerate Members and Properties

Here's the code for this sample:

```
<HTML>
<BODY BGCOLOR=WHITE>
<FONT FACE=ARIAL SIZE=3>
<B>
Enumerate Members and Properties
</B>
<HR SIZE=1>
</FONT>
<FONT FACE=ARIAL SIZE=2>
<%
Dim objADs
Dim objADsContainer
Dim objADsClass
Dim varAttribute
```

```
' Connect to the Site Server Directory
' ***********************************
Set objADsContainer = GetObject("LDAP://localhost:1003/o=Wrox/ou=members")

' Enumerate Items in the members container
' ***********************************
For Each objADs In objADsContainer
  ' Grab the class of the object in the container
  ' ***********************************
  Set objADsClass = GetObject(objADs.Schema)

  ' Ignore items if we get an error
  ' ***********************************
  On Error Resume Next

  ' Display the cn of the item
  ' ***********************************
  Response.Write "<B>" & objADs.Get("cn") & "</B><BR>"

  ' Enumerate through optional attributes
  ' ***********************************
  For Each varAttribute In objADsClass.optionalProperties
    If Len(objADs.Get(varAttribute)) <> 0 Then
```

```
        Response.Write "<I>" & varAttribute & "</I> : "  & objADs.Get(varAttribute)
    "<BR>"
        End If
    Next

    Response.Write "<P>"

    ' Clear any errors
    ' ***********************************
    Err.Clear
Next
%>
</FONT>
</BODY>
</HTML>
```

After running this script, we should see something similar to:

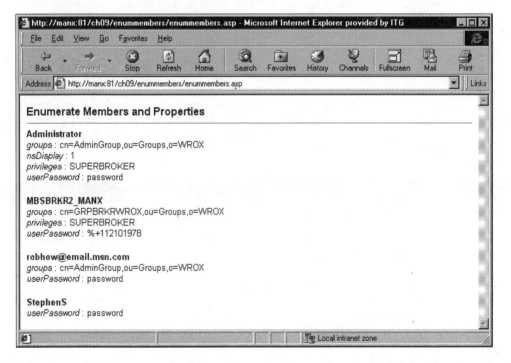

Whether we realize it or not, we've been using a property cache to store information about members when we request it. In the previous sample, the Membership Directory only needs to retrieve the data for each member once. Once the initial request has been made, the member attributes and values are in a property cache living in the requesting application. In Chapter 3 we read about data caching and the ADSI cache, which is used for all the values of an ADSI object. When we first bind to an object, we can use the GetInfo() method to access and populate the cache.

The GetInfo() Method

We use the `GetInfo()` method to refresh or retrieve the information in the ADSI cache. Any object that uses ADSI interfaces to access a directory has a cache that provides the requested information to the client. Instead of asking the LDAP Service to retrieve a value from the Membership Directory when it is requested, the entire contents of the attributes of the object are immediately available after the first `Get` of an individual attribute, or after calling `GetInfo()`.

Whenever a change has been made to the directory, for example from outside the application, the ADSI cache can become dirty. A **dirty cache** is a cache that contains information that does not coincide with the actual information in the Membership Directory.

Let's cover a couple of example situations here, to better understand the use of the `GetInfo()` method as it relates to a dirty cache. The first example involves a dynamic directory. If we're using a dynamic directory, where a member object has a time-to-live (TTL), the TTL of the object changes over time. Before we try to access this object, we want to call `GetInfo()` to re-check the TTL value. If the TTL value falls below an acceptable value, we either need to reset the TTL or not ask for the information from the object.

A second example of using `GetInfo()` involves changes to the AUO. Say we've created an instance of the Active User Object that points to a specific member in an Active Server Page and want to add this member to a group. Assuming that the member doesn't have SUPERBROKER privileges in the directory, and that the directory is secured, we need to make the modifications indirectly through ADSI via the LDAP namespace. After we make these modifications, we need to refresh the Active User Object so that its cache receives these modifications. Here's a simple ASP script that uses this example scenario – handling a modification from outside the AUO. In fact, parts of this code are borrowed from a piece of production code that I wrote for a Site Server Membership/Commerce integration site.

Code Sample – The GetInfo Method of IADs

We create the Active User Object and pass some of the AUO information – namely the `ADsPath` property – to the `SecuredAddMemberToGroup()` method. Assuming the Membership Directory has been secured – which we'll read about in Chapter 13 – the `SecuredAddMemberToGroup()` method uses a special user to add the current AUO to a Membership group.

In this example, we'll use a special user that has permissions to accomplish actions such as adding a member to a group or creating a new member. The `CreateMember` can't add security permissions, and ideally we should store the password for the `CreateMember` in the registry (or the IIS metabase) rather than the ASP. We'll talk more about the `CreateMember` concept in Chapter 13.

```
<HTML>
<BODY BGCOLOR=WHITE>
<FONT FACE=ARIAL SIZE=3>
<B>
IADs - GetInfo Method
</B>
<HR SIZE=1>
</FONT>
<FONT FACE=ARIAL SIZE=2>
<%
' *****************************************
' FUNCTION: SecuredAddMemberToGroup
'
```

```
' PURPOSE: Adds the currently-authenticated member (via the AUO)
'          to a specified group.
'
' REQUIRES:    A userid (here AddtoGroupMember) that has the
'              necessary ACEs for adding the logged-on member to a
'              group.
'
' PARAMETERS: strUserADsPath
'             ADs Path to member we wish to add
'
'             strGroupADsPath
'             Name of the group to add to
'
' RETURNS:    boolean - true success / false failure
'
Public Function SecuredAddMemberToGroup(strUserADsPath,strGroupADsPath)
  On Error Resume Next

  Dim objIADsContainer
  Dim strUserDNPath
  Dim strGroupGUID
  Dim objGuidGen

  ' Assume failure
  ' *****************************
  SecuredAddMemberToGroup = False
```

```
    ' Userid and password that has the authority
    ' to add a member to a group
    ' For a secured directory the userid should
    ' have the ACEs:
    '    Create Child - object Member - No Inheritance
    '    Read - all objects in the Members container
    '
    ' Ideally this information should be in the registry
    ' not in an active server page
    ' *****************************
    Const ADDTOGROUPMEMBER_NAME = "cn=AddToGroupMember, ou=Members, o=Wrox"
    Const ADDTOGROUPMEMBER_PASSWORD = "password"

    ' Bind to the LDAP Service
    ' *****************************
    Set objLDAP = GetObject("LDAP:")

    ' Do a secured bind to the group
    ' as a user that has permissions to
    ' add members to this group
    ' *****************************
    Set objIADsContainer = objLDAP.OpenDSObject(strGroupADsPath,CREATE_MEMBER_NAME,
CREATE_MEMBER_PASSWORD, 1)

    ' Create the GUIDGen object
    ' *****************************
    Set objGuidGen = Server.CreateObject("Membership.GuidGen.1")

    ' Generate the GUID for the group
    ' *****************************
    strGroupGUID = objGUIDGen.GenerateGuid
```

```
' Create a new memberof object
' *******************************
Set objAddMember = objIADsContainer.Create("memberof", "cn=" &
                                                  strGroupGUID)

If Err.Number <> 0 Then
  Err.Clear
  Exit Function
End If

' Get the MembershipInfo object to help convert ADsPath to DN
' *******************************
Set objMemInfo = Server.CreateObject("Membership.MembershipInfo.1")
If Err.Number <> 0 Then
  Err.Clear
  Exit Function
End If

' Convert user object's ADs path to DN path
' *******************************
strUserDNPath = objMemInfo.ADsPathToDN(strUserADsPath)

' Store user object's DN path in group object
' *******************************
objAddMember.Put "memberobject", CStr(strUserDNPath)
If Err.Number <> 0 Then
  Err.Clear
  Exit Function
End If

' SetInfo and trap errors
' *******************************
objAddMember.SetInfo
If Err.Number <> 0 Then
  Err.Clear
  Exit Function
Else
  SecuredAddMemberToGroup = True
End If
End Function
```

To test this function out we'll set a constant for the group to which we want to add members. This group should be a group you've already created; we'll use the group Premium. The other parameter we pass to our `SecuredAddMemberToGroup()` method, using the AUO, is the ADsPath of the current user. The add-to-group will be carried out by the special member `AddToGroupMember` we defined above.

```
' *******************************
' Example Use
' *******************************
Dim objAUO
Dim blnSuccess

' Create Active User Object
' *******************************
Set objAUO = Server.CreateObject("Membership.UserObjects.1")
If Err.Number <> 0 Then
```

```
      Response.Write "Can't create AUO"
      Response.Write "End"
   End If

   ' Set ADsPath of the group to which we want to add a member
   ' **********************************
   Const GROUPS_ADS_PATH = "LDAP://localhost:1003/o=Wrox/ou=Groups/cn=Premium"

   ' Add the member who is currently authenticated (using the AUO)
   ' to the specified group
   ' *******************************
   blnSuccess = SecuredAddMemberToGroup(objAUO.ADsPath, GROUPS_ADS_PATH)

   ' If blnSuccess is true the
   ' Active User Object has a dirty cache
   ' *******************************
   If blnSuccess Then
      Response.Write "Update AUO, call GetInfo()"
      objAUO.GetInfo
   Else
      Response.Write "Add Member to group failed."
   End If
   %>
   </FONT>
   </BODY>
   </HTML>
```

Since we've made our modifications to the member from outside the AUO, we have to call GetInfo() to refresh the property cache of the current member.

Next, we'll take a look at how to add information to the Membership Directory through the IADs Put() method.

The Put() Method

Once we've created the AUO, we use the Put() method to add values to the attributes of the Members class. The Put() method updates the ADSI cache for the Active Directory provider. Let's look at the two parameters for the Put() method:

❑ bstrName – represents the name of the attribute to be updated. If we wanted to update the givenName of a member, we would pass givenName as the bstrName parameter value.

❑ vProp – after specifying the attribute to update, we pass the value for the attribute through the vProp parameter.

Note that we can use the Put() method explicitly, like this:

```
objAUO.Put "givenName", "StephenS"
```

or implicitly, like this:

```
objAUO.givenName "StephenS"
```

Code Sample – The Put() Method of IADs

Let's take a look at the code:

```
<HTML>
<BODY BGCOLOR=WHITE>
<FONT FACE=ARIAL SIZE=3>
<B>
IADs - Put
</B>
<HR SIZE=1>
</FONT>
<FONT FACE=ARIAL SIZE=2>
<%
On Error Resume Next
Dim objAUO

' Create the Active User Object
' ********************************************************
Set objAUO = Server.CreateObject("Membership.UserObjects.1")
If Err.Number <> 0 Then
  Response.Write "Unable to create the AUO."
  Response.End
End If

' Use the Put Method
' ********************************************************
Response.Write "The Put add values "
Response.Write "for mustContain or "
Response.Write "mayContain attributes "
Response.Write "for members.<P>"

objAUO.Put "givenName", "Rob" ' First Name
objAUO.Put "sn", "Howard" ' Last Name
' Read from the ADSI cache
' ********************************************************
Response.Write "First Name: " & objAUO.Get("givenName") & "<BR>"
Response.Write "Last Name: " & objAUO.Get("sn")
%>
</FONT>
</BODY>
</HTML>
```

The attribute values from the Put() sample code are never written to the directory; the attribute values reside only in the ADSI cache, not in the Membership Directory. For the values to be written back to the Membership Directory, we have to call the SetInfo() method. There are one or two things that the Put() method can't do – such as delete values in attributes and add values for a multi-valued attributes. This is where the PutEx() method comes in handy.

The PutEx() Method

We use the PutEx() method to remove attributes, and manage multi-valued attributes. The PutEx() method is simply an extension of the Put() method. The rules of COM state that once an interface is published it can't be changed. Somebody came up with the idea of providing extended methods when functionality needed to be added. More often than not, these extended methods are called by the old methods – such as PutEx() being called by Put() – since the extended method usually supports the functionality of the original, and we don't want to duplicate our efforts.

Let's start by looking at the parameters that `PutEx()` expects:

❑ `lnControlCode` – the control code tell the method what action to perform with the data passed in the `bstrName` and `vProp` parameters. They are summarized in the following table:

Flag Name	Value	Description
ADS_PROP_ERASE	1	We use the `ADS_PROP_ERASE` constant, or 1, to set the value of an attribute to nothing. However, rather than setting the value of the attribute to null, the `PutEx` method will remove the attribute from class instance. This saves us from storing an empty value in the Membership Directory.
ADS_PROP_UPDATE	2	`ADS_PROP_UPDATE` provides the identical functionality of the `Put` method call. When it is used, it either adds the attribute with the appropriate value to the class instance, or changes the current value of the attribute.
ADS_PROP_APPEND	3	We'll use the final constant, 3, to modify multi-valued attributes. Although we can't remove values from multi-valued attributes, we can add to them. `ADS_PROP_APPEND` allows us to append values to multi-valued attributes.

❑ `bstrName` – the second parameter accepted by `PutEx()` is the same as the `Put()` method. It is the attribute whose value we wish to modify based on the `lnControlCode` parameter.

❑ `vProp` – again, similar to the `Put()` method, the `vProp` represents the value of the attribute specified by `bstrName`.

Now that we've looked at the parameters, let's see how they are used.

Removing Attribute Values

When I was learning how to use the Membership Directory, I experienced the frustration of trying to figure out how to set the value of an attribute to null. For example, try to set the `givenName` to null (assuming some value already exists), by using either the line:

```
objAUO.givenName = ""
```

or:

```
objAUO.put "givenName", ""
```

You won't get an error, but you won't get the expected behavior either. The value remains the same! Actually, we don't ever delete the value. We remove the attribute and the value from the Membership Directory.

The solution to this problem is to use the `PutEx()` method. The `PutEx()` method differs from the standard `Put()` in that we have several flags that can be used to modify the behavior of the method call. In Chapter 10, we'll use the `PutEx()` method for a personalized form to add or remove values for attributes. We'll call our personalized form `Request.Form`. If a value in the `Request.Form` collection has no value, we need to remove the attribute from the class instance.

Code Sample – The PutEx() Method of IADs

Using the example of a personalized form, let's take a look at a snippet of this code to see how we use the `PutEx()` method and its different parameters to remove attributes.

```
' Has the forms collection been
' populated?
' *****************************
If Request.Form("SUBMIT") <> "" Then

   ' Enumerate through Request.Form()
   ' *****************************
   For Each item in Request.Form()
      ' Ignore submit values
      ' *****************************
     If Not LCase(item) = "submit" Then
        ' If the item has data
        ' *****************************
        If Len(Request.Form(item)) <> 0 Then
           objAUO.Put CStr(item), CStr(Request.Form(item))
        Else
           ' If the item has no data
           ' *****************************
           If Len(objAUO.Get(CStr(item))) <> 0 Then
              ' Or the property doesn't exist yet
              ' *****************************
              If Err.Number = E_ADS_PROPERTY_NOT_FOUND Then
                 Err.Clear
              Else
                 ' No data to set, but the property
                 ' exists, remove it
                 ' *****************************
                 objAUO.PutEx ADS_PROP_ERASE, CStr(item), ""
              End If
           End If
        End If
     End If
   Next

   ' Handle errors / SetInfo
   ' *****************************
   If Err.Number <> 0 Then
      Response.Write "Error: Problem occured while putting data"
      Response.End
   Else
      objAUO.SetInfo
   End If
End If
```

We enumerate through the items on the form, using the `Put()` method to write new member data if we find any. If the attribute exists, but we have no data for it we use `PutEx()` to remove the attribute.

The `PutEx()` method can also be used to add or append multi-valued attributes. When we add a multi-valued attribute, such as the description for a member, to an object instance we need to be careful how we create and populate the array to ensure that all the values for the array are populated. A multi-valued attribute is programmatically treated as an array (variant safe-array). We can set a variable to the attribute type, by requesting it through `Get()` or `GetEx()` methods, modifying the array, and finally saving the attribute value back by using the `PutEx()` method.

> **If all the dimensioned values in an array are not used we will get an error. If we dimension an array in Visual Basic Script: Dim arrDescription(1) we need to make sure that both arrDescription(0) and arrDescription(1) have values before we attempt to call PutEx() to add the multi-valued attribute back to the class instance.**

Code Sample – Putting Multi-Valued Attributes

Let's look at some code to show this.

```
<HTML>
<BODY BGCOLOR=WHITE>
<FONT FACE=ARIAL SIZE=3>
<B>
Put Multi-valued Attribute
</B>
<HR SIZE=1>
</FONT>
<FONT FACE=ARIAL SIZE=2>
<%
On Error Resume Next

Dim objAUO
Dim arrDescription(1)

arrDescription(0) = "Hello"
arrDescription(1) = "World"

' Create the Active User Object
' *******************************************************
Set objAUO = Server.CreateObject("Membership.UserObjects.1")
If Err.Number <> 0 Then
  Response.Write "Unable to create the AUO."
  Response.End
End If

' Put multivalued attribute arrDescription
' *******************************************************
objAUO.PutEx 2, "description", (arrDescription)

' Update Membership Directory
' *******************************************************
objAUO.SetInfo
If Err.Number <> 0 Then
  Response.Write "Failed to call SetInfo"
  Response.End
Else
```

```
      Response.Write "Done!"
   End If
%>
</FONT>
</BODY>
</HTML>
```

This code sample was originally emailed back and forth between a Microsoft consultant and myself while we tried to figure out the behavior related to adding a multi-valued attribute to an object. It turned out that the *real* trick was making sure that all the values of a dimensioned array had been assigned values – this is actually a bug with how ADSI or the AUO implementation of IADs handles the bounds of a variant safe array.

So the real problem is that we need to check the array bounds before we call PutEx(). To do this we can use the ValidateArray() method, which when passed an array will return a new valid array after performing some bounds checking.

Code Sample – ValidateArray() Method

```
<HTML>
<BODY BGCOLOR=WHITE>
<FONT FACE=ARIAL SIZE=3>
<B>
ValidateArray
</B>
<HR SIZE=1>
</FONT>
<FONT FACE=ARIAL SIZE=2>
<%
' **************************************************
' FUNCTION:    ValidateArray
'
' DESCRIPTION:There is a problem with the way
'             PutEx handles a variant safe array
'             this method will take an array
'             and redim preserve to remove any
'             unused elements
'
' PARAMETERS: arrArray - passed array to modify
'
' RETURNS:     array
'
Public Function ValidateArray(arrArray)
   On Error Resume Next

   Dim nUbound
   Dim nLbound
   Dim arrFixed
   Dim nArrayLoop
   Dim nValidElement

   ' Is this a valid array?
   ' ****************************
   If Not IsArray(arrArray) Then
     Exit Function
   End If
```

```
    ' Get array bounds
    ' ****************************
    nLbound = LBound(arrArray)
    nUbound = UBound(arrArray)

    ' Set valid element
    ' ****************************
    nValidElement = 0

    ' Check array
    ' ****************************
    For nArrayLoop = nLbound to nUbound
      If Not arrArray(nArrayLoop) = "" Then
        If Not IsArray(arrFixed) Then
          ReDim arrFixed(nValidElement)
        Else
          nValidElement = nValidElement + 1
          ReDim Preserve arrFixed(nValidElement)
        End If

        arrFixed(nValidElement) = arrArray(nArrayLoop)
      End If
    Next

    If Err.Number = 0 Then
      ValidateArray = arrFixed
    End If
End Function
```

The method iterates through the array checking all elements and eliminating null values. You can incorporate this method into other scripts just by passing it the array you want to check, as shown below.

```
    ' ****************************
    ' Example use
    ' ****************************
    Dim arrSomeArray(2)

    arrSomeArray(0) = "hello"
    arrSomeArray(1) = "world"

    arrValidArray = ValidateArray(arrSomeArray)

    Response.Write "The UBound was: " & UBound(arrSomeArray) & "<P>"
    Response.Write "The new UBound is: " & UBound(arrValidArray) & "<P>"
    %>
    </FONT>
    </BODY>
    </HTML>
```

When we use Put() or PutEx() to update the ADSI cache, we also need to call the SetInfo() method when we have finished making changes.

The SetInfo() Method

We use the `SetInfo()` method to update the Membership Directory with only the items we change in the ADSI cache. There are two points we should remember about a `SetInfo()` call:

- ❑ Not all attributes are updated. The *only* attributes updated by `SetInfo()` are those for which `Put()` or `PutEx()` was called. This means that if an attribute has changed and `SetInfo()` is not called, the value won't be changed in the Membership Directory.

- ❑ Only one trip is made to the directory to update the information. This saves network traffic (if the Membership Directory is on another machine), because there's no need to use the network for every single `Put()` or `PutEx()` performed.

The `SetInfo()` method has to be one of the more frustrating calls for any developer working with the AUO or with raw ADSI objects. Personally, I have spent a good deal of time debugging applications that worked just fine until the `SetInfo()` method was called. It's one of the unfortunate things about working with the ADSI cache – it's something of an *idiot savant* when we're adding information. We don't know if we've populated all the mustContain values, or if the values are valid, until `SetInfo()` is called.

We can `Put()` values and then call `SetInfo()`, but if we haven't added values for all the mustContain attributes or if we've improperly set a value, the `SetInfo()` will fail with an invalid procedure call error. When we create a member through the New User Wizard in the Membership Directory Manager we never see a GUID value so we assume that to create a new member, we just need to set a common name (cn) attribute. However, this simple assumption can lead to some real problems. If we don't `Put()` a value for the member instance mustContain attribute of GUID, the `SetInfo()` will fail. Imagine doing a presentation for a senior executive and having the code blow up on `SetInfo()`! Here is some plausible code that we might want to run to create a member.

Code Sample – What's Wrong?

See if you can work out what's wrong with it!

```
<HTML>
<BODY BGCOLOR=WHITE>
<FONT FACE=ARIAL SIZE=3>
<B>
Fail to Call SetInfo
</B>
<HR SIZE=1>
</FONT>
<FONT FACE=ARIAL SIZE=2>
<%
On Error Resume Next

Dim objIADs
Dim objLDAP
Dim strCn

strCn = "billg"

' Do the bind
' *********************
Set objLDAP = GetObject("LDAP://localhost:1003/o=Wrox/ou=Members")
If Err.Number <> 0 Then
```

```
      Response.Write "Oops - couldn't bind to the directory!"
      Response.End
   End If

   ' Create the member
   ' *********************
   Set objIADs = objLDAP.Create("member", "cn=strCn")
   If Err.Number <> 0 Then
      Response.Write "Error: Couldn't create member"
      Response.End
   End If

   ' All Done! - (or so we think)
   ' *********************
   objIADs.SetInfo()
   If Err.Number <> 0 Then
      Response.Write "Error: unable to call SetInfo<BR>"
      Response.Write Err.Number & " - " & Err.Description
   Else
      Response.Write "There's no way we'll see this message!"
   End If
%>
</FONT>
</BODY>
</HTML>
```

The `Create()` *method that appears in this code sample will be covered a little later in the chapter, in the* `IADsContainer` *section. Please suspend belief until then...*

If we run this code, we should get the following results:

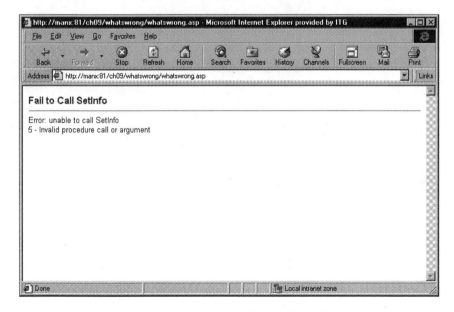

'Invalid procedure call' is a great error message... What we're really missing here is a value for a mustContain property, specifically the GUID attribute of a member class instance.

Code Sample – What's Wrong? – Fixed

Here's how to fix the problem:

```
[code cut out]
' Create the member
' *********************
Set objIADs = objLDAP.Create("member", "cn=strCn")
If Err.Number <> 0 Then
  Response.Write "Error: Couldn't create member"
  Response.End
End If

' Create a guid object
' *********************
Dim objGUID
Set objGUID = Server.CreateObject("Membership.GUIDGen.1")
If Err.Number <> 0 Then
  Response.Write "Unable to create the GuidGen object"
  Response.End
End If
' Put a guid for the member
' *********************
objIADs.put "GUID", CStr(objGUID.GenerateGuid)

' All Done! - (or so we think)
' *********************
objIADs.SetInfo()
If Err.Number <> 0 Then
  Response.Write "Error: unable to call SetInfo<BR>"
  Response.Write Err.Number & " - " & Err.Description
Else
  Response.Write "SetInfo called successfully!"
End If
[code cut out]
```

Now we should see the following result:

Finally, before we wrap up our discussion of `SetInfo()` you also should know that the `MemRightsChanged` cookie is sent after every `SetInfo()` performed and thus you will get the following dialog:

The `MemRightsChanged` cookie tells the P&M system that it needs to refresh the ADSI cache.

> *We first introduced the* `MemRightsChanged` *cookie in Chapter 3 – we'll discuss it in detail in Chapter 12.*

Now that we've learned how to put information into the directory, let's talk about how we get individual values for attributes from the Membership Directory or the ADSI cache.

The Get() Method

We use the `Get()` method to retrieve the value of an attribute. This value is either retrieved directly from the directory, for the first call, or from the ADSI cache for every subsequent call. We've already discussed the `GetInfo()` method, and how it refreshes the ADSI cache containing the object attributes and values when called. If we don't call this method when we first bind to an object, we have nothing in our cache. However, the first `Get()` essentially has the same functionality as `GetInfo()`. It updates the entire cache for all attributes. Each subsequent call reads from this cache.

> If `GetInfo()` **has not been called, then the first** `Get()` **updates the ADSI cache for the calling object.**

Like the `Put()` method, we can use the `Get()` method explicitly, like this:

```
objAUO.Get("givenName")
```

or implicitly, like this:

```
objAUO.givenName
```

We'll use an example of ADSI Caching for our code sample showing the `Get()` method. If we have a Membership Directory on machine A, and a client on machine B, we can bind to the Membership Directory on machine A from machine B and view a disconnected cache in action. If we used the following code, and have debugging turned on, we disconnect the physical network connection between the two machines when we encounter the stop directive. After disconnecting the physical network wire, we can continue our code and still view attribute values. However, before we look at a code sample, let's review the parameter required by `Get()`:

❑ `bstrName` – The `Get()` method allows us to retrieve the value that an attribute contains, but to retrieve the value, we have to specify the attribute. `bstrName` represents the name of the attribute whose value we wish to retrieve.

Code Sample – Active Directory Caching

To use the code sample we need to have debugging turned on, which we should have in a development environment. You can read about that in Chapter 3. When we encounter the stop directive, we can disconnect the network cable and still read from the ADSI cache.

```
<HTML>
<BODY BGCOLOR=WHITE>
<FONT FACE=ARIAL SIZE=3>
<B>
Active Directory Caching
</B>
<HR SIZE=1>
</FONT>
<FONT FACE=ARIAL SIZE=2>
<%
On Error Resume Next

Dim objAUO

' Create AUO
' ***************************
Set objAUO = Server.CreateObject("Membership.UserObjects.1")
If Err.Number <> 0 Then
  Response.Write "Error creating AUO"
  Response.End
End If

Response.Write "The cn of the user is: " & objAUO.Get("cn")
Response.Flush

' Disconnect network here
' ***************************
stop

Response.Write "Your password is: " & objAUO.Get("userPassword")
%>
</FONT>
</BODY>
</HTML>
```

We'll still be able to access the password attribute value for the AUO in our cache, although we no longer have access to the Membership Directory

The GetEx() Method

The GetEx() method works in a similar manner to the Get() method. GetEx() is an extension of the Get() method, and is specifically designed for accessing and modifying multi-valued attributes (although it works just as well with single value attributes). The GetEx() method requires just a single parameter:

❑ bstrName – represents the same value as the bstrName parameter specified in the Get() method.

Code Sample – The GetEx() Method of IADs

```
<HTML>
<BODY BGCOLOR=WHITE>
<FONT FACE=ARIAL SIZE=3>
<B>
IADs - GetEx
</B>
<HR SIZE=1>
</FONT>
<FONT FACE=ARIAL SIZE=2>
<%
On Error Resume Next

Dim objAUO
Dim nLoop
Dim arrDescription

Const E_ADS_PROPERTY_NOT_FOUND = &H8000500D

' Create AUO
' ***************************
Set objAUO = Server.CreateObject("Membership.UserObjects.1")
If Err.Number <> 0 Then
  Response.Write "Error creating AUO"
  Response.End
End If

' Use the GetEx
' **********************************************************
Response.Write "The GetEx is used to "
Response.Write "return a value from an "
Response.Write "attribute or a variant "
Response.Write "array from a multi "
Response.Write "valued attribute.<P>"

' Description must be set as a multi-valued attribute
' **********************************************************
arrDescription = objAUO.GetEx("description")
If Err.Number = E_ADS_PROPERTY_NOT_FOUND Then
  Response.Write "Description must be set as a multi "
  Response.Write "valued attribute...with values."
  Response.End
Else
  ' Loop through multi-valued attributes
  ' **********************************************************
  For nLoop = LBound(arrDescription) to UBound(arrDescription)
```

```
      Response.Write "Value " & nLoop & " - " & arrDescription(nLoop) & "<BR>"
   Next
End If
%>
</FONT>
</BODY>
</HTML>
```

Here, we are getting the multi-valued attribute, that we added to the current user earlier in this chapter. The attribute was `description`, and it had two attributes ("hello" and "world"). As `GetEx()` deals with multi-valued attributes, it returns an array with those values in it. You can then use `LBound` and `UBound` to find out how many items are in the array, and loop through it accessing the values.

You might have noticed the definition of `E_ADS_PROPERTY_NOT_FOUND`. This code is actually an error code that we can test for and trap if we encounter a property (attribute) not found error. To see a complete list of the error codes reference Appendix F. It is safe to assume that using the `Get()` method, covered earlier, will return the same pointer to a variant-safe array as if we had asked for a multi-valued attribute with `GetEx()` – which in fact it does.

We now have more than a cursory knowledge of the `IADs` interface. We've taken a close look at both the properties and the methods of the interface and shown some examples of how to use the interface with the Membership Directory. The knowledge gleaned from the `IADs` interface doesn't only apply to the Active User Object. The AUO just happens to support this interface; any directory provider that wants to take advantage of the Active Directory Service Interface model must support the `IADs` and `IADsContainer` interfaces. Now let's look at the other Active Directory Service Interface that the Active User Object exposes – the `IADsContainer`.

The IADsContainer Interface

We've covered the ADSI `IADs` interface, which is used for working with class instances in the Membership Directory. However, we haven't talked about how we deal with containers in the Membership Directory, or how we can programmatically create or delete class instances. We can do all of this, and more, with the Active Directory `IADsContainer` interface. This interface is used to bind to containers (such as the ou=Members container), and to create, delete, move and get objects in the container. In particular, the `IADsContainer` is used for a key role in member management for the Membership Directory: moving anonymous users to the ou=Members container.

There are several `IADsContainer` *properties that are not supported by the Membership Directory. They include the* `Filter` *and* `Hints` *properties.*

The properties of the `IADsContainer` we'll be examining include:

Property	Description
Count	Returns the available number of AUO providers for the Membership Server instance

IADsContainer also features the following four methods:

Method	Description
GetObject()	Used to update the values that have been modified in the ADSI cache
Create()	When passed the name of an attribute, it returns the value that the attribute contains
Delete()	Deletes class instances
MoveHere()	Moves class instances

Our exploration of the IADsContainer will begin with a look at the Count property. This property is used to enumerate through the available AUO providers available through the current Membership Server.

The Count Property

The Count property of the IADsContainer for the AUO returns the number of AUO providers for the Membership Server instance. We can use it to enumerate through the AUO providers available. The Count property can *only* be accessed through the Active User Object IADsContainer. If we bind directly to the IADsContainer through the LDAP namespace, we won't be able to return a count of the available AUOs since the interface by itself is not an AUO provider.

Code Sample – The Count Property of IADsContainer

Let's look at a code sample for this property.

```
<HTML>
<BODY BGCOLOR=WHITE>
<FONT FACE=ARIAL SIZE=3>
<B>
IADsContainer - Count
</B>
<HR SIZE=1>
</FONT>
<FONT FACE=ARIAL SIZE=2>
<%
On Error Resume Next

Dim objAUO

' Create the Active User Object
' ********************************************************
Set objAUO = Server.CreateObject("Membership.UserObjects.1")
If Err.Number <> 0 Then
  Response.Write "Unable to create the AUO."
  Response.End
End If

' Use the Count
' ********************************************************
Response.Write "The Count property returns "
Response.Write "the available number of AUO "
```

```
Response.Write "providers for the Membership "
Response.Write "server instance.<P>"
Response.Write "Number of AUO providers " & objAUO.Count
%>
</FONT>
</BODY>
</HTML>
```

This ASP simply returns the number of available AUO providers – not too terribly useful unless we programmatically create a new provider and want to test if any new providers do in fact exist.

We've looked at the GetObject() before when discussing the IADs interface, but we haven't yet looked at it in detail. Let's examine it next.

The GetObject() Method

We use the GetObject() method to bind from a container directly to an object by passing in the ClassName type to bind to, such as member, and the relative distinguished name (RelativeName) of the object, such as cn=Administrator. Here are its two parameters:

- ❑ ClassName – specifies the name of the class object to bind to – such as member or organizationalUnit.
- ❑ RelativeName – specifies the name of the class instance to bind to – such as cn=StephenS or ou=Members. This parameter is the same as the value returned by the Name property of the IADs interface.

For example, suppose that we already have an object called objIADsContainerMember bound to the ou=Members container. Then we can bind to a member in the container – such as StephenS – by calling:

```
Set objIADsMember = objIADsContainerMember.GetObject("member", "cn=StephenS")
```

We can show this in a code sample by using some of the IADs properties to walk down the Membership Directory to the root container, and then walk back up the directory to the ou=Members container and bind to the Administrator account.

Code Sample – The GetObject() Method of IADsContainer

Note that this sample code will only work with a directory that has not been secured.

```
<HTML>
<BODY BGCOLOR=WHITE>
<FONT FACE=ARIAL SIZE=3>
<B>
IADsContainer - GetObject()
</B>
<HR SIZE=1>
</FONT>
<FONT FACE=ARIAL SIZE=2>
<%
On Error Resume Next

Dim objAUO
```

```
' Create the Active User Object
' ********************************************************
Set objAUO = Server.CreateObject("Membership.UserObjects.1")
If Err.Number <> 0 Then
  Response.Write "Unable to create the AUO."
  Response.End
End If

Response.Write "AUO - " & objAUO.Name
Response.Write "<P>Use GetObject to bind to the Administrator<P>"

Set objLDAPRoot = objAUO

' Loop to get ldap root
' ************************************************
Do While Not (objLDAPRoot.class = "organization") OR (Err.Number <> 0)
  Set objLDAPRoot = GetObject(objLDAPRoot.parent)Loop

' Use the IADs GetObject to bind to the members container
' ********************************************************
Set objIADsContainer = objLDAPRoot.GetObject("organizationalUnit", "ou=Members")

' Use the IADs GetObject to bind to the member
' ********************************************************
Set objAUO = objIADsContainer.GetObject("member", "cn=Administrator")

' Now we're the Administrator!
' ********************************************************
Response.Write objAUO.Name
%>
</FONT>
</BODY>
</HTML>
```

This sample takes the current user, works its way back up the organizational structure, and then works down to find the Administrator user. This is what you should see after running this ASP:

The `IADsContainer` interface's `GetObject()` method is used to bind to *any* object in the directory.

Now that we know how to bind to containers, we can use the `IADsContainer`'s `Create()` method to create new objects in them.

The Create() Method

The `Create()` method creates new instances of classes in the directory. This includes new attributes and new classes, not just instances – remember even these objects are classes that we can create. This method takes the same two parameters as the the `GetObject()` method defined above: `ClassName` and `RelativeName`.

If we wanted to write a script to create a new container under the members container we would bind to the ou=Members container and use the `Create()` method on this IADsContainer object to create a new organizationalUnit (ou) object. Passing the `ClassName` of organizationalUnit and the `RelativeName` value of the new container, would create the appropriate container for us. In Chapter 14, we'll see the `Create()` method again when we look at creating members, attributes, and classes.

Code Sample – The Create() Method of IADsContainer

Let's review a code sample that uses the `Create()` method to create a new container called ou=Premium under the ou=Members container.

```
<HTML>
<BODY BGCOLOR=WHITE>
<FONT FACE=ARIAL SIZE=3>
<B>
IADsContainer - Create
</B>
<HR SIZE=1>
</FONT>
<FONT FACE=ARIAL SIZE=2>
<%
On Error Resume Next

Dim objAUO

' Create the Active User Object
' ********************************************************
Set objAUO = Server.CreateObject("Membership.UserObjects.1")
If Err.Number <> 0 Then
  Response.Write "Unable to create the AUO."
  Response.End
End If

Set objLDAPRoot = objAUO

' Loop to get ldap root
' ***********************************************
Do While Not objLDAPRoot.class = "organization"
  Set objLDAPRoot = GetObject(objLDAPRoot.parent)
Loop
```

```
' Use the IADs GetObject to bind to the members container
' ********************************************************
Set objIADsContainer = objLDAPRoot.GetObject("organizationalUnit", "ou=Members")

' Use the IADs Create to create a new container called Premium
' ********************************************************
Set objIADsContainer = objIADsContainer.Create("organizationalUnit", "ou=Premium")

' Call SetInfo
' ********************************************************
objIADsContainer.SetInfo

If Err.Number <> 0 Then
  Response.Write "Error: New container not created!"
Else
  Response.Write "New container created!"
End If
%>
</FONT>
</BODY>
</HTML>
```

We can see the new container that's been created in the Membership Directory:

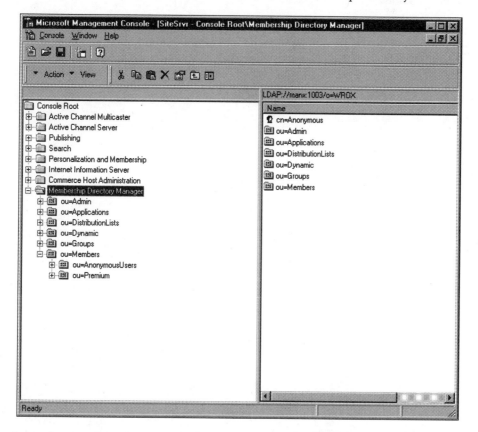

Now that we've seen how to create objects, let's talk about deleting them.

The Delete() Method

Just as we use the `Create()` method to create instances, the `Delete()` method exists to delete class instances. This method takes two parameters which are identical to the parameters defined for the `GetInfo()` method, although the parameter names are slightly different: `bstrClassName` and `bstrRelativeName`. The `bstrClassName` value represents the type of class to be deleted – such as member – and the `bstrRelativeName` represents the name of the objects – such as cn=StephenS.

A container must be empty before it can be deleted – this is simple referential integrity. If we attempt to delete a container that has children (either subcontainers or entries), we will get an error (0x80007002). However, this is not the case when we delete containers through the Membership Directory Manager (MDM). If we delete a container that has children, the MDM will delete all subcontainers and entries in the container to be deleted. Instead of enforcing the referential integrity it will recursively delete all entries below itself before finally deleting the item selected. To do the same thing programmatically, we'll use the `DeleteContainer()` method.

Code Sample – The DeleteContainer() Method of IADsContainer

The following code sample – `DeleteContainer()` – does what the MDM does through a recursive method and simple directory navigation. It recursively deletes all containers, entries, and finally the container to which it points.

```
<HTML>
<BODY BGCOLOR=WHITE>
<FONT FACE=ARIAL SIZE=3>
<B>
IADsContainer - Delete
</B>
<HR SIZE=1>
</FONT>
<FONT FACE=ARIAL SIZE=2>
<%
Public Function DeleteContainer(strADsPathToContainer)
  On Error Resume Next

  Const ISCONTAINER_TRUE  = 1
  Const ISCONTAINER_FALSE = 0
  Const E_ADS_PROPERTY_NOT_FOUND = &H8000500D

  Dim objADs
  Dim objADsContainer
  Dim objADsParent
  Dim blnIsContainer

  ' Assume failure
  ' ***********************************
  DeleteContainer = False

  ' Connect to the Site Server Directory
  ' ***********************************
  Set objADsContainer = GetObject(strADsPathToContainer)
  If Err.Number <> 0 Then
    Exit Function
  End If

  ' Enumerate Items in the members container
```

```
' **************************************
For Each objADs In objADsContainer

  ' Is this object a container
  ' **************************************
  blnIsContainer = objADs.Get("isContainer")
  If Err.Number = E_ADS_PROPERTY_NOT_FOUND Then
    Err.Clear

    ' Handle special DS cases
    ' **************************************
    Select Case objADs.Class
      Case ("organizationalUnit")
        blnIsContainer = ISCONTAINER_TRUE
      Case ("organization")
        blnIsContainer = ISCONTAINER_TRUE
      Case Else
        blnIsContainer = ISCONTAINER_FALSE
    End Select
  End If

  ' Recursive if we encounter a container
  ' **************************************
  If blnIsContainer = ISCONTAINER_TRUE Then
    DeleteContainer(objADs.ADsPath)
  Else
    ' Grab the class and name of the
    ' object in the container
    ' **************************************
    ADsClassType = objADs.Class
    ADsDN = objADs.Name

    ' Delete the object
    ' **************************************
    objADsContainer.Delete ADsClassType, ADsDN
    If Err.Number <> 0 Then
      Exit Function
    End If
  End If
Next

' Bind to the parent container
' **************************************
Set objADsParent = GetObject(objADsContainer.Parent)
If Err.Number <> 0 Then
  Exit Function
End If

' Deleted all items in the container
' now delete the container itself
' **************************************
objADsParent.Delete objADsContainer.Class, objADsContainer.Name
If Err.Number <> 0 Then
  Exit Function
Else
  DeleteContainer = True
End If
End Function
```

```
' **************************
' Example Use
' **************************
Dim blnDeleted

' Path to object to delete
' **************************
strADsToDelete = "LDAP://localhost:1003/o=Wrox/ou=Members/ou=Premium"

' Call the DeleteContainer method
' **************************
blnDelete = DeleteContainer(strADsToDelete)

' Dispaly results
' **************************
If blnDelete = False Then
  Response.Write "Container not deleted."
Else
  Response.Write "Container deleted."
End If
%>
</FONT>
</BODY>
</HTML>
```

Now that we've looked at how to delete entries, let's look at how we can move them to different locations.

The MoveHere() Method

We use the last method of the IADsContainer, the MoveHere() method, to move objects from one container to another. The primary use of the MoveHere() method for member management is the progression of a member account from the ou=AnonymousUsers to the ou=Members container. Here's the list of parameters:

- ❑ SourceName – represents the Active Directory path – LDAP://localhost/o=Wrox/ou=Members/ou=AnonymousUsers – from where the object to be moved exists. We could also use the ADsPath parameters from the IADs interface to retrieve this value.
- ❑ NewName – represents the new name of the object – such as cn=UsedToBeAnonymous.

The MoveHere() method allows us to move a member that was anonymous to another container, such as the ou=Members container, while retaining all of the members properties. This is especially important since we can migrate this member without losing all the member information that is being stored about the member.

Code Sample – The MoveMember() Method of IADsContainer

```
<HTML>
<BODY BGCOLOR=WHITE>
<FONT FACE=ARIAL SIZE=3>
<B>
IADsContainer - MoveHere
</B>
<HR SIZE=1>
</FONT>
```

```
<FONT FACE=ARIAL SIZE=2>
<%
' ********************************************************
' FUNCTION:    MoveMember
'
' PURPOSE:     Move member from one container to another.
'
' PARAMETERS: strADsPathToMember
'                  Path to the member to move
'
'             strADsPathToContainer
'                  Path to move member to
'
'             strNewMemberCn
'                  New common name for member if necessary
'
' RETURNS:     object - object exists / object nothing
'
Public Function MoveMember(strADsPathToMember, strADsPathToContainer,
strNewMemberCn)
  On Error Resume Next

  Dim objIADsContainer
  Dim objIADsMember

  ' Assume failure
  ' ************************
  Set MoveMember = Nothing

  ' Bind to the strADsPathToContainer
  ' ************************
  Set objIADsContainer = GetObject(strADsPathToContainer)
  If Err.Number <> 0 Then
    Err.Clear
    Exit Function
  End If

  ' Bind to the strADsPathToMember
  ' ************************
  Set objIADsMember = GetObject(strADsPathToMember)
  If Err.Number <> 0 Then
    Err.Clear
    Exit Function
  End If

  ' Are we passing a new cn?
  ' ************************
  If Len(strNewMemberCn) > 0 Then
    strNewMemberCn = "cn=" & strNewMemberCN
  Else

    ' Get Member Name (RDN)
    ' ************************
    strNewMemberCn = objIADsMember.Name
  End If

  ' Move the AUO user to the
  ' appropriate container
  ' ************************
  objIADsContainer.MoveHere objIADsMember.ADsPath, strNewMemberCn
```

```
    If Err.Number <> 0 Then
      Err.Clear
      Exit Function
    End If

    ' SetInfo
    ' ************************
    objIADsContainer.SetInfo
    If Err.Number <> 0 Then
      Err.Clear
      Exit Function
    Else
      Set MoveMember = objIADsContainer.GetObject("member",strNewMemberCn)
    End If
End Function


' ********************************
' Example Use
' ********************************
Dim objAUO
Dim objNewAUO

' Create the Active User Object
' ********************************************************
Set objAUO = Server.CreateObject("Membership.UserObjects.1")
If Err.Number <> 0 Then
  Response.Write "Unable to create the AUO."
  Response.End
End If

Set objLDAPRoot = objAUO

' Loop to get ldap root
' *********************************************
Do While Not objLDAPRoot.class = "organization"
  Set objLDAPRoot = GetObject(objLDAPRoot.parent)
Loop

' Use the IADs GetObject to bind to the members container
' *********************************************************
Set objIADsContainer = objLDAPRoot.GetObject("organizationalUnit", "ou=Members")

' Use the MoveMember function to migrate the member
' *********************************************************
Set objNewAUO = MoveMember(objAUO.ADsPath, objIADsContainer.ADsPath, "Rob")
If objNewAUO Is Nothing Then
  Response.Write "Failed to move Member"
Else
  Response.Write "Member moved successfully"
End If
%>
</FONT>
</BODY>
</HTML>
```

We'll look at the MoveHere() method some more in Chapter 14 when we discuss managing the Membership Directory programmatically. Next, let's look at the third and last interface definition that we use: the IUserObjects interface.

The IUserObjects Interface

The `IUserObjects` interface provides methods for binding to a directory, as well as methods for retrieving interface pointers to objects in the directory as the user who is running the Active User Object. `IUserObjects` is the first interface called when an AUO instance is created in an Active Server Page, and the last one called when the ASP cleans up its memory. Among the properties and methods of the `IUserObjects` are the following methods:

Method	Description
OnStartPage()	Allow the passing of context from the calling object to the called object
OnEndPage()	Called when the object is no longer needed
Init()	Method called to bind to the Membership Directory – called implicitly by OnStartPage()
SetUserName()	Moves class instances
BindAs()	Allows for binding as a specific member other than the one authenticated as to obtain special access to resources
GetObjectAsUser()	Similar to using GetObject() but allows for the bind to be performed in the context of the authenticated member
GetObjectEx()	Used to provide explicit access for secondary providers

We can also use the `IUserObjects` interface to bind the AUO to a directory from an ASP – or other application in VB/C++ – not mapped to a Membership Server.

The OnStartPage() Method

When the Active User Object is created in an ASP, the `OnStartPage()` method of the object is called. `OnStartPage()` is an ASP event to allow the passing of context from the calling object to the called object. Context is the concept of the state of a running object – the object creator's identity and execution environment. When the Active User Object's `OnStartPage()` method is called, the context of the calling object – the ASP – passes a pointer to its context. The AUO uses this context to switch its running thread's user to the same user and shared memory space of the ASP. The `OnStartPage()` method has a single parameter:

❑ pContext – the context object passed from the ASP to the object being created (in this case the AUO).

> The `OnStartPage()` **should never be called directly from an ASP – such as**
> **objAUO.OnStartPage().**

Order of Events

When a user first attempts to access a resource from an IIS 4.0 web, authentication happens first. Either the user is authenticated as the IUSR_*[server name]* or the appropriate Security Support Provider is called for Windows NT authentication or Membership authentication. The Security Support Providers are the authentication methods used by either Windows NT or Membership authentication that then pass off the credentials to the Security Support Provider Interfaces (SSPI) of Internet Information Server 4.0. The SSPI decides whether or not the Windows NT user exists – the MemProxyUser for Membership authentication or a valid Windows NT account for Windows NT authentication – and either returns an "access denied" error or switches the thread serving the IIS 4.0 request to the valid Windows NT account.

If the initial request was for an ASP page, and the ASP contained a CreateObject() method call for the AUO, the creation of the AUO will receive the context of the user from the ASP via the OnStartPage() method call. Finally, using this context, the AUO will call the Init() method passing the Internet Information Server 4.0 server instance id –
Request.ServerVariables("INSTANCE_ID") – and the user –
Request.ServerVariables("REMOTE_USER") – to bind to the appropriate member in the Membership Directory.

Similarly the OnEndPage() is also called by the ASP page.

The OnEndPage() Method

The OnStartPage() method is called by the Server CreateObject() method of an Active Server Page to pass context to the object being created – in our case the Active User Object. Similarly, the OnEndPage() is called when the object is no longer needed, and releases the memory held by the object.

> The OnEndPage() **should also never be called directly from an ASP.**

The Init() Method

The Active User Object can be bound to a member in one of two ways. First, if the AUO is created from an ASP served by an IIS 4.0 web mapped to a Membership Server, the IUserObjects' OnStartPage() method calls the Init() method passing the information obtained from the context of the ASP. However, if the AUO is created from an ASP not mapped to a Membership Server or from another application that either has not obtained the user context or cannot pass it, we can call the Init() method ourselves. To do this, we need some basic information about the web server – specifically the web server instance id.

Here are the parameters of the Init() method:

- ❑ bszHost – represents the IIS instance id of the web that the AUO should be initialized to. Init() uses bszHost to discover which Membership Server is mapped to the IIS 4.0 web – this value corresponds to the Request.ServerVariables("INSTANCE_ID") server variable.
- ❑ bszUserName – identifies the name of the member that was authenticated by IIS. This value corresponds to the Request.ServerVariables("REMOTE_USER") server variable.

The Init() uses the instance id – bszHost – to look up the Membership Server mapped to the IIS 4.0 web. From this Membership Server the Init() binds to the directory and reads the Root DSE – DSA Specific Entry – and finds the base distinguished name value to bind to members. Finally, the Init() method uses the username to bind to – bszUserName – in conjunction with the base distinguished name to bind to the appropriate IADs object – the member.

ASP/VBS

We can use the Init() method from an Active Server Page – not mapped to a membership server – if we know the correct server instance id and user to bind as. In the code below we've hard-coded the values with which we want to call Init() for clarity. We'll assume our server instance ID is 3, and we'll use the Administrator as the user to which we want to bind. In the example a little further on, when we look at the BindAs() method, we'll see how to retrieve the IIS server instance ID. Note that we create our AUO instance with CreateObject(), instead of Server.CreateObject().

Code Sample – Init from ASP/VBS

```
<HTML>
<BODY BGCOLOR=WHITE>
<FONT FACE=ARIAL SIZE=3>
<B>
IUserObjects - Init
</B>
<HR SIZE=1>
</FONT>
<FONT FACE=ARIAL SIZE=2>
<%
On Error Resume Next

Dim objAUO

' Create the Active User Object
' *******************************************************
Set objAUO = CreateObject("Membership.UserObjects.1")
If Err.Number <> 0 Then
  Response.Write "Unable to create the AUO."
  Response.End
End If

' If this page uses anonymous access or is called from
' an ASP not in an IIS/Membership Server bound web, but
' we know the IIS Instance ID and Username we wish to bind as
' *******************************************************
objAUO.Init "3", "Administrator"
If Err.Number <> 0 Then
  Response.Write "Unable to initialize the AUO : "
  Response.Write Hex(Err.Number)
  Response.End
End If

Response.Write objAUO.ADsPath
%>
</FONT>
</BODY>
</HTML>
```

We could easily port this code over to VB with minor modifications. However, let's look at what this would look like with C++:

C++

We can use the Active User Object just as easily from C++ as long as we use the correct header files. You should find that `iostream.h` is installed by default with your C++ compiler. The other two files are available from the Site Server 3.0 SDK – which you can download from http://msdn.microsoft.com/developer/sdk/platform.htm.

You'll find files called `auo.h` and `auo.idl` in the `/include` directory of the SDK. If you're running Visual C++, this is how to create `auo_i.c`:

1 Start an MS-DOS session, and navigate to the directory containing `vcvars32.bat` (this is probably in `/vc/bin` or `/vc98/bin`, under your Visual C++ installation. Run `vcvars32`.

2 Compile `auo.idl` using your MIDL compiler. You should find `midl.exe` in the same directory as `vcvars32.bat`. As a result of the compilation, you get `auo_i.c`.

> *You may find that it's necessary to ensure that* `auo.h` *and* `auo_i.c` *are contained in the* `/vc/include` *or* `/vc98/include` *directory, under your Visual C++ installation. There's more about using C++ with Personalization and Membership in Chapter 15.*

We will call `Init()` with a IIS Instance ID of 1 and bind as the Administrator – you would need to replace these values as we discussed in relation to the previous example.

Code Sample – Init() from C++

```cpp
// The following files should be added to this project:
//
// iostream.h
// auo.h
// auo_i.c

#include "iostream.h"
#include "auo.h"
int main()
{
  CoInitialize(NULL);

  IUserObjects* pIUserObj = NULL;

  HRESULT hr = CoCreateInstance(
               CLSID_UserObjects,
               NULL,
               CLSCTX_ALL,
               IID_IUserObjects,
               (PVOID*)&pIUserObj
               );

  if (FAILED(hr))
    cout << "CoCreateInstance failed" << endl;

  hr = pIUserObj->Init(L"1", L"Administrator");

  if (FAILED(hr))
  {
    cout << "Init call failed" << endl;
  }
  else
```

```
    {
        cout << "Init call succeeded" << endl;
    }

    return 0;
}
```

Now that we've learned how to use the `Init()` method, let's look at the `SetUserName()` method.

The SetUserName() Method

The `SetUserName()` method allows us to bind as a different member with the AUO other than the one authenticated as – as long as the originally binding member has the security rights in the Membership Directory to do so. A user that would have such permissions would be the Administrator. The `SetUserName()` method takes a single parameter:

❑ `bszUserName` – the name of the member to bind as

The most useful thing for the `SetUserName()` method is for authenticating as the Administrator and then viewing settings for other members – such as the display of the page.

Code Sample – SetUserName() Method

For this `SetUserName()` method code sample, we configure the ASP serving the data to use an authentication mechanism such as Basic/Clear Text authentication. Next, we bind as any member and the code will bind as the administrator – this will only work on a Membership Directory that has not been secured.

```
<HTML>
<BODY BGCOLOR=WHITE>
<FONT FACE=ARIAL SIZE=3>
<B>
IUserObjects - SetUserName
</B>
<HR SIZE=1>
</FONT>
<FONT FACE=ARIAL SIZE=2>
<%
On Error Resume Next

Dim objAUO

' Create the AUO
' **************************************
Set objAUO = Server.CreateObject("Membership.UserObjects.1")
If Err.Number <> 0 Then
    Response.Write "Unable to create the AUO"
    Response.End
End If

' Use Setinfo to bind as another member
' **************************************
objAUO.SetUserName("Administrator")

' Display the ADsPath
```

```
' *****************************************
Response.Write objAUO.ADsPath
%>
</FONT>
</BODY>
</HTML>
```

Once we run this code, we'll be returned with the ADsPath to the Administrator rather than the member we authenticated as – remember this will only work on a non-secured Membership Directory.

Next, let's look at another method for connecting as a different member.

The BindAs() Method

The BindAs() method is used to bind the AUO as a specific member. When BindAs() is used, we have to call the Init() method ourselves, as well as passing the username (DN) and password with which to bind to the AUO. We can use the BindAs() method to allow members to connect to pages and perform actions that they ordinarily would not have credentials to perform. This is faster than adding the member to a group to get access to a resource for only a limited amount of time. BindAs() could be used on a resource that the member has paid for and is only allowed to view once. Rather than assigning the member to a group or assigning an ACE, it might be easier simply to allow the user in and BindAs() a member that has the correct credentials for the information or action requested.

Here's the parameter list:

- ❑ bszAlias – The Active User Object alias to manipulate. In most cases we'll be working with the default AUO provider, so we'll pass an empty string "" for this value.
- ❑ bszUserName – Represents the name of the member to bind as – this is the full distinguished name (DN) of the member.
- ❑ bszPassword – Represents the password of the member to bind as.

Code Sample – BindAs() Method

Let's look at a code sample to illustrate the BindAs() method. Note we can use the Request.ServerVariables("INSTANCE_ID") call to retrieve the ID for our IIS server instance.

```
<HTML>
<BODY BGCOLOR=WHITE>
<FONT FACE=ARIAL SIZE=3>
<B>
IUserObjects - BindAs
</B>
<HR SIZE=1>
</FONT>
<FONT FACE=ARIAL SIZE=2>
<%
On Error Resume Next

Dim objAUO
Dim strUsername
```

```
    Dim strPassword
    Dim nInstanceID

    strUserpath = "cn=StephenS, ou=Members, o=Wrox"
    strUsername = "StephenS"
    strPassword = "password"

    ' Create the AUO - use the CreateObject
    ' so that the OnStartPage() event is not
    ' called and we can initialize the object
    ' our self
    ' *************************************
    Set objAUO = CreateObject("Membership.UserObjects.1")
    If Err.Number <> 0 Then
      Response.Write "Unable to create the AUO"
      Response.End
    End If


    ' Get the IIS instance ID
    ' *************************************
    nInstanceID = Request.ServerVariables("INSTANCE_ID")

    ' Call the init method of the AUO
    ' *************************************
    objAUO.Init nInstanceID, strUsername

    ' Use BindAs to bind as another member
    ' than the member the auo thinks we are
    ' *************************************
    objAUO.BindAs "", strUserpath, strPassword

    Response.Write "We're now bound as: "
    Response.Write objAUO.cn
    %>
    </FONT>
    </BODY>
    </HTML>
```

You might notice that we're doing something a little out of the ordinary here – we're using the CreateObject() method without using the ASP intrinsic Server object. Site Server provides us with the ability to do this so that the OnStartPage() method call will be skipped when the AUO – or other objects – are created. If OnStartPage() is skipped we have to provide the initialization of the AUO and the bind ourselves.

Next, let's look at another method that allows us to get an ADSI as the member the AUO is bound to.

The GetObjectAsUser() Method

The GetObjectAsUser() method allows us to bind to any object in the Membership Directory from a passed LDAP namespace path as the member authenticated and bound to the AUO. If we needed to bind to the cn=Schema, but we need to bind as a valid member – remember if we simply use GetObject() and the ADsPath to bind to we'll bind anonymously – we'll use the GetObjectAsUser() method.

Essentially, `GetObjectAsUser()` is like doing an authenticated bind through the `OpenDSObject()` method (covered in Chapter 12) without the extra parameters. There's just a single parameter involved:

❑ `bszADsPath` – the ADsPath of the object to be bound to as the current member.

Code Sample – GetObjectAsUser() Method

Let's take a look at a sample that shows how to use the `GetObjectAsUser()` method:

```
<HTML>
<BODY BGCOLOR=WHITE>
<FONT FACE=ARIAL SIZE=3>
<B>
IUserObjects - GetObjectAsUser
</B>
<HR SIZE=1>
</FONT>
<FONT FACE=ARIAL SIZE=2>
<%
On Error Resume Next

    Dim objAUO
    Dim objGroups
    Dim strGroupADsPath

    ' Create the AUO
    ' ****************************************
    Set objAUO = Server.CreateObject("Membership.UserObjects.1")
    If Err.Number <> 0 Then
      Response.Write "Unable to create the AUO"
      Response.End
    End If

    ' Build ADsPath to group
    ' ****************************************
    strGroupADsPath = "LDAP://localhost:1003/o=Wrox/ou=Groups"

    ' Use the GetObjectAsUser to bind to the
    ' groups container
    ' ****************************************
    Set objGroups = objAUO.GetObjectAsUser(strGroupADsPath)
    If Err.Number <> 0 Then
      Response.Write "Unable to bind to: " & strGroupADsPath
    Else
      Response.Write "Bound to: " & objGroups.ADsPath
      Response.Write " as " & objAUO.cn
    End If
%>
</FONT>
</BODY>
</HTML>
```

`GetObjectAsUser()` is very useful, and we'll see more possibilities for this further on in the book. There are also other methods of binding securely to objects in the Membership Directory as we'll see in Chapter 14.

The GetObjectEx() Method

The `GetObjectEx()` method is a seldom used method for working with secondary providers – additional providers created for the Membership Directory. It takes only one provider:

❑   `bszEntryName` – the name of the secondary provider to be accessed through the main provider.

The Site Server SDK covers this method really well. `GetObjectEx()` provides us with an explicit means to access the secondary provider through the AUO. If we have a secondary provider for a Membership Server named 'Dynamic' we access the secondary provider through the main provider by specifying the name of the secondary provider implicitly:

```
Dim objAUO

' Create the AUO
' **************************
Set objAUO = Server.CreateObject("Membership.UserObjects.1")

' Access secondary provider to return the
' common name of the corresponding
' dynamic object.
' **************************
Response.Write objAUO("dynamic").cn
```

However, if we wanted to explicitly obtain access to the secondary provider, we do so with `GetObjectEx()`:

```
Dim objAUO

' Create the AUO
' **************************
Set objAUO = Server.CreateObject("Membership.UserObjects.1")

' Access secondary provider to return the
' common name of the corresponding
' dynamic object using GetObjectEx()
' **************************
Response.Write objAUO.GetObjectEx("dynamic").cn
```

The `GetObjectEx()` method is nice, but we'll rarely use it.

We've taken a very in-depth code-centric view of the Active User Object. Hopefully by now, any questions or curiosities you've had about the AUO have been answered. Next, we'll look at the `Membership.GUIDGen` object used to generate the all-important GUIDs we use in the Membership Directory.

The Membership.GUIDGen Object

We use GUIDs (Globally Unique Identifiers) in the Membership Directory for uniquely identifying objects, as well as for the mustContain GUID attribute of a new instance of a member class. Site Server 3.0 installs an object specifically for generating GUIDs that provides a single interface `IGuidGen` and a single method, `GenerateGuid()`. We'll use the `GenerateGuid()` method to return a GUID, which is treated as a string.

> *The GUIDGen object is designed to support IDispatch and provides similar functionality to the*
> *C++ CoCreateGuid method. However, CoCreateGuid returns a GUID data structure*
> *type, while the GenerateGuid method returns a string type.*

Instantiating

We instantiate the GUIDGen object in an ASP page with the intrinsic
Server.CreateObject([PROGID]) method, passing the PROGID and returning a pointer to the
newly created object. The programmatic id (PROGID) for the GUIDGen object is
Membership.GuidGen.1, and the complete syntax for creating the object is:

```
Dim strGuid
Set objGuidGen = Server.CreateObject("Membership.GuidGen.1")
```

Let's take a look at the IGUIDGen interface, the only one of importance to us:

IGuidGen

Looking through the interface definition of IGuidGen in Appendix C, we'll notice that there are
three methods available – OnStartPage(), OnEndPage() and GenerateGuid(). We've covered
the functionality and purpose of the first two in the interface definition of the Active User Object's
IUserObjects interface, so we won't be spending any more time on those two. However, we will
discuss the third method GenerateGuid() which we'll use to return a new GUID.

The GenerateGuid() Method

The GenerateGuid() method is a very simple method to use. Calling it simply returns a new
GUID with the decorations removed:

Code Sample – Generate a GUID

```
<HTML>
<BODY BGCOLOR=WHITE>
<FONT FACE=ARIAL SIZE=3>
<B>
IGuidGen - GenerateGuid
</B>
<HR SIZE=1>
</FONT>
<FONT FACE=ARIAL SIZE=2>
<%
On Error Resume Next

Dim objGuidGen
Dim strGuid
Set objGuidGen = Server.CreateObject("Membership.GuidGen.1")
If Err.Number <> 0 Then
  Response.Write "It appears that the Membership.GuidGen "
  Response.Write "object is not available from this machine "
  Response.Write "GuidGen is installed with Site Server 3.0."
  Response.End
End If

' Return a new GUID value and display it
```

```
' ****************************************
strGuid = objGuidGen.GenerateGuid()

Response.Write "The new GUID that was generated: " & strGuid
%>
</FONT>
</BODY>
</HTML>
```

After running this ASP, we should see something similar to:

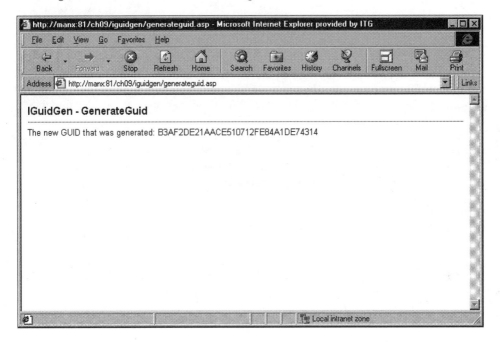

The GUID that you will see will be different of course – since the GUID is guaranteed to be globally unique. You'll never get the same GUID twice.

Summary

We've covered a lot in this chapter, but hopefully with the explanations and the code samples provided you can now more easily understand and use the Active User Object.

The AUO is an amazing object, and we've only scratched the surface of what it can be used for. We'll be using the AUO fairly extensively throughout the remainder of this book, so the understanding of what the AUO does is critically important.

To summarize, we covered the following:

- First, we introduced and discussed the AUO, and – in advance of learning about the AUO's interfaces – we covered how to create instances of the AUO. We saw how important it is to use the AUO from an ASP served by an IIS 4.0 web mapped to a Membership Server.
- There are three key interfaces provided by the AUO: Two of them, IADs and IADsContainer, are in fact ADSIs that are exposed by the AUO. The third, IUserObjects, is used by the AUO to connect to the correct Membership Directory. We've seen examples of code that uses these interfaces.
- The Membership GUIDGen object is simpler than the AUO object. We learned how to create the Membership GUIDGen object, and learned why we need it.
- The GenerateGuid() method of the IGuidGen interface is the only key method of the GUIDGen object. We've learned how to generate a new GUID and display its value.

In the next chapter, we'll build on the knowledge presented in this chapter by performing some personalization using the Active User Object.

10

Personalizing ASP Content

Personalization is deciding what action to take, or what content to display, based on the values associated with a member. Once the Active User Object (AUO) is instantiated, we can construct code to provide content to the user based on any of the user's attributes. We'll use the AUO in this chapter to see how, based on member attributes, we can change the functionality of the page. Objects like the AUO provide an easy means of getting to member data in an inexpensive manner. As we saw in Chapter 3, we can use authentication and ADSI caching to help improve performance, as we don't require a network round-trip for each request.

In this chapter we'll look at some simple ASP personalization. We'll provide some code examples of how custom content can be provided to members based on their attributes. Some of this code comes from the Wall Street Investing demonstration website, and we'll see many further examples of personalization when we look at the demo in Appendix A.

So here's a breakdown of what we'll be looking at in this chapter.

- ❑ **Simple Customization.** Building on our Chapter 9 Active User Object knowledge, we'll start with some simple examples, such as greeting the member.
- ❑ **Personalizing HTML Forms**. We'll look here at how to implement and use a personalized HTML form.
- ❑ **Customized Redirection.** In this section we'll discuss when and how we would want to direct users to different pages based on their attributes.

This chapter is an introduction to personalizing ASP; how you want to further implement and develop personalization will depend on your own custom setup. In the following chapters we'll learn how to retrieve and manage the data our personalization is based upon. Let's start off with a look at some simple ways to customize content with the AUO.

Simple Customization

Since authentication is the first thing that occurs within an IIS 4.0 Personalization and Membership enabled site, the context of the authenticated member is available through the Active User Object. Through the AUO we have access to all the information we have available about the member.

Greeting the Member

Greeting the member is one of the simplest tasks that can be done with the AUO. It's simply a matter of retrieving the common name attribute (cn) or, if available, the first name attribute (givenName). We can add attributes either through the Membership Directory Manager (see Chapter 7) or programmatically (see Chapter 9). Either way, we can view the member attributes and values from the Membership Directory Manager by double-clicking on the member in the ou=Members container, to bring up the following dialog:

From this screen shot, we can see what member attributes have been set, as well as their values. So how would we read the first name attribute value from the Membership Directory and display it in HTML?

Implementation

We can very easily implement code to display the first name attribute by using the AUO Get() method. Here's an example of a simple ASP that displays the member's cn attribute.

Code Sample – Simple.asp

```
<HTML>
<BODY>
<%
Option Explicit
On Error Resume Next

' ************************************************
' Simple ASP to display the current member's
' common name (cn) attribute
' ************************************************

Dim objAUO
Dim strMemberName
```

```
' Create the Active User Object
' ************************************************
Set objAUO = Server.CreateObject("Membership.UserObjects.1")
If Err.Number <> 0 Then
  Response.Write "Unable to create AUO. Make sure the "
  Response.Write "web is mapped to a Membership Server, "
  Response.Write "and that authentication is enabled."
  Response.End
End If

' Assign the member's common name value to the
' variable strMemberName. This is faster than
' requesting objAUO.cn each time.
' ************************************************
strMemberName = objAUO.Get("cn")

' Display the member's cn
' ************************************************
Response.Write strMemberName
%>
</BODY>
</HTML>
```

After we've run this code you should see something similar to:

> **If this script returns an error you will need to check your IIS authentication settings.**

My particular configuration here was with Clear Text/Basic authentication. Note that if authentication for this page had been set to anonymous we would have got an AUO error, since if we are logged on with an anonymous user account (IUSR_*[servername]*) there is no information available to initialize the AUO. If we had logged on with Automatic Cookie authentication we would exist in the Membership Directory as an object in the Anonymous Users container, and therefore the cn value returned would be a GUID string.

For more information on setting IIS authentication methods see Chapter 8.

Once we've requested the information you could assign it to a variable to save the system from having to request the information from the directory cache again. Although the cache does provide a fast mechanism for accessing information without having to talk to the Membership Directory, the application memory for the ASP is much faster.

Now that we have the `strMemberName` value, how difficult could it be to integrate this in a more 'personalized' fashion? The flow for our example is simple, we create the Active User Object, request and assign the common name attribute to a variable, and display the contents of the variable in the resulting HTML. The differences between our previous example, and a personalized display, is integrating the above code into the context of another ASP, such as the `default.asp` provided by IIS 4.0:

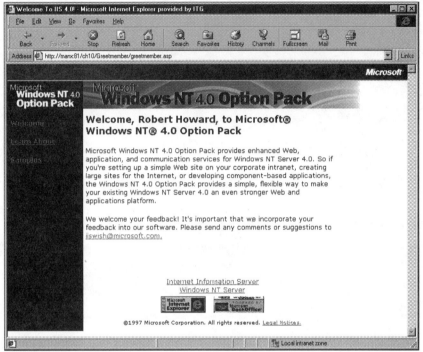

You may be wondering what needed to be done for this page to display the greeting. The `Simple.asp` logic was cut and pasted into the `default.asp`, and a single line of code was modified to display `strMemberName` in the welcome:

```
Welcome, <%=strMemberName%>, to Microsoft® Windows NT® 4.0 Option Pack
```

Just to make sure we always displayed something for the welcome message, I also made a minor modification to the `Simple.asp` code to determine if we even had a member name – in case we wanted to also support anonymous:

```
' Determine if we have a valid member name
' **************************************************
If Len(strMemberName) = 0 Then
  strMemberName = "valued customer"
End If
```

We've seen a very simple demonstration of how easy it is to personalize a page. Once a Membership Server is mapped to an IIS 4.0 web, and we've configured an authentication type, we only need to add a few lines of custom code to display attributes back to the browser through HTML. However what about using HTML as a mechanism for updating information in the Membership Directory?

Personalizing HTML Forms

Using HTML forms, the Active User Object, and a little Visual Basic Script we can build an Active Server Page that makes use of a personalized form. Members – or administrators – can use this 'personalized' form to enter or update information related to their attributes. These forms make it easy for the user to manage their own information:

Implementation

Putting the information in the HTML form for display is simple. You simply pass the value for the field as a form value, and when the HTML is rendered the appropriate value is displayed:

```
<INPUT TYPE=TEXT NAME=givenName VALUE="<%=objAUO.givenName%>">
```

You'll see this line of code in context in the complete example. First however, what about updating the member attributes? If a member changes their first name, the ASP should be able to update the information. We'll use the Put() and PutEx()methods of the AUO's IADs interface to add or delete values after the information is POSTed back to itself:

```
If Request.Form("SUBMIT") <> "" Then

  ' Enumerate through Request.Form()
  ' ******************************
  For Each item in Request.Form()
    ' Ignore submit values
    ' ******************************
    If Not LCase(item) = "submit" Then
      ' If the item has data
      ' ******************************
      If Len(Request.Form(item)) <> 0 Then
        objAUO.Put CStr(item), CStr(Request.Form(item))
      Else
        ' If the item has no data
        ' ******************************
        If Len(objAUO.Get(CStr(item))) <> 0 Then
```

```
                  ' Or the property doesn't exist yet
                  ' *****************************
               If Err.Number = E_ADS_PROPERTY_NOT_FOUND Then
                  Err.Clear
               Else
                  ' No data to set, but the property
                  ' exists, remove it
                  ' *****************************
                  objAUO.PutEx ADS_PROP_ERASE, CStr(item), ""
               End If
            End If
         End If
      End If
   Next

   ' Handle errors / SetInfo
   ' *****************************
   If Err.Number <> 0 Then
      Response.Write "Error: Problem occurred while putting data"
      Response.End
   Else
      objAUO.SetInfo
   End If
End If
```

In the above code I've actually cheated and made my application a little more efficient by using the names of the attributes as the values in the form, i.e. givenName, sn, telephoneNumber, and 1. Once the POST is performed a loop simply walks through the Request.Form() collection. Next, if the value contains data, the value is updated in the ADSI cache. If the value doesn't exist, it is created. Next, if the value is set to NULL or empty string, the attribute is removed from the ADSI cache. Finally, once all the ADSI cache updates are complete, SetInfo() is called and the ADSI cache data is written back to the Membership Directory.

Before we write the code and include the fragments we've just seen, we need to decide the order of what needs to be accomplished. First we need to create an instance of the Active User Object. The AUO reads all the member attributes from the Membership Directory and makes them available. Next, we need to pre-populate the HTML form with the existing values. And finally we need to either set or change the attributes posted back to the Active Server Page, again using the Active User Object.

So here's all the pieces put together in code:

Code Sample – Personalized HTML Forms

```
<% Option Explicit %>
<HTML>
<BODY BGCOLOR=WHITE>
<TITLE>Personalized Form</TITLE>
<FONT FACE=ARIAL SIZE=3>
<B>
Personalized Form Example
</B>
<HR SIZE=1>
</FONT>
<FONT FACE=ARIAL SIZE=2>
<%
```

```
On Error Resume Next

Dim objAUO
Dim strTemp
Dim item

Const ADS_PROP_ERASE = 1
Const E_ADS_PROPERTY_NOT_FOUND = &H8000500D

' Create the Active User Object
' ****************************
Set objAUO = Server.CreateObject("Membership.UserObjects.1")
If Err.Number <> 0 Then
  Response.Write "Error: Can't create the AUO<BR>"
  Response.Write "Suggestion: Make sure the IIS web is mapped "
  Response.Write "to a Membership Directory<BR>"
  Response.End
End If

' Has the forms collection been
' populated?
' ****************************
If Request.Form("SUBMIT") <> "" Then

  ' Enumerate through Request.Form()
  ' ****************************
  For Each item in Request.Form()
    ' Ignore submit values
    ' ****************************
    If Not LCase(item) = "submit" Then
      ' If the item has data
      ' ****************************
      If Len(Request.Form(item)) <> 0 Then
        objAUO.Put CStr(item), CStr(Request.Form(item))
      Else
        ' If the item has no data
        ' ****************************
        If Len(objAUO.Get(CStr(item))) <> 0 Then
          ' Or the property doesn't exist yet
          ' ****************************
          If Err.Number = E_ADS_PROPERTY_NOT_FOUND Then
            Err.Clear
          Else
            ' No data to set, but the property
            ' exists, remove it
            ' ****************************
            objAUO.PutEx ADS_PROP_ERASE, CStr(item), ""
          End If
        End If
      End If
    End If
  Next

  ' Handle errors / SetInfo
  ' ****************************
  If Err.Number <> 0 Then
    Response.Write "Error: Problem occurred while putting data"
    Response.End
  Else
    objAUO.SetInfo
```

```
   End If
End If
%>
<FORM METHOD=POST>
  <TABLE CELLPADDING=0 CELLSPACING=3 BORDER=0>
    <!-- UserID (cn) -->
    <TR>
      <TD ALIGN=RIGHT>
        User ID:
      </TD>

      <TD WIDTH=5>
      </TD>

      <TD ALIGN=LEFT>
        <%=objAUO.cn%>
      </TD>
    </TR>

    <!-- First Name (givenName) -->
    <TR>
      <TD ALIGN=RIGHT>
        First Name:
      </TD>

      <TD WIDTH=5>
      </TD>

      <TD ALIGN=LEFT>
        <INPUT TYPE=TEXT NAME=givenName VALUE="<%=objAUO.givenName%>">
      </TD>
    </TR>

    <!-- Last Name (sn) -->
    <TR>
      <TD ALIGN=RIGHT>
        Last Name:
      </TD>

      <TD WIDTH=5>
      </TD>

      <TD ALIGN=LEFT>
        <INPUT TYPE=TEXT NAME=sn VALUE="<%=objAUO.sn%>">
      </TD>
    </TR>

    <!-- Phone Number (telephoneNumber) -->
    <TR>
      <TD ALIGN=RIGHT>
        Phone Number:
      </TD>

      <TD WIDTH=5>
      </TD>

      <TD ALIGN=LEFT>
        <INPUT TYPE=TEXT NAME=telephoneNumber VALUE="<%=objAUO.telephoneNumber%>">
      </TD>
    </TR>
```

```
        <!-- City (city) -->
        <TR>
          <TD ALIGN=RIGHT>
            City:
          </TD>

          <TD WIDTH=5>
          </TD>

          <TD ALIGN=LEFT>
            <INPUT TYPE=TEXT NAME=mail VALUE="<%=objAUO.1%>">
          </TD>
        </TR>

        <!-- Submit -->
        <TR>
          <TD ALIGN=RIGHT>
          </TD>

          <TD WIDTH=5>
          </TD>

          <TD ALIGN=LEFT>
            <INPUT TYPE=SUBMIT NAME=Submit>
          </TD>
        </TR>
      </TABLE>
    </FORM>
  </BODY>
</HTML>
```

We now have the knowledge to build simple personalization ASP pages to greet the member, and we can easily handle other cases depending upon the attribute values for the member. The examples we've looked at so far are related to basic display information. Let's look at something a little more complex.

Customized Redirection

We've already shown how we can easily customize data within the page, but what if we didn't want to provide dynamically customized pages, but rather static pages that we sent the user to dynamically? Not to say that these pages couldn't be dynamically generated, but there are some cases where we want to send a user to a page based on their attributes.

For instance, large organizations like to 'suggest' the installed behavior for many applications, such as pointing the default home page for the browser to the start of the Intranet web. However, this isn't necessarily what all the business groups within an organization need. The marketing group might want all the members of the marketing department to start off on the marketing page, rather than the Internal home page. With Personalization and Membership we can still allow the Administrator to pre-configure the browser, but include the flexibility needed by the various business units. The default home page can be used as a re-direction point where, based on a member attribute such as 'businessUnit', the page can re-direct the user to the appropriate page for that member.

To expand on the example above, let's look at a large content site that has several template ASP home pages to which the member is redirected. If it is a sports-based site, templates may be provided for football, ice hockey, or basketball. Members that love football would want a football-based template. The template would be personalized with graphics from their favorite team, e.g. the Seattle Seahawks. Members that were interested in ice hockey would get a template for ice hockey teams. However, rather than providing one ASP to handle all of this functionality – which could be done, but would be very complex – why not provide a series of templates? When the user selects their own personalized sports page type, we could write code to capture and store this type in their profile. Later, when the user visited the site again, they could get redirected to the appropriate 'personalized' home page template. Let's see how we could implement this.

Implementation

To determine where we need to direct the user, we first need to get some information about the user. To do this, we need to create an instance of the Active User Object and ask for the appropriate attribute. Next, we need to selectively direct the member to the appropriate page based on this information. We'll do this by adapting the code from the personalized HTML form:

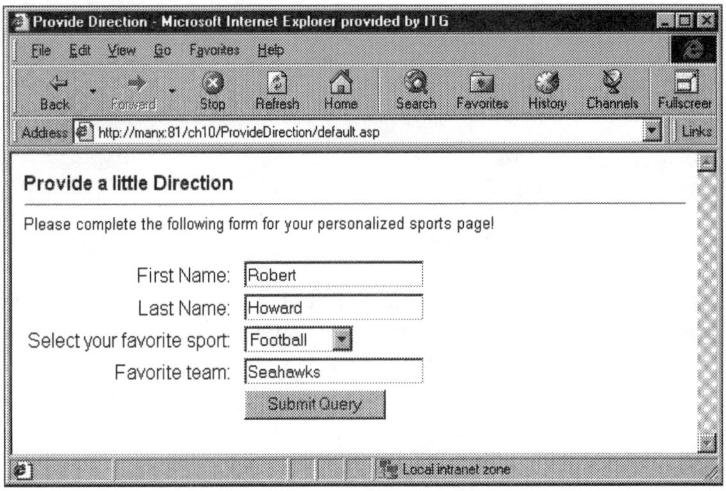

In the screenshot above (as in the previous form), we request information from the member and write the data back to the Membership Directory. Next, we need to determine where to redirect the member. We'll redirect the member if they have already selected a favorite sports team and are merely revisiting the site, or once they complete the initial form.

Here's the code we do this with:

```
' Determine if we need to redirect
' ****************************
nTeam = objAUO.Get ("age")
If Err.Number = E_ADS_PROPERTY_NOT_FOUND Then
    Err.Clear
Else
    Select Case nTeam
      Case 0
        Response.Redirect "football.asp"
```

```
     Case 1
        Response.Redirect "hockey.asp"

   End Select
End If
```

The member is then redirected to the appropriate location. In this case it is `football.asp`, our football template:

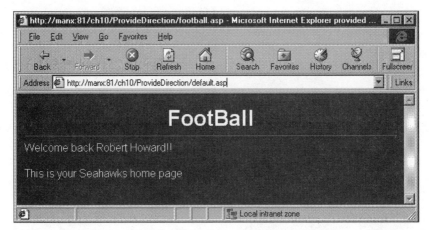

Had we selected Ice Hockey, we would have been redirected to the `hockey.asp` template. Once we have a member, personalization is easy. The Wall Street Investing website in Appendix A provides a demonstration of personalizing website content. You can download the Wall Street Investing demonstration website from the Wrox site, and you'll find a walkthrough of the website and installation instructions in Appendix A. To examine any of the examples in the Wall Street Investing demo click on the View the Code button at the bottom of the screens, and you'll see the commented ASP page that is producing the customized content. You should be able to recognize some of the examples from this chapter!

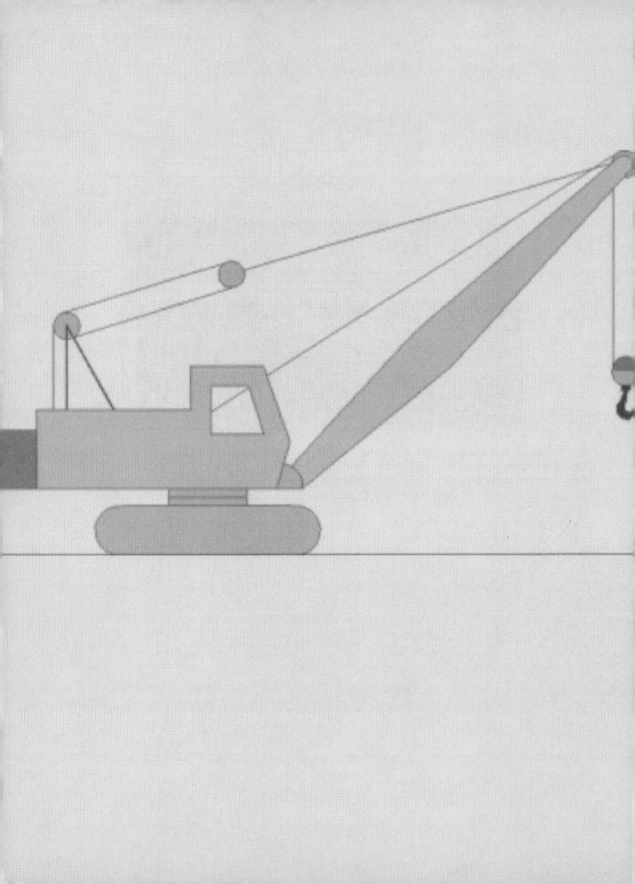

Integrating Personalization and Membership

11

We define integration, as it relates to software, as the ability for separate systems or services to work together to provide common services. The ability to integrate products together is what really adds value to a system. We're going to discuss two different forms of integration with Site Server Personalization and Membership in this Chapter: existing integration, and non-existing integration. We'll start with existing integration.

Site Server 3.0, as we said in the first chapter of this book, is a collection of useful tools and utilities. However, what we neglected to mention was that the level of integration provided between these tools and utilities is equally useful. The tool we'll be looking at as an example of this is Site Server Direct Mailer. Next, we'll look at how we can use Site Server 3.0's Membership Directory to provide Membership and Personalization to other services. We've already seen how Site Server Personalization and Membership is integrated with Internet Information Server 4.0. But, in this chapter, we'll also read how we can integrate these technologies with other services – such as the Microsoft Site Server Commerce Edition, and Microsoft Windows NT NetShow Services.

So here's a high-level overview of what we'll be discussing in this chapter.

❑   **Site Server Direct Mailer.** Site Server 3.0 installs a tool – and services – that we can use to generate personalized emails to our members. We'll look at how to configure this tool, as well as some ASP code used to generate a Direct Mailing.

❏ **Microsoft Site Server Commerce Edition.** Site Server Commerce Edition is an add-on to the base installation of Site Server 3.0 and provides all the necessary tools and components to easily create an Internet Commerce solution. We'll take a look at how we can integrate Site Server Membership with Site Server Commerce to provide a pay-for-membership (or pay-per-view) solution.

❏ **Personalized Windows Media Streams.** Using the XML based format called ASX, which describes the content that a Media Player can display, we'll look at how we can generate personalized Windows Media Streams using member attributes from the Membership Directory to dynamically generate ASX data using ASP and Site Server Personalization.

❏ **Windows NT NetShow Services Authentication.** After learning how to personalize streams, we'll examine how we can provide secure access to streams using Windows NT NetShow Services authentication against a Membership Directory. Additionally, we'll look at how we can extend our previous Commerce Edition integration discussion to provide pay-per-view streaming media.

❏ **Advanced Concepts.** Finally, we'll look at a special component that we can use from the Commerce Pipeline to dump the orderform dictionary variables to a file. This allows us to know exactly what's happening at each stage of the pipeline.

By the end of this chapter, you should have a clear picture of how flexible a solution Site Server Personalization and Membership is. Extending this framework for working with other applications and services is simple, and provides a common data store for all Internet authentication needs. Let's start by looking at the Site Server Direct Mail Integration.

Site Server Direct Mail Integration

Site Server 3.0 Direct Mail is a tool we can use to automatically generate and send personalized emails to members. These mailings are sent to a predefined distribution list of members. Distribution lists are contained in a **distributionList** class instance in the ou=DistributionLists container of our Membership Directory (which we saw in Chapter 7). We can define our own distribution lists in the ou=DistributionLists container, or use the distribution list instance, KMBriefList, installed by default in this container. If we double-click on the KMBriefList instance in the Membership Directory Manager we can add members to the instance. The email address attribute should be defined for each member in the distribution list (you can define this attribute by double-clicking on the member object in the Membership Directory). The Direct Mail then uses an ASP page that we provide to email each member on the distribution list. We can also generate mail content based on information from the Analysis system – we'll touch on this as it relates to direct Mail, but we won't be covering Analysis in any detail. Let's read a little about how to set up Direct Mail.

Configuring Direct Mail

To use the Direct Mail features we have must have created a Direct Mail instance when we created our Membership Server. We would have done this by selecting the M̲essage Builder Service from the New Membership Server Wizard's third screen (in Chapter 6).

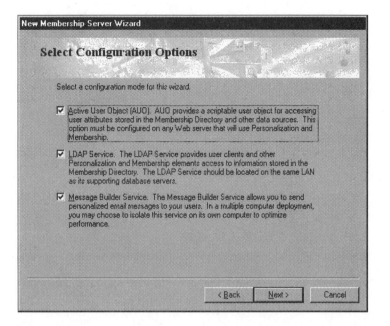

To add Direct Mail to a Membership Server that does not use Direct Mail, you will have to delete the Membership Server, and create a new Membership Server, and select the **Message Builder Service**. However you won't need to create a new Membership Directory; you can easily reconnect your new Membership Server to the existing Membership Directory.

Once we have a Direct Mail instance the next step is to configure the SMTP Service. There are three services used by Direct Mail: the SMTP service, the List Builder service and the Message Builder service. All we need to do for the List Builder and the Message builder is to make sure they're running. The first time we access them we'll be prompted to provide a username and password – we'll see this when we look at the Direct Mailer tool in a moment. First however we need to confirm our SMTP Service configuration.

The SMTP Service

To use the Direct Mail features a Simple Mail Transfer Protocol (SMTP) service must be provided. We can use the SMTP service provided with IIS 4.0, or we can set the SMTP service to use another machine (we specify this other machine in the Properties dialog, below). If we use the SMTP service provided with IIS 4.0 we need to configure the SMTP smart host setting, since it is only a relayer – i.e. the SMTP service relays to either a POP3 server or another mail server package, such as Exchange. The smart host is the name of a host that is able to receive email from a relayer – our SMTP service – and send it to the proper destination – i.e. the email address.

To configure the smart host, expand the Internet Information Server snap-in from the Site Server Service Admin (MMC) and right-click on the Default SMTP Site. Select Properties, and then navigate to the Delivery tab. Next enter the name of an Exchange Server (or other) mail server relay into the Smart host text box:

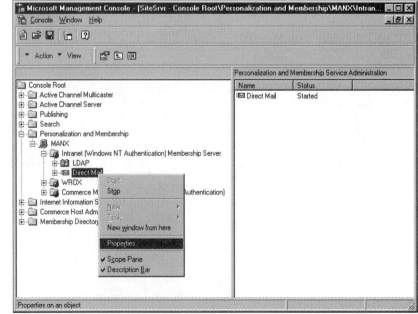

Once we have entered a value here, any email sent to this SMTP service will be directed to the smart host that knows where the email needs to go to be delivered.

To read more about the SMTP service and the smart host, see the IIS 4.0 documentation.

We can now go on to review the properties of a Direct Mail instance.

Properties of a Direct Mail Instance

To view the properties of a Direct Mail instance, open the Membership Server that the Message Builder Service was created with and right-click on the Direct Mail service, and select Properties:

After selecting Properties, you should see the Direct Mail Properties dialog:

You'll see two tabs, General and Logging.

The General Tab

The General tab is used to configure general settings for the Direct Mail service. From here we can specify the SMTP server name, or modify values for the Membership Directory used by Direct Mail.

- ❏   SMTP server name: We enter the name of the machine providing the SMTP service that we discussed above. This can either be a local machine or another machine on the network.

Membership Directory connection

Here we specify the information necessary to use when accessing the Directory Service containing the data we need for Direct Mailings.

- ❏   LDAP server name: The name of the LDAP service exposing the Membership Directory.
- ❏   TCP port: The TCP port of the LDAP service through which to communicate.
- ❏   User name: This should be a user who has the permissions in the Membership Directory necessary to perform binds to other members and read their attributes. The Direct Mail Administrators group in the Membership Directory has the necessary permissions, and the member should belong to this group. Fortunately for us, rather than having to configure and manage these settings, the Membership Server creates a member – see the screen shot – already part of this group. Note: for a Membership Directory using Windows NT (Intranet) Authentication a user account is created in the Windows NT Security Accounts Manager database.
- ❏   Password: The password that corresponds to the username above.

The Logging Tab

The logging feature of the Direct Mail properties allows for logging of Direct Mail services. We can choose to start a new log daily, weekly, monthly, or when the log file reaches a predetermined size. Additionally, we can change the path that the log file is written to.

Now that we know what's required to configure the Direct Mail service, let's see how we use it.

Using the Direct Mailer Tool

You open up the Direct Mailer tool from Programs I Microsoft Site Server I Tools I Direct Mailer:

However, assuming that we haven't used the Direct Mail tool yet, we'll be presented with the Direct Mail Settings dialog. Before we use the Direct Mailer, we need to specify some of the default settings and the Direct Mail service to use (if you've already used and/or configured the tool, you can find these under Tools I Settings from the toolbar of the Direct Mailer).

Direct Mail Settings

The Direct Mail Settings dialog provides us with the tabs necessary to configure the Direct Mailer. We'll look at each in turn.

The Defaults Tab

The Defaults tab lets us specify the defaults settings used by the Direct Mailer. We have three different options in this tab that we need to set values for:

- ❑ Sender Name – Specifies the email address of sender. This is the default value for any new Direct Mailing we create. Later, when we create a new Direct Mailing we'll replace the default sender name.
- ❑ Status recipient – Specifies the email address that a status email is sent to by the tool.
- ❑ Message type – Specifies the message type to be sent, we can choose to use plain text, or HTML.

The Direct Mail Tab

The Direct Mail tab defines the servers and accounts used for the message builder and list builder services. To review what these services are see Chapter 5:

The accounts used for the various services must have administrative capabilities on the machine specified in the server name for both services. Additionally, the accounts need to be members of the **SiteServer DirectMail Administrators** Windows NT group.

The Analysis Integration Tab

The Analysis Integration tab allows us to target members from an Analysis database of our choice for the mailing, instead of using members from a distributionList class instance.

In addition to selecting the appropriate database, we also can select the Application server for Rule Builder. If we are creating mails using analysis we will use the rule builder to determine which data is selected to be included in the mail. The Direct Mailer requires a definition of where to find the Rule Builder we want to use:

❑ Application server for Rule Builder – The name of the server providing the Rule Builder – generally the local machine.

After we properly configure the various services and settings for the Direct Mailer tool, we can create a new Direct Mailing. After configuring the distributionList class instance in the Membership Directory that we want to use – let's assume you've created one called: NewProducts – select Schedule | Create Direct Mailing... from the Direct Mailer to open the Create New Direct Mailing wizard.

The Create New Direct Mailing Wizard

We'll use the Create New Direct Mailing Wizard to create a new Direct Mailing for members from our NewProducts distributionList. Using this wizard will allow us to specify the Active Server Page used to generate the Direct Mail and select the distributionList class instance containing the list of member to be emailed.

Let's look at the three different screens available through the Create New Direct Mailing Wizard.

Screen 1: Direct Mail Name and Template

Unlike other Site Server wizards we've seen throughout the book, the Create New Direct Mailing Wizard cuts straight to the chase – no splash screen:

The first screen, Direct Mail Name and Template, enables us to configure the name of the Direct Mailing as well as the template used to generate the email to be sent:

❑ Name – The name of the Direct Mailing as it appears in the Direct Mailer.

❑ Template URL – The path to the Active Server Page used to generate the email contents. We'll look at a sample ASP after we've created the Direct Mailing.

Site Server 3.0 Personalization and Membership

❑   Specify Personalization... – We can choose to email the same message to all users, or we can choose to personalize – we'll select personalization. Choosing to personalize will allow the account specified in the Direct Mail property settings we configured for the Membership Server to impersonate each member of the distributionList instance in the Membership Directory. The Active Server Page used as the template for the Direct Mailing can then personalize using the attribute(s) of the member that is accessing the page.

Screen 2: Select Users

The second screen of the Create New Direct Mailing Wizard allows us to select the members to be mailed:

We could either enter an email address or generate our list from Analysis:

❑   Use existing distribution list(s) – We'll choose this option to use a distributionList class instance from the Membership Directory. However, rather than entering the LDAP path to the distributionList entry to be used, we'll enter an email address. The Direct Mailer interprets the email address to bind to the appropriate distributionList class instance to discover the members to be mailed. We can see this email address when we double-click on the distributionList instance to see its properties. If we created a NewProducts distributionList entry in the Membership Directory on the same machine, we could use NewProducts@localhost as our value.

❑   Create list dynamically using Site Server Analysis – If we wanted to use members from the Analysis database, we could select this option – see the Site Server 3.0 documentation for more information on Analysis and Direct Mail integration.

Screen 3: Sender Name and Schedule

Screen 3 of the wizard allows us to select the value of the *from* field of the email, as well as the subject, and how often the email should be sent:

- ❑ Sender name – The default value of the Sender name will be the setting we chose for the default settings of the Direct Mailer. Sender name represents the name that the email will be from. If the recipient chooses to reply to the mailing, or if a reply is required, ensure that this is a valid email account.
- ❑ Subject line – The subject line of the email that the recipient will receive.
- ❑ Schedule time – In addition to specifying the sender and the subject of the email, we can also schedule how often it is sent. Be careful with this setting. You want to send the email to provide the user with information they requested. Don't bombard them with random email, or you will soon find you distribution list shrinking.

This is the final screen of the wizard, and afterwards we should see our new Direct Mailing (New Products) displayed in the Direct Mailer:

The Site Server Message Builder and List Builder services will then take over and generate the emails. The Message Builder service accesses an Active Server Page as the current member on the list and emails the results to the SMTP service we configured earlier, which should relay them to the appropriate mail server. Let's look at the Active Server Page used to define our sample Direct Mailing:

Direct Mail ASP Code Sample

The following ASP code is used by the Direct Mailer to generate the email to members. It reads the member list from the distributionList class instance configured for the service. Next, it authenticates to the Active Server Page as each member in the list to personalize and generate the email:

> The Active Server Page used for the Direct Mailer must use Automatic Cookie Authentication, as this is the mechanism used by the Message Builder service to impersonate each member.

Code Sample – NewProducts.asp

Let's look at the code, and then discuss what it's doing:

```
<%
Option Explicit

On Error Resume Next

Dim objAUO
Dim strName
Dim nProductID

Const ADS_TYPE_PROPERTY_NOT_FOUND = &H8005000D

' Handle any encountered errors
' ************************************************
Set objAUO = Server.CreateObject("Membership.UserObjects.1")
If Err.Number <> 0 Then
  ' Get the members first name
  ' ************************************
  strName = objAUO.Get("givenName")

  ' If we don't have a first name use
  ' the common name value
  ' ************************************
  If Err.Number = ADS_TYPE_PROPERTY_NOT_FOUND Then
    Err.Clear
    strName = objAUO.Get("cn")
  End If

  ' Get the members favorite product
  ' ************************************
  nProductID = objAUO.Get("favProduct")
  ' If we don't have a favProduct default to 0
  ' ************************************
  If Err.Number = ADS_TYPE_PROPERTY_NOT_FOUND Then
    Err.Clear
    nProductID = 0
  End If

Else
  ' Default values
  ' ************************************
  strName = "Valued member"
  nProductID = 0
End If
```

```
' Write out the MIME type
' **********************************************
Response.Write "<META NAME=""DMailFormat"" "
Response.Write "CONTENT=""MIME"">" & vbNewLine

' Write the message
' **********************************************
Response.Write strName & "," & "<BR>"
Response.Write "Thanks for taking an interest "
Response.Write "in our products!"
Response.Write "<P>"
Response.Write "Here's the information you requested:"
Response.Write "<BR>"

' Send member appropriate information
' **********************************************
Select Case nProductID
  Case 1
    Response.Write "Product 1 Information here"
  Case 2
    Response.Write "Product 2 Information here"
  Case 3
    Response.Write "Thank you for requesting a product coupon. "
    Response.Write "Please find the coupon attached."
    Response.Write "<META NAME=""DMailAttachment"" "
    Response.Write "CONTENT=""http://webserver/discounts/coupon.doc"">"
  Case Else
    Response.Write "Default product information here"
End Select

Response.Write "<P>"
Response.Write "Thanks!"
Response.Write "<BR>"
Response.Write "The Product Management Team"
%>
```

What the Code Sample Does

The Message Builder service will access this page in the context of a member from the available members of the distributionList. Then, using the AUO, the ASP is able to generate a personalized document based on member settings. You might notice we're doing some defensive coding here. Just in case an error occurs, either with reading the member's name, or their favorite product, we are still able to generate an email for the service – albeit not personalized. Additionally, we're specifying the MIME type of the message with the HTML meta tag value of MIME.

The two settings that we require from members are: strName and nProductID. These values are used to store the name of the member (either the **givenName** or **cn** attribute values) as well as the **favProduct** attribute value. Based on the values from both these variables we first greet the member, and then determine what content to send them. If their favorite product happens to be product number 3, we'll send them a coupon for a discounted purchase of the product as an attachment.

What the Member Receives

Finally, once the ASP has been personalized and generated, it is finally emailed to the member. Here's what the final product should look like – if we had a member named Bill at Microsoft who was on our New Product distributionList:

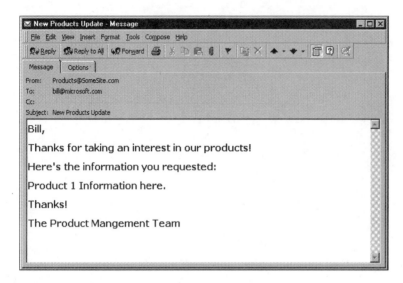

We could adapt our sample to many other situations, or integrate it with other web applications. Direct Mailings can be powerful tools, as long as they are not abused.

Site Server Commerce Integration

We could spend an entire book writing about all the possibilities of using Personalization and Membership with the Commerce Edition of Site Server, in fact there's a book on the way from Wrox focusing specifically on Site Server Commerce Edition. The Commerce Edition is an add-on to the base installation of Site Server 3.0, which provides all of the COM objects and applications necessary to build a complete Internet commerce application. Because of Site Server Commerce's flexible design, we can easily integrate solutions such as Site Server Personalization and Membership, which unfortunately is not integrated with Site Server Commerce out of the box.

We'll focus on the clearest, most applicable implementation by using the Membership System of Site Server Personalization and Membership (Membership Authentication) to show how we can build a store that offers Membership as a product – i.e. pay for membership. A web site that wants to provide secured access to content that can be accessed after paying for membership could easily implement the solution outlined in this section. Using the Site Server Commerce system and the Site Server Membership features together we can build a system where after validating payment we can either create the member or add the member to the appropriate group – or both. The way we'll do this is through the Site Server Commerce Pipeline using a Scriptor component (which we'll discuss later) that will be run after the payment stage has been approved.

To run this example you'll need to have installed Site Server Commerce Edition, including the Volcano Coffee sample site component. Have a look at the Commerce Edition website, at http://www.microsoft.com/siteserver/commerce.

> *You'll find that the Volcano Coffee sample site needs an SQL Server or Oracle database – set one up (and a system DSN) before you install*

Commerce Pipeline

The Pipeline is a staged series of components that is run to process a payment or accomplish other commerce related tasks. If we've installed the Site Server Commerce Edition, and have additionally installed the Volcano Coffee 3.0 demo site, we can open up the `Purchase.pcf` found in the Config directory of the Vc30 site (Vc30 is created under wwwroot by default) using the Commerce Server Pipeline Editor.

> The Commerce Server Pipeline Editor can be found under the program group **Microsoft Site Server | Commerce | Pipeline Editor.**

After opening `Purchase.pcf`, we should see:

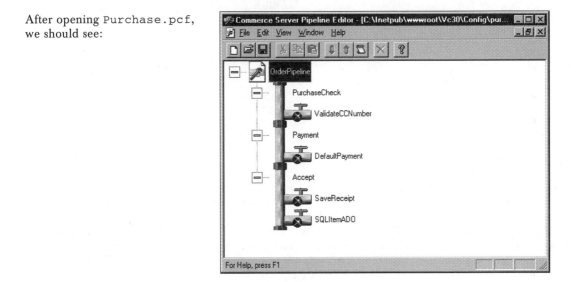

What is the Pipeline?

Some might think that the pipeline is a GUI for managing the processing of a payment. This is only partially correct however; the pipeline only determines the order in which separate components get executed. Each component provides a distinct role, for instance calculating the tax. Each pipeline component is simply a COM object that uses a shared dictionary object, known as the orderform, to modify values in its respective stage.

Since these components are COM objects – and tend to be quite complex and specific for individual business needs – they can be built in any language that supports automation (VB, C++, Java, etc.). But, they can also be purchased from various venders on the Internet. Some service providers, such as CyberCash, provide a component that can be integrated into the Commerce Pipeline to allow CyberCash to handle the credit card transactions.

The Pipeline is a COM object

The pipeline itself is a COM object used by Site Server Commerce from Active Server Pages. In the ASP code provided with the VC30 site, you'll see references where the pipeline component is created, and the appropriate pipeline configuration file, i.e. Purchase.pcf, is passed.

The xt_orderform_purchase.asp *passes the* Purchase.pcf *value as a parameter for a method called* UtilRunTxPipe() *defined in* util.asp.

However, rather than creating a new component, we'll use a special provided component called the Scriptor component.

Scriptor Component

Sometimes a full blown component is not necessary, especially for simple straight-forward business logic, such as adding members to the Membership Directory, or when prototyping an application. For these situations we'll use the Commerce Scriptor component. The Scriptor component is a special pipeline component that lets us run a segment of Visual Basic Script code (actually we could use any installed scripting language, including PERL) to accomplish a specific purpose. Anything that is possible from Visual Basic Script can be done within the Scriptor component, including creating and adding members to groups.

In Chapter 14 we'll examine creating new members and adding members to groups in more detail.

Now that we have the basics down, let's look at the system design we'll use for our Site Server Commerce driven membership site.

System Design

The system design will be such that a customer will use the Site Server Commerce system to purchase a product – in our case membership, but it could be any other product. Membership will be granted by purchasing an existing product at full price, or purchasing a membership for a lesser price. When the Purchase pipeline is run, a Scriptor component will take the information provided by the Commerce orderform – a dictionary object used to store the information about the customer and purchase – such as the customer's name and create a new member in the Membership Directory. Additionally, the new member will be added to an appropriate group – such as Premium. This group will have its corresponding Windows NT Group Site_*[Membership Directory Name]*_Premium Access Control Entry written on the folder that contains the members-only content. Once the member has purchased the membership and has been added to the correct group, the member/customer will then be able to gain access to the secured content.

We can make these changes to the Volcano Coffee Site such that when a customer purchases a product they automatically become a member and gain access to a member's only section – or they can purchase the membership independently. We won't discuss any error handling here since the VC30 site already handles errors, and if any component in the pipeline fails, the entire pipeline fails.

Let's take a look at this in a diagram:

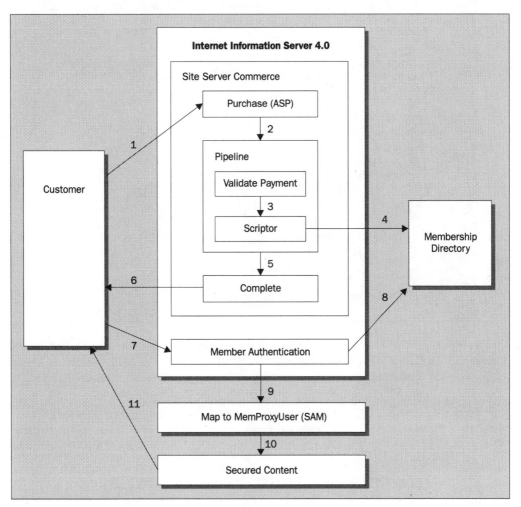

This diagram shows the progression of a purchased membership through the Commerce system. Let's break it down and explain each piece individually:

1. **Purchase** – The customer has visited our site and decided to pay for the premium content or services we provide. They navigated to the Purchase (or similar – in the case of Vc30 `checkout-pay.asp`) Active Server Page, which is simply a form that they must fill out with some information. This information includes name, password, credit card number, credit card expiration, address, etc.

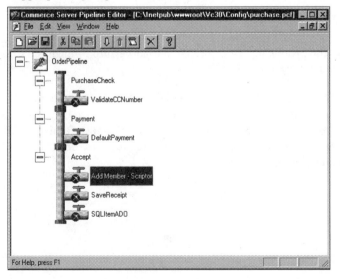

2. **Start Pipeline** – Upon submitting the Purchase Active Server Page, the information entered is passed to the Commerce Pipeline representing the transaction. For VC30 this would be the Purchase.pcf. The Pipeline would process and validate the information provided and bill the credit card in the ValidateCCNumber component of the Purchase Pipeline.

3. **Scriptor Component** – Upon the successful completion of the appropriate sections of the Purchase Pipeline, the Scriptor component will be run. The Scriptor component's primary purpose in this scenario is to create a new member in the Membership Directory and add that member to the appropriate group.

4. **Add Member** – Once the Scriptor component begins executing, the information passed from the orderform dictionary object is used inside the component to create a new member. The new member's cn and userPassword attributes are based on the customer's **_shopper_email** and **_shopper_password** values from the orderform already assigned to the user – which can be changed at a later time. (Note that this information is stored in the Commerce database, but could alternatively be stored in the Membership Directory – but that's a whole different book.)

5. **Pipeline Completion** – If the Commerce Pipeline Scriptor component successfully completes – along with any remaining components – then the Pipeline will hand back off to an ASP page. If the Scriptor component does not complete successfully, or an error occurs in another component, then the pipeline fails and it is the responsibility of the ASP to gracefully handle the failure.

6. **Complete Purchase** – Upon successful completion, the customer is directed to an ASP page that informs the customer that the purchase succeeded – in VC30, this page is `confirmed.asp`:

In addition, this page could display the username and password assigned to the member to access the privileged content.

7. **Request Content** – Once the member has purchased the product to gain access to the privileged content, the member can request this content. The privileged content is protected by Windows NT Access Control Entries that specify which Windows NT Security Principals can have access to the resources:

8. **Validate Membership** – Upon the request for the secured content, the Membership authentication system binds to the Membership Directory with the broker account and attempts to validate the credentials passed by the member. If the credentials are invalid the member is denied access, but if the credentials are valid the member is mapped to the impersonation account – MemProxyUser (note that we're using Membership authentication for our system).

9. **Map Member to MemProxyProxy** – Since our member has been added to the appropriate group (or groups), their security context – once authenticated – will contain the Security IDs of the Windows NT groups that correspond to the Membership groups (Site_WROX_Premium). That will then allow them to gain access to the requested content.

10. **Gain Access to Content/Services** – Once the thread executing the request has been mapped to the MemProxyUser with the appropriate Security Ids of the Window's NT groups, access to the content or services requested is allowed.

11. **Display Content/Services** – Finally, the information is displayed back to the member, and every subsequent request (before the authentication times out) will go directly to Step 10.

We'd expect the member to see something similar to this:

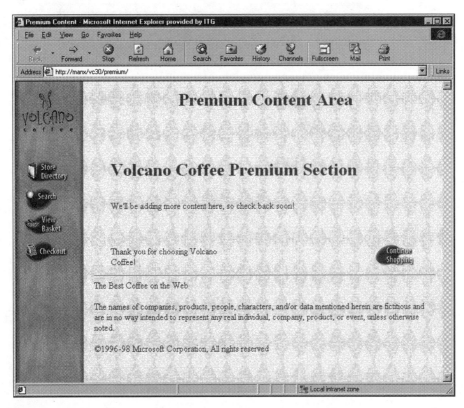

Now we've considered the system design, let's look at how we to build the system.

Building the System

If we wanted to build this system into the existing Volcano Coffee 3.0 site – to add the user as a member and also to the appropriate groups – we would first need to add a new Scriptor component to the `Purchase.pcf` Pipeline. Remember we can find the `Purchase.pcf` file in the `vc30\Config` directory under the `wwwroot` if we selected to install it when we installed Site Server Commerce Edition.

Adding a New Scriptor Component

To add a Scriptor component that adds and modifies a member after the purchase is completed, open the `Purchase.pcf` in the Commerce Pipeline Editor and highlight the **Accept** section of the graphical pipeline. The Accept section occurs after the PurchaseCheck and Payment sections are completed. The PurchaseCheck and Payment sections are responsible for validating information and billing the credit card. We want to run our Scriptor component after we have verified the purchase and completed the payment – hence the accept section representing the acceptance of the payment.

After highlighting the Accept section of the pipeline, right click and select Insert Component....

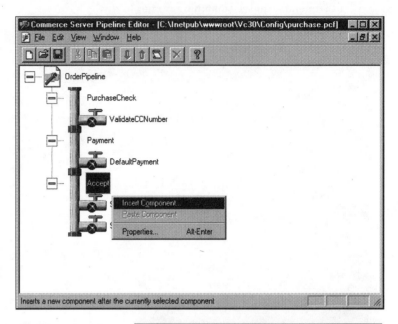

Selecting Insert Component... will bring up the Choose a component dialog:

Choosing a Component Dialog

The Choose a component dialog lets us select components for the Commerce Pipeline that can be run in the Accept section. The component we want is the Scriptor component.

After pressing OK from the Choose a component dialog, the new Scriptor component is added to the Accept section of the Commerce Pipeline. To modify the Scriptor component, first highlight the component, right click, and select Properties, or Edit I Properties from the Pipeline Editor.

Once the Properties option is selected, the Component Properties dialog box is displayed. From the Component Properties dialog, we have two tabs that allow for the configuration of various options for the component.

The Scriptor Tab

The first tab, Scriptor, displays options for the language the engine will use, the source of the script, and any configuration parameters we need to pass to the component upon execution. We can choose either to use script from a file, or to type the script directly in as part of the Scriptor component properties. We'll read more about internal script when we add actual script to the component.

The Component Properties Tab

The second tab, Component
Properties, lets us specify some
information about the component. For
our Scriptor component, we'll change
the Label to Add Member – Scriptor.
This label is the identifier for the
Scriptor in the Commerce Pipeline,
and simply makes it more convenient
to identify our Scriptor in the
pipeline. We can also add a
description for our Scriptor
component:

Adding Code to the Scriptor

After we've renamed the Scriptor component, we can turn our attention back to the first Component
Properties tab: Scriptor. If we select the Edit button from this tab, we'll be able to access the Scriptor
– Source Code Edit dialog. The Scriptor – Source Code Edit dialog specified two sub routines and
one function:

Default Methods

MSCSOpen(config) and MSCSClose() are both used to initialize or release variables or objects
needed by the main routine MSCSExecute(config, orderform, context, flags). The
config parameter passed by both the MSCSOpen() method and the MSCSExecute() method is
used to pass configuration information between methods – config is merely a dictionary object that
we can use to pass values to MSCSExecute() from MSCSOpen().

The only method we need to concern ourselves with is the `MSCSExecute()` method. When this method is called, one of the parameters passed is the `orderform`, which is the dictionary object containing all of the user information we need to create the member and add them to the appropriate group.

Membership Scriptor Code

If we put the following code into the `MSCSExecute()` method, we'll have the necessary code to create new members and add them to the appropriate group (Premium) after they have purchased something from our store. You'll need to change the values in this code to suit your own Directory Structure and Administrator password, for instance change o=Wrox to o=yourDirectoryName. In addition make sure that you have already created the group Premium, to which you want to add users, in the Membership Directory. Although some of the code we've seen in this integration demonstration has yet to be covered, you should be able to see what is happening – we'll be covering these functions in detail in the next few chapters. Cut and paste the Scriptor component code (available from the Wrox website as usual) into the end of the `MSCSExecute()` method.

Code Sample – Commerce Scriptor

```
' Create LDAP namespace object
' *******************************
Set objLDAP = GetObject("LDAP:")

' Do a secured bind to the directory
' as a user that has permissions to
' create new members in the members container
' *******************************
Set objIADsContainer = objLDAP.OpenDSObject( _
                    "LDAP://localhost:1003/o=Wrox/ou=Members", _
                    "cn=Administrator, ou=Members, o=Wrox", _
                    "password", 1)

' Create GUID gen object
' *******************************
Set objGUIDGen = CreateObject("Membership.GuidGen.1")

' Create Member
' *******************************
Set objIADsMember = objIADsContainer.Create("member", CStr("cn=" & _
                                    orderform.value("_shopper_email")))

' Add mustContain attributes
' *******************************
objIADsMember.Put "GUID",  Cstr(objGUIDGen.GenerateGuid)

' Add mayContain attributes
' *******************************
objIADsMember.Put "userPassword", CStr(orderform.value("_shopper_password"))

' SetInfo For user information
' *******************************
objIADsMember.SetInfo

' *******************************
' Add User to Premium group
' *******************************
```

```
' Do a secured bind to the group
' as a user that has permissions to
' add members to this group
' ********************************
Set objIADsContainer = objLDAP.OpenDSObject( _
                     "LDAP://localhost:1003/o=Wrox/ou=Groups/cn=Premium", _
                     "cn=Administrator, ou=Members, o=Wrox", "password", 1)

' Generate the GUID for the group
' ********************************
strGroupGUID = objGUIDGen.GenerateGuid

' Create a new memberof object
' ********************************
Set objAddMember = objIADsContainer.Create("memberof", "cn=" & strGroupGUID)

' Get the MembershipInfo object to help convert ADsPath to DN
' ********************************
Set objMemInfo = CreateObject("Membership.MembershipInfo.1")

' Convert user object's ADs path to DN path
' ********************************
strUserDNPath = objMemInfo.ADsPathToDN(objIADsMember.ADsPath)

' Store user object's DN path in group object
' ********************************
objAddMember.Put "memberobject", CStr(strUserDNPath)

objAddMember.SetInfo
```

What the Membership Scriptor Code Does

The above code first binds to the Membership Directory securely, and then creates a new member object in the ou=Members container of the Membership Directory. The members common name value is the email address specified by the shopper – we use the email address since it must be unique. Additionally, we set the userPassword to the value specified by the user's shopper password, and generate a new GUID for the member's guid attribute. After calling SetInfo() the member is created.

Next, we once again bind to the Membership Directory as a secured member, but instead of binding to the ou=Members container, we bind to the group (which is also a container) the member needs to be added to; in this case the group is premium. We then create a new memberof object in the premium group and point that memberof object to the new member we created in the ou=Members container.

Finally, we call SetInfo(), and the member is now part of the cn=Premium group, which is required to gain access to the premium portion of the VC30 site – the premium area being any content underneath a premium directory created in the VC30 root.

We can view the new member in the Membership Directory Manager in the MMC. Implementing this solution is really this simple. The only thing we've done is to add one component to the Commerce Pipeline, integrated with Membership authentication. We now have a protected, premium section of our website, and an implentation which you can build on in many different ways.

Personalized Windows Streaming Media Integration

We can use the personalization information that we have stored for members in the Membership Directory in many different ways. In Chapter 10 we looked at generating customized ASP pages to tailor the display of web content. We can also just as easily apply the same logic to tailor the display of Windows Media Streams. To run the next examples you will need to install the Windows Media Player – have a look at the Media Player website, at http://www.microsoft.com/windows/mediaplayer/. For the next section, where we discuss authenticating Media Streams, you will also need to have installed Windows NT NetShow Services. For more information see http://www.microsoft.com/windows/downloads/contents/Updates/NTNetShowServices.

ASXs for the Media Player

The Microsoft Streaming Media player (formerly known as NetShow) is able to read an ASX file format, an XML-based definition used to describe media streams. The code below shows a simple ASX file, which displays an ASF file on the Windows Media Player. (If **iigsdcmm.asf** is not on your system, you will need to modify the path to a different asf file).

ASF (Advanced Streaming Format) is a multimedia file format. For more information read the articles or download the ASF Professional Developers Kit from http://www.microsoft.com/asf. *If you have installed Windows NT NetShow Services you will also have some sample ASF files and information.*

Code Sample – Simple.asx

```
<ASX VERSION = "3">
<ENTRY>
<TITLE>Display a simple ASF</TITLE>
<REF HREF = "C:\WINNT4\Help\iis\htm\mm\iigsdcmm.asf" />
</ENTRY>
</ASX>
```

If we open `simple.asx` from the Windows Media Player, we should see something similar to the screenshot below:

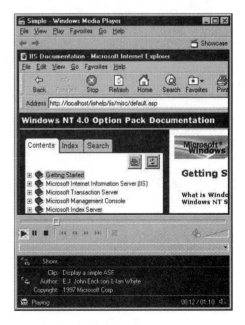

The Windows Media Player can read this XML description of the stream and modify the Windows Media Player's display, as well as fetch the stream. You'll notice that the Clip: displayed by the media player reflects the <TITLE> that we defined in the ASX.

To read more about the ASX file format, see the Windows Media Player SDK – you can download it from http://www.microsoft.com/ntserver/nts/mediaserv/.

ASP Pages for the Media Player

ASX files can easily be generated from ASP. The only factor is that we need to specify a Content Type. In this example ASP page we'll set a content type for the Windows Media Player.

Code Sample – Simple.asp

```
<%
' Send the header format so that if
' this is read from a browser the
' browser knows to start the
' Windows Media Player
' ********************************
Response.ContentType = "video/x-ms-asf"
Response.Expires = 0

' Write the ASX XML
' ********************************
Response.Write "<ASX VERSION = ""3"">" & vbNewLine
Response.Write "<ENTRY>" & vbNewLine
Response.Write "<TITLE>Display a simple ASF - from ASP!</TITLE>" & vbNewLine
Response.Write "<REF HREF = ""C:\WINNT4\Help\iis\htm\mm\iigsdcmm.asf"" />" &
vbNewLine
Response.Write "</ENTRY>" & vbNewLine
Response.Write "</ASX>" & vbNewLine
%>
```

This ASP code will generate the ASX file we looked at above. If you run it through your browser from your web directory, it will start the Windows Media Player and display the specified ASF file.

So, now that we know that we can generate an ASX from an ASP, we can obviously write logic in the ASP to dynamically change the display, streams, or stream order displayed to the Windows Media Player. If we can write logic – and of course create components – why not generate an ASX dynamically based on member properties? Sounds fairly straightforward, but of course there's an unexpected caveat – unfortunately, the Media Player and Site Server Membership don't like each other too much. If we were to request an ASP for the Media Player from a web server using Personalization and Membership, it won't work since the Media Player can't accept cookies and doesn't know how to authenticate the ASX. To allow the Windows Media Player to read an ASP from an IIS 4.0 web server mapped to a Membership Server, mark the ASP as Allow Anonymous only.

Marking the ASP as <u>A</u>llow Anonymous lets the Windows Media Player gain access to the stream – as long as the file level access control lists allow the IUSR_*[server name]* user account access. Now we're ready to learn how to personalize an ASX using ASP.

Personalizing ASX Through ASP

We'll use an example of a play list to show how we can personalize ASX. The Media Player uses ASX files to build play lists for media streams. These play lists can be dynamically generated with ASP, using the knowledge from the beginning of this topic. We can then use them in conjunction with Personalization and Membership to build personalized media streams, based on attributes in the Membership Directory for the member viewing the stream. However, you might be wondering how we personalize an ASP page that authenticates anonymously, instead of authenticating as a member. We can pass values to an ASP page by using the query string to pass member attributes.

In the PlayList.asp file included with the Wall Street Investing (WSI) demo – Appendix A – we pass member attributes to the ASP page using the query string. The ASP page uses these passed parameters to generate the appropriate ads and news streams to the member based on their preferred type of investments. For the WSI demo, we define three preferred types: technology, sporting goods, and entertainment. One of these types is selected as the member's preferred type when they personalize.

> *Unfortunately when I wrote the demo, the only good ASF streams I had readily available were general ads, and technology ads. So, when you use the WSI – and the* PlayList.asp *after modifying the stream names – you'll only see a 'targeted' stream if you select your investing type as technology. That is, until you've modified the code for your own needs!*

Code Sample – Generating a Dynamic Personalized ASX

Let's review `PlayList.asp` from the WSI demo:

```
<%
Option Explicit
' **************************************************************
' Name:
'   PlayList.asp
'
' Purpose:
'   Generates an ASX file for NetShow to play
'

' Send Header
' ********************************
Response.ContentType = "video/x-ms-asf"
Response.Expires = 0

' Define Global Constants
' ********************************
Const ADS_TOTAL_GEN = 8              ' The number of available general ads
Const ADS_TOTAL_TECH = 5            ' The number of tech ads available
Const ADS_TOTAL_INDUSTRY = 1        ' The number of industry ads available

Const STORY_TOTAL_TECH = 2          ' The number of technical stories available

Const TYPE_GEN = "Gen"              ' General Ad type
Const TYPE_TECH = "Tech"            ' Technology Ad type

Const PERS_TECH = 1                 ' Personalized type technology

' Define Global Variables
' ********************************
Dim nMainType
Dim g_GenAdsPlayed
Dim nClipNum

' Assign variable values
' ********************************
If Request.QueryString("ShowType") <> "" Then
  nMainType = Int(Request.QueryString("ShowType"))
Else
  nMainType = 0
End If

' **************************************************************
' Start Stream Format
' **************************************************************

' Start ASX
' ********************************
Response.Write ("<ASX VERSION = ""3"">" & vbNewLine)

If nMainType = 0 Then
  Response.Write ("<TITLE>Not - Personalized</TITLE>")
Else
  Response.Write ("<TITLE>Personalized</TITLE>")
End If
```

```
' Display Personalized Ad
' *******************************
Select Case nMainType
  ' Display tech ad
  ' *******************************
  Case Int(PERS_TECH)
    nClipNum = GenerateRnd(ADS_TOTAL_TECH)
    GenerateAd TYPE_TECH, nClipNum, 1

  ' Display General Ad
  ' *******************************
  Case Else
    ' Display gen ad
    ' *******************************
    nClipNum = GenerateRnd(ADS_TOTAL_GEN)
    GenerateAd TYPE_GEN, nClipNum, 0
End Select

' Display general ad
' *******************************
nClipNum = GenerateRnd(ADS_TOTAL_GEN)
GenerateAd TYPE_GEN, nClipNum, 0

' Display Personalized Info
Select Case nMainType
  ' Display tech Story
  ' *******************************
  Case Int(PERS_TECH)
    nClipNum = GenerateRnd(STORY_TOTAL_TECH)
    GenerateStory TYPE_TECH, nClipNum, 1

  ' Display General Story
  ' *******************************
  Case Else
    ' Display gen Story
    ' *******************************
    nClipNum = GenerateRnd(ADS_TOTAL_GEN)
    GenerateStory TYPE_GEN, nClipNum, 0
End Select

' Display general ad
nClipNum = GenerateRnd(ADS_TOTAL_GEN)
GenerateAd TYPE_GEN, nClipNum, 0

' End ASX
' *******************************
Response.Write ("</ASX>" & vbNewLine)


' ****************************************************************
' Define Functions
' ****************************************************************


' ****************************************************************
' Function:
'   GenerateRnd
'
' Purpose:
```

```
' Generates a random number to display ads with
Public Function GenerateRnd(nUBound)
  ' Randomly Choose a number between 1 and ADS_TOTAL_GEN
  Randomize
  Dim nRndNum
  GenerateRnd = Int((nUBound - 1 + 1) * Rnd + 1)
End Function

' **********************************************************
' Sub:
'   GenerateAd
'
' Purpose:
'   Generates an add based on type and clip number
Public Sub GenerateAd(strADType, nAdClipNum, nPersonalized)
  Response.Write ("<ENTRY>" & vbNewLine)
  If nPersonalized = 1 Then
    Response.Write ("<TITLE>Personalized Ad - " & strADType & "</TITLE>" &
vbNewLine)
  Else
    Response.Write ("<TITLE>Not - Personalized Ad - " & strADType & "</TITLE>" &
vbNewLine)
  End If

  Response.Write ("<REF HREF = ""http://localhost/NetShow/ads/" & strADType & "_"
& nAdClipNum & ".asf"" />" & vbNewLine)
  Response.Write ("</ENTRY>" & vbNewLine)
End Sub

' **********************************************************
' Sub:
'   GenerateStory
'
' Purpose:
'   Generates a story based on type and clip number
Public Sub GenerateStory(strADType, nAdClipNum, nPersonalized)
  Response.Write ("<ENTRY>" & vbNewLine)
  If nPersonalized = 1 Then
    Response.Write ("<TITLE>Personalized Story - " & strADType & "</TITLE>" &
vbNewLine)
  Else
    Response.Write ("<TITLE>Not-Personalized Story - " & strADType & "</TITLE>" &
vbNewLine)
  End If

  Response.Write ("<REF HREF = ""http://localhost/NetShow/story/" & strADType &
"_" & nAdClipNum & ".asf"" />" & vbNewLine)
  Response.Write ("</ENTRY>" & vbNewLine)
End Sub
%>
```

Results of PlayList.asp

After creating some constants and variables, we read the value passed by ShowType from the
QueryString and assigned its value to nMainType. This variable represents the personalization type
that the stream should be formatted to. Next, we write out some basic XML definition for the stream
and display in the title whether or not the stream is personalized based on the value from
nMainType. Next, we display a personalized ad, generating the ad based on a random number of the
available ads on the system.

We then generate a general ad, i.e. no personalization, display a personalized or non-personalized story – again based on the number of available new stories related to type specified by nMainType. Finally, we display another generalized ad before ending the stream. You can view the output of playlist.asp by commenting out the line defining the content type:

```
Response.ContentType = "video/x-ms-asf"
```

When playlist.asp has executed select View | Source in your browser.

Not Personalized

If we pass no values to PlayList.asp – i.e. no personalization information – then the ASX should look something like this:

```
<ASX VERSION = "3">
<TITLE>Not - Personalized</TITLE><ENTRY>
<TITLE>Not - Personalized Ad - Gen</TITLE>
<REF HREF = "http://localhost/NetShow/ads/Gen_6.asf" />
</ENTRY>
<ENTRY>
<TITLE>Not - Personalized Ad - Gen</TITLE>
<REF HREF = "http://localhost/NetShow/ads/Gen_5.asf" />
</ENTRY>
<ENTRY>
<TITLE>Not-Personalized Story - Gen</TITLE>
<REF HREF = "http://localhost/NetShow/story/Gen_3.asf" />
</ENTRY>
<ENTRY>
<TITLE>Not - Personalized Ad - Gen</TITLE>
<REF HREF = "http://localhost/NetShow/ads/Gen_6.asf" />
</ENTRY>
</ASX>
```

Personalized

However, if we pass a value to PlayList.asp via the QueryString – i.e. PlayList.asp?ShowType=1 – then we should see something similar to this:

```
<ASX VERSION = "3">
<TITLE>Personalized</TITLE><ENTRY>
<TITLE>Personalized Ad - Tech</TITLE>
<REF HREF = "http://localhost/NetShow/ads/Tech_5.asf" />
</ENTRY>
<ENTRY>
<TITLE>Not - Personalized Ad - Gen</TITLE>
<REF HREF = "http://localhost/NetShow/ads/Gen_8.asf" />
</ENTRY>
<ENTRY>
<TITLE>Personalized Story - Tech</TITLE>
<REF HREF = "http://localhost/NetShow/story/Tech_2.asf" />
</ENTRY>
<ENTRY>
<TITLE>Not - Personalized Ad - Gen</TITLE>
<REF HREF = "http://localhost/NetShow/ads/Gen_3.asf" />
</ENTRY>
</ASX>
```

Personalizing a stream is easy. It is ASP development that simply creates a different type of content. We've shown how we personalize a stream, but what if we need to authenticate a stream?

Windows NT NetShow Services Authentication Integration

If we take the time to investigate the NetShow SDK, we might notice the mention of the 'integration of Site Server Membership'. At one point Windows NT NetShow Services was part of the Site Server product and was to be tightly integrated with the Membership Authentication system. However, the cards falling as they do, the Membership integration with Site Server was never included in either the regular documentation or the SDK. Since the group I work with (the Developer Relations Group at Microsoft) works with Internet Content Providers, and is responsible for 'evangelizing' Site Server 3.0 and the Windows Media Technologies, I took it as my personal responsibility to integrate Membership Authentication and the Windows NT NetShow Services.

> **If you wanted to control – or for that matter sell – access to Windows Media Streams, you could easily do so with the technology presented in this chapter – in fact, organizations are using these same bits to sell access to content.**

Before I began this particular problem, there was no intention whatsoever to include C++ examples in this book. However, since the majority of the work I did was with C++ to get this particular NetShow 'plug-in' to work, I thought the readers should share in the wealth of knowledge!

The NSMemberAuthentication.dll Filter

The filter, or plug-in, as the NetShow SDK document calls them, is simply a DLL that is called when media is streamed by the Windows NT NetShow Services. This plug-in has methods that are called by the services when certain events occur, such as an authentication request. In order for this authentication filter to function properly several methods have to be supported and within these methods, we handle the authentication process of the member.

> *To run this example, you'll need to have installed Windows NT Netshow Services. For information on Netshow – and more details on the methods needed to support a Windows NT NetShow Services 'plug-in' – see* http://www.microsoft.com/windows/downloads/contents/Updates/NTNetShowService s.

The NetShow Member Authentication filter is a C++ DLL built using the Active Template Library in Microsoft Visual Studio 6.0. The compiled DLL and source code can be found at http://webdev.wrox.co.uk/books/1940.

> **The authentication does not work on multicast streams, only unicast streams.**

Registering the Authentication Filter

Before we can start using the NSMemberAuthentication.dll filter, we need to register it as a COM object in the registry. To register the DLL simply run: `Regsvr32 NSMemberAuthentication.dll` from the command prompt. If you receive an error while attempting to register the DLL, ensure that you have completed the following steps:

- ❑ Install the ADSI SDK (to make sure you have all the necessary header and library files for all the code examples in this book, it is best to download the Build Environment SDK, the ADSI SDK and the Site Server SDK. For more information, see http://msdn.microsoft.com/developer/sdk/platform.htm)
- ❑ Register the DLL atl.dll
- ❑ Move the NSMemberAuthentication.dll to the same directory from where you run Regsvr32 (usually winnt\system32)

You have Administrative rights to the server.

Registry Entry

In order for the NetShow server to use the registered filter, we need to provide some information about the filter for the server. In addition, we need to provide the DLL with the necessary information to authenticate members from the appropriate Membership Directory container. This is done through a registry entry under the following registry key:

[HKLM]\Software\Microsoft\NetShow\Servers\Default\Authentication

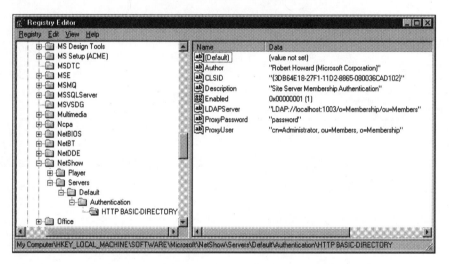

We can add the new registry entry in of two ways. We can either modify and run the NSMemberAuthentication.reg file (saved with the extension .reg) by simply double clicking on the file, or we can enter it by hand.

Here is the NSMemberAuthentication.reg file (supplied with the DLL when you download the code for this chapter) that we could use:

```
REGEDIT4

[HKEY_LOCAL_MACHINE\Software\Microsoft\NetShow\Servers\Default\Authentication\HTTP
BASIC-DIRECTORY]
"CLSID"="{3DB64E18-27F1-11D2-8865-080036CAD102}"
"Description"="Site Server Membership Authentication"
"Author"="Robert Howard (Microsoft Corporation)"
"LDAPServer"="LDAP://localhost:1003/o=Membership/ou=Members"
```

```
"ProxyUser"="cn=Administrator, ou=Members, o=Membership"
"ProxyPassword"="password"
"Enabled"=dword:00000001
```

Alternatively, we can add the registry information by hand. We create a new registry key under HKEY_LOCAL_MACHINE called HTTP-BASIC-DIRECTORY under \Software\Microsoft\NetShow\Servers\Default\Authentication. Next we create the following strings and DWORD entries in the new key with the appropriate values:

Type: STRING	
Entry	**Value**
CLSID	{3DB64E18-27F1-11D2-8865-080036CAD102}
Description	Site Server Membership Authentication
Author	Robert Howard (Microsoft Corporation)
LDAPServer	LDAP://localhost:1003/o=Membership/ou=Members
ProxyUser	Cn=Administrator, ou=Members, o=Membership
ProxyPassword	Password

Type: DWORD	
Entry	**Value**
Enabled	1

Here's a brief description of each of these entries:

❑ **CLSID** – Represents the class id of the DLL to be used for the authentication
❑ **Description** – Display text used by the NetShow server for showing the available authentication filters
❑ **Author** – Person who wrote the filter – yours truly!
❑ **LDAPServer** – The LDAP path to the container that has the members to be used for authentication in the Membership Directory
❑ **ProxyUser** – This space can be left blank for sites that have not secured the Membership Directory. Otherwise it needs to be the full distinguished name (DN) to the member that has permissions for viewing all properties of other members

Ideally, the ProxyUser should be a broker account that only has enough permission to view other user's usernames and passwords in the container specified by LDAPServer.

❑ **ProxyPassword** – The password of the ProxyUser
❑ **Enabled** – Determines whether or not the filter is enabled for the NetShow server: 1 enabled / 0 not enabled

Finally, we need to 'refresh' the Windows NT NetShow Unicast Service by stopping and starting the service from the control panel services applet. This will allow for the Windows NT NetShow Service to start using the new Membership Directory authentication DLL.

Authentication

After refreshing the Windows NT NetShow Unicast Service, any stream that we attempt to access will be authenticated against the Membership Directory. If for example we run the same `simple.asp` file that we saw in the previous section, before the Media Player displays the ASF file we have specified we will be prompted to authenticate ourselves to the Membership Directory with the following dialog:

For some of us it might end here. The filter works, we can authenticate our members, end of story. But we should take a look behind the scenes to better understand what's going on.

Behind the Scenes

The NSMemberAuthentication.dll is a plug-in written in C++. In addition to supporting the necessary Windows NT NetShow methods to trap events, there is also a special class call `CLDAPAccess` used to provide LDAP access through ADSI. `CLDAPAccess` provides the implementation for binding to the Membership Directory and authenticating requestors of the stream. This class has two methods `InitLDAP()` and `AuthenticateUser()`.

InitLDAP()

The first method we'll look at is `InitLDAP()`. This method is called when the Unicast service is first started, and is responsible for binding to the Membership Directory container used to authenticate members from specified in the registry. Let's look at the method parameters of `InitLDAP()`:

- ❑ **pszLDAPServer** – This parameter is a pointer to the value read from the registry for the full path to the container to authenticate members from.
- ❑ **pszProxyUser** – Represents the proxy user that has enough permissions in the Membership Directory to bind to and view the password value of other members. Similar to the broker account for the Membership Authentication Service. Also read from the value set in the registry.
- ❑ **pszProxyPassword** – The password for the ProxyUser. Also read from the value set in the registry.

Code Sample – InitLDAP()

Now that we've reviewed the parameters let's take a look at the code, and then explain what it does:

```
HRESULT CLDAPAccess::InitLDAP(WCHAR * pszLDAPServer,
                             WCHAR * pszProxyUser,
                             WCHAR * pszProxyPassword)
{
    CComBSTR bstrLDAPServer( pszLDAPServer );
    CComBSTR bstrProxyUser( pszProxyUser );
    CComBSTR bstrProxyPassword( pszProxyPassword );

    HRESULT hr;

    if (pszProxyUser == NULL)
    {
      hr = ADsGetObject(bstrLDAPServer,
                        IID_IADsContainer,
                        (void**)&m_pIADsContainer);
    }
    else
    {

      hr = ADsOpenObject(bstrLDAPServer,
                         bstrProxyUser,
                         bstrProxyPassword,
                         ADS_SECURE_AUTHENTICATION,
                         IID_IADsContainer,
                         (void**)&m_pIADsContainer);
    }

    return hr;
}
```

InitLDAP() uses the parameters passed to decide how to bind to the Membership Directory. We'll read more about binding with C++ in Chapter 15. However, the code makes a decision whether or not to bind as a member or bind anonymously. After attempting to bind, we will either have a m_pIADsContainer (defined in the header file for CLDAPAccess) or a failed connect. Regardless, the HRESULT hr is passed back to the caller to determine whether or not InitLDAP() was successful – HRESULTs specify error or success codes returned by the method.

If InitLDAP() was successful, then we have a pointer (m_pIADsContainer) to the container in the Membership Directory where we need to authenticate members from. Later, when a user requests a stream, we'll call the AuthenticateUser() method to determine whether the member exists in the Membership Directory.

AuthenticateUser()

AuthenticateUser() uses the bound m_pIADsContainer object to attempt to bind to the member who has provided credentials when challenged by the authentication for the stream. Before we look at the code, let's examine the parameters of AuthenticateUser():

❑ **bstrUser** – The name of the member that is attempting to authenticate.

❑ **bstrPwd** – The password of the member that is attempting to authenticate.

❑ **pfUserAuthenticated** – Boolean pointer used to return whether to allow (TRUE) or deny (FALSE) the member.

Now let's look at the code:

```
HRESULT CLDAPAccess::AuthenticateUser(BSTR bstrUser,
                                      BSTR bstrPwd,
                                      BOOL* pfUserAuthenticated)
{
        CoInitialize(NULL);

        *pfUserAuthenticated = FALSE;

        IADs * pIADs = NULL;
    HRESULT hr;

    CComBSTR bstrRDNMember(_T("cn="));
    bstrRDNMember.Append(bstrUser);

    hr = m_pIADsContainer->GetObject(L"member",
                                     bstrRDNMember,
                                     (IDispatch**)&pIADs);
    if ( FAILED( hr ) )
    {
      return S_OK;
    }

    VARIANT varPassword;
    hr = pIADs->Get(L"userPassword", &varPassword);

    if (FAILED(hr))
    {
      if (bstrPwd == NULL)
      {
        *pfUserAuthenticated = TRUE;
        return S_OK;
      }
      else
      {
        return S_OK;
      }
    }

    if ((_bstr_t)varPassword == (_bstr_t)bstrPwd)
    {
      *pfUserAuthenticated = TRUE;
    }
    else
    {
      *pfUserAuthenticated = FALSE;
    }
      return S_OK;
}
```

AuthenticateUser() uses the passed parameters to attempt to bind to a member with the name of the value in bstrUser. We set the *pfUserAuthenticated = FALSE so that if we encounter an error, we only need to return E_FAIL to indicate failure. Next, rather than binding as the member attempting to be authenticated, we use the context from m_pIADsContainer – where we can use a Proxy member that has permissions to all member attributes in the appropriate container.

If the Proxy member binds successfully to the member object – by testing the HRESULT after calling `m_pIADsContainer->GetObject()` – we'll have a `pIADs` pointer to the member in the Membership Directory. Next, we use the `pIADs` pointer to retrieve the value of the member's password and compare it to the password of the user attempting to be authenticated. If the passwords match, we set `*pfUserAuthenticated = TRUE` and return `S_OK` to indicate success. The plug-in then decides whether or not to stream the media to the user based on the return values of the `HRESULT` and `pfUserAuthenticated`.

Although not included in our discussion of the two methods, there is code used to write a log file of what is taking place written to `c:\temp\MemberAuth` log by default.

Integration with Site Server Commerce

Earlier, we looked at a way to control access to premium content through the use of the Site Server Membership Authentication system, but what if we wanted to do the same thing with Windows Media Streams? We obviously can't leverage Site Server Membership Authentication since the service is specific to Internet Information Server 4.0. However, how difficult would it be to re-purpose the code sample provided to provide pay-per-view along with authentication against the Membership Directory? Not too difficult at all. In fact, there are two separate strategies you could follow to accomplish this.

❑ Use another container for pay-per-view members, and only members that existed in this container would be granted access. Of course this would mean changing the registry entry for NSMemberAuthenticaiton, but that isn't difficult at all.

❑ A more elegant approach would to be to write another component for authorizing a Windows Media Stream request. After authenticating, the request would be handed off to the authorization component which could look for a member attribute that determined whether or not the member is allowed to view the stream – note, you could modify `AuthenticateUser()` to do this.

Although not included in this book, there is such a plug-in available that allows us to authorize streams. You might have noticed that we didn't discuss authorization – i.e. does the member have the necessary rights to view the stream. I have actually written another plug-in called NSMemberAuthorization used for authorization, but unfortunately was not able to include it in the book in time. However, I hope to have the plug-in available from the Wrox web site for this book as soon as possible.

Advanced Concepts

A little known gem included with the Site Server Commerce Edition is a Scriptor component called `DumpOrder.vbs`. `DumpOrder.vbs` is able to dump the values of the orderform at any stage in the pipeline, so we can see exactly what values it contains. In this *Advanced Concepts* section we'll take a look at a how to use `DumpOrder.vbs`.

DumpOrder.vbs

When designing a Commerce solution, sometimes it helps to know what's in the orderform dictionary object so that you can use it settings. The `DumpOrder.vbs` script provides this exact functionality.

> **In order to use** `DumpOrder.vbs` **you must have installed the Site Server Commerce Edition SDK.**

To use the `DumpOrder.vbs`, create a new Scriptor component in the desired pipeline – such as the `purchase.pcf` discussed earlier. Next, open up the new Scriptor component and select **External** as the source of the code. Next, navigate to the installation point of the Site Server Commerce Edition SDK samples\commerce folder and select DumpOrder.vbs. Finally, set the Config parameter name value pair to filename=*[full path to file]*:

The Config name/value pair is used by `DumpOrder.vbs` as the location and file to use to dump the orderform values. Choosing an External file rather than an Internal code source, as we looked at earlier, simply tells the Scriptor component to run this file and let it modify the order form as it sees fit. However, we still have to implement the `MSCSExecute()` method, as this is what will be called by the Scriptor component.

Examining the Dumped Orderform

If we set the name/value pair in the Scriptor component to filename=c:\DumpPurchase.txt, ran the VC30 `purchase.pcf` (by using VC30 to purchase a product), and examined the resulting file, we should see something similar to this:

```
Order Key [shopper_id] {String} Value [BWVULMVFCHS12NE800GPQPQEFD500439] {String}
Order Key [date_changed] {String} Value [10/11/98 8:55:45 PM] {Date}
Order Key [bill_to_name] {String} Value [Robert Howard] {String}
Order Key [bill_to_street] {String} Value [One Microsoft Way] {String}
Order Key [bill_to_city] {String} Value [Redmond] {String}
Order Key [bill_to_state] {String} Value [WA] {String}
Order Key [bill_to_zip] {String} Value [98053] {String}
Order Key [bill_to_country] {String} Value [USA] {String}
Order Key [bill_to_phone] {String} Value [425 882 8080] {String}
Order Key [ship_to_name] {String} Value [Robert Howard] {String}
Order Key [ship_to_street] {String} Value [One Microsoft Way] {String}
Order Key [ship_to_city] {String} Value [Redmond] {String}
Order Key [ship_to_state] {String} Value [WA] {String}
Order Key [ship_to_zip] {String} Value [98053] {String}
Order Key [ship_to_country] {String} Value [USA] {String}
Order Key [ship_to_phone] {String} Value [425 882 8080] {String}
Order Key [cc_name] {String} Value [Robert Howard] {String}
Order Key [order_id] {String} Value [FRVULMVFCHS12NE800GPQPQEF5] {String}
```

Note that this is only a fragment of `DumpPurchase.txt`.

Summary

This chapter provided some interesting ideas as to how you can easily extend the provided framework of Site Server 3.0 Personalization and Membership to other applications and services. Many of the examples and solutions provided in this chapter came from real-world implementations of these integration solutions.

Here's a brief summary of what we covered in this chapter.

- ❑ **Site Server Direct Mail.** We took a look at the Direct Mail tool installed by Site Server 3.0 used to generate personalized emails to select members. Additionally, we looked at a sample ASP used to generate the mailing.

- ❑ **Microsoft Site Server Commerce Edition.** Here we examined Site Server Commerce Edition and learned how we could easily provide a pay-for-membership solution. We introduced the Site Server Pipeline and showed how we could solve complex problems using the provided Scriptor component inserted in the Pipeline.

- ❑ **Personalized Windows Media Streams.** Using the XML based format called ASX, which describes the content that a Media Player can display, we looked at how we can generate personalized Windows Media Streams using member attributes from the Membership Directory.

- ❑ **Windows NT NetShow Services Authentication.** After learning how to personalize streams, we examined how we can provide secure access to streams using Windows NT NetShow Services by authenticating against a Membership Directory. Additionally, we looked at how we can extend our previous Commerce Edition integration discussion to provide pay-per-view streaming media.

- ❑ **Advanced Concepts.** Finally, we looked at a special component that we can use from the Commerce Pipeline to dump the orderform dictionary variables to a file. This allowed us to know exactly what's happening at each stage of the pipeline.

Additional ADSI and P&M Objects

In Chapter 9, we looked at the Active User Object and learned about two ADSIs supported by the Membership Directory, `IADs` and `IADsContainer`. These are not the only objects or interfaces available to us, and we'll be covering the most useful of them in this chapter. We'll discuss two further ADSIs supported by the Membership Directory, and we'll take a look at some of the other objects installed with Site Server 3.0 Personalization and Membership. These objects include the Membership Information object, and Membership Administration object used to configure the Membership Server and the AUO. We'll be looking at the methods and properties available in relation to ASP.

Here are the chapter topics.

- **Additional Supported Active Directory Service Interfaces.** We'll take a look at two more ADSI interfaces – `IADsClass` and `IADsOpenDSObject`. Although there are quite a few other ADSIs, only a handful may be used on the Membership Directory. The others are reserved for Windows NT 5.0 Active Directory.

- **Membership Information.** Here we'll explore the `ADsPathToDN()` and `DNToADsPath()` methods exposed by the `IMembershipInfo` interface. We'll learn how we can use these methods for managing groups and binding with the DNs.

- **Membership Administration Broker and Config.** We'll examine both the broker and the config methods and properties used to return values about the Membership Server. We'll learn how we can programmatically modify IIS 4.0 authentication methods, and how to determine the server and port where the LDAP Service is available from.

- **Membership Verify User.** The Membership Verify User provides us with some methods for managing member authentication settings for cookies and HTML Forms Authentication. We'll explore how we can use these methods to better manage our members.

- **Advanced Concepts.** Here we'll see how to tie some of the different features together – we'll look at secure binding and programmatic determination of the server and port of the LDAP. In addition, we'll create and use a special object to provide a higher level of security to your ASP applications.

So, let's start by looking at two further ADSI interfaces that we can use with the Membership Directory.

Additional Supported Active Directory Service Interfaces

Windows NT 5.0's Active Directory will use all of the Active Directory Service Interfaces as the primary API for programming against the Active Directory. Some of these interfaces include: `IADsComputer`, `IADsGroup`, and `IADsMembers`. We'd expect the `IADsGroup` and `IADsMembers` ADSIs to work fine with the Membership Directory – but they don't. The Membership Directory supports only the core ADSIs necessary to work with a directory: `IADs`, `IADsContainer`, `IADsClass`, `IADsProperty` and `IADsOpenDSObject`.

> *To read more about ADSI, see* http://www.microsoft.com/adsi.

We've already seen the first two in the list – `IADs` and `IADsContainer` – in chapter 9. In this chapter, we'll explore the `IADsClass` and `IADsOpenDSObject` interfaces. We won't look at the `IADsProperty` ADSI, because (after working with `IADsClass`, `IADs` and `IADsContainer`) we should have enough information to understand what `IADsProperty` provides – an ADSI for working with attributes in the schema. Let's look at `IADsClass`.

The IADsClass Interface

The Active Directory Service Interface `IADsClass` is used to view and modify definitions for the schema class objects that define a directory service, including interfaces, properties, methods, containment relationships and provider-specific rules. Specifically, we can use the `IADsClass` for working with **classSchema** objects in the cn=Schema, ou=Admin, o=*[organization]* container of the Membership Directory.

`IADsClass` provides several of the same methods and properties as `IADs` – such as `Name`, `ADsPath`, and `Class` – so we'll only focus on the new ones. For a complete definition of all the available properties and methods of the `IADsClass`, see Appendix C.

The simplest way to get an `IADsClass` interface is to create an instance of the Active User Object and bind to its `Schema` property – the `Schema` property returns the path to the class object in the cn=Schema:

```
Set objAUO = Server.CreateObject("Membership.UserObjects.1")
Set objIADsClass = GetObject(objAUO.Schema)
```

Once we've done this, we can use the properties and methods provided by the `IADsClass` interface. However, we'll only discuss the properties and methods that apply to the Membership Directory.

The MandatoryProperties Property

Whenever you see `MandatoryProperties`, think **mustContain** – they're one and the same. However, the `MandatoryProperties` are only available from a `IADsClass` interface. If we bind to a classSchema using an `IADs` interface, we would still need to use the mustContain attribute array. However, when we bind with `IADsClass` we can ask for the `MandatoryProperties` value of the class bound to. The returned value of a request for the `MandatoryProperties` property should be treated as an array.

Although, in Chapter 9, we used the mustContain multi-valued attribute of the members object to list attributes for the member, we could have used MandatoryProperties.

Code Sample – MandatoryProperties.asp

We use the MandatoryProperties in much the same way as we use the mustContain array:

```
<HTML>
<BODY BGCOLOR=WHITE>
<FONT FACE=ARIAL SIZE=3>
<B>
IADsClass - MandatoryProperties
</B>
<HR SIZE=1>
</FONT>
<FONT FACE=ARIAL SIZE=2>
<%
On Error Resume Next

Dim objAUO
Dim objIADsClass
Dim objIADsProperty
Dim arrMProps
Dim nIndex

' Create the Active User Object
' ********************************************************
Set objAUO = Server.CreateObject("Membership.UserObjects.1")
If Err.Number <> 0 Then
  Response.Write "Unable to create the AUO."
  Response.End
End If

' Bind to the member class in the schema
' ********************************************************
Set objIADsClass = GetObject(objAUO.Schema)

' Assign the value to a local variable
' ********************************************************
arrMProps = objIADsClass.MandatoryProperties

' Display the contents of the MandatoryProperties array
' ********************************************************
For nIndex = LBound(arrMProps) to UBound(arrMProps)
  Response.Write arrMProps(nIndex) & "<BR>"
Next
%>
</FONT>
</BODY>
</HTML>
```

Just as easily as we use the MandatoryProperties for mustContain attributes, we can use its counterpart, OptionalProperties, for mayContain attributes.

The OptionalProperties Property

As MandatoryProperties represents mustContain attributes, the OptionalProperties of an IADsClass represents the mayContain attributes. We won't spend a great deal of time examining OptionalProperties, since their use is identical to the previous property we examined.

Code Sample – OptionalProperties.asp

If you wanted to use the `OptionalProperties` in code, here's what it would look like:

```
' Assign the value to a local variable
' *********************************************************
arrOProps = objIADsClass.OptionalProperties

' Display the contents of the OptionalProperties array
' *********************************************************
For nIndex = LBound(arrOProps) to UBound(arrOProps)
   Response.Write arrOProps(nIndex) & "<BR>"
Next
```

Create `OptionalProperties.asp` by replacing the shaded section of `MandatoryProperties.asp` with this fragment. Running `OptionalProperties.asp` dumps out all of the member class's `OptionalProperties`:

Next, let's look at a very important property that tells us which ADSI to use with a specific class in the Membership Directory.

The PrimaryInterface Property

The `PrimaryInterface` returns the ADSI identifier used for the object in the schema. If we were to create an instance of the AUO, use its `Schema` property to bind to the schema definition of the class, and ask for the `PrimaryInterface` property, we would be returned a GUID value:

PrimaryInterface :{FD8256D0-FD15-11CE-ABC4-02608C9E7553}

Like the `MandatoryProperties` and `OptionalProperties` we've already reviewed, retrieving the `PrimaryInterface` is simply a matter of asking for it:

```
Response.Write "<B>PrimaryInterface: </B>" & objIADsClass.PrimaryInterface
```

Code Sample – PrimaryInterface.asp

Let's look at some code that can return all the `PrimaryInterface`(s) of all the objects in the Schema:

```
<HTML>
<BODY BGCOLOR=WHITE>
<FONT FACE=ARIAL SIZE=3>
<B>
IADsClass - PrimaryInterface
</B>
<HR SIZE=1>
</FONT>
<FONT FACE=ARIAL SIZE=2>
<%
On Error Resume Next

Dim objIADsSchema
Dim objIADsClass
Dim varPI

Const E_ADS_PROPERTY_NOT_FOUND = &H8000500D

' Bind to the schema
' ********************************************************
Set objIADsSchema = GetObject("LDAP://localhost:1003/Schema")

' Enumerate all possible value for the Primary Interface
' ********************************************************
For Each objIADsClass in objIADsSchema
  ' Assign varPI to the Primary Interface value
  ' ********************************************************
  varPI = objIADsClass.PrimaryInterface

  If Err.Number = E_ADS_PROPERTY_NOT_FOUND Then
    Err.Clear
  Else
    Response.Write objIADsClass.Name
    Response.Write "'s <B>PrimaryInterface</B>"
    Response.Write " is :" & varPI & "<BR>"
  End If
Next
%>
</FONT>
</BODY>
</HTML>
```

After binding to the Schema, the script enumerates each class or attribute and then displays the PrimaryInterface:

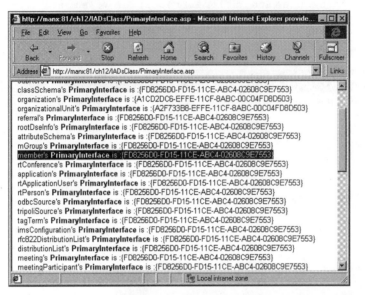

The GUID returned represents an interface identifier for an ADSI interface. If we were to perform a search in the registry for this GUID value, we would find that it is the ADSI interface identifier for IADs:

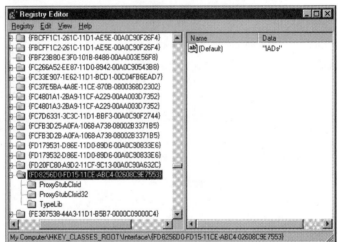

The `PrimaryInterface` tells us the ADSI that is best suited for the structure represented by the class. Nearly all the `PrimaryInterface` values returned by the Membership Directory will be of type `IADs`.

The IADsOpenDSObject Interface

As we've seen in the previous examples, you can access the directory in a non-secure way by simply passing the LDAP namespace path to the directory using `GetObject()`. However, to access the directory securely you need to use the `IADsOpenDSObject` ADSI to bind to a particular object. Binding securely to the directory is critically important once the directory has been secured – which we'll read about in Chapter 13. Once we've bound securely to an object, any further accesses we do with that object will use the security context of the member we used to bind. `IADsOpenDSObject` has several methods, but we'll only look at one of them here: `OpenDSObject()`.

The OpenDSObject() Method

Using `OpenDSObject()` is no different from using the `GetObject()`, in that we still pass the LDAP namespace path. However, we'll also pass the member we want to use to bind, the member's password, and a flag. We'll be returned a pointer to an `IADs` object. Here's the list of `OpenDSObject()`'s parameters:

- **lpszDNName** – The full LDAP namespace path of the object to bind to – such as `LDAP://localhost:1003/o=Wrox`.

- **lpszUserName** – One of the more confusing parameters. We don't pass the username – hey we can't assume the object knows where the members live – but instead the DN (distinguished name) of the member. For instance, to bind as the Administrator in the default ou=Members container of the o=Wrox organization, we would pass cn=Administrator, ou=Members, o=Wrox.

- **lpszPassword** – We simply need to pass the password of the member we want to use for the bind, since we already know the DN of that member.

- **lnReserved** – lnReserved is just what it says, reserved. However, just in case the Interface and method definition doesn't change, we'll pass the values to tell the method that we want to additionally encrypt our username and password information. The value is 1, but we should define and use the constant `ADS_SECURE_AUTHENTICATION = 1` – more definitions can be found in the file `iads.h`:

```
#define        ADS_SECURE_AUTHENTICATION        ( 0x1 )
#define        ADS_USE_ENCRYPTION               ( 0x2 )
#define        ADS_READONLY_SERVER              ( 0x4 )
#define        ADS_PROMPT_CREDENTIALS           ( 0x8 )
```

The semantics of the `OpenDSObject()` method is a little different from a normal `GetObject()` call. Rather than passing the full namespace path, we first bind to the LDAP service using only the moniker:

```
Set objIADsOpenDSObject = GetObject("LDAP:")
```

Next, we'll use the bound object to return an interface pointer to an `IADs` through the `OpenDSObject()` method.

```
Set objIADs = objIADsOpenDSObject.OpenDSObject("LDAP://localhost", _
                        "cn=Administrator, ou=Members, o=Wrox", _
                        "password", _
                        ADS_SECURE_AUTHENTICATION)
```

There – we've successfully bound to the root object as the Administrator. How is this useful, you ask? Well let's take a look.

For example, if we had a system where membership was a commodity that we sold, such as the Site Server Commerce integration example we provided in Chapter 11, we wouldn't want users to have the ability to add themselves to a group without having the appropriate security permissions. If members had the authority to add themselves to groups, they could easily give themselves access to anything else they needed by assigning themselves to an Administrative group – not good! Additionally, if a packet-sniffing device was used to examine packets as they sailed across the network, username and password information might be sniffed.

We'll examine some packet-sniffing scenarios in Chapter 13.

We can avoid these scenarios by only allowing a specific member, a proxy, to perform all security-related functions. We then pass the username and password of the proxy member – using ADS_SECURE_AUTHENTICATION passes username and password information securely when doing an ADSI OpenDSObject() bind.

Simple DirectoryBind() Method

Let's take a look at a sample method that binds either securely or anonymously to a Membership Directory, depending on the parameters passed. The parameters that the DirectoryBind() method takes are:

- ❑ **strUserName** – The distinguished name of the member to bind securely as. If no strUserName is passed, the bind will be done anonymously.
- ❑ **strPassword** – If a strUserName parameter is passed the strPassword parameter corresponds to the username
- ❑ **strPath** – The LDAP namespace path to bind to. This parameter is required to specify the Membership Directory to bind to either securely or anonymously.
- ❑ **pObjIADs** – the pObjIADs passed represents the object to bind to if the method succeeds – we can test whether the bind succeeds by the return value of the boolean parameter. If the bind is successful, we can use the passed object (by reference) to navigate the Membership Directory.

Code Sample – DirectoryBind() Method

Let's have a look at the code to the DirectoryBind() method:

```
<HTML>
<BODY BGCOLOR=WHITE>
<FONT FACE=ARIAL SIZE=3>
<B>
IADsOpenDSObject - OpenDSObject
</B>
<HR SIZE=1>
</FONT>
<FONT FACE=ARIAL SIZE=2>
<%
Const ADS_SECURE_AUTHENTICATION = 1

' **********************************************************
' METHOD:      DirectoryBind()
'
' PURPOSE:     Binds to a directory securly if a user
'              name and password is passed, if not binds
'              anonymously
'
' PARAMETERS:  strUserName
'              Username to bind with
'
'              strPassword
'              password to bind with
'
'              strPath
'              Path to bind to - full LDAP namespace path
'
'              pobjIADs
'              IADs interface to return
'
```

```
' RETURNS:    boolean - True Success / False Failure
'
Public Function DirectoryBind(strUserName, strPassword, strPath, ByRef pobjIAds)
  On Error Resume Next

  Dim objIADsOpenDSObject

  ' Assume failure
  ' *******************************************
  DirectoryBind = False

  ' Did we pass an LDAP path?
  ' *******************************************
  If Len(strPath) = 0 Then
    Exit Function
  End If

  ' Did we pass a username?
  ' *******************************************
  If Len(strUserName) <> 0 Then
    ' Bind securly
    ' *******************************************
    Set objIADsOpenDSObject = GetObject("LDAP:")
    If Err.Number <> 0 Then
      Exit Function
    End If

    ' Use OpenDSObject method
    ' *******************************************
    Set pObjIADs = objIADsOpenDSObject.OpenDSObject(strPath, _
                             strUserName, _
                             strPassword, _
                             ADS_SECURE_AUTHENTICATION)
    If Err.Number <> 0 Then
      Exit Function
    End If
  Else
    ' Bind anonymously
    ' *******************************************
    Set pObjIADs = GetObject(strPath)
    If Err.Number <> 0 Then
      Exit Function
    End If
  End If

  ' All done
  ' *******************************************
  DirectoryBind = True
End Function
```

The example code below demonstrates using the `DirectoryBind()` method firstly to bind anonymously and then to bind as the administrator. In order for both of these method calls to succeed you must have the correct authentication methods set to access your Membership Directory (you can set these through the LDAP Service Properties dialog for the appropriate Membership Server as we saw in Chapter 6 – the appropriate Membership Server will be the one to which you have mapped your IIS 4.0 web).

Remember, you will only be able to bind anonymously if you have enabled anonymous authentication for the Membership Directory, and you'll only be able to bind as the administrator if you have a password authentication method enabled.

You will also need to replace the values in the code below with the correct DN and password for your administrator account:

```
' ************************************************************
' Example Use
' ************************************************************

Dim objIADs
Dim blnSuccess

' Bind anonymously
' ******************************************
blnSuccess = DirectoryBind("", "", "LDAP://localhost:1003", objIADs)

If blnSuccess = True Then
 Response.Write "Bound anonymously to: " & objIADs.AdsPath & "<P>"
Else
 Response.Write "Anonymous bind failed<P>"
End If

' Bind Securely
' ******************************************
blnSuccess = DirectoryBind("cn=Administrator,ou=Members, o=Wrox", _
                   "password", _
                   "LDAP://localhost:1003", _
                   objIADs)

If blnSuccess = True Then
 Response.Write "Bound securly to: " & objIADs.AdsPath & "<P>"
Else
 Response.Write "Secure bind failed<P>"
End If
%>
</FONT>
</BODY>
</HTML>
```

The `DirectoryBind()` is a handy little method that allows you to use one method for all your binding needs, based on the values of the parameters that are passed. In the first example, no parameters were passed for the username or password:

```
blnSuccess = DirectoryBind("", "", "LDAP://localhost:1003", objIADs)
```

However, we *do* pass the `IADs` object to return and the `ADsPath` to which we bind. When `DirectoryBind()` is used, and since no username exists, the bind is done anonymously with the `GetObject()` method using the passed `ADsPath` value. When in the second call we defined the values for the username and password, the bind was performed with the `OpenDSObject()` method and the `ADS_SECURE_AUTHENTICATION` flag:

```
blnSuccess = DirectoryBind("cn=Administrator, _
                   ou=Members, o=Wrox", "password", _
                   "LDAP://localhost:1003", _
                   objIADs)
```

Using the ADS_SECURE_AUTHENTICATION flag signifies to ADSI to perform the bind securely.

DirectoryBind() proves to be a useful method for developing with an unsecured Membership Directory, and later modifying the code to use delegation to perform actions using the returned IADs reference (objIADs). Simply define constants, such as DELEGATE_BIND_USER, and DELEGATE_BIND_PWD as null strings:

```
Const DELEGATE_BIND_USER = ""
Const DELEGATE_BIND_PWD = ""
```

Passing these values to DirectoryBind() will bind anonymously. Later, when you've determined a secure mechanism for retrieving username and password information with which to bind and you don't want to store usernames or passwords in ASP, you can pass values for these parameters. In the *Advanced Concepts* section of this chapter, we'll explore a way to design a special COM object that holds this necessary information, and to expose it for the DirectoryBind() method.

Now that we've covered the most useful aspects of the ADSI interfaces we can use with P&M, let's turn to examine some further Membership-specific COM objects.

The Membership Information Object

The only interface of the Membership Information object (ProgID Membership.MembershipInfo) that we'll look at in detail is the interface IMembershipInfo.

The IMembershipInfo Interface

Although the IMembershipInfo interface provides several properties, they're not altogether very useful. However, the IMembershipInfo interface does provide one wonderfully useful method for converting ADsPaths to distinguished names.

> **Note the** DNToADsPath() **does not work as intended. If the ADsPath requires a port, the** DNToADsPath() **conversion does not include it.**

The ADsPathToDN() Method

The ADsPathToDN() method returns the distinguished name of an object when passed its Active Directory service Path. The ADsPath for a member could be LDAP://localhost:1003/o=Wrox/ou=Members/cn=Robert Howard. If we want to refer to a member from within the Membership Directory, for instance to represent members in a group, we would need that member's DN: cn=Robert Howard, ou=Members, o=Wrox. The diagram should make this a little clearer:

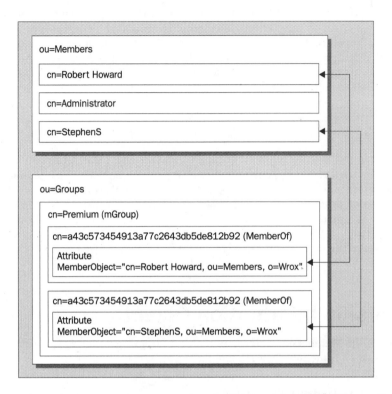

The MemberOf object for Robert Howard in the Groups container has as an attribute the distinguished name of the Robert Howard member object. The distinguished name points back to the Robert Howard member object in the ou=Members container. If we bound to an mGroup object, such as Premium, we could then enumerate and bind to each member. Likewise, if we wanted to add a member to this group, we would first convert the ADsPath property of the member to a DN, and then save that property as an attribute for the MemberOf object.

Now that we've examined why we use the ADsPathToDN() method, let's look at its parameters, as well as some sample code to see how it is used. The ADsPathToDN() method accepts one parameter:

- **bstrADsPath** – The ADsPath (LDAP namespace path) to be returned as a distinguished name to uniquely identify the object in the Membership Directory.

In Chapter 14 we'll discuss the AddUsertoGroup() method, where we'll use the ADsPathToDN() method to convert the ADsPath of the user – passed as the parameter strADsPathToUser – to a distinguished name value for a new MemberObject.

Code Sample – Snippet of AddUserToGroup()

The following snippet of code is from the AddUsertoGroup() method.

```
' Get the MembershipInfo object to help convert ADsPath to DN
' ********************************
  Set objMemInfo = Server.CreateObject("Membership.MembershipInfo.1")
```

```
      If Err.Number <> 0 Then
         Err.Clear
         Exit Function
      End If

      ' Convert user object's ADs path to DN path
      ' ******************************
      strUserDNPath = objMemInfo.ADsPathToDN(strADsPathToUser)

      ' Store user object's DN path in group object
      ' *********************************
      objAddMember.Put "memberobject", CStr(strUserDNPath)
      If Err.Number <> 0 Then
         Err.Clear
         Exit Function
      End If
```

You can see that we create an instance of the `Membership.MembershipInfo.1` object, and then use its `ADsPathToDN()` method to convert the ADsPath value passed as the `strADsPathToUser` parameter. We then add this DN as the value of the MemberObject. If the value of `strADsPathToUser` is `LDAP://localhost:1003/o=Wrox/ou=Members/cn=Administrator`, then `strUserDNPath` would contain the following value `cn=Administrator, ou=Members, o=Wrox`.

So we have a method for converting from an ADsPath to a DN, but what do we do if we need to go back? `IMembershipInfo` provides another method to do this: `DNToADsPath()` – however there is a problem.

The DNToADsPath() Method

Unfortunately, the `DNToADsPath()` method does not work as provided. It should return the full ADsPath when passed a distinguished name. For example, examine the following code:

Code Sample – DNToADsPath() Method

```
<HTML>
<BODY BGCOLOR=WHITE>
<FONT FACE=ARIAL SIZE=3>
<B>
IMembershipInfo - DNToADsPath
</B>
<HR SIZE=1>
</FONT>
<FONT FACE=ARIAL SIZE=2>
<%
Dim objIADs
Dim objMemInfo
Dim strMemberDN
Dim strMemberADsPath
Dim objBadADsBind

Const MEMBER_PATH = "LDAP://manx:1003/o=Wrox/ou=Members/cn=Robert Howard"

' Create the Membership Information object
' *******************************************
Set objMemInfo = CreateObject("Membership.MembershipInfo.1")
```

```
   If Err.Number <> 0 Then
      Response.Write "Unable to create MembershipInfo object"
      Response.End
   End If

   ' Bind to a member
   ' *******************************************
   Set objIADs = GetObject(MEMBER_PATH)
   If Err.Number <> 0 Then
      Response.Write "Invalid object: " & MEMBER_PATH
      Response.Write "<P>You need a valid member."
      Response.End
   End If

   ' Convert to DN and covert back to ADsPath
   ' *******************************************
   strMemberDN = objMemInfo.ADsPathToDN(objIADs.ADsPath)
   strMemberADsPath = objMemInfo.DNToADsPath(strMemberDN)

   ' Display correct and incorrect member adspath values
   ' *******************************************
   Response.Write "Before Member ADsPath: "
   Response.Write objIADs.ADsPath & "<P>"
   Response.Write "After Member ADsPath: "
   Response.Write strMemberADsPath

   ' Attempt to bind with
   ' *******************************************
   Response.Write "<P>Attempt to bind with new ADsPath: "

   ' Perform bind
   ' *******************************************
   Set objBadADsBind = GetObject(strMemberADsPath)

   If Err.Number <> 0 Then
      Response.Write "Error: " & Hex(Err.Number)
   Else
      Response.Write "No error...only if on port #389"
   End If
%>
</FONT>
</BODY>
</HTML>
```

This code sample uses the ADsPath of a member and passes it through the `ADsPathToDN()` method to convert it to a DN. Next, the DN is passed back through the `DNToADsPath()` method, but here it loses the port number:

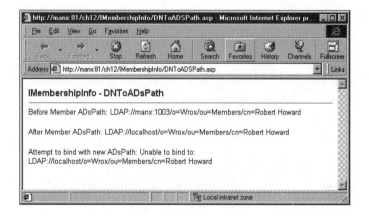

As you can see, the `DNToADsPath()` method is fairly useless unless the LDAP Service we need happens to be on the default port (389). However, that's perfectly all right, if you already have the context of a bound Membership Directory object.

A Resolution to DNToADsPath()

Later, we'll see how we can programmatically determine the server and port name of the LDAP Service from an ASP. Until then, let's assume we have that information available, and let's see how the following code would bind directly to the DN of our Robert Howard member. (Don't forget to change the values of the two constants to reflect your Membership Directory when you run this code for yourself.)

Code Sample – Bind Using the DN

```
<HTML>
<BODY BGCOLOR=WHITE>
<FONT FACE=ARIAL SIZE=3>
<B>
Bind Using the DN
</B>
<HR SIZE=1>
</FONT>
<FONT FACE=ARIAL SIZE=2>
<%
On Error Resume Next

Dim objIADs
Dim objMemInfo
Dim strMemberDN
Dim objBindDN

Const MEMBER_PATH = "LDAP://manx:1003/o=Wrox/ou=Members/cn=Robert Howard"
Const DIRECTORY_PATH = "LDAP://manx:1003/"

' Create the Membership Information object
' **********************************************
Set objMemInfo = CreateObject("Membership.MembershipInfo.1")
If Err.Number <> 0 Then
  Response.Write "Unable to create MembershipInfo object"
  Response.End
End If

' Bind to a member
' **********************************************
Set objIADs = GetObject(MEMBER_PATH)
If Err.Number <> 0 Then
  Response.Write "Invalid object: " & MEMBER_PATH
  Response.Write "<P>You need a valid member."
  Response.End
End If

' Obtain the DN
' **********************************************
strMemberDN = objMemInfo.ADsPathToDN(objIADs.ADsPath)

' Display correct ADsPath, and the correct DN
' **********************************************
Response.Write "Member ADsPath: "
Response.Write objIADs.ADsPath & "<P>"
```

```
Response.Write "Member DN: "
Response.Write strMemberDN

' Attempt to bind with
' ********************************************
Response.Write "<P>Attempt to bind with the DN:<BR>"

' Perform bind
' ********************************************
Set objBindDN = GetObject(DIRECTORY_PATH & strMemberDN)

If Err.Number <> 0 Then
  Response.Write "Unable to bind to: " & strMemberDN
Else
  Response.Write "Bound to: " & objBindDN.ADsPath
End If
%>
</FONT>
</BODY>
</HTML>
```

After running this code, you should see something similar to this:

As you can see, the DNToADsPath() is not critical to our application, and it is possible to bind using the DN of the member. So why is binding with the DN useful?

Enumerating Members of Groups

If you wanted to display all the members of a group, you could enumerate through each MemberOf object using the MemberObject attribute value (the DN) to bind to the Member. You could then display the member's common name (cn).

Code Sample – Bind To And Display Members of a Group

```
<HTML>
<BODY BGCOLOR=WHITE>
<FONT FACE=ARIAL SIZE=3>
<B>
Display Members of a Group
</B>
<HR SIZE=1>
</FONT>
<FONT FACE=ARIAL SIZE=2>
```

```
<%
Dim objIADs
Dim objIADsContainer
Dim objMemInfo
Dim strMemberDN
Dim objMemberOf

  Const GROUP_PATH = "LDAP://manx:1003/o=Wrox/ou=Groups/cn=Premium"
  Const LDAP_SERVER = "localhost"
  Const LDAP_PORT = "1003"

  ' Create the Membership Information object
  ' ********************************************
  Set objMemInfo = CreateObject("Membership.MembershipInfo.1")
  If Err.Number <> 0 Then
    Response.Write "Unable to create MembershipInfo object"
    Response.End
  End If

  ' Bind to group
  ' ********************************************
  Set objIADsContainer = GetObject(GROUP_PATH)
  If Err.Number <> 0 Then
    Response.Write "Invalid object: " & GROUP_PATH
    Response.Write "<P>You need a valid object."
    Response.End
  End If

  ' Enumerate throgh MemberOf Object
  ' ********************************************
  For Each objMemberOf in objIADsContainer
    ' Obtain the DN
    ' ********************************************
    strMemberDN = objMemberOf.Get("MemberObject")

    ' Bind to member
    ' ********************************************
    Set objIADs = GetObject("LDAP://" & LDAP_SERVER & ":" _
                            & LDAP_PORT & "/" & strMemberDN)

    ' Display Member cn
    ' ********************************************
    Response.Write "Member of group: " & objIADs.Get("cn") & "<BR>"
  Next
%>
</FONT>
</BODY>
</HTML>
```

However, you should consider whether or not the overhead associated with each bind is worth the value that displaying member information provides. In Chapter 13, we'll compare groups and containers and learn how we can use these to organize and manage members more effectively.

Membership Administration Broker and Config

The Membership Administration Broker COM object (ProgID: `MemAdmin.BrokServers`) exposes the `IBrokServers` interface that allows you to configure information as it relates to Membership Servers. Using the `MappedTo()` method, we can determine the Membership Server instance id. Then, using the Membership Server instance id, we can use another Membership Administration object (ProgID: `MemAdmin.BrokConfig`) to programmatically determine the server and port name to be used in an LDAP bind, with methods exposed through its interface, `IBrokConfig`.

We won't be examining all of the methods provided by of `IBrokServers` or `IBrokConfig`, but I do suggest you examine the source of PMAdmin.vbs (found in the Site Server \Bin\P&M directory) as a resource. PMAdmin.vbs uses all of the provided methods and properties of `IBrokServers` and `IBrokConfig`.

IBrokServers

`IBrokServers` exposes methods used to configure, stop, and start the services contained in a Membership Server. However, we'll only look at some of the more relevant methods. The first of these methods allow you to programmatically determine the authentication method used on an IIS 4.0 resource.

The GetAuthTypes() Method

The `GetAuthTypes()` method tells us the authentication method used by a resource for IIS 4.0. In Chapter 8, we configured these settings with the Membership Authentication tab for an IIS 4.0 web server mapped to a Membership Server using Membership Authentication.

The `GetAuthTypes()` method returns a numerical value indicating the authentication type to use for an IIS 4.0 resource. The values may be OR(ed) together, (see Chapter 13 for a thorough explanation of OR[ing]), to allow for multiple authentication types to be supported. In the example code I've provided for `GetAuthTypes()` I've defined the various authentication types as constants:

```
Const AUTH_MBS_AUTO_COOKIE     = 1      ' Automatic Cookie Authentication
Const AUTH_MBS_HTML_FORM       = 2      ' HTML Forms Authentication
Const AUTH_MBS_CLEAR_BASIC     = 4      ' Clear Text/Basic Authentication
Const AUTH_MBS_DPA             = 8      ' Distributed Password Authentication
Const AUTH_ANONYMOUS           = 16     ' IIS Anonymous IUSR_servername
```

An example of this would be supporting both Allow Anonymous and Clear Text/Basic Authentication, which would mean an authentication value of 20 (4 and 16, ORed together), as is configured in our previous screenshot.

You can then use the GetAuthTypes() method, passing the appropriate IIS metabase path to your IIS 4.0 web, to return the authentication value. We've defined the IIS metabase path as a constant in the sample code:

```
Const IIS_RESOURCE = "/LM/W3SVC/Root/3"
```

> **To determine the appropriate path, you can either replace the numerical value in the metabase path above with the correct instance id, or use the Directory Walker tool discussed in Chapter 15 binding with**
> IIS://localhost/W3SVC. **Remember you can retrieve the IIS instance id with** Request.ServerVariables ("INSTANCE_ID").

The GetAuthTypes() method requires a single parameter:

❑ **bszPath** – The path in the IIS metabase to the resource whose authentication type will be returned.

Code Sample – GetAuthtypes.asp

Let's look at GetAuthTypes.asp, which displays the authentication type used by an IIS 4.0 web server mapped to a Membership Server:

```
<HTML>
<BODY BGCOLOR=WHITE>
<FONT FACE=ARIAL SIZE=3>
<B>
IBrokServers - GetAuthTypes()
</B>
<HR SIZE=1>
</FONT>
<FONT FACE=ARIAL SIZE=2>
<%
On Error Resume Next
Dim objBrokServers
Dim nAuthType

' The various authentication types
' which may be OR(ed) together
' ********************************
Const AUTH_MBS_AUTO_COOKIE     = 1      ' Automatic Cookie Authentication
Const AUTH_MBS_HTML_FORM       = 2      ' HTML Forms Authentication
Const AUTH_MBS_CLEAR_BASIC     = 4      ' Clear Text/Basic Authentication
Const AUTH_MBS_DPA             = 8      ' Distributed Password Authentication
Const AUTH_ANONYMOUS           = 16     ' IIS Anonymous IUSR_servername
```

367

```
' The metabase path to  the IIS Resource
' ********************************
Const IIS_RESOURCE = "/LM/W3SVC/Root/3"

' Create the Membership Admin object
' ********************************
Set objBrokServers = Server.CreateObject("MemAdmin.BrokServers")
If Err.Number <> 0 Then
  Response.Write "Unable to create MemAdmin.BrokServers."
  Response.End
End If

' Discover the authentication type
' used by the resource
' ********************************
nAuthType = objBrokServers.GetAuthTypes(IIS_RESOURCE)

Response.Write "The selected resource is authenticated by: <BR><B>"
Select Case nAuthType
  Case AUTH_ANONYMOUS
     Response.Write "IIS Anonymous IUSR_[servername] anonymous<BR>"

  Case AUTH_MBS_AUTO_COOKIE
     Response.Write "Membership Automatic Cookie Authentication<BR>"

  Case AUTH_MBS_HTML_FORM
     Response.Write "Membership HTML Forms Authentication<BR>"

  Case AUTH_MBS_CLEAR_BASIC
     Response.Write "Membership Clear Text/Basic Authentication<BR>"

  Case AUTH_MBS_DPA
     Response.Write "Membership Distributed Password Authentication<BR>"

  ' Handle multiple auth types
  ' ********************************
  Case (AUTH_ANONYMOUS OR AUTH_MBS_AUTO_COOKIE)
     Response.Write "IIS Anonymous IUSR_[servername] anonymous<BR>"
     Response.Write "Membership Automatic Cookie Authentication<BR>"

  Case (AUTH_ANONYMOUS OR AUTH_MBS_HTML_FORM)
     Response.Write "IIS Anonymous IUSR_[servername] anonymous<BR>"
     Response.Write "Membership HTML Forms Authentication<BR>"

  Case (AUTH_ANONYMOUS OR AUTH_MBS_CLEAR_BASIC)
     Response.Write "IIS Anonymous IUSR_[servername] anonymous<BR>"
     Response.Write "Membership Clear Text/Basic Authentication<BR>"

  Case (AUTH_ANONYMOUS OR AUTH_MBS_DPA)
     Response.Write "IIS Anonymous IUSR_[servername] anonymous<BR>"
     Response.Write "Membership Distributed Password Authentication<BR>"

  Case (AUTH_ANONYMOUS OR AUTH_MBS_DPA OR AUTH_MBS_CLEAR_BASIC)
     Response.Write "IIS Anonymous IUSR_[servername] anonymous<BR>"
     Response.Write "Membership Clear Text/Basic Authentication<BR>"
     Response.Write "Membership Distributed Password Authentication<BR>"

  Case (AUTH_MBS_DPA OR AUTH_MBS_CLEAR_BASIC)
     Response.Write "Membership Clear Text/Basic Authentication<BR>"
```

```
        Response.Write "Membership Distributed Password Authentication<BR>"
    End Select

    Response.Write "</B>"
    %>
    </FONT>
    </BODY>
    </HTML>
```

Essentially, this ASP page is one large case statement that determines the display by comparing the ORed values of the authentication types to the variable nAuthtype. nAuthType is the value returned by GetAuthTypes().

After running this script on a resource configured with Allow Anonymous and Clear Text/Basic Authentication, you would see the following results:

Displaying the authentication values is simple, but what if we wanted to change the authentication method from Anonymous Authentication and Clear Text/Basic Authentication to Automatic Cookie Authentication?

Easy, we would use SetAuthTypes().

The SetAuthTypes() Method

The SetAuthTypes() method allows you to modify the configured authentication type programmatically. Again, we'll use the constants defined above to configure the authentication type to use. To set the authentication method to Automatic Cookie Authentication, we simply need to pass this value.

Let's examine the parameters of SetAuthTypes(), and then look at a small sample used to modify the authentication method on our resource. Again we'll use a constant for the IIS metabase path:

```
Const IIS_RESOURCE = "/LM/W3SVC/Root/3"
```

Here's the parameter list:

- ❑ **bszPath** – bszPath represents the same value as GetAuthTypes(), the path in the IIS metabase for the resource whose authentication method we wish to configure.
- ❑ **lTypes** – The values of our authentication methods, ORed together.

369

The values we'll use for lTypes (under Membership authentication) are as follows:

```
Const AUTH_MBS_AUTO_COOKIE      = 1     ' Automatic Cookie Authentication
Const AUTH_MBS_HTML_FORM        = 2     ' HTML Forms Authentication
Const AUTH_MBS_CLEAR_BASIC      = 4     ' Clear Text/Basic Authentication
Const AUTH_MBS_DPA              = 8     ' Distributed Password Authentication
Const AUTH_ANONYMOUS            = 16    ' IIS Anonymous IUSR_servername
```

Code Sample – SetAuthTypes.asp

Here's what the code would look like to make the modification to IIS_RESOURCE to support
Automatic Cookie Authentication:

```
<HTML>
<BODY BGCOLOR=WHITE>
<FONT FACE=ARIAL SIZE=3>
<B>
IBrokServers - SetAuthTypes()
</B>
<HR SIZE=1>
</FONT>
<FONT FACE=ARIAL SIZE=2>
<%
On Error Resume Next
Dim objBrokServers
Dim nAuthType

' The various authentication types
' which may be OR(ed) together
' ********************************
Const AUTH_MBS_AUTO_COOKIE      = 1     ' Automatic Cookie Authentication
Const AUTH_MBS_HTML_FORM        = 2     ' HTML Forms Authentication
Const AUTH_MBS_CLEAR_BASIC      = 4     ' Clear Text/Basic Authentication
Const AUTH_MBS_DPA              = 8     ' Distributed Password Authentication
Const AUTH_ANONYMOUS            = 16    ' IIS Anonymous IUSR_servername

' The IIS Resource's authentication type
' ********************************
Const IIS_RESOURCE = "/LM/W3SVC/3/Root"

' Create the Membership Admin object
' ********************************
Set objBrokServers = Server.CreateObject("MemAdmin.BrokServers")
If Err.Number <> 0 Then
  Response.Write "Unable to create MemAdmin.BrokServers."
  Response.End
End If

' Define the authentication type to use
' ********************************
nAuthType = AUTH_MBS_AUTO_COOKIE

' Write the Authentication type on
' the resource
' ********************************
objBrokServers.SetAuthTypes IIS_RESOURCE, nAuthType
If Err.Number <> 0 Then
  Response.Write "Unable to Write authentication information for: "
  Response.Write IIS_RESOURCE
Else
```

```
        Response.Write "Authentication method information changed for: "
        Response.Write IIS_RESOURCE
    End If
%>
</FONT>
</BODY>
</HTML>
```

Afterwards, if we look at the resource that was modified, we should see the following:

The Membership Authentication type is now set to **Automatic Cookie Authentication** per our code!

Now that you know how to configure the authentication method, let's see how to programmatically determine whether or not the IIS 4.0 web server is using Windows NT (Intranet) or Membership Authentication.

The GetSecurityMode() Method

The GetSecurityMode() method returns either a 0 or a 1, which tells us the type of authentication used by a specified service and instance. I've defined the following constants to make it easier to determine the authentication type:

```
' Constants for our security types
' *********************************
Const AUTH_TYPE_WINNT   = 1
Const AUTH_TYPE_MEMBR   = 0
```

Hence, if the GetSecurityMode() method returns 0, the site uses Membership Authentication. If the method returns 1, the site uses Windows NT (Intranet) Authentication. Although the sample code we'll look at for this method returns the authentication type of the IIS 4.0 web server from which the ASP code is run, it is possible to specify other services and instances.

Here's the parameter list for the `GetSecurityMode()` method:

- ❑ **bszServiceName** – The name of the service whose authentication type we are curious about. The most common value is of course for IIS, `W3SVC`.

- ❑ **lVirtServId** – The specific instance of the service whose authentication type is to be returned. We can ascertain this value for IIS from an ASP by requesting the `Request.ServerVariables("INSTANCE_ID")` value.

Code Sample – GetSecurityMode.asp

Let's look at some code that displays the authentication type used by the web server the following ASP is run under:

```
<HTML>
<BODY BGCOLOR=WHITE>
<FONT FACE=ARIAL SIZE=3>
<B>
IBrokServers - GetSecurityMode
</B>
<HR SIZE=1>
</FONT>
<FONT FACE=ARIAL SIZE=2>
<%
On Error Resume Next
Dim objBrokServers
Dim nInstanceID
Dim nSecurityMode

' Constants for our security types
' ********************************
Const AUTH_TYPE_WINNT  = 1
Const AUTH_TYPE_MEMBR  = 0

' Create the Membership Admin object
' ********************************
Set objBrokServers = Server.CreateObject("MemAdmin.BrokServers")
If Err.Number <> 0 Then
  Response.Write "Unable to create MemAdmin.BrokServers."
  Response.End
End If

' Get the Instance ID
' ********************************
nInstanceID = Request.ServerVariables("INSTANCE_ID")

' Get the Security Mode
' ********************************
nSecurityMode = objBrokServers.GetSecurityMode("W3SVC", nInstanceID)

' Case Statement to display the
' authentication type used by this ASP
' ********************************
Response.Write "This site uses: "
Select Case nSecurityMode
  Case AUTH_TYPE_WINNT
    Response.Write "<B>Windows NT (Intranet) Authentication</B>"
  Case AUTH_TYPE_MEMBR
```

```
      Response.Write "<B>Membership Authentication</B>"
   End Select
%>
</FONT>
</BODY>
</HTML>
```

After creating the `MemAdmin.BrokServers` object, we determine the `INSTANCE_ID` of the IIS web server. Next, we pass the instance id value to the `GetSecurityMode()` method, where we've already hard-coded the value for the service.

```
nSecurityMode = objBrokServers.GetSecurityMode("W3SVC", nInstanceID)
```

Finally, a case statement is used to compare `nSecurityMode` to the defined constants to determine, and display, the authentication type used by the web server.

The HasNTAdminPrivilege() Method

This method determines whether the user has NT Administrator level privileges. To use this method, you must support error trapping. `HasNTAdminPrivilege()` fails if the user in context does not have Windows NT Administrator level privileges, but returns no error if it succeeds.

Code Sample – HasNTAdmin.asp

There are no parameters, and using the method is as follows:

```
<HTML>
<BODY BGCOLOR=WHITE>
<FONT FACE=ARIAL SIZE=3>
<B>
IBrokServers - HasNTAdminPrivelege()
</B>
<HR SIZE=1>
</FONT>
<FONT FACE=ARIAL SIZE=2>
<%
On Error Resume Next

Dim objBrokServers

' Create the Membership Admin object
' ********************************
Set objBrokServers = Server.CreateObject("MemAdmin.BrokServers")
If Err.Number <> 0 Then
  Response.Write "Unable to create MemAdmin.BrokServers."
  Response.End
End If

' Determine if we have the NT Admin
' Priveleges necessary to make modifications
' ********************************
objBrokServers.HasNTAdminPrivilege
If Err.Number <> 0 Then
  Response.Write "User/Member does not have NT Admin Privilege."
Else
```

```
     Response.Write "User/Member does have NT Admin Privilege."
  End If
%>
</FONT>
</BODY>
</HTML>
```

Most of the modifications made with `IBrokServers` require that the user context have Windows NT Administrator privileges.

The MappedTo() Method

The `MappedTo()` method enables us to programmatically discover the instance id of the Membership Server which is mapped to the service whose name we pass as a parameter. The method returns populated values for two of its parameters – `plVirtMemInstId` and `pbszComment`. The `plVirtMemInstId` parameter represents the instance id of the Membership Server that is mapped to the service, and the `pbszComment` parameter represents the name of that Membership Server.

> *We use the value of the Membership Server instance id to bind to that Membership Server and get configuration information with the `IBrokConfig` interface that we'll read about in the next section.*

Before we take a look at some example code using this method, let's review the parameter definitions:

❑ **bszServiceName** – The name of the service to which the Membership Server is mapped. To find the Membership Server information from an Internet Information Server 4.0 web use `W3SVC` as the service name.

❑ **lVirtServInstId** –The virtual service instance id of the Internet Information Server 4.0 web. The instance id is always numeric, and can be determined by the server variable `Request.ServerVariables("INSTANCE_ID")`.

❑ **plVirtMemInstId** – The `MappedTo()` method is a sub routine rather than a method that returns a single value, thus enabling for multiple return values. This is accomplished by passing empty variants, such as `plVirtMemInstId`. When the subroutine completes successfully the passed variant contains the return value. The value that this parameter contains is the instance id of the Membership Server mapped to the service specified by (`bszServiceName`) and (`lVirtServInstId`).

❑ **pbszComment** – the `pbszComment` parameter is also used to return a value from the `MappedTo()` subroutine and should be treated in a similar fashion to the `plVirtMemInstId` parameter. The returned value represents the name of the Membership Server that the service is mapped to.

Code Sample – ServerInstance() Method

The sample code for `MappedTo()` is another method that can be used from an ASP page.

```
<HTML>
<BODY BGCOLOR=WHITE>
<FONT FACE=ARIAL SIZE=3>
<B>
ServerInstance()
</B>
<HR SIZE=1>
```

```
</FONT>
<FONT FACE=ARIAL SIZE=2>
<%
' ********************************************************
' FUNCTION:ServerInstance()
'
' PURPOSE:      The Membership Server instance id number
'               that this script is run under.
'
' RETURNS: long - number
'
Public Sub ServerInstance(nInstanceId, strServerName)
  On Error Resume Next

  Dim nVirtualServer     ' IIS Instance ID
  Dim objBrokServers     ' BrokServers
  Dim objBrokConfig      ' BrokConfig
  Dim strComment         ' Membership Server Name

  ' Assume failure
  ' ********************************************************
  nInstanceId = ""
  strServerName = ""

  ' Find out which membership server we're mapped to
  ' ********************************************************
  nVirtualServer = Request.ServerVariables("INSTANCE_ID")

  ' Create an instance of a Membership Admin Server object
  ' ********************************************************
  Set objBrokServers = CreateObject("MemAdmin.BrokServers")
  If Err.Number <> 0 Then
    Err.Clear
    Exit Sub
  End If

  ' Connect to the server instance
  ' ********************************************************
  objBrokServers.MappedTo "W3SVC", nVirtualServer, nInstanceId, strServerName
  If Err.Number <> 0 Then
    Err.Clear
    Exit Sub
  End If
End Sub

' ********************************************************
' Example Use
' ********************************************************
Dim nMemServerID
Dim strMemServerName
Call ServerInstance(nMemServerID, strMemServerName)
If nMemServerID > 0 Then
  Response.Write "This web is bound to Membership Server #" & nMemServerID
  Response.Write " (" & strMemServerName & ")"
Else
  Response.Write "Unable to determine the server mappings."
End If
%>
</FONT>
</BODY>
</HTML>
```

Whereas the `MappedTo()` method tells us which Membership Server a particular IIS 4.0 web (or other service) is mapped to, the `MapToBroker()` method allows us to map a Membership Server to an IIS 4.0 web (or other service) programmatically.

The MapToBroker() Method

The `MapToBroker()` method allows for Membership Servers to be mapped to services programmatically. If we know the name of the service to be mapped to the Membership Server, i.e. `W3SVC` for the web, and the service instance ID, i.e. `Request.ServerVariables("INSTANCE_ID")`, and finally the id of the Membership Server, we have all the information we need to map a Membership Server to an IIS 4.0 web.

The functionality of mapping a Membership Server to a service – usually Internet Information Server 4.0 – is provided through the MMC, which we reviewed in Chapter 8:

The same functionality is also provided through the `PMAdmin.vbs` tool, discussed in Appendix B.

The parameter list for the `MapToBroker()` method is as follows:

❑ **bszServiceName** – The service name to which we want to map a Membership Server. The service that will most often be mapped is the W3SVC or Internet Information Server 4.0 service.

❑ **lVirtServId** – The numeric id of the service to be mapped – this number corresponds to the `Request.ServerVariables("INSTANCE_ID")`.

❑ **lVirtBrokId** – The ID of the Membership Server to map.

Code Sample – SetMapping() Method

```
<HTML>
<BODY BGCOLOR=WHITE>
<FONT FACE=ARIAL SIZE=3>
<B>
IBrokServers - MapToBroker()
</B>
<HR SIZE=1>
</FONT>
<FONT FACE=ARIAL SIZE=2>
<%
' ************************************************************
' FUNCTION:    SetMapping
'
' PURPOSE:     Calls the broker MapToBroker method of the
'              IBrokServer interface. This method has
'              been redefined for ASP - the original is
'              in PMAdmin.vbs
'
' PARAMETERS:
'              strServiceName - Name of the service to be
'                               mapped to the Membership
'                               Server (i.e. - W3SVC)
'
'              lServiceInstance - The service instance number
'                                 of the service to be mapped
```

```
'                              (i.e. - INSTANCE_ID)
'
'               lVirtServId - The service instance number of
'                           the membership server to map
'
' RETURNS:       True - success / False - failure
'
Function SetMapping(strServiceName, lServiceInstance, lVirtServId)
  On Error Resume Next

  ' Assume failure
  ' ****************************
  SetMapping = False

  ' Create broker object
  ' ****************************
  Set objBroker = Server.CreateObject("MemAdmin.BrokServers")
  If Err.Number <> 0 Then
    Err.Clear
    Exit Function
  End If

  Call objBroker.MapToBroker(strServiceName, lServiceInstance, lVirtServId )
  If Err.Number <> 0 Then
    Err.Clear
    Exit Function
  Else
    SetMapping = True
  End If
End Function


' *********************************************************
' Example Use
' *********************************************************
Dim blnMapService
Dim lServiceID
Dim lMemServID

lServiceID = Request.ServerVariables("INSTANCE_ID")
lMemServID = 2

' Map this web to the following Membership Server
' **************************************************
blnMapService = SetMapping("W3SVC", lServiceID, lMemServID)

If blnMapService = True Then
  Response.Write "Mapped this web to the Membership Server"
Else
  Response.Write "Unable to map this web to the Membership Server"
End If
%>
</FONT>
</BODY>
</HTML>
```

IBrokConfig

The `IBrokConfig` interface provides the methods and properties for viewing and changing the configuration information for the Membership Authentication system. Many methods and properties are defined by this interface, which we'll access through the ProgID of `MemAdmin.BrokConfig`. We'll only look at three of the properties exposed by `MemAdmin.BrokConfig`, starting with the `GetConfig()` method.

The GetConfig() Method

To use `MemAdmin.BrokConfig`, we first have to specify the Membership Server instances to view. To do this, we use the `GetConfig()` method. The `GetConfig()` method accepts one parameter, `lVirtServId`:

- ❑ **lVirtServId** – The service instance id of the Membership Server to which to bind the `MemAdmin.BrokConfig` object. We can programmatically determine this from the context of an ASP page, shown below.

Code Sample – Programmatically Determine the lVirtServId

To programmatically determine the **lVirtServId** parameter use the `MappedTo()` method of the `MemAdmin.BrokServers` object:

```
<HTML>
<BODY BGCOLOR=WHITE>
<FONT FACE=ARIAL SIZE=3>
<B>
IBrokConfig - GetConfig
</B>
<HR SIZE=1>
</FONT>
<FONT FACE=ARIAL SIZE=2>
<%
On Error Resume Next

Dim nVirtualServer      ' IIS Instance ID
Dim objBrokServers      ' BrokServers
Dim objBrokConfig' BrokConfig
Dim nVirtBrokId         ' ID of broker value
Dim strComment          ' extra

' Find out which membership server we're mapped to
' *******************************************************
nVirtualServer = Request.ServerVariables("INSTANCE_ID")

' Create an instance of a Membership Admin Server object
' *******************************************************
Set objBrokServers = CreateObject("MemAdmin.BrokServers")
If Err.Number <> 0 Then
  Response.Write "Unable to create BrokServer"
  Response.End
End If

' Connect to the server instance
' *******************************************************
objBrokServers.MappedTo "W3SVC", nVirtualServer, lVirtBrokId, strComment
```

```
' User membership broker to determine BaseDN
' **********************************************************
Set objBroker = CreateObject("MemAdmin.BrokConfig")
If Err.Number <> 0 Then
  Response.Write "Unable to create BrokConfig"
  Response.End
End If

' Display lVirtBrokId
' **********************************************************
Response.Write "The Membership Server instance id is: " & lVirtBrokId
%>
</FONT>
</BODY>
</HTML>
```

The `MappedTo()` method returns the `lVirtBrokId` variable with a value. After creating the `MemAdmin.BrokConfig`, you can then pass the `lVirtBrokId` value as the parameter for `GetConfig()`:

```
' Get the configuration information
' **********************************************************
objBroker.GetConfig(lVirtBrokID)
```

We'll be using the above code again and again in the rest of our discussion of `MemAdmin.BrokConfig`. You've just learned 99% of all you need to know to use the `MemAdmin.BrokConfig` object. Next, let's use this information to determine the BaseDn, port, and finally the server that the Membership Server is on.

The bszBaseDN Property

In Chapter 8's *Advanced Concepts* area, we used the `PMAdmin.vbs` tool to change the base distinguished name (BaseDN) value for a Membership Server. To do this, `PMAdmin.vbs` used `MemAdmin.BrokConfig`. Although we're not going to look at how to change the BaseDN programmatically, we will look at how you can discover the BaseDN programatically.

The ability to discover the BaseDN programmatically allows for us to always find the root container from where members are authenticated or stored. We could then modify our `DirectoryBind()` method, or any other method that has dependencies upon the location of a member, to use the BaseDN value. Let's see how we can programmatically determine this value:

Code Sample – bszBaseDN Property

```
<HTML>
<BODY BGCOLOR=WHITE>
<FONT FACE=ARIAL SIZE=3>
<B>
IBrokConfig - bszBaseDN
</B>
<HR SIZE=1>
</FONT>
<FONT FACE=ARIAL SIZE=2>
<%
On Error Resume Next
```

```
Dim nVirtualServer      ' IIS Instance ID
Dim objBrokServers      ' BrokServers
Dim objBrokConfig' BrokConfig
Dim nVirtBrokId         ' ID of broker value
Dim strComment          ' extra

' Find out which membership server we're mapped to
' *******************************************************
nVirtualServer = Request.ServerVariables("INSTANCE_ID")

' Create an instance of a Membership Admin Server object
' *******************************************************
Set objBrokServers = CreateObject("MemAdmin.BrokServers")
If Err.Number <> 0 Then
  Response.Write "Unable to create BrokServer"
  Response.End
End If

' Connect to the server instance
' *******************************************************
objBrokServers.MappedTo "W3SVC", nVirtualServer, lVirtBrokId, strComment

' User membership broker to determine BaseDN
' *******************************************************
Set objBroker = CreateObject("MemAdmin.BrokConfig")
If Err.Number <> 0 Then
  Response.Write "Unable to create BrokConfig"
  Response.End
End If

' Get the configuration information
' *******************************************************
objBroker.GetConfig(lVirtBrokID)

' Display the BaseDN
' *******************************************************
Response.Write objBroker.bszBaseDN
If Err.Number <> 0 Then
  Response.Write "Unable to display BaseDN"
  Response.End
End If
%>
</FONT>
</BODY>
</HTML>
```

So, after calling GetConfig(), the bszBaseDN property is available and it may be displayed. Now that we have the BaseDN, we know the default container to find members. If only we could have the port and server to the LDAP Server to build an ADsPath dynamically...Let's do that next!

The lPort Property

The lPort property represents the port number that the LDAP server listens to. We can either get or set the value for the lPort property. However, the best use of the lPort property is for dynamically discovering the port that the website is mapped to – i.e. the Membership Server. So we won't show any examples of updating the lPort value through code – to see examples of this look at the code in the PMAdmin.vbs file.

Code Sample – lPort Property

```
<HTML>
<BODY BGCOLOR=WHITE>
<FONT FACE=ARIAL SIZE=3>
<B>
IBrokConfig - lPort
</B>
<HR SIZE=1>
</FONT>
<FONT FACE=ARIAL SIZE=2>
<%
On Error Resume Next

Dim nVirtualServer        ' IIS Instance ID
Dim objBrokServers        ' BrokServers
Dim objBrokConfig         ' BrokConfig
Dim nVirtBrokId           ' ID of broker value
Dim strComment            ' extra

' Find out which membership server we're mapped to
' ******************************************************
nVirtualServer = Request.ServerVariables("INSTANCE_ID")

' Create an instance of a Membership Admin Server object
' ******************************************************
Set objBrokServers = CreateObject("MemAdmin.BrokServers")
If Err.Number <> 0 Then
  Response.Write "Unable to create BrokServer"
  Response.End
End If

' Connect to the server instance
' ******************************************************
objBrokServers.MappedTo "W3SVC", nVirtualServer, lVirtBrokId, strComment

' User membership broker to determine LDAP server and PORT
' ******************************************************
Set objBroker = CreateObject("MemAdmin.BrokConfig")
If Err.Number <> 0 Then
  Response.Write "Unable to create BrokConfig"
  Response.End
End If

' Get the configuration information so we can view
' LDAP Server properties
' ******************************************************
objBroker.GetConfig(lVirtBrokID)

' Display the LDAP Port Number
' ******************************************************
Response.Write objBroker.lPort
If Err.Number <> 0 Then
  Response.Write "Unable to display lPort"
  Response.End
End If
%>
</FONT>
</BODY>
</HTML>
```

It's very simple to find the port number, and it's just as easy to find the server name – which we'll see next.

The bszServer Property

As you may have guessed, we can determine the server programmatically. It is simply exposed as a property called `bszServer`. Rather than showing you how to determine the value, let's see how we can combine the `bszServer` and the `lPort` values into a method that enables the ASP to programmatically determine the LDAP Service to which to bind. Non-hardcoded examples such as this make moving solutions from development to production easier. However, performance is sacrificed since a objects have to be created to do the look up. In the Advanced Concepts section we'll look at some code to optimize this process a little more using application state.

To programmatically determine the LDAP Service we want we will use the `ServerAndPort()` method. The `ServerAndPort()` method returns the server name and the port number separated by a colon, e.g. `Wrox:1003`.

Code Sample – ServerAndPort() Method

```
<HTML>
<BODY BGCOLOR=WHITE>
<FONT FACE=ARIAL SIZE=3>
<B>
ServerAndPort()
</B>
<HR SIZE=1>
</FONT>
<FONT FACE=ARIAL SIZE=2>
<%
Public Function ServerAndPort()
  On Error Resume Next

  ' Assume failure
  ' ********************************************************
  ServerAndPort = ""

  Dim nVirtualServer    ' IIS Instance ID
  Dim objBrokServers    ' BrokServers
  Dim objBrokConfig     ' BrokConfig
  Dim nVirtBrokId       ' ID of broker value
  Dim strComment        ' extra

  ' Find out which membership server we're mapped to
  ' ********************************************************
  nVirtualServer = Request.ServerVariables("INSTANCE_ID")

  ' Create an instance of a Membership Admin Server object
  ' ********************************************************
  Set objBrokServers = CreateObject("MemAdmin.BrokServers")
  If Err.Number <> 0 Then
    Exit Function
  End If

  ' Connect to the server instance
  ' ********************************************************
  objBrokServers.MappedTo "W3SVC", nVirtualServer, lVirtBrokId, strComment
```

```
   ' User membership broker to determine LDAP server and PORT
   ' ***********************************************************
   Set objBroker = CreateObject("MemAdmin.BrokConfig")
   If Err.Number <> 0 Then
     Exit Function
   End If

   ' Get the configuration information so we can view
   ' LDAP Server properties
   ' ***********************************************************
   objBroker.GetConfig(lVirtBrokID)

   ' get the LDAP server and port number
   ' ***********************************************************
   If Err.Number <> 0 Then
     Exit Function
   Else
     ServerAndPort = objBroker.bszServerName & ":" & objBroker.lPort
   End If
End Function

' Example Use bind to the Membership Directory
' ***********************************************************
Dim objIADsContainer         ' IADsContainer Object
Dim strLDAPPathToRoot        ' Path to the Root of the directory

strLDAPPathToRoot = ServerAndPort()

If strLDAPPathToRoot <> "" Then
  Set objIADsContainer = GetObject("LDAP://" & strLDAPPathToRoot)
  If Err.Number <> 0 Then
    Response.Write "Unable to bind to: " & strLDAPPathToRoot
  Else
    Response.Write "Successfully bound to: " & objIADsContainer.ADsPath
  End If
End If
%>
</FONT>
</BODY>
</HTML>
```

We can use this function to bind dynamically to the Membership Directory without ever needing to explicitly write this information into our code – this adds a great deal of flexibility to our code base.

Storing the value of the `strLDAPPathToRoot` value in an ASP application state variable would be a great idea!

Membership Verify User

The Membership Verify User Object (ProgID: `Membership.VerifUsr`) provides an interface `IVerifUsr` which exposes methods for verifying user credentials and managing member cookies. Several of these methods are used for HTML Forms Authentication to validate the username and password information passed by the POST from the `FormsLogin.asp` page.

> **The Membership Verify User Object is only used for Membership Authentication.**

Several of the methods provided are also used to expire or reset/send member cookies.

The IVerifUsr Interface

The interface of the `Membership.VerifUsr` object that provides the methods we'll be looking at is `IVerifUsr`. `IVerifUsr` provides a total of 11 methods, two of which are the `OnStartPage()` and `OnEndPage()` which we're already familiar with from the `IUserObject`'s interface of the Active User Object from Chapter 9. Six of the remaining nine methods are used specifically for cookies, and the others serve the purpose of validating credentials. We won't be looking at any methods that we've already covered: for a complete list of the methods exposed, see Appendix C. The first method we'll examine is the `VerifyCredentials()` method.

The VerifyCredentials() Method

The `VerifyCredentials()` method accepts a username, password and URL (`bszUserName`, `bszPassword` and `bszUrl` respectively) as parameters. This is the same method used by the `VerifPwd.asp` that we re-wrote in Chapter 8.

> `VerifPwd.asp` – *the ASP called by the* `FormsLogin.asp` *used for HTML Forms Authentication – uses the* `VerifyCredentials()` *method to authenticate members via HTML Forms Authentication.*

Upon successful completion, the URL is returned by the `bszURL` parameter, telling the client to redirect. The `VerifyCredentials()` method will return the URL passed every time. The URL is not used for security checking or validation, but rather is just the path from where the authentication originated. The method attempts to bind as the member whose credentials are passed. It is important to note that `bszURL` has no effect on whether or not the authentication succeeds.

Here's the parameter list for `VerifyCredentials()`:

- ❑ **bszUserName** – The Membership Directory member attempting to be authenticated. The path to the user or member is dependent upon the BaseDN value from where authentication should occur.
- ❑ **bszPassword** – The password of the Membership Directory member attempting to be authenticated.
- ❑ **bszUrl** – `bszUrl` represents the URL from which the authentication request originated. Once the `VerifyCredentials()` method has been called, a redirect can be done to this URL.

Code Sample – VerifPwd.asp

For the code sample to demonstrate the `VerifyCredentials()` method, we'll revisit our old friend `VerifPwd.asp` from Chapter 8.

```
<%
Option Explicit
On Error resume next

' ****************************************
```

```
' Use the Membership.VerifUsr object to
' verify the Member's credentials
' **************************************

Dim objVerif
Dim strURL
Dim strUserName
Dim strPassword

' Grab passed form items
' **************************************
strUrl = Request.Form("URL")
strUsername = Request("Username")
strPassword = Request("Password")

' Create the VerifUsr object
' **************************************
Set objVerif = Server.CreateObject("Membership.verifusr.1")
If Err.Number <> 0 Then
  Response.Write "Authentication failed. Please try logging in again.<br>"
  Response.Write "The URL " & strUrl & " cannot be accessed.<br>"
  Response.Write "Use the back button on your browser to try again."
End If

' Call the VerifyCredentails method
' to validate the account
' **************************************
strUrl = objVerif.VerifyCredentials(strUsername, strPassword, strUrl)

' Handle errors or redirect
' **************************************
If (Err.Number <> 0) Or (strURL = "") Then
  Response.Write "Authentication failed. Please try logging in again.<br>"
  Response.Write "The URL " & strUrl & " cannot be accessed.<br>"
  Response.Write "Use the back button on your browser to try again."
Else
  Response.Redirect strUrl
End if
%>
```

The only case where the redirection will not occur is when there is an invalid parameter passed. Otherwise we will always be redirected to the URL requesting the HTML Forms Authentication. In the case of invalid credentials or access denied errors, the ISAPI authentication filter will trap these and attempt to re-authenticate or direct the user to an error page – most likely PrivilegedContent.asp. Next, before we start looking at the various methods used to manage member cookies, let's look at the VerifyPassword() method that can tell us whether or not the password passed by the member is valid.

The VerifyPassword() Method

The VerifyPassword() method accepts the username and password and returns either a 1 for a valid password or a 0 for an invalid username–password combination. On the surface, the functionality of VerifyPassword() and VerifyCredentials() appear similar. However, the VerifyPassword()method merely verifies whether or not a username and password is valid, whereas the VerifyCredentials() method also authenticates the member. Using the VerifyPassword() method, we can provide a way for members – or administrators – to validate username and password combinations.

The parameter values of the `VerifyPassword()` method are identical to the `VerifyCredentials()` method, except that the `bszUrl` is not required. So the parameter list is as follows:

❑ **bszUserName** – The Membership Directory member attempting to be authenticated. The path to the user or member is dependant upon the BaseDN value from where authentication should occur.

❑ **bszPassword** – The password of the Membership Directory member attempting to be authenticated.

Let's look at a code sample that uses the AUO to bind to the current member and validate the username and password – if the member does not have a password (i.e. anonymous) this script will return a message stating **Your username and password is no longer valid.** However, if the account has a valid username and password, the script will return **Valid username/password.** Remember, the AUO is able to pick up the context of the authenticated member through its `IUserObjects` `OnStartPage()` method.

Code Sample

```
<HTML>
<BODY BGCOLOR=WHITE>
<FONT FACE=ARIAL SIZE=3>
<B>
IVerifPwd - VerifyPasswords
</B>
<HR SIZE=1>
</FONT>
<FONT FACE=ARIAL SIZE=2>
<%
On Error Resume Next

Const VALID_PWD_TRUE    = 1
Const VALID_PWD_FALSE   = 0

Dim objAUO

' Create the Active User Object
' *****************************************************
Set objAUO = Server.CreateObject("Membership.UserObjects.1")
If Err.Number <> 0 Then
  Response.Write "Unable to create the AUO."
  Response.End
End If

' Create the VerifUsr object
' *****************************************************
Set objVerif = Server.CreateObject("Membership.VerifUsr.1")
If Err.Number <> 0 Then
  Response.Write "Unable to create the Verif object."
  Response.End
End If

' Verify the current user's password
' *****************************************************
blnVerif = objVerif.VerifyPassword(objAUO.cn, objAUO.userPassword)

  If blnVerif = VALID_PWD_TRUE Then
```

```
   Response.Write "Valid username/password"
 Else
   Response.Write "Your username and password is no longer valid"
 End If
%>
</FONT>
</BODY>
</HTML>
```

This script could easily be re-purposed to allow a means for members to find out the status of their account – i.e. submit username and password, and if the member is valid display the value of the accountStatus attribute. Now that we've learned how to verify the member credentials, let's look at how we manage the cookies used by the P&M system.

The IssueCookie() Method

The IssueCookie() method provides a method for writing cookies to the client machine. We use the IssueCookie() method when a member has lost their cookies (!) or the cookies' expiration date has arrived. We'll most often use the IssueCoookie() method to reset member cookies.

Here's the parameter list:

- ❑ **bszCookieName** – The bszCookieName parameter represents the name of the cookie. If we wanted to send a new MEMUSER cookie, we would pass MEMUSER as the value for this parameter.
- ❑ **bszCookieValue** – bszCookieValue represents the value we wish to set for the bszCookieName parameter. Cookies store information in a name/value pair relationship. If we wanted to set a new value for our MEMUSER cookie, we could pass in the Name property of the current user – i.e. objAUO.Name. Remember the Name property returns the relative distinguished name of the object which the IADs object points to.

The easiest and most obvious way to employ the IssueCookie() method is to create an ASP page protected by a method of authentication that requires credentials – such as Clear Text/Basic Authentication. After the member has presented their credentials we can send them their correct cookies.

Code Sample – IssueCookie() Method

```
<%
' Protect this page behind a method of authentication
' other than Automatic Cookie Authentication.
'
' If the user looses their cookies we can send them to
' this page. Once they've authenticated we can create
' an AUO that's bound to the correct user
'
' This file needs to write to the headers - don't write
' any HTML until the very end
'

On Error Resume Next

Dim objAUO
Dim objVerif
```

```
Dim strRedirect

' Grab the redirect path if passed
' ********************************************
If Request.QueryString("Redirect") Then
  strRedirect = Request.QueryString("Redirect")
End If

' Create the AUO
' ********************************************
Set objAUO = Server.CreateObject("Membership.UserObjects.1")
If Err.Number <> 0 Then
  Response.Write "An error occured while trying to create "
  Response.Write "the AUO - Please check the mappings."
  Response.End
End If

' Create the VerifUsr
' ********************************************
Set objVerif = Server.CreateObject("Membership.VerifUsr.1")
If Err.Number <> 0 Then
  Response.Write "An error occured while trying to create "
  Response.Write "the VerifUsr."
  Response.End
End If

' Issue the correct cookies
' ********************************************
objVerif.IssueCookie "SITESERVER", "GUID=" & objAUO.Get("guid")

' Don't issue a MEMUSER to an anonymous member
' ********************************************
If objAUO.Get("guid") <> objAUO.Get("cn") Then
  objVerif.IssueCookie "MEMUSER", objAUO.name
End If

' Redirect?
' ********************************************
If Len(strRedirect) <> 0 Then
  Response.Redirect strRedirect
Else
  Response.Write "Appropriate cookies written for "
  Response.Write "member: " & objAUO.Get("cn")
End If
%>
```

Now that we've learned how to write cookies, let's take a look at how to remove them.

The CancelCookie() Method

Just as the IssueCookie() method allows us to issue new cookies, the CancelCookie() method allows us to remove cookies. If we pass the name of the cookie we wish to delete, the CancelCookie() method will tell the browser to delete the cookie – values and all. The CancelCookie() method is especially useful for the InvalidCookie.asp discussed in Chapter 8. Additionally, if you wanted to provide a mechanism for a member to 'sign-off' from their account, CancelCookie() would be used to remove the SITESERVER and MEMUSER cookies.

The `InvalidCookie.asp` is displayed to a member whenever the ISAPI AuthFilter finds a SITESERVER cookie that it cannot recognize – i.e. corrupted – or contains information for a member that no longer exists. Since we want to minimize the frequency of errors that users receive, we can modify the `InvalidCookie.asp` to first delete all SITESERVER site-specific cookies (we can't touch cookies on the user's machine that don't belong to us). Then, we'll redirect to a roaming profile page where we present the user with the opportunity to allow the system to write a new cookie – a.k.a. a roaming user profile (we'll expand upon this in Chapter 14) – if so desired. This method takes one parameter, `bszCoookieName`:

❑ **bszCookieName** – The `bszCookieName` property represents the name of the cookie to be removed from the browser. If we wanted to remove the MEMUSER and SITESERVER cookies we would pass these names as parameter values.

Code Sample – InvalidCookie.asp

The code sample we'll look at for this method is a reworked `InvalidCookie.asp`.

```
<%
' **********************************
' InvalidCookie
' **********************************

' Accepts passed values as well
' **********************************
If Request.QueryString("Redirect") <> "" Then
  strRedirect = Request.QueryString("Redirect")
ElseIf Request.Form("Redirect") <> "" Then
  strRedirect = Request.Form("Redirect")
Else
  ' Previous URL
  ' **********************************
  strRedirect = Request.QueryString()
End If

' Remove all Site Server member cookies
' **********************************
If RemoveSSCookies() = True Then
  Response.Redirect strRedirect

' If we had an 'issue'
' **********************************
Else
  Response.Write "<TITLE>Incorrect Personalization Information</TITLE>"
  Response.Write "<BODY bgcolor=#FFFFFF>"
  Response.Write "<H2><IMG SRC=""/_mem_bin/ERROR.GIF"">"
  Response.Write "Incorrect Personalization Information.</H2>"
  Response.Write "The site cannot recognize the cookie "
  Response.Write "stored on your machine to identify "
  Response.Write "you to the site.<P>Plese close your "
  Response.Write "browser and remove all cookies."
End If

' **********************************************************
' METHOD:     RemoveSSCookies()
'
' PURPOSE:    Removes all cookies - but
'             still behaves if we encounter
'             an error
```

```
'
' RETURNS:    Boolean true - success / false - failure
'
Public Function RemoveSSCookies()
  On Error Resume Next

  Dim objVerif
  Dim strCookie

  ' Assume failure
  ' **********************************
  RemoveSSCookies = False

  ' Create the VerifyUser object
  ' **********************************
  Set objVerif = Server.CreateObject("Membership.VerifUsr.1")
  If Err.Number <> 0 Then
    Exit Function
  End If

  ' Enumerate through all cookies
  ' but only delete P&M specific cookies
  ' **********************************
  For each strCookie in Request.Cookies()
    If (strCookie = "SITESERVER") OR (strCookie = "MEMUSER") Then
      ' Use the CancelCookie() method
      ' to remove this cookie
      ' **********************************
      objVerif.CancelCookie(CStr(strCookie))
    End If

    If Err.Number <> 0 Then
      Exit Function
    End If
  Next

  ' Looks good
  ' **********************************
  RemoveSSCookies = True
End Function
%>
```

This reworked `InvalidCookie.asp` deletes the cookies that cause the ISAPI AuthFilter to redirect to the `InvalidCookie.asp` page and redirects back to the page that caused the error. Since the page causing the error apparently supports Anonymous Cookie Authentication (otherwise, how would we be at the `InvalidCookie.asp`?), we should create a new valid cookie for the user in the ou=AnonymousUsers container. We can do this, or better yet, we can code in an ASP application variable (or hardcode it into the `InvalidCookie.asp`) to redirect the ASP page, such that the member is reauthenticated. After the member is reauthenticated, your application will have the correct member credentials. We'll do this in Chapter 14 when we take a look at the `RoamingProfile.asp`, that allows members' cookies to be reissued.

IssueCookieToNewUser() Method

The `IssueCookieToNewUser()` method is used to send the SITESERVER and MEMUSER cookies to a user that has been created programmatically. However, if the member already exists the GUID value set for the SITESERVER cookie does not match the member's GUID. There's just one parameter here:

❑ **bszUserName** – The value to be set in the MEMUSER value of the new cookie to be written to the user's browser.

`IssueCookieToNewUser()` is a misleading method, don't let it confuse you. The following code sample demonstrates how an existing member can't use the `IssueCookiesToNewUser()` method. The method doesn't return the GUID value that the member has, but instead creates a new GUID (which is the return value of the method).

Code Sample – IssueCookiesToNewUser() Method

```
<%
On Error Resume Next
' Create the AUO
' ************************************************************
Set objAUO = Server.CreateObject("Membership.UserObjects.1")
If Err.Number <> 0 Then
  Response.Write "Unable to create the AUO."
  Response.End
End If

strMember = objAUO.cn

' Create the VerifUsr object
' ************************************************************
Set objVerif = Server.CreateObject("Membership.VerifUsr.1")
If Err.Number <> 0 Then
  Response.Write "Unable to create the Verif object."
  Response.End
End If

' Grab the different GUID values
' ************************************************************
strCookie = objVerif.IssueCookiesToNewUser(strMember)
userguid = objAUO.Get("GUID")
%>
<HTML>
<BODY BGCOLOR=WHITE>
<FONT FACE=ARIAL SIZE=3>
<B>
IVerifPwd - IssueCookiesToNewUser
</B>
<HR SIZE=1>
</FONT>
<FONT FACE=ARIAL SIZE=2>
<%
Response.Write "New cookie issued: " & strCookie
Response.Write "<P>"
Response.Write "Current member's cookie: " & userGuid
%>
</FONT>
</BODY>
</HTML>
```

To properly use this method, we would have to run it to retrieve the value of the GUID, and then replace the member's GUID in the Membership Directory. If we don't do this we'll get bounced to the `InvalidCookie.asp` since our cookie and the member's GUID are not in sync. We'll look at a better solution in Chapter 14, in which we move the anonymous member to the ou=members container without having to create new GUIDs for the member or the MEMUSER cookie; we saw a little of this in Chapter 9 with the `MoveHere()` method of the `IADsContainer`.

IssueRecentChangesCookie() Method

We read about the caching that takes place in the Membership Server in Chapter 3. The Membership Server caches all information about an object that we have bound to in the Membership Directory – such as a member. Once we've bound to an `IADs` object and called either `GetInfo()` or `Get()` on an item the cache contains the values of the object. If any changes are made to this cache – i.e. `Put()` – the data is changed in the cache, but is not reflected in the Membership Directory until the `SetInfo()` method is called.

Large scale sites that serve content from multiple machines each with their own Membership Server behind a DNS round-robin can't guarantee what machine the user will be sent to for the next request. Several Membership Servers on these machines can each have their own cache with valid data. However, if the `SetInfo()` is done on one machine, how do the other Membership Servers know that the data in their cache is no longer valid? This is done through a special cookie called **MemRightsChanged**. If a user has a `MemRightsChanged` cookie, the Membership Server knows to refresh the ADSI cache. A `MemRightsChanged` cookie is issued by default whenever a `SetInfo()` is performed:

However, if we aren't using the AUO to do the `Put()` but instead have done a direct ADSI modification – such as through the `LDAPNamespace` object – we need to issue this cookie ourselves. The `IssueRecentChangesCookie()` method allows us to force this cookie to be sent to the browser.

There's just a single parameter to `IssueRecentChangesCookie()`:

❑   **bszUserName** – The name of the membership user for whom the MemRightsChanged cookie should be issued for.

Code Sample – IssueRecentChangesCookie() Method

We can easily force this cookie by calling the `IssueRecentChangesCookie()` method with the value of the current AUO's cn:

```
<%
On Error Resume Next

' Create the AUO
' *********************************************************
Set objAUO = Server.CreateObject("Membership.UserObjects.1")
If Err.Number <> 0 Then
  Response.Write "Unable to create the AUO."
  Response.End
End If

strMember = objAUO.cn

' Create the VerifUsr object
' *********************************************************
Set objVerif = Server.CreateObject("Membership.VerifUsr.1")
If Err.Number <> 0 Then
  Response.Write "Unable to create the Verif object."
  Response.End
End If

' Issue the MemRightsChanged Cookie
' *********************************************************
objVerif.IssueRecentChangesCookie(strMember)
%>
```

As I've said throughout the book, everything that is done by the Membership system can be done programmatically – including issuing cookies.

Advanced Concepts

If you intend to provide secured access to any resources through ASP, you should never expose your username and password. This is also true for secured binds to the Membership Directory. Although we'll go into more detail as to security in the next chapter, the following is a simple idea that anyone can implement to help secure a site.

Building Security.SecureInfo

Security.SecureInfo is a ProgID for a simple COM object that you can easily build to help strengthen the security of your site. Rather than storing the username and password values directly in an ASP, where they run the risk of being exposed by any user that has access to the ASP, compile them down into a DLL. The DLL, since it is compiled, provides a mechanism so that usernames and passwords cannot be easily guessed. By exposing two properties, username and password, and hardcoding the values of a username and password into this DLL, data can only be retrieved when the ASP page is executed.

Ideally, the object should be instantiated in the global.asa, and exposed as a variable that has application level scope throughout the site. My suggested approach is for the Membership Directory, and for strict delegation, which we'll talk about in the next chapter. Here's what the code could look like:

Code Sample – Security.SecureInfo (VB Class)

```
' Recompile for your own needs if IIS crashes, or your ASP code is exposed
' the username and password stored in this VB COM object is unaccessible
' *********************************
Public bszUser
Public bszPassword

Private Sub Class_Initialize()
    ' Set the value for the user and password
    ' to use for secured binds
    ' *********************************
    bszUser = "cn=Administrator, ou=Members, o=Wrox"
    bszPassword = "password"
End Sub
```

When a username or password needed to be used to make Administrative level modifications in the Membership Directory, such as adding a member to a group, we would see something similar to the following in our ASP code (using `DirectoryBind()` from the beginning of the chapter).

Code Sample – Sample.asp

You need to add the function definitions for `DirectoryBind()` and `ServerAndPort()`:

```
<SNIP>
On Error Resume Next

Dim blnBindSuccess
Dim strLDAPPath
Dim objIADs

' Do we have application state yet?
' *********************************
If IsObject(Application("SecureInfo")) Then
   Set SecureInfo = Application("SecureInfo")
Else
   ' Create the SecurityInfo object
   ' *********************************
   Set SecureInfo = Server.CreateObject("Security.SecureInfo")

   ' Add to application state
   ' *********************************
   Application.Lock
     Set Application("SecureInfo") = SecureInfo
   Application.Unlock
End If

' Use broker objects to bind to the Membership
' Directory this ASP is mapped to
' *********************************
strLDAPPath = "LDAP://" & ServerAndPort()

' Bind securly to the Membership Directory
' using context from SecureInfo application object
' *********************************
blnBindSuccess = DirectoryBind(SecureInfo.bszUser, _
                              SecureInfo.bszPassword, _
```

```
                            strLDAPPath, _
                            objIADs)

' Write ADsPath
' **********************************
Response.Write objIADs.ADsPath
</SNIP>
```

> You'll notice that we're also using the `ServerAndPort()` method to determine at runtime the LDAP namespace path to bind with.

If the code source to this ASP page is breached, the hacker would not be able to ascertain the LDAP server or port number. Additionally, the username and password used to access the LDAP is secured in our COM object.

Summary

In this chapter, we've taken a look at some of the other key objects installed with Site Server 3.0 Personalization and Membership.

❑ We started by examining two ADSIs you can use with the Membership Directory. We've used IADsOpenDSObject() in the previous chapter in the discussion of authentication, but here we explained what the ADSI did. It's important to remember that although there is a number of ADSIs, most are reserved for Windows NT 5.0 Active Directory.

❑ After exploring the ADSIs, we turned our attention to the `Membership.MembershipInfo` object that provided a method for converting an ADsPath to a DN. We examined how this is useful for working with groups, since are containers that container MemberOf objects used to represent group members. Additionally, we learned that the `DNToADsPath()` method only worked if the LDAP Service is on port 389 – the default LDAP port. We then provided some work-arounds for this problems, and showed how we can bind with the DN just as easily.

❑ Next, we introduced the `MemAdmin.BrokServers` and `MemAdmin.BrokConfig` objects used to return values about the Membership Server. We learned how you can programmatically modify IIS 4.0 authentication methods, and how to determine the server and port where the LDAP Service is available from.

❑ After the MemAdmin object, we discussed the Membership Verify User object, which provides methods for managing member authentication settings for cookies and HTML Forms Authentication. We explored how we can use these methods to better manage our members.

❑ Finally, in the Advanced Concepts we explored how we can tie some of the different features together, such as secure binding and programmatically determining the server and port of the LDAP.

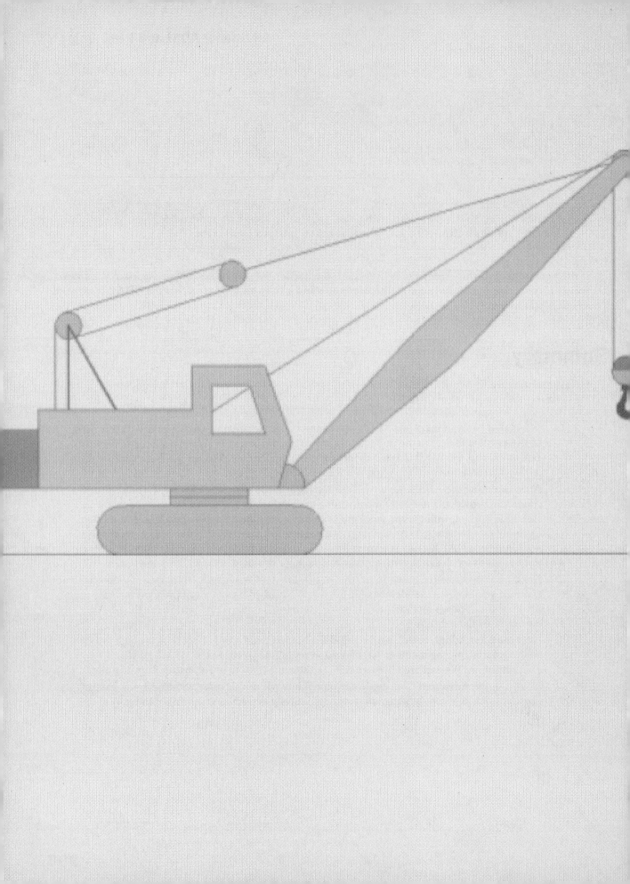

13

Directory and File System Security

When I bought a new car this year, I was given *two* different utilities to manage my car's security – a set of keys and a keyless entry remote. These two access methods accomplish similar (but not identical) actions. With the keyless remote, there are three buttons. With the first button, I can unlock only the driver's door; or clicking twice, I can unlock all the doors. With the second button, I can lock all the doors by clicking once, and turn on the alarm by clicking twice. The third button is a special panic button that will start the alarm in case of emergencies.

Using the keys I can open the driver and passenger doors, trunk and rear hatch, and start the car. I can't do all the fancy things I can do with the remote keyless entry, but I *can* do the most important thing – start the car!

Site Server Membership Security also uses keys. Site Server keys come in two forms: **Windows NT authentication** and **Membership authentication**. Windows NT authentication is like the main set of car keys – with a Windows NT security account, users can be allowed or denied access to the system, and to the system's resources.

Membership authentication is more like the keyless entry remote, which still needs in the car key in order to start the car. A membership-authenticated user still needs to use a Windows NT security account either to gain or to be denied access to systems resources (even though the user may not realize it). This is accomplished through impersonation, in which a single Windows NT security account can be used by *all* the Membership accounts and permissions to requested resources are granted or denied dynamically.

This chapter is the cornerstone for understanding Site Server Membership and providing secure access to resources. We've tackled security topics elsewhere in the book, but we've made regular references to the material in this chapter. We'll take a very detailed look at just how Site Server Membership, file system, and directory security are affected by the various settings and options that can be configured for Site Server Personalization and Membership.

Here's what we'll be covering in this chapter.

- ❑ **Architecture Security.** We'll start this chapter by examining the security between the various pieces of the architecture. First, we'll look at how applications (such as IIS 4.0) connect to the LDAP Services from the network. After examining the network-to-LDAP connection, we'll look at the LDAP-to-Membership Directory security. We'll look at how an LDAP Service denies access to a specific account or IP address.

- ❑ **Basic Windows NT Security.** We'll examine the basics of Windows NT security, focusing mainly upon Access Control Lists and Access Control Entries. We'll give a couple of code samples that modify Windows NT ACLs and ACEs programmatically.

- ❑ **Membership Directory Security.** After discussing Windows NT security, we'll turn our attention to the Site Server Membership Directory. We'll examine how the Membership Directory also uses the concept of ACLs and ACEs, and we'll provide more code for modifying ACLs programmatically.

- ❑ **Authentication Methods and NT Resource Access.** Here we'll look at how Windows NT authentication and Membership authentication gain access to Windows NT resources. In particular, we'll focus on the aspects of Membership authentication.

- ❑ **Advanced Concepts.** Finally, in the *Advanced Concepts* section we'll briefly examine how to support members and groups for domains in Membership Authentication.

As we've seen throughout the book, there are two important and distinct concepts that raise their heads time and again. The first is **authentication** – the process of validating information used to identify a security principal. In the following discussion, the most common security principal we'll refer to is a **user** (under Windows NT authentication) or a **member** (under Membership authentication). The information that validates a user or member is a username–password combination. If the username and password are valid, we consider the security principal authenticated; if they're invalid, the security principal is denied access.

The second concept is **authorization** – the process of deciding whether the security principal is allowed to access the requested resource.

In terms of Personalization and Membership, one important difference between these two security concepts is in the way they're handled. Authentication can be handled via Windows NT authentication *or* via Membership authentication; however, authorization is *always* handled by the Windows NT security system.

OK. Let's begin our discussion of Site Server Personalization and Membership security, starting with a discussion of architectural security.

Architecture Security

In the early chapters of the book we looked at LDAP, the Membership Directory, and the n-tier architecture of Site Server Personalization and Membership. However, the discussion of how to secure the P&M architecture has been deferred until now.

Security – as it relates to the Internet or to any n-tier architecture – is a complex beast, and involves thinking about both presentation-to-business logic security *and* business logic-to-data storage security. We won't be discussing presentation security between a web browser and your business logic (i.e. SSL or certificates). If you're interested in that, I recommend Alex Homer's book *Professional ASP Techniques for Webmasters* (Wrox Press, 1-861-00-1797) – he covers SSL and certificates in detail as they relate to the browser and the business logic, from an IIS perspective.

However, we will look at the different levels of security between the network and the LDAP Service, and between the LDAP Service and the data storage layer (SQL Server). We'll also look at how we can use blacklisting to control account security policies. Let's start our discussion with the communication between the network and the LDAP Service.

Securing Network–LDAP Communications

We've already (see Chapter 12) had a glimpse of why the IADsOpenDSObject ADSI interface is important. It allows us to bind securely to the Membership Directory as a member. Secure Sockets Layer may be used to encrypt data as it moves across the wire, but this tends to cause a dramatic reduction in the efficiency of the application – this latency is due to the encryption and decryption steps and increased network packet size.

In some cases, the trade-off doesn't pay – that is, the reduction in efficiency isn't worth the extra security. Of course, username/password information is important in some cases – for example, in a banking environment – and then, SSL or certificates should be used stringently. However, when username and password information isn't absolutely critical, you can design your site's security model to use a **loose authentication/strict delegation** architecture only.

Information that is not highly sensitive can be loosely authenticated (e.g. via Clear Text/Basic Authentication, where username and password information is passed in the clear), and strictly delegated (that is, by using another account to perform the desired actions). This architecture allows you to scale the site easily and efficiently, while also protecting sensitive actions. We need to discuss the concept of loose authentication and strict delegation in more detail.

Loose Authentication

We'll use the term **loose authentication** to cover all authentication methods other than DPA or NTLM. We'll use this term to reflect the fact that authentication data sent by one of these methods could be sniffed out using a **packet sniffer**.

Sniffing Packets

Sniffing packets is actually quite easy, but it's finding the data you're looking for that's difficult. Monitoring all the packets sent to a particular server requires that every packet is searched; it also requires knowledge of what the username/password combination is (or what it should look like).

So how is it done, and how does it affect you? We can learn more by looking at a clever little tool called Network Monitor. The tool is available as a standalone utility; there's also a more powerful version (available as part of Microsoft Systems Management Server) which allows you to look at network packets sent to machines other than your own.

We're not going to discuss how to configure or use Network Monitor; I'll leave that up to you. However, we will look at some of the resulting packets sniffed between a client machine and a web server machine. (A little later we'll look at network sniffs between the LDAP and SQL Server.)

The following screenshot shows a Network Monitor session, where packets pass between a client and a web server (the actual capture was a Membership authentication type, HTML Forms Authentication login):

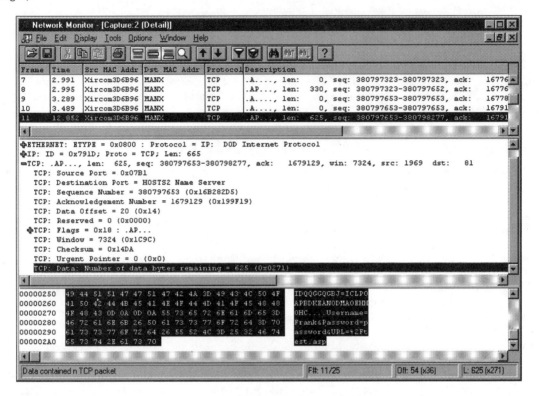

As you can see, the username and password (Frank and Password respectively) are passed in the packet. If a third party uses a packet sniffer to gain access to this information, they could then gain access to Frank's account in the Membership Directory, and cause havoc!

HTML Forms use POST, rather than GET, so data is sent in the header rather than along with the URL. If this authentication data were sent via GET, it would be just as easy – if not easier – to secure.

Surprisingly, we can repeat this sniff for any non-HTTP scenario that accesses the Membership Directory with a GetObject() call from a machine separate from the LDAP Service. In another example, consider a Visual Basic application on a client machine, that is binding to the Administrator account and setting the account's password. In this example, the Membership Directory has not been secured and this modification is done anonymously:

```vb
Private Sub Form_Load()
  Dim objIADs As Object

  Const LDAP_PATH = "LDAP://manx:1003/o=Wrox/ou=Members/cn=Administrator"

  Set objIADs = GetObject(LDAP_PATH)
  objIADs.Put "userPassword", "password"
  objIADs.SetInfo
End Sub
```

The following screenshot shows a Network Monitor session that sniffs the packet:

Notice how many packets are actually sent for this to occur – nine! Imagine trying to monitor a single server, and trying to sniff all packets, then searching for the values you are looking for!

Again, you can clearly see the credentials passed in the clear. However, this time it's the distinguished name of the member, the userPassword attribute, and the userPassword value. Obviously, it's not good. If you wanted to add Frank to a new group, or change a member's password, would you accept this security problem? Of course not!

Strict Delegation

In the above, ordinary users had been given the power to make security-related modifications. When given the opportunity, I prefer to employ a broker or proxy account to perform security-related tasks such as adding a member to a group, or changing a member's password. I refer to this as **strict delegation**. Let's look at the two examples from the previous section again.

Wrapping Functionality into a COM Object

In the first example, a server-side Visual Basic COM object would be a much more secure way of adding Frank to a group. Our COM object would wrap the functionality of adding a member to a group, and use the security context of a member that had the rights to add Frank to the appropriate group. Of course, the security context and privileges would be dependent upon how the Membership Directory is secured – we'll look at that a little later.

Although Frank's username and password could still easily be discovered, the system's security could not be as easily compromised.

The ADS_SECURE_AUTHENTICATION Parameter

How do we make our second sample more secure? There's a special ADSI interface, the IADsOpenDSObject, that we've already mentioned in Chapter 12. The IADsOpenDSObject interface has a method, OpenDSObject(), that allows us to bind to a Membership Directory as a specific member. OpenDSObject() also allows us to pass a parameter, ADS_SECURE_AUTHENTICATION (hex code 0x1) that specifies how the bind should be performed. Specifying this parameter allows ADSI to perform a secured bind to a directory (in our case, the Membership Directory).

In Chapter 11, the Windows NT NetShow Services authentication plug-in uses ADS_SECURE_AUTHENTICATION to bind as the ProxyUser specified in the Windows Registry:

```
HRESULT CLDAPAccess::InitLDAP(WCHAR * pszLDAPServer,
                             WCHAR * pszProxyUser,
                             WCHAR * pszProxyPassword)
{
    CComBSTR bstrLDAPServer( pszLDAPServer );
    CComBSTR bstrProxyUser( pszProxyUser );
    CComBSTR bstrProxyPassword( pszProxyPassword );

    HRESULT hr;

    if (pszProxyUser == NULL)
    {
      hr = ADsGetObject(bstrLDAPServer,
                        IID_IADsContainer,
                        (void**)&m_pIADsContainer);
    }
    else
      {

        hr = ADsOpenObject(bstrLDAPServer,
                           bstrProxyUser,
                           bstrProxyPassword,
                           ADS_SECURE_AUTHENTICATION,
                           IID_IADsContainer,
                           (void**)&m_pIADsContainer);
    }

    return hr;
}
```

In fact, we could perform the same logic in ASP:

```
Public Function InitLDAP(pszLDAPServer, pszProxyUser, pszProxyPassword, pobjIADs)

  Const ADS_SECURE_AUTHENTICATION = &h1

  If Len(pszProxyUser) = "" Then
    ' Perform an anonymous bind
    ' ***************************
    pobjLDAP = GetObject(pszLDAPServer)
  Else
```

```
' Perform an secured bind
' ****************************
pobjLDAP = GetObject("LDAP:")
Set pobjLDAP = pobjLDAP.GetObject(pszLDAPServer, pszProxyUser, _
                              pszProxyPassword, ADS_SECURE_AUTHENTICATION)
    End If
End Function
```

The ProxyUser has the necessary permissions in the Membership Directory to view the passwords of other members. When these other passwords are passed, they are passed in clear text – that is, they're available through the packet sniffer. Although these passwords are passed in the open, and could possibly be obtained, the ProxyUser and ProxyPassword are never made available.

Now that we've looked at how to better secure the communication between the network and the LDAP Service, let's see how security is provided between the LDAP Service and the Membership Directory.

Securing LDAP–Membership Directory Communications

When you're running your P&M site in a real-life production environment, then you're likely to be using SQL Server to represent the Membership Directory. Communication between the LDAP Service and SQL Server is fairly secure, and should only cause concern if the LDAP Service is accessing a SQL Server across the Internet.

Security is provided by two keys – the PEkey and the KEkey. These keys are used together to encrypt passwords in the SQL Server database. We'll look at the PEkey first, and then see where the KEkey comes into the equation.

> Note that this section only applies to Membership Directories running under Membership authentication. Windows NT authentication uses the highly secure Windows NT Security subsystem.

The Password Encryption Key (PEkey)

The **Password Encryption Key** (or **PEkey**) is a randomly-generated 42-character hexadecimal value, that is used to encrypt the userPassword attribute of a member. The encrypted value of the userPassword attribute is then stored in the Membership Directory. This encryption provides two levels of security – security in the Membership Directory, and security across the Wire. Let's explore these security features.

Security in the Membership Directory

If an unwelcome visitor succeeds in accessing the Membership Directory database, then he might be able to obtain members' userPassword attributes. However, in order to decrypt the password, the intruder would need the PEKey. So while the visitor can gain access to attributes and members, he can't impersonate a member's security context because he can't obtain an unencrypted version of the userPassword attribute.

We can better understand this by following an example, in which we attempt to view a userPassword attribute in a Membership Directory that uses Microsoft Access. First, we'll determine the member whose userPassword attribute we wish to view; do this by opening the Object_Lookup table and finding the member. In this example, we'll use the cn=Administrator member:

We can make a note of the administrator's i_DSID value – in this example, it's 65. Next, we'll open the attributes table:

From this table we'll look up userPassword in the vc_Name column, and take a note of its i_AID value – in this case, it's 41. Finally, we open the Object_Attributes table, and search for the i_DSID value that represents the member and the i_AID of the userPassword attribute (in this example, 65 and 41 respectively):

Found them? In this row, the userPassword attribute for the cn=Administrator account is found in the vc_Val column. However, we can only see the *encrypted* value of the administrator's userPassword attribute – in the example above, it's **58549148BF672F823**. From this alone, we can't deduce that the administrator's password is (rather unimaginatively) password. Thus, we're unable to impersonate the administrator.

> *If access is gained to your Membership Directory database, you're in big trouble anyhow! If a 'rogue' user gains access to the database, he can always initiate a **denial of service attack**, by changing the value of the userPassword attribute, or other data. The bottom line is this: make sure your SQL Server is well secured, especially if it exposed on the Internet. One thing you should do immediately is to change the default TCP/IP port from 1433 to another value. This will help to prevent hackers from discovering your SQL Server service.*

In addition to security in the Membership Directory database, transport level security is also provided.

Security Across the Wire

When the LDAP Service makes a request for the userPassword from the Membership Directory it's actually the PEkey-encrypted value of version the userPassword that's retrieved. Moreover, when the userPassword is set, its value is also PEkey-encrypted before it is sent to the Membership Directory. Thus, the unencrypted value of the password is never sent across the wire.

Take a look at an example. The following Network Monitor session has managed to sniff a packet that has been sent across the wire. The originator was the Administrator member modifying his own password, i.e. modifiying the cn=Administrator's userPassword attribute to the new value, password:

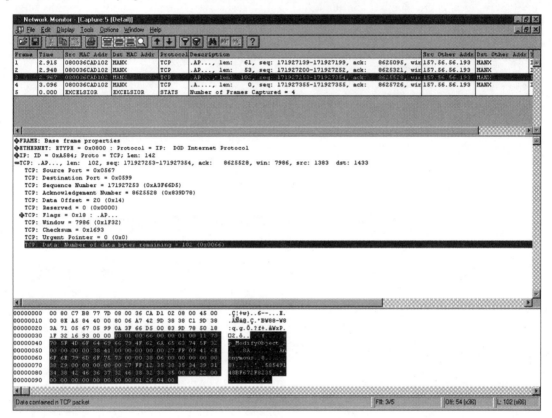

You may notice the reference to Anonymous *in this packet. This is simply the name of the user making the modification – in this case the Membership Directory is not secured, and the access was done anonymously (i.e. using* GetObject() *rather than* OpenDSObject()*).*

Notice that the packet-sniff has only captured the *encrypted* userPassword: **58549148BF672F823** – and not the password value itself. Even if a potential intruder managed to sniff the right packet, he wouldn't be able to do anything with the encrypted password information that is captured.

The Key Encryption Key (KEkey)

As we've seen, the LDAP Service prepares to send the value of the userPassword attribute by encrypting it with the PEkey. How does the Membership Directory store the PEkey? In fact, in order to secure the value of PEkey in the Membership Directory, the PEkey must *also* be encrypted – and this is done using the **Key Encryption Key** (or **KEkey**).

The value of PEkey in the Membership Directory is KEkey-encrypted. Even if an intruder manages to obtain PEkey-encrypted password and the KEkey-encrypted PEkey from the Membership Directory, he still can't decode the password without the KEkey itself. However, the KEkey value is *not* stored in the Membership Directory – it's part of the LDAP Service.

In order to see this more clearly, let's look at how the PEkey and KEkey fit into the process of authenticating a member:

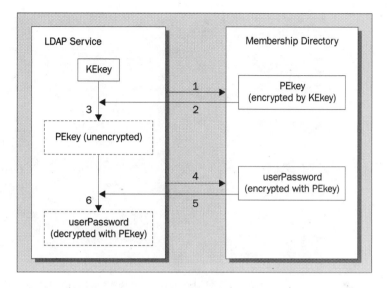

When the LDAP Service starts, it requests the PEkey value from the Membership Directory (1). The KEkey-encrypted value of PEkey is returned to the LDAP Service (2). Next, the LDAP service decrypts the PEkey value, using the KEkey. Later in the session, when the LDAP Service requests the value of a userPassword attribute from the Membership Directory (4), it's the PEkey-encrypted value of the userPassword attribute that is returned (5) to the LDAP Service. Finally, the LDAP Service decrypts the userPassword value (6) using the already-decrypted PEkey.

Changing the KEkey

The KEkey value may be modified, and should be if the Membership Directory database is accessed over the Internet. Every LDAP Service installed by Site Server uses the same initial KEkey value. So, any LDAP Service could then connect to a Membership Directory database and be able to decrypt userPassword values.

The KEkey for an LDAP Service instance can be changed by using the kekey.exe command line application, found in the \Microsoft Site Server\Bin\P&M directory.

To change the KEkey, first determine the LDAP Service instance to modify. The instance number may be determined by running the PMAdmin.vbs command line utility (again, found by navigating to the Microsoft Site Server\Bin\P&M directory):

```
PMAdmin list instance
```

This command returns a list of the available LDAP Service instances running on the Windows NT Server. You must also know the name of the Membership Server, which is also returned by the above command:

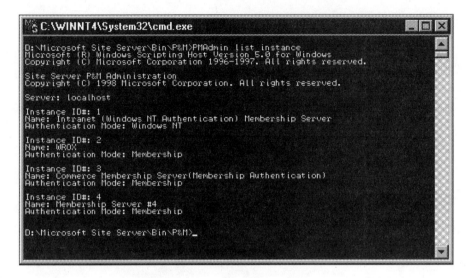

Once you have the instance ID of the appropriate LDAP Service, use the kekey.exe application. Here's the syntax you should use if you want to set a new KEkey:

```
KEkey [instance id] set [new key]
```

The [new key] parameter is a string of up to 255 characters. So an example use would look something like this:

```
KEkey 2 set 10293WROX84756
```

The LDAP Service instance then needs to be stopped and restarted for the modification to take effect. When the LDAP Service is re-started, the PEkey is re-encrypted.

If you are using multiple LDAP Service instances for the Membership Directory, each LDAP Service's KEkey must use the same KEkey value, i.e. if you change one KEkey, you must change all LDAP Service KEkey values shared by that Membership Directory.

> **When you set up a new LDAP Service, be sure to change the value of the KEkey. If you're using multiple LDAP services to service a Membership Directory, they must all have the same KEkey.**

IPDeny and AccountDeny

In Chapter 8 we discussed how a malicious user could initiate a denial of service attack by repeatedly POSTing to an Membership HTML Forms-authenticated resource. This could be done simply by determining where the HTML Form POSTed its information, and what information is required by the POST; all this of course available from the HTML code in the HTML Form.

The LDAP Service provides the ability to deny an IP address, or an account. Both the IP address and account denial settings are configured programmatically, but the functionality is already encapsulated in the PMAdmin.vbs command line tool.

Configuring IPDeny and AccountDeny

Here's how to use the PMAdmin.vbs command line tool to deny an IP address or account after a specified period of time, and to lock the account for a specified period of time. First, open up a command line session, and navigate to Microsoft Site Server\bin\P&M\. Next, determine the LDAP Service instance ID to modify, as we described in the previous section:

```
PMAdmin list instance
```

Next, check whether or not IP address denial or account denial is already activated. To do this, run the PMAdmin.vbs tool again, this time specifying the instance ID of the LDAP Service:

```
PMAdmin get LDAP /ID:[instance_id]
```

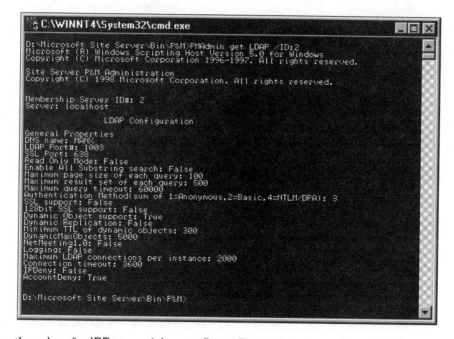

Examine the values for IPDeny and AccountDeny. True represents that the feature is activated, False represents that it's deactivated. In the above screenshot, AccountDeny is set to True – this means that if an authentication is attempted with an incorrect password in a specific time period, the account will be denied.

In order to turn the IPDeny and AccountDeny features on and off, use the PMAdmin.vbs tool again, with the following syntax:

```
PMAdmin set LDAP /ID:[instance_id] /IPDeny:[boolean]
PMAdmin set LDAP /ID:[instance_id] /AccountDeny:[boolean]
```

Here, [boolean] should be True if you're turning the feature on, and False if you're turning it off.

If you want to read more about timeout values and various other settings, see the discussion of the PMAdmin get master *command in Appendix B.*

Now it's time to turn our attention to a brief examination of Windows NT security.

Basic Windows NT Security

Later in this chapter we'll look at how you apply Windows NT security to provide authorization to resources for Personalization and Membership. But before we look at how to configure authorization, it's important to be familiar with some of the basics of Windows NT security.

We won't be looking at all of the details. However, we will be examining security as it relates to our discussion of securing resources for Personalization and Membership; and more specifically, how Windows NT Access Control Lists and Access Control Entries (ACLs and ACEs) are used. Site Server Personalization and Membership relies on Windows NT security ACLs and ACEs on the file system to authorize (i.e. grant permissions to) users and groups.

This section is not intended to be the end-all of security discussions – we simply can't cover all the possible Windows NT security scenarios here. If you want to read more about Windows NT security take a look at the Windows NT Server Resource Kit *(Microsoft Press, ISBN 1-572-31-3447) or refer to* http://www.microsoft.com/security.

ACLs and ACEs

Before we start explaining the importance of these two security items, let's formally define them. It's important that you understand the relationship between ACLs and ACEs, because these security concepts are used both in NT security and in Membership Directory security.

An **Access Control Entry** (**ACE**) is a resource descriptor used by the Windows NT Security system to allow or deny access to resources. The ACE contains a security ID (SID) and a set of access permissions (e.g. Read, Write). An **Access Control List** (**ACL**) is simply a list of ACEs. Every object (or resource) has an ACL, and a resource's ACL defines the permissions that different users can be granted when access to the resource is requested.

Before the end of the section, we'll see where security descriptors come into the equation, and how to modify ACLs and ACEs. First, let's examine the ACLs and ACEs themselves in more detail.

Access Control Lists

An ACL is a container for ACEs. A resource's ACL contains a series of ACEs, which collectively list the SIDs of users and groups, and the permissions that those users/groups have to the resource.

When a security principal (i.e. a user) requests a resource, the Windows NT security subsystem begins a search to find an ACE (in the ACL) that matches the user's SID. If a match is found, then the user is granted or denied access to the resource – depending on what access the user requested and what permissions the ACE says he's entitled to. If the user's SID can't be matched against the entries in the ACL, then access is denied.

Access to things like the machine or network, the registry, and file system, in Windows NT 4.0 are protected by ACLs. In addition, all classes, attributes and class instances in Site Server's Membership Directory are also protected by ACLs.

Some resources, such as those on the Windows NT File System, have two ACLs – a Direcretionary ACL (DACL) and a Systems ACL (SACL).

The Discretionary ACL

The most common type of ACL is the **Discretionary ACL** (or DACL). This is the type of ACL used by the Windows NT 4.0 file system (NTFS format) to verify credentials before granting access. When you modify permissions on a file system resource, for example through Windows NT Explorer, you're modifying the resource's DACL.

The Systems ACL

The second type of ACL is the **Systems Access Control List** (SACL), which provides the ability to audit certain security events per the C2-level security requirements for Windows NT system security.

> *The C2-level security requirements meet the United States' National Security Agency's (NSA's) definition of what the US Department of Defense lists as a 'secure' system. Basically, this means that all users must be held accountable for their actions, i.e. actions and actors are logged, and allows for other users to be granted access to their resources, etc.*

The SACL defines what actions should be logged to the security log file whenever a event (such as the deletion of a resource) occurs. Every object has its own SACL, that is used to log various actions by users.

Access Control Entries

Each entry in an SACL or DACL defines a set of permissions that allow or deny different types of access to a particular user or group – each of these entries is an **Access Control Entry** (ACE). It's possible that an ACL will have many ACEs for a given security principal (in this case, they are represented collectively through ORing the representative values for the permission together).

Let's take a look at some ACEs. In the screenshot below, the File Permissions dialog for a text file resource called cmlog.log shows that the resource has two ACEs:

The first allows 'read' and 'execute' permissions (but not 'delete') for the security principal Everyone, and the second allows 'full' permissions for the security principal Administrators. It's also important to realize that only the requested permissions are granted. If a user requests 'read' access, and the ACL on the resource gives the Everyone group 'full' access, only 'read' access will be granted.

411

How an ACE Can Describe Multiple Permissions

In the above example, we use a single ACE that defines *two* permissions ('read' and 'execute') for the Everyone group. These permissions are represented in binary form, where each bit is set to 0x0 or 0x1 to represent whether the corresponding permission is off or on (respectively).

These bitwise representations are then ORed together to represent the mask for the permission. Let's look at a simple example: suppose that the 'read' permission and 'execute' permission are represented as bits 1 and 2 respectively (reading right-to-left). Then we can represent the combination of both permissions to on by specifying 0x11. Alternatively, we can specify read but not execute by specifying 0x01.

The DACL and SACL on a resource, along with several other security-related properties, are collectively known as a **security descriptor**.

Security Descriptors

Each resource has a security descriptor, that defines specific security-related properties about the resource. The properties of the security descriptor consists of:

- ❑ **Owner/creator** – stores the Windows NT security principal that created (or 'owns') the resource.
- ❑ **Primary group security identification** – the primary group that has access to the resource.
- ❑ **Discretionary ACL** – contains the ACEs that allow security principals to gain access to the resource.
- ❑ **System ACL** – contains the ACEs that write information back to the event security log when a pre-defined threshold is reached – for example, when a user accesses a resource, this event will be written to the security logs (if enabled in the SACL).

When we talk about resources, we mean items that exist on the Windows NT system. This can include anything that can be secured in the system, or the registry. Later, we'll examine resources in the Membership Directory; they too have security descriptors.

We won't study Windows NT security descriptors in great detail in this book; however, we will briefly discuss how to access and modify the elements of a security descriptor.

Modifying Security Descriptors

How do we modify the security descriptor for a file system resource? One way is through Windows NT Explorer. Let's look at an example. Select a resource (such as the **Inetpub** folder, say) from the Windows NT Explorer, and select File | Properties. On the resulting Properties dialog, choose the Security tab: this allows us to view the various options for modifying the security descriptor of the resource (note that we'll only see this if the drive is formatted as NTFS):

On a Windows NT Server NTFS partitioned drive, we can modify both the DACL and SACL of any file or directory resource from the Security tab. The DACL for a resource may be modified through the Permissions button, and the SACL is modified through the Auditing button.

Modifying the DACL

To access the Directory Permissions dialog used to modify a file system resource DACL, select the Properties of an object from Windows Explorer, and then select the Permissions button from the Security tab:

In the resulting dialog box, we see the ACEs in the DACL – in this case, we see that the Everyone group has 'full' permissions for both the file and directory.

Later in this chapter, we'll discuss the differences between Windows NT authentication and Membership authentication, and how permissions should be modified for resources for each authentication type.

Modifying the SACL

To modify the SACL, select <u>A</u>uditing from the security descriptor applet (select a file system object in Windows NT Explorer, then select File | Properties | Security tab) and select the options to be logged:

```
Directory Auditing                                    [X]

Directory:     C:\Inetpub                          [   OK   ]

[ ] Replace Auditing on Subdirectories             [ Cancel ]
[x] Replace Auditing on Existing Files
Name:                                              [  Add... ]

┌──────────────────────────────────────┐          [ Remove ]
│                                      │
│                                      │          [  Help  ]
│                                      │
│                                      │
└──────────────────────────────────────┘

┌ Events to Audit ──────────────────────────────────┐
│                                 Success    Failure │
│   Read                            [ ]        [ ]   │
│   Write                           [ ]        [ ]   │
│   Execute                         [ ]        [ ]   │
│   Delete                          [ ]        [ ]   │
│   Change Permissions              [ ]        [ ]   │
│   Take Ownership                  [ ]        [ ]   │
└────────────────────────────────────────────────────┘
```

Modifying ACLs and ACEs Programmatically

We can modify the ACEs of a file system resource DACL programmatically – and this is especially useful if we need to grant access to a resource *dynamically*. This can be done using the `Commerce.AdminSecurity` object, which is installed with Site Server 3.0. (Even though we haven't installed the Commerce Edition of Site Server 3.0, several key COM objects with 'Commerce' in their name are installed on the system.)

The Commerce.AdminSecurity Object

The `Commerce.AdminSecurity` object provides several methods to modify security permissions on Window NT resources such as files, directories, the IIS 4.0 metabase and the registry. The following ASP page modifies the DACL of a resource called `C:\temp\test.txt`.

> *You can find this code, with a selection of other functions that are used to modify security permissions (both in the Membership Directory and on the NT system), can be found on the Wrox web site at* http://webdev.wrox.co.uk/books/1940.

This code can easily be re-purposed to modify registry and Internet Information Server 4.0 metabase security properties as well.

Code Example – Modifying the DACL on a Directory

In order to run this script, or similar scripts that modify permission, the application running the script must be running under the *context* of a Windows NT group or user that has enough permission to make modifications to the resource:

```
<HTML>
<BODY BGCOLOR=WHITE>
<FONT FACE=ARIAL SIZE=3>
<B>
AddFileSystemACL
</B>
<HR SIZE=1>
</FONT>
<FONT FACE=ARIAL SIZE=2>
<%
' *************************************************
' Constant Definitions for NTFS File System
' *************************************************
Const GENERIC_READ               = &H80000000   ' Read
Const GENERIC_WRITE              = &H40000000   ' Write
Const GENERIC_EXECUTE            = &H20000000   ' Execute
Const GENERIC_ALL                = &H10000000   ' All


' *******************************************
' METHOD:  AddFileSystemACL
'
' PURPOSE: Modifies the DACL on a file
'          system resource
'
' PARAMETERS:
'          strResource
'            Path to resource
'
'          nFile
'            Whether or not resource
'            is a file
'
'          strNTPrincipal
'            The principal used for the ACE
'
'          hexPermissions
'            Mask of permissions to add
'
' RETURNS: Boolean (true success)
'
Public Function AddFileSystemACL(strResource, nFile, strNTPrincipal,
hexPermissions)
  On Error Resume Next

  ' Assume failure
  ' *************************************************
  AddFileSystemACL = False

  Dim objSecurity

  ' Create the Commerce AdminSecurity object
  ' *************************************************
  Set objSecurity = Server.CreateObject("Commerce.AdminSecurity")
  If Err.Number <> 0 Then
    Err.Clear
    Exit Function
  End If

  ' Add the Permissions
  ' *************************************************
  objSecurity.AddPermission CStr(strNTPrincipal), hexPermissions
```

```
    ' Write the new security descriptor
    ' ************************************************
    If nFile = 1 Then ' It's a file
       objSecurity.WriteSecurityFile strResource
    Else
       objSecurity.WriteSecurityDirectory strResource, 0
    End If

    ' Did an error occur on the method?
    ' ************************************************
    If Err.Number <> 0 Then
       Err.Clear
       Exit Function
    Else
       AddFileSystemACL = True
    End If
End Function

' Example Use - Add Administrators group to a
' text file called test.txt in c:\temp. Give
' Administrator Full permissions
' ************************************************
Dim blnSuccess

Const RESOURCE = "c:\temp\test.txt"
Const FILE = 1
Const PRINCIPAL = "Administrators"

' Attempt to modify the DACL
' ************************************************
blnSuccess = AddFileSystemACL(RESOURCE, FILE, PRINCIPAL, GENERIC_ALL)

If blnSuccess = True Then
   Response.Write RESOURCE & " DACL modified successfully"
Else
   Response.Write RESOURCe & " DACL not modified successfully"
End If
%>
</BODY>
</HTML>
```

Obviously, before running the ASP page from your browser, you'll need to create the file test.txt. After running the ASP page, you can use the NT Explorer to check that the permissions of test.txt consist of a single ACE that allows full permissions to the Administrators.

> *Note that this code overwrites the existing DACL – that is, it does not add to the existing DACL, but instead replaces it. Later, we'll learn how to modify a DACL by adding a new ACE to the existing DACL.*

The script begins by creating a new ACE based on the security principal (user or group) adding the security principal and the ACE mask. (Note that if we wanted to create a mask allowing 'read' and 'execute' permissions, we can do so by ORing GENERIC_READ and GENERIC_EXECUTE together.) Finally, the ACE is written to the DACL of the specified resource.

Why is this important? With this, we can write applications that self-install and programmatically modify the ACEs on a resource. Later, we'll look at why this becomes important if we're using Membership authentication. You now have the knowledge (and code) to modify file system security through applications or script with the Commerce.AdminSecurity object.

Understanding Windows NT security is *critically* important to building a secure web site. It is also important that you understand that the Windows NT security system uses ACLs and ACEs to authorize access to content after authenticating the security principal. We can modify these permissions both through the dialogs provided by the system, or programmatically through script (or applications) by taking advantage of the objects installed by Site Server 3.0.

Now that we've covered the groundwork on ACEs and ACLs, let's look at Membership Directory security. The Membership Directory also uses ACEs and ACLs to secure resources, but their behavior is a little different than their Windows NT counterparts.

Membership Directory Security

The Membership Directory takes advantage of parts of the Windows NT 5.0 Access Control Model. The **Access Control Model** defines how access to resources are authorized, and how authorization is configured.

In particular, we can configure the ACLs and ACEs for *all* items in the Membership Directory. Moreover, these ACLs and ACEs have some extra capabilities that provide greater access control.

The security model of the Membership Directory is completely distinct from the Windows NT security model. Site Server Personalization and Membership provides the bridge to integrate the two together.

The Access Control Model

The Membership Directory's access control model allows for object-level control and attribute-level control, and objects and attributes that can inherit ACEs (inside the Membership Directory).

When a member accesses the Membership Directory, he can request access to objects (containers, distribution lists, other members, and so on) and – of course – he can request access to the attributes of these objects.

Of course, there are some attributes values that the member should not have access to – for example, attributes that describe another member (such as membership level, password, or other information stored in the member profile). We can take care of this using the access control model. Although programmatically this shouldn't be a problem, what happens when the advanced user/member decides to write his or her own application to access the Membership Directory? They should be able to connect and access the Membership Directory, and view their profile information, but they shouldn't be able to view certain other properties such as security settings and other sensitive site data stored about themselves and other users.

The ACEs in the Membership Directory provide a more granular level of control over how resources are authorized, such as creating or deleting *specific instances* of an object. Unlike Windows NT 4.0's access control model, we can specify whether or not a member in the Membership Directory has the right to create (or use other permissions on) other members. Like modifying DACLs in Windows NT, we can modify ACLs for Membership Directory objects either through a GUI (in this case, the Membership Directory Manager) or programmatically.

Let's first look at how we configure ACEs using the Membership Directory Manager.

Defining ACEs from the Membership Directory Manager

The first thing to check is that we've connected to the correct LDAP Service from the Membership Directory Manager. Now, right-click on an object (any object other than items in the cn=Schema) – and select Properties. This brings up the properties of the selected object. In this illustration, we'll use the cn=Administrator object:

We're presented with the Properties dialog, which has a Security tab. The Security tab represents the Access Control List for the Membership Directory resource – it's similar to a DACL for a file system resource:

The Security tab presents us with an abundance of information:

- ❑ The Name field indicates the distinguished name of the object that is being displayed.
- ❑ The Access control entries table lists the individual ACEs that together make up the ACL. ACEs can be added or removed using the Add... and Remove buttons.

- ❏ The Type of permission box indicates whether the highlighted ACE Allows or Denys the permissions it specifies.
- ❏ The Permission field indicates the permission assigned to the ACE. We'll examine all the permissions in a moment. The access control model allows us to specify permissions for tasks other than reading and writing, such as creating and deleting objects within a container.
- ❏ The Granularity field says what the permissions apply to. These can include the Membership Directory, or individual objects.
- ❏ The Inheritance field determines whether or not the ACE can be inherited to child objects. ACEs in the Membership Directory may be fully inherited, inherited to one level, or not inherited.
- ❏ If the Apply permission to child objects only box is checked, then only children of this object (i.e. objects belonging to this container) will have this permission applied to them. This is particularly useful for configuring permissions to members that exist in a container. The permission won't apply to the container itself, but it will apply to the members within.
- ❏ The Add... button allows us to add new ACEs to the object.
- ❏ The Remove button allows us to remove ACEs from an object.
- ❏ The Protect this object from inheritance checkbox – when checked – specifies that all inherited ACEs should be ignored for this object.

We can use an object's Security tab to configure and specify the security settings for the object. We'll continue by reviewing the Permission and Granularity settings, and then we'll look at how ACEs are applied in the Membership Directory.

Permissions

The permissions define the rights that are to be granted (or denied) by an ACE in the resource's ACL. Here are the different permission settings:

- ❏ Create Child – Permits the ability to create child objects. For example, we can create an ACE on the ou=Members container that denies a member the Create Child right (specified by Permissions) on all objects (specified by Granularity, see later). Then that member would be unable to create objects beneath the ou=Members container.
- ❏ Delete Child – Controls whether or not child objects can be deleted beneath the container on which the ACE is specified.
- ❏ Create/Delete Child – A combination of the Create Child and Delete Child permissions. In the Windows NT NetShow Server plug-in example of Chapter 11, the ProxyUser would ideally have this permission on ou=Members. The ACE would be set for granularity of the member class, preventing the ProxyUser from creating or deleting members in the ou=Members container.
- ❏ Search – Controls the ability to view (or list) the child objects of the specified object.
- ❏ Read – Controls the ability to view (or list) the attributes of the specified object.
- ❏ Write – Controls the ability to change or add to the attributes of the specified object.
- ❏ Read/Write – A combination of Read and Write.
- ❏ Delete – Controls the ability to delete an object.
- ❏ View/Set Security – Determines whether or not the security setting may be viewed. Members of the Membership authentication Public group, or the Windows NT authentication Everyone group don't necessarily need the ability to set or view security permissions for objects. This ACE permission does not have any granularity settings.
- ❏ Full – ACE permission that specifies all rights (depending upon the granularity), which maybe set to All. The Administrator has full rights, but not because of the Full ACE. In fact, the Administrator has the Bypass ACL checking privilege set to SUPERBROKER.

Granularity

We've alluded to what granularity is above, but waited to define it until now. The **granularity** of a permission is unique since it defines specifically what object the permission applies to. A permission may apply to an entire resource, but can also be applied on a more 'granular' level (hence the term), to specific attributes or classes within the resource.

To make this clearer, we can step through the creation of the ProxyUser for our Chapter 11 Windows NT NetShow Services integration example. First, create a new member, called ProxyUser – either programmatically or via the New User Wizard. For now, just assign the userPassword attribute with the value password – that's the only necessary attribute for this example.

Next, go to the Membership Directory Manager snap-in, right-click on the ou=Members container and select Properties. Then view the Security tab:

Now, let's crank down the security so that the ProxyUser *only* has permissions to read other members, and then to view *only* their passwords.

> *In the case of the ProxyUser, these permissions are approptiate because the ProxyUser is an administrative account, that is used to* authenticate *credentials.*

We'll do this by adding a couple of ACEs to the ou=Members container, which will grant these permissions and granularity levels. First, click the Add... button to bring up the Add/Remove dialog. Select the ou=Members container for the Membership Directory, and then select ProxyUser from the available items:

Once you've done that, hit OK to return to the Properties dialog. This adds a new line to the Access control entries table. This line will form the first of our new ACEs – the read ACE – which will allow the ProxyUser to read all the members underneath the ou=Members container. At the bottom-right of the dialog, select Read in the Permission field, member-object in the Granularity field and Full Inheritance in the Inheritance field:

Then hit OK and wait for the changes to take effect.

Now let's add one more ACE. Start as we did before, by clicking on the Add... button to get the Add/Remove dialog; selecting the ou=Members container, Adding the ProxyUser and clicking OK – this gives us another new line in our Access control entries table. This time, select Read in the Permission field, user-password in the Granularity field and Full Inheritance in the Inheritance field:

Then hit OK, and we're done! Our new ProxyUser is ready to roll. Our ProxyUser will be able to read all members, i.e. view their common name value, and their passwords. All the functionality our ProxyUser needs for strict delegation.

So that's how to configure ACEs in the Membership Directory. We must now consider how ACEs are applied to determine the rights assigned to a security principal.

Determining Rights and Permissions

You may have noticed that when we added the ACEs to the ACL in the above example, the ACE is first added to the bottom of the ACL as we make our modifications. After pressing OK on the Properties dialog, the Membership Directory Manager automatically reorders the ACEs, according to a predefined set of rules. This is known as **canonicalization** – we'll take a look at the rules of ACL canonicalization in a moment.

The order of a resource's ACEs has a direct effect on how the security permissions are applied on a resource in the Membership Directory. This is particularly necessary when an ACL contains two ACEs that specify conflicting permissions – the Membership Directory uses the order of ACEs to resolve the conflict. For example, suppose we have an ACE that *grants* a user the 'read' permission, and another ACE that *denies* the same user the 'read' permission. The order of the ACEs will determine what permissions this user will receive.

Note that we can override the rules of canonicalization if we choose – for example, if we need special security restrictions. Let's have a look at the canonicalization rules, and then we'll consider a couple of examples.

Canonicalized ACLs – The Rules

Here are the three rules that we use to canonicalize the order of ACEs in an ACL.

1. **Explicit ACEs override inherited ACEs.** The security implementation allows for security to be inherited; this rule dictates that an explicit ACE has priority over an inherited ACE.

2. **Deny overrides Allow.** When there are two ACEs that both allow and deny permission to an object, and Rule 1 has not resolved the conflict, then the deny ACE has priority over the allow ACE.

3. **An ACE that applies to a user overrides an ACEs that applies to a group.** When an ACE specifies certain permissions to a user, which conflict with prmissions specified by a group ACE (and the user belongs to the group), and Rules 1 and 2 do not resolve the conflict, then the user ACE has priority ove rthe group ACE.

Canonicalized ACLs – Examples

So let's consider some examples – in which permission conflicts are resolved by consulting a canonicalized ACL.

Suppose that the ou=Members container in the Membership Directory specifies that all members will be denied the SELF permission of 'read' on the userPassword attribute, and that this rule is inherited. All members created under the ou=Members container will inherit this ACE. However, we could then create a new member under the ou=members container, and explicitly assign this new member an ACE specifying permission to Read the userPassword attribute. The inherited ACE and the explicit ACE are in direct conflict. However, the ACL is canonicalized; so (by Rule 1) the explicit ACE wins and our new member is granted Read access.

How about a different example – where again the ACL is canonicalized. A member under the ou=Members container is assigned two ACEs from group permissions – 'allow write' on a text resource inherited from the authors group, and 'deny write' on the same resource inherited from the general_users group. In this case, we can guess where the conflict came from – it looks like the member has been promoted to 'author', and the administrator simply forgot to remove the member from the general_users group. To resolve the conflict, we check the canonicalized order of the ACL. Rule 1 doesn't resolve the conflict, but Rule 2 dictates that 'deny write' overrides the 'allow write'. The member will need to contact the administrator!

Now that we've discussed how security is applied in the Membership Directory, let's examine how we can tighten it down.

Securing the Membership Directory

When a new Membership Directory is created, it is not secured. If the Membership Directory is created to support Windows NT authentication, there's a special group – Everyone – created in the ou=Groups container. Under Membership authentication, there's a special group called Public created in the ou=Groups container. The Everyone and Public groups represent the set of all members. For a Membership Directory that uses Windows NT authentication, the Everyone group corresponds to the group of the same name in Windows NT.

When a new Membership Directory is created, the Everyone or Public group has an ACE created on the root (o=*[organization]*) container, specifying Full permission.

It is very important that you understand what this means for securing the system. Whenever a new directory is created – under Windows NT authentication *or* under Membership authentication – this ACE means that *all* users have *full* permissions – inherited from the Public-group ACE or the Everyone-group ACE applied on the root container.

In previous chapters, have you wondered how it is that we've been allowed to use `GetObject()` (rather than `OpenDSObject()`) to bind to the Membership Directory, and that we've had permission to do almost anything we like? It's because the anonymous member also has full permissions! The full permissions or course inherited from the ACE on the root container.

> *Why is this ACE created by default? In my opinion, it's so that understanding and using the Membership Directory is less confusing for developers starting out with Site Server Personalization and Membership.*

So before you use the Membership Directory in a production environment, you need to secure the directory. Otherwise, any hacker who knows the name/IP and port of the LDAP Service can gain access to your system.

> **When a new Membership Directory is created, the Everyone group (in Windows NT authentication) or the Public group (for Membership authentication) is granted full permissions with full inheritance for the entire directory. You need to secure the Directory by deleting the relevant ACE.**

Closing this security hole is very simple: remove the ACE that grants full permissions to the Public or Everyone group.

Removing the Public or Everyone Group ACE

To remove the Public group ACE, we first need to connect the Membership Directory Manager to the appropriate LDAP Service by modifying the properties of the Membership Directory Manager. The property settings we need to change include the server and port name of the LDAP Service. Then, right-click on Membership Directory Manager folder (which represents the root container of the Membership Directory) and select Properties.

A dialog box should appear – it's the same one that we used just now to point to the appropriate Membership Directory, but instead of modifying the server and port information, click on the Security tab:

In this dialog, we are looking at a Membership Directory that is using Membership authentication and has the Membership Directory group Public (highlighted in the screenshot). To secure the Membership Directory, all we need to do is remove this group ACE from the root container of the Membership Directory. To do this, select the appropriate ACE (highlighted in the screenshot) and press the Remove button. It may take several minutes – since the group needs to be removed from every container and object below the root container – but afterwards, the Membership Directory will be secured from giving all users full permissions.

If you're using Membership authentication, removing the Public group is as easy as that. If you're using Windows NT authentication, you need to remove the Everyone group instead – this is done by following the same procedure we've just outlined above.

Delegated Administration

Although the security issue presented above is quite concerning, there is a key concept buried within it. We've seen how, by assigning the Public group or Everyone group full permissions on the root container with full inheritance, we can give all members of those groups full permissions *anywhere* in the directory. What if we created a similar ACE that can do the same thing, but only within *specific* containers with *specific* members – rather than the entire directory? We can, and it's called **delegated administration**.

Delegated administration is the concept of allowing certain security principals – but not others – the ability to administer sections of the Membership Directory. Delegated administration removes responsibility from one administrator and splits the load between other users, who might have more of a 'vested' interest in their own objects and members.

Let's look at some different scenarios, which illustrate how delegated administration could be applied.

An Internet Service Provider

An Internet Service Provider might implement a single Membership Directory to manage all web sites that wanted to make use of Site Server Membership. We could arrange for each web site to have its own dedicated container, underneath the ou=Members container – and its own LDAP Service that authenticates members against this container. In addition, we can assign one 'administrative' user to each site – this user would have full permissions for that container (the container itself would provide full inheritance for everything created underneath the container).

An Internet Content Provider

Suppose an Internet content provider receives content from a variety of sources. It could delegate containers in much the same way as we described for the ISP scenario above. The containers could be divided between different types of authors, and other types of content providers (such as advertisers).

An Intranet or Enterprise Site

An Intranet or Enterprise site could delegate administrative tasks to the departments within the organization – marketing, sales, administration, etc. This means that the IT administrator doesn't have to administer all the users – the delegated department administrator manages the users within his or her own department. The rights could be the ability to create new members, or simply the ability to change passwords or expire accounts.

Planning and Implementing Delegated Administration

Planning for delegated administration is relatively straightforward, and unlike some aspects of planning the Membership Directory, we can make changes as our needs change. The only planning required is to decide how the delegated administration should be granted. It may be that some members need to administer objects in the Membership Directory, while others will need to be able to add other members to groups.

The easiest way to implement delegated administration is with a combination of groups and containers. We'll use containers to group objects to be administrated together in a logical fashion, and groups to grant or deny permissions to users within these containers. Take a look at the following example:

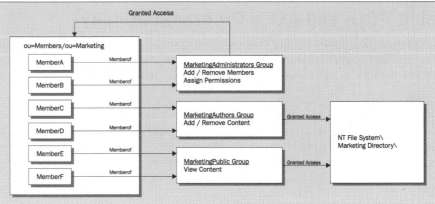

In the diagram, we're using delegated administration to grant certain permissions to MemberA and MemberB of the MarketingAdminstrators group. These permissions are full access to create, add, and modify members of the ou=Members/ou=Marketing container in the Membership Directory, and to add members to other groups.

Moreover, we're adding MemberC and MemberD to the MarketingAuthors group, which has a corresponding group in Windows NT that is assigned to the directory on the file system. Members of the MarketingAuthors group have the permissions on the Marketing file system directory to add and remove content.

Depending on the authentication method, the MarketingAuthors and MarketingPublic groups will either be accessed directly with by Windows NT user, by Windows NT authentication, or by the MemProxyUser, Membership authentication.

Finally, all other members of the marketing department will need to view content in the Marketing Directory, so they are added to the MarketingPublic group; members of this group only have permission to read the content in the directory.

Groups and Containers

There's a dilemma that many developers often get hung up on – namely, when to use groups and when to use containers. In principal, the answer is this:

Use groups to assign security permissions. Groups in the Membership Directory are special, because we can use them to also authorize (i.e. grant access to) resources on Windows NT.
Use containers to logically organize similar information together. The ou=Members container groups members together; take this one step further by using containers to collect together members with a common interest.

For example, if you create a new group called cn=MarketingAdministrators, you would assign the administrators of the marketing department to this group. A MarketingAdministrators ACE could then be assigned to resources, to dictate permission for members of the cn=MarketingAdministrators group. Members of the marketing department of your organization could exist within a container called ou=Marketing, underneath the ou=Members container. Using delegated administration, we could assign a cn=MarketingAdministrators ACE on the ou=Marketing container, permitting members of the cn=MarketingAdministrators group to manage members in the ou=Marketing group (that is, members of the marketing department).

Assigning ACLs and ACEs Programmatically

At the beginning of our discussion of Membership Directory security, we used the Membership Directory manager to modify the ACL of the ou=Members container for our ProxyUser. At that stage I allured you with the promise that I'd explain how to do the same thing programmatically.

We'll step through segments of the code that *add* an ACE to an ACL (rather than *replacing* the old ACL, as we did in our Windows NT example). We'll then look at some code that canonicalizes the ACL programmatically, after we've added the ACE. The Membership Directory Manager canonicalized the ACE we added through the Membership Directory Manager, but when we add ACEs programmatically, we have to do this canonicalization ourselves.

The ModifyPermissions() Method

The `ModifyPermissions()` method adds an ACE permission for a specified security principal on a specified resource. The `ModifyPermission()` method relies upon two other methods – `CanonicalizeACL()` and `CompareACEs()`. We won't be looking at all the code, but we'll examine `ModifyPermissions()` and important parts of the other two methods.

Here's the list of parameters for the `ModifyPermissions()` method:

❑ **strADsPathToEntry** – The Active Directory Service path to the object whose Membership Directory ACL is to be modified.

❑ **strADsPathToTrustee** – The Active Directory Service path to the security principal – the trustee – for whom an ACE will be added to the ACL specified by `strADsPathToEntry`.

❑ **hexAccessMask** – The hexadecimal code of the access permission for the ACE. Hexadecimal values are used to represent the available permissions (much as we saw when setting permissions within the Windows NT environment) – these values are specific to the Membership Directory object. We'll also define the following constants for the methods:

```
' hexAccessMask
' ********************************************************
Const DSRIGHT_CREATE_CHILD       = &H00000001  ' Create Child
Const DSRIGHT_DELETE_CHILD       = &H00000002  ' Delete Child
Const DSRIGHT_CREATE_DELTE_CHILD = &H00000003  ' Create OR Delete Child
Const DSRIGHT_SEARCH             = &H00000004  ' Search
Const DSRIGHT_READ               = &H00000010  ' Read
Const DSRIGHT_WRITE              = &H00000020  ' Write
Const DSRIGHT_READ_WRITE         = &H00000030  ' Read OR Write
Const DSRIGHT_DELETE_SELF        = &H00010000  ' Delete Self
Const DSRIGHT_WRITE_DACL         = &H00040000  ' Write DACL
Const DSRIGHT_FULL               = &H0005003F  ' Full
```

❑ **hexAceType** – The hexadecimal code used to determine whether the ACE will allow or deny the permission defined by the `hexAccessMask`. The following constants are defined in the library for the methods:

```
' hexAceType
' ********************************************************
Const DSRIGHT_ALLOW              = &H0         ' Allow permission
Const DSRIGHT_DENY               = &H6         ' Deny permission
```

❑ **hexAceFlags** – The hexadecimal code used to identify whether or not the ACE is to be inherited in the Membership Directory. Again, constants are defined in the library for the methods:

```
' hexAceFlags
' ********************************************************
Const DSINHERITANCE_NONE         = &H00        ' No Inheritance
Const DSINHERITANCE_FULL         = &H03        ' Full Inheritance
Const DSINHERITANCE_ONE_LEVEL    = &H07        ' One Level
Const DSINHERITANCE_CHILD_ONLY   = &H08        ' Child objects only
Const DSINHERITANCE_ACE          = &H10        ' ACE Inherited
```

❑ **hexFlags** – The hexadecimal code used to determine what type of granularity is supported for the ACE. In this version of the method, the only granularity supported is full. However, you could add the necessary functionality to support object granularity. Here are the available constants:

```
' hexFlags
' ************************************************
Const DSGRANULARITY_ALL          = &H0       ' Granularity applied to all
objects
Const DSGRANULARITY_SPECIFIC     = &H1       ' Granularity set on specific
objects
```

❑ **vNextVer** – The GUID value used to identify the object for granularity to be applied to. This
parameter is not implemented, so just pass 0.

Code Sample – ModifyPermissions() Method

As I said, we won't print the full method – it's too long! – but we will examine some of the more
interesting parts. The full code is available from Wrox's web site, at
http://webdev.wrox.co.uk/books/1940.

```
<SNIP>
  ' Grab Entry object
  ' ************************************************
  Set objDSEntry = GetObject(strADsPathToEntry)
  If Err.Number <> 0 Then
    Err.Clear
    Response.Write "Cannot get ADsPath to entry <p>"
    Exit Function
  End If
<SNIP>
  ' Grab NT Security Descriptor
  ' ************************************************
  Set objSecurityDesc = objDSEntry.Get("ntSecurityDescriptor")
  If Err.Number <> 0 Then
    Err.Clear
    Response.Write "Cannot get Security Descriptor <p>"
    Exit Function
  End If
<SNIP>
```

We first bind to the object in the Membership Directory and get the `ntSecurityDescriptor`
attribute of the object. The `ntSecurityDescriptor` is a binary attribute that defines the security
descriptor for the object.

```
  ' Grab Discretionary ACL
  ' ************************************************
  Set objDescACL = objSecurityDesc.DiscretionaryAcl
  If Err.Number <> 0 Then
    Err.Clear
    Response.Write "Cannot get discretionary ACL <p>"
    Exit Function
  End If
```

After obtaining the security descriptor of the object, we ask for the DACL containing the ACEs used
to define what security principals are allowed or denied access to the object.

```
  ' Create and Access Control Entry
  ' ************************************************
  Set objACE = CreateObject("AccessControlEntry")
  If Err.Number <> 0 Then
```

```
      Err.Clear
      Response.Write "Cannot create Access control entry <p>"
      Exit Function
   End If


   ' Determine Trustee for new ACE
   ' ************************************************
   If objDSEntry.ADsPath = objSPEntry.ADsPath Then
      strDNToTrustee = "SELF"
   Else
      ' Create Membership object
      ' ************************************************
      Set objMembershipInfo = Server.CreateObject("Membership.MembershipInfo.1")
      If Err.Number <> 0 Then
         Err.Clear
         Response.Write "Cannot create Membership object <p>"
         Exit Function
      End If


      ' Needs to be in DN format
      ' ************************************************
      strDNToTrustee = objMembershipInfo.ADsPathToDN(objSPEntry.ADsPath)
   End If

   ' Build ACE
   ' ************************************************
   objACE.Trustee = strDNToTrustee
   objACE.AccessMask = hexAccessMask
   objACE.AceType = hexAceType
   objACE.AceFlags = hexAceFlags
   objACE.Flags = hexFlags
```

Next, we create a new ACE, and then use the `Membership.MembershipInfo` object to convert the ADsPath of the security principal to a distinguished name. Then we build the new ACE, setting the trustee to the distinguished name of the security principal, and setting the various properties of the ACE using the hex values we passed through the method.

```
   ' Call function to canonicalize the ACL with the
   ' new ACE
   ' ************************************************
   Set objDescACL = CanonicalizeACL(objDescACL, objACE, strADsPathToTrustee)
   If Err.Number <> 0 Then
      Err.Clear
      Response.Write "Cannot get canonicalize the ACL <p>"
      Exit Function
   End If
```

After building the ACE, we pass the ACE to the `CanonicalizeACL()` method – which canonicalizes the ACL, and returns the new ACL.

```
   ' Put the new NT Security Descriptor
   ' ************************************************
   objDSEntry.Put "ntSecurityDescriptor", (objSecurityDesc)

   ' Call Set Info
   ' ************************************************
   objDSEntry.SetInfo
```

Finally, we set some properties for the security descriptor (not shown here), put the new security descriptor back into the object, and call `SetInfo`.

Example Use

If you wanted to use this programmatic approach to add the Administrator to the ou=Members container of a specific Membership Directory, you would call the `ModifyPermissions()` method as follows:

```
' Example Use
' ***************************************
Dim blnWriteACE
Const ADS_PATH = "LDAP://localhost:1003/o=Wrox/ou=Members"
Const ADS_MEMBER = "LDAP://localhost:1003/o=Wrox/ou=Members/cn=Administrator"


blnWriteACE = ModifyPermissions(ADS_PATH, ADS_MEMBER, _
                                DSRIGHT_FULL, DSRIGHT_ALLOW, _
                                DSINHERITANCE_NONE, _
                                DSGRANULARITY_ALL, 0)

Response.Write "New ACE Added: " & blnWriteACE
```

The method returns `True` or `False`, depending upon whether it succeeded or failed. Next, let's look at the `CanonicalizeACL()` method; we'll start by explaining its purpose.

Programmatically Canonicalizing the ACL

When we use the Membership Directory Manager to add an ACE to an object in the Membership Directory, the Membership Directory Manager automatically canonicalizes the ACL. In other words, the Membership Directory Manager determines the proper order of the ACEs, per the canonicalization rules that we listed earlier in this chapter, and rewrites the ACL accordingly.

If an ACE is added to a Membership Directory ACL by a means other than the Membership Directory Manager – either from an application or from script – the ACL for the entry is *not* automatically canonicalized. This means that the security permissions will not be applied according to the canonicalization rules, when trying to determine security privileges for a member trying to access the modified resource in the Membership Directory.

Moreover, the next time the security is viewed on the entry, an error dialog will appear stating that the ACL is not properly canonicalized:

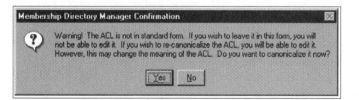

To avoid this message, and to provide for the ability to canonicalize an ACL through code, we can use a little method that I've called `CanonicalizeACL()`. The `CanonicalizeACL()` method relies upon the `CompareACEs()` method, which enforces the three canonicalization rules we defined earlier.

The CanonicalizeACL() and CompareACEs() Methods

We won't examine the parameters of either of these methods, but we will look at the code to help you understand the purpose and role of each method.

The `CanonicalizeACL()` method enumerates the ACEs in the ACL passed by the `ModifyPermissions()` method. Next, the `CompareACEs()` method is called to determine whether or not the new ACE to be added should be added before the current ACE.

Here's the code from `CanonicalizeACL()` that is responsible for looping through the ACL:

```
' Loop through each ACE in the ACL
' ************************************************
For Each objACE in objACL

  ' Has the new ACE been added?
  ' ************************************************
  If blnNewAceAdded = False Then

    ' Determine ACE Trustee Type
    ' ************************************************
    Set objACETrustee = GetObject(strLDAPServer & objAce.Trustee)
    If Err.Number <> 0 Then
      ' Trustee's that are SELF will generate an error
      ' ************************************************
      strACETrustee = "SELF"
      Err.Clear
    Else
      If LCase(objACETrustee.class) = "mgroup" Then
        strACETrustee = "GROUP"
      Else
        strACETrustee = "MEMBER"
      End If
    End If

    ' Determine ACE to add Trustee Type
    ' ************************************************
    Set objACEToAddTrustee = GetObject(strLDAPServer & objAceToAdd.Trustee)
    If Err.Number <> 0 Then
      ' Trustee's that are SELF will generate an error
      ' ************************************************
      strACEToAddTrustee = "SELF"
      Err.Clear
    Else
      If LCase(objACEToAddTrustee.class) = "mgroup" Then
        strACEToAddTrustee = "GROUP"
      Else
        strACEToAddTrustee = "MEMBER"
      End If
    End If

    ' Call the CompareACEs function to determine
    ' if the new ace should be added yet
    ' ************************************************
    blnAddNewACE = CompareACEs(objACE, objACEToAdd, _
                       strACETrustee, strACEToAddTrustee)

    ' If CompareACEs returns true then ace should be
    ' added, otherwise add the current ace to the new acl
```

```
' ************************************************
      If blnAddNewACE = True Then
         objNewACL.AddACE objACEToAdd
         objNewACL.AddACE objACE
         blnNewAceAdded = True
      Else
         objNewACL.AddACE objACE
      End if
   Else
      ' New Ace had been added, add all other aces
      ' ************************************************
      objNewACL.AddAce objAce
   End If
Next
```

A flag blnNewAceAdded is used in the loop to determine if the new ACE has been added. If it *has* been added (blnNewAceAdded = True) then we don't need to perform the comparison on each of the remaining ACEs in the ACL. Instead, we simply write the remainder of the new ACL with the remaining values of the old ACL.

However, if blnNewAceAdded = False, we call the CompareACEs() method to determine whether the ACE to be added belongs before the current ACE in the existing ACL. Here's a snippet of the logic from the CompareACEs() method that is responsible for ACE comparisons for group security principals:

```
' Handle GROUP ACEs
' ************************************************
If strACE1Trustee = "GROUP" AND strACE2Trustee = "GROUP" Then
   If (objACE1.AceType = DSRIGHT_DENY OR _
          objACE1.AceType = DSRIGHT_DENY_OTHER) AND _
       (objACE2.AceType = DSRIGHT_DENY OR _
          objACE2.AceType = DSRIGHT_DENY_OTHER) Then
     CompareACEs = True
     Exit Function
   ElseIf (objACE1.AceType = DSRIGHT_ALLOW OR _
             objACE1.AceType = DSRIGHT_ALLOW_OTHER) AND _
          (objACE2.AceType = DSRIGHT_DENY OR _
             objACE2.AceType = DSRIGHT_DENY_OTHER) Then
     CompareACEs = True
     Exit Function
   ElseIf (objACE1.AceType = DSRIGHT_ALLOW OR _
             objACE1.AceType = DSRIGHT_ALLOW_OTHER) AND _
          (objACE2.AceType = DSRIGHT_ALLOW OR _
             objACE2.AceType = DSRIGHT_ALLOW_OTHER) Then
     CompareACEs = True
     Exit Function
   End If
End If
```

This code snippet from the CompareACEs() method compares two ACEs, the current ACE from the CanonicalizeACL() ACL loop, and the new ACE defined by ModifyPermissions(). In this particular case, we're checking what do to in the situation that ACEs are group ACEs. The various comparisons are made between the properties of the two group ACEs, to determine which has precedence based on the rules defined for canonicalization.

The End Result

After creating the new ACE, examining the ACL and comparing the ACEs, the new ACL must be written. Finally, the new ACL is passed back to the `ModifyPermissions()` method and the new ACL is written back to the object, as per our example:

I've shown you some really powerful code that you can use to modify the security of objects in the Membership Directory programmatically. Ideally, this logic should be wrapped in a COM object, exposing only the `ModifyPermissions()` method.

Next, we'll complete our discussion of file system and directory security by looking at how Windows NT authentication and Membership authentication use the Membership Directory, and how you secure the file system to authorize resources using both authentication types.

Authentication Methods and NT Resource Access

We're not going to spend a great deal of time discussing Windows NT (Intranet) authentication, because – as it relates to authentication and authorization – it's not any different to what you could read in the *Windows Internet Information Server 4.0 Resource Kit* or any other reputable work on Windows NT; and also because Membership authentication is rather more complex.

Windows NT Authentication

Internet Information Server provides the authentication mechanisms, as we covered in Chapter 8, and once a value is added through the AUO (i.e. via `objAUO.Put "givenName", "Jon"`), a member is created in the Membership Directory. This member account has no bearing on whether the user will be authenticated, because the user must exist in the Windows NT Security Accounts Manager. However, it does have a bearing on resources in the Membership Directory. We can still use all of the other features we discussed in this chapter, such as delegation and programmatic administration.

Let's take a look at the more interesting and definitely more complex features of Membership authentication.

Membership Authentication

Membership authentication authenticates the credentials against the Membership Directory. It uses Windows NT ACLs and ACEs to grant and deny permissions to resources, just like Windows NT authentication. However, unlike Windows NT authentication, Membership authentication uses an impersonation account to gain access to the Windows NT system. Once a member is authenticated from the Membership Directory, the Security Support Provider Interface (SSPI) creates a new security context for the user, as the Windows NT MemProxyUser impersonation account. The SSPI then switches the running application's thread to the MemProxyUser's security context.

The verified MemProxyUser security context now 'owns' the thread running the application. Any time the thread requests a Windows NT resource, the security ID (SID) of the thread is compared with the ACEs of the requested resource, to determine what permissions the user has to that particular resource.

The MemProxyUser

When you create a Membership Directory that uses Membership authentication, an impersonation account – MemProxyUser – is created in the Windows NT SAM. One MemProxyUser is created for each Membership Server instance on the computer:

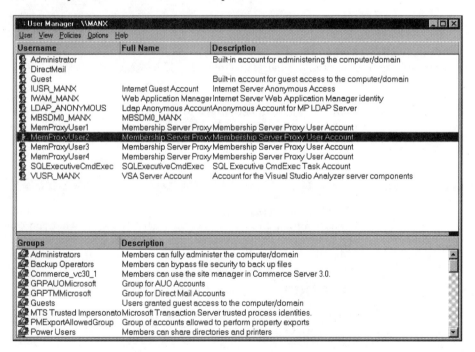

The role of the MemProxyUser is to allow access to resources provided by Windows NT 4.0 Server, to users that *don't exist* in the Windows NT SAM. When an authenticated member requests a resource (such as the root page in an IIS 4.0 web), the MemProxyUser context is used to impersonate the member in the Membership Directory. No security privileges or permissions are carried over from the Membership Directory, other than the group mappings, which we'll cover in a moment.

Which Impersonation Account am I Using?

To determine the impersonation account that a particular Membership Directory is using, open the Microsoft Management Console, right-click on the Membership Directory instance and select Properties. Listed under the Windows NT impersonation account section of the Authentication Service tab, you'll find the the username and password of the user that this Membership Directory instance uses as its impersonation account:

However, since a common account is used to access all resources – the MemProxyUser – you can't simply assign this security principal to resources needing to be authorized in the Membership Directory.

> **Don't use the MemProxyUser security principal as part of an ACE on any resource you want to secure. Since every member uses the MemProxyUser as its impersonation account, this would simply grant access to *all* members!**

If we can't use the MemProxyUser as the security principal to authenticate resources under Membership authenrtication, how *do* we authorize users to access Windows NT resources?

The trick is to authorize access to resources through the use of **proxy groups**. Proxy groups are groups that exist in both the Membership Directory and in the Windows NT SAM. Members of the group in the Membership Directory receive the corresponding Windows NT proxy group's SID. The proxy group can then be assigned the appropriate permissions to your secure resources. If the MemProxyUser requesting the resources has the SID of the appropriate proxy group, access will be granted.

Group Permissions

When a new group is created in a Membership Directory under Membership authentication, a corresponding group called Site_[Membership Server Name]_[Directory Service Group Name] is created in the Windows NT SAM. We call this group a Windows NT proxy group since the Windows NT group corresponds to a Membership Directory group:

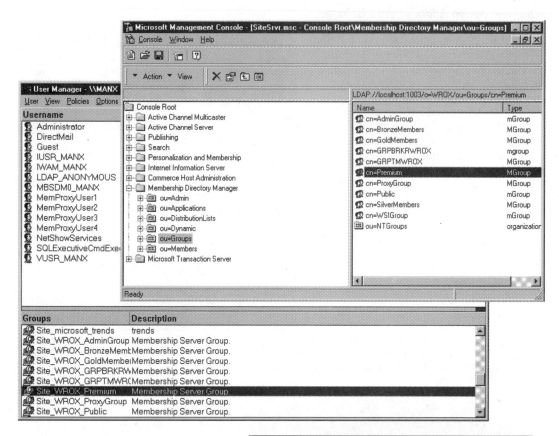

This Windows NT proxy group is then added to the system resource that the group needs access to:

The member (in the Membership Directory) then needs to be added to that group. Then, when the member is authenticated, the MemProxyUser will dynamically be granted the rights and privileges assigned to the group in the Membership Directory by the relevant ACEs. (We added members to groups through the Membership Directory Manager in Chapter 7, and we'll see how it's done programmatically – through ASP script – in Chapter 14.)

Automatic Creation and Poll Time

Proxy groups are created automatically by Site Server. However, after creating a new membership group, don't expect the corresponding Windows NT group to be created right away. There is a 10-minute **poll time** for any changes and updates to the Membership Directory. It is possible to speed the process, up by stopping and restarting the LDAP Service.

An Example Using Proxy Groups

To make use of the Windows NT proxy groups, first create several new groups in the Membership Directory Manager: GoldMembers, SilverMembers and BronzeMembers. Next, create some new members in the ou=Members container: GoldMember, SilverMember and BronzeMember. Set each member's password to the value password. GoldMember should be a member of all groups; SilverMember should be a member of the SilverMembers and BronzeMembers groups, and finally, BronzeMember should be a member of the BronzeMembers group only.

Here's a screenshot from the New User wizard, that shows the groups that SilverMember belongs to:

Next, create three files that are accessible from a web using Membership authentication, call these files Gold.txt, Silver.txt and Bronze.txt. Inside each of these files, enter some identifying text.

After creating the files, use IIS 4.0 to change the Membership authentication method for these three files to Clear Text/Basic Authentication.

Now – assuming we've given the Membership Directory about 10 minutes to create the proxy groups – let's modify the DACL for each resource. For the Gold.txt remove the Everyone ACE, and add only the Site_*[Membership Server Name]_*Gold ACE. For Silver.txt, add the proxy groups relating to both gold and silver. Finally for Bronze.txt, add all three groups:

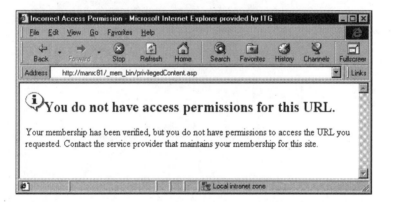

Now, whenever you access any of these resources from the web, you have to provide credentials for one of the three members that we created. For example, if you try to access Gold.txt using the correct user–password combination for the BronzeMember account, you will receive the following error:

However, if you use the GoldMember account to access any of these three resources, you'll be authorized since the necessary ACE for the proxy group is on the resource.

Advanced Concepts

This advanced concepts discussion will be relatively short; we'll simply look at how to change the settings so that the Membership Server can use a domain – rather than the Windows NT local SAM – for groups and security principals in Membership authentication.

Domain Authentication

Windows NT shadow groups are (by default) created as local NT groups. Therefore, any NT machine that is going to support Membership authentication must have its *own* set of groups to represent the groups in the Membership Directory. If the organization makes use of Windows NT domains, then Membership should also be able to take advantage of domain groups, so that it doesn't need to create local groups on every machine.

In fact, this can be done. However, unlike the local groups that are automatically created, a little more is involved in creating Membership NT domain shadow groups. To inform the Personalization and Membership authentication service that domain groups will be used instead of local groups, use the PMAdmin Windows Scripting Host to set the service to map Membership Directory groups to Windows NT domain groups. (There's more about the PMAdmin WSH script command line interface in Appendix B). Also, the new Windows NT shadow groups have to be created through the Windows NT User Manager, so the Auto Create NT Group feature should also be turned off.

To use the PMAdmin command line tool, drop to a command prompt, navigate to the `Microsoft Site Server\bin\P&M` directory, and type:

```
PMAdmin set authSvc /GroupDomain:[Domain Name] /ID:[Membership Instance ID]
```

where `[Domain Name]` is the name of the Windows NT domain name to use, and `[Membership Instance ID]` is the instance of the Membership Directory to be modified. The `[Membership Instance ID]` is the same number used to identify the MemProxyUser, and is one of the only references to the Membership Directory instance ID.

Summary

This chapter provided an inside look at security from several different angles. Here's what we covered in the chapter.

❑ **Architecture Security.** We started this chapter by examining security issues behind the network-to-LDAP connection, and the LDAP-to-Membership Directory connection, and we took a look at AccountDeny and IPDeny policies. We saw some packet sniffing and examined how the PEKey and KEkey are used to help secure the Membership Directory.

❑ **Basic Windows NT Security.** We examined the basics of Windows NT security, focusing mainly upon Access Control Lists and Access Control Entries. We also looked at some code used to modify Windows NT ACLs and ACEs programmatically.

❑ **Membership Directory Security.** We looked at security in the Membership Directory; we examined how the Membership Directory also uses the concept of ACLs and ACEs, and met canonicalized ACLs. We also looked at a piece of code that you can use to modify ACLs programmatically.

❑ **Authentication Methods and NT Resource Access.** Here we looked at how Windows NT authentication and Membership authentication gain access to Windows NT resources, focusing in particular on how Membership authentication uses the MemProxyUser and proxy groups.

❑ **Advanced Concepts.** Finally, we saw how we can use the PMAdmin tool to adjust the settings so that a Membership Directory under Membership authentication can use domains other than the local Windows NT SAM.

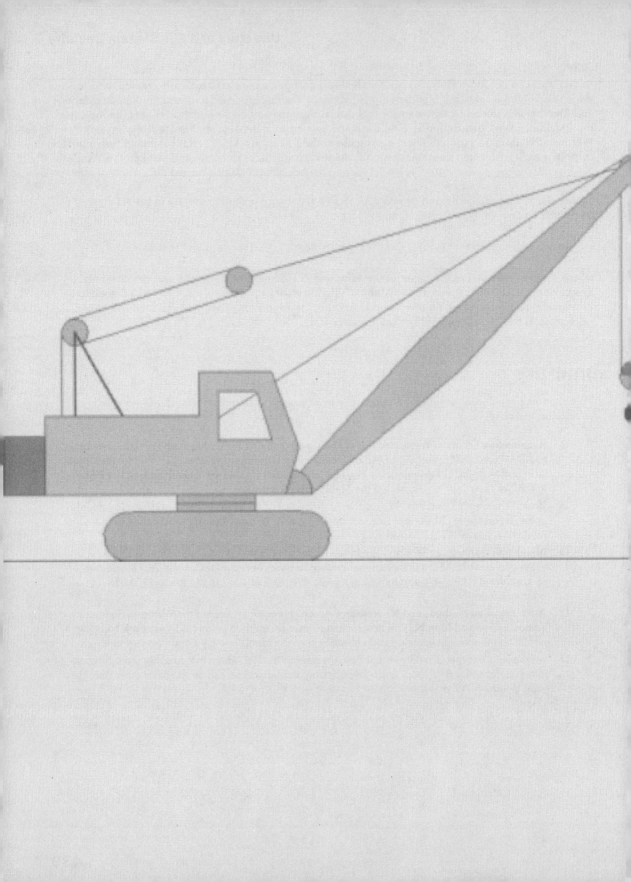

Managing the Membership Directory with Active Server Pages

As we've already noted, all the administrative tasks that can be done from the Microsoft Management Console can also be accomplished programmatically. We can write our own custom COM objects in either C++ or Visual Basic; alternatively, with Active Server Pages we can rapidly build a custom solution and tweak it as we go.

So why would we want to manage the Membership Directory programmatically? To begin with, it means our administrative capabilities are much more easily distributed and accessible from a number of platforms. In addition, if we have specific business problems or administrative tasks that we can automate, we can do this with our own code. A great example of this would be an ASP page that could bind to a database containing users and migrate those users into the Membership Directory. This is easier than having to use the wizards that we looked at in Chapter 7; it's also much, much faster.

It's important to realize that many of the solutions presented in this chapter shouldn't be made available to the public users of the site. However, administrators, content managers and developers working on the back-end servers will find the topics covered perfect for building administrative tools using Active Server Pages and Visual Basic Script. One way to secure this content is to use the techniques learned in Chapter 13 to secure file system resources through Membership authentication and authorization.

Here's how this chapter is organized:

❑ **Using Script Instead of Wizards.** We'll look here at the basic tasks involved in administering the Membership Directory. This includes programmatically creating attributes and classes, adding these attributes to classes, and creating members.

❑ **Other Membership Directory Tasks.** We'll also look at some other Membership Directory tasks that can be performed through the Membership Directory Manager, that we can also do through script. We'll also look at how to manage a roaming user profile, in case a member loses or attempts to access his profile, and the site does not recognize him.

❑ **Advanced Concepts.** Finally, we'll extend the DeleteObject() method, in order to solve some specific problems. These problems include removing expired members, and removing anonymous members from the ou=AnonymousUsers container.

By the end of this chapter, we'll be able to use Active Server Pages and Visual Basic Script to perform the tasks that – up to now – we've performed in the Membership Directory Manager; and so we'll be able to do them more quickly and efficiently.

Using Script Instead of Wizards

Many of the concepts presented in this chapter already exist in the ASP pages that Site Server provides for administering the Personalization and Membership system. The aim here is to enable you to gain a deeper understanding of the available functionality, so that you can build solutions tailored to your particular requirements and use the existing ASP pages more effectively. I have isolated some of the functionality into sets of VB Script functions, that you can download from the Wrox web site – you'll find them at http://webdev.wrox.co.uk/books/1940. With these generic functions you'll rapidly be able to build customized solutions, similar to the ones presented in the Site Server P&M Administrative ASPs.

> *For more information on classes and attributes, and a description of the attributeSchema and classSchema classes, refer back to the discussion in Chapter 2.*

Let's begin with creating new attributes programmatically.

Creating New Attributes

Creating new attributes in the Membership Directory through ASP script is very easy. You'll recall that in Chapter 2 we looked at the attributeSchema and classSchema classes. All we need to do is create a new attributeSchema class in the cn=Schema, ou=Admin, o=[*organization name*] container of the Membership Directory, and populate its mustContain attributes.

Why do we want to create new attributes programmatically? One reason is so that we can write a setup script, application, or object for our Membership Directory that will automatically create all the attributes specific to our organization. Although we could just as easily create attributes through the Membership Directory Manager, it is much faster to do so with script. This is true for two reasons:

❑ We don't have to use the wizards. Although the wizards work very well, they do require us to step through them – which takes time. We need another approach if we want to create a large number of attributes at the same time.

❑ We can predefine the attributes and let the application take the responsibility of creating them. Predefining and adding attributes programmatically gives us an easy mechanism to replicate a Membership Directory. For example the Wall Street Investor demo (in Appendix A) uses an ASP page, setup.asp, to add several new attributes to the Membership Directory, and then adds these new attributes to the member class. Through script, the demo site can be installed without having to edit the directory schema through the Membership Directory Manager. The attributes are simply pre-defined and read into an array that is then passed to a function that can read the array values and create attributes.

If we were to look at the properties of the givenName attribute in the Membership Directory Manager, here's what we would see:

In this screen shot,

     ❑   Name represents the mustContain value of the attributeSchema's cn value

     ❑   Syntax represents the mustContain value of the attributeSchema's attributeSyntax value.

     ❑   Multi-valued represents the mustContain value of the attributeSchema's isSingleValued value.

Note that the isSearchable value is not displayed in the attribute property dialog, but it still exists.

Before we create a new attribute, we need to have the proper permissions in the Membership Directory. Binding to the directory is dependent upon the security of the directory. If the Membership Directory has been secured, we have to bind to the Membership Directory as a known and privileged user (see Chapter 13 for more details).

For the sake of simplicity, we'll bind to the directory here by using a global variable, g_objSchema. I'm not particularly a fan of using global objects, but example code is a lot clearer if we make some assumptions, so we'll go for the easiest option here.

Code Sample – Bind With Global Object

The sample code for binding securely to the directory looks like this:

```
Dim g_objSchema
Dim strPathToSchema
Dim strSecureUser
Dim strSecurePassword

strPathToSchema = "LDAP://localhost:1003/o=Wrox/ou=Admin/cn=Schema"
strSecureUser = "Administrator"
strSecurePwd = "Password"

If SecuredBind(strPathToSchema, g_objSchema, strSecureUser, strSecurePwd) = False
Then
    ' ...Handle unable to bind error here
End If
```

First we define our global variable, g_objSchema. Next, we do the same for three other parameters, that we'll need for the SecuredBind() method (we'll look at this method in Chapter 15). These three parameters represent the path to the object to which we will bind; a username to bind as; and a password for that user. We set values for these variables – here, we're going to bind using the Administrator account.

Finally, we call the SecuredBind() method with the four parameters. We would need to add some error handling if we wanted to build upon this code, but we'll leave it out for the purposes of this example. Upon the successful completion of this method, the specified g_objSchema object will be bound to the Membership Directory.

In all the code examples here, you may find that it's necessary to replace localhost *with your own server name – depending on your system setup.*

So, now we can bind successfully to the Membership Directory, we'll see how to create an attribute.

The CreateAttribute() Method

The **CreateAttribute()** method creates a new attribute based on the parameters passed to the function. Let's look at the parameters required by this method:

- ❑ **strCN** – The strCN parameter represents the common-name value of the attribute. The common-name is a mustContain attribute, and *must* be defined in order for the attribute to be created. For example, if we wanted to create a new attribute to track the number of visits for a member, we could choose the common-name value 'numVisits' for the attribute.

- ❑ **strName** – The strName parameter represents the display name value of the attribute. The display name is a user-friendly name for the attribute, used when it is displayed on the screen. For example, if the common-name of the attribute is 'numVisits', the display name might be 'Number of Visits'. The display name is a mayContain attribute.

- ❑ **strDesc** – The description value of the attribute is defined by the strDesc parameter. Using our example from the strName parameter, the description is a more verbose way of describing the attribute, including any relevant extra information. For example, if the display name is 'Number of Visits', then the description might be "The number of times a user has visited this site".

❑ **strType** – The `strType` parameter defines the type of the attribute. There are five possible types available. These five types are defined for the function as constants – using constants allows us to keep a reference of the available options within the program code for quick lookup. For our 'numVisits' example, this value would be an integer, or CREATEATTRIBUTE_TYPE_INTEGER. The five types of constant for `strType` are:

```
Const CREATEATTRIBUTE_TYPE_INTEGER    = "Integer"

Const CREATEATTRIBUTE_TYPE_STRING     = "UnicodeString

Const CREATEATTRIBUTE_TYPE_DATE       = "GeneralizedTime"

Const CREATEATTRIBUTE_TYPE_DN         = "DN"

Const CREATEATTRIBUTE_TYPE_BINARY     = "Binary"
```

The `strType` is a mustContain attribute.

❑ **nSingle** – `nSingle` is another mustContain attribute for a new attribute and defines whether or not the new attribute will be multi-valued. A multi-valued attribute is capable of holding multiple values stored as an array in a single attribute. In our 'number of visits' example we only need to store a single value, so we would pass CREATEATTRIBUTE_MULTIVALUED_FALSE as the parameter for `nSingle`. The two possible constants are:

```
Const CREATEATTRIBUTE_MULTIVALUED_TRUE     = 1

Const CREATEATTRIBUTE_MULTIVALUED_FALSE    = 0
```

❑ **nSearch** – The last parameter of the `CreateAttribute()` method is used for determining whether or not the attribute can be searched on. This is useful once we need to search for a value in the Membership Directory. For our example, the `numVisits` attribute should be searchable in case we need to run a report to tell us the number of visits per member, so we would pass CREATEATTRIBUTE_SEARCHABLE_TRUE to the `CreateAttribute()` method. The two possible constants are:

```
Const CREATEATTRIBUTE_SEARCHABLE_TRUE      = 1

Const CREATEATTRIBUTE_SEARCHABLE_FALSE     = 0
```

Code Sample – CreateAttribute Method

Now that we've defined the parameters, let's take a look at the code. You'll want to turn on debugging for the web site it is being run under.

```
<HTML>
<BODY BGCOLOR=WHITE>
<FONT FACE=ARIAL SIZE=3>
<B>
Function CreateAttribute(strCN, strName, strDesc, strType, nSingle, nSearch)
</B>
<HR SIZE=1>
</FONT>
<FONT FACE=ARIAL SIZE=2>
```

```
<%
' ****************************************************
' Constants for CreateAttribute Function
' ****************************************************
Const CREATEATTRIBUTE_TYPE_INTEGER         = "Integer"
Const CREATEATTRIBUTE_TYPE_STRING          = "UnicodeString"
Const CREATEATTRIBUTE_TYPE_DATE            = "GeneralizedTime"
Const CREATEATTRIBUTE_TYPE_DN              = "DN"
Const CREATEATTRIBUTE_TYPE_BINARY          = "Binary"
Const CREATEATTRIBUTE_MULTIVALUED_TRUE     = 1
Const CREATEATTRIBUTE_MULTIVALUED_FALSE    = 0
Const CREATEATTRIBUTE_SEARCHABLE_TRUE      = 1
Const CREATEATTRIBUTE_SEARCHABLE_FALSE     = 0


' ****************************************************
' FUNCTION: CreateAttribute
'
' PURPOSE: Creates new attriubtes
'
' PARAMETERS:
'     strCN - Common name of attribute
'
'     strName - Display name of attribute
'
'     strDesc - Description of attribute
'
'     strType - Attribute type, valid values defined by contants
'
'     nSingle - Multivalued attitbe, defined by contants
'
'     nSearch - Is attribute searchable, defined by contants
'
' REQUIRES: g_objSchema - Global object that points to the
'                         cn=Schema, ou=Admin, o=[organization name]
'                         container
'
' RETURNS: Boolean (True = success / False = failure)
'
```

After the headers for the HTML page, we'll define the constants we need for this method. We'll keep a description of the methods and its parameters in the code file for reference. Now let's look at the method itself.

```
Public Function CreateAttribute(strCN, strName, strDesc, strType, nSingle,
Search)
    On Error Resume Next

    CreateAttribute = False

    ' Create objects used to work with attributes
    ' *******************************
    Dim objSchemaAttribute

    Set objSchemaAttribute = g_objSchema.Create("attributeSchema", "cn=" & strCN )
```

First we define our function and set the default return value to indicate a failure. This ensures that, if the function terminates abnormally, the correct value is returned.

Next we want to create our new attribute object, objSchemaAttribute, and define it as a new instance of the attributeSchema class, with a common name of the value of the strCN parameter.

```
' We'll get an error if the attribute exists
' or if we haven't defined g_objSchema
' *******************************
If Err.Number <> 0 Then
   Err.Clear
   Exit Function
End If

objSchemaAttribute.put "displayname", Array(strName)
objSchemaAttribute.put "description", Array(strDesc)
objSchemaAttribute.put "attributeSyntax", Array(strType)
objSchemaAttribute.put "isSingleValued", Array(nSingle)
objSchemaAttribute.put "isSearchable", Array(nSearch)
```

After dealing with any errors, we define the attributes that will make up our new attributeSchema object.

```
' Call SetInfo to update directory
' *******************************
objSchemaAttribute.setInfo

If Err.Number <> 0 Then
   Err.Clear
   Exit Function
End If

' Everything looks good!
' *******************************
CreateAttribute = True
End Function
```

We update the Membership Directory, check that this has been successful and exit if not, and there we have our new attributeSchema object. Now that we have our createAttributes method we'll test it out.

```
' ***************************************************
' Example use of CreateAttributes Function
On Error Resume Next

Dim g_objSchema
Dim blnAddedNewAttribute

' Bind to the schema
' *******************************
Set g_objSchema = GetObject("LDAP://localhost:1003/o=Wrox/ou=Admin/cn=Schema")
If Err.Number <> 0 Then
   Response.Write "Unable to bind to schema."
   Response.End
End If
```

```
' Add new attribute - Example
' *******************************
blnAddedNewAttribute = CreateAttribute("numVisits", "Number of Visits", "The
number of times a user has visited this site", CREATEATTRIBUTE_TYPE_INTEGER,
CREATEATTRIBUTE_MULTIVALUED_FALSE, CREATEATTRIBUTE_SEARCHABLE_TRUE)

If blnAddedNewAttribute = True Then
  Response.Write "Added new attribute."
Else
  Response.Write "Failed to add new attribute"
End If
%>
</FONT>
</BODY>
</HTML>
```

We bind to the Membership Directory using the global object we discussed before looking at this method. We call the `CreateAttribute()` method with all the necessary parameters, and assign its return value to the variable `blnAddedNewAttribute`. We can then test this variable for the success of the method.

Don't forget to enable debugging (see Chapter 3) for the web site under which this is being run! The best way to see how the sample works is to either set a break point, or use the stop directive to step through the code in the debugger and watch the values while it executes, as in the screenshot below.

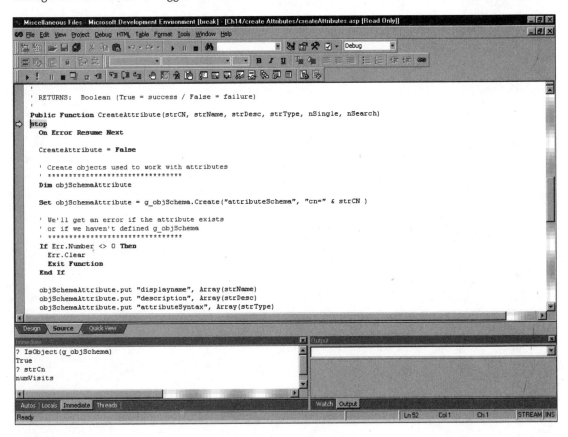

Now that we've learned how to create attributeSchema objects programmatically, let's do the same with classSchema objects.

Creating New Classes

The attributeSchema class was one of the two basic class types. To create new classes programmatically, we need to use the second of these two basic class types: we need to create a new classSchema instance for a new class. Again, similar to the reason for programmatically creating new attributes, we want to be able to create new classes programmatically so that we can manage the Membership Directory independently from the Membership Directory Manager. Of course, we can add new classes just as easily from the Membership Directory Manager, but if we have to add a large number of complex classes then it's much faster with script. Moreover, if we wanted to write our own web-based administration tools specific to our organization, we would want to be able to make modifications to classes through script.

For example, to populate a Membership Directory with a specific schema, it is much easier to maintain an 'installation' script that automatically creates and adds the correct attributes to classes, as opposed to trying to remember the details for each class. This is especially useful in a development-to-production environment, where the schema might change as the product is developed. The attributes and classes could exist in a script, and when the site is ready to be put into production the script can be run once to populate the Membership Directory with the correct information. If we sold a product that took advantage of the Membership Directory to track customers, we would want our product to create and install a new object class of customers that we would use.

Once again, we need to bind to the Membership Directories' cn=Schema, ou=Admin, o=[*organization name*] container and create a new entry, this time for a classSchema object rather than an attributeSchema object. We can use the same method to bind that we saw in the previous section, using a global variable, g_objSchema, so we won't repeat the code sample again here.

The CreateClass() Method

The **CreateClass()** method creates a new class based on the parameters passed to the function. Let's take a look at the necessary parameters:

- ❑ **strCN** – The strCN parameter represents the common-name value of a new class. The common-name is a mustContain attribute and must be defined for the class to be created. For example, if we wanted to create a new class to represent Windows Media streams, we might create a new class with a cn value of 'WMStreams'.
- ❑ **strName** – The strName parameter represents the display name value of the class, and is a user-friendly name for the class. For example, if the common-name of the attribute is 'WMStreams', the display name might be 'Windows Media Streams'. The display name is not a mustContain attribute.
- ❑ **strDesc** – The description value of the class is defined by the strDesc parameter. The description is a more verbose way of describing the class. For example, if the display name is 'Windows Media Streams', the description might be 'Class to represent Windows Media Streams'.

- ❑ **nIsContainer** – The `nIsContainer` parameter represents the mustContain attribute of isContainer which determines whether or not the new class can act as a container for other classes. We'll use constants defined in the function to determine whether or not this class can be a container. In our example, the 'WMStream' class is not a container, and we would therefore set the `nIsContainer` attribute to `CREATECLASS_ISCONTAINER_FALSE`. The constants available for this parameter are:

```
Const CREATECLASS_ISCONTAINER_TRUE        = 1

Const CREATECLASS_ISCONTAINER_FALSE       = 0
```

- ❑ **nIsSecPrincipal** – The `nIsSecPrincipal` parameter is a mustContain attribute of a new class and determines whether or not the attribute can be used as a security principal. A security principal is any object in the Membership Directory that can be used to define an Access Control Entry for other objects. An example of a security principal in the Membership Directory is the member class. For our 'WMStream' class, we don't need to make it a security principal so we'll use the constant that defines whether or not the new class will be a security principal, `CREATECLASS_ISSECPRINCIPAL_FALSE`. The constants for this parameter are:

```
Const CREATECLASS_ISSECPRINCIPAL_TRUE    = 1

Const CREATECLASS_ISSECPRINCIPAL_FALSE   = 0
```

- ❑ **arrMustContain** – The `arrMustContain` parameter is a one-dimensional array that we pass to the function: the array contains the common-name values of all the attributes that the new class mustContain. The `arrMustContain` attribute is a mustContain attribute of a new class, so it must be defined. Moreover, the `rdnAttId` has to be an attribute included in this array (its value is defined through the `strRDNId` parameter we'll see below). For our 'WMStream' class example we could use common name, companyName and description as the attributes in this array, meaning that any instance of the 'WMStream' class that is created must contain these values.

> **The rdnAttId, which defines the naming type of instances of the new class, must be an attribute defined in the arrMustContain attribute array**

- ❑ **arrMayContain** – Somewhat like the `arrMustContain` array, the `arrMayContain` is an array of attributes used to describe an instance of a class. The `arrMayContain` attributes do not need to be defined to create a new instance of the class. Using our 'WMStream' example, we could use `creatorsName` as a mayContain attribute to track. Any new instance of the WMStream class may or may not choose to define this attribute for the class.

- ❑ **strRDNId** – The `strRDNId` parameter of the function defines the mustContain value rdnAttId. The `rdnAttId` (the relative distinguished name attribute id) is one of the mustContain attributes for a classSchema and is used to identify instances of the new class. The most common attribute used for the `rdnAttId` is the common name (cn) attribute. For our 'WMStream' example, we'll use the cn to represent new instances of the class.

- ❑ **ArrPossSuperiors** – Finally, the `arrPossSuperiors`, another mustContain attribute of a new classSchema entry in the Membership schema, is used to define the possible superior objects that instances of this class can be created under. The `arrPossSuperiors` is a list of classes that can be containers of the new class. For our 'WMStream' class, the organization (o=) and the organizationalUnit (ou=) classes are used since the new class should be able to be created under an organization or an organizationalUnit.

Code Sample – CreateClass Method

Now that we've defined the parameters, let's take a look at the code:

```
<HTML>
<BODY BGCOLOR=WHITE>
<FONT FACE=ARIAL SIZE=3>
<B>
Function CreateClass(strCN, strDesc, strName, nIsContainer, nIsSecPrincipal,
arrMustContain, arrMayContain, strRDNID, arrPossSuperiors)
</B>
<HR SIZE=1>
</FONT>
<FONT FACE=ARIAL SIZE=2>
<%
' **************************************************
' Constants for CreateClass Function
' **************************************************
Const CREATECLASS_ISCONTAINER_TRUE      = 1
Const CREATECLASS_ISCONTAINER_FALSE     = 0

Const CREATECLASS_ISSECPRINCIPAL_TRUE   = 1
Const CREATECLASS_ISSECPRINCIPAL_FALSE  = 0

' **************************************************
' FUNCTION: CreateClass
'
' PURPOSE: Creates new classes
'
' PARAMETERS:
'     strCN - Common name of class
'
'     strDesc - Description of class
'
'     strName - Display name of class
'
'     nIsContainer - boolean whether or not this class can be a container
'
'     nIsSecPrinicipal - boolean whether or not this class can be
'                               a security principal
'
'     arrMustContain - array of must contain attributes
'
'     arrMayContain - array of may contain attributes
'
'     strRDNId - RDN for new instances of this class
'
'     arrPossSuperiors - Classes that can be containers for this class
'
' REQUIRES: g_objSchema - Global object that points to the
'                               cn=Schema, ou=Admin, o=[organization name]
'                               container
'
' RETURNS: Boolean (True = success / False = failure)
'
```

As before, after the HTML headers we define the constants we need and describe the method. Then, below, we can go on to define our `CreateClass()` method.

```
Public Function CreateClass(strCN, strDesc, strName, nIsContainer,
nIsSecPrincipal, arrMustContain, arrMayContain, strRDNID, arrPossSuperiors)
  On Error Resume Next

  CreateClass = False

  ' Create objects used to work with classes
  ' ********************************
  Dim objSchemaClass

  Set objSchemaClass = g_objSchema.Create("classSchema", "cn=" & strCN )

  ' We'll get an error if the attribute exists
  ' or if we haven't defined g_objSchema
  ' ********************************
  If Err.Number <> 0 Then
    Err.Clear
    Exit Function
  End If
```

As before, we set the default return value of our `CreateClass()` method in case of an abnormal failure. We then create a new instance of the classSchema class, with a common name value of the `strCN` parameter, and check that this hasn't failed. Now we have a new object, we can go on to populate its attributes:

```
  objSchemaClass.put "displayname", CStr(strName)
  objSchemaClass.put "description", CStr(strDesc)
  objSchemaClass.put "isContainer", CStr(nIsContainer)
  objSchemaClass.put "isSecurityPrincipal", CStr(nIsSecPrincipal)
  objSchemaClass.mustContain = arrMustContain
  objSchemaClass.put "rdnAttID", CStr(strRDNID)
  objSchemaClass.possSuperiors = arrPossSuperiors
  objSchemaClass.mayContain = arrMayContain

  ' Call SetInfo to update directory
  ' ********************************
  objSchemaClass.SetInfo

  If Err.Number <> 0 Then
    Err.Clear
    Exit Function
  End If

  ' Everything looks good!
  ' ********************************
  CreateClass = True
End Function
```

We've set all the other attributes that we'll want to be included in our new class object, updated the Membership Directory, and checked that we've successfully created our new class. Now we can try the method out:

```
' **************************************************
' Example use of function
On Error Resume Next

Dim g_objSchema
Dim blnAddedNewClass

' Create local arrays for the must
' contain and the may contain
' attributes of this class
' *******************************
Dim l_arrMayContain(0)
Dim l_arrMustContain(2)

' Create local array to represent
' possible superiors of this object
' *******************************
Dim l_arrPossSuperiors(1)

' Populate may contain array
' *************************
l_arrMayContain(0) = "creatorsName"

' Populate must contain array
' *************************
l_arrMustContain(0) = "cn"
l_arrMustContain(1) = "companyName"
l_arrMustContain(2) = "description"

' Populate possible superiors array
' *************************
l_arrPossSuperiors(0) = "organization"
l_arrPossSuperiors(1) = "organizationalUnit"
```

A number of the attributes for this new class take an array of values. We need to create these arrays locally in order to store the values with which we want to create our new class instance. We can then pass the local arrays as parameters when we call the method, below:

```
' Bind to the schema
' *******************************
Set g_objSchema = GetObject("LDAP://localhost:1003/o=Wrox/ou=Admin/cn=Schema")
If Err.Number <> 0 Then
  Response.Write "Unable to bind to schema."
  Response.End
End If

' Add new Class - Example
' *******************************
blnAddedNewClass = CreateClass("WMStream", "Class to represent Windows Media
streams", "Windows Media Stream", CREATECLASS_ISCONTAINER_FALSE,
CREATECLASS_ISSECPRINCIPAL_FALSE, l_arrMustContain, l_arrMayContain, "cn",
l_arrPossSuperiors)

If blnAddedNewClass = True Then
  Response.Write "Added new class."
Else
```

```
      Response.Write "Failed to add new class."
End If
%>
</FONT>
</BODY>
</HTML>
```

As before, we bind to the Membership Directory and check that this has worked, call the method and test the return value. We should then have a populated instance of our new class.

Creating classes programmatically is very useful. However, we may also want to change existing classes.

Adding Attributes to Classes

We've created both new classes and new attributes, and we know how we could add these new attributes to a new class. But how do we add attributes to existing classes? The mustContain and mayContain attributes of a class are already populated since the class already exists.

To add attributes to an existing class, first we need to read out the existing attributes and compare them to the attributes we want to add. If there is a match, we don't need to add the attribute. However, if the attribute doesn't exist then we need to add it to the array representing either the mustContain or mayContain array of valid values, and save it back to the class. As we discovered in Chapter 7, it's relatively simple to add an attribute to an existing class through the Membership Directory Manager. If we want to manage these classes from script, to automate the process, we can do so with the AddAttributesToClass() method.

The AddAttributesToClass() Method

The AddAttributesToClass() method takes three parameters:

an array of attributes that are to be added to a class, the name of the class that is to be modified, and an indication of whether or not the attributes are to be added to the mayContain or mustContain attribute of the class.

- ❑ **arrAttributesToAdd** – The arrAttributesToAdd parameter is a one-dimensional array listing the attributes that are to be added to the class. For example, if we want to add a new attribute to the member class (such as an existing attribute 'education'), we would pass an array with this one value.

- ❑ **strClassName** – The strClassName parameter is used to pass the name of the class to which we want to add the new attributes. Using our member class and 'education' attribute example, we would want to pass the string 'member' – to tell the method that we want to make modifications to the 'member' class.

- ❑ **nMayContain** – The nMayContain parameter is used to tell the AddAttributesToClass() method whether the attributes are to be added as the mayContain or the mustContain attributes. To do this, we'll use the following constants:

```
      Const ADDATTRIBUTESTOCLASS_MAYCONTAIN_TRUE  = 1

      Const ADDATTRIBUTESTOCLASS_MAYCONTAIN_FALSE = 0
```

In the code sample we'll use ADDATTRIBUTESTOCLASS_MAYCONTAIN_TRUE, since the attribute 'education' isn't a required attribute for a new member. If we were to use ADDATTRIBUTESTOCLASS_MAYCONTAIN_FALSE then the method would set the attribute 'education' as a mustContain attribute for the member class. Consequently, any new member that was created would have to declare values for the cn, GUID and education attributes.

Code Sample – AddAttributesToClass Method

Just as in the other two methods that we've covered so far, the AddAtrributesToClass() method depends upon a global object, g_objSchema, that is a reference to the cn=Schema container.

```
<HTML>
<BODY BGCOLOR=WHITE>
<FONT FACE=ARIAL SIZE=3>
<B>
Function AddAttributesToClass(arrAttributesToAdd, strClassName, nMayContain)
</B>
<HR SIZE=1>
</FONT>
<FONT FACE=ARIAL SIZE=2>
<%
Const ADDATTRIBUTESTOCLASS_MAYCONTAIN_TRUE = 1
Const ADDATTRIBUTESTOCLASS_MAYCONTAIN_FALSE = 0

' ************************************************
' FUNCTION: AddAttributesToClass
'
' PURPOSE: Adds attributes to the specified class
'
' RETURNS: True - Success / False - Failure
'
' Parameters:
'      arrAttributesToAdd - Array of attributes to be added to the class
'
'      strClassName - The name of the class in the schema to add the attributes to
'
'      MayContain - boolean determines whether the attributes
'                   are mayContain (true) or mustContain (false)
'
Function AddAttributesToClass(arrAttributesToAdd, strClassName, nMayContain)
   On Error Resume Next

   Dim objClass
   Dim arrContain
   Dim nExistingItems
   Dim arrAddAttributes
   Dim nArrayLoop
   Dim nArrayLoop2
   Dim blnMatch


   ' Assume failure
   ' ************************************************
   AddAttributesToClass = False
```

As with our previous samples, we define the constants and the function name, and set the default return value:

```
' Attempt to bind to the classSchema type
' fail if classSchema type doesn't exist
' ***********************************************
Set objClass = g_objSchema.GetObject("classSchema", "cn=" & strClassName)
If Err.number <> 0 Then
  Err.Clear
  Exit Function
End If

' Populate arrays for must and may contain attributes
' based on nMayContain parameter
' ***********************************************
If nMayContain = ADDATTRIBUTESTOCLASS_MAYCONTAIN_TRUE Then
  ' modify may contain attributes
  ' *******************************************
  arrContain = objClass.Get("mayContain")
Else
  ' modify must contain attributes
  ' *******************************************
  arrContain = objClass.Get("mustContain")
End If
```

First we bind to the supplied schema. Then we need to find out whether the attribute that we're adding is of type mayContain or mustContain, so that we can get the correct attribute array to modify.

```
' Get the number of existing items
' ***********************************************
nExistingItems = UBound(arrContain) - LBound(arrContain)

' Populate the arrAddAttributes array with all
' of the items in arrContain
' ***********************************************
ReDim arrAddAttributes(nExistingItems)
For nArrayLoop = LBound(arrContain) to UBound(arrContain)
  arrAddAttributes(nArrayLoop) = arrContain(nArrayLoop)
Next
```

We copy all existing attributes into the array that will be the new complete list of attributes, arrAddAttributes. Next we have to establish whether we have any new attributes to add to this array.

```
' Compare new properties in existing. If there is not a match then
' add them to arrAddAttributes
' ***********************************************
For nArrayLoop = LBound(arrAttributesToAdd) to UBound(arrAttributesToAdd)
  blnMatch = False

  ' Loop through and compare
  ' ***********************************************
  For nArrayLoop2 = LBound(arrContain) to UBound(arrContain)
```

```
      If LCase(arrAttributesToAdd(nArrayLoop)) = LCase(arrContain(nArrayLoop2))
Then
        blnMatch = True
        Exit For
      End If
    Next

    If Not blnMatch Then
      nExistingItems = nExistingItems + 1
      ReDim Preserve arrAddAttributes(nExistingItems)
      arrAddAttributes(nExistingItems) = arrAttributesToAdd(nArrayLoop)
    End If
  Next
```

We compare each attribute in the array we were passed as a parameter, `arrAttributesToAdd`, with the list of existing attributes we have in `arrContain`. We exit the loop if we find that the attribute already exists in the class. If there isn't a match for that attribute we add it to our new complete list of attributes, `arrAddAttributes`.

```
' Set either must or may contain array to
' our new array with our desired values
' *********************************************
If nMayContain = ADDATTRIBUTESTOCLASS_MAYCONTAIN_TRUE Then
  ' Put may contain attributes
  ' *********************************************
  objClass.Put "mayContain",(arrAddAttributes)
Else
  ' Put must contain attributes
  ' *********************************************
  objClass.Put "mustContain",(arrAddAttributes)
End If

' Error putting new array
' *********************************************
If Err.number <> 0 Then
  Err.Clear
  Exit Function
End If

' Save changes
' *********************************************
objClass.setInfo
If Err.number <> 0 Then
  Err.Clear
  Exit Function
Else
  AddAttributesToClass = True
End If
End Function
```

We can then store the new complete array of attributes in the class and save the class in the Membership Directory, checking for errors as we go. Let's look at some example code to call this method.

```
' ****************************************************
' Example use of function
On Error Resume Next

Dim g_objSchema
Dim blnAddedAttributesToClass

' Create local arrays for the must
' contain and the may contain
' attributes of this class
' ********************************
Dim l_arrMayContain(0)

' Populate may contain array
' *************************
l_arrMayContain(0) = "education"
```

First, we set up the local array with the one attribute that we're going to add to the member class. Then we bind to the schema and call the method as we've seen in the previous examples:

```
' Bind to the schema
' ********************************
Set g_objSchema = GetObject("LDAP://localhost:1003/o=Wrox/ou=Admin/cn=Schema")
If Err.Number <> 0 Then
  Response.Write "Unable to bind to schema."
  Response.End
End If

' Add attributes to class
' ********************************
blnAddedAttributesToClass = AddAttributesToClass(l_arrMayContain, "member",
ADDATTRIBUTESTOCLASS_MAYCONTAIN_TRUE)

If blnAddedAttributesToClass = True Then
  Response.Write "Added attributes to class."
Else
  Response.Write "Failed to add attributes to class."
End If
%>
</FONT>
</BODY>
</HTML>
```

We now have the knowledge necessary to create and modify both attributeSchema and classSchema objects in the Membership Directory. Let's now spend some time looking at how to create members programmatically.

Creating New Members

Creating new instances of the member class for new members is nothing new. We've shown several examples of creating new members throughout the book; however, when it comes to creating new members, programmatically is the only way to go. As easy as the Microsoft Management Console Membership Directory Manager snap-in and wizards are to use, nothing beats writing a script to create all those new users automatically – especially when we have a set of pre-existing members to add.

There may be other reasons to use code to create new members. What if membership for the site is gained simply by asking for it? It's a lot easier to write an ASP page that can auto-register and create new members after successfully completing a membership registration form, than having every individual user email the site administrator and apply for his or her own separate membership account. Not only does this take precious time away from the site administrator, but worse, users have to wait before they can get the information they want!

Where to Create New Members

Although new members – like any other object – can be created anywhere in the Membership Directory, they *should* be created in the ou=Members container, or in a container under the ou=Members container.

The reasoning for this is simple. The Membership Directory already provides this container and all of the Site Server tools that work with the Membership Directory, such as Personalization and Membership, know how to 'look' in the ou=Members container for members. If we wanted P&M to use another container to authenticate members, we would have to modify the base distinguished name (BaseDN). We covered this in Chapter 8.

> **Members should be created in or under the ou=Members container for the Personalization and Membership system to work with the default settings.**

This doesn't mean however that all members have to exist in the same container. The ou=Members container can be divided into sub-containers (which themselves can be further divided into sub-containers) to logically group members together in groups such as marketing, administration, or engineering:

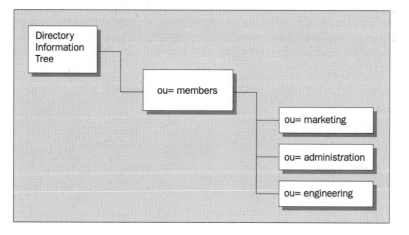

We won't look at sub-classing the ou=members container here. It's easily done through the Membership Directory Manager, since it is more of a planned necessity than one driven by immediate user needs.

Now that we've learned where members should be created, let's look at the CreateMember() method used to create members programmatically.

The CreateMember() Method

The `CreateMember()` method requires the LDAP path from the Membership Directory root to the container where the new member needs to be created. Additionally, the new member name and password is required. The method returns a member object back to the caller, and this object should be tested with `Is Nothing` to determine whether or not the method call succeeded.

As with the previous examples, we need to bind to the Membership Directory. However, unlike binding to the cn=Schema, for the `CreateMember()` method we need a global object bound to the Membership Directory root – `g_objLDAPRoot`. This object's ADsPath value should be:

```
LDAP://[server name]:[port number]/o=[organization name]
```

An example of this is provided in the code sample. Now let's have a look at `CreateMember()`'s parameters:

- ❑ **strPathToContainerFromRoot** – The `strPathToContainerFromRoot` is used by the method to determine what container the new member should be created under. For example, to create a new member in a subcontainer of ou=Members, called ou=NewMembers, we would pass a `strPathToContainerFromRoot` value of 'ou=NewMembers, ou=Members'. This path information would then be used in conjunction with a global `g_objLDAPRoot` to bind to.

- ❑ **strMemberName** – The `strMemberName` parameter represents the new member to be created in the `strPathToContainerFromRoot`. If we wanted to create a new member, 'Jon', we would pass this value for this parameter, and if successful, Jon will be created in the container described by `strPathToContainerFromRoot`.

- ❑ **strMemberPassword** – Similar to `strMemberName`, `strMemberPassword` is used for the new member to be created. While `strMemberName` represents the cn value of the new member object, `strMemberPassword` represents the userPassword value.

Code Sample – CreateMember() Method

Now that we've reviewed the parameters, let's take a look at the code. We'll begin by defining everything we need, as we've seen before:

```
<HTML>
<BODY BGCOLOR=WHITE>
<FONT FACE=ARIAL SIZE=3>
<B>
Function CreateMember(strPathToContainerFromRoot, strMemberName,
strMemberPassword)
</B>
<HR SIZE=1>
</FONT>
<FONT FACE=ARIAL SIZE=2>
<%
' ****************************************************
' FUNCTION: CreateMember()
'
' PURPOSE: Creates new membership members
'
' RETURNS: Object representing new member (IADs)
'
' PARAMETERS:
```

```
'       strPathToContainer - Path to container to create new member in... such as:
'                   ou=Members, ou=NewMembers
'
'       strMemberName - The username (cn) of the new member
'
'       strMemberPassword - The password (userPassword) of the new member
'
' REQUIRES:
'       g_objLDAPRoot - Root of the Membership Directory:
'                   such as g_objLDAPRoot = GetObject(LDAP://server:port)
'
Public Function CreateMember(strPathToContainerFromRoot, strMemberName,
strMemberPassword)
    On Error Resume Next

    Dim objGUIDGen
    Dim strGUID
    Dim objMemberContainer
    Dim objNewUser

    ' Assume Failure
    ' ****************************
    Set CreateMember = Nothing
```

Next we set up the body of the method:

```
' Connect to the container to
' create new objects in
' ****************************
    Set objMemberContainer  = GetObject(g_objLDAPRoot.ADsPath & "/" &
strPathToContainerFromRoot)
    If Err.Number <> 0 Then
        Err.Clear
        Exit Function
    End If
```

Here we point to the container into which the new member will be placed.

```
' Create the Membership GUID Generator
' ****************************
    Set objGUIDGen = Server.CreateObject("Membership.GUIDGen.1")
    If Err.Number <> 0 Then
        Err.Clear
        Exit Function
    End If

' Create the GUID
' ****************************
    strGUID = objGUIDGen.GenerateGuid
```

Members have to have a GUID, to uniquely identify them in the directory, so we use the GUID generator to create this for us.

```
   ' Create the new user
   ' ****************************
   Set objNewUser = objMemberContainer.Create("member", "cn=" & strMemberName)
   If Err.Number <> 0 Then
     Err.Clear
     Exit Function
   End If

   ' Set some user attributes
   ' ****************************
   objNewUser.put "GUID", CStr(strGUID)                    ' must contain
   objNewUser.put "userPassword", CStr(strMemberPassword)  ' may contain

   ' Call SetInfo
   ' ****************************
   objNewUser.SetInfo
   If Err.Number <> 0 Then
     Err.Clear
     Exit Function
   End If

   ' Pass back the new user
   ' ****************************
   Set CreateMember = objNewUser
End Function
```

So, the function will create a new member with two attributes – a GUID and a password – and pass this new member back. Note we use Set to assign the return value of the function, since it returns an object. We can call this function, as we've seen before.

```
   ' ****************************************************
   ' Example use of function
   On Error Resume Next

   Dim g_objLDAPRoot
   Dim objNewMember

   ' Bind to root of directory
   ' ****************************
   Set g_objLDAPRoot = GetObject("LDAP://localhost:1003")
   If Err.Number <> 0 Then
     Response.Write "Unable to bind to directory"
     Response.End
   End If

   ' Create new member
   ' ****************************
   Set objNewMember = CreateMember("ou=Members", "Robert", "password")
```

We've created a new member called 'Robert'. Finally, we need to test for the new member's existence.

```
' test for new member existance
' ****************************
If objNewMember Is Nothing Then
  Response.Write "New Member not created."
Else
  Response.Write "New Member created : " & objNewMember.cn
End If
%>
</FONT>
</BODY>
</HTML>
```

Assuming that the public group has been removed from the root of the Directory Information Tree and that anonymous users have the necessary rights to create new members, this script will work on a secured site (although you probably want to limit the permissions that new users have).

Code Sample – Creating New Members in C++

Another solution for creating new members on a secured site is to create a COM object, either in VB or C++. Let's look at a C++ example that creates new members – we could do the same thing in VB by using the same logic and code from the previous ASP sample with minor modifications.

```cpp
//Add the files activeds.lib and adsiid.lib to this project
#include <comdef.h>
#include <iostream.h>
#include <activeds.h>
#include <winerror.h>

HRESULT CreateMember(BSTR bstrADsParentPath, BSTR bstrMemberName,
                                             BSTR bstrMemberPassword)
{
  HRESULT hr;

  IADsContainer * pIADsContainer;
  IADs * pIADsNewMember;
  GUID guid;
  wchar_t szGUID[39];

  // Bind to the parent container
  // **********************************
  hr = ADsGetObject(bstrADsParentPath,
                    IID_IADsContainer,
                    (void**)&pIADsContainer
                    );
  if (FAILED (hr))
  {
    return (hr);
  }

  // Generate a guid
  // *******************************
  hr = CoCreateGuid(&guid);
  int r = ::StringFromGUID2(guid,szGUID, 39);
  if (FAILED (hr))
  {
    return (hr);
  }
```

```
   // Create the new user
   // ********************************
   hr = pIADsContainer->Create(L"member",
                               bstrMemberName,
                               (IDispatch**)&pIADsNewMember
                               );
   if (FAILED (hr))
   {
     return (hr);
   }

   // Set some new user attributes
   // ********************************
   hr = pIADsNewMember->Put(L"GUID", (_variant_t)szGUID);
   hr = pIADsNewMember->Put(L"userPassword",
                            (_variant_t)bstrMemberPassword
                            );

   // SetInfo on new member
   // ********************************
   hr = pIADsNewMember->SetInfo();
   if (FAILED (hr))
   {
     return (hr);
   }

   return hr;
}

int main()
{
   CoInitialize (NULL);

   HRESULT hr = NULL;

   // Function returns HRESULT
   // ********************************
   hr = CreateMember(L"LDAP://manx:1003/ou=members,o=Wrox", L"cn=Rob",
L"password");

   // Success or Failure message
   // ********************************
   if (FAILED(hr))
   {
     if (hr == -2147024713)
     {
       cout << "Failed: User already exists." << endl;
     }
     else
     {
       cout << "Failed: Unknown error." << endl;
     }
   }
   else
   {
     cout << "New user created." << endl;
   }

   return 0;
}
```

Now that we've covered the primary tasks of the Membership Directory Manager wizards, let's look at how we can do some other membership management tasks.

Other Membership Directory Tasks

In addition to creating new attributes, classes, and members, we sometimes need to manage other items in the Membership Directory – such as reissuing cookies to members that have lost the cookies which identify them, or creating new groups and adding members to those groups. Let's take a look first at how we can support a roaming user profile.

The Roaming User Profile

When using Cookie Authentication to authenticate members, we may encounter certain problems. The cookies can sometimes get corrupted or can be deleted by the member. Some members want to access their profile from different machines, from home as well as the office. Say you've taken the time to personalize a site at home – for example an investment site. If you wanted to view the information from a friend's computer, how do you get to it? For a site using Clear Text/Basic Authentication, this won't be much of a problem, but for a site using Cookie Authentication, how do you get the appropriate cookie back to the user?

To do this we need to provide an alternative form of authentication – such as Site Serve HTML Forms or Clear Text/Basic Authentication. After authenticating the member through the alternative form of authentication, the Membership System now knows who the member is. After re-establishing who the member is, we can validate the cookies on their machine. If the cookies are invalid we can send the new cookies and if the cookies are valid we can send them on their merry way.

Cookie Authentication uses the SITESERVER cookie to store the member GUID, and the MEMUSER cookie to store the member relative distinguished name (relative to the base distinguished name). To change these values, we can use the Membership.VerifUsr object and the IssueCookie() method. The new cookies we'll issue are the values of the Name property and the GUID attribute of the member.

> *Remember – don't ask for the GUID implicitly, i.e. through* objAUOUser.Guid *– this returns the IADs* Guid *property, not the GUID value of the member attribute.*

Let's review a method called SendCookies() that sends the appropriate cookies to the member. To use this method, we need to create an instance of the Active User Object behind a page that has been authenticated (with one of the other authentication methods we discussed). The AUO will then send the correct cookies using the member profile with which the member authenticated the page.

Code Sample – SendCookies() Method

Here's the code:

```
<%
' ****************************************************
' FUNCTION: SendCookies()
'
' PURPOSE: Send correct cookie to member
'
```

```
' RETURNS: True - success / False - failed
'
Public Function SendCookies()
  On Error Resume Next

    ' Assume failure
    ' ***********************************
    SendCookies = False

    Dim objAUO        ' Active User Object
    Dim strGuid       ' Value of GUID attribute
    Dim strCn         ' Value of common name
    Dim objNewCookie  ' Verify User Object
```

This method doesn't take any parameters, so all we have to do is define the variables we're going to need in the method.

```
    ' Create the AUO
    ' ***********************************
    Set objAUO = Server.CreateObject("Membership.UserObjects.1")
    If Err.Number <> 0 Then
      Err.Clear
      Exit Function
    End If

    ' Retrieve User values
    ' ***********************************
    strGuid = objAUO.Get("guid")
    strCn = objAUO.Get("cn")

    ' Remove decoration from GUID
    ' (hold over from the beta)
    ' ***********************************
    strGuid = Replace(strGuid, "-", "")
    strGuid = Replace(strGuid, "{", "")
    strGuid = Replace(strGuid, "}", "")
```

Now that we've created our AUO instance and retrieved two attributes (the GUID and the cn values for this user) we can issue the cookies if they're required.

```
    ' Do we have the correct cookie
    ' ***********************************
    If (Request.Cookies("SITESERVER") <> "GUID=" & strGuid) OR
 (Request.Cookies("MEMUSER") = "") OR (Request.Cookies("MEMUSER") <> Strcn) Then
      ' Create a new VerifyUser object
      ' ***********************************
      Set objNewCookie = Server.CreateObject("Membership.verifusr.1")

      If Err.Number <> 0 Then
        Err.Clear
        Exit Function
      Else
        ' Everythings looks good...set the cookies
        ' ***********************************
        objNewCookie.IssueCookie "SITESERVER", "GUID=" & strGuid
        objNewCookie.IssueCookie "MEMUSER", strCn
```

```
        ' Did we update?
        ' ********************************
        If Err.Number <> 0 Then
           Err.Clear
           Exit Function
        Else
           SendCookies = True
        End If
      End If
   End If
End Function
```

Notice that we don't do any of the cookie creation if it already exists as part of the browser's cookies collection. This would happen for those people who have successfully got cookies from previous use.

Next we need to test out our method.

```
' ****************************
' Example Use of SendCookies()
If SendCookies() Then
   blnSent = True
Else
   blnSent = False
End If
%>

<FONT FACE=ARIAL SIZE=3>
<B>
Function SendCookies()
</B>
<HR SIZE=1>
</FONT>
<FONT FACE=ARIAL SIZE=2>
<%
If blnSent Then
   Response.Write "New cookies written!"
Else
   Response.Write "Error - New cookies not written!"
End If
%>
</FONT>
</BODY>
</HTML>
```

Make sure the SendCookies() method is called before writing any HTML back to the browser. The SendCookies() method sends cookies back to the browser and will fail if the server has already written the headers.

Adding Members to Groups

In Chapter 9, we saw how we can easily create groups using the Create() method of the IADsContainer interface. Let's now take it a step further and learn how we can programmatically add members to groups.

The AddUserToGroup() Method

The `AddUserToGroup()` method accepts parameters that define the member to be added and the group the member will be added to:

❑ **strADsPathToUser** – The `strADsPathToUser` parameter defines the full path to the member in the Membership Directory. We can retrieve this value for this parameter by passing the `ADsPath` property of the member to be added.

❑ **strGroupName** – In addition to passing the ADsPath to the member to add, we also have to pass the name of the group that the member is to be added to. `strGroupName` represents the name of the group in the ou=Groups container to add the member to. Note that we're not passing the `Name` property of the group, but rather the value of the cn of the group – for example, we're passing Premium rather than cn=Premium.

Now that we've read over the parameters, let's look at the code.

Code Sample – AddUserToGroup() Method

`AddUserToGroup()` requires a pre-bound global object. `g_objLDAPRoot`. `g_objLDAPRoot` is an object that is already bound to the root container – such as `LDAP://localhost:1003/o=Wrox` – before the `AddUserToGroup()` method is called.

```
<FONT FACE=ARIAL SIZE=3>
<B>
Function AddUsertoGroup(strADsPathToUser, strGroupName)</B>
<HR SIZE=1>
</FONT>
<FONT FACE=ARIAL SIZE=2>
<%
'*************************************************
' FUNCTION: AddUsertoGroup
'
' PURPOSE:  Adds a user to a specified group
'
' PARAMETERS:
'     strADsPathToUser - ADsPath to user in DS
'     strGroupName - Name of Group to add user to
'
' REQUIRES: g_objLDAPRoot - Root path to Membership Directory
'
' RETURNS: True - Success
'          False - Failure
'
Public Function AddUsertoGroup(strADsPathToUser, strGroupName)
  On Error Resume Next

  ' Set intial return value of function
  ' ***************************
  AddUsertoGroup = false

  Dim objGroupContainer     ' Object used to point to group container
  Dim objMembersContainer   ' Object used to point to the members container
  Dim objGroup              ' Object uset to point to the group
  Dim objGuidGen            ' Object used to generate GUIDS
  Dim strGroupGUID          ' Guid used for creating a memberof group property
```

```
Dim objAddMember           ' Object used to add user to a group
Dim objMemInfo             ' Membership Info Object
Dim strUserDNPath          ' User's DN Path
```

Here, we've defined the method heading, and dimensioned all the variables we're going to need. Next we need two objects, one bound to the members container and the other bound to the groups container:

```
' Connect to Groups Container
' ****************************
Set objGroupContainer = g_objLDAPRoot.GetObject("organizationalUnit",
"ou=Groups")
If Err.Number <> 0 Then
  Err.Clear
  Exit Function
End If

' Connect to Members Container
' ****************************
Set objMembersContainer = g_objLDAPRoot.GetObject("organizationalUnit",
"ou=Members")
If Err.Number <> 0 Then
  Err.Clear
  Exit Function
End If

' Point the Group that we passed in
' ****************************
Set objGroup = objGroupContainer.GetObject("mGroup", "cn=" & strGroupName)
If Err.Number <> 0 Then
  Err.Clear
  Exit Function
End If
```

We've defined a group object for the group value, which was passed to the method as a parameter. Next we need to establish the GUID for the group to which we want to add a member. We can then use this GUID as a parameter for the `Create()` method of our group object, to create a new `memberof` object.

```
' Create GUID Creation object
' ******************************
Set objGUIDGen = Server.CreateObject("Membership.GUIDGen.1")
If Err.Number <> 0 Then
  Err.Clear
  Exit Function
End If

' Generate the GUID for the group
' ******************************
strGroupGUID = objGUIDGen.GenerateGuid

' Create a new memberof object
' ******************************
Set objAddMember = objGroup.Create("memberof", "cn=" & strGroupGUID)
If Err.Number <> 0 Then
```

```
            Err.Clear
            Exit Function
       End If
```

Finally, we use the `MembershipInfo` object to find the user's DN path (we looked at the details of this in Chapter 12). All information can now be stored back into the Membership Directory.

```
    ' Get the MembershipInfo object to help convert ADsPath to DN
    ' *******************************
    Set objMemInfo = Server.CreateObject("Membership.MembershipInfo.1")
    If Err.Number <> 0 Then
      Err.Clear
      Exit Function
    End If

    ' Convert user object's ADs path to DN path
    ' *******************************
    strUserDNPath = objMemInfo.ADsPathToDN(strADsPathToUser)

    ' Store user object's DN path in group object
    ' *******************************
    objAddMember.Put "memberobject", CStr(strUserDNPath)
    If Err.Number <> 0 Then
      Err.Clear
      Exit Function
    End If

    ' Commit the info into the DS
    ' *******************************
    objAddMember.SetInfo
    If Err.Number <> 0 Then
      Err.Clear
      Exit Function
    End If

    ' Everything looks good
    ' **************************
    AddUserToGroup = True
End Function
```

Now let's put this method into practice:

```
' **************************************************
' Example use of function
On Error Resume Next

Dim g_objLDAPRoot
Dim blnAddedUserToGroup

' Bind to the root object
' **************************
Set g_objLDAPRoot = GetObject("LDAP://localhost:1003")
If Err.Number <> 0 Then
```

```
        Response.Write "Unable to bind to directory."
        Response.End
    End If

    ' Add user to group
    ' ***************************
    blnAddedUserToGroup =
    AddUserToGroup("LDAP://localhost:1003/o=Wrox/ou=Members/cn=Administrator",
    "public")

    If blnAddedUserToGroup = True Then
        Response.Write "Added user to group"
    Else
        Response.Write "Failed to Add user to group"
    End If
%>
</FONT>
```

The method binds to the appropriate group, creates a new `memberof` object used to represent members of a group, and finally associates the `memberof` object with the member passed as a parameter.

Next, let's look at how to create new containers.

Creating New Containers

Creating new containers in the Membership Directory (organizational units, in our case) is easy with the Membership Directory Manager, but this is not the most effective or efficient way of doing things – especially when we need to modify the directory information tree specific to our own application requirements. Creating containers can be done programmatically by using the `LDAPNamespace` provider object or the Active User Object – both support the necessary `Create()` method through the `IADsContainer` interface. Since we already know how to use `Create()` from the AUO, let's see how we do it using the `LDAPNamespace` object.

To create new containers in the Membership Directory using script, first create a new instance of the LDAP namespace object by calling:

```
Set LDAPRoot = GetObject("LDAP://[server]:[port]")
```

Then navigate to the appropriate container and use the `Create()` method to create a new entry, whose class is organizationalUnit, with the name of the new container. For example, the following code creates a new container under the members container called PremiumMembers:

```
Set objMemberContainer = LDAPRoot.GetObject("organizationalUnit", "ou=members")
Set objNewUser = objMemberContainer.Create("organizationalUnit",
"ou=PremiumMembers")
```

It's fairly simple, so now let's encapsulate this into a method that we can call to abstract some of the complexity and make container creation easier: `CreateContainer()`. This method will accept a name – such as `PremiumMembers` – and the path of the parent of this new object, and will create a new organizationalUnit container underneath the parent.

First let's review the parameters of the method:

❑ **strADsParentPath** – The first parameter, `strADsParentPath`, represents the `ADsPath` property of the parent of the new object. If we desired to create a new container underneath the `ou=Members` container, we would pass the `ADsPath` property – e.g. `LDAP://localhost:1003/o=Wrox/ou=Members`.

❑ **strContainerName** – Represents the name of the new organizationalUnit container to be created – such as PremiumMembers.

Code Sample – CreateContainer() Method

Now that we've reviewed the parameters, let's take a look at the code:

```
' *******************************************************
' FUNCTION:    CreateContainer
'
' PURPOSE:  Create new container in Directory Service
'
' PARAMETERS:
'     strADsParentPath - ADs Path to parent object
'     strContainerName - Name of the container to be created
'
' RETURNS: true - container created
'          false - container not created
'
' HISTORY: 6/98 Robert Howard Created
Public Function CreateContainer(strADsParentPath, strContainerName)
   On Error Resume Next

   ' Assume failure
   ' *****************************************
   CreateContainer = false

   Dim objParentContainer
   Dim objNewContainer
```

We start the code as we have seen in the previous samples. Next, we bind to the parent container and create our new container below it:

```
   ' Bind to the container passed
   ' *****************************************
   Set objParentContainer = GetObject(strADsParentPath)
   If Err.Number <> 0 Then
     Exit Function
   End If

   ' Create the new container with the passed container name
   ' *****************************************
   strContainerName = "ou=" & strContainerName
   Set objNewContainer = objParentContainer.Create("organizationalUnit",
strContainerName)
   If Err.Number <> 0 Then
     Exit Function
   End If

   ' Call SetInfo
```

```
' *****************************************
objNewContainer.SetInfo
If Err.Number <> 0 Then
  Exit Function
End If

' No errors
' *****************************************
CreateContainer = true

End Function
```

After the successful completion of this method, we can test the return value to determine if our new organizationalUnit has been created. If so, we can then use the values from the parameters passed to bind to our new container and begin using it.

So we've learned how to create a container, and we already know how to create new entries – such as members – in the appropriate container. Now, let's look at how we can delete entries.

Deleting Entries

In Chapter 9, we learned how to use the `Delete()` method of the `IADsContainer` to remove items from the Membership Directory – but the method provided in Chapter 9 was used to delete a container, rather than a specific class type in the container. In this chapter, we'll look at a method for removing entries from the Membership Directory – it encapsulates the same functionality as the method examined in Chapter 9, but instead it gives us the option of whether or not we want the deletion to be recursive.

Before we look at the code, let's review the parameters required:

❑ **strADsPathToContainer** – The `strADsPathToContainer` passes the ADsPath to the container in which the entry to be deleted currently exists. If we wanted to delete member objects, we would provide the ADsPath to the ou=Members container. Likewise, if we wanted to delete a container underneath the ou=Members container we would pass the same ADsPath.

❑ **strClassType** – Specifies the class type of the object to be removed. An example we'll look at later is for cleaning the ou=AnonymousUsers container.

❑ **blnRecursive** – a boolean flag that specifies whether or not the method should recursively delete the class types specified in `strClassType`.

Code Sample – DeleteObjects() Method

Let's look at the code sample:

```
<HTML>
<BODY BGCOLOR=WHITE>
<FONT FACE=ARIAL SIZE=3>
<B>
DeleteObjects(strADsPathToContainer, strClassType, blnRecursive)
</B>
<HR SIZE=1>
</FONT>
<FONT FACE=ARIAL SIZE=2>
```

```
<%
Public Function DeleteObjects(strADsPathToContainer, strClassType, blnRecursive)
  On Error Resume Next

  Const ISCONTAINER_TRUE  = 1
  Const ISCONTAINER_FALSE = 0
  Const E_ADS_PROPERTY_NOT_FOUND = &H8000500D

  Dim objADs
  Dim objADsContainer
  Dim objADsParent
  Dim blnIsContainer

  ' Assume failure
  ' ***********************************
  DeleteObjects = False
```

After defining the variables and the function, as before, we bind to the Membership Directory and begin iterating through the items in the ou=members container. We need to test each item to see whether it is a container, and set the appropriate constant. When we find a container we need to iterate through it recursively, looking for members or further containers.

```
  ' Connect to the Site Server Directory
  ' ***********************************
  Set objADsContainer = GetObject(strADsPathToContainer)
  If Err.Number <> 0 Then
    Err.Clear
    Exit Function
  End If

  ' Enumerate Items in the members container
  ' ***********************************
  For Each objADs In objADsContainer

    ' Is this object a container
    ' ***********************************
    blnIsContainer = objADs.Get("isContainer")
    If Err.Number = E_ADS_PROPERTY_NOT_FOUND Then
      Err.Clear

      ' Handle special DS cases
      ' ***********************************
      Select Case objADs.Class
        Case ("organizationalUnit")
          blnIsContainer = ISCONTAINER_TRUE
        Case ("organization")
          blnIsContainer = ISCONTAINER_TRUE
        Case Else
          blnIsContainer = ISCONTAINER_FALSE
      End Select
    End If

    ' Recursive if we encounter a container
    ' ***********************************
    If (blnIsContainer = ISCONTAINER_TRUE) AND (blnRecursive = True) Then
      blnSuccess = DeleteObjects(objADs.ADsPath, strClassType, blnRecursive)
```

```
      If blnSuccess = False Then
         Exit Function
      End If
   Else
```

If the object matches the type that was passed in the `strClassType` parameter, we will delete it:

```
      ' Grab the class and name of the
      ' object in the container
      ' ***********************************
      ADsClassType = objADs.Class
      ADsDN = objADs.Name

      ' Delete the object if we match
      ' ***********************************
      If AdsClassType = strClassType Then
         objADsContainer.Delete ADsClassType, ADsDN
         If Err.Number <> 0 Then
            Err.Clear
            Exit Function
         End If
      End If
   End If
Next

If Err.Number <> 0 Then
   Err.Clear
   Exit Function
Else
   DeleteObjects = True
End If
End Function
```

As an example, the objects we'll delete are anonymous members. We call the method with the path to the anonymous users container, the class type "member", and recursive set to true, so that we will also delete any users in subcontainers of the AnonymousUsers container.

```
' ************************
' Example Use
' ************************
Dim blnDeleted

' Path to object to delete
' ************************
strADsToDelete = "LDAP://localhost:1003/o=Wrox/ou=Members/ou=AnonymousUsers"

' Call the DeleteContainer method
' recursively delete members (anonymous)
' ************************
blnDelete = DeleteObjects(strADsToDelete, "member", True)

' Display results
' ************************
If blnDelete = False Then
```

```
      Response.Write "Objects not deleted."
   Else
      Response.Write "Objects deleted."
   End If
%>
</FONT>
</BODY>
</HTML>
```

We now have the ability – and the code – to do anything in the Membership Directory related to administrative tasks. Let's next look at some advanced concepts for some more specific problems.

Advanced Concepts

In the *Advanced Concepts* section of this chapter, we'll look at how we can expire members and how we can remove the members from the ou=AnonymousUsers container. First we'll look at how we can expire a member.

Expiring Members

In Chapter 8, we read about the accountStatus attribute that the Membership system uses to determine whether or not an account should gain access to the requested resource. The accountStatus attribute settings are as follows: 1= active, 2= pending, 3= disabled, 4= to be removed. The default value for the accountStatus is 1, active.

The Problem

Programmatically, we can modify this attribute; however, if the attribute value is set at 4 (to be removed), the member will not be automatically removed from the Membership Directory. We have to do this ourselves.

The Solution

To do this, we'll make some modifications to the DeleteObjects() method that already knows how to work recursively with objects and how to delete them. However, we'll extend this method to suit our own needs. More specifically, we'll change the DeleteObjects() method so that it only deletes members whose accountStatus attribute is 4. Only one parameter for this method is required:

❑   **strADsPathToContainer** – The starting point for the method to start looking for member objects with the accountStatus attribute of 4 to be deleted.

Code Sample – DeleteExpiredMembers.asp

In the code below, we've modified the DeleteObjects() method – the new method is called DeleteExpiredMembers().

```
<HTML>
<BODY BGCOLOR=WHITE>
<FONT FACE=ARIAL SIZE=3>
<B>
```

```
DeleteExpiredMembers(strADsPathToContainer)
</B>
<HR SIZE=1>
</FONT>
<FONT FACE=ARIAL SIZE=2>
<%
Public Function DeleteExpiredMembers(strADsPathToContainer)
  On Error Resume Next

  Const ISCONTAINER_TRUE  = 1
  Const ISCONTAINER_FALSE = 0
  Const E_ADS_PROPERTY_NOT_FOUND = &H8000500D

  Dim objADs
  Dim objADsContainer
  Dim objADsParent
  Dim blnIsContainer

  ' Assume failure
  ' **********************************
  DeleteExpiredMembers = False

  ' Connect to the Site Server Directory
  ' **********************************
  Set objADsContainer = GetObject(strADsPathToContainer)
  If Err.Number <> 0 Then
    Err.Clear
    Exit Function
  End If

  ' Enumerate Items in the members container
  ' **********************************
  For Each objADs In objADsContainer

    ' Is this object a container
    ' **********************************
    blnIsContainer = objADs.Get("isContainer")
    If Err.Number = E_ADS_PROPERTY_NOT_FOUND Then
      Err.Clear

      ' Handle special DS cases
      ' **********************************
      Select Case objADs.Class
        Case ("organizationalUnit")
          blnIsContainer = ISCONTAINER_TRUE
        Case ("organization")
          blnIsContainer = ISCONTAINER_TRUE
        Case Else
          blnIsContainer = ISCONTAINER_FALSE
      End Select
    End If

    ' Recursive if we encounter a container
    ' **********************************
    If (blnIsContainer = ISCONTAINER_TRUE) Then
      blnSuccess = DeleteExpiredMembers(objADs.ADsPath)

      If blnSuccess = False Then
        Exit Function
      End If
```

```
      Else
        ' Grab the class and name of the
        ' object in the container
        ' **********************************
        ADsClassType = objADs.Class
        ADsDN = objADs.Name
        nAccntStatus = objADs.accountStatus
```

The function so far is the same as above. Here however we have also retrieved the account status for the current member. We need to handle the error we will get if this property has not yet been set for a user: here we will just set the status to 0. If the account status has been set, and matches the value we are looking for, here 4, we can go ahead and delete that member.

```
        ' Delete the object if we match
        ' **********************************
        If Err.Number = E_ADS_PROPERTY_NOT_FOUND Then
          nAccntStatus = 0
        End If

        ' Delete the object if we match
        ' **********************************
        If (AdsClassType = "member") AND (nAccntStatus = "4") Then
          objADsContainer.Delete ADsClassType, ADsDN
          If Err.Number <> 0 Then
             Err.Clear
             Exit Function
          End If
        End If
      End If
    Next

    If Err.Number <> 0 Then
      Err.Clear
      Exit Function
    Else
      DeleteExpiredMembers = True
    End If
End Function
```

This is how we would put the method into practice:

```
' *************************
' Example Use
' *************************
Dim blnDeleted

' Path to object to delete
' *************************
strADsToDelete = "LDAP://localhost:1003/o=Wrox/ou=Members"

' Call the DeleteContainer method
' recursivley delete members (anonymous)
' *************************
blnDelete = DeleteExpiredMembers(strADsToDelete)
```

```
' Display results
' ************************
If blnDelete = False Then
  Response.Write "Expired objects not deleted."
Else
  Response.Write "Expired objects deleted."
End If
%>
</FONT>
</BODY>
```

This simple example shows how we can easily modify the existing methods provided in this book to solve our specific problems with only minor modifications. We might want to use a similar approach to remove members from the ou=AnonymousUsers container

Cleaning the ou=AnonymousUsers Container

Anonymous Cookie Authentication creates new member objects in the ou=AnonymousUsers container for members that are allowed to access an IIS 4.0 web server anonymously, and still want to receive personalized content. Remember, we can't personalize the experience for the IUSR_*[server_name]* account.

The Problem

At some point, the number of these members grows beyond an acceptable level – such as 300+ – and consumes resources in our Membership Directory.

The Solution

To solve this problem, we need some way of periodically cleaning out the ou=AnonymousUsers container. We can use the DeleteObjects() method to do this. In fact, we can choose to build either an ASP or simple VB application that we can run to clean the directory periodically. We *could* perform this action through the Membership Directory Manager by simply selecting all these members and pressing delete: this is a simple, straightforward solution, but what if we want only to delete members that haven't been to the site in 30 days? We can only do this programmatically (we'd have to ensure that each member carried an attribute, called lastvisit, say, that stores the last visit date of the member).

So, with that said, let's look at a simple script that uses the DeleteObjects() method by including it from a file. In the sample code below the DeleteObjects() method removes all anonymous users in this container. Later, you can modify this script to look for and delete only those members with the required attributes and values specific to your site's design.

Code Sample – DeleteAnonymousMembers.asp

Here's the code:

```
<HTML>
<BODY BGCOLOR=WHITE>
<FONT FACE=ARIAL SIZE=3>
<B>
DeleteAnonymousMembers.asp
```

```
</B>
<HR SIZE=1>
</FONT>
<FONT FACE=ARIAL SIZE=2>
<%
' Include the DeleteObject.inc which is the method
' provided by DeleteObjects.asp
' **************************************************
%>
<!--#include file="DeleteObjects.inc"-->
<%
On Error Resume Next

Dim blnRemove
Dim blnSuccess

' Define constants for our DeleteObjects() method
' used to remove the members from the
' AnonymousUsers container
' **************************************************
Const ADS_PATH_TO_ANONMEMBERS =
"LDAP://localhost:1003/o=Wrox/ou=Members/ou=AnonymousUsers"
Const ADS_CLASS_TO_REMOVE = "member"
Const ADS_RECURSIVE_DELETE = FALSE
```

We've defined values for this script so that it will always remove members in the anonymous
members container. We call the method as seen in the previous example.

```
' Do we need to run the method?
' **************************************************
If (Request.QueryString("Remove")) > 0 Then
  blnRemove = True
Else
  blnRemove = False
End If

If blnRemove = True Then
  blnSuccess = DeleteObjects(ADS_PATH_TO_ANONMEMBERS, _
                     ADS_CLASS_TO_REMOVE, _
                     ADS_RECURSIVE_DELETE)

  ' Was the call to DeleteObjects succesful?
  ' **************************************************
  If blnSuccess = True Then
    Response.Write "All anonymous members were "
    Response.Write "successfully deleted."
  Else
    Response.Write "Anonymous members were not "
    Response.Write "successfully deleted."
  End If
Else
  Response.Write "To remove all of the anonymous members "
  Response.Write "press Remove Anonymous Members."
  Response.Write "<P>"
  Response.Write "<FORM METHOD=GET>"
  Response.Write "<INPUT TYPE=SUBMIT NAME=Remove "
  Response.Write "VALUE=""Remove Anonymous Members"">"
```

```
      Response.Write "</FORM>"
   End If
   %>
   </FONT>
   </BODY>
   </HTML>
```

You can modify these example scripts so that they best suit your specific administrative needs.

Summary

We've mirrored a majority of the capabilities of the Membership Directory Manager through script to show how we can easily manage the Membership Directory through ASP. We've also looked at a series of methods that can easily be re-purposed for our own needs. Let's take a look at exactly what we covered:

❑ **Common Classes and Attributes.** We started by reviewing some of the common attributes and classes that we need to be familiar with to work with the Membership Directory. We learned that the classSchema and attributeSchema are the two most fundamental class types that all other classes and attributes are created from. We also spent some time with the mayContain and mustContain attributes, which together determine what attributes a new class may or must have in order to be created.

❑ **Using Script instead of Wizards.** After reviewing some of the common classes and attributes, we turned our attention to how we perform the tasks accomplished by the wizards in the Membership Directory Manager through Script. This included programmatically creating attributes and classes, adding these attributes to classes, and finally creating members. Rather than just showing simple ASP scripts we reviewed methods that you can later use in your own site to rapidly build solutions.

❑ **Other Membership Directory Tasks.** After reviewing some of the more common Membership Directory tasks, we looked at some other more complicated tasks – such as deleting objects – that can also be performed through script. Again, we also encapsulated this knowledge into methods that you can take and use in your own applications.

❑ **Advanced Concepts.** Finally, in the Advanced Concepts section of this chapter, we extended the DeleteObjects() method, in order to solve some specific problems – removing expired members and anonymous members from the ou=AnonymousUsers container.

The concepts in this chapter were presented in ASP/VBScript. However, this code could easily be ported to Visual Basic. In the next chapter, we'll look at how we can apply a majority of the solutions presented in this book through Visual Basic and C++.

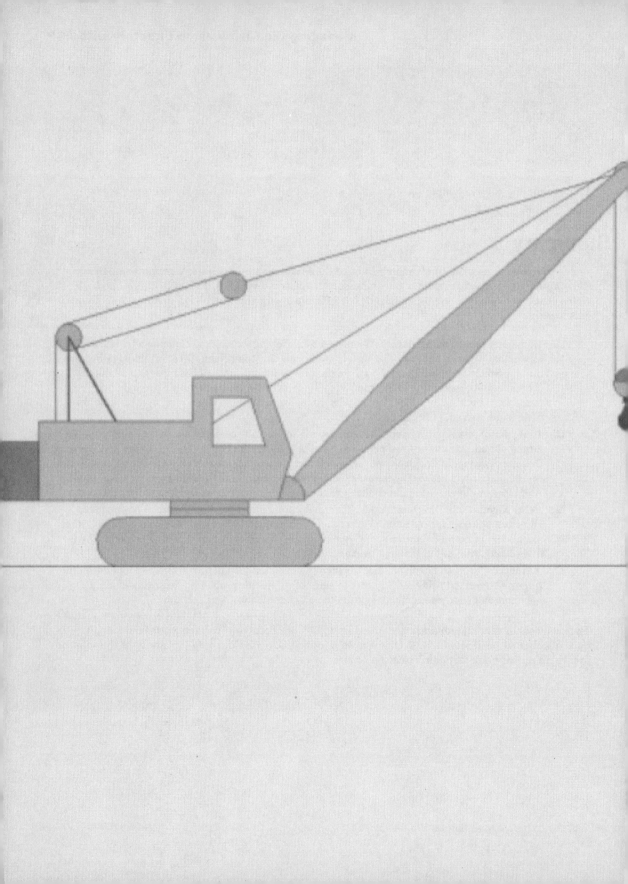

15

Managing the Membership Directory with Visual Basic and C++

In this chapter we'll cover Visual Basic and C++ and discuss how we can use each to access and manage resources in the Membership Directory. Throughout the book, we have often mentioned that Active Server Pages with Visual Basic Script is not the only way to access the Membership Directory. An example application would be the Windows Media Player – formerly Netshow – plug-in that we encountered in Chapter 11. In this chapter we'll cover how automation can be implemented in C++ or Visual Basic, and what each language supports.

Most of the points we'll cover will be in reference to Visual Basic, however we will touch on some of the C++ highlights as necessary. If you're not familiar with C++, take a look at *Beginning Visual C++* (Wrox, 1-861-00-012X) and *Beginning ATL COM* (Wrox, 1-861-00-0111) – they'll help to get you started with the foundation you need to apply ADSI knowledge to C++ components and programs.

Here's what we'll be covering in this chapter.

- ❑ **Implementing VB and C++.** We're not going to cover the differences between the two languages, but we will compare how these two languages are used to access the Membership Directory. These differences include early and late binding in Visual Basic, and the type libraries and header files required for C++.
- ❑ **Binding to the Membership Directory.** In this section we'll discuss the two possible types of authentication against a Membership Directory: Anonymous and Member. We'll learn how to bind to the Membership Directory anonymously with the GetObject() in Visual Basic and the ADsGetObject() method in C++. Next, we'll look at how to bind to the Membership Directory as a member with the OpenDSObject() method in Visual Basic and the ADsOpenObject() method in C++.

❑ **Walking the Membership Directory with Visual Basic.** Here we'll discuss how we can easily reassign VBScripts and ASPs for Visual Basic. We'll also take it one step further, and show a fully-fledged Visual Basic application called Directory Walker, where we'll use all of our knowledge of binding and ADSI to mimic the Membership Directory Manager.

❑ **Advanced Concepts.** Here we'll explore the OLE/COM Object Viewer to examine the interface definitions of some Membership objects. These are all defined in Appendix C.

This is the last chapter of the book and concludes the section on *Advanced Personalization and Membership*. By the end of this chapter, you should have all the necessary knowledge to build an advanced Personalization and Membership application.

Implementing VB and C++

Whether we are using Visual Basic or C++ we access the Membership Directory in a similar manner. For example, with Visual Basic, we'll use the GetObject() method while in C++ we'll use the ADsGetObject() method. Both of these methods serve identical purposes – binding to the LDAP namespace path passed as a parameter. The difference is in how the bind is achieved, and the information that we need to provide – such as providing three parameters for the ADsGetObject(), but only one for GetObject(). The way that variables are typed – or defined in the code – differs greatly from Visual Basic Script. In Visual Basic Script all variables are treated as variants, whether dimensioned or not. Although this gives us a great deal of flexibility, Visual Basic – and especially C++ – are a little more particular about how variables are declared.

We'll start with a look at how we use the Active DS Type Library to allow Visual Basic to early bind to objects, and in the C++ section we'll discover where we can find the ADSI SDK necessary for building C++ applications that use ADSI. But before we begin, let's look at why we won't be discussing the Active User Object in this chapter.

Why we Won't use the AUO in VB and C++

The Active User Object could be used from VB and C++ – and will still take advantage of the Membership authentication cache – but this isn't necessarily the most efficient way of doing things. All the AUO really does is provide a nice wrapper around the ADSI interfaces and abstract away the complexity of binding to the Membership Directory – either anonymously or securely – through the IUserObjects interface. As familiar as we are with the AUO, it doesn't make a lot of sense to use the object from VB or C++. It makes more sense to use straight ADSIs – the same ones implemented by the AUO. The reasoning for this is simple. The AUO is designed for an Active Server Page environment used in conjunction with the security support providers (SSPs) for authentication.

In Chapter 9, we learned how we can create the AUO by using the Init() method of the IUserObjects interface without depending upon the OnStartPage() method to pass our member context. Using this knowledge we could create an instance of the AUO passing in the member to bind as, and the IIS instance id, from Visual Basic or C++. However, in the end we wind up using the same ADSIs that we could access directly. If we use straight ADSIs our code will also be much more flexible as we won't have to depend on a web server for an IIS instance id. So, with that said, let's spend our time learning how to use the ADSIs through VB and C++, rather than rehashing the AUO.

Let's look at when we should use VB and when we should use C++ for our component development choice.

When to use VB/C++

There are many advantages and disadvantages to choosing one development language over another. In fact, there are so many that we couldn't possibly cover them all in full detail. However, we will look at some of the more general reasons.

The most obvious reason for using Visual Basic as the language of choice for component development is its ease of development. There are a number of other reasons for choosing VB over C++, including these:

❑ **Time** – It can take half the time (or less) to write, test and debug a component using VB – compared to the similar process in C++.

❑ **Portability** – ASP pages often use Visual Basic Script for their logic, and this can easily be ported to Visual Basic components. Porting business logic from ASP to a C++ component is, however, no small task, and usually means re-writing the entire logic in C code.

❑ **Financially** – More developers use Visual Basic than any other language. C++ developers are more expensive, and good ones are difficult to find.

Visual Basic is great for building components, and for 90% of your Site Server Personalization and Membership-related development, Visual Basic will work fine. However, for those of you writing other services – such as the Member authentication plug-in, from Chapter 11 – you'll want to use C++. In some cases there's no choice. For example, the Windows Media Services require a threading model that is not available in Visual Basic.

There are other advantages that come with choosing C++ over VB:

❑ **Performance** – Because C++ allows us to do everything at a lower level, we can fine-tune our component to perform better. Not only because we have to write the code ourselves, but also because C++ is compiled into more optimized code than could be written with VB.

❑ **Threading Model** – This goes hand-in-hand with performance, because C++ allows us to use any threading model we want (i.e. single, apartment, both, free). However, we also have to write the code to handle any possible contention between threads. Some applications do require that we use a free threading model so that the component can scale better – that is, each request uses its own thread. Visual Basic only allows for single and apartment model threaded components. The threading model affects how an application or component runs. With single threading, all requests are serviced on a single thread. This means that requests are executed in the order in which they are received. Apartment model threading requires that all objects are created in the same thread, but still have their own memory space – so as not to conflict with global variables.

We could summarize by suggesting that you use Visual Basic if you want it done quickly, and C++ if you want the application to perform. My personal preference is to use VB whenever possible, and only use C++ when I have to, or when the application requires it. Now, let's move on and take a look at how we would use ADSI in Visual Basic.

ADSI from Visual Basic

Using Active Directory Service Interfaces from Visual Basic is just as easy as when we used Visual Basic Script in an Active Server Page. See the later sections of Chapter 9 for examples of this. We use the Active Directory Service Interfaces in one of two ways from VB; either the object type library can be used to early bind to the ADSIs, or the `CreateObject()` method can be used to late bind to the ADSIs. The difference being that early binding is more expensive in the beginning and faster after that, whereas late binding is fast on startup but slow for every `CreateObject()` used to bind to the object at run-time.

> *Whether early or late binding is used depends entirely on the way variables are declared. It has nothing to do with the way objects are created.*

Don't worry, we're not going to go into too much detail here. I'll save that discussion for when you decide to dip into *Professional VB Business Objects* (Wrox, ISBN 1-861001-07X). Let's start with early binding.

Early Binding

Early binding simply means that Visual Basic knows the type of the object before the application is compiled. In other words, we explicitly declare the variable and type it before using it. Declaring the variables as being of a specific type means that the application does not have to look up the method or property via `IDispatch` at run time. Instead, the code knows how objects of the specified type should be created. We can implement this by using a type library.

A type library simply defines the interfaces, properties, and methods supported by an object. Binding to the Active Directory Service Interfaces early from Visual Basic means that a reference to the ADSI type library needs to be made. This is so that Visual Basic knows the object type of the variables to be declared. So rather than saying:

```
Dim objIADs
```

as we do in Visual Basic Script inside an ASP page, we can declare our variables as:

```
Dim objIADs as IADs
```

However, before we can perform this magical feat, we need to let Visual Basic know what type library to use. In our case this will be the Active DS Type Library.

Active DS Type Library

The Active DS Type Library defines the ADSIs that we want to use in our component. To bind to the appropriate type library from Visual Basic select Project | References on the toolbar. This brings up a plethora of available type libraries, some of which are already selected. Just select the one required by ticking in the appropriate box. We can see this below in the screenshot of the Project Reference window:

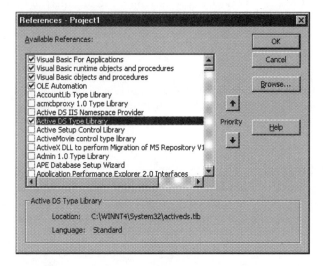

Using this type library we can now define variable types as IADs, IADsContainer, etc. If you happen to be developing on a machine where Site Server 3.0 is not installed, you might not see the **Active DS Type Library**. To install the necessary files download and install the ADSI SDK from http://msdn.microsoft.com/adsi.

Now that we have bound to the type library, we can take full advantage of some of the advanced features in Visual Basic to make our development easier. One of my favorite features of Visual Basic 5.0 (and now 6.0) is the IntelliSense listing of object's properties and methods. This provides a quick and easy means of using the correct methods or properties, without ever having to reference either the Visual Basic Object Browser or OLE/COM Object Viewer.

> *We'll look at the OLE/COM Object Viewer in the Advanced Concepts section at the end of this chapter.*

You can see IntelliSense in action in the adjacent screenshot:

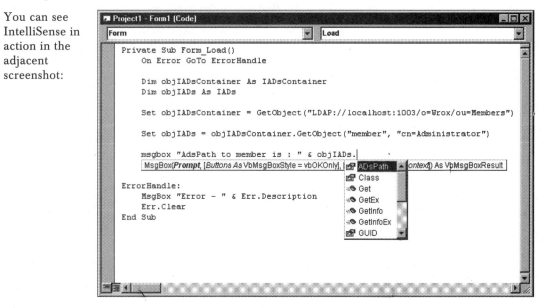

Because we've used the type library to declare the variables, IntelliSense can provide us with the methods and properties of the object we're using by looking up the declared variable. Where we know that the method we want is exposed from the IADs ADSI, we can type the name of the object followed by a period and then select from a list of all of the available properties and methods.

Early binding, therefore, means that the application does not have to check at run time whether or not a property or method exists. It already has this information through the type library we've provided, and can instead go straight to the call being made. If we don't use a type library, Visual Basic has to query the object at run time to determine method or property support. This is known as late binding.

Late Binding

Sometimes early binding doesn't provide the functionality we want. For instance, an object that needs to stay in memory constantly, and that aggregates several different objects (such as ActiveX Data Objects and Active Directory Service Interfaces) should make use of late binding. Late binding allows the object to only use required objects and then to release them. This helps save on the most precious resource of all, memory.

> Late Binding requires 50% more work for the system and gets more expensive for out-of-process calls.

However, it is very rare to use late binding as opposed to early binding from Visual Basic. Most objects don't hold onto that much memory and the speed difference of early binding vs. the resource usage of late binding is like comparing a Porsche 911 to a Honda Civic. They both get the job done, but the Porsche gets there a quite a bit earlier and uses more resources, while the Honda arrives a bit later, but uses fewer resources.

Active Server Pages make use of late binding – i.e. `Server.CreateObject(ProgID)`.

Since late binding doesn't bind to the object until the very last moment, we can't take advantage of the IntelliSense features – or be type specific of the variables we use. If we wanted to use the same example as we used in the IntelliSense screen shot, we would have to make the following modifications:

```
Dim objIADsContainer as Object ' We'll late bind

Set objIADsContainer = GetObject("LDAP://localhost:1003/o=Wrox/ou=Members")
```

In this example, we've declared `objIADsContainer` as an object – an intrinsic Visual Basic type – and we'll let it determine its type at run time.

To read more about late and early binding from Visual Basic, visit http://premium.microsoft.com/msdn/library/devprods/vb/vb50docs/f1/d5/s1af2d.htm.

Next, let's turn our attention to C++.

ADSI from C++

To use Active Directory Service Interfaces from C++, we need to download the platform SDK from http://msdn.microsoft.com/developer/sdk/platform.htm. To make sure that you have all the necessary header and library files, it is best to download the Build Environment SDK first, followed by the ADSI SDK, and finally the Site Server SDK. You can also check out the ADSI site at http://www.microsoft.com/adsi.

To use ADSI from C++ we need to add the `adsiid.lib` and `activeds.lib` files to our project. We also need to #include the `activeds.h` header file in our code and make sure that it too is included in our project. The `activeds.h` header file includes the other necessary header files required for ADSI. The IID (Interface ID) definitions can be found in `adsiid.h`. Here's what the `activeds.h` file looks like, with the comments removed:

```
#include "iads.h"
#include "adshlp.h"
#include "adserr.h"
#include "adsiid.h"
#include "adssts.h"
#include "adsnms.h"
#include "adsdb.h"
```

We won't be covering the details of C++ in this book. There are plenty of good books, but a couple of excellent tomes are *Beginning Visual C++ 6.0* (Wrox, 1-861-00-088X) and the wonderful *Beginning ATL COM Programming* (Wrox, 1-861-00-0111). Together, these should provide you with the foundation to understand how to develop C++ components.

Now that we have the information necessary to use ADSI from both Visual Basic and C++, let's examine how we bind – or connect – to the Membership Directory.

Binding to the Membership Directory

We know that Active Directory Service Interfaces are used to bind to the Membership Directory, and that any application we build using either Visual Basic or C++ has to use ADSI to talk to the Membership Directory. In Visual Basic, we can use nearly identical syntax and structure as from Visual Basic Script in Active Server Pages. This is actually very advantageous for a developer because it allows us to prototype an application or business logic solution in ASP and Visual Basic Script, and quickly port it to a Visual Basic COM object, which we can then share amongst other applications. From C++ we need to be more specific about what we're requesting from ADSI – i.e. specifying the return types when we attempt to bind to an LDAP namespace path.

However, even after we work out the implementation differences in the different languages we develop in, we still need to decide how to bind to the Membership Directory. If the Membership Directory has not been secured we can bind anonymously with the `GetObject()` method. Binding anonymously is useful for public information that is shared for all users. For instance, we could store information on how to connect to an organization's product database in a central repository, so that anonymous users could look up product information.

Once the Membership Directory has been secured we will need to pass credentials that identify us as a valid member in order to perform administrative tasks. We can still bind anonymously, but we will only be able to read basic information about the Membership Directory from the **RootDSE**.

The RootDSE object or Root Directory Service Agent Specific Entry is public information about the Membership Directory that is shared with all requestors. The RootDSE provides information such as the root container of the Membership Directory.

If we wanted to perform a task such as creating a new member we could bind as the Broker. The broker has the attribute **DS-PRIVELEGES** with the value **SUPERBROKER** that we learned about in detail in Chapter 13. If the Membership Directory has been secured then we cannot bind as the member attempting to obtain access. This is because the member might not exist or might not have enough security permissions in the Membership Directory to obtain the userPassword attribute. The broker has these privileges and performs the role of binding to the member and verifying password information.

We saw an example of this process in Chapter 11. Customers requesting Windows Media Streams are first authenticated by the Windows NT Netshow Services and then verified by the NSMemberAuthentication.dll *plug-in. The plug-in binds to the Membership Directory as a member that has the appropriate permissions to view other member's information. Next, using this securely bound object, an attempt is made to bind to the member in the Membership Directory trying to be authenticated.*

Binding Anonymously

If we bind to the Membership Directory through a simple GetObject() method call passing only the LDAP namespace path to bind to, ADSI assumes that we want to bind anonymously, and the LDAP Service uses anonymous credentials to bind to the Membership Directory. To bind anonymously we will use either the cn=Anonymous account in the root container of the Membership Directory (if the Membership Directory is using Membership authentication), or the LDAP_ANONYMOUS account from the Windows NT SAM (if the Membership Directory is using Windows NT authentication).

We've seen how to bind anonymously using the LDAPNamespace object with the GetObject() call from an Active Server Page in Visual Basic Script:

```
Set objLDAP = GetObject("LDAP://localhost:1003/o=Wrox/ou=Members")
```

We can do almost the same thing in Visual Basic (5.0 or 6.0) and from C++, as long as the machine has ADSI installed. First we'll see how to use GetObject() from Visual Basic.

Using GetObject() from Visual Basic

In Visual Basic, as with VB Script, we only need to pass the LDAP namespace path to the Membership Directory object to which we want to bind. With VB Script we'd use the following:

Visual Basic Script in an Active Server Page

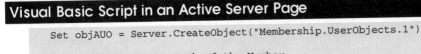

```
Set objAUO = Server.CreateObject("Membership.UserObjects.1")

' Bind using the ADsPath of the Member:
' LDAP://server:port/o=org/ou=Members/cn=MemberName (or similar)
' ***********************************************
Set objIADs = GetObject(objAUO.ADsPath)
```

In Visual Basic we can bind to the Membership Directory using the `GetObject()` method by passing an LDAP namespace path.

The GetObject() Method

Visual Basic's MSDN help files define the `GetObject()` method as: Returns a reference to an object provided by an ActiveX component. `GetObject()` is different from `CreateObject()` in that it allows us to connect to a running object if necessary. We use `GetObject()` to bind to an LDAP Service rather than using `CreateObject()` because the LDAP Service is already running, and does not need to be created.

Calling the `GetObject()` method creates an `LDAPNamespace` object by passing the pathname specified after the `LDAP://` moniker. The `LDAPNamespace` object attempts to communicate with the LDAP Service that points to the Membership Directory. If the `LDAPNamespace` object finds the appropriate LDAP Service, the LDAP Service returns a pointer to the root container of the Membership Directory – the organization (o=) container by default. The LDAP Service is able to return a pointer to the root container since this information is available through the Membership Directory Root Directory Service Agent Specific Entry (Root DSE).

We'll take a look at two code samples so that we can compare both early and late binding to the Membership Directory.

Visual Basic Application

For the first sample we've early bound to the correct type library:

```
Private Sub Form_Load()
    ' Assume we've early bound to the Active DS Type Library
    ' ***************************************************
    Dim objIADs as IADs
    Dim strLDAPPath as String

    strLDAPPath = "LDAP://localhost:1003"

    ' Perform the bind
    ' ***************************************************
    Set objIADs = GetObject(strLDAPPath)
End Sub
```

Code Sample – Using Visual Basic's GetObject() Method

The second sample uses late binding. Here we've also included some handling for cases where we want to use the default port.

```
' ***************************************************
' FUNCTION: BindToDirectory
'
' PARAMETERS:
'           strServer - LDAP Service name to bind to
'           nPort     - Port of LDAP Service to bind to.
'
' RETURNS:  Reference to directory if successful,
'             otherwise returns nothing
'
```

```
Public Function BindToDirectory(ByRef strServer As String, _Optional ByRef nPort
s Integer _) As Object
    On Error Resume Next

    ' nPort will be 0 if nothing has been passed
    ' call for bind will default to port 389
    ' *******************************************
    If nPort = 0 Then
        Set BindToDirectory = GetObject("LDAP://" & strServer)
    Else
        Set BindToDirectory = GetObject("LDAP://" & strServer & ":" & nPort)
    End If

    ' Set object to nothing if there was an error
    ' *******************************************
    If Err.Number <> 0 Then
        Set BindToDirectory = Nothing
    End If
End Function
```

Next let's look at an alternative method of binding.

The AdsGetObject() Method

Believe it or not, binding to a directory from C++ isn't all that difficult. The ADSI SDK includes a helper method called `ADsGetObject()` that has similar behavior to its Visual Basic counterpart `GetObject()`. However, unlike the `GetObject()` method, the `ADsGetObject()` method requires some more information. We'll look first at this method in Visual Basic code, so that we can relate it to the code we've just discussed.

The ADsGetObject() Method in Visual Basic

The `ADsGetObject()` method is defined in the `adshlp.h` file, which is included with the `activeds.h` header file from the ADSI SDK that should be included in our project. `ADsGetObject()` allows us to bind to the Membership Directory and return an ADSI pointer to the object in the Membership Directory identified by the namespace path. In addition to passing the LDAP namespace path, we also need to pass a reference interface id (a `riid`) and a pointer to the object to which we want to bind (a `void**`). Passing the `riid` tells the `ADsGetObject()` method what type of ADSI to return. If we were to specify `IID_IADS` as the interface id, the method would return a pointer to an `IADs` ADSI. Additionally, the method returns an `HRESULT`, which is simply a return code that indicates either the success or failure of the method call. Passing the `void**` is similar to passing an `IADs` that we have not called `Set` on yet in a Visual Basic through a sub or function `ByRef` and returning an `IADs` that points to a Membership Directory entry (or other valid object).

Sample Code – Pseudo ADsGetObject() Method

To make this a little clearer, let's review the following code sample:

```
Const IID_IADS = 0
Const IID_IADSCONTAINER = 1

' ***********************************************
' METHOD:    ADsGetObject
'
```

```
'  PURPOSE:   VB representation of what a call to
'             C++ ADsGetObject() might look like
'
'  PARAMETER:
'    lpszPathName -        LDAP namespace path to
'                          bind to.
'
'    riid -                Object type to return
'
'    ppObject -            Object returned
'
Public Function ADsGetObject(ByVal lpszPathName As String, _
                        ByVal riid As Integer, _
                        ByRef ppObject As Object) As Boolean
    On Error Resume Next

    ' Assume failure
    ' **********************
    ADsGetObject = False

    ' In c++ we would QueryInterface for the
    ' interface
    ' ****************************
    Select Case riid
        Case IID_IADS
            Dim objIADs As IADs

            Set objIADs = GetObject(lpszPathName)
            If Err.Number <> 0 Then
                Err.Clear
                Exit Function
            Else
                ADsGetObject = True
                Set ppObject = objIADs
            End If
        Case IID_IADSCONTAINER
            Dim objIADsContainer As IADsContainer

            Set objIADsContainer = GetObject(lpszPathName)
            If Err.Number <> 0 Then
                Err.Clear
                Exit Function
            Else
                ADsGetObject = True
                Set ppObject = objIADsContainer
            End If
    End Select
End Function

Private Sub Form_Load()
    Dim strLDAPPath As String
    Dim objIADs As Object


    ' Bind to the Membership Directory Using our
    ' Pseduo C++ ADsGetObject() method
    ' *************************************
    strLDAPPath = "LDAP://localhost:1003"
```

```
      If ADsGetObject(strLDAPPath, IID_IADS, objIADs) = True Then
          Debug.Print objIADs.ADsPath
      End If
End Sub
```

After calling our `ADsGetObject()` function, `objIADs` now points to the root container of the specified Membership Directory on the localhost port 1003.

The AdsGetObject() Method from C++

It is a little more involved to bind to the Membership Directory in C++, but with this extra involvement comes greater of control over what is happening. For example, in Visual Basic we don't truly know what interface is passed back from a `GetObject()` method call; it could be an `IADs` or it could be an `IADsContainer` – it does in fact return an `IADs`. Using C++ we can specify the ADSI pointer to return – in this case we'll return an `IADsContainer` and bind to a member in the ou=Members container. The prototype for the `ADsGetObject()` method in C++ is defined as:

```
HRESULT WINAPI
ADsGetObject(
    LPWSTR lpszPathName,
    REFIID riid,
    VOID * * ppObject
    );
```

You may have noticed that we used the `ADsGetObject()` method call from inside the `LDAPAccess.cpp` file, in the example provided in Chapter 11, *Authenticating Windows Media Streams against the Membership Directory*. To show a simple example of using the `ADsGetObject()` method here, we'll create a simple C++ program to bind to a Membership Directory and display the `ADsPath` property. We'll pass a LDAP namespace path to the root container: `LDAP://localhost:1003`. We'll also specify the return type of the pointer that the `ADsGetObject()` method will return to us, `IID_IADsContainer`, and the pointer itself, `&pIADsContainer`.

Code Sample – Using C++ To Get the AdsPath (anonymous bind)

```
//You need to add the following files to this project:
//comdef.h
//activeds.h
//adsiid.lib
//activeds.lib

#include <iostream.h>
#include <comdef.h>
#include "activeds.h"

int main()
{
  CoInitialize(NULL);

  IADsContainer * pIADsContainer = NULL;
  IADs * pIADs = NULL;

  HRESULT hr;
  BSTR bstrADsPath = NULL;
```

```
// Connect to the Membership Directory
// ***********************************
hr = ADsGetObject(L"LDAP://localhost:1003",
                  IID_IADsContainer,
                  (void**)&pIADsContainer);
if (FAILED(hr))
{
  cout << "Failed to get object." << endl;
}

// Connect to the ou=members container
// ***********************************
hr = pIADsContainer->GetObject(L"organizationalUnit",
                               L"ou=members",
                               (IDispatch**)&pIADs);
if (FAILED(hr))
{
  cout << "Failed to get members container." << endl;
}

// Get the ADsPath of the members container
// ***********************************
hr = pIADs->get_ADsPath(&bstrADsPath);
if (FAILED(hr))
{
  cout << "failed!" << &pIADsContainer;
}

// Display the ADsPath
// ***********************************
cout << "ADsPath is: " << (_bstr_t)bstrADsPath << endl;

char ch;
  cout << "Enter something to finish:" << endl;
cin >> ch;

return (0);
}
```

After running this code, modified with the parameters specific to your LDAP Service and
Membership Directory, you should see something similar to this:

Now we can bind anonymously, we'll look at what we would need to do if the Membership Directory
has been secured. Resources in the Membership Directory are protected by Access Control Entries –
as we read about in Chapter 13 – and we need to explicitly tell the Membership Directory who we
are so we can get access to the resources we need.

Binding as a Member

In Chapter 11 we showed an example of how to sell Membership access using the Site Server Commerce Edition pipeline. Once the customer was approved for the purchase of the Membership, we used a scriptor component in the pipeline to bind to the Membership Directory. The customer was bound as a member that could create new members and add those members to the Premium group for gaining access to file system resources.

We did this by using an ADSI that could pass member credentials to the LDAP Service, and attempt to bind with those credentials.

If we need to perform similar tasks from a Visual Basic or C++ application we need to specify who we are when we bind to the Membership Directory. Once we've presented our member credentials and they have been approved, we are able to access protected resources in the Membership Directory as the bound member. In addition, we can walk up and down the Membership Directory using the properties and methods of the `IADs` and `IADsContainer` interfaces, such as the `Parent` property. Unlike binding anonymously, binding as a member is a little more complicated. This applies to both Visual Basic and C++.

Binding as a Member from Visual Basic

We still need to use the `GetObject()` method and `LDAPNamespace` object, but instead of binding to the Membership Directory we'll create an instance of the `LDAPNamespace` object without passing a namespace to bind to:

```
GetObject("LDAP:")
```

We can then use the `LDAPNamespace` object's `IDispatch` interface and the ADSI `IADsOpenDSObject`'s `OpenDSObject()` method to perform the bind as a member. As we saw when we used the `OpenDSObject()` method from ASP in Chapter 12, it enables us to pass the member credentials with which to bind as well as the LDAP path.

For more information on the `OpenDSObject()` *method refer to Chapter 12.*

Code Sample – Visual Basic OpenDSObject()

Here's what using this method looks like in Visual Basic:

```
Set objLDAP = GetObject("LDAP:")
Set objIADsContainer = objLDAP.OpenDSObject("LDAP://localhost:1003", _
                                 "cn=Administrator, ou=Members, o=Wrox", _
                                 "password", _
                                 1)
```

Let's examine a method called `SecuredBind()` used from within Visual Basic and incorporating `OpenDSObject()`. This will bind securely to a member using the BaseDN, so that we won't require the full DN of the member. The method builds the ADsPath from the `LDAP_ROOT_PATH` and `LDAP_BASE_DN`, which can either be constants or global references to these values. It also takes the following parameters:

- ❏ **strName** – The name of the member to bind as, e.g. Administrator.
- ❏ **strPassword** – The password of the member to bind as.
- ❏ **pIADsContainer** – The object type to return, we'll return a pIADsContainer – by reference – when passed a NULL IADsContainer object instance.
- ❏ **pblnSuccess** – Similar to pIADsContainer. This is a passed variable that returns whether or not the method succeeded. We should test success with this variable.

Code Sample – SecuredBind() Method

Now that we've examined the parameters, let's look at the code:

```
' ***********************************************
' SUB:          SecuredBind()
'
' PURPOSE:      Performs as secured bind to a Membership Directory without
'               requiring the full DN of the Member - uses the BaseDN. Binds
'               to the root container
'
' PARAMERS:     strName
'               Name of the member to bind to from the BaseDN (ou=Members)
'
'               strPassword
'               Password of the member to bind as
'
' RETURNS:      pblnSuccess
'               Passed value to test for success as boolean
'
'               pIADsContainer
'               Valid IADsCOntainer if pblnSuccess
'
Public Sub SecuredBind(ByVal strName As String, ByVal strPassword As String, _
                ByRef pIADsContainer As IADsContainer, _
                ByRef pblnSuccess As Boolean)

    On Error GoTo Failed

    Dim objLDAP As Object
    Set objLDAP = GetObject("LDAP:")

    Set pIADsContainer = objLDAP.OpenDSObject(LDAP_ROOT_PATH, _
                                        "cn=" & strName & ", " &
LDAP_BASE_DN, _
                                        strPassword, _
                                        ADS_SECURE_AUTHENTICATION)

    ' No Errors
    '***********************************************
    pblnSuccess = True
    Exit Sub

Failed:
    ' Failed somewhere - unable to bind as the member
    ' ***********************************************
    Set pIADsContainer = Nothing
    pblnSuccess = False
End Sub
```

The `SecuredBind()` method returns a boolean value indicating whether or not the passed object was successfully bound to the specified LDAP path using the member name and password provided. We can then use this object for tasks within the Membership Directory.

Binding as a Member from C++

To bind securely from C++ we'll use the `ADsOpenObject()` method from the `adshlp.h` header file.

ADsOpenObject() Method

The `ADsOpenObject()` method accomplishes a similar role to that of the `OpenDSObject()` method but was designed for C++ rather than the `IDispatch` world of VB. We once again need to pass the reference interface id (`riid`) and the pointer type that's returned to the caller. The prototype for the `ADsOpenObject()` method is:

```
HRESULT WINAPI
ADsOpenObject(
    LPWSTR lpszPathName,
    LPWSTR lpszUserName,
    LPWSTR lpszPassword,
    DWORD  dwReserved,
    REFIID riid,
    void FAR * FAR * ppObject
    );
```

The definitions for the six parameters are:

❑ **lpszPathName** – The LDAP namespace path to the Membership Directory or Membership Directory object to bind to. This is the same path that we used from the `GetObject()` method call from Visual Basic Script in an Active Server Page – i.e. LDAP://localhost:1003/o=Wrox/ou=Members to return a bound ADSI to the ou=Members container.

❑ **lpszUserName** – Similar to the `OpenDSObject()`, the `lpszUserName` specifies the member we'll use to bind to the Membership Directory. However, we can't pass just the member name – we need to pass the full distinguished name to the member in the Membership Directory. i.e. to bind as the Administrator in the ou=Members container we would pass cn=Administrator, ou=Members, o=Wrox as the value for the `lpszUserName`.

❑ **lpszPassword** – The password of the member we're using to bind. If we were binding as the Administrator member in the Membership Directory we would pass the Administrator's password value.

❑ **dwReserved** – The `dwReserved` parameter corresponds to the same value as the `lnReserved` in the `OpenDSObject()` method, and is reserved for future use. However, the following definitions are available in the `IADS.H` file for the future definition of the `dwReserved` parameter:

```
#define    ADS_SECURE_AUTHENTICATION    ( 0x1 )
#define    ADS_USE_ENCRYPTION           ( 0x2 )
#define    ADS_READONLY_SERVER          ( 0x4 )
#define    ADS_PROMPT_CREDENTIALS        ( 0x8 )
```

❑ **riid** – The interface id to be returned by the method call. If the LDAP namespace path passed pointed to a container in the Membership Directory we would want to specify a value of `IID_IADSCONTAINER` as the return type. If the namespace path pointed to a member in the ou=Members container we would specify `IID_IADS` as the return type. The return types are defined in the `ADSIID.H` header files.

❑ **ppObject** – The last parameter in the `ADsOpenObject()` method definition is the `ppObject`. The `ppObject` parameter is a pointer to a pointer (`void**`). This parameter passes an empty pointer and, after the method call, returns a pointer to the object specified in the `lpszPathName` parameter of the type specified in the `riid` parameter.

Code Sample – Using C++ To Get the AdsPath (bind as a member)

We can easily take our `ADsGetObject()` anonymous bind C++ example, and change it to use `ADsOpenObject()`, so that we'll bind as a specific member:

```
// You'll need to ensure that the following files are added to the project:
// comdef.h
// activeds.h
// adsiid.lib
// activeds.lib

#include <iostream.h>
#include <comdef.h>
#include "activeds.h"

int main()
{
  CoInitialize(NULL);

  IADsContainer * pIADsContainer = NULL;
  IADs * pIADs = NULL;

  HRESULT hr;
  BSTR bstrADsPath = NULL;
  BSTR bstrMember = L"cn=Administrator, ou=Members, o=Wrox";
                                            // change this for your own purposes
  BSTR bstrPassword = L"password";          //change this value


  // Connect to the Membership Directory
  // ***********************************
  hr = ADsOpenObject(L"LDAP://localhost:1003",
                     bstrMember,
                     bstrPassword,
                     ADS_SECURE_AUTHENTICATION,
                     IID_IADsContainer,
                     (void**)&pIADsContainer);
  if (FAILED(hr))
  {
    cout << "Failed to get object." << endl;
  }

  // Connect to the ou=members container
  // ***********************************
  hr = pIADsContainer->GetObject(L"organizationalUnit",
                                 L"ou=members",
                                 (IDispatch**)&pIADs);
  if (FAILED(hr))
  {
    cout << "Failed to get members container." << endl;
  }

  // Get the ADsPath of the members container
  // ***********************************
```

```
hr = pIADs->get_ADsPath(&bstrADsPath);
if (FAILED(hr))
{
   cout << "failed!" << &pIADsContainer;
}

// Display the ADsPath
// ***********************************
cout << "ADsPath is: " << (_bstr_t)bstrADsPath << endl;

return (0);
}
```

If we successfully bind to the Membership Directory (after the necessary modifications for your LDAP Service and Membership Directory), you should see the ADsPath property value of the bound object displayed on the command line:

Supporting both Anonymous and Authenticated Binds

In our Windows NT NetShow Services plug-in from Chapter 11, we used a combination of both of our C++ binding methods to provide the capability to allow for anonymous or authenticated binds:

```
HRESULT CLDAPAccess::InitLDAP(WCHAR * pszLDAPServer,
                             WCHAR * pszProxyUser,
                             WCHAR * pszProxyPassword)
{
   CComBSTR bstrLDAPServer( pszLDAPServer );
   CComBSTR bstrProxyUser( pszProxyUser );
   CComBSTR bstrProxyPassword( pszProxyPassword );

   HRESULT hr;

   if (pszProxyUser == NULL)
   {
      hr = ADsGetObject(bstrLDAPServer,
                        IID_IADsContainer,
                        (void**)&m_pIADsContainer);
   }
      else
   {
      hr = ADsOpenObject(bstrLDAPServer,
                         bstrProxyUser,
                         bstrProxyPassword,
                         ADS_SECURE_AUTHENTICATION,
                         IID_IADsContainer,
                         (void**)&m_pIADsContainer);
   }

   return hr;
}
```

If the value for the ProxyUser is undefined in the registry, we attempt to bind to the Membership Directory anonymously. Otherwise, we use the credentials found in the registry.

At this point we have all the knowledge required to bind to a Membership Directory securely from both Visual Basic and C++. Now we're going to expand on the Visual Basic methods we have discussed, in order to see how we can walk the Membership Directory programmatically.

Walking the Membership Directory with Visual Basic

We can navigate through the Membership Directory with Visual Basic as easily as we do with Visual Basic Script in Active Server Pages. In fact, we can easily convert much of the ASP code we examined and translate it into Visual Basic code. First we'll look at a simple method to enumerate the members in a container.

Enumerating Members

We can use the information provided by the DumpMemberData() method to enumerate all the IADs objects in a container. This method dumps the member, the member attributes and the member values to the Visual Basic immediate debug window. The method takes one parameter:

❑   **StrMemContainer** – with this parameter we pass the path to the container whose contents we want to enumerate.

Sample Code – DumpMemberData() Method

For this example we'll assume that we're enumerating the contents of the members container:

```
' ********************************************************
' FUNCTION:     DumpMemberData()
'
' PURPOSE:      Dumps the member variables of the Membership
'               directory.
'
' PARAMETERS:   strMemContainer
'               The LDAP path to bind to
'
Public Function DumpMemberData(ByVal strMemContainer As String)
    On Error Resume Next

    Const E_ADS_PROPERTY_NOT_FOUND = &H8000500D

    Dim objMembersIADS As IADs
    Dim objMemCntrIADsContainer As IADsContainer
    Dim objIADsClass As IADsClass
    Dim objIADsProperty As IADsProperty
    Dim strLDAPServer As String
    Dim nPropertyLoop As Integer

    ' Bind to the Membership Directory
    ' ********************************************
    Set objMemCntrIADsContainer = GetObject(strMemContainer)
    If Err.Number <> 0 Then
      MsgBox "Unable to bind to the Membership Directory: " & strMemContainer
      Exit Function
    End If
```

The method starts with a simple GetObject() bind to the appropriate container – ideally the ou=Members container. Note that for simplicity we're not implementing any security checks. This functionality could easily be added by allowing for a username and password to be passed as a method parameter. After binding, the method enumerates through all the objects in this container.

```
' Enumerate Members
' *****************************************
For Each objMembersIADS In objMemCntrIADsContainer

    Debug.Print objMembersIADS.Name

    ' Bind to the schema object to find all the
    ' attributes that the member has
    ' *****************************************
    Set objIADsClass = GetObject(objMembersIADS.Schema)
```

Each IADs schema object is used to bind to the class type in the cn=Schema, ou=Admin, o=[organization] container. Once we've bound to the schema object, we can go on to enumerate through the mayContain properties by passing the value of the optionalProperties properties of the schema object.

```
        ' Enumerate the may contain properties of
        ' the members class
        ' *****************************************
        For nPropertyLoop = LBound(objIADsClass.OptionalProperties) To _
                            UBound(objIADsClass.OptionalProperties)
            Set objIADsProperty = GetObject(objIADsClass.Parent & "/" & _
                            objIADsClass.OptionalProperties(nPropertyLoop))

            Debug.Print " " & objIADsProperty.Name & "(" & _
                            objMembersIADS.Get(objIADsProperty.Name) & ")"

            If Err.Number = E_ADS_PROPERTY_NOT_FOUND Then
                ' This member doesn't have this property
                ' *****************************************
                Err.Clear
            End If
        Next
    Next
End Function
```

Finally, after enumerating through all the optionalProperties and trapping any errors when we use the current optionalProperty value to bind to the member, we display each attribute and its value for each member. After running the DumpMemberData() method, we should see something similar to the following in the immediate window of Visual Basic:

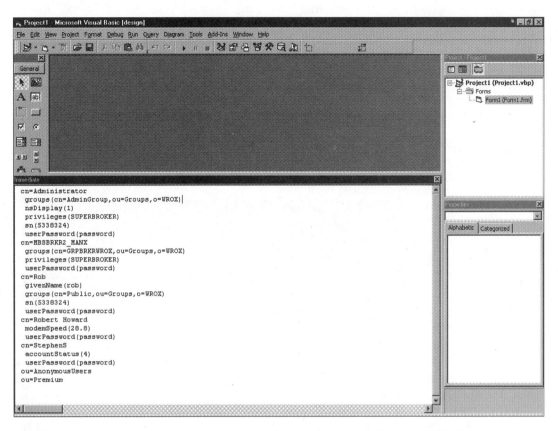

Now that we know how easy it is to write Visual Basic applications that use ADSI, let's see how we could create a more powerful application. We'll look at an application to mimic the view of the Membership Directory we have through the Membership Directory Manager.

The Directory Walker

The Directory Walker tool gives us an idea of the possibilities open to us in developing Visual Basic applications for use with Personalization and Membership, and builds on what we've learned so far in this chapter. The Directory Walker is a Visual Basic program that can bind either to a Membership Directory through the LDAPNamespace object, or the IIS metabase through the IISNamespace object. The complete source code for the Directory Walker is available for download from the Wrox website, along with the rest of the code for this chapter. Before we use the Directory Walker, let's view the different paths we can use for binding.

Binding with the Directory Walker

To bind to a Membership Directory we would pass a namespace path of LDAP://server:port. If the name of our machine was manx (or localhost), we provided an LDAP Service exposed through port 1003, and the Membership Directories root container is o=Wrox, we could use the following ADsPaths:

❑ LDAP://manx:1003 or LDAP://manx:1003/o=Wrox – Binds to the Membership Directory and displays all information. Displays more data about attributes, classes, and objects than the Membership Directory Manager

❑ LDAP://manx:1003/RootDSE – Displays the RootDSE information for the Membership Directory.

To bind to an IIS 4.0 metabase we would pass a namespace path of IIS://server/W3SVC. Continuing with our example server name, we would use the following ADsPaths:

❑ IIS://manx/W3SVC – Displays the IIS metabase directory. Displays all information related to the IIS web servers configured on the machine.

❑ IIS://manx/Schema – Displays the schema of the IIS metabase.

We can also bind securely to Membership Directories:

The Directory Walker can be used to bind securely to a Membership Directory when credentials are entered in the **Bind as Name:** and **Bind as Password:** textboxes. If credentials are not entered, the bind is done anonymously. The IIS metabase is exposed through Windows NT credentials and is a whole other book. It can, however, still be bound to by using this tool.

After entering credentials – if desired – and the namespace path to bind to, pressing the **Connect** button will initiate a GetObject() or a OpenDSObject() method call to either the Membership Directory or the Internet Information Server 4.0 metabase. Once we've successfully bound, the left window of the Directory Walker employs a tree control to browse the structure of the directory, and the right window displays information on particular objects. If we click on the object in the left window all the attributes and values of the object are displayed in the right hand window.

Binding to and populating the tree control is an expensive one-off operation – it takes about 20 seconds to complete. It would have been much more efficient to use C++, but VB appeals to a larger audience.

The UpdateList Method

The sample snippet we'll focus on is the UpdateList() method. UpdateList() updates the list control that displays the attributes and values of the pobjIADs parameters passed – if pobjIADs is not available the bind and list generation is done on the root object g_objIADs. g_objIADs is the root object we bound to defined in the LDAP Server text box.

Code Sample – UpdateList() Method

```
' *************************************************
' SUB:          UpdateList()
'
' PURPOSE:      Method responsible for updating
'               the list view control
'
'
' PARAMETERS:   pobjIADs
'               Optional passed pointer to display
'               contents of current object
'
'
' RETURNS:      Nothing
'
Public Sub UpdateList(Optional ByRef pobjIADs As IADs)
    ' Inline Error Handling
    ' ***********************
    On Error Resume Next

    Dim strAttribute As String
```

```vb
        Dim varValue As Variant
        Dim objIADsClass As IADsClass
        Dim objIADs As IADs
        Dim objListItem As ListItem
        Dim arrMayContain As Variant
        Dim arrMustContain As Variant
        Dim nPropertyLoop As Integer
        Dim nLoopArray As Integer

        ' Clear current values
        ' ************************
        lstVwProps.ColumnHeaders.Clear
        lstVwProps.ListItems.Clear

        ' Set up the columns of the list
        ' ************************
        lstVwProps.ColumnHeaders.Add , , "Attribute", lstVwProps.Width / 2
        lstVwProps.ColumnHeaders.Add , , "Value", lstVwProps.Width / 2
        lstVwProps.View = lvwReport

        ' Use the globabl g_objIADs if we
        ' don't have a reference to pobjIAds
        ' ************************
        If pobjIADs Is Nothing Then
            Set pobjIADS = g_objIADS
        End If

        ' Bind to the schema of the
        ' current object
        ' ************************
        Set objIADsClass = GetObject(pobjIADs.Schema)

        ' Handle special cases
        ' ************************
        If Err.Number = E_ADS_PROPERTY_NOT_SUPPORTED Then
            Err.Clear

            Select Case pobjIADs.Name
                Case "rootdse"
                    Set objIADs =
GetObject("LDAP://manx:1003/o=Wrox/ou=Admin/cn=Schema/cn=RootDseInfo")
                    arrMayContain = objIADs.Get("mayContain")
                    arrMustContain = objIADs.Get("mustContain")
            End Select
        Else
            ' Get the mayContain array
            ' ************************
            arrMayContain = objIADsClass.OptionalProperties

            ' Get the mustContain array
            ' ************************
            arrMustContain = objIADsClass.MandatoryProperties
        End If

        ' Loop through the OptionalProperty
        ' items and display results
        ' ************************
        For nPropertyLoop = LBound(arrMayContain) To UBound(arrMayContain)
            ' Get the attribute name
            ' ************************
```

```vb
        strAttribute = arrMayContain(nPropertyLoop)

        ' Get the attribute value
        ' ************************
        varValue = pobjIADs.Get(strAttribute)

        ' Handle error if attribute
        ' contains no value
        ' ************************
        If (Err.Number = E_ADS_PROPERTY_NOT_FOUND) Or (Err.Number = 91) Then
          Err.Clear
        Else
            ' Are we multi-valued?
            ' ***************************
            If IsArray(varValue) Then
                Set objListItem = lstVwProps.ListItems.Add(, , CStr(strAttribute))
                objListItem.SubItems(1) = CStr(varValue(0))

                ' Loop through and display multi
                ' valued attribute values
                ' ****************************
                For nLoopArray = LBound(varValue) To UBound(varValue)

                    ' Do we need to add a blank
                    ' attribute name?
                    ' ****************************
                    If nLoopArray = UBound(varValue) Then
                      ' Display blank for attribute since
                      ' the value belongs to the previous
                      ' *********************************
                      Set objListItem = lstVwProps.ListItems.Add(, , CStr(""))
                      objListItem.SubItems(1) = CStr(varValue(nLoopArray))
                    End If
                Next
            Else
                ' Looks like we're not mulit-valued
                ' ********************************
                Set objListItem = lstVwProps.ListItems.Add(, , CStr(strAttribute))
                objListItem.SubItems(1) = CStr(varValue)
            End If
        End If
    Next

    ' Loop through the MandatoryProperty
    ' items and display results, following the same proceedure as for the
OptionalProperties array
    ' ******************************************
    For nPropertyLoop = LBound(arrMustContain) To UBound(arrMustContain)
        ' Get the attribute name
        ' ************************
        strAttribute = arrMustContain(nPropertyLoop)

        ' Get the attribute value
        ' ************************
        varValue = pobjIADs.Get(strAttribute)

        ' Handle error if attribute
        ' contains no value
        ' ************************
        If (Err.Number = E_ADS_PROPERTY_NOT_FOUND) Or (Err.Number = 91) Then
```

```
            Err.Clear
        Else
            ' Are we multi-valued?
            ' ****************************
            If IsArray(varValue) Then
                Set objListItem = lstVwProps.ListItems.Add(, , CStr(strAttribute))
                objListItem.SubItems(1) = CStr(varValue(0))

                ' Loop through and display multi
                ' valued attribute values
                ' ****************************
                For nLoopArray = LBound(varValue) To UBound(varValue)

                    ' Do we need to add a blank
                    ' attribute name?
                    ' ****************************
                    If nLoopArray = UBound(varValue) Then
                        ' Display blank for attribute since
                        ' the value belongs to the previous
                        ' ********************************
                        Set objListItem = lstVwProps.ListItems.Add(, , CStr(""))
                        objListItem.SubItems(1) = CStr(varValue(nLoopArray))
                    End If
                Next
            Else
                ' Looks like we're not mulit-valued
                ' ********************************
                Set objListItem = lstVwProps.ListItems.Add(, , CStr(strAttribute))
                objListItem.SubItems(1) = CStr(varValue)
            End If
        End If
    Next
End Sub
```

Advanced Concepts

Before we end this chapter, let's look at a tool you can use to work with objects: the OLE/COM Object Viewer.

The OLE/COM Object Viewer

The OLE/COM Object Viewer happens to be one of my favorite tools when using COM objects. If you've never used it and you're doing any serious development work with COM, you're spinning your wheels! This section isn't an end-all for the OLE/COM Object Viewer, but I would like to share with you how I use it and make it an effective part of my development arsenal.

Finding OLE/COM Object Viewer

The OLE/COM Object Viewer is installed with C++ 5.0 and with Visual Studio 6.0. However, you don't need to know C to use the tool. The tool is available from the start menu (Visual Studio 6.0 install): Microsoft Visual Studio 6.0 | Microsoft Visual Studio 6.0 Tools | OLE View.

Use Expert Mode

OK, don't let your head swell too much, but we'll use this tool in expert mode. Once you're comfortable with the tool in this mode, you'll find that it's more useful than non-expert mode. To set **OLE/COM Object Viewer** to expert mode select <u>V</u>iew | <u>E</u>xpert Mode.

Expert mode simply means that we'll distinguish between Object Classes, Application IDs, Type Libraries and Interfaces. In addition, expert mode groups all the objects together, so that you don't have to flip back and forth between containers to view objects.

Viewing Membership Objects

Let's use the OLE/COM Object Viewer to look at some Membership COM objects, such as the `Membership.UserObjects` (the AUO). To view the AUO's methods and properties, first expand the **Object Classes** container, followed by the **All Objects** container and scroll all the way down to **UserObjects Class** and expand it:

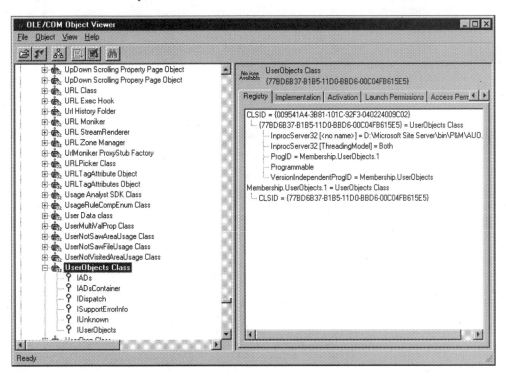

> **Expanding the object actually creates an instance of the object.**

You may notice that objects aren't necessarily listed by their PROGID, i.e.
`Membership.UserObjects`. Instead objects are listed by the default value that corresponds to the
CLISD (Class ID) in the registry, here the UserObjects Class.

Finding the Class ID Default Value

The easiest way to determine what the representation of an object will be in the OLE/COM Object
Viewer is to look up the PROGID in the registry under [HKEY_CLASSES_ROOT]. To find the
CLISD default name of the `Membership.UserObjects` PROGID, use regedit.exe to expand the
[HKEY_CLASSES_ROOT] hive and scroll down to the PROGID of `Membership.UserObjects`.
Items in this hive are listed in alphabetical order, and you might notice two representations of the
object: `Membership.UserObject` and `Membership.UserObjects.1`. Both represent the same
object, but one displays the version number of the object in the PROGID as specified by COM:

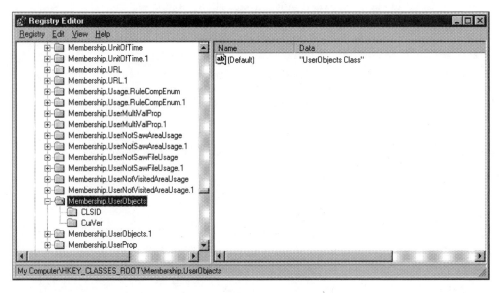

After finding the appropriate PROGID for the object, examine the default value in the folder. This
will be the name of the object we need to use when we look it up with the OLE/COM Object Viewer.

Viewing Methods and Properties

Now that we know how to find all the different objects used for Personalization and Membership, we
can use the OLE/COM Object Viewer tool to view the methods and properties exposed by the
object. For example, if we wanted to examine the methods and properties of the
`Membership.VerifUsr` object we would look up the default name of the object in the registry and
then find the matching name (verfiusr Class) in OLE/COM Object Viewer:

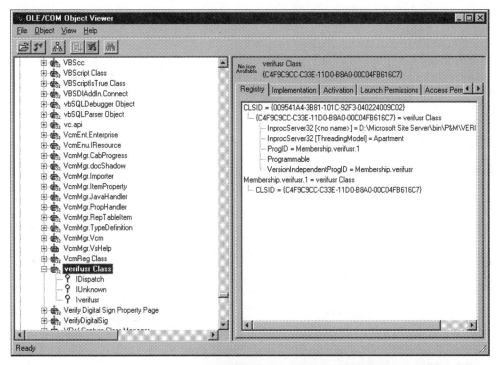

If we then double click on the `Iverifusr` interface the Default Interface Viewer dialog asks us if we would like to view the type info:

Pressing the View Type Info button will then open the ITypeInfo Viewer window:

We can then expand the method container and find a listing of the various method definitions.

The OLE/COM Object Viewer is extremely useful when you're trying to determine how to use a method exposed by an object, and it's definitely not limited just to the Membership Objects. We could easily do the same thing with the Active Data Object or `LDAPNamespace` objects. Appendix C contains all of the interface, method, and property definitions for all the ADSIs and objects we've read about for reference, but you can also find them in the OLE/COM Object Viewer.

Summary

In this final chapter, we took an in-depth look at how to use Personalization and Membership from both Visual Basic and C++ viewpoints. Here's what we learned:

- ❑ **Implementation Differences.** We compared how Visual Basic and C++ are used to access the Membership Directory. These differences included early and late binding in Visual Basic, and the type libraries and header files required for C++.
- ❑ **Binding to the Membership Directory.** Here we discussed two possible types of authentication against a Membership Directory: Anonymous and Member. We learned how to bind to the Membership Directory anonymously with the `GetObject()` in Visual Basic, and the `ADsGetObject()` method in C++. Additionally, we looked at how to bind to the Membership Directory as a member with the `OpenDSObject()` method in Visual Basic and the `ADsOpenObject()` method in C++.
- ❑ **Walking the Membership Directory with Visual Basic.** Here we discussed how we can easily re-purpose the Active Server Page code covered in earlier chapter to Visual Basic. We also went one step further, and showed a full-fledged Visual Basic application called Directory Walker. Directory Walker used all of our knowledge of binding and ADSI to mimic the Membership Directory Manager's output.
- ❑ **Advanced Concepts.** Finally, in the Advanced Concepts section of this chapter, we explored the OLE/COM Object Viewer used to examine the interface definitions of COM objects.

With this final section of the book under your belt, you should be well equipped to maintain your Membership Directory programmatically, using ASP, or VB, and – if you like – a smidgen of C++.

We've worked up to this from the basic concepts and architecture, and hopefully I've gone some way to showing the potential of Site Server, and – in particular – its Personalization and Membership solution. There's much more to Site Server that we haven't covered in this book – there simply isn't enough room to cover *all* the aspects of Site Server Commerce, Analysis, Search, Direct Mail... but it's all there for you to exploit, now you've taken the decision to go with Site Server. Good luck!

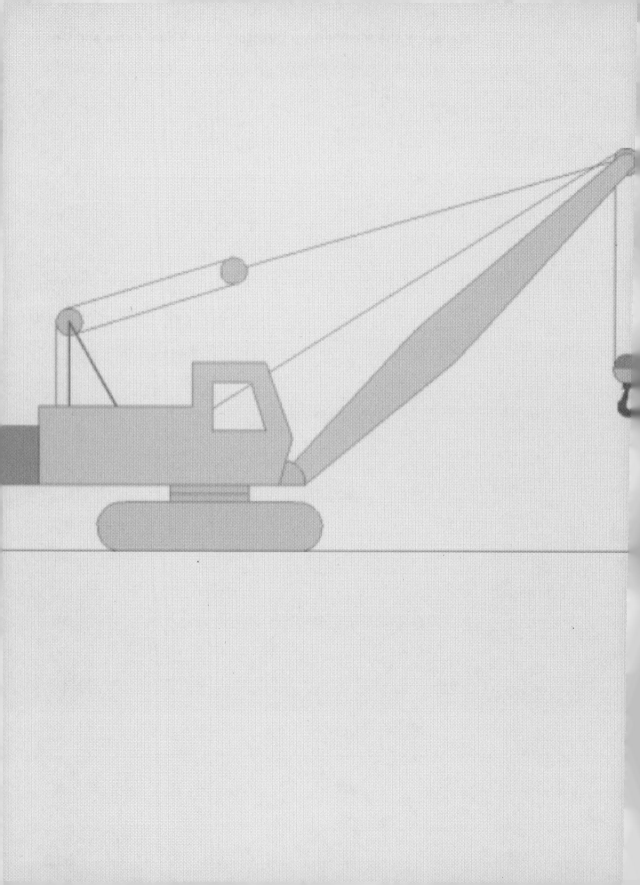

Appendix A – Wall Street Investing

The Wall Street Investing Demo demonstrates several different Microsoft technologies. It focuses mainly on Site Server Personalization and Membership, but we'll also see Microsoft Transaction Server, Internet Information Server, Internet Explorer 4, Dynamic HTML and the Windows Media Player. We've used the Wall Street Investing Demo to provide examples for several of the concepts we've covered in previous chapters, and we've discussed excerpts of the code in Chapters 9, 10, 11 and 14. Since we've already covered the most important features we won't be going over the code line by line here. However, in the Wall Street Investing website you'll find links to View the Code, so you can see what's happening behind the scenes.

We'll begin with a walkthrough of the Wall Street Investing demo, to see the structure of the site that we're going to set up. Once we know where we're heading, we'll move on to the installation process.

Introduction

Wall Street Investing is a fictional investing business that uses Site Server 3.0 Personalization and Membership to serve its customers more effectively. Authentication is performed using Automatic Cookie Authentication. For two areas of the site that have more sensitive content, such as purchasing stocks or changing the member profile, Clear Text/Basic Authentication is implemented.

> **Although for the sake of simplicity this demo does not use SSL to protect areas of the site, you should consider implementing SSL when transmitting sensitive data.**

Also demonstrated are the different possibilities of how we can integrate with other technologies such as the Windows Media Player, and how profiling can be done explicitly through HTML forms, or implicitly such as with the DHTML Windows Media Player.

The design goal of this site was to show the capabilities of Site Server 3.0 Personalization and Membership. However, another important consideration was to build upon libraries of reusable code, that a developer could use to rapidly build their own solution. The demo uses a database to store data that changes frequently, but can be associated with a personalization profile, i.e. only member data is stored in the Membership Directory, so that all content is separate from the member profile. Additionally, the site is not 'optimized' for performance, and has some expensive characteristics. Some objects and data could be put in application state, and some data, such as the stocks, could be stored in a dictionary object in memory. Before you even ask… the site is 'optimized' for Internet Explorer 4.0, meaning that it won't look too good in IE 3.0 or Netscape Navigator.

Browsing the Site

We begin by navigating to the home page of the Wall Street Investing site, `default.asp`. Site Server will send you a cookie used to identify you as an anonymous member in the ou=AnonymousUser, ou=Members container of your Membership Directory.

Membership

A profile on the server will be immediately built with your member account, storing information such as the number of times you've visited the site 'anonymously'. We do this by capturing a numVisits attribute that we increment every time you visit the home page. After the page has completed executing, you should see:

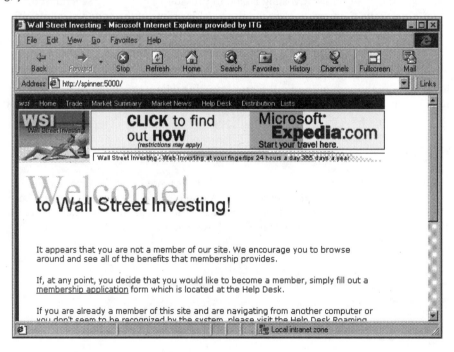

The site welcomes you to the Wall Street Investing Site, and notifies you that it appears that you are not a member of the site. Additionally, you are encouraged to browse around the site to see all the benefits that membership brings. However, you'll soon notice that all the features – other than registering or reading the information about the site – require you to become a member, imagine that!

New Member

Clicking on either the membership application or Help Desk | New Member links will take you to the new member registration page (Don't pay any attention to the Roaming Profile link yet, we'll cover that a little later):

Purpose

The new member registration page, NewMember.asp, requires you to select a member id and a password to use for your membership account. After selecting a member id and a password and pressing **Create New Account** the new account is created in the Membership Directory and you will be re-directed to the HelpDesk to complete your membership information. Since the member profile in the HelpDesk uses Clear Text/Basic Authentication, you must enter your new credentials when prompted.

Member Profile

After providing the necessary credentials to gain access, the page `MemberProfile.asp` will be displayed:

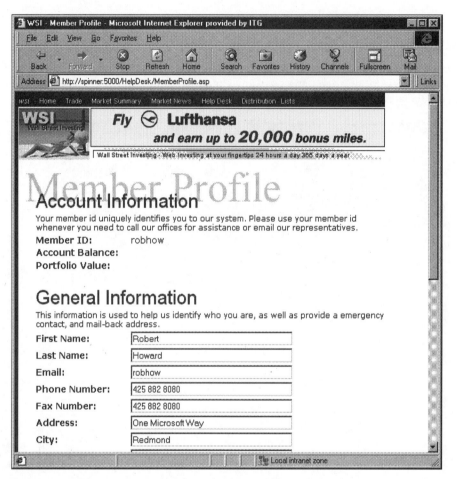

The member profile has two separate sections: General Information and Personalization information.

General Information

The General Information portion of the member profile asks for your first and last name, as well as your email and snail-mail address, i.e. general information. We'll use some of this information for personalization purposes in various parts of the site, but it's not absolutely critical.

Personalization Information

The Personalization Information section states that the information you provided will be used to assist you while navigating the site. Providing this information lets you concentrate on the business of investing, rather than navigating the site! Remember, a key part of using personalization is to provide your users with an easier means of finding the information they are looking for. Don't force your users to sift through all your data just to find information that you could have provided them with through personalization.

Five Explicit Personalization Options

If we do opt to personalize the site, we can choose from five different options that affect the behavior of the site:

❑ Purchase Stock – This setting will determine whether or not the stocks displayed in the Trade section will display only personalized stocks or all stocks available for purchase.

❑ Preferred Type – The preferred type option is probably the most important option we can select when using the Wall Street Investing Site. Preferred type lets us select the preferred investing type that we are most interested in: Technology, Entertainment, or Sporting Goods – I'll suggest you select Technology as there is more interesting content for this type.

❏ Display NetShow – This option determines whether or not we wish to have a Windows Media Stream updating us with the day's news – of course personalized for our preferred type. Additionally, we can select to view the Windows Media Player as a free-floating window, or as a fixed window. We'll discuss this in more detail a little later.

❏ Market Ticker and Market Graph – Both the Market Ticker and Market Graph are used to dynamically replace display elements within the site. Selecting the Market Ticker will removed the banner underneath the ads at the top of every page and replace it with a scrolling stock ticker. The Market Graph, if selected, will display a Java applet charting stock performance. Again, we'll discuss their relevance a little later.

After entering the General and Personalization information, and pressing the Update Information button, your member profile is updated in the Membership Directory. Additionally, you will be redirected back to the main page where you may access all of the additional links, such as purchasing stocks. Later, if you come back to the Member Profile, the form is auto-populated with the values you entered earlier. How this is accomplished is explained in detail in Chapter 10's Personalized HTML Forms topic. If you purchased a stock and returned to the default page, you would additionally see the stock you purchased displayed along with the personalized 'targeted' news stories.

Personalized Home Page

In the following screenshot, I've purchased a single stock, and have selected technology as my preferred type:

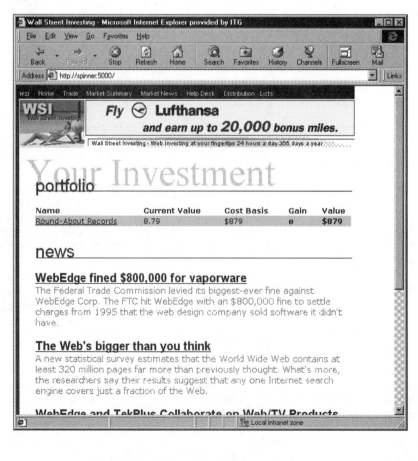

This screen is the same page we saw earlier – `default.asp` – but this time it is personalized using the information from the Membership Directory to tailor the display of the data. The news stories displayed are personalized to technology, my preferred type.

The new articles are read from a database, and then passed into an array – this is done in the `NavBar.inc` file. Let's step through this code to see what's happening:

```
If CreateWSIObject() = true Then
```

`CreateWSIObject()` determines if the WSI object has been instantiated. If it has, the method returns true. If it hasn't, the object will be instantiated, and the method will return true. The method should only return false, if there is a problem creating the object.

```
On Error Resume Next
' Set the database name property
' ***********************************************************
g_objWSIContent.strDBName = AUTO_DB_NAME
```

The `AUTO_DB_NAME` constant identifies the system DSN: WSIDB, and sets the `strDBName` property of the WSI object. AUTO_DB_NAME is defined in another included file: `libConst.inc`.

```
' Call the GetContentType Method of the WSI Component
' IContent Interface to return the content type specified
' ***********************************************************
' GetContentType(Type of content, Number of records to return)
Set g_objWSIRS = g_objWSIContent.GetContentType(AUO_USER_OBJECT_INVTYPE, 3)
```

Next, the `GetContentType()` method of the WSI object is called to return a record set of three news articles. The number of records and the type of records are specified by parameters. `AUO_USER_OBJECT_INVTYPE` defines the member's value for the invType attribute. Afterwards, the `g_objWSIRS` variable contains an ADO record set containing the articles to be displayed.

```
' Handle Errors - If there are no errors display the data
' ***********************************************************
If Err.Number = 0 Then
    ' Populate the content array
    ' ***********************************
Dim nArrayIndex
nArrayIndex = 0
ReDim g_ArrContent(3, nArrayIndex)
' Handle Errors
' **********************
If Err.Number <> 0 Then
    Set g_ArrContent = Nothing
    Err.Clear
End If

' Populate
' **********************
Do While Not g_objWSIRS.EOF
    g_ArrContent(0, nArrayIndex) = g_objWSIRS(CONTENT_ID)
    g_ArrContent(1, nArrayIndex) = g_objWSIRS(CONTENT_TITLE)
    g_ArrContent(2, nArrayIndex) = g_objWSIRS(CONTENT_LEAD)
    g_ArrContent(3, nArrayIndex) = g_objWSIRS(CONTENT_BODY)
```

The `g_ArrContent` is populated with the select values of the ADO record set. `g_ArrContent` is used in several different places, and is less expensive than using an entire record set. The values used by the array from the record set, are defined by constants, such as `CONTENT_TITLE`, that specify the column named to be retrieved.

```
    ' Move to the next item in the recordset
    ' ******************************************
    g_objWSIRS.MoveNext

    ' Increase Array Index?
    ' ******************************************
    If Not g_objWSIRS.EOF Then
      nArrayIndex = (UBound(g_ArrContent, 2)) + 1
      ReDim Preserve g_ArrContent(3, (nArrayIndex))
    End If
  Loop

    ' Must have an error
    ' ******************
  Else
    Err.Clear          ' Handle failure gracefully
  End If
End If
```

Next, let's see how some of the other personalization settings available from the Member Profile affect the display of the site.

Market Ticker and Market Graph

Both of these personalization options change the display of the page by adding or removing elements. To see this in action, first visit the Trade menu and select the Buy option. From this page, select a stock, such as: Round-About Records, to view its Stock datasheet:

Next, revisit the Member Profile page and modify your member settings to display the Market Ticker and Market Graph. When you then return to the stock page, you should see something like this:

The replacement of the banner bar is performed by the following code:

```
If AUO_USER_OBJECT_MTICKER = 0 Then
```

`AUO_USER_OBJECT_MTICKER` is a variable used to contain the value of the marketTicker attribute. Based on this value, 0 or 1, the ticker will either be displayed (1), or the graphic banner is displayed (0).

```
   Response.Write ("<IMG SRC=""/images/banner.gif"">")
Else
   Response.Write ("<FONT FACE=ARIAL SIZE=2><B>" & vbNewLine)
   Response.Write ("<MARQUEE ID=marketTicker ")
   Response.Write ("BGCOLOR=WHITE WIDTH=465 HEIGHT=20>" & vbNewLine)
   Response.Write ("All prices delayed 15 min. :   " & vbNewLine)
   ' Call function from libAccount.inc to
   ' display market ticker items
   DisplayPurchaseAccounts(G_ACCNT_DIS_TICKER)
   Response.Write ("</MARQUEE>" & vbNewLine)
```

```
      Response.Write ("<SCRIPT LANGUAGE=VBSCRIPT>" & vbNewLine)
      Response.Write ("marketTicker.scrollDelay = 150" & vbNewLine)
      Response.Write ("</SCRIPT>" & vbNewLine)
   End If
```

Now we've looked at personalization for the Market Ticker and Market Graph personalization selections, let's see how the site applies personalization to other technologies.

Windows Media Personalization

The media player for the WSI demo is displayed in a DHTML dynamic window that can be moved and positioned around the site. Additionally, as we covered in Chapter 11, the WSI site will display a personalized media stream based on the preferred type of investing style of the member. We're implicitly profiling the member as this window is being moved around, by writing its X and Y coordinates back to the Membership Directory. For this we use an IFRAME and JavaScript to call back to another page:

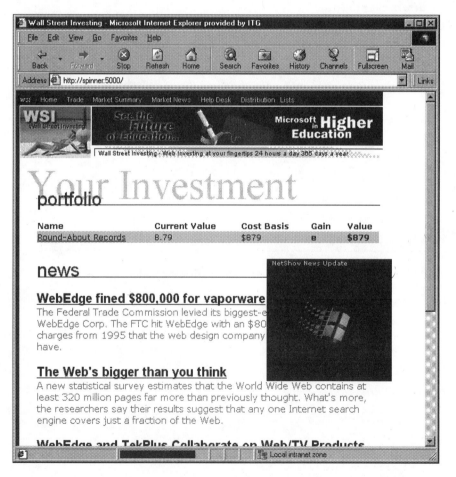

Whenever the DHTML NetShow News Update window is moved our JavaScript calls ModifyAUO.asp, passing all the necessary information.

At this point, we can close the browser and open a new browser, navigating back to our WSI demo. You'll notice that the state of the entire page, DHTML windows and all, remains the same. We're retaining this state by using the SITESERVER and MEMUSER cookies to know which member is currently on the site; however what would happen if the user were to lose or delete this cookie?

Roaming User Profile

The Roaming Profile is a feature to allow a member access to the site in both the following cases:
- ❑ They have lost their cookie identifying them as a member of the site (remember we are using Automatic Cookie Authentication)
- ❑ They are accessing the site from another machine and still want their profile information.

We covered the code and discussed how this works in Chapter 14.

Once you return to the site, an anonymous cookie will be written to your browser automatically, which will incorrectly authenticate you as an anonymous member. To circumvent this, and write the correct cookie back to the browser, we need to obtain the correct member credentials – which we can do by reauthenticating the member and comparing the current member cookie's values to the values for the authenticated member.

Method

To perform this re-authentication we'll use an ASP page, `RoamProfile.asp`, protected by Clear Text/Basic Authentication. Using a method other than Automatic Cookie Authentication on this ASP page requires you to formally authenticate. After properly authenticating, the `RoamProfile.asp` creates an instance of the AUO which has the correct user context.

Next, the code in `RoamProfile.asp` compares the cookie on your machine – sent via the header – to the member common name stored in the Membership Directory:

```
Your Profile
<%
If Request.Form("SUBMIT") <> "" Then
   Response.Write(" - has been Updated")
ElseIf Request.Cookies("MEMUSER") = AUO_USER_OBJECT_CN Then
   Response.Write(" - Is Current")
Else
   Response.Write(" - Is not current")
End If
%>
```

After running the entirety of this code, the ASP reports back whether the cookie of the member and the context of the member match. If they don't, you would see the following screen:

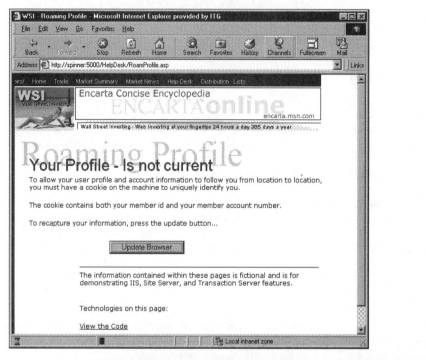

If the values don't match, pressing the **Update** button will programmatically issue a new cookie to the member. This is done with the `SendCookiesToNewUser()` method defined in the `libDSUtils.inc` file. We covered a similar method in Chapter 14's Roaming User Profile discussion. Afterwards, you will be 'properly' recognized by the site.

Now that you've seen what the WSI demo does, let's install it!

Installation

Installing the Wall Street Investing demo is no small chore. However, it's somewhat easier with an installation script called `setup.asp` found in the Setup directory. Here are the steps you need to follow to successfully install the Wall Street Investing Demo.

Create the Directory Structure

❑   Create the following directories and copy the respective files to these locations (the InetPub location is not critical, but rather an organizational suggestion to help keep all your webs together). When the files are unzipped, the zip will rebuild the directory structure of the site.

❑   \InetPub\WSI\Include - Copy all files from the include.zip to this sub directory. Their respective folders should be created by the unzip utility. These files represent the libraries used by the site.

❑   \InetPub\WSI\WallStreetInvesting - Copy all files from the WSI.zip to this sub directory. Again, their respective folders should be created by the unzip utility. These files represent the main files of the site. The Setup.asp page mentioned earlier will be installed in a Setup directory off the WallStreetInvesting directory.

❑   \InetPub\WSI\Components – Finally, copy all files from Components.zip to this sub directory. These files contain the source code for demo components.

The source code for the demo components is written in Visual Basic 5.0 – if you don't yet have Visual Basic 6.0 you'll still be able to build the components. Visual Basic 6.0 will 'upgrade' the Visual Basic 5.0 code.

After creating this directory structure, you should see something like this in Windows NT Explorer:

Build the WSI Server Component

After creating and uncompressing the necessary files, you need to set up the WSI component used by the site. You have two options here.

To register the compiled `WSI.DLL` that you'll find in the `\InetPub\WSI\Components\VB\WSI\Projects` directory, do the following:

- ❑ Copy `WSI.dll` into the default DLL directory (normally drive:\WINNT\SYSTEM32)
- ❑ From the command line run `regsvr32 WSI.dll`

To build the WSI component yourself do the following (you will need Visual Basic 5.0 or 6.0 installed):

- ❑ From Visual Basic open the project WSI.vbp, in the directory \InetPub\WSI\Components\VB\WSI\Projects
- ❑ Make the `WSI.DLL`. This creates the WSI.IContent component used by the WSI site to access and relate information stored in a database with member attributes. You can create the DLL in the same directory as the project.

...

Configuring the Web Site

Now that the component has been built, we're ready to configure the web site.

- ❑ **Create a new virtual web site** – Create a new virtual web site on port 5000 (any port will do, but I always use 5000) that points to \InetPub\WSI\WallStreetInvesting. Make sure the virtual server has execute for scripts, and name the virtual web server Wall Street Investing.
- ❑ **Create a new virtual directory** – Create a new virtual directory in the Wall Street Investing web called include that points to \InetPub\WSI\Include. Make sure that include virtual directory has execute for scripts
- ❑ **Other** – To view the Windows Media Player personalization, you must have the most recent Windows Media Player installed. For more information on this see the discussion in Chapter 11.

Configure the Site Database

You can use either Microsoft Access or SQL Server for the WSI site. If you want to use Access, you can leave the database to be created during the Membership Server setup. However, you will be unable to buy or sell stocks in the demo if you are using Microsoft Access. Purchasing stocks in the WSI site utilizes Microsoft Transaction Server, and we therefore need to set up SQL server as the site database (with Microsoft Access we can't roll back transactions). To use SQL Server you will need to set up an empty database following the procedure below, before you create a Membership Server. You can of course migrate your data from Access to SQL Server at a later stage, but this is an added complication! To create the SQL Server database:

- ❑ **Create a new device** – WSIDATA (25MB). We'll use the new data device for our database and the log files.

❑ **Create a new database** – using the WSIDATA device name the database WSIDB. Use 20mb for the data and 5mb for the logs:

❑ **Check Truncate logs** – Make sure truncate log on check point is selected for the database, using Edit database I Options. This means that the logs will simply be overwritten once full.

Setup Membership Server

Now that the web site is properly configured, we need to create the Membership Server that will be mapped to the site. If you attempt to access the site before mapping the Membership Server, you will get an AUO error.

❑ **Create the Membership Server** – Create a new Membership Server instance named WSI using either an Access or SQL Server database. Choose create new Membership Directory and create an LDAP service instance. Finally choose Membership Authentication as the authentication type to use. We discussed creating a new Membership Server in Chapter 6.

❑ **Map the Membership Server** – Map the new Membership Server to the WSI virtual web server. We discussed mapping in Chapter 8.

After creating the new web server, and the new virtual directory, and mapping the Membership Server, your MMC should look something like this:

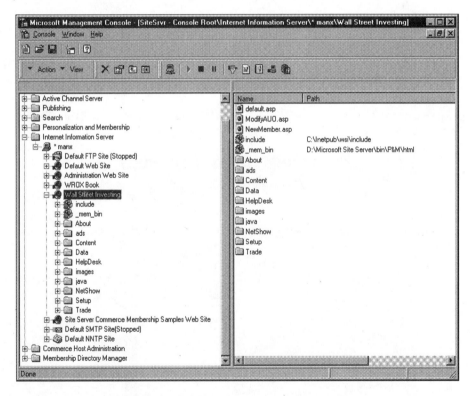

❑ **Open Internet Explorer 4.x** – Open IE 4.x and run
`http://localhost:5000/setup/setup.asp`. Login with the Administrator account and the password, created when we created the Membership Server. `Setup.asp` will automatically create attributes in the Membership Directory, and add these attributes to the members class in the cn=Schema. The output showing the attributes created will appear in the browser:

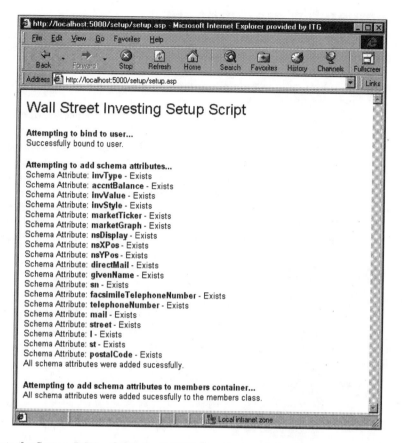

❑ **Create the System DSN** – Open the ODBC Data Source Administrator from the Control Panel, and create a new system DSN for the WSI database. (If you chose Access this will be located at: \InetPub\WSI\WallStreetInvesting\Data\WSI.MDB). Name the System DSN **WSIDB**.

Configure Membership Authentication

Almost done! The only thing left to do is configure the different Membership Authentication methods to use with IIS 4.0.

❑ **Open the Site Server Service Admin MMC** – Expand the Internet Information Server folder, and find the Wall Street Investing web server.

❑ **Select Properties** – Select the properties of the root web server, and select the Membership Authentication tab.

❑ **Automatic Cookie Authentication** – Select Automatic Cookie Authentication as the authentication type to use on all resources in the IIS 4.0 web. Make sure that you uncheck Anonymous Authentication. Applying these settings from the root will affect all sub directories and files.

❑ **Clear Text/Basic Authentication** – Next, select the HelpDesk and Trade subdirectories, choose Properties, and in the Membership Authentication tab apply Clear Text/Basic Authentication. This will force members to log in, since a member name and password is required. The authentication settings for the Helpdesk and Trade subdirectories should look like this:

All done! Yes, you should now be able to access the Wall Street Investing Demo at http://localhost:5000.

PMAdmin.vbs

PMAdmin.vbs is a command line tool for administrating various Personalization and Membership services. The tool is written in Visual Basic Script for the Windows Scripting Host (WSH), and the script can be opened and scrutinized for how information is obtained.

This administration tool can do much of what the Microsoft Management Console Personalization and Membership and Membership Directory Manager snap-ins can do... and more. The documentation provided with Site Server covers this tool very well – well enough, in fact, to mean that we don't need to review all the components and features of the tool. However, we will look at its most relevant uses as applied to this book.

To find the documentation for PMAdmin.vbs, open the online documentation under **Programs | Microsoft Site Server | Site Server Documentation**. After the documentation window opens, expand **Personalization and Membership | P&M System Reference | P&M Command Line Interface**.

To use the PMAdmin tool, open a command line window and switch to the
[Default Site Server Directory]\bin\P&M directory:

```
Command Prompt

Microsoft(R) Windows NT(TM)
(C) Copyright 1985-1996 Microsoft Corp.

D:\>cd microsoft site server

D:\Microsoft Site Server>cd bin

D:\Microsoft Site Server\Bin>cd "p&m"

D:\Microsoft Site Server\Bin\P&M>_
```

Using the PMAdmin Tool

The PMAdmin tool is used by specifying verbs and attributes to both return and set information relative to Site Server 3.0 Personalization and Membership. The verbs represent the actions that we can perform, and the attributes represent the objects on which we can perform these actions. We can also specify a particular parameter by using the switch representing that parameter and a value, separated by a colon. The syntax for using the PMAdmin tool looks like this:

```
PMAdmin verb attribute [[/switch:value]...]
```

Each verb may only be used to perform actions on specific attributes. The following is a list of the attributes that may be used in conjunction with each verb.

Valid verb/attribute Combinations

Verb	Attribute
Add	Auo
	Dbserver
Check	Account
Clear	Mapping
Create	Instance
	Directory
	Partition
Delete	Instance
Fix	Directory
Get	Master
	Instance
	Authsvc
	Mapping
	Ldap
	Directory
	Auo
	Dmail
	Authmethod
	Dbserver

Verb	Attribute
List	Instance
	Dbserver
	Auo
	Partition
	Dynamicreplication
Pause	Ldap
Remove	Auo
Set	Master
	Instance
	Authsvc
	Mapping
	Ldap
	Directory
	Auo
	Dmail
	Authmethod
	Dbserver
Start	Ldap
	Dbserver
Status	Ldap
	Dmail
Stop	Ldap
	Dmail

Valid True/False Values

A number of settings have boolean values. This table contains a list of the permitted boolean values:

True	False
True	False
Yes	No

Table Continued on Following Page

True	False
Y	N
On	Off
T	F
1	0

We'll explore this tool by grouping common actions together.

The Master Configuration

The master configuration values and settings apply global settings for all Membership Servers on the machine.

Getting/Setting the Master Configuration

To return the master settings for all LDAP Services on the server, we type the following on the command line:

```
pmdmin get master
```

To set any of the parameters for the master, we type:

```
pmdmin set master
```

followed by the switch for that parameter and the new value. For instance, to set the parameter **LdapIPDenyThreshold** to a value of 2012, we would type:

```
pmdmin set master /LdapIPDenyThreshold:2012
```

When the set has been completed successfully, we will see the following message:

```
Windows NT Registry updated
```

The following table shows the parameters of the master configuration and for each parameter, the switch (in most cases, this is the parameter name preceded by a slash), the value type, the default value, and a description of that parameter.

Parameter Name /SWITCH	Valid Value	Default Value	Description
LdapIPDenyThreshold /LdapIPDenyThreshold:	Integer	2024	The number of failed authentications allowed before the IP address is denied. The number of authentication failures must occur within the time limit specified by the `LdapIPDenyWindow` setting.

Parameter Name / SWITCH	Valid Value	Default Value	Description
LdapIPDenyWindow /LdapIPDenyWindow:	minutes	10	The time, in minutes, allowed for failed authentications if the number of failed authentications is less than the value in `LdapIPDenyThreshold`.
LdapIPDenyTimeout /LdapIPDenyTimeout:	minutes	3	The time, in minutes, that an account will be denied access after the `LdapIPDenyThreshold` is reached in the time limit specified by `LdapIPDenyWindow`.
LdapAccountDeny Threshold /LdapAccountDeny Threshold:	Integer	10	If short term access denial is enabled, this value represents the number of failed account logins allowed before the account is temporarily disabled – all failures must occur within the time limit specified by `LdapAccountDenyWindow`.
LdapAccountDeny Window /LdapAccountDeny Window:	minutes	10	The time, in minutes, that failed account logins must occur within before the account is temporarily disabled.
LdapAccountDeny Timeout /LdapAccountDeny Timeout:	minutes	3	The time, in minutes, that an account will be disabled after the `LdapAccountDenyThreshold` is reached in the time specified by `LdapAccountDenyWindow`.
Bypass ACL checking /AuthenticationACL Bypass:	Boolean	On	Determines whether or not accounts with the attribute and value pair of **DS-PRIVILEGES / SUPERBROKER** will be allowed to bypass Access Control List (ACL) checking in the Membership Directory.
NTAutoMap /NTAutoMap:	Boolean	On	For Membership Directories that use Membership Authentication, this value determines if the groups listed in the ou=Groups, ou=NTGroups will map to the impersonation account for Windows NT authorizations.
AUOCacheAccess /AUOCacheAccess:	Boolean	On	Determines whether or not user properties from the authentication cache are used.

Table Continued on Following Page

Parameter Name /SWITCH	Valid Value	Default Value	Description
FormsAuthTimeout /FormsAuthTimeout:	Boolean	On	Determines if the user is periodically issued a new FORMSAUTH cookie to keep a session active.
FormsAuthReissue: /FormsAuthReissue:	Seconds	60	The length of time that the system waits before issuing a new FORMSAUTH cookie
AuthAccountDeny Threshold /AuthAccountDeny Threshold:	Integer	25	The number of failed authentications allowed before the account is temporarily disabled for the time period specified in AuthAccountDenyTimeout.
AuthAccountDeny Timeout /AuthAccountDeny Timeout:	Minutes	3	The time, in minutes, that an account is temporarily disabled due to failed login attempts.
DPACookies /DPACookies:	Boolean	On	Determines whether or not DPA authentication will use cookies – necessary for proxy authentications.
CookieScope /CookieScope:	Integer	0	The number of segments – of a domain – used for the identification cookie. If set to 0 the system will determine the setting on its own. If set to 2 the cookie will be called – mydomain.com – if set to 3 the cookie will be called www.mydomain.com. This is useful for sites that use a same domain name, but different prefixes. A CookieScope setting of 2 will allow these domains to share a common cookie.

Oddly enough, the modification made for the cookiescope is made under
`[HKEY_LOCAL_MACHINE]\Software\Microsoft\SiteServer\3.0\`
`Analysis\UA\UAS Filter\Cookies\Cookie domain scope\Value`
– Analysis!

Managing LDAP Services

These are the verbs and attributes used for managing the LDAP Services.

Getting/Setting the LDAP Service parameters

We can get or set the LDAP Service configuration information with:

```
pmadmin get ldap
```

or

```
pmadmin set ldap
```

as appropriate. This will return the LDAP configuration information for the first Membership Server (an ID of 1). If we have more than one Membership Server running on the machine we can specify which Membership Server we want with the following switch:

Switch	Valid Value	Default Value	Description
/ID:	Integer	1	The Membership Server instance id to display directory values for

To return configuration information for Membership Server number 2 we enter on the command line:

```
PMAdmin get ldap /ID:2 /AccountDeny:ON
```

We should get the following return value:

```
LDAP configuration set
```

The following table shows the parameters of the LDAP configuration and for each parameter, the switch (in most cases this is the parameter name preceded by a slash), the value type, the default value, and a description of that parameter.

Parameter /Switch	Valid Value	Default Value	Description
Membership Server ID# /ID:	Integer	1	The service instance id
Server		localhost	Name of the server providing the services
DNS Name			Domain Name Server for the server above
LDAP Port# /LdapPort:	Integer	1001 + instance id	The port used to provide the LDAP Service. The default LDAP port is 389
SSL Port /LdapSSLPort:	Integer	636 + instance id	SSL should only be supported on 636

Table Continued on Following Page

Parameter /Switch	Valid Value	Default Value	Description
Read Only Mode /ReadOnly:	Boolean	Off	Determines whether or not the LDAP Service works in read-only mode.
Enable All Substring search /SubStringSearches:	Boolean	On	Whether searches will be performed on all substrings.
Maximum Page size of each query /MaxPageSize:	Integer	100	Maximum page size of an LDAP query
Maximum result set of each query /MaxResults:	Integer	500	Maximum number of results to display per LDAP query
Maximum query timeout /MaxQueryTime:	Integer	60	Period in milliseconds before an LDAP query times out
Authentication Method /LdapAuth:	Integer	3: Membership Authentication 7: Windows NT (Intranet) Authentication	Sum of numbers provided to determine authentication mechanism used to access the Membership Directory from the LDAP service: 1=Anonymous 2=Clear Text/Basic 3=Anonymous and Clear Text/Basic 4=DPA or Windows NT Challenge/Response 5=Anonymous and DPA or Windows NT Challenge/Response. 7=ALL
SSL support /LdapSSL:	Boolean	Off	Whether or not SSL is enabled for this Membership Directory.

Parameter /Switch	Valid Value	Default Value	Description
128bit SSL support /SSL128:	Boolean	Off	Whether 128bit SSL is enabled.
Dynamic Object support /Dynamic:	Boolean	On	Whether or not dynamic objects are supported.
Dynamic replication /DynamicReplication:	Boolean	Off	Whether dynamic information is shared between servers providing LDAP services.
Minimum TTL of dynamic objects /DynamicMinTTL:	Integer	300	The time to live (TTL) of a dynamic object in milliseconds
DynamicMaxObjects /DynamicMaxObjects:	Integer	5000	The maximum number of dynamic objects that can be created.
NetMeeting1.0 /NetMeeting1:	Boolean	Off	Whether or not NetMeeting1.0 is supported for the Membership Directory.
Logging /Logging:	Boolean	Off	Whether or not logging is turned on for the LDAP service.
Maximum LDAP connections per instance /MaxConnections:	Integer	2000	Maximum number of connections provided through the LDAP service
Connection timeout /ConnectionTimeout:	Integer	3600	Connection timeout in seconds, 60 minutes here
IPDeny /IPDeny:	Boolean	Off	Whether or not IP deny is turned on
AccountDeny /AccountDeny:	Boolean	Off	Whether or not account deny is turned on

Status of the LDAP Service

The `status ldap` command returns the status of the LDAP Service defined by the following switch:

Switch	Valid Value	Default Value	Description
/ID:	Integer	1	The service instance number

To return the status of LDAP Service 2 enter:

```
PMAdmin status ldap /ID:2
```

A sample return value is:

```
LDAP Server Status: Server has been started.
```

Starting the LDAP Service

The `start ldap` command is used to **start** LDAP Services that are stopped or paused. The LDAP Service is specified with the switch:

Switch	Valid Value	Default Value	Description
/ID:	Integer	1	The service instance number

To start LDAP Service 2 enter:

```
PMAdmin start ldap /ID:2
```

This returns:

```
LDAP Server Status: Server is starting.
```

Stopping the LDAP Service

The `stop ldap` command allows us to stop the LDAP Service specified by the switch:

Switch	Valid Value	Default Value	Description
/ID:	Integer	1	The service instance number

To stop LDAP Service 2 enter:

```
PMAdmin stop ldap /ID:2
```

This returns:

```
LDAP Server Status: Server has been stopped.
```

Pausing the LDAP Service

The `pause ldap` command pauses the LDAP service specified by the switch:

Switch	Valid Value	Default Value	Description
/ID:	Integer	1	The service instance of the provided service parameter.

To pause LDAP Service2 enter:

```
PMAdmin pause ldap /ID:2
```

No message is returned from this command.

Managing Membership Directories

Verb and attribute combinations used to return settings for Membership Directories, as well as create new Membership Directories.

Creating a new Membership Directory

The `create directory` command is used to create new Membership Directories. These are the switches we can specify in conjunction with this command:

Switch	Valid Value	Default Value	Description
/ID:	Integer	1	The Membership Server instance id to create
/AuthMode:	Type	1	Determines the authentication mode used by the Membership Directory. Valid values include: 0=Windows NT Authentication 1=Membership Authentication
/Realm:	String		The realm of the instance
/DBType:	Integer	2	Determines the database type used for the Membership Directory 1=Microsoft SQL Server 2=Microsoft Access
/DBSource:	String	%root%\ Microsoft Site Server\ Data\mpinst# \<instance>	The source of the database. This value is automatically created for Access databases, but must be specified by \\server\database for SQL Server

Table Continued on Following Page

Switch	Valid Value	Default Value	Description
/DBUsername:	String		Username value for the database used for the Membership Directory. Only required for SQL Server.
/DBPassword:	String		Password value for the database used for the Membership Directory. Only required for SQL Server.
/DnPrefix:	String	Null	Prefix (c=) value for new Membership Directory. Not used by default.
/SuperPassword:	String		The password of the Administrators account that is created in the new Membership Directory
/Dirroot:	String	Microsoft	Name of the root node

To create a new directory with a Membership Server Instance id of 3 and the administrator password set to 'password', we enter:

```
PMAdmin create directory /ID:3 /SuperPassword:password
```

We are returned the parameters in the table above, and the following messages:

Create directory completed
Status message that the Membership Directory has successfully been created. Next, the services are rolled so that the new Membership Directory is available.

LDAP Server Status: Server is Stopping
LDAP Server Status: Server is Starting
The LDAP Service is started and stopped to make the new Membership Directory available

Creating Default Groups
Default groups are being created in the new Membership Directory

Creating Default AUO Provider
Creating the default AUO provider

Creating Broker Account
Creating the broker account for Membership Authentication

Broker is turned on for authentication.
Whether or not the broker will be used for authentication

Creating Direct Mail Account
Direct Mail account is created in the Membership Directory

Setting Default ACLs
Default Groups and users created and ACLs set
Security permissions are set for the Membership Directory

DS Setup Complete
Configuration complete – New Membership Directory created.

Getting/Setting Membership Directory parameters

The get directory command returns information about the Membership Directory. We can use one switch with this command:

Switch	Valid Value	Default Value	Description
/ID:	Integer	1	The Membership Server instance id for which to display directory values

To retrieve information for the Membership Directory for Membership Server 2, we enter:

```
PMAdmin get directory /ID:2
```

We are returned the parameters listed in the table below. The set directory command sets information about the Membership Directory. We can use the following switches with this command:

Parameter /Switch	Valid Value	Default Value	Description
Membership Server ID# /ID:	Integer	1	The Membership Server instance id to create
Server		localhost	The server on which the Membership Server resides.
Root Data Store Type /DBType:	Integer	2	Determines the database type used for the Membership Directory 1=Microsoft SQL Server 2=Microsoft Access
DBSource /DBSource:	String	%root%\ Microsoft Site Server\ Data\mpinst#<instance>	The source of the database. This value is automatically created for Access databases, but must be specified by \\server\database for SQL Server

Table Continued on Following Page

Parameter /Switch	Valid Value	Default Value	Description
Root Name			The name of the root container (usually organization o=) of the Membership Directory
Authentication Mode	Type		Authentication type used by the Membership Directory
Authentication Method	Integer	3: Membership Authentication 7: Windows NT (Intranet) Authentication	Sum of numbers provided to determine authentication mechanism used to access the Membership Directory from the LDAP service: 1=Anonymous 2=Clear Text/Basic 3=Anonymous and Clear Text/Basic 4=DPA or Windows NT Challenge/Response 5=Anonymous and DPA or Windows NT Challenge/Response. 7=ALL
/DBUsername:	String		Username value for the database used for the Membership Directory. Only required for SQL Server.
/DBPassword:	String		Password value for the database used for the Membership Directory. Only required for SQL Server.
DNPrefix /DnPrefix:	String	Null	Prefix (c=) value for new Membership Directory. Not used by default.

To set the database username to 'sa' for the Membership Directory with a Membership Server instance id of 2, enter:

```
PMAdmin set directory /ID:2 /DBUsername:sa
```

Setting directory information returns:

```
DS Setup Complete
```

to show Membership Directory configuration complete.

Managing Membership Servers

These are the verb and attribute combinations used to manage Membership Server settings.

Listing Membership Server instances

The list instance command returns all the Membership Server instances available on the server. On the command line enter:

```
PMAdmin list instance
```

You will see the following return values:

Instance ID#: 2
The instance id of the Membership Server. Note list instance displays the same three bits of detail for each Membership Server on the server.

Name: WROX
The name of the Membership Server

Authentication Mode: Membership
The authentication type used by the Membership Directory for this Membership Server instance.

Getting/Setting Membership Server Instance information

The get instance command returns the servers and ports configured for the various services supported by the Membership Server specified by the instance id switch:

Switch	Valid Value	Default Value	Description
/ID:	Integer	1	The Membership Server instance id to display directory values for

To return server and port information for Membership Server 2 enter:

```
PMAdmin get instance /ID:2
```

This returns the following values:

Membership Server ID#: 2
The Membership Server instance passed by the /ID:# switch

Name: WROX
The name of the Membership Server

Realm:
The realm displayed for authentications

Authentication Mode: Membership
Membership or Windows NT authentication

LDAP Server and Port:
LDAP: Server=MANX Port=1003 SSL=False SSLPort=638
AUTHSVC : Server=MANX Port=1003 SSL=False SSLPort=0
AUO: Server=MANX Port=1003
Configurations for the supported services: server, port, Secure Sockets Layer (SSL), and SSL port.

The `set instance` command allows for various settings to be modified for a Membership Server. We can use the following switches with this command:

Switch	Valid Value	Default Value	Description
/ID:	Integer	1	The Membership Server instance id to modify
/Name:			The name of the Membership Server instance – displayed in the Personalization and Membership snap-in
/LdapServer:		Localhost	The server that the LDAP Service lives on
/LdapPort:			The port that the LDAP Service lives on
/LdapSSL:			The port used for Secure Sockets Layer communications
/Realm:			The organization o= name of the Membership Directory

To set the name of Membership Server 2 to Wrox, enter:

```
PMAdmin set instance /ID:2 /Name:WROX
```

This returns:

Name: WROX
The new name of the Membership Server – viewable from the Personalization and Membership Server.

Getting/Setting Membership Server Mapping Information.

The `get mapping` command returns the mapping information for Membership Servers. We can use the following switches:

Switch	Valid Value	Default Value	Description
/ServiceInstance:	Integer	1	Instance number of the application server.
/Service:	String	W3SVC	The service to return configuration information for, i.e. W3SVC.

To return the mapping information for the service with an instance id of 3, enter:

```
PMAdmin get mapping /ServiceInstance:3
```

This returns:

Membership Server ID#: 2
The instance id of the Membership Server that this service is using

Name: WROX
The name of the Membership Server that this service is using

The set mapping provides a means for changing the mapping settings for various services (usually IIS 4.0 webs). We can use the following switches:

Switch	Valid Value	Default Value	Description
/ServiceInstance:	Integer	1	The service instance of the provided service parameter.
/Service:	String	W3SVC	The service to return configuration information for
/ID:	Integer	1	The Membership Server instance to map the specified service instance to

To map the service with an instance id of 3 to Membership Server 2, enter:

```
PMAdmin set mapping /ID:2 ServiceInstance:3
```

This returns:

Service Name: W3SVC
Service type the Membership Server is mapped to

Service Instance#: 3
Service instance the Membership Server is mapped to

Mapped To: 2
Membership Server the service is mapped to

Clearing a Membership Server mapping

The clear mapping command removes the mapping of a Membership Server from another service, such as IIS 4.0.

Switch	Valid Value	Default Value	Description
/ServiceInstance:	Integer	1	The service instance of the provided service parameter.
/Service:	String	W3SVC	The service to return configuration information for

To unmap the service with an instance id of 3 from a Membership Server enter:

```
PMAdmin clear mapping /ServiceInstance:3
```

This returns:

Mapping cleared
The service, in this case 3, is no longer mapped to a Membership Server.

Authentication Service

These are the verbs and attributes used to modify an authentication service. You can only use these commands if the Membership Directory for the Membership Server we are querying uses Membership Authentication.

Getting/Setting Authentication Service information

The get authsvc command returns the authentication information for the Membership Server instance, specified by the switch:

Switch	Valid Value	Default Value	Description
/ID:	Integer	1	The Membership Server instance id to display authentication service values for

To return authentication information for Membership Server 2 enter:

```
PMAdmin get authsvc /ID:2
```

The parameters this returns are listed in the table below. The set authsvc command sets authentication information for the Membership Server instance. The switches we can use in conjunction with this command are listed in the table below.

Switch	Valid Value	Default Value	Description
Membership Server ID /ID:	Integer	1	The Membership Server instance id
Name	String		The name of the Membership Server
The broker is turned on for authentication			The broker is being used for authentication
LDAP Server Name /LdapServer:	String	Localhost	The name or IP of the LDAP server

552

Switch	Valid Value	Default Value	Description
LDAP Port# /LdapPort:	Integer	1002	The port from which LDAP services are available
Using SSL /LdapSSL:	Boolean	Off	Does the LDAP Server use secure sockets layer
SSL Port /LdapSSLPort:	Integer	0	The port of the SSL used to communicate with the LDAP Server securely
LDAP Search TimeLimit /TimeLimit:	Seconds	60	The amount of time that will be spent on an LDAP search before timing out.
LDAP Search SizeLimit /SizeLimit:	Bytes	0	If the search limit has a size limit. 0 = no limit
Group Prefix /GroupPrefix:	String	Site_MDName_	Groups that are created in the Membership Directory are also created in the Windows NT SAM with the following prefix to insure that the group name is unique.
Auto create NT group /CreateGroups:	Boolean	On	Determines whether or not the NT groups will be created automatically
Group Domain /GroupDomain:	String		If groups are to be created on the domain SAM
Authentication Service Account /DsUser:	String		The broker account used to bind to and look up members in the Membership Directory.
/DsPasssword:	String		The password of the broker account
Windows NT Impersonation Account /ProxyName:	String	MemProxyUser + Instance ID	The name of the impersonation account used to gain access to the Windows NT file system – MemProxyUser by default
/ProxyPassword:	String		Password of the impersonation account

Table Continued on Following Page

Switch	Valid Value	Default Value	Description
Proxy Domain /ProxyDomain:	String		Domain the impersonation account is on
FormAuthTimeout **(Timeout when** **using Cookie** **authentication)** /FormAuthTimeout:	minutes		The amount of time in minutes before a cookie authenticated logon times out.
/Restart:	Boolean	Off	Whether to restart the authentication service when changes are made without prompting the user
Realm			The realm value displayed for dialog-based authentication (Basic/Clear text Authentication and DPA). If left blank defaults to Membership Server name
BaseDN /BaseDN:	String	ou=Members	The base distinguished name setting for the Membership Server. Additionally covered in Chapter 8.

To set the authentication for Membership Server 2 so that members will be authenticated from the Premium container (see Chapter 8 for details), enter:

```
PMAdmin set authsvc /ID:2 /BaseDN:"ou=Premium, ou=Members"
```

There is no return message.

Getting/Setting the Authentication Method

The get authmethod command returns the authentication method used by a resource (such as an IIS Server instance) mapped to a Membership Server. We specify the IIS server instance with the switch:

Switch	Valid Value	Default Value	Description
/MetabasePath:	String	None	The metabase path in IIS, such as IIS://localhost/W3SVC/Root/3. "/LM/W3SVC/Root/#" corresponds to the value of the appRoot value of a IIS 4.0 server. '#' is the number of the IIS 4.0 server instance. We can view these values using the Directory Walker tool from Chapter 15.

To return the authentication method used by the IIS 4.0 server instance 3, enter:

```
PMAdmin get authmethod /MetabasePath:"/LM/W3SVC/Root/3"
```

This returns the authentication type as an integer, for example:

```
Authentication Type: 16
```

We'll see the authentication type values in the table below.

The `set authmethod` command sets the authentication method used by an IIS 4.0 server mapped to a Membership Server. We use the following switches:

Switch	Valid Value	Default Value	Description
/MetabasePath:	String	None	The metabase path in IIS, such as IIS://localhost/W3SVC/Root/3. "/LM/W3SVC/Root/#" corresponds to the value of the `appRoot` value of a IIS 4.0 server. '#' is the number of the IIS 4.0 server instance. We can view these values using the Directory Walker tool from Chapter 15.
/Types:	Integer	20	The authentication types are represented by integer values.
			1=Automatic Cookie Authentication
			2=HTML Forms Authentication
			4=Clear Text/Basic Authentication
			8=DPA Authentication
			16=IIS 4.0 IUSR_[server name] Anonymous Authentication
			To combine authentication types, use the sum of the values.

To set the authentication method of the IIS 4.0 server instance 3 to Clear Text/Basic Authentication enter:

```
PMAdmin set authmethod /MetabasePath:"/LM/W3SVC/Root/3" /Types:4
```

There is no return message.

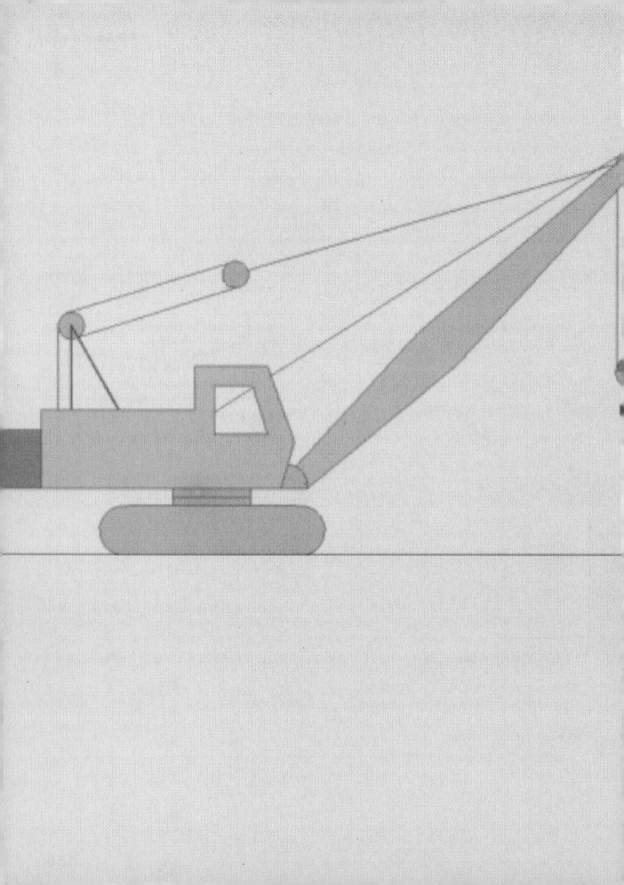

Object and Interface Reference for the Membership Directory

The following interface definitions are from the OLE/COM Object Viewer and are the interface definitions for objects used to work with the Personalization and Membership system.

For an explanation of the Active User Object see Chapter 9, for many of the other object definitions and example uses see Chapter 12.

Supported Active Directory Service Interfaces

The IADs and IADsContainer are exposed through all Active Directory providers – such as the LDAPNamespace and the Active User Object.

IADs

Properties	Methods
BSTR Name()	void GetInfo()
BSTR Class()	void SetInfo()
BSTR GUID()	VARIANT Get(BSTR bstrName)
BSTR ADsPath()	void Put(BSTR bstrName, VARIANT vProp)
BSTR Parent()	VARIANT GetEx(BSTR bstrName)
	void PutEx(long lnControlCode, BSTR bstrName, VARIANT vProp);
	void GetInfoEx(VARIANT vProperties, long lnReserved);

IADsClass

Properties	Methods
BSTR Name()	void GetInfo()
BSTR Class()	void SetInfo()
BSTR GUID()	VARIANT Get(BSTR bstrName)
BSTR ADsPath()	void Put(BSTR bstrName, VARIANT vProp)
BSTR Parent()	VARIANT GetEx(BSTR bstrName)
BSTR Schema()	void PutEx(long lnControlCode, BSTR bstrName, VARIANT vProp)
	void GetInfoEx(VARIANT vProperties, long lnReserved);
BSTR PrimaryInterface()	
BSTR CLSID()	void CLSID(BSTR rhs)
BSTR OID()	void OID(BSTR rhs)
VARIANT_BOOL Abstract()	void Abstract(VARIANT_BOOL rhs)
VARIANT_BOOL Auxiliary()	void Auxiliary(VARIANT_BOOL rhs)
VARIANT MandatoryProperties()	void MandatoryProperties(VARIANT rhs)
VARIANT OptionalProperties()	void OptionalProperties(VARIANT rhs)
VARIANT NamingProperties()	void NamingProperties(VARIANT rhs)
VARIANT DerivedFrom()	void DerivedFrom(VARIANT rhs)
VARIANT AuxDerivedFrom()	void AuxDerivedFrom(VARIANT rhs)
VARIANT PossibleSuperiors()	void PossibleSuperiors(VARIANT rhs)
VARIANT Containment()	void Containment(VARIANT rhs)
VARIANT_BOOL Container()	void Container(VARIANT_BOOL rhs)
BSTR HelpFileName()	void HelpFileName(BSTR rhs)
long HelpFileContext()	void HelpFileContext(long rhs)
IADsCollection* Qualifiers()	

IADsContainer

Properties	Methods
long Count()	
IUnknown* _NewEnum()	
VARIANT Filter()	void Filter(VARIANT rhs)

Properties	Methods
VARIANT Filter()	void Filter(VARIANT rhs)
VARIANT Hints()	void Hints(VARIANT rhs)
	IDispatch* GetObject(BSTR ClassName, BSTR RelativeName)
	IDispatch* Create(BSTR ClassName, BSTR RelativeName)
	void Delete(BSTR bstrClassName, BSTR bstrRelativeName)
	IDispatch* CopyHere(BSTR SourceName, BSTR NewName)
	IDispatch* MoveHere(BSTR SourceName, BSTR NewName)

IADsOpenDSObject

Method
IDispatch* OpenDSObject(BSTR lpszDNName, BSTR lpszUserName, BSTR lpszPassword, long lnReserved)

IADsProperty

Properties	Methods
BSTR Name()	void GetInfo()
BSTR Class()	void SetInfo()
BSTR GUID()	VARIANT Get(BSTR bstrName)
BSTR ADsPath()	void Put(BSTR bstrName, VARIANT vProp)
BSTR Parent()	VARIANT GetEx(BSTR bstrName)
BSTR Schema()	void PutEx(long lnControlCode, BSTR bstrName, VARIANT vProp)
	void GetInfoEx(VARIANT vProperties, long lnReserved)
BSTR OID()	void OID(BSTR rhs)
BSTR Syntax()	void Syntax(BSTR rhs)
long MaxRange()	void MaxRange(long rhs)

Table Continued on Following Page

559

Properties	Methods
long MinRange()	void MinRange(long rhs)
VARIANT_BOOL MultiValued()	void MultiValued(VARIANT_BOOL rhs)
IADsCollection* Qualifiers()	

Membership User Objects

Active User Object: IUserObjects

> The Active User Object also supports the Interfaces IADs and IADsContainer

PROGID: *Membership.UserObject.1*

CLSID: *{77BD6B37-B1B5-11D0-BBD6-00C04FB615E5}*

Methods
void OnStartPage(IUnknown* pContext)
void OnEndPage()
void Init(BSTR bszHost, BSTR bszUserName)
void SetUserName(BSTR bszUserName)
void BindAs(BSTR bszAlias, BSTR bszUserName, BSTR bszPassword)
IDispatch* GetObjectAsUser(BSTR bszADsPath)
IDispatch* GetObjectEx(BSTR bszEntryName)

GUID Generator Class: IGuidGen

PROGID: *Membership.GuidGen.1*

CLSID: *{CB7865A2-E677-11D0-BDC7-00C04FB6163F}*

Properties	Methods
BSTR GenerateGuid()	void OnStartPage([in] IUnknown* piUnk)
	void OnEndPage()

Broker Config Class: IBrokServers

PROGID: MemAdmin.BrokServers

CLSID: {CD8F114E-C4AC-11D0-BBDA-00C04FB615E5}

Properties	Methods
void Init()	void CreateServer(VARIANT* plVirtServId)
void HasWritePrivilege()	void DeleteServer(long lVirtServId)
void HasNTAdminPrivilege()	void StartServer(long lVirtServId)
	void StopServer(long lVirtServId)
	void GetServers(VARIANT* plVirtServIds, VARIANT* pComments);
	void MapToBroker(BSTR bszServiceName, long lVirtServId, long lVirtBrokId);
	void ClearMapping(BSTR bszServiceName, long lVirtServId)
	void MappedTo(BSTR bszServiceName, long lVirtServId, VARIANT* plVirtBrokId, VARIANT* pbszComment)
	void SetAuthTypes(BSTR bszPath, long lTypes)
	long GetAuthTypes(BSTR bszPath)
	long GetSecurityMode(BSTR bszServiceName, long lVirtServId)

Broker Admin Class: IBrokConfig

PROGID: MemAdmin.BrokConfig

CLISD: {C78FA6E6-C4AC-11D0-BBDA-00C04FB615E5}

Properties	Methods
void SetConfig()	void LoadDefaults(long lVirtServId)
	void GetConfig(long lVirtServId)
	void CheckAcct(BSTR bszDomain, BSTR bszName, BSTR bszPassword)
long lVirtServId()	void lVirtServId(long rhs)

Table Continued on Following Page

Properties	Methods
long bLocal()	void bLocal(long rhs)
BSTR bszServerName()	void bszServerName([in] BSTR rhs)
long lPort()	void lPort(long rhs)
long bSecure()	void bSecure(long rhs)
long lSecurePort()	void lSecurePort(long rhs)
long lTimeLimit()	void lTimeLimit(long rhs)
long lSizeLimit()	void lSizeLimit(long rhs)
BSTR bszBaseDN()	void bszBaseDN([in] BSTR rhs)
long lCacheTimeout()	void lCacheTimeout(long rhs)
BSTR bszGroupPrefix()	void bszGroupPrefix(BSTR rhs)
long bCreateGroups()	void bCreateGroups(long rhs)
BSTR bszDomain()	void bszDomain(BSTR rhs)
BSTR bszDsName()	void bszDsName(BSTR rhs)
BSTR bszDsPwd()	void bszDsPwd(BSTR rhs)
BSTR bszProxyName()	void bszProxyName(BSTR rhs)
BSTR bszProxyPwd()	void bszProxyPwd(BSTR rhs)
BSTR bszProxyDomain()	void bszProxyDomain(BSTR rhs)
long bUseTrackCookie()	void bUseTrackCookie([in] long rhs)
long lPwdCookieTimeout()	void lPwdCookieTimeout(long rhs)
long bEnabled()	void bEnabled(long rhs)
BSTR bszComment()	void bszComment(BSTR rhs)
long bPwdCookiePersist()	void bPwdCookiePersist(long rhs)
BSTR bszRealm()	void bszRealm(BSTR rhs)
long lTokenCacheTimeout()	void lTokenCacheTimeout(long rhs)
BSTR bszTokenCreatorDll()	void bszTokenCreatorDll(BSTR rhs)
long bDirty()	

MembershipInfo Class: IMembershipInfo

PROGID: Membership.MembershipInfo

CLSID: {CB7865AC-E677-11D0-BDC7-00C04FB6163F}

Properties	Methods
BSTR bszServerDirectory()	void OnStartPage(IUnknown* piUnk)
BSTR bszClientDirectory()	void OnEndPage()
BSTR bszComputerName()	BSTR ADsPathToDN(BSTR bstrADsPath)
BSTR bszSiteServerInstallDirectory()	

MembershipSchema Class: ISchemaObjects

PROGID: Membership.SchemaObjects

CLSID: {C642753E-B74B-11D0-BBD7-00C04FB615E5}

Methods
void OnStartPage(IUnknown* pContext)
void OnEndPage()
BSTR GetRelativeName(IUnknown* pUnk)
BSTR GetEntrySchemaPath(BSTR bszEntryName)
void InitEx(BSTR bszHostName, VARIANT_BOOL fPromptCredentials)
void BindAs(BSTR bszAlias, BSTR bszUserName, BSTR bszPassword)

MembershipSchema Class: IAuoConfig

PROGID: Membership.SchemaObjects

CLSID: {C642753E-B74B-11D0-BBD7-00C04FB615E5}

Methods
void GetInfo(long lVirtServId)
void SetInfo()

Table Continued on Following Page

Methods
void SetEntry(BSTR bszName, BSTR bszADsPathPrefix, BSTR bszSchema, BSTR bszClass, long lSuffix, BSTR bszDepObject, BSTR bszDepProp, BSTR bszBindAsName, BSTR bszBindAsPassword);
void GetEntry(BSTR bszName, VARIANT* pbszADsPathPrefix, VARIANT* pbszSchema, VARIANT* pbszClass, VARIANT* plSuffix, VARIANT* pbszDepObject, VARIANT* pbszDepProp, VARIANT* pbszBindAsName, VARIANT* pbszBindAsPassword)
void RemoveEntry(BSTR bszName)
void GetEntries(VARIANT* pNames, VARIANT* pProviders)
void DeleteInstance()

Directory Service Configuration

DSConfig: DSAccounts

PROGID: DSConfig.DSAccounts

CLSID: {6AA33FD1-B917-11D1-B63A-00A0C99F1831}

Properties	Methods
short AUO_ACCOUNT()	void AUO_ACCOUNT(short rhs)
short BROKER_ACCOUNT()	void BROKER_ACCOUNT(short rhs)
short DM_ACCOUNT()	void DM_ACCOUNT(short rhs)
	VARIANT CreatePMAccount(BSTR ServerName, short Port, short AcctFlag, VARIANT* AcctName, VARIANT* AcctPassword, BSTR Username, BSTR password, short UniqueID)

DSConfig: DSPrep

PROGID: DSConfig.DSPrep

CLSID: {6AA33FD3-B917-11D1-B63A-00A0C99F1831}

Methods
VARIANT CheckOnBDC(BSTR* ServerName, BSTR* PDCName, VARIANT* DomainName)
VARIANT CheckOnPDC(BSTR* ServerName, BSTR* DomainName)

Methods
VARIANT SetDefaultACLs(BSTR* ServerName, short* Port, BSTR* Username, BSTR* password)
VARIANT GetRootContext(BSTR* SvrName, short* Port, VARIANT* DirName)
VARIANT GetSecurityMode(BSTR* SvrName, short* Port, VARIANT* SecurityMode)
VARIANT CreateDefaultGroups(BSTR* SvrName, short* Port, BSTR* Username, BSTR* password)

DSConfig: RegReader

PROGID: DSConfig.RegReader

CLSID: {6AA33FD5-B917-11D1-B63A-00A0C99F1831}

Methods
VARIANT InitializeGroupNameEnumerator()
long GetNextGroupName([in, out] VARIANT* theValue)
BSTR GetRegKeyLocalMachine(BSTR* sKeyName, BSTR* sValue)
BSTR GetRegKey(BSTR* ServerName, BSTR* sKeyName, BSTR* sValue)

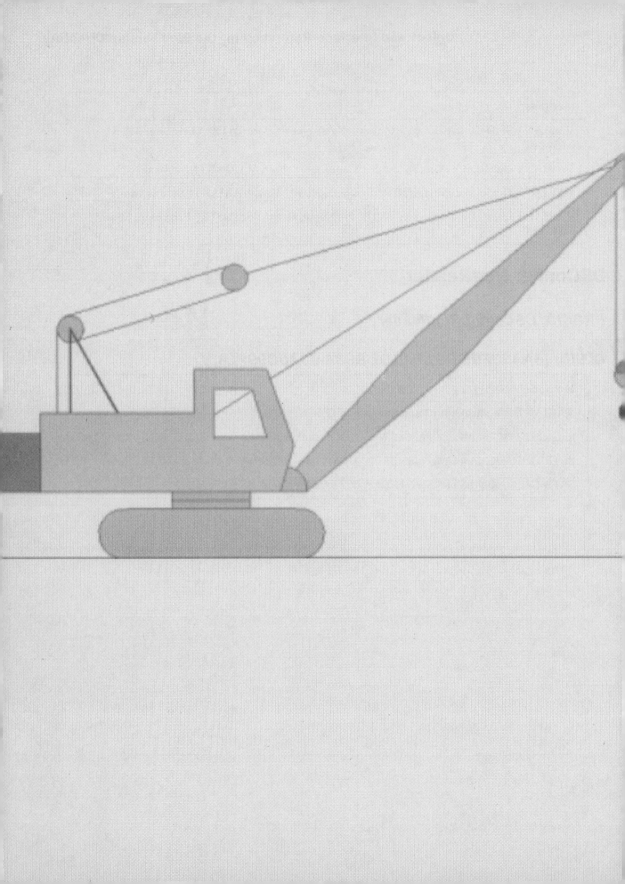

LDAP Event Messages

The LDAP server writes event messages to the event log of the Windows NT 4.0 machine it runs on. There are three different categories of errors: error, warning, and informational, decreasing in severity in that order.

Severity: Error

Event Number Constant Definition; Action (if applicable)	Notes
396 LDAP_EVENT_TIMEBOMB The evaluation period for this product has expired and could no longer be started.	Uninstall this beta version and purchase the retail version of Site Server 3.0
400 LDAP_EVENT_CANNOT_INITIALIZE _SECURITY Site Server LDAP Service cannot initialize its security. **Action**: Check Windows NT configuration and reboot the server.	Check the broker account and the account used to run the LDAP service on the computer. Either the broker or the account running the service does not have the proper permissions configured.

Table Continued on Following Page

Event Number Constant Definition; Action (if applicable)	Notes
401 LDAP_EVENT_CANNOT_INITIALIZE_WINSOCK Site Server LDAP Service cannot initialize the socket library. **Action**: Check the TCP/IP configuration.	LDAP uses TCP/IP to communicate across the network. TCP/IP must be installed and properly configured to use LDAP.
402 LDAP_EVENT_MAX_CONNECTION_REACHED Site Server LDAP Service rejected the connection attempt because there are too many users connected.	The maximum number of users that can be connected to the system has been reached. Use the P&M snap-in to configure support for more connections or add another service.
404 LDAP_EVENT_CANNOT_LOCATE_LDAP Site Server LDAP Service cannot open the LDAP/TCP service. The data area contains the return error code.	The LDAP service is unavailable due to problems with the TCP/IP configurations. Check the machine's settings.
405 LDAP_EVENT_CANNOT_CREATE_CONNECTION _SOCKET Site Server LDAP Service cannot create the main connection socket. The data area contains the return error code.	The LDAP service is unavailable due to problems with the TCP/IP configurations. Check the machine's settings.
406 LDAP_EVENT_CANNOT_CREATE_CONNECTION _THREAD Site Server LDAP Service cannot create the main connection thread. The data area contains the return error code.	The LDAP service is unavailable due to problems with the TCP/IP configurations. Check the machine's settings.
407 LDAP_EVENT_CANNOT_CREATE_CLIENT_CONN Virtual Server %1: Site Server LDAP Service cannot create a client connection object for user at host %2. The connection to this user is terminated. The data area contains the return error code.	A connection was refused on virtual server number %1 (Membership Server #) for the user at %2 (IP address).

Event Number Constant Definition; Action (if applicable)	Notes
408 LDAP_EVENT_SYSTEM_CALL_FAILED A call to a system service failed unexpectedly. The data area contains the return error code.	System error.
409 LDAP_EVENT_CLIENT_TIMEOUT User %1 at host %2 timed out after %3 seconds of inactivity.	The threshold for the user session (named) at host (IP address) has timed out – default set for 10 minutes.
417 LDAP_EVENT_CANNOT_OPEN_SVC_REGKEY Site Server LDAP Service cannot open the LDAP registry key %1.	Ensure that the registry key is available and that the ACEs on this key allow for the account running the LDAP service to gain access.
418 LDAP_EVENT_CANNOT_READ_SVC_REGKEY Site Server LDAP Service cannot read registry key %1.	Ensure that the registry key is available and that the ACEs on this key allow for the account running the LDAP service to gain access.
481 LDAP_EVENT_CANNOT_INITIALIZE_OBJECT Site Server LDAP Service cannot initialize the following object: %1.	Check the security requirements of the object and insure that the LDAP service account has the proper permissions for this object.
1003 LDAP_EVENT_GLOBAL_ERROR Error %1 Solution	Dependent upon returned error code.
2133 LDAP_BOOT_ERROR The server has detected a previous instance and will not boot until the old instance goes away. **Action**: After waiting some time, try to start the service. The data is the error code. Error description is %1.	Apparently another instance of the LDAP service attempting to be started is already running. Check the LDAP instance configurations through the PMAdmin.vbs utility for duplicate instance.

Table Continued on Following Page

Event Number Constant Definition; Action (if applicable)	Notes
2500 LDAP_DSCORE_INIT_ERROR The server failed to start due to an initialization error. **Action**: Verify the configuration. Error description is %1.	See the returned error code.
2501 LDAP_DSCORE_RUNTIME_ERROR The server failed due to a runtime error. Error description is %1.	See the returned error code.
2503 LDAP_SECURITY_BAD_SD The Security Descriptor data was not valid. %1	The security descriptor for the object is corrupt. Use the commerce security objects to check the security descriptor for problems.
2600 LDAP_REPL_INIT_ERROR Dynamic replication for the Site Server LDAP. Service failed due to an initialization error. **Action**: Verify the configuration. Error description is %1.	Dynamic data replication failed. Insure that all RPC services are accessible for the machine needing to communicate – additionally check firewall settings if on separate segments.
2601 LDAP_REPL_RUNTIME_ERROR Dynamic replication for the Site Server LDAP. Service failed due to a runtime error. Error description is %1.	See the returned error code.
2700 LDAP_EVENT_GENERIC_LDAP_ERROR General error for the Site Server LDAP Service: %1 (where %1 is name of the error).	See the returned error code.

Event Number Constant Definition; Action (if applicable)	Notes
2701 LDAP_EVENT_CANT_MONITOR_IPBLIST There was a problem monitoring the IP blacklist file for changes.	The IP blacklist text file is either corrupt or missing.
2703 LDAP_EVENT_ERROR_UPDATING_IPBLIST There was a problem monitoring the IP blacklist file for changes.	The IP blacklist text file is either corrupt or missing.
2708 LDAP_EVENT_KEKEY_INVALID The Key Encryption Key needs to be updated for the instance number %1.	The key encryption key for a Membership Server Instance has been changed, and needs to be changed in other Membership Server Instances. Use the kekey.exe utility found in the \bin\P&M directory.
2711 LDAP_EVENT_KEKEY_UPDATE_FAILED The Key Encryption Key has failed to be updated for Site Server LDAP Service instance number %1.	Make sure the LDAP service is stopped before attempting to change the key.
2712 LDAP_EVENT_KEKEY_UPDATE_DS_FAILED The Encrypted Password Encryption Key failed to be updated for the database for Site Server LDAP Service instance number %1.	Check the value of the PE – the PE in the database should never be changed.

Severity: Warning

Event Number Constant Definition; Action (if applicable)	Notes
397 LDAP_EVENT_SSL_FAILED Site Server LDAP Service could not establish Secure Sockets Layer (SSL) channel. **Action:** Verify that a proper certificate is installed correctly. The data area contains the return error code.	See the data returned for specific error information. Insure that port 636 is used for SSL communications.
398 LDAP_EVENT_OUT_OF_MEMORY Cannot allocate %1 because there is not enough memory available.	Install more memory.
399 LDAP_EVENT_OUT_OF_POOL Cannot allocate %1 because the pre-allocated limit has been reached.	Check the number of accounts used to access the database providing the services for the Membership Directory – more open accounts may need to be added.
482 LDAP_EVENT_COMMAND_TOO_BIG The Site Server LDAP Service command that was requested is too big for this server to process.	Trim the LDAP service command into smaller segments.
485 LDAP_EVENT_NT_CALL_FAILED A system call (%1) failed unexpectedly. The data area contains the return error code.	The system call to the specified NT item, event, or service failed.
2603 LDAP_REPL_RUNTIME_LOG Dynamic replication warning for Site Server LDAP Service %1.	The specified LDAP service is having problems replicating the dynamic data. Check the data being replicated for any unnecessary information.
2502 LDAP_DSCORE_RUNTIME_LOG Site Server LDAP Service directory server %1.	Internal error.

Event Number Constant Definition; Action (if applicable)	Notes
2704 LDAP_EVENT_SHORTTERM_IPBLACKLISTED Rejected connection attempt from IP address %1. Address is on short-term blacklist.	The IP address requesting LDAP service has been rejected since it is on the short-term IP blacklist – either remove the IP address from the blacklist or ignore.
2706 LDAP_EVENT_SHORTTERM_ACCT_BLACKLISTED Rejected binding attempt to account %1. Account is on short-term blacklist.	The account requesting LDAP service has been rejected since it is on the short-term blacklist – either remove the account from the blacklist or ignore.
2707 LDAP_EVENT_BLACKLISTING_INITIALIZE_ERROR %1 blacklisting failed to initialize. This feature will be turned off for the current session.	No blacklist files found – blacklist disabled.

Severity: Informational

Event Number Constant	Notes
483 LDAP_EVENT_SET_MAX_SIZE_ACCEPTED	Virtual Server %1: The maximum accepted message size is set to %2.
484 LDAP_EVENT_SET_MAX_SIZE_BEFORE_CLOSE	Virtual Server %1: The maximum message size accepted before the socket is forced closed is set to %2.
530 LDAP_EVENT_SERVICE_STARTED	Site Server LDAP Service has been started.
531 LDAP_EVENT_SERVICE_STOPPED	Site Server LDAP Service has been stopped.

Table Continued on Following Page

Event Number Constant	Notes
532 LDAP_EVENT_SERVICE_INSTANCE_STARTED	Site Server LDAP Service instance %1 has been started.
533 LDAP_EVENT_SERVICE_INSTANCE_STOPPED	Site Server LDAP Service instance %1 has been stopped.
534 LDAP_EVENT_SERVICE_INSTANCE_PAUSED	Site Server LDAP Service instance %1 has been paused.
535 LDAP_EVENT_SERVICE_INSTANCE_UNPAUSED	Site Server LDAP Service instance %1 has been un-paused.
536 LDAP_EVENT_SERVICE_INSTANCE_CREATED	Site Server LDAP Service instance %1 has been created.
537 LDAP_EVENT_SERVICE_INSTANCE_DELETED	Site Server LDAP Service instance %1 has been deleted.
538 LDAP_EVENT_SSL_NEGOTIATION_FAILED	Site Server LDAP Service failed to negotiate Secure Sockets Layer (SSL) connection.
539 LDAP_EVENT_CONNECTION_TIMED_OUT	The connection timed out.
2602 LDAP_REPL_RUNTIME_INFO	Dynamic replication information for the Site Server LDAP Service: %1.
2699 LDAP_EVENT_LONGTERM_BLACKLIST_DISABLED	The %1 file could not be found. Permanent blacklisting for the instance is disabled.
2702 LDAP_EVENT_CAN_MONITOR_IPBLIST	The problem with monitoring the IP blacklist file has been resolved. Will resume monitoring the file for changes.

Event Number Constant	Notes
2705 LDAP_EVENT_LONGTERM_IPBLACKLISTED	Rejected connection attempt from IP address %1. Address is on permanent blacklist.
2709 LDAP_EVENT_KEKEY_UPDATED	The Key Encryption Key has been successfully updated for the Site Server LDAP Service instance number %1.
2710 LDAP_EVENT_KEKEY_UPDATED_DS	The Key Encryption Key has been successfully updated for the database for Site Server LDAP Service instance number %1.

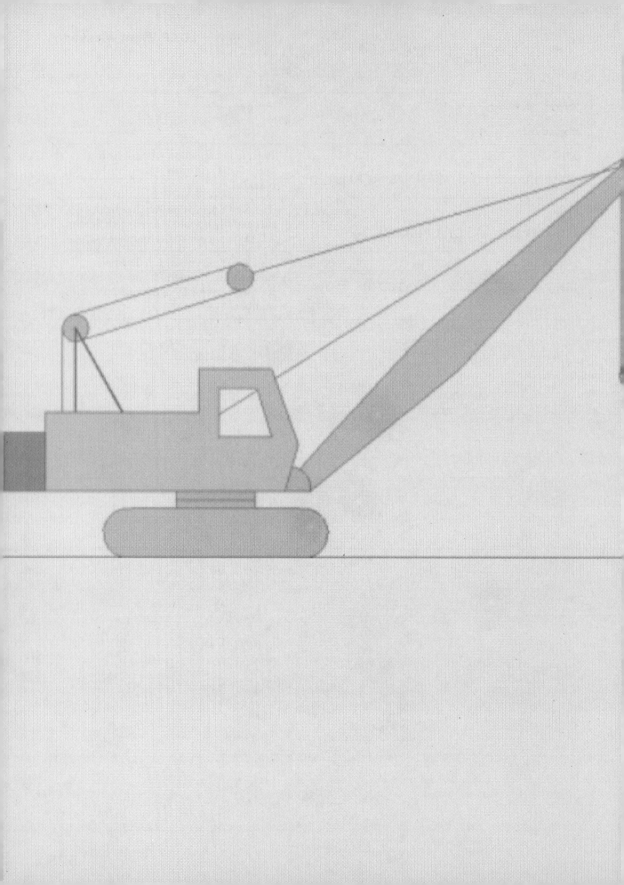

ADSI Error Codes

Active Directory Service Interfaces return the following error codes. These error codes can originate from the Active User Object – an ADSI provider – or from direct use of ADSI interfaces.

To trap these errors properly in an Active Server Page, we either need to define the constants in the ASP, or include the `ads_error.inc` – available from the Wrox web site:

> http://webdev.wrox.co.uk/books/1940

Additionally, these error codes can be found in the `adserr.h` file installed with the ADSI SDK, which defines the errors.

Hex Error Code Constant Name Description	Notes
0x80005000 E_ADS_BAD_PATHNAME An invalid Active Directory pathname was passed	The Active Directory Path, i.e. `LDAP://Wrox/o=Wrox`, is invalid. Check the ADsPath value passed to ensure it points to a valid directory service.
0x80005001 E_ADS_INVALID_DOMAIN_OBJECT An unknown Active Directory domain object was requested	Not applicable to the Site Server Membership Directory.

Table Continued on Following Page

Hex Error Code Constant Name Description	Notes
0x80005002 E_ADS_INVALID_USER_OBJECT An unknown Active Directory user object was requested	The user object requested is invalid. Check the list of available user objects that the directory supports.
0x80005003 E_ADS_INVALID_COMPUTER_OBJECT An unknown Active Directory computer object was requested	Not applicable to the Site Server Membership Directory.
0x80005004 E_ADS_UNKNOWN_OBJECT An unknown Active Directory object was requested	The Active Directory object requested does not exist. Please check the validity and type of the object and try again.
0x80005005 E_ADS_PROPERTY_NOT_SET The specified Active Directory property was not set	The ADSI property was not set and will not be updated in the directory.
0x80005006 E_ADS_PROPERTY_NOT_SUPPORTED The specified Active Directory property is not supported	The ADSI property you are attempting to use is not supported.
0x80005007 E_ADS_PROPERTY_INVALID The specified Active Directory property is invalid	The ADSI property is invalid. This will usually occur in a Membership Directory when a request is made for a user property and that property does not exist.
0x80005008 E_ADS_BAD_PARAMETER One or more input parameters are invalid	The parameter value passed for the property is invalid. Check the property type of the object and pass the correctly typed value for this property.

Hex Error Code Constant Name Description	Notes
0x80005009 **E_ADS_OBJECT_UNBOUND** The specified Active Directory object is not bound to a remote resource	The Active Directory object is not bound to a remote object. To use the object, it must first be bound to an ADs object – such as the ou=members container in the Membership Directory.
0x8000500A **E_ADS_PROPERTY_NOT_MODIFIED** The specified Active Directory object has not been modified	The ADs property has not been modified.
0x8000500B **E_ADS_PROPERTY_MODIFIED** The specified Active Directory object has been modified	The ADs property has been modified.
0x8000500C **E_ADS_CANT_CONVERT_DATATYPE** The Active Directory datatype cannot be converted to/from a native DS datatype	Check the data types supported by the directory provider. Next make sure the object type passed matches the acceptable object types for the provider.
0x8000500D **E_ADS_PROPERTY_NOT_FOUND** The Active Directory property cannot be found in the cache.	Either the property does not exist, or the cache needs to be refreshed. To refresh the cache, call `GetInfo()` from the object whose properties need to be refreshed.
0x8000500E **E_ADS_OBJECT_EXISTS** The Active Directory object exists.	The Active Directory object attempting to be created already exists – i.e. use a different naming value for the new object.
0x8000500F **E_ADS_SCHEMA_VIOLATION** The attempted action violates the DS schema rules.	The schema of the directory does not support this action.

Table Continued on Following Page

Hex Error Code Constant Name Description	Notes
0x80005010 E_ADS_COLUMN_NOT_SET The specified column in the Active Directory was not set.	The column for the search was not set, therefore the search cannot continue.
0x00005011 S_ADS_ERRORSOCCURRED One or more errors occurred	Unknown error has occurred.
0x00005012 S_ADS_NOMORE_ROWS No more rows to be obtained by the search result.	Occurs if a request is made past the number of available rows.
0x00005013 S_ADS_NOMORE_COLUMNS No more columns to be obtained for the current row.	Occurs if a request is made past the number of available columns.
0x80005014 E_ADS_INVALID_FILTER The search filter specified is invalid	The search filter specified for the search is invalid. Please examine the syntax of the query – additionally check the allowed types set by the Membership Server.

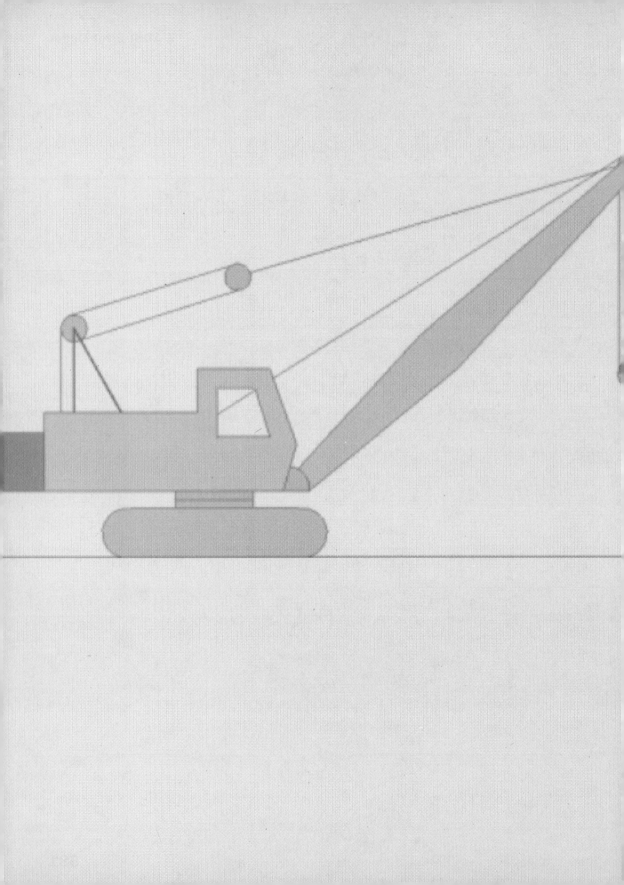

Miscellaneous Resources

ConfigView.asp

ConfigView.asp is a simple ASP that I designed and used while I was writing this book. It allows you use your browser to view the values of authentication settings and some lower -level settings (such as the BaseDN):

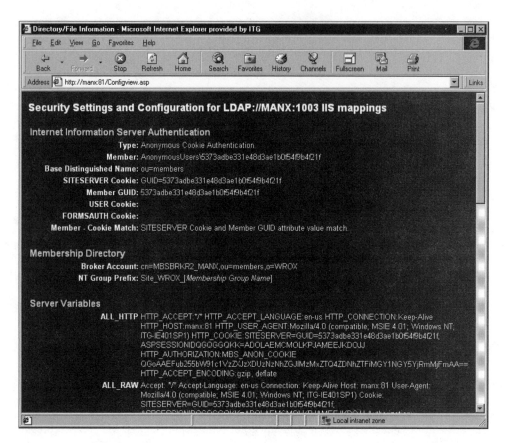

It is designed for use with an IIS 4.0 web server using Membership authentication. However, it could easily be re-purposed to support Windows NT authentication. This resource is available with the download files for this book, from the Wrox Press web site at http://webdev.wrox.co.uk/books/1940.

Books

Here's a list of resources that you may find useful. All the books and websites that are mentioned in this book are gathered together here for quick reference. The list also includes books and websites that I use all the time, as they provide some great resources on some very technical issues.

General Programming

Debugging the Development Process: Practical Strategies for Staying Focused, Hitting Ship Dates, and Building Solid Team (Microsoft Press, ISBN 1-556-15-6502)

Code Complete: A Practical Handbook of Software Construction (Microsoft Press, ISBN 1-556-15-4844)

Writing Solid Code: Microsoft's Techniques for Developing Bug-Free C Programs (Microsoft Press, ISBN 1-556-15-5514)

Windows NT Server 4.0

Microsoft Windows NT Server 4.0 Resource Kit (Microsoft Press, ISBN 1-572-31-3447)
Professional NT Services (Wrox, ISBN 1-861-00-1304)

Internet Information Server 4.0

Microsoft Internet Information Server 4.0 Resource Kit (Microsoft Press, ISBN 1-572-31-6381)

Active Server Pages

Beginning Active Server Pages 2.0 (Wrox, ISBN 1-861-00-1347)
Professional Active Server Pages 2.0 (Wrox, ISBN 1-861-00-1266)
Professional ASP Techniques for Web Masters (Wrox, ISBN 1-861-00-1797)

COM

Beginning ATL COM Programming (Wrox, ISBN 1-861-00-0111)
Inside COM (Microsoft Press, ISBN 1-572-31-3498)
Essential COM (Addison Wesley, ISBN 0-201-63-4465)

C/C++

C++ Pointers and Dynamic Memory Management (Wiley, ISBN 0-471-04-9980)
Algorithms in C (Addison Wesley, ISBN 0-201-51-4257)

Web Sites

http://www.microsoft.com/siteserver
http://www.siteserver.com
http://www.siteserver101.com
http://www.15seconds.com
http://www.amazon.com
http://info.internet.isi.edu/in-notes/rfc/files/rfc1777.txt (to review LDAP documentation)
http://www.microsoft.com/security
http://www.microsoft.com/backoffice/siteserver/site/30/gen/cpa.htm (Site Server Capacity and
Performance Analysis)
http://www.microsoft.com/workshop/server/nextgen/sessiondata.asp (Session State)
http://msdn.microsoft.com/developer/sdk/platform.htm (for SDKs)
http://www.microsoft.com/siteserver/commerce
http://www.microsoft.com/windows/mediaplayer
http://www.microsoft.com/windows/downloads/contents/Updates/NTNetShowServices
http://www.microsoft.com/asf
http://www.microsoft.com/ntserver/nts/mediaserv (for the Windows Media Player SDK)
http://www.microsoft.com/adsi
http://premium.microsoft.com/msdn/library/devprods/vb/vb50docs/f1/d5/s1af2d.htm (VB late and
early binding)

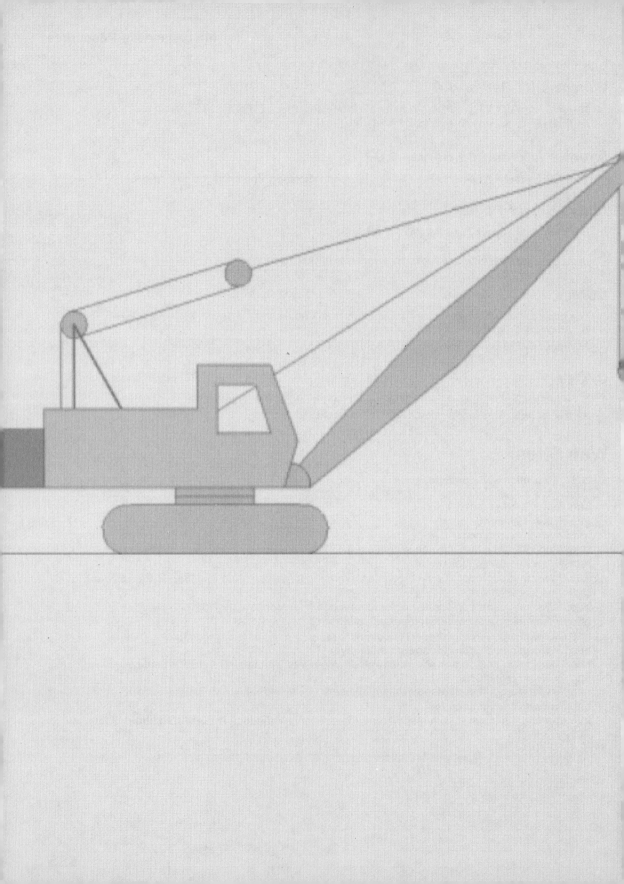

Appendix G Support and Errata

One of the most irritating things about any programming book can be when you find that bit of code you've just spent an hour typing in simply doesn't work. You check it a hundred times to see if you've set it up correctly and then you notice the spelling mistake in the variable name on the book page. Grrr! Of course, you can blame the authors for not taking enough care and testing the code, the editors for not doing their job properly, or the proofreaders for not being eagle-eyed enough, but this doesn't get around the fact that mistakes do happen.

We try hard to ensure no mistakes sneak out into the real world, but we can't promise that this book is 100% error free. What we can do is offer the next best thing by providing you with immediate support and feedback from experts who have worked on the book and try to ensure that future editions eliminate these gremlins. The following section will take you step by step through the process of posting errata to our web site to get that help. The sections that follow, therefore, are:

- ❑ Wrox Developers Membership
- ❑ Finding a list of existing errata on the web site
- ❑ Adding your own errata to the existing list
- ❑ What happens to your errata once you've posted it (why doesn't it appear immediately?)

There is also a section covering how to e-mail a question for technical support. This comprises:

- ❑ What your e-mail should include
- ❑ What happens to your e-mail once it has been received by us

So that you only need view information relevant to yourself, we ask that you register as a Wrox Developer Member. This is a quick and easy process, that will save you time in the long-run. If you are already a member, just update your membership to include this book.

Wrox Developer's Membership

To get your FREE Wrox Developer's Membership click on Membership in the navigation bar of our home site

`www.wrox.com.`

This is shown in the following screen shot:

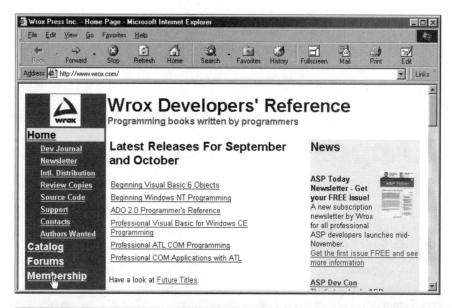

Then, on the next screen (not shown), click on **New User**. This will display a form. Fill in the details on the form and submit the details using the **submit** button at the bottom. Before you can say 'The best read books come in Wrox Red' you will get this screen:

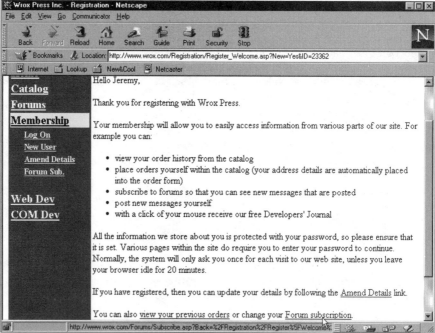

Finding an Errata on the Web Site.

Before you send in a query, you might be able to save time by finding the answer to your problem on our web site: http:\\www.wrox.com.

Each book we publish has its own page and its own errata sheet. You can get to any book's page by clicking on support from the left hand side navigation bar.

From this page you can locate any books errata page on our site. Select your book from the pop-up menu and click on it.

Then click on Enter Book Errata. This will take you to the errata page for the book. Select the criteria by which you want to view the errata, and click the apply criteria button. This will provide you with links to specific errata. For an initial search, you are advised to view the errata by page numbers. If you have looked for an error previously, then you may wish to limit your search using dates. We update these pages daily to ensure that you have the latest information on bugs and errors.

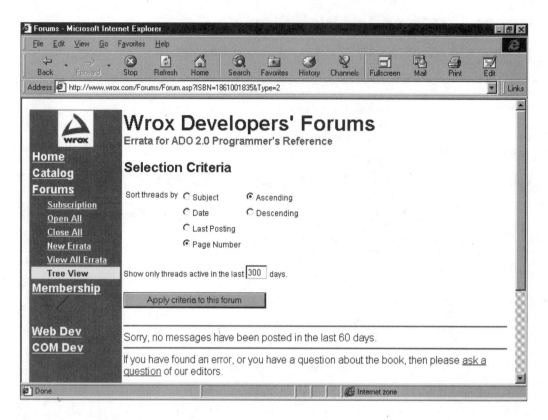

Adding an Errata to the Sheet Yourself.

It's always possible that you may find that your error is not listed, in which case you can enter details of the fault yourself. It might be anything from a spelling mistake to a faulty piece of code in the book. Sometimes you'll find useful hints that aren't really errors on the listing. By entering errata you may save another reader hours of frustration, and of course, you will be helping us provide even higher quality information. We're very grateful for this sort of advice and feedback. You can enter errata using the 'ask a question' of our editors link at the bottom of the errata page. Click on this link and you will get a form on which to post your message.

Fill in the subject box, and then type your message in the space provided on the form. Once you have done this, click on the Post Now button at the bottom of the page. The message will be forwarded to our editors. They'll then test your submission and check that the error exists, and that the suggestions you make are valid. Then your submission, together with a solution, is posted on the site for public consumption. Obviously this stage of the process can take a day or two, but we will endeavor to get a fix up sooner than that.

E-mail Support

If you wish to directly query a problem in the book with an expert who knows the book in detail then e-mail support@wrox.com, with the title of the book and the last four numbers of the ISBN in the subject field of the e-mail. Your e-mail **MUST** include the title of the book the problem relates to, otherwise we won't be able to help you. The diagram below shows what else your e-mail should include:

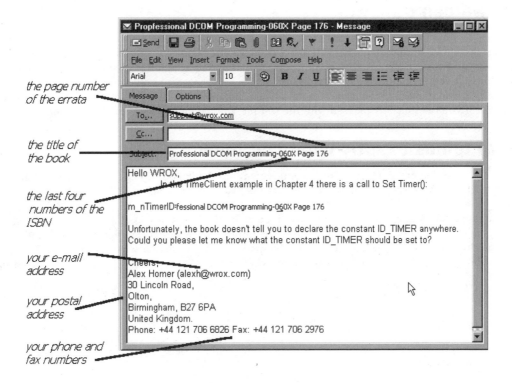

the page number of the errata

the title of the book

the last four numbers of the ISBN

your e-mail address

your postal address

your phone and fax numbers

We won't send you junk mail. We need the details to save your time and ours. If we need to replace a disk or CD we'll be able to get it to you straight away. When you send an e-mail it will go through the following chain of support:

Customer Support

Your message is delivered to one of our customer support staff who are the first people to read it. They have files on most frequently asked questions and will answer anything general immediately. They answer general questions about the book and the web site.

Editorial

Deeper queries are forwarded to the technical editor responsible for that book. They have experience with the programming language or particular product and are able to answer detailed technical questions on the subject. Once an issue has been resolved, the editor can post the errata to the web site.

The Authors

Finally, in the unlikely event that the editor can't answer your problem, s/he will forward the request to the author. We try to protect the author from any distractions from writing. However, we are quite happy to forward specific requests to them. All Wrox authors help with the support on their books. They'll mail the customer and the editor with their response, and again all readers should benefit.

What we can't answer

Obviously with an ever growing range of books and an ever-changing technology base, there is an increasing volume of data requiring support. While we endeavor to answer all questions about the book, we can't answer bugs in your own programs that you've adapted from our code. So, while you might have loved the help desk systems in our Active Server Pages book, don't expect too much sympathy if you cripple your company with a live adaptation you customized from Chapter 12. But do tell us if you're especially pleased with the routine you developed with our help.

How to tell us exactly what you think.

We understand that errors can destroy the enjoyment of a book and can cause many wasted and frustrated hours, so we seek to minimize the distress that they can cause.

You might just wish to tell us how much you liked or loathed the book in question. Or you might have ideas about how this whole process could be improved. In which case you should e-mail feedback@wrox.com. You'll always find a sympathetic ear, no matter what the problem is. Above all you should remember that we do care about what you have to say and we will do our utmost to act upon it.

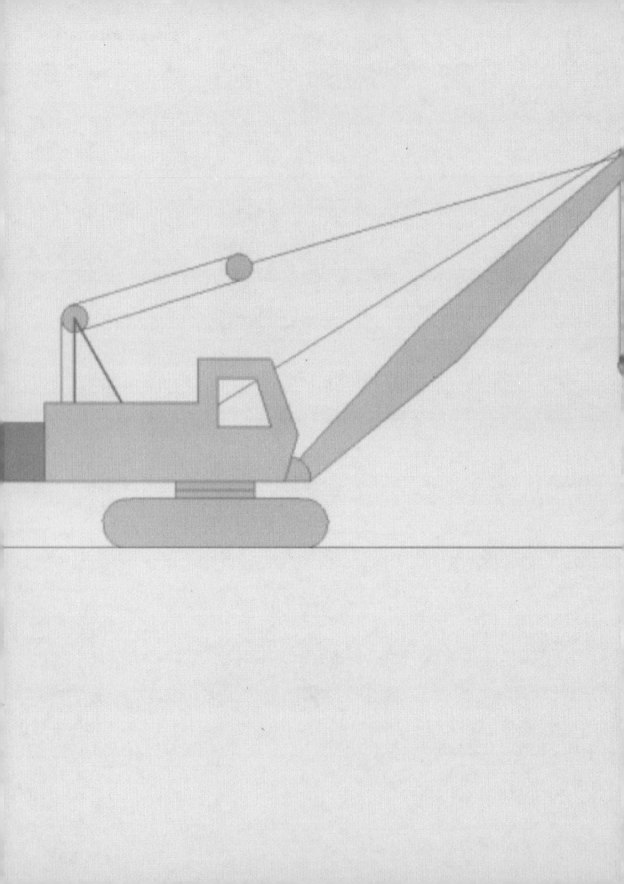

Index

Wrox writes books for you. Any suggestions, or ideas about how you want information given in your ideal book will be studied by our team. Your comments are always valued at Wrox.

Free phone in USA 800-USE-WROX
Fax (773) 397 8990

UK Tel. (0121) 687 4100   Fax   (0121) 687 4101

Site Server 3.0 Personalization and Membership

Name _____

Address _____

_____

_____

City _____ State/Region _____

Country _____ Postcode/Zip _____

E-mail _____

Occupation _____

How did you hear about this book? _____

☐ Book review (name) _____

☐ Advertisement (name) _____

☐ Recommendation _____

☐ Catalog _____

☐ Other _____

Where did you buy this book? _____

☐ Bookstore (name) _____ City _____

☐ Computer Store (name) _____

☐ Mail Order _____

☐ Other _____

What influenced you in the purchase of this book?

☐ Cover Design

☐ Contents

☐ Other (please specify) _____

How did you rate the overall contents of this book?

☐ Excellent   ☐ Good

☐ Average   ☐ Poor

What did you find most useful about this book? _____

What did you find least useful about this book? _____

Please add any additional comments. _____

What other subjects will you buy a computer book on soon? _____

What is the best computer book you have used this year? _____

Note: This information will only be used to keep you updated about new Wrox Press titles and will not be used for any other purpose or passed to any other third party.

wrox
PROGRAMMER TO PROGRAMMER™

NB. If you post the bounce back card below in the UK, please send it to:

Wrox Press Ltd., Arden House, 1102 Warwick Road,
Acocks Green, Birmingham B27 9BH, UK.

Computer Book Publishers

NO POSTAGE
NECESSARY
IF MAILED
IN THE
UNITED STATES

BUSINESS REPLY MAIL
FIRST CLASS MAIL   PERMIT#64   CHICAGO, IL

POSTAGE WILL BE PAID BY ADDRESSEE

WROX PRESS INC.,
29 S. LA SALLE ST.,
SUITE 520
CHICAGO IL 60603-USA